D1088118

ADAM MICKIEWICZ

ADAM MICKIEWICZ

The Life of a Romantic

ROMAN KOROPECKYJ

CORNELL UNIVERSITY PRESS

Ithaca and London

First published 2008 by Cornell University Press

Printed in the United States of America

Library of Congress Cataloging-in-Publication Data

Koropeckyj, Roman Robert.
Adam Mickiewicz : the life of a romantic / Roman Koropeckyj.
p. cm.
Includes bibliographical references and index.
ISBN 978-0-8014-4471-5 (cloth : alk. paper)
1. Mickiewicz, Adam, 1798–1855. 2. Poets, Polish—19th century—Biography.
I. Title.

PG7158.M51K643 2008
891.8'516—dc22
[B]

2008016785

Cornell University Press strives to use environmentally responsible suppliers and materials to the fullest extent possible in the publishing of its books. Such materials include vegetable-based, low-VOC inks and acid-free papers that are recycled, totally chlorine-free, or partly composed of nonwood fibers. For further information, visit our website at www.cornellpress.cornell.edu.

Cloth printing 10 9 8 7 6 5 4 3 2 1

To Volod'ka

Abundant and pure are the tears that I shed
Over my childhood, idyllic, angelic,
Over my youth, brash and sublime,
Over my prime, my age of defeat;
Abundant and pure are the tears that I shed.

—Adam Mickiewicz

If Mickiewicz was alive today, he'd be a good rapper.

—Doniu

CONTENTS

PREFACE

Upon hearing of Adam Mickiewicz's death in Istanbul in 1855, his sometime friend and rival Zygmunt Krasiński proclaimed, "We all stem from him."[1] Like all of his fellow Poles, Krasiński understood at that moment that with his works, no less than through his tempestuous life, Mickiewicz had come to define the very essence of modern Polish national consciousness. For nearly two hundred years, his name has served as a point of reference whenever the survival of the Polish nation was at stake, and whenever ideas about its fate needed legitimation. His words inspired insurrections against Poland's nineteenth-century partitioners as well as efforts to accommodate them; they informed the foundation of every party and ideology struggling to reconstitute an independent Poland, and then those that succeeded in doing so; they gave hope to the Polish resistance against Nazi occupation, and were used by the postwar Communist regime to prop up its authority. In the spring of 1968, the decision by those same Communist authorities to ban the performance of his 1832 drama *Forefathers' Eve*, part 3, radicalized a generation, initiating the country's march toward the revolution of 1989. As Poland endeavors to define itself in the twenty-first century, Mickiewicz's countrymen find themselves, much to their own amazement, still "asking" the poet for guidance.[2]

As Poland's "strong poet," his legacy conditioned every successive literary generation, down to the rappers of Poland's postsocialist *bloks*, who can somehow still declare that "if Mickiewicz was alive today, he'd be a good rapper."[3] Despite a literary tradition that stretches back to the sixteenth century, it is Mickiewicz whom Poles consider their *wieszcz*—at once their national bard, poet-prophet, and embodiment of the Polish ethos, "the first and the greatest." Monuments to him stand prominently in Poznań, Cracow, and Warsaw, in Lviv and Vilnius, once Polish cities, and overlook the Seine in Paris, where he spent nearly half his life. Practically every Polish town has a Mickiewicz street or square.

Schools, societies, and organizations bear his name. Snippets of his verse punctuate a Pole's daily discourse. His remains are interred among those of Poland's kings and heroes in the vaults of Cracow's Royal Cathedral, an *acknowledged* legislator of at least that corner of the world.

Mickiewicz? "Mickey-witz," rather. To the non-Pole the name means very, very little, if anything at all. Perhaps such is the fate of all Eastern European national bards, from the Ukrainian Taras Shevchenko and the Hungarian Sándor Petőfi to the Romanian Mihai Eminescu and the Belarusian Ianka Kupala. Concerned as they all were with the exigencies of national survival and self-determination, their poetry operates with myths, symbols, and affects that for their countrymen resonate on the most elemental, "tribal" level but are largely incomprehensible to those outwith the culture. (How much their translators should be held to account for this is another matter.)

Why, then, this biography?

Leaving aside both personal predilection and the pretext of the recent bicentennial of his birth in 1998 and sesquicentennial of his death in 2005, it bears stressing that Mickiewicz was not always an unknown quantity to non-Polish audiences. Throughout much of the nineteenth century, his poetry attracted enthusiastic readers in France, Germany, Russia, Italy, England, and even America. Like today's Western consumers of Polish literature, they too were drawn by its "exoticism." By this I mean not so much strange-sounding names and curious modes of behavior, or evocations of distant lands and inhospitable climates. Rather, they saw in Mickiewicz's poetry a visceral and at the same time ethically provocative attachment to a cause. For European readers imbued with the same romantic sensibility, his works spoke with unusual power on behalf of a people that dared resist the brutal might of reactionary empires and, as "Satan's-Imitator,"[4] even God himself.

Although this goes far in accounting for Mickiewicz's prominence during his lifetime, it was no less his physical—some may say charismatic—presence, his intellect, his confidence, his forcefulness of expression and belief that drew such admirers as Pushkin, Goethe, James Fenimore Cooper, Lamennais, George Sand, Daniel Stern, Gogol, Sainte-Beuve, Quinet, Michelet, Mazzini, and Margaret Fuller. For several decades, this exiled poet from Europe's backwater became a fixture in some of the most prominent salons of Russia and Europe. His 1840–1844 lectures on Slavic literature at the Collège de France, an exposition of a liberation theology *avant la lettre*, attracted an international audience. He used his name to rally Italians in their untimely struggle for liberation in 1848, and in 1855 to try to organize in Turkey a contingent of Jewish fighters to do battle against a common Russian oppressor. Like his heroes Napoleon and Byron, Mickiewicz saw life itself as a page upon which one must write a poetry of deed. He was the quintessential European romantic.

There is relatively little about Mickiewicz in English. Apart from articles and book chapters on specialized topics, several 1955 jubilee collections, and a couple of monographs devoted to his poetry,[5] only five book-length biographies have been published to date.

Three are translations from Polish meant for popular consumption;[6] of the two written by non-Poles, one, by Marion Moore Coleman (1956), is confined to the story of Mickiewicz's youth;[7] the other, by Monica Gardner, narrates his entire life and first appeared in 1911.[8] In addition, there exists a substantive biographical article by Wiktor Weintraub, the twentieth century's leading Mickiewicz scholar in the West.[9] To state that there is a lacuna to be filled is to state the obvious.

Of course, biographies of Mickiewicz in Polish, scholarly and otherwise, could fill a good shelf or two, to say nothing of the dozens of monographs and hundreds of articles devoted to various aspects of his life. Over the past two centuries Polish scholars have tracked down every possible material trace of the poet's life, and of much and many associated with him. New discoveries that might shed additional light on it have by now become very few and very far between. Yet for all their merits, most of these biographies remain unsatisfying. Although this body of work cannot but consider Mickiewicz's life within the wider European and Russian context, its attention ultimately centers on his significance as a Pole for Poles, for whom his poetry is as familiar, and as meaningful, as Goethe's is for Germans or Pushkin's for Russians and for whom he is an inexhaustible source of national pride. At the same time, precisely because of Mickiewicz's status as a national icon, there has always been a tendency to mythologize and, concomitantly, often downplay or even suppress certain moments in his life—be it for ideological ends or out of a misguided sense of discretion. For readers not familiar with his poetry, for those in whom the figure of Poland's national poet evokes no emotional associations, this is irrelevant. What they find compelling, rather, is the human Mickiewicz, at once victim and beneficiary of tsarist repression, Polish patriot and habitué of cosmopolitan salons, pious Catholic and heterodox sectarian, womanizer and feminist, egotist and devoted friend, Bonapartist, mystic politician, and revolutionist. It is this life, as misguided as it was sublime, that I shall narrate here. To this end, my biography engages Mickiewicz's poetry only insofar as it exemplifies or clarifies the life. My hope is that this will encourage readers to explore what is available of Mickiewicz's writing in English, or better still, inspire one or two of them to learn Polish and produce a few decent translations.

This biography does not pretend to be exhaustive or to present new archival materials. It is based in good part on the magnificent, albeit still incomplete, *Chronicle of Mickiewicz's Life and Work*, wherein practically every day of the poet's life and his immediate world is accounted for.[10] In consulting it, however, I have sought out all of the printed sources upon which it draws, references to which are provided in the footnotes. At the same time, I have supplemented and updated the *Chronicle* with an array of other published materials as well as with an edition of correspondence to Mickiewicz that is still under preparation. It goes without saying that in formulating my own views on Mickiewicz I have absorbed and gleaned much from an extraordinarily rich critical tradition, the most relevant texts of which are listed in the selected bibliography.

Although the recent bicentennial occasioned the publication of a new, superbly edited and annotated edition of Mickiewicz's complete writings (*Dzieła*, 17 volumes, 1998–2006), one still awaits a definitive critical edition of his works. The lack of such is particularly acute in the case of Mickiewicz's many French-language texts, which this most recent edition of his works, like those preceding it, have, with the exception of his correspondence, chosen to render into Polish. Alongside references to *Dzieła*, then, I provide references to the French originals from a variety of older editions. Unless otherwise noted, all translations into English are mine.

The writing of this biography was made possible by grants from the American Council of Learned Societies, the National Endowment for the Humanities, the International Research and Exchanges Board, and the UCLA Faculty Senate. Besides freeing me from teaching duties in order to write, these grants also helped subsidize two journeys in Mickiewicz's footsteps that took me to Europe, Russia, and Turkey. Throughout, I was received with kindness and solicitude by a host of curators and scholars of his legacy: at the Mickiewicz museums in Zaosie and Navahrudak in Belarus; the Mickiewicz Museum in Vilnius; the Pushkin Museum in St. Petersburg; the Nechui-Levyts'kyi Museum in Stebliv, Ukraine; the Odessa Museum of Literature; the Śmiełów Museum and the Kórnik Library in western Poland; the Polish Library and Mickiewicz Museum in Paris; the Polish Museum in Rapperswil, Switzerland; and the Mickiewicz Museum in Istanbul. To all of them, I am most grateful. I would like to extend special thanks to Dr. Janusz Odrowąż-Pieniążek, director of the Adam Mickiewicz Museum of Literature in Warsaw, together with Drs. Emilia Tomasik and Grażyna Grochowiakowa, for help in putting together the illustrations for this volume as well as to Drs. Krystyna Kulig-Janarek and Aleksandra Oleksiak of the National Museum in Cracow for the same. Thanks, too, to the staff of the library of the Institute of Literary Research of the Polish Academy of Sciences for providing me with copies of a number of hard-to-come-by texts as well as to Professor Joanna Niżyńska and Mr. Zdzisław Niżyński for helping with occasional requests for materials. I am no less grateful in this regard to Drs. Aleksander Nawarecki, Dorota Siwicka, Marek Zaleski, and Marek Bieńczyk of the Institute of Literary Research, yet my gratitude to them far transcends practical considerations. Without the intellectual as well as gastronomical stimulation they served up for me on my visits to Warsaw, and without the encouragement they offered on these occasions, who knows whether I would be writing this book.

It would have been impossible to complete this project without the help of the Interlibrary Loan services of UCLA's Charles Young Research Library. To Jennifer Lee, Sandra Farfan-Gracia, Reynoir I, Cindy Hollmichel, Kevin Balster, Kimberly Sanders, and Dinah Ortiz, my sincerest thanks, together with apologies for episodes of impatience and frustration.

I would like to thank my colleagues Aleksandr Ospovat and David Frick for reading portions of the manuscript and offering valuable suggestions, Michael Heim for providing the sound advice of a seasoned translator, and Larry Kruger for the lightbulb to embark on this task. I am especially indebted to Boris Dralyuk of UCLA for compiling the index and at the same time proofreading the manuscript, which he did with patience, meticulousness, and wit, and to my no less patient and meticulous editors at Cornell University Press, Bruce Acker and Karen Laun. Above all, I am deeply grateful to Dr. Marta Zielińska and to my parents, Professor Emeritus Iwan S. and Dr. Natalia B. Koropeckyj, for their willingness to read the manuscript in its entirety. Each in their own way—the first as one of Poland's leading Mickiewiczologists, the second as a nonspecialist but well-informed and critical audience—sought to improve my scribblings. If in this they did not succeed, it is through no fault of theirs.

ABBREVIATIONS

AMaydF	*Adam Mickiewicz aux yeux des Français*, ed. Zofia Mitosek (Warsaw: PWN, 1992).
AMwppo	*Adam Mickiewicz w poezji polskiej i obcej 1818–1855–1955 (Antologia)*, ed. Jerzy Starnawski (Wrocław: Ossolineum, 1961).
AMwm	*Adama Mickiewicza wspomnienia i myśli*, ed. Stanisław Pigoń (Warsaw: Czytelnik, 1958).
AF K	*Archiwum Filomatów: Korespondencja*
AF M	*Archiwum Filomatów: Materiały*
AF P	*Archiwum Filomatów: Poezja*
AF Lzw	*Archiwum Filomatów: Listy z więzienia*
AF Nz	*Archiwum Filomatów: Na zesłaniu*
AF Lzz	*Archiwum Filomatów: Listy z zesłania*
DpM	Stanisław Szpotański, *Działalność polityczna Mickiewicza*, vol. 3 of *Adam Mickiewicz i jego epoka* (Warsaw: J. Mortkowicz, 1922).
Dz.	Adam Mickiewicz, *Dzieła* (Wydanie Rocznicowe), 17 vols. (Warsaw: Czytelnik, 1993–2006).
Dziennik SB	Seweryn Goszczyński, *Dziennik Sprawy Bożej*, ed. Zbigniew Sudolski et al., 2 vols. (Warsaw: PAX, 1984).
DzW	Adam Mickiewicz, *Dzieła wszystkie*, vols. 1.1–4, 4 (Wrocław: Ossolineum, 1969–).
HZZP	Paweł Smolikowski, *Historia Zgromadzenia Zmartychwychstania Pańskiego. Podług źródeł rękopiśmiennych*, 4 vols. (Cracow: Spółka Wydawnicza Polska, 1892–1896).
Kallenbach, AM (1897)	Józej Kallenbach, *Adam Mickiewicz*, 2 vols. (Cracow: Spółka Wydawnicza Polska, 1897).
Kallenbach, AM (1923)	Józej Kallenbach, *Adam Mickiewicz*, 2 vols., 3d ed. (Lviv: Ossolineum, 1923).
Kallenbach, AM (1926)	Józef Kallenbach, *Adam Mickiewicz*, 2 vols., 4th ed. (Lviv: Ossolineum, 1926).

K biografii	Teodor Wierzbowski [Verzhbovskii], *K biografii Adama Mitskevicha v 1821–1829 godakh* (St. Petersburg: Imperatorska Akademiia Nauk, 1898).
Korespondencja	Korespondencja Adama Mickiewicza (manuscript).
Korespondencja AM	Adam Mickiewicz, *Korespondencja*, ed. Władysław Mickiewicz, 4 vols. 2d ed. (Paris: Księgarnia Luxemburgska, 1875–1876 [1880–1889]).
Korespondencja JBZ	Józef Bohdan Zaleski, *Korespondencja*, ed. Dyonizy Zaleski, 5 vols. (Lviv: H. Altenberg, 1900–1904).
Kronika 1798–1824	Maria Dernałowicz, Ksenia Kostenicz, and Zofia Makowiecka, *Kronika życia i twórczości Mickiewicza. Lata 1798–1824*, Kronika Życia i Twórczości Mickiewicza (Warsaw: PIW, 1957).
Kronika 1832–1834	Maria Dernałowicz, *Od "Dziadów" części trzeciej do "Pana Tadeusza." Marzec 1832–czerwiec 1834*, Kronika Życia i Twórczości Mickiewicza (Warsaw: PIW, 1966).
Kronika 1834–1840	Maria Dernałowicz, *Paryż, Lozanna. Czerwiec 1834–październik 1840*, Kronika Życia i Twórczości Mickiewicza (Warsaw: IBL, 1996).
Kronika 1840–1844	Zofia Makowiecka, *Mickiewicz w Collège de France. Październik 1840–maj 1844*, Kronika Życia i Twórczości Mickiewicza (Warsaw: PIW, 1968).
Kronika 1844–1847	Zofia Makowiecka, *Brat Adam. Maj 1844–grudzień 1847*, Kronika Życia i Twórczości Mickiewicza (Warsaw: PIW, 1975).
Kronika 1848–1849	Ksenia Kostenicz, *Legion Włoski i "Trybuna Ludów." Styczeń 1848–grudzień 1849*, Kronika Życia i Twórczości Mickiewicza (Warsaw: PIW, 1969).
Kronika 1850–1855	Ksenia Kostenicz, *Ostatnie lata Mickiewicza. Styczeń 1850–26 listopada 1855*, Kronika Życia i Twórczości Mickiewicza (Warsaw: PIW, 1978).
LdDP	Zygmunt Krasiński, *Listy do Delfiny Potockiej*, 3 vols., ed. Zbigniew Sudolski (Warsaw: PIW, 1975).
"Listy o AM"	"Listy o Adamie Mickiewiczu w zbiorach rękopiśmiennych Biblioteki PAN w Krakowie," ed. Zbigniew Jabłoński, *Rocznik Biblioteki Polskiej Akademii Nauk w Krakowie* 1 (1955): 48–185.
Listy SG	Seweryn Goszczyński, *Listy Seweryna Goszczyńskiego (1823–1875)*, ed. Stanisław Pigoń, Archiwum do Dziejów Literatury i Oświaty w Polsce, 19 (Cracow: PAU, 1937).
Listy SW	Stefan Witwicki, *Listy . . . do Józefa Bohdana Zaleskiego*, ed. Dionizy Zaleski (Lviv: Dionizy Zaleski, 1901).
Ll	*Listy legionistów Adama Mickiewicza z lat 1848–1849*, ed. Hanna Lutzowa (Wrocław: Ossolineum, 1963).
LS	Adam Mickiewicz, *Cours de littérature slave professé au Collège de France*, 5 vols. (Paris: L. Martinet, 1860).
Lzp	Antoni Edward Odyniec, *Listy z podróży*, ed. Marian Toporowski, 2 vols. (Warsaw: PIW, 1961).
Mémorial	Władysław Mickiewicz, *Mémorial de la Légion Polonaise de 1848 créée en Italie par Adam Mickiewicz*, 3 vols. (Paris: Libraire du Luxembourg, 1877).
"Mm"	Władysław Mickiewicz, "Moja matka," *Przegląd Współczesny* 5.18 (1926): 145–75, 395–406; 5.19 (1926): 119–31, 280–90, 380–409.

MP	Adam Mickiewicz, *Mélanges posthumes*, 2 vols., ed. Władysław Mickiewicz (Paris: Librairie du Luxembourg, 1872–1879).
"MwkN"	Leon Płoszewski, "Mickiewicz w korespondencj i zapiskach Leonarda Niedźwieckiego," *Pamiętnik Biblioteki Kórnickiej* 6 (1958): 189–285.
Mwow	Witold Bilip, *Mickiewicz w oczach współczesnych. Dzieje recepcji na ziemiach polskich w latach 1818–1830. Antologia* (Wrocław: Ossolineum, 1962).
"Prawda"	Ksenia Kostenicz, "Prawda i nieprawda w relacjach o śmierci Mickiewicza," *Blok-Notes Muzeum Literatury im. Adama Mickiewicza* 1 (1975): 42–95.
Przemówienia	Adam Mickiewicz, *Dzieła wszystkie* (Wydanie Sejmowe), vol. 13, *Przemówienia*, ed. Stanisław Pigoń (Warsaw: Skarb Rzeczypospolitej Polskiej, 1936).
PSB	*Polski słownik biograficzny* (Cracow: Gebethner and Wolff, 1935–).
PS	Sudolski, Zbigniew, *Panny Szymanowskie i ich losy. Opowieść biograficzna* (Warsaw: LSW, 1986).
Rekonstrukcja	Jerzy Borowczyk, *Rekonstrukcja procesu filomatów i filaretów 1823–1824*, Uniwersytet im. Adama Mickiewicza w Poznaniu, Filologia Polska, 75 (Poznań: UAM, 2003).
Rozmowy	Adam Mickiewicz, *Rozmowy z Adamem Mickiewiczem*, ed. Stanisław Pigoń, vol. 16 of *Dzieła wszystkie* (Wydanie Sejmowe) (Warsaw: Skarb Rzeczypospolitej Polskiej, 1933).
Ss	Adam Mickiewicz [Mitskevich], *Sobranie sochinenii*, vol. 5, ed. M. S. Zhivov et al. (Moscow: Khudozhestvennaia Literatura, 1954).
TP	Adam Mickiewicz, *La Tribune des Peuples*, ed. Władysław Mickiewicz (Paris: E. Flammarion, 1907).
TP (f)	*La Tribune de Peuples. Édition phototypique*, ed. Henryk Jabłoński (Wrocław: Ossolineum, 1963).
WAM	*Współudział Adama Mickiewicza w sprawie Andrzeja Towiańskiego. Listy i przemówienia*, 2 vols. (Paris: Księgarnia Luksemburgska, 1877).
Wspomnienie	Antoni Edward Odyniec, in K. W. Wójcicki, *Wspomnienie o życiu Adama Mickiewicza* (Warsaw: J. Jaworski, 1858).
Żywot	Władysław Mickiewicz, *Żywot Adama Mickiewicza podług zebranych przez siebie materiałów oraz z własnych wspomnień*, 4 vols. (Poznań: Dziennik Poznański, 1892–1895).
Żywot^2	Władysław Mickiewicz, *Żywot Adama Mickiewicza podług zebranych przez siebie materiałów oraz z własnych wspomnień*, 2d ed., 2 vols. (Poznań: Poznańskie Towarzystwo Przyjaciół Nauk, 1929–1931).

CHAPTER ONE

CHILDHOOD (1798–1815)

As family legend would have it, on 24 December 1798/6 January 1799,* a midwife lay Mikołaj and Barbara Mickiewicz's second-born on a book and cut his umbilical cord, hoping in this way to "predestine him to be an intelligent man." Where, exactly, this happened—an inn? a home?—will probably never be known, but if it did, it was somewhere on or near a farmstead called Zaosie in a far northeastern corner of Europe known then as Lithuania. The midwife's superstitious gesture would prove providential.[1]

I

Adam Mickiewicz was born and raised in what is now western Belarus, at the time a recently acquired province of the Russian Empire. Until 1795 the land had been part of the Grand Duchy of Lithuania, which in 1569 united with the Kingdom of Poland to constitute the Polish-Lithuanian Commonwealth. As a consequence, both the Baltic peoples inhabiting the grand duchy's north and the East Slavic peoples in its south came under intensifying Polish cultural influence. Over the century or so following the union, most of the native gentry had assimilated into the religious (Roman Catholic, to a lesser extent Protestant) and sociolinguistic culture of Poland; peasants, the ancestors of today's Lithuanians and Belarusians, continued to lead their traditional lives as the gentry's neofeudal subjects. By the end of the eighteenth century, the Nowogródek (Navahrudak) region where Mickiewicz was born was thus populated by an Orthodox or Uniate Belarusian peasantry and a

*Although Mickiewicz's culture was Roman Catholic and thus used the Gregorian calendar, the Julian calendar was the official calendar of the Russian Empire. Henceforth, until Mickiewicz leaves the empire's confines in 1829, both dates are provided side by side, New Style (Gregorian) first, Old Style (Julian) second.

gentry (about 9 percent of the population) whose religious, linguistic, and cultural orientation was for the most part Polish, albeit with a strong sense of regional—Lithuanian—particularism that distinguished it from the inhabitants of the kingdom. Except for a patent and the right to own land, the majority of the gentry nonetheless enjoyed a way of life only marginally different from that of a peasant: their women, as Mickiewicz would write in his epic poem *Pan Tadeusz* (1834), wore gloves when harvesting or spinning cloth. The grand duchy was also home to a large number of Jews, who made up about 14 percent of the population, and in towns, where they lived side by side with Christian inhabitants, sometimes well over 50 percent. With the third partition of the Polish-Lithuanian Commonwealth in 1795, when Russia, Prussia, and Austria finally erased the once mighty state from the political map of Europe, this region of Belarusian villages, mostly modest Polish gentry estates and farmsteads, and an occasional town, was absorbed into the Russian Empire. It was probably in this year that Mickiewicz's parents were married.

At the time of Mickiewicz's birth in 1798, the imperial mode of administration was just beginning to be felt and in any case was hardly burdensome. The newly acquired Lithuanian provinces were allowed to retain many of the traditional institutions unique to the grand duchy, thus securing for the empire a modicum of loyalty from most of its citizens—but by no means love. Memories of the 1792–1793 Russo-Polish War were still all too fresh, as were, indeed, those of the great anti-Russian uprising of 1794, which was supported with particular enthusiasm in what was then left of the grand duchy. Although its defeat marked the end of the commonwealth, the uprising engendered a powerful patriotic narrative, made all the more resonant for the inhabitants of the region by the fact that the leader of the uprising, Tadeusz Kościuszko, was a native son. This narrative was only one among the many that kept Polish hopes for the restoration of their state continually alive.

2

Not much more than a cottage with a few outbuildings and 154 acres of land, Zaosie lay some 40 kilometers south of the town of Nowogródek, the regional center. The farmstead had been in Mickiewicz's family since 1784, when his paternal granduncles apparently took it by force from a debtor. In 1798, they invited their thirty-four-year-old nephew Mikołaj, a lawyer working out of Nowogródek, to administer it. Like his uncles Bazyli and Adam, both of whom were killed in brawls shortly after Mickiewicz's birth,* Mickiewicz's father was a fractious sort, but no different in this respect than most of his fellow gentrymen. Being a pettifogger in a society known for its litigiousness only increased the

*The name of Bazyli's killer was Saplica *vel* Soplica, whom Mikołaj kept hounding through the courts and with whom, as a result, the Mickiewicz family subsequently had trouble for a number of years. It is this name that Mickiewicz chose for the eponymous hero of *Pan Tadeusz*.

chances of violent confrontation. In 1799, for example, he was badly beaten as a result of his involvement in a divorce proceeding.

But practicing law also had its advantages, particularly when questions arose about the bona fides of one's gentry status, and Mikołaj Mickiewicz was forced to answer such questions more than once. The stakes were enormous: however minimal the difference between an impoverished Lithuanian gentryman and a Belarusian serf may have been economically, socially it meant being either a freeman or a bondman. Against accusations that the Mickiewiczes were in fact runaway serfs, Mikołaj's efforts proved successful (although not necessarily trustworthy), and thanks to them we have some ostensible idea about Adam Mickiewicz's paternal lineage. According to documents Mikołaj submitted to patent commissions, the Mickiewiczes, of the Poraj branch of the Rymwid clan, were petty gentry landowners in the Nowogródek region whose patriarch settled there at the end of the seventeenth century from the Lida region just to the north. Of course, the very fact that their bona fides came under suspicion is a good indication of the clan's socio-economic status. By the time Adam was born, Mikołaj's family (which already included one son, Franciszek, born two years earlier) appears to have owned little or no land and depended on rent from some property in Nowogródek in addition to the unpredictable and rather paltry income from the father's law practice.

If Mickiewicz's paternal lineage raised questions of a social nature, questions of a different sort have been raised concerning his mother's side. In his 1832 drama *Forefather' Eve*, part 3, a character has a vision of Poland's "savior," who, among such attributes as "three faces" and "the name forty-four," is identified as being "of a foreign mother" (Dz. 3:190–91). Even when one assumes that this savior is a projection of the author himself, all this might be written off as but the vague symbolism of biblically inspired mystical prophetism—were it not for persistent rumors among his contemporaries as well as comments supposedly made by Mickiewicz himself to the effect that his mother was descended from Jews.

One may dismiss in this connection the statements of his acquaintance Zygmunt Krasiński, the conservative author of a drama that blamed European revolutions on a Jewish conspiracy, who hysterically insisted in 1848 that Mickiewicz's mother "was a Jew who had converted before marrying his father." Yet according to the eccentric magnate Ksawery Branicki, financier of Mickiewicz's revolutionist activities in 1848, the poet "often" claimed, "My father came from Mazovian stock, my mother Majewska from converts; I'm thus half Lechite and half Israelite, and I'm proud of it." For her part, Karolina Jaenisch-Pavlova, the woman Mickiewicz almost married while in exile in Russia, once confided to a friend that "Mickiewicz was a Jew." There is nothing in the extant, but very meager, archival records that would suggest that Barbara née Majewska came from a family of Jewish converts be it on her paternal or her maternal side (just as there is no evidence that Mikołaj's family was from Mazovia). Her father, for many years a steward at an estate not far from Nowogródek, was apparently of gentry origins (of the Starykoń clan, Murawiec branch); her mother (Orzeszko), the daughter of a petty gentry functionary in the region.[2]

It is a fact, nonetheless, that there were lines of Majewskis in Lithuania who were converted Jews, just as there are certain moments in Mickiewicz's biography that cannot but give pause. Celina Szymanowska, the woman the poet married in 1834 and with whose mother he was on particularly close terms when in Russia, was from a family of Frankists, a messianic sect of Polish Jews who in the mid-eighteenth century had converted en masse to Catholicism. Jews and Israel were essential references, mystical and otherwise, in Mickiewicz's own messianic sectarianism, articulated most fully in his demand for the full emancipation of Polish Jews in his 1848 protoconstitution for a future Poland as well as in his attempt to organize a Jewish legion during the Crimean War. More telling, though, are the little things, the seemingly spontaneous reflexes, such as Mickiewicz's first impressions of Rome communicated to one of his closest friends, wherein he focused on "the Jerusalem candelabra on Titus's arch of triumph"; or when, in connection with the Jewish legion, someone "ironically" referred to "filthy Jews" and in response the poet "glowered, . . . grew angry." Was it possible, a witness asked, to "so love something that is alien?"[3]

These are facts, open to interpretation, but facts all the same. As such, they suggest something akin to a "Jewish complex"* on the part of someone who, if anything, perhaps suspected his origins but was unsure. After all, it was Mickiewicz's father who in 1801 gathered signatures certifying the gentry pedigree of Barbara's father Mateusz. In any case, the question of Mickiewicz's "Jewishness" remains unresolved, but it persists, and that it does bespeaks, more than anything else, the complex, and complexed, relationship between Poles and Jews over the last two centuries. That it should be played out through the figure Poles consider their national poet makes it especially salient.

3

Mickiewicz spent only part of his first three years at the homestead in Zaosie, although he would often visit it and the surrounding countryside thereafter. It is this land of simple beauty—of "wooded hills" and "green meadows, / Spread out along the azure Niemen," of "fields painted by various grains, / Gilded with wheat, silvered with rye, / Where amber mustard and buckwheat white as snow, / Where clover like a blushing maiden grows, / And everything is girded with a ribbon of green / Meadow, whereon the occasional quiet pear trees stand" (Dz. 4:11)—that he will describe in such breathtaking, nostalgic detail in

*I borrow the term from Oberlaender, "Kompleks żydowski."

Pan Tadeusz as "the land of childhood years" (without, however, mentioning its harsh winters). Perhaps it was with Zaosie that the future poet associated his first memory, of how he enjoyed "sitting on the train of his mother's dress so she could drag him around the room."[4]

But it was in the town of Nowogródek that Mickiewicz was baptized Adam Bernard and where he spent most of his early life. The town was small, in all some 1,500 inhabitants, of which about 50 percent were Jews and another 20 percent Tatars. It was founded in the thirteenth century by the Lithuanian grand duke Mindaugas, the ruins of whose castle, towering over the town, could inspire a child's imagination. Besides the crumbling historical monuments, Nowogródek had little else to offer: a bazaar in the small square, a handful of brick dwellings, the requisite houses of worship to serve the various faiths, an inn that doubled as a performance space for visiting theatrical troupes, a few shops and offices, and the regional Polish school. The family settled there more or less permanently in 1801, the year the next of the Mickiewiczes' children, Aleksander, was born, and where two more would come into this world, Jerzy in 1804, and the short-lived Antoni in 1805. By 1806, the Mickiewiczes owned two houses in the town, apparently renting out one or the other. As Mikołaj's law practice withered, they became their most important source of income. What this amounted to can best be gauged by Franciszek's lament some years after his father's death, "Clothes, clothes, O shoes, shoes," and the plea of his "coatless" brother Aleksander that Adam rip up letters in which he writes about the family's desperate straits, "because should someone find them, why should they laugh at our poverty?"[5]

Until the age of ten, Mickiewicz was educated at home, first by his mother, then by a series of unremarkable tutors. He began attending school together with Franciszek in 1807. The school was run by Dominicans, but like other educational institutions of the grand duchy it was under the jurisdiction of a recently formed secular school district centered in Vilnius and headed by Prince Adam Czartoryski, at that time, at least, Emperor Alexander I's favorite Pole. Its curriculum incorporated many of the reforms introduced by the progressive Commission of National Education (1773–1794), one of the great achievements of the Polish Enlightenment.

Aside from religious instruction (this was, after all, a parochial school), as the boys progressed through the six years of their education in Nowogródek they studied mathematics, from fractions to logic; the natural as well as applied sciences, including zoology, botany, agriculture, physics, and chemistry; and geography—that of Russia, Europe, and the remainder of the known world (in that order)—which prepared them for the study of history, first of the preclassical world, then of ancient Greece and Rome, finally of Russia and Poland. Lessons in moral science drew largely from classical authors and in the higher grades addressed such topics of Enlightenment interest as natural law and economics, together with notions of the basic rights of man and of collectives. Although the study of Latin remained the mainstay of education, it not only focused on mastery of the language, but utilized passages by authors ranging from Cicero, Horace, and Quintillian to Pliny, Cornelius Nepos, and Columella to illustrate material for the other subjects. By the third grade, though, the study of Polish assumed greater prominence, encompassing grammar, word formation, syntax, rhetoric, poetics, as well as the history of Polish literature, all based on a rich canon of writers from the sixteenth century to authors only a generation or so removed from that of the schoolboys. If Mickiewicz's primary education left him with a solid command of the classics (and after completing university, it would be superb), it also provided him with a knowledge no less sound of Polish literature, a knowledge that quickly grew into love. On top of these required subjects, Mickiewicz apparently also learned the rudiments of Russian and French, although he read Marmontel's *Les Incas; ou, La Destruction de l'empire du Pérou* in Polish translation.[6]

More than anything else, the study of Latin and Polish constituted something of a workshop in writing. Through memorization, translation, and imitation, the foundations of classicist pedagogy, Mickiewicz became familiar with a stock of rhetorical and poetic devices and like every schoolboy thus achieved a basic level of proficiency in the art of writing. Although this method of instruction led to a tide of graphomania among his contemporaries, it also made them relatively intelligent readers, sensitive to literary allusions and conventions and to writing that subverted them. Mickiewicz's own first attempts at poetry may have received a further impulse from his father Mikołaj, who apparently was himself something of a versifier, but, it seems, no encouragement: fear of criticism, as Mickiewicz would later recall, kept him from showing his efforts to his father. It is curious, then, that the one boyhood poem to which family legend as well as Mickiewicz's own reminiscences attest was written about a fire in Nowogródek that eventually cost Mikołaj his life.

Mickiewicz's report cards from his years at the Dominican school indicate that he was a good student, at times even outstanding, especially in the natural and moral sciences and in history. But he was also in perpetually feeble health, which is perhaps why he had to repeat his third as well as fifth years. The one subject that he could not master was penmanship. Mickiewicz later claimed that as a child "those arabesques reminded [him] of the squashed innards of spiders, and spiders in particular always disgusted [him]." His mother apparently admonished him for his "chicken scratches," adding that if he were a rich gentleman, he could count on a secretary, but since he was only a poor squire he would have to learn how to manage by himself. Mickiewicz never fully succeeded in improving his scrawl: his hand is often difficult to decipher.[7]

4

In the fall of 1811, the Great Comet became visible to the naked eye in Lithuania. Its appearance was immediately assumed to be an omen. As if in confirmation, a large fire broke out in Nowogródek that November (such fires were common enough in a town built largely of wood). Mikołaj Mickiewicz helped fight the blaze, and as a result of his efforts fell ill. Within a few months, on 16/28 May 1812, he died, leaving his wife and three sons (the youngest, Antoni, had died in 1810) in miserable financial circumstances. Many years later Mickiewicz would recall that on the day of his father's death "a mirror hanging in their home cracked." Whether he made a connection between these two events and the appearance of the comet—or, for that matter, with the poem he supposedly wrote about the fire—is uncertain, but they became firmly associated in his mind with what was the most memorable experience of his childhood, Napoleon Bonaparte's campaign against Russia.[8]

Four years earlier, less than 200 kilometers west of Nowogródek on the other side of the Niemen River, a restored Polish statelet had come into existence. Carved largely out of what Prussia had acquired through its three partitions of the commonwealth, the Duchy of Warsaw was Napoleon's strategically calculated "gift" to the Poles, many of whom had gone west after 1795 in the belief that their support of revolutionary France's struggle against its enemies would in turn lead to the liberation of Poland. In 1797, their leader, General Henryk Dąbrowski, managed to form a Polish legion of several thousand men in Italy to fight against Austria under Napoleon's command. Courageous and loyal as the legionnaires were—in the words of their fight song (and now Poland's national anthem), "Bonaparte set us an example of how we should overcome"—their dream of restoring the commonwealth with France's help ran up against their idolized commander's own plans for Europe, and for Poland's place in it. Although the creation of the nominally independent duchy was a moment in which the aims of the two ostensibly coincided, in reality it proved to be a nasty disappointment. It was not until 1812, when Napoleon finally moved against Russia, that the Poles' faith in the emperor seemed to avail.

In June, as the French armies made their way east across the Niemen into Lithuania to wage what Napoleon proclaimed was "the second Polish war," the parliament in Warsaw declared the restoration of the Kingdom of Poland and its reunification with the Grand Duchy of Lithuania. Contingents of the *Grande armée* entered Nowogródek near the end of the month, led by King Jérôme Bonaparte and Prince Józef Poniatowski, the commander of the Polish forces. The king stayed briefly in the Radziwiłł mansion just a few streets up from the Mickiewiczes'. In August, the town celebrated the birthday of Poland's "savior," "miraculously appointed" and "blessed by Providence," with a mass, a dinner for the gentry, and fireworks. A banner hung out on the frontal of the Franciscan church depicted a fiery comet with the letter "N" and the words "Maximus in Magno Napoleone Deus." Like everyone else in town, little Adam was overjoyed by the arrival of the French and their Polish allies, but the black he was still wearing in mourning for his father made a rather different impression on the townsfolk: they accused him of harboring sympathies for the departed Russians. "This accusation," he recalled years later, "hurt me deeply, and I couldn't forget it for a long, long time."[9]

Six months later, during the brutal winter of 1812, what was left of the *Grande armée* straggled back through Nowogródek. "Every place was full of them," Mickiewicz later recounted to a French friend, "homes, public buildings, the school.... Fires were lit for the soldiers in halls, vestibules, everywhere." Their suffering, their hardiness, their courage, but above all their unshakable loyalty to the emperor, even in humiliating defeat, left an indelible impression on the fourteen-year-old boy. Not long afterward, Mickiewicz added the name "Napoleon" to his; with time, the figure of Bonaparte would grow into an obsession.[10]

Disruptive as the events of 1812 were for Mickiewicz and for Nowogródek as a whole, they did not interrupt the boy's education (for some reason, only moral science was not taught that year). Mickiewicz graduated from school in 1815, having finished all six grades. His diploma noted that "Master Adam Mickiewicz... did not countenance anything contrary to good morals; and indeed stood out on account of his deep faith in God, sound morals, and diligent application." In September of that year, at the age of sixteen, he set off to Vilnius, the provincial capital some 150 kilometers north of Nowogródek, in order to continue his education at the university. Although he would return to his family home for summer vacations, it served primarily as a base for excursions into the surrounding countryside. Indeed, one gets the impression from his years in Vilnius and Kowno (Kaunas) of a certain distance toward his mother and brothers: even as he tried to help them financially in his own straitened circumstances, he rarely wrote. Mickiewicz found more emotionally satisfying substitutes among his university brethren in Vilnius—and with an older woman in Kowno.[11]

CHAPTER TWO

YOUTH (1815–1824)

On 12/24 September 1815, "his head filled with stories about bandits," the sixteen-year-old Mickiewicz set out from Nowogródek in a Jewish wagonnette for the day-long trip to Vilnius. Within a few days of his arrival there, he registered at the university and settled in with a distant relative, who also happened to be the dean of the Faculty of Physics and Mathematics. Mickiewicz was to live in the university-owned building for the next two years. Before long he became fast friends with a few of its other young residents, like him petty gentrymen from the provinces for whom a university education constituted the only path to a decent livelihood.[1]

I

Founded as a Jesuit academy in 1578, the University of Vilnius was revived, after a period of decline, in 1803 as the Imperial University of Vilnius under the superintendentship of Prince Czartoryski. During the tenure of rector Jan Śniadecki (1807–1815), a mathematician, astronomer, Benthamite utilitarian, and unreconstructed rationalist, it became a beacon of Lithuania's belated Enlightenment. With Czartoryski's encouragement, Śniadecki managed to attract a stable of outstanding professors to the university, including his brother Jędrzej, a professor of chemistry and medicine, and also a talented satirist; the renowned pathologist Józef Frank; Leon Borowski, a professor of aesthetics, poetics, and rhetoric; the classical philologist Gottfried Ernest Groddeck; and the historian Joachim Lelewel. (The latter two were also instrumental in developing a program of Orientalist studies that eventually produced some of the Russian Empire's leading Orientalists.) Over the course of about three decades, the university, well endowed and an imposing physical presence in the heart of Vilnius, became the focus of the city's cultural life. Its professors were involved in publishing periodicals, organizing charitable societies, and since practically all were members, reforming the city's Masonic movement. The high-spirited among them joined a few of their more enlightened gentry compatriots in founding the Society of Rogues, which through its organ, *The Sidewalk News*, hoped to jolt the backward province into modernity with mockery and satire. At the time of Mickiewicz's enrollment, the university had emerged as the most progressive institution of higher learning in the Polish lands.

Aside from the university, though, Vilnius itself was not much to speak of: "A lot of pride... and few amenities," as one memoirist put it. From the perspective of Warsaw, the capital of the Congress Kingdom and the center of Poland's cultural establishment, it was little more than an occasion for a witticism about the sticks. A provincial capital, Vilnius was indeed provincial, with a population of about 46,000 that had grown little over the previous two centuries. To be sure, the presence in the city of the regional high court drew gentry from the surrounding countryside, particularly during Carnival. Yet few streets were paved, there were no sidewalks, and the city was illuminated only on special occasions, such as the visit that fall of Emperor Alexander I, the new king of the recently created Congress Kingdom of Poland. In the years Mickiewicz lived there, Vilnius did not even have a decent theater, but it did, thanks again to the university, have a botanical garden. There were also a few salons, most prominently that of Salomea Bécu, the mother of Mickiewicz's future rival in poetry Juliusz Słowacki. Although many of the buildings were still wooden (hence the periodic fires that over time destroyed many vestiges of its medieval and Renaissance past), the city's central core consisted of a remarkably uniform collection of stone buildings dating back to the seventeenth and eighteenth centuries. Above all, Vilnius was a city of churches, Protestant, Uniate, Orthodox, Catholic, as well as monasteries, reflecting the city's diverse religious and ethnic history. Germans, Belarusians, Lithuanians, Russians, and Poles lived side by side with a large Jewish community (some 40 percent of the population) as well as some Tatars—quite literally, since in Mickiewicz's time Vilnius was just beginning to expand beyond what had once been the walls of a compact medieval city. Of these, only one gate remained, the one housing the miracle-working icon of the Virgin of Ostrabrama.[2]

By virtue of its responsibility for public education in the lands of the grand duchy, the University of Vilnius had the task of training teachers for the district. An incentive in this regard was a stipend for prospective candidates, who for every year of study subsidized by the university were expected to teach two years in a district school after completing their education. For indigent students such as Mickiewicz, this arrangement was really the only viable option. Shortly after arriving in Vilnius, the sixteen-year-old youth from Nowogródek took the entrance exam to the teachers' program and was accepted, thanks in part to the protection of a distant kinsman.

Fig. 1 Adam Mickiewicz in 1823. Drawing by Kazimierz Kowalewski after a drawing by Walenty Wańkowicz. Courtesy of the National Museum in Cracow.

As part of his training, Mickiewicz was required to spend his first year taking courses in the faculty of mathematics and physical sciences, but from the beginning his chosen track was philology. His four years at the university thus consisted primarily of courses in the classics, which aside from Latin now included Greek; world history and historiography; aesthetics, literary theory, and rhetoric, which were at the same time courses in Polish literature as well as translation; French, English, German (the former two languages he mastered quite well while a student, the latter only after finishing the university); and classes in Russian language and literature, which, as his transcript notes, "he rarely attended."[3]

Three of his professors in Vilnius—Groddeck, Borowski, and Lelewel—left a lasting impression.

With the first, a partially polonized German from Gdańsk, Mickiewicz seems to have had something of a love-hate relationship. Groddeck could be imperious, rude, and thin-skinned (which is perhaps why he complained once that a "young man" such as Mickiewicz "should be a bit more polite"). He at one point suggested, to his student's amusement, that "devoting one's entire life to a commentary" on some unpublished classical author "would be the highest achievement, a supreme contribution." Nevertheless, Groddeck provided his students with a solid and in some respects innovative education in the classics. Thanks to him, Mickiewicz absorbed a classicist sensibility, replete with a stock of literary devices and references, that is palpable in all of his poetry. Even at its most romantic, it remains robust, lucid, and apprehensible.[4]

The relationship Mickiewicz had with his professor of aesthetics, poetics, and rhetoric was of a different nature. Although a neoclassicist at heart, Borowski was open to the newest (that is, romantic) literary currents seeping in from the West (England as well as Germany) and even polemicized on this account with Jan Śniadecki and the conservative literary establishment in Warsaw. Mickiewicz began attending his classes as an auditor during his first year and quickly drew Borowski's attention with the quality of his translations. "I remember," Mickiewicz recalled in 1844, "how powerfully moved I was when once in class he read, loudly and with feeling, one such translation and referred to me by name." Borowski devoted many hours outside of class helping Mickiewicz with pieces that the young writer never hesitated to bring for his perusal. That Mickiewicz continued to seek Borowski's opinion of the poetry he was writing in Kowno—by now radically romantic—and then later in Russia says much about how highly he valued his professor's advice, particularly when it came to "form and language." "Every time he sat down to write a poem," one of Mickiewicz's friends recalled, "he felt... the figure of Borowski beside him, who without any mercy for rhyme or poetic harmony... would chase down every unlogical thought, every unclear expression, every word used incorrectly."[5]

In Borowski, Mickiewicz found an understanding paternal figure who, unlike some others of his generation, did not feel threatened either by the young poet's brashness or talent. In the person of the historian Joachim Lelewel he found someone more akin to an older brother (he was twelve years Mickiewicz's senior), whose sensibility, particularly in matters concerning the nation's destiny, he shared. Romantic Poland's most outstanding historian—but less than outstanding politician—Lelewel was an adjunct instructor when Mickiewicz began attending his classes. Like his fellow students, he scrupulously recorded the historian's lectures and devoured his works. To what degree Lelewel conditioned the poet's views on history, both native and universal, is perhaps best evinced by the poem Mickiewicz wrote in honor of the historian upon the latter's appointment as a professor in 1822, a decision that electrified the entire Vilnius student body. In it, Mickiewicz condenses centuries of world history into a narrative marked by the struggle between forces of freedom and forces of tyranny and aggression, at one point addressing his professor:

> LELEWEL! each and everyone genuine pride expresses
> That the Polish fatherland produced a one like you.
> Radiating in the sacred office of historian,
> You show us what was, what is, and what will be.
>
> (Dz. 1:144)

But beyond his impact as a teacher, Lelewel became with time Mickiewicz's trusted protector, helping him publish his earliest efforts, recommending him for travel abroad and an appointment somewhere other than in Kowno (unsuccessfully in both instances), and posting bail after his arrest. As his plenipotentiary in Warsaw, he continued to watch over Mickiewicz's affairs during the latter's exile in Russia.

That Mickiewicz would go on to be a schoolteacher and later himself a professor of classic and then Slavic philology is indication enough of the kind of education he received at the University of Vilnius. His native intelligence and curiosity, bolstered by a prodigious memory, were at once guided and firmly anchored by an impressive command of the fundamentals of philology, historiography, philosophy, aesthetics, and even the natural sciences, something that only a first-class institution with first-rate professors can instill. This notwithstanding, Mickiewicz never actually graduated. Although he passed his qualifying exams, Groddeck refused to accept his master's thesis in 1821, "largely," Mickiewicz claimed, "because it had orthographic errors." There must surely have been other issues at stake here: a day after Mickiewicz's arrest in 1823, Groddeck "broke down in tears" in front of his class as he was commentating a passage in one of Demosthenes' *Philippics* describing Philip's arrests of Athenian notables. He was aware that his pupil had been working on a drama about the orator.[6]

But as decisive as Mickiewicz's academic training was for his intellectual development, the university provided him with something incalculably more valuable: a surrogate family.

2

"To my friends Jan Czeczot, Tomasz Zan, Józef Jeżowski, and Franciszek Malewski, as a souvenir of the happy moments of youth that I spent with them" (Dz. 1:52). The artlessness of this dedication in Mickiewicz's first volume of poetry (1822) is perhaps the most eloquent testimony to the intensity of feeling that bound the cohort of 1815. Czeczot, whom Mickiewicz befriended when the two were still attending school in Nowogródek, put the nature of this relationship more explicitly, in Ciceronian terms:

> We have the purest and most beautiful friendship, founded on what most links . . . persons who confide in each other in everything, and I mean everything: sincerity and frankness, the basis of which is genuine virtue, which sincerity, frankness, and the capacity to elicit them, that is, some similarity in upbringing, mores, education, and to a certain extent inclinations, engender.[7]

But Czeczot's was also a peculiar friendship, teetering uncomfortably between devotion and insecurity, hence often tinged with envy, jealousy, and self-righteousness. Zan's friendship, on the other hand, was as self-confident as it was blissfully selfless. A "gentle" but psychologically unstable youth with a propensity for "the mystical" (Dz. 3:123), he struck up a friendship with Mickiewicz when the two took the exam for the teachers' scholarship, which both agreed went to Mickiewicz because of his relative's pull. Mickiewicz, Czeczot (a.k.a. "Mentor"), and Zan (a.k.a. "Supremo") were soon joined by Jeżowski (a.k.a. "Hedgehog"), a talented classicist who was as sickly as he was Spartan and at times overbearingly pedantic; Malewski (a.k.a. "Vegetarian"), the son of the recently appointed rector of the university and perhaps the most balanced of them all, who in time became Mickiewicz's closest friend; and also by the earthy Onufry Pietraszkiewicz (a.k.a. "Onufr"/"Nufr"), thanks to whose instincts as an archivist we know so much about these friendships and this entire period in Mickiewicz's life.*

All of them came from similar provincial, for the most part impecunious, petty gentry backgrounds. A good education was their only hope for survival in a society still dominated by old blood, if not necessarily money. Although they ranged rather widely in age (Pietraszkiewicz was born in 1793, Malewski in 1800), for all of them the final partition of Poland was a painful albeit consummated fact, and its predicament weighed heavily on the course and contours of their development. The Napoleonic adventure of 1812, with its grandiloquent promise of reversing Polish history, affected them all profoundly—Mickiewicz was not the only one to add the emperor's name to his. But

*Pietraszkiewicz presciently hid the entire archive of the group after its members' arrests, thus preserving a remarkably detailed picture of their activities from 1817 to 1824.

more than just a cohort, they represented the first Polish generation to consciously and programmatically acknowledge itself as such; indeed, the first to transform the attributes of *youth* into a signifier of *generation* and thus imbue both notions with radically new meaning.

As the students gravitated toward each other in search of help with course work and in meeting everyday material needs, each recognized in the others a kindred sensibility, in literature and philosophy, in humor and forms of entertainment, in friendship, and in matters of love, and the same aspirations when it came to defining their duties as citizens of a stateless nation. Situated in the interstice between the Napoleonic generation of neoclassicists and those for whom Byron was already a given, they worshipped Horace ("'most gentleman-like of Roman poets'"), Marcus Aurelius ("the father of a million children, [who] himself restrains the fire of his intensity" [Dz. 3:282]), Voltaire (as author of *La Pucelle d'Orléans*), Rousseau (as author of *Émile* and *La Nouvelle Héloïse*), and the Polish classicist Stanisław Trembecki ("a joy to memorize"), while at the same time discovering Schiller (who "affects youth through emotion"), Goethe's *Werther* (full of "ardor and tears" [Dz. 3:48]), and Byron (whose "passions, like the *fatum* of the ancients, . . . governed his entire physical and moral life" [Dz. 5:178]).[8]

Just as saliently, though, theirs was a vision of Poland that in many ways differed little from the program espoused by their enlightened Masonic elders: that the nation's survival depended not on pedigree, but on civic responsibility and moral uprightness, which, in turn, was a function of education. Rector Malewski himself drove this point home in one of his first directives. He forbade his students to "frequent inns, billiard parlors, coffee houses, parties, soirées, and similar public establishments," to hunt, to gamble, or to duel, that is, engage in any activity that might distract them from their studies. But where the old diverged from the young, and diverged fundamentally, was in the question of who was to effect this program and how. The immediate answer of Mickiewicz and his cohort—the answer of youth—was to formalize their informal circle into a secret fraternity independent of their elders, something that Rector Malewski's directive forbade no less categorically.[9]

"As we got to know each other closer," confessed Jeżowski during his interrogation in 1824,

> and talked about our studies, about writers, and about books, Adam Mickiewicz, Tomasz Zan, Onufry Pietraszkiewicz, and I came to constitute a rather tight group or society. These contacts were so pleasant, made time go by so quickly, that often we would forget about our various troubles, particularly those resulting from our straitened circumstances. . . . So that our conversations would not be simply a pleasant form of idleness, we tossed around at various times the idea of drawing up some sort of statute so as to assume the character of a genuine society.

Their efforts led to the creation in the fall of 1817 of what the friends decided to call the Society of Philomaths (Lovers of Learning), its name inspired by the Parisian Societé de Philomatique, its form more by Prussian *Tugenbunden*. The society's inner circle, headed by the somewhat dictatorial Jeżowski, soon also included Malewski and Czeczot. Although it was not the only one of its kind in Vilnius, it was—and programmatically strove to be—the driving force of extracurricular life among the students of the university and even beyond. In its halcyon days between 1817 and 1819, the society was the focus of, quite literally, Mickiewicz's everyday existence. There were periods when meetings of one sort or another were held practically every evening. Its history is inextricably intertwined with his life in those years, and in the context of the society's activities, Mickiewicz evolved as a thinker, organizer, and writer. Indeed, the Philomaths remained a constant, and in some respects even more indispensable, presence during his time in Kowno. His closest friends, they were always a principal point of reference, a source of moral (and often financial) support, and, at times, annoyingly cloying constraint.[10]

The aims of the society, largely unchanged over the course of some six years, are best summed up by the opening paragraph of its statute for the 1819/1820 academic year:

> To inculcate among Polish youth feelings of pure morality; to maintain among them a love for things native; to awaken in them a desire for learning; to support them in the difficult avocation of intellectual improvement by providing all possible mutual help; to further strengthen the salutary ties engendered by coincidence in age and upbringing; to raise, to the best of one's power, the level of national education, and in this way work for the good and prosperity of the land.

These principles were not altogether inconsistent with the general program of Vilnius's Freemasons nor, for that matter, with Alexander I's initially relatively liberal policies in the grand duchy. To be sure, outsiders occasionally attempted to influence the Philomaths in a more conspiratorial direction, and individual members, including Mickiewicz, showed some interest in cooperating with the secret societies of their elders, although fear of cooptation restrained them. There is no evidence, however, that the Philomaths were themselves involved in any conspiratorial activity. Nevertheless, they insisted on secrecy, aware that their aims could be construed as threatening—be it to the local power structure, dominated as it was by conservative as well as clerical elements, or, more perilously, to imperial rule in Lithuania. To this end, the Philomaths remained exclusive, never growing beyond the original inner circle of bosom friends and a dozen or so close associates.[11]

Besides expending inordinate amounts of energy on tinkering with their bylaws, proposing new projects, and reassessing the society's program, the Philomaths devoted their twice and sometimes thrice-weekly meetings to formal presentations by members. These were then critiqued, discussed, and voted on, all according to strict protocol. This was, in essence, a society of young scholars or, as their contemporaries preferred to call them, "pedants," who "could solve every math problem, . . . commentate Homer, Plato, and Aristotle, and enter into theological and philosophical disputes with Spinoza, Wolff, Leibnitz, or Locke." Organized into two sections—literature and the liberal arts, and mathematics, physics, and medicine—they lectured each other on topics ranging from originality, Provençal poetry, "the influence of Greek religion on the state of society in the heroic period," and "how one should choose a scholarly discipline in order to be constantly devoted to it and what care one should take so that the discipline be effectively assimilated" to theories of electricity and color, the classification of the mathematical sciences, and tails of comets. There were group projects as well: summaries of articles from foreign journals, commentaries on classical authors intended, eventually, for use in regional schools, the translation of Johann Georg Sulzer's *Allgemeine Theorie der schönen Künste*, and so forth. And then there were *belles lettres*—poems, stories, tragedies, translations—at which, for better or worse, most members tried their hand. These were critiqued, discussed, and approved in the same "pedantic" manner as the scholarly reports. In order to underscore the egalitarian principles of the society, the members were ordered (by Jeżowski, of course) to wear to their meetings "a black dress coat with either black or cloth buttons, with a waistcoat of black cloth and buttons of the same, a black ascot around the neck, black pants, and shoes without tassels." (Since most of the cohort could barely afford a pair of nankeen underwear, this directive was probably not strictly enforced.) All of these proceedings were recorded with obsessive scrupulousness, as if in inverse proportion to their actual importance.[12]

Together with Jeżowski and Malewski, Mickiewicz was particularly active in formulating the society's objectives, suggesting projects, instructions, and revisions of statutes that were almost bureaucratic in their attention to organizational formalities—the son of a lawyer, after all. Like other members, he too prepared scholarly reports ("How to derive synonyms," "On the best way of solving geometrical problems and theorems," "The goal we should set in cultivating our mind," "On beauty"), literary analyses (of Voltaire, d'Arnaud), and critiques of fellow members' contributions. Among his efforts in this arena was a rather scathing review of a Polish neoclassicist epic that, upon Lelewel's recommendation, Mickiewicz managed to place in a Warsaw journal in 1819, a coup considering that Warsaw was still the unchallenged capital of neoclassicist correctness. But it was Mickiewicz's own poems, stories, translations, and improvisations that secured his reputation among the Philomaths.[13]

As early as 1817, in his report on the Philomaths' activities during that year, Jeżowski singled out Mickiewicz for his poetic talents. His praise was occasioned by his colleague's translation of excerpts from Voltaire's blasphemous *Pucelle* (*Dz.* 2:223–32): "Anyone," he noted, "who could translate such a poem into our native language with ease . . . must possess a bit of that creative fire which burned in the author of the original." Indeed,

Fig. 2 Franciszek Malewski. Rotograph after a drawing by Walenty Wańkowicz, ca. 1823. From *Z filareckiego świata. Zbiór wspomnień z lat 1816–1824*, ed. Henryk Mościcki (Warsaw, 1924).

a good portion of the poetic work Mickiewicz submitted for the society's approval in the first two years of its existence was either explicitly "in imitation of Voltaire" (e.g., "Mieszko, Prince of Nowogródek" [Dz. 2:207–17] and "Lady Aniela" [Dz. 2:119–22], both based on stories from *Contes en vers*) or inspired by him (the unfinished mock-epic "The Potato" [Dz. 2:233–51], in which the tuber literally weighs in on deciding Columbus's voyage to the New World). As for all of his brethren, the writings of this most impenitent of the French rationalists constituted for Mickiewicz a provocatively liberating vehicle for expressing his own oppugnance to the sociocultural backwardness still gripping Lithuania, his own sense of freedom, and a kind of sophisticated cosmopolitanism. The fact that this same Voltaire was the intellectual soulmate of Catherine II and fawningly "praised the partition of Poland as 'noble' and 'useful' work" did not, somehow, seem to bother the Philomaths.[14]

But there were other inspirations and other creative solutions: the poem "City Winter" (Dz. 1:35–37), a deft exercise in neoclassicist poetics à la Trembecki and the first of Mickiewicz's works to appear in print (in 1818); the mock-heroic "Checkers" (Dz. 1:130–39), written for Malewski and inspired by Marco Girolamo Vida's *Scacchia Ludus* (1527);* the tragedy "Demosthenes," over which Mickiewicz labored for some four years before never finishing it; the Petrarchan sonnet "Remembrance" (Dz. 1:139–40), an intimation of a formal predilection that would effloresce during the poet's exile in Russia; and the short story "Żywila" (Dz. 5:63–68), whose eponymous heroine was the first in a series of Mickiewicz's literary depictions of strong, patriotic Polish-Lithuanian women willing to sacrifice themselves for their people. Purporting to be an excerpt from a medieval Slavic chronicle—such mystifications were common enough at the time—it is not surprising that "Żywila" should draw on local Lithuanian color. But then so too did Mickiewicz's reworkings of Voltaire, which brim with references to regional historic and natural landmarks. Although not quite yet a programmatic statement, this decidedly unclassicist fascination with the provincially native as well as the medieval foreshadowed what would become programmatically romantic soon enough.

All of these early efforts—with the exception, perhaps, of the clever, and overtly patriotic, advertisement Mickiewicz composed for a brand of Polish sealing-wax in 1819 (Dz. 1:452)—were to a large extent written as exercises, classicist *imitatio* in the best sense of the word, to be evaluated, however, not so much by professors, by authoritative elders, but rather by peers with similar sensibilities, those whose attention and approbation mattered most to the young poet. And pay attention they did—to a voice that was remarkably mature, self-confident, and at times daring, certainly head and shoulders above the puerile stammerings of Pietraszkiewicz, Czeczot, and Zan. Most important, this voice belonged

*There was also a Polish version of Vida's *Game of Chess* written in the 1560s by Poland's greatest Renaissance poet, Jan Kochanowski, a great favorite of Mickiewicz.

to one of the cohort, to *their* poet, to someone who spoke for and about *their* generation—a poet, as Jeżowski proclaimed, for whom "laurels were undoubtedly waiting."[15]

And it was in this connection that yet another side to Mickiewicz's early work emerged. It was produced exclusively for the Philomaths, in most cases with no thought of eventual publication.

As befitted a fraternity devoted to shaping the well-rounded individual—intellectually, morally, through friendship, and through appeals to civic duty—the Philomaths also developed modes of play that were envisaged as no less an integral part of their program than scholarly reports and debates about organizational matters. Each member's name-day became an occasion for a fête, to which everyone contributed according to his talents and means. In warm weather they were held in the glades that surrounded the city, where the Philomaths liked to go for walks and (apparently unregulated) horseplay; in the winter—Mickiewicz's name-day fell on 24 December—at some convenient locale within the city walls. For Pietraszkiewicz's, on 30 May 1819, Mickiewicz and another Philomath intimate prepared

> a lean-to of branches in the forest leading up the hill along steps made of tamped-down earth and illuminated with lanterns up to [a depiction of] Onufry's age, which was woven out of leaves and wildflowers and hung from a tree; opposite the lean-to, on a hill between bushes, there could be seen by the light of a lamp a painting depicting Onufry and Tomasz doing Onufry's well-known dance, which they were wont to perform when drink renders the head gay and the feet nimble. From the painting, in the direction of a glen filled with water, there led a path made especially for the occasion, called the Roman Road.

Everyone hid in the forest. As Pietraszkiewicz was led to the site, Zan, unseen, began playing a flute, whereupon the entire company jumped out yelling "Vivat Onufr!" Wine, more "vivats," and then Czeczot, Zan, and Mickiewicz began singing songs and reciting "iambs," poems written especially for such occasions. Like all such adolescent wordplay, they poked fun at the name-day boy, more often than not in terms that were comprehensible only to the initiated, while at the same time constituting a kind of informal review of his activity in the fraternity.[16]

For all of their seemingly spontaneous gaiety, these fêtes were rituals, as regular, and in a sense as regulated, as the Philomaths' weekly meetings. They served as a periodic reminder, and hence guarantee, of what bound the group together. It was for just such a fête that Mickiewicz, inspired by Masonic ritual, wrote a hymn that by its very context no less than content captured the Philomath experience:

> Hey, eyes will flash with joy,
> A wreath our brows adorn,

And all will lovingly embrace:
We're brothers all! All one!

Flattery, duplicity, and excess,
Let everyone deposit at the door,
Because here we make a shrine eternal
To knowledge, fatherland, and virtue.

Bound by the torch of brotherhood,
Let us unveil our hearts,
Let us disclose our feelings and our fancies.
What is revealed here is a sacred trust!

Here common ills are soothed:
By friendship, gaiety, and song.

But whosoever be a member of our circle,
Be it in work or when at play,
Be it when plowing or in glory,
He shall our *Bylaws* all the while obey!
(Dz. 1:41)

Not surprisingly, when in 1820 Mickiewicz learned that this particular hymn had leaked out of the tight circle of his Philomath intimates and was being sung openly ("stupidly," as he said) at "May fêtes" that Zan had organized for a wider student public, he was not particularly pleased; that at these same fêtes students were overheard talking "about freeing the fatherland from its chains" disquieted him.[17]

This notwithstanding, since 1819 the Philomaths, nudged in part by Mickiewicz himself, had been seeking, cautiously and in secrecy, to disseminate their program among the student masses. To this end, they either moved to co-opt existing student societies or, more forcefully, began sponsoring affiliates of their own—the Club, the Literary Society, the Association of Friends, the Association of Philadelphists, the Scholarly Association, the Association of Local Naturalists—with a view toward exploiting them as a pool from which to recruit potential members. The success of Zan's fêtes—in effect happenings, held openly, that combined play and lecture and drinking milk with mystically tinged *communitas*—forced them to reassess their initial caution. Taking advantage of the unexpected resonance of their message among the students of Vilnius, they acted quickly to organize them in their own image.

The most successful undertaking in this respect was the creation in 1820 of a society called the Philareths (Lovers of Virtue), with Zan at its head. Mickiewicz, for his part, proposed the statutes and even wrote a song they could call their own, one explicitly modeled on the drinking songs of German *Burschenschaften*, with no less radical implications:

> Hey, let's live life to its fullest!
> After all, we only have one life to live. . . .
>
> Why all the foreign tongues here,
> We're drinking Polish mead;
> Far better is our folk's song
> Far better, too, our kith and kin.
>
> You've crawled into piles of Greek
> And Roman books, not to rot,
> But to play just like the Greeks did
> And like the Romans to smite and fight. . . .
>
> Apply your compass, scale, and ruler
> To move this unmovable mass;
> Measure your strengths against your aspirations,
> Not your aspirations against your strengths.
>
> (Dz. 1:44–46)

Before long, Philomath notions of virtue, learning, civic duty, love of country, friendship, and generational solidarity, or, as Mickiewicz put it, of "simplicity of manner, familiarity, and sincerity," became, in the words of a student of the time, "a stimulus . . . not only for improving academic work, but . . . a model for moral behavior"—and an articulation of youthful rebellion. However it was ultimately interpreted, what the Philomaths had to offer found avid buyers among a Lithuanian youth eager to create their own narrative of Poland's future.[18]

It is this narrative that Mickiewicz adumbrated most explicitly in his 1820 hymn "To Youth":

> Bereft of heart, bereft of spirit, these are but skeletons of men;
> Youth! give me wings!
> So I can soar above this lifeless world
> Into illusion's Edenic realm:
> Where ardor miracles creates. . . .
>
> Let him whom age befuddles,
> Bowing down his furrowed brow,
> See only that horizon
> Which he inscribes with earthbound eyes. . . .

Together, youthful friends!...
The happiness of all is everybody's aim;
Strong in unity, wise in madness,
Together, youthful friends!...

Reach where vision reaches not;
Force what the mind will not force;
Youth! Your power is your eagles' flight,
Like thunder is your arm....

The impassive ice is vanishing,
So are the superstitions which dim the sun;
Welcome, O morning star of liberty,
What comes now is salvation's sun!
(Dz. 1:42–44)

Although replete with familiar allusions to classical mythology and Masonic symbolism, the hymn nonetheless contained images that at first baffled Mickiewicz's friends. "I read it out loud," wrote Czeczot to Mickiewicz,

> it's a bit unreadable and even hinders such a reading; I read it to myself, and even this is an *impedimentum*. I read it, biased. So I think to myself: why is that Adam exerting himself so, why is he forcing such peculiar thoughts and expressions. I finished reading.

"I don't understand it," Czeczot admitted to Malewski. The latter, though, familiar as he was with German culture, grasped the import of the poem immediately, describing it as "Schiller's goddaughter," full of "*Andacht*." "This is what I call ardor, thought, poetry!" he told Czeczot,

> You won't find stuff like this even on a bon-bon. No Pole has ever written this way before. It captures Schiller perfectly. The latter always soars toward the ideal, everything on earth for him is ugly, leaden, unpleasant; he builds for himself a world of imagination and would prefer to always inhabit it.[19]

Copied and recopied among the youths of Vilnius, and soon enough beyond, what came to be known as "Ode to Youth" became the hymn of a generation. Paraphrased, reconfigured, and adapted to the circumstances, critiqued and parodied and scoffed at, it midwifed generations of young Poles to come. In its impatience with the status quo and its insistence on the capacity of an idealistic few to transform it through the power of imagination, the poem defines the very essence of Polish romanticism—and, as such, of the modern Polish mind.

3

In the late summer of 1819, as he was exploring the countryside around Nowogródek with his friends, Mickiewicz learned that he had been appointed to teach "literature, history, and law" in the district school in Kowno. This was by no means a choice assignment, considering that he had been entertaining more prestigious possibilities. Situated some 130 kilometers northeast of Vilnius, with views of the Niemen River and the Congress Kingdom on the opposite bank, Kowno was not much larger than Nowogródek, and no less provincial. As a teacher there Mickiewicz would earn 300 rubles a year. Board cost him about 10 rubles a month; a dress coat, about 21 rubles; the trip from Kowno to Vilnius, almost 3.[20]

The new schoolteacher settled into a room in the former Jesuit Collegium situated in the town's main square. With the exception of the 1821/1822 academic year, he would live there until 1824.

The school in Kowno was of the same type as the one Mickiewicz had attended in Nowogródek, hence he was familiar with the general program, and his training at the university provided him with a solid foundation for educating provincial schoolboys. Nonetheless, the burden of organizing and teaching his own courses in grammar; ancient, world, and Polish history; natural and political law; rhetoric, poetics, and Latin and Roman literature to some fifty pupils in the upper four grades six days a week, every morning and every other afternoon, proved daunting. That the students were uncommonly "lacking in talent," "utterly Samogitian [i.e., hick] heads," made Mickiewicz's task thankless. But good Philomath that he was, he persevered, determined "to give the best lectures possible." He would get up at four in the morning—"and, by God, sometimes before four"—to prepare lessons, and his letters to his friends in Vilnius are full of requests not only for any books that could help him improve his courses, but also for material—above all commentaries to classical authors—that the Philomaths themselves might be interested in preparing (and thus also put at least one aspect of their program into practice). As the teacher in charge of the school library, he ordered books and subscribed to periodicals. At one point he persuaded his fraternity brethren to contribute books that could be given out as prizes at graduation. For the annual inspections by university officials, his students performed as well as could be expected, and the inspectors were invariably pleased, often singling out the new teacher for his dedication. There were days, however—many, in fact—when Mickiewicz would "come home from school . . . fretting about either the indocility or, more often, the imbecility of the students, . . . throw [himself] on the bed, and lie there for a few hours thinking nothing.... Add a few more ounces of this and one could go crazy or hang oneself."[21]

Separation from friends, with whom he had spent practically every day of his life for the past four years, as well as from Vilnius itself, made Mickiewicz's days in provincial Kowno especially depressing. "Boredom, tediousness, languor, sluggishness, etc.," he wrote to Jeżowski in the late fall of 1819; "what's certain is that if I remain [here] for another year or two—*requiem aeternam.*" He was quick to complain, with obvious relish, about various ailments: bad teeth, hemorrhoids, varieties of coughs, headaches, chest pains, and sore throats. "My cough is dry," Mickiewicz informed Jeżowski, so that the latter should know what to tell the pharmacist in Vilnius, "every now and again I bring up a piece of phlegm and then I experience relief." Smoking a pipe (a habit he indulged until the end of his life) was one remedy; and during a particularly bad spell so too was a five-day diet of herring and caviar. The state of his health, both physical and mental, worried his friends, perhaps more even than Mickiewicz himself. All soon came to believe that his only salvation was travel abroad, and barring this, at least transfer to a more hospitable teaching environment. To this end, they massaged the question of health for all it was worth.[22]

Despite the expense of traveling to Vilnius, Mickiewicz made every effort to spend holidays with his Philomath brethren; his summers in the Nowogródek area were devoted to seeing more of them than his family. Indeed, as Pietraszkiewicz reminded him, the Philomaths *were* his "family." But burdened by their own cares and responsibilities, his friends managed to make it to Kowno only rarely. They compensated, though—many times over—with correspondence. Over the course of four years, letters—at about 14 kopecks apiece—were dispatched and arrived almost daily, sometimes several at a time, from wherever members of the cohort happened to find themselves: Czeczot to Mickiewicz; Mickiewicz to Czeczot; Czeczot to Pietraszkiewicz; Pietraszkiewicz to Malewski; Malewski to Pietraszkiewicz and Jeżowski; Mickiewicz to Czeczot and Zan; Zan to the Philomaths; Zan, Jeżowski, Malewski, Pietraszkiewicz, and Czeczot to Mickiewicz; and then he to them. When Pietraszkiewicz moved to Warsaw to continue his studies or when Malewski received a scholarship to study in Germany, it was only the workings of postal services—as well as the nosiness of imperial postal inspectors—that affected the frequency of their correspondence. Even the cohort's imprisonment in 1823–1824 did not interrupt the flow.[23]

The letters were often numbingly prolix ("five sheets," "three and a half half-quires," "a sheet," "half a quire") and at times painfully, embarrassingly frank (particularly those between Czeczot and Mickiewicz and Mickiewicz and Zan). They touched on practically every aspect of their lives, from health and material worries to flirtations, Philomath matters, and the literature they were both consuming and producing, from musings about friendship to the newest gossip and weather, from mutual praise, encouragement, and moralistic lecturing to petty rivalries and envy. The most common refrain involved complaints that one or another was not writing as often or as much as he should, in response to which they would even "write for the sake of writing":

> But it's time to explain why I haven't written to you for so long. It's not those who are angry that don't write to you..., but those who have nothing to write to you about.... But maybe write one should. I've become disused to writing. There is no other reason to write to you except to write. For that reason I haven't written. I have nothing important to tell you, for there are others who know more and can tell you more; I don't feel like babbling god knows what and beginning the letter, as so often happens, with: *I want to write and don't know what to write.*

Thanks to this compulsion, no other period in Mickiewicz's life is as well documented—with the exception, tellingly enough, of his years as a sectarian, which were also marked by a sense of intense *communitas.*[24]

4

Although incessant communication with the Philomaths went a long way toward relieving Mickiewicz's "spleen," the first two years in Kowno were actually not as monotonously bleak as he so often made them out to be (like most sensitive young men, he knew how to play for sympathy and attention). In fact, they proved to be extremely productive. As Malewski wrote to his friend in January 1821, "The more despondent you are, the more you create."[25]

Mickiewicz continued to take an active part in Philomath affairs in his correspondence as well as on his occasional visits to Vilnius, contributing with earnestness and zeal to the society's organizational well-being. Concerned now especially with matters of outreach, he encouraged Zan to routinize his May happenings into a formal student society, for which he himself compiled the statutes. It was in this context too, at once of scholarship and civic duty, that he continued to work on his translation of *La Pucelle,* on his play "Demosthenes," on commentaries to classical as well as Polish authors, and planned a textbook of poetics for use in schools. None of this activity, however, proved as effective in articulating and disseminating Philomath ideals than the songs and hymns he composed at this time. "Hey, Eyes Will Flash with Joy...," "Ode to Youth," and "Song of the Philareths" imbued the Philomath program with a pithiness and an affective power that at once intuited and inspired the collective mood of Lithuania's youth. Yet alongside these expressions of late Enlightenment sensibility, another set of inspirations began to shape Mickiewicz's aesthetic disposition.

In June 1820, hoping to cheer his splenetic friend, Malewski wrote to Mickiewicz, "Schiller's youth was similar to yours!... Maybe Kowno will be for you what the oppression and poverty in the military academy were for Schiller." A flattering comparison, particularly for someone who since at least 1818, and with a still rather anemic command of German, had been captivated by one of the genitors of European romanticism. A collection of Schiller's songs and ballads in Polish translation appeared that year in Lwów (Lviv) and Mickiewicz, it seems, had written a letter to the translator expressing his gratitude for introducing him to the poet. As his German improved, he would refuse to part with the copies of Schiller that Malewski would send him from Vilnius, claiming that "reciting [the German poet] distracts [his] agitated imagination." "Ode to Youth" was one upshot of this engagement; a series of ballads written between 1819 and 1821 was another.[26]

Mickiewicz was not the first in his circle to begin exploring this quintessentially romantic genre. Zan, then Czeczot and Pietraszkiewicz, increasingly fascinated with the culture of the Belarusian and Lithuanian peasant as well as by the nature and historical artifacts of the Lithuanian countryside, produced ballads that as early as 1818 were presented for discussion at Philomath meetings. They drew their inspiration in part from stylizations of English ballads by Polish pre-romantics, but they were also familiar with the ballads of Goethe, with Gottfried August Bürger's "Lenore" (as well as recent Russian reworkings of the latter) and, of course, with Schiller. Mickiewicz was quick to grasp the possibilities of the genre. He tried his hand at rendering Schiller's "*Handschuh*" [The glove] into Polish and, as if engaging in some sort of contest, wrote several ballads on topics already treated by his friends: the mysterious Lake Świteź near Nowogródek; the necromancer Twardowski, a kind of Polish Dr. Faustus. In doing so, he not only surpassed them with the inventiveness, vitality, and sophistication of his poetic language, but transformed the genre into a vehicle for articulating a radically new sensibility.

In the 1821 ballad entitled, appropriately enough, "Romanticism" and, no less appropriately, with an epigraph from Shakespeare ("Methinks I see... where?—In my mind's eyes"), the narrator turns to address "an old man" mockingly skeptical of folk superstitions:

> "Affect and faith speak more strongly to me
> Than the lens and the eye of a wise man.
>
> You know but dead truths, unknown to the folk,
> You observe the world in speckles of dust, in every flash of a star.
> You can't grasp living truths, you will never a miracle see!
> Have a heart and gaze into the heart!"
>
> (Dz. 1:57)

Written as a programmatic riposte to a vitriolic 1819 critique of romanticism by the Vilnius professor Jan Śniadecki, Lithuania's paragon of enlightened rationalism, "Romanticism," like "Ode to Youth," constituted a brash youth's challenge to a sociocultural elite whose lessons he had internalized only to question their premise. Many years later, Mickiewicz

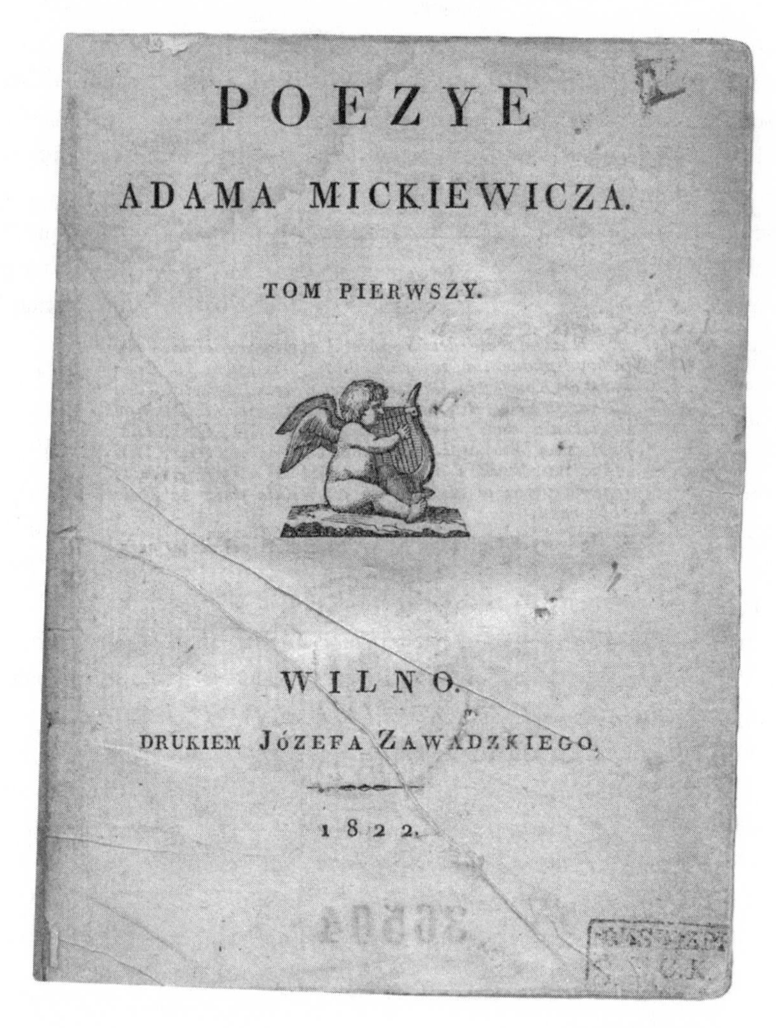

POEZYE

ADAMA MICKIEWICZA.

TOM PIERWSZY.

WILNO.

DRUKIEM JÓZEFA ZAWADZKIEGO.

1822.

Fig. 3 Title page of Mickiewicz's *Poems*, volume 1. Courtesy of the Adam Mickiewicz Museum of Literature, Warsaw.

confided that "the seed of [his] future poetry [may] already [be found] in 'Romanticism': 'affect and faith.'" This was said, to be sure, with the benefit, as well as blindness, of hindsight. Yet this notwithstanding, all of the ballads he wrote during those first two years in Kowno—and "Romanticism" is simply the most explicit in this regard—evoked a world in which the rational and the arational share the same space, their boundaries blurred and even provocatively transgressed. Although the justification for this dialectic of reason and affect derived from a recognition of the "savage mind" on the part of a child of the Enlightenment, refracted through the idealism of early German romanticism, it adumbrated what is arguably the pith of Mickiewicz's psyche—an intuitive openness to the supernatural.[27]

The ballads—ten in all—together with two sentimentalist idylls subtitled "romances," came to constitute *Ballads and Romances*, the first part of Mickiewicz's debut volume, entitled simply *Poems*, volume 1. They were prefaced by yet another programmatic poem, "The Primrose," which signaled the novelty of the collection with weighted oppositions familiar from "Ode to Youth": winter and springtime, ice and ardency, quiescence and energy. The second part of the volume consisted of "Various Poems" (four of them), including the early "Checkers" and "Remembrance." Mickiewicz wanted to include "Ode to Youth" here as well, but the censor, not surprisingly, demurred. The entire collection was introduced by an extensive foreword (later entitled "On Romantic Poetry"), which offered a learned young man's overview of poetic systems from ancient Greece to Mickiewicz's present in order to legitimate romanticism as a mode of poetic expression. Although the essay was meant to be an intervention into the intensifying Polish debate about the meaning and implications of romanticism, it refrained from responding directly to its detractors. Mickiewicz, it seems, felt more comfortable—and more confident—letting his poetry speak for itself—which, in any case, it did far more convincingly, as a *fait accompli*.

The appearance of the first volume of *Poems*, and quite possibly even the very idea of the book, was an enterprise that involved the entire Philomath cohort, but above all Czeczot, who was particularly solicitous in guiding the book through print. Since its eventual publisher, the Vilnius bookseller Józef Zawadzki, was at first none too eager to purchase the manuscript outright—"You see," he told Mickiewicz, "people don't write poetry in Vilnius but in Warsaw"—Mickiewicz organized a subscription drive, albeit without any public fanfare, afraid, as a friend put it, of "caustic gibes" from Vilnius's cultural establishment. To this end, the Philomaths mobilized dozens of their Philareth acolytes and in this way managed to penetrate not only the Lithuanian market, but also the Congress Kingdom and even Galicia. The cost was 10 złotys for what was projected to be a three-volume set. All told, the poet and his friends enlisted 383 subscribers, including even a few established literary figures from Warsaw. Complimentary copies were promised to the superintendent of Vilnius schools Prince Czartoryski, to Professors Borowski and Lelewel, but not, for some reason, to Groddeck. The drive's success impressed Zawadzki, who finally agreed to pay for the printing by advancing Mickiewicz 100 rubles for his (never completed) textbook on poetics. On 25 May/6 June 1822 the censor signed off on the manuscript, and *Poems*, volume 1, appeared in Vilnius a few days later in a printing of some 500 copies.[28]

A month later, Mickiewicz could already report to Malewski that from what he had heard, *Ballads and Romances* "were pretty well received and read." This was a modest understatement: within five months, only a few copies of the volume remained. In August, Pietraszkiewicz wrote to Mickiewicz that he had had to order fifteen more copies for Warsaw, since "the one copy" that was circulating among the capital's *haute monde* "was snatched up, read, and liked immensely." In early December, Czeczot informed Mickiewicz that the volume was quite a hit in Warsaw, where they were calling the poet "a Lithuanian Walter Scott."[29]

Although the comparison is a good indication of the Varsovites' perspective on Vilnius, it was in Warsaw that Mickiewicz's volume rated its first and only review:

> Originality, simplicity, a beautiful and robust composition of verse, a lively, fiery imagination and a daring imagination expressed in a way that is remarkable—these are the main features of this young and very promising poet's work.

Malewski, who at this time was traveling in Europe on a scholarship, wrote from Prague to tell his friend, "You won't believe how that one volume of mine circulated. . . . It was copied helter-skelter." By 1823, *Poems* had made its way to Russia, where it "interested Russian writers in the extreme, including [the father of the Russian romantic ballad Vasilii A.] Zhukovskii, who [was] in raptures over the inventiveness and formal grace of . . . the poetry; everyone [was] eagerly awaiting the next volumes." Mickiewicz, for his part, was pleased to remember years later that "the first person who sincerely liked these poems was the typesetter printing them; his name was Bończyk."[30]

But to rephrase an old saw, the highest form of appreciation is imitation. The appearance of *Ballads and Romances*, a collection that in effect sought to legitimate a new sensibility by showcasing the genre that in many ways defined it, triggered an outbreak of balladomania in Polish letters. For better or, as these things usually go, for worse, aspiring poets—and composers—began pumping out ballads as a manifestation of both literary rebellion and sophistication. At the same time, the fashion impelled them to explore, however superficially, medieval chronicles, regional geography, and above all the songs and legends of the Polish as well as Lithuanian, Belarusian, and Ukrainian folk. The ballad became an adit to the Polish unconscious.

Whether out of smugness or bemusement, Warsaw's neoclassicist arbiters of literary taste chose at first to ignore Mickiewicz's debut. But as a second printing of *Poems* appeared in early 1823, and as ballads from all over the Polish lands began flooding into editorial offices, it became increasingly clear that this thing called romanticism was more than just some misguided fad from the provinces. Slight would no longer be an option when later that year Mickiewicz published *Poems*, volume 2. The works it contained not only returned defiantly to the world of the folk imagination and of medieval chronicles, but provoked even further with an exploration of romantic love.

5

Mickiewicz wrote what appears to be his first ballad, the humorously self-referential "I Like It," at the very end of 1819. It was addressed (at that time) to a certain Johasia. But who this Johasia (Johalka, Joasia, Johanka, Joanka) was, what her relationship with the poet may have been, even her last name, remain obscure. In a letter of May 1820 the poet expressed a desire to have the ballad printed separately, since he "had to send [a copy] to Johasia, for whom [he] had written it." Much later in life, Mickiewicz reminisced about a certain Józia, whom still as a schoolboy he "espied sitting on a sheaf with a guitar, singing with a strong, pure voice." "My love for [her]," he maintained, "had nothing lustful about it: I liked sitting next to her, exuding as she did so much freshness and life." But whether this Józia is yet another hypostasis of Johasia, this, too, is not altogether clear.[31]

There was also a certain Aniela (again, last name unknown), with whom the poet became involved during his first year in Vilnius. Her love, however, was more than he was prepared for. "I found her overjoyed at my arrival," Mickiewicz informed Czeczot about one particularly emotional encounter, but "that joy frightened me terribly: I had to destroy it." Aniela, it seems, was pressuring Mickiewicz into marriage before her departure from Vilnius, and it was only after an afternoon of recriminations, tears, and kisses that he managed to persuade her that they should simply wait out their separation. There is a palpable sense of relief in his description of the scene, although Czeczot still refers to Aniela as the poet's "beloved" as late as 1819, when Mickiewicz was already in Kowno. But this appears to be the last reference to her. In any case, this was the first, but certainly not the last, time that Mickiewicz's unwillingness to commit would be the cause of a woman's distress.[32]

Commitment, though, but only of a sort, was never an issue in Mickiewicz's relationship with Karolina Kowalska, the poet's first serious erotic attachment, whose affections proved even more efficacious in alleviating his melancholy in Kowno than correspondence with his friends. Née Wegner, from a prosperous Vilnius burgher family, she was either three or five years older than Mickiewicz and a mother of four when he arrived in Kowno. With her husband, the regional doctor, she lived directly across the square from Mickiewicz's room in the collegium, whence he could thus see who from the Kowalski household was coming or going.

The Kowalskis quickly adopted the brooding but quick-witted and handsome twenty-year-old. They often invited him to supper, and he would spend evenings with them listening to Karolina on the piano and playing cards. On Sundays and holidays the threesome would go on excursions to the surrounding countryside. But Dr. Kowalski's duties had him going and coming a great deal of the time—and Karolina, by all accounts, was stunning. Upon meeting her for the first time, Malewski confessed that he "had nowhere to hide [his] eyes, for having glanced at her once, [he] was afraid to raise them again." As Antoni Edward Odyniec, a younger friend of Mickiewicz who would later position himself in the role of the poet's Eckermann, remembered it sixty years later, "It would be difficult to imagine a more beautiful woman than her."

> Her figure, features, glance, and smile could serve as a model for a sculptor or painter, all the more so since her very dress seemed to imitate artistic Greek tunics rather than

designs in fashion journals. She hardly ever went out socially, and at home she dressed according to her own tastes.

The cohort called her the Venus of Kowno; but they also referred to her as Cleopatra.[33]

In a letter to Czeczot, written in the winter of 1820, Mickiewicz described one of those weekend excursions, an aim of which was to pick up a packet of correspondence from his Vilnius friends:

> I sat [in the sleigh] with the beautiful Kowl. and drove her myself for half the trip. True, I didn't say much, but I peeked at her often beneath that damned hat of hers. We got out.... Anxious to read your letters, I run..., pick up the packet, return to my beautiful companion, whom not without regret I had abandoned in the tavern, rip open the packet, and read. In the meantime, they took utensils for making coffee out of the sleigh and made it in fancy pots, but I wasn't watching. Now they're pouring it, laughing and joking, and I won't forget to add that because there were not enough glasses to go around I drank out of the same cup with Kow. Your half-read letters, the peculiar contrast of the dirty tavern with the fête and, most of all, with... all sorts of associations and memories... put me into a truly romantic mood.

The letter crackles with joy, "so happy" was Mickiewicz in Kowno that day. It was in fact the sight of Kowalska preparing coffee herself one day that finally sealed the poet's attraction:

> Kow. never made much of an impression on me until the time I espied her blowing at the embers under a coffee pot! How's this? The intemperate blush, or, rather, the flush on her face would appear to the delicate eye to be lacking in romance, to be not all that prepossessing, but for me it revealed in her person an angel, a Venus, etc., etc.

This revelation was so powerful that Mickiewicz resolved not to visit the Kowalskis for the next two months. Within a year, however, he was sleeping with her regularly. "Imagine if you can," the poet wrote to Pietraszkiewicz after a night spent with Kowalska, "a goddess with hair playing down her shoulders, amidst white muslins, on a magnificent bed, in a beautiful room. I look at this goddess every day: all traces of aesthetics have vanished."[34]

The mention here of aesthetics has little to do with the treatises—Latin, Polish, German, French—that Mickiewicz the writer, scholar, and teacher was reading voraciously at the time. Rather, the term refers to the system, and vocabulary, of affect that Zan had developed out of his interest in Mesmerian animal magnetism. "Rays," that is, the invisible medium connecting two beings; "radiants," that is, adepts of Zan's theory; degrees on an "erotometer," that is, the measure of those rays (Kowalska's, apparently, rated 50°);

and "aesthetics," that is, affect pure and chaste—these were terms that thanks to Zan entered the Philomath lexicon of eros, male and female alike.[35]

And as much as he tried to assure his friends to the contrary, Mickiewicz's feelings toward Kowalska were anything but "aesthetic." On the contrary, they were, as he almost defiantly confessed to Jeżowski in the late fall of 1820, "very physical":

> I return a sign of affection with a sign of affection, but very calmly, and charms only tickle me and by no means make it to my heart. I return from a romantic conversation calmly. Since my organism, albeit a bit unrestrained, settles more easily than my imagination.[36]

Exactly how unrestrained may best be gauged by what occurred a few months later, on the first day of the Easter holidays in April 1821. Annoyed by the attention that another regular at the Kowalskis, a certain Nartowski, was paying to Karolina, Mickiewicz, son of Mikołaj and grandnephew of Bazyli and Adam, found a pretext during a game of boston to slap the fellow upside the head. As Nartowski was getting up to return the blow, Mickiewicz hurled a lantern at him. Mrs. Kowalska fainted, and when Dr. Kowalski ran into the room, Nartowski began accusing Mickiewicz of having an affair. The next day the poet received two challenges, one from Kowalski for offending his home, the other from Nartowski for personal insult and injury. After living "for three days on strong wine, tobacco, and bitter cheese," Mickiewicz wrote to his friends what he said might be his last letter from Kowno. But by the time several of them arrived from Vilnius to act as seconds, Karolina had managed to placate her husband. Nartowski, for his part, lost his nerve. No duel was fought, and Kowalska ordered Nartowski and Mickiewicz to avoid each other at her home. From descriptions of the entire episode, it is clear that Mickiewicz emerged the victor. "Adam was angelic, divine," wrote Malewski recounting the events to Jeżowski,

> his eyes shone with a brighter gleam, too, his person was somehow magnificent, pleased that peace had once again returned, proud that he had such a lover that he could show off so wonderfully in front of his friends, like a husband. At last our people got into the carriage, Kowalska came out to say good-bye; Adam, embracing his friends for the last time, said so that she could hear him: "*Peut-être, je combattrais pour vous.*" [Perhaps I fought for you all].[37]

There is something peculiar in this last declaration, just as there was, in fact, in Mickiewicz's description of his first moment of joy with Kowalska, with its curious juxtaposition of reading correspondence from his friends, the dirty tavern, and sharing a cup with Karolina. And indeed, a week after the aborted duel, the Philomaths received a poem from their friend that was anything but delicate in expressing an ostensible shift in his interests, if not necessarily affections. Increasingly larger doses of Byron at this time at once facilitated and sharpened its articulation. Entitled "The Sailor," the poem describes the struggles of an allegorical solo sailor with an allegorical storm and ends with the following lines:

> If I hurtle myself where flings me despair,
> There'll be tears at my madness, complaints that I'm thankless
> Because for you these storm clouds are much harder to see,
> Barely audible from afar are the winds that tug at the rigging,
> The thunder that resounds here is to you but a flash.
>
> And what I feel beneath these peals of thunder,
> Others would feel with me together, but in vain!
> Except for God, our fate is no one's to determine.
> If to judge me is what you want, not with me must you be but here inside me
> —You go on home, I'm sailing on.
>
> (Dz, 1:129–30)

"Unaesthetic" as Mickiewicz's entire affair with Kowalska may have been, the Philomaths had let it be, tolerating it insofar as it made their friend's life easier in Kowno and created an atmosphere conducive to creativity. They were even to some extent vicariously titillated by his erotic adventures. But the aborted duel was a bit too much, and they admonished him in their own self-righteous way, hoping "to extricate" him from what they perceived as the "meretricious" "clutches" of "a married woman." The poem, however, constituted a breach, a slight to values that lay at the very foundations of their community—friendship, civic devotion to the fatherland, and the capacity for sacrificing self for the good of the collective. Jeżowski was particularly blunt in his reaction:

> There is nothing easier than to play a hero of love. Half the world could take the stage if we had the time to list them all, from David on. What we need are not sofas, not cushions, not soft sheets, not bed curtains, not caresses. Friendship, work, tenacious and in common, self-discipline, perseverance, citizen-youths, the country, the fatherland, all these we should have before our eyes when sleeping and when awake. We need Brutuses, not Antonys.

Hence, Cleopatra.[38]

An erotic attachment to a married woman (or, for that matter, to any sexually active woman) was something the Philomaths could not quite fit into their program. Zan's vocabulary of love was, after all, but a puerile sublimation, meant more, perhaps, as a bond between male friends than a language for attracting the young ladies some of them taught and flirted with and fell hopelessly in love with at Mr. Deybel's *pension* in Vilnius. Thanks to Kowalska, Mickiewicz experienced a different, mature love, and by the same token came to understand that there were emotional needs that a collective could not satisfy. But he also learned that, like a mistress, a collective could be jealous and uncompromising in its demands.

6

As productive as the first two years in Kowno were creatively, with one exception there are no allusions to either the town nor its beautiful inhabitant in Mickiewicz's work from the period (the ballads are largely set amid the nature of the Nowogródek countryside). The exception is a reminiscence in the poetic tale *Grażyna*, which features Żywila's more mature literary sister, a heroic Lithuanian princess who, disguised in the armor of her husband, sacrifices her life defending her people against the Teutonic Knights.* At one point the poet describes a glen in Kowno, "Where a water nymph's palm, in spring and in summer, / Spreads greensward, embroidered with colorful flowers; / This is the most beautiful glen in the world" (Dz. 2:23). For some reason, Mickiewicz felt compelled to reiterate this fact in a note he appended to these lines: "A few versts from Kowno, in the mountains [in actuality, more like steep hills], there stretches a glen, decked with flowers and through which flows a stream. One of the most beautiful places in Lithuania" (Dz. 2:59)—to which one may add the following commentary from an 1821 letter to Czeczot: "I was at the glen yesterday . . . at two in the sweltering heat with a lady, who arrived later, having left the carriage by the road. I was this far from going crazy, and perhaps only the traipsing of peasants cutting twigs delivered me from unaesthetic temptations."[39]

Mickiewicz probably began writing *Grażyna* sometime in the summer of 1822. He did not finish it until December of that year, when after a year's sabbatical in Vilnius he was obliged to return to his teaching duties in Kowno. His work on the poem was interrupted by efforts to complete yet another piece he had begun writing as early as 1820, but which in the course of two years had grown and branched and mutated into the several parts of a poetic drama entitled *Forefathers' Eve*. Odyniec, who knew both Mickiewicz and his Kowno lover, suggested many years later that in the figure of Grażyna one can discern certain features reminiscent of Karolina Kowalska. However this may be, there is—and already at the time there was—no doubt as to the identity of the woman that the figure of Maryla in *Forefathers' Eve*, part 4, was meant to evoke. *Grażyna* and *Forefathers' Eve* appeared in 1823 side by side in *Poems*, volume 2. This may have not been a coincidence,

*Like the early Russian romantic Vasilii A. Zhukovskii, who made up the name *Svetlana* (from the Slavic root for "light," "bright") for his eponymous 1808 reworking of Bürger's "Lenore" and which subsequently became one of the most popular names for Russian women, Mickiewicz also made up the name *Grażyna* (from the Lithuanian root for "beauty"), which then too became an extremely popular name for Polish women.

since Mickiewicz's attraction to the two women whom the works ostensibly portray was also a parallel affair.[40]

During an excursion to the Nowogródek countryside in the summer of 1820, Mickiewicz and Zan paid a week-long visit to Tuhanowicze, the estate of the well-to-do Wereszczaka family. At the time the family consisted of a widowed matriarch, two sons, and a daughter. The older of the two brothers, Michał (or, rather, *Michel* to a family that communicated in French as much as they did in Polish), was an amateur historian, a collector of antiquities, a lover of flowers, and in general something of an eccentric. It is to him that Mickiewicz dedicated the ballad "Świteź," in which an expedition led by a character based on Wereszczaka fishes out "a creature" from a lake rumored to contain a sunken town (*Dz.* 157–64). But as much as both Mickiewicz and Zan enjoyed the company of Wereszczaka, his sister Maria—Marie, Maryla—also drew their attention. As Zan reported to Pietraszkiewicz in his naïvely earnest way:

> I had to . . . go to Tuhanowicze, where together with Adam an entire week went by most pleasantly, most happily. . . . In Tuhanowicze, not only with Adam, but with the genuinely kindhearted, radiant [in Zan's specific use of the word] Wereszczakas, with the radiant and oh-so-kind Maria, whom Adam himself admires, with whom Master Tomasz [Zan] learned several . . . songs and performed them, with whom he played chess, won and lost, to whom he sent the laws of radiance, who is kind and beautiful and pleasant. . . . A truly comfortable life: there are pears, there's coffee, there are apples, there's wine, there are sumptuous dinners, there's tea, there are horses, there's Maria. . . . Adam himself envied me a few times.[41]

That Maria made an impression on Mickiewicz as well is evident from a letter he addressed to Jeżowski, but only several months later. "Write to me, please," he asked his friend, "whether you can make it to the Wereszczakas."

> But take a lorgnette with you, the best one you have, and be a rigorous observer *qua* moral philosopher and *Kunstrichter*, and then write to me about every object! . . . If you could capture a characteristic feature, I'll like that feature, since it signifies a beautiful soul.

That same November, Mickiewicz wrote "Maryla's Grave Mound," one of the "romances" that appeared in *Poems*, volume 1. A sentimentalist pastoral, it depicts several rustics lamenting the death of the young shepherdess Maryla with the words, "You are no more, Maryla, no more" (*Dz.* 1:79–83). Yet until the summer of 1821, there is nothing in Mickiewicz's correspondence that would indicate that Maria Wereszczaka was really anything at all. His letters at this time are full of breathless references only to Kowalska, for whom he was all set, presumably, to fight and die. Nonetheless, there was something

Fig. 4 Maria Puttkamer née Wereszczaka. Contemporary miniature. Courtesy of the National Museum in Cracow.

in Maria that had stirred his imagination, and by all accounts, quite powerfully. According to Czeczot, who was none too kindly disposed to Kowalska, his friend's attraction to the good doctor's wife was in fact little more than compensation "for the absence of his beloved Maria, in whom he has recognized rays of up to 80° for some time now." Malewski too made note of Mickiewicz's fascination with the girl. In the same April 1821 letter in which he described the ado with Nartowski, he observed "that Maria has lodged in [Mickiewicz's] heart most powerfully, that for all his love for K., he can't rid himself of the other one." It would appear that Maria Wereszczaka's marriage two months earlier to Count Wawrzyniec Puttkamer (to whom she had been engaged since 1815) had worked like an aphrodisiac: a romantic object of desire precisely because it was unobtainable—and hence also unlikely to entail commitment.[42]

Maria Wereszczaka-Puttkamer was a year younger than Mickiewicz, but born on the same day. This in itself must have seemed tantalizingly significant to two young people who were both discovering the mysteries of love through the prism of *Young Werther*, *Valérie*, *La Nouvelle Héloïse* as well as Zan's theories of mutually attractive rays. As the love-stricken hero of *Forefathers' Eve*, part 4, puts it, "An identical star shown for us at birth" (Dz. 3:82). In contrast to Kowalska, Maria was by no means a beauty—plain, in fact, if one is to judge by portraits of her (including a miniature she gave Mickiewicz in 1821) and by descriptions of those who knew her: petite, with blue eyes, light curly hair, and a somewhat tuberous nose; there was, nonetheless, "a peculiar charm to her [round] mouth and gaze." From her letters, written in both passable French and slightly less passable Polish, she comes off as naïve and not particularly bright. Her "charm" appears to have been in part a function of her romantic pose, much of it assumed from sentimental novels and romantic poetry, although there were peculiar limits in this respect: told that Mickiewicz was thinking of undertaking a new translation of *Werther*, she let it be known that he should "fix Goethe's shortcomings in this work, who spoiled a most beautiful romance with a bad ending." In any case, as all who met her at the time attest, there was something captivating about this sensitive young woman who smoked a pipe, played chess with men, rode horses in solitude, had planted for her "a forest of somber firs and pines, trees of the tomb," and in general shared the Philomaths' sensibilities. They visited her often, exchanged books, sent her verses, which often contained allusions to "Maryla." They nicknamed her "Peri," a reflection of their growing interest in things oriental, in this case via Thomas Moore's *Lalla Rookh*.[43]

Her marriage in February 1821 to the slightly older Puttkamer, whose estate in Bolcieniki some 40 kilometers south of Vilnius became their primary residence, was dictated by financial considerations. Although the count was, by all accounts, kind, liked, and respected by all who knew him (including Mickiewicz), Maria did not love him. Now suddenly, "as [her] material envelope was chained" in Bolcieniki, her "restless soul flew toward" the figure of the poor schoolteacher from Kowno, in whom, she now realized, she had at last found a kindred spirit. With his dark good looks and propensity for melancholy, the young poet fueled fantasies already primed by various Werthers, Gustaves, and Saint-Preuxs. The two were ready to enact their own romantic narrative of transgressive love.[44]

Mickiewicz, as usual, spent the summer of 1821 in the Nowogródek region, but this time the circumstances were dramatically different, and not only because his purpose now was to explore the charms of Maria. In early October 1820, his mother Barbara had died. Afraid of exacerbating what they believed to be their friend's depression, the Philomaths as well as Mickiewicz's own brothers kept the news from him until his holiday visit to Vilnius two months later. The poet's reaction, at least as expressed in a February 1821 letter to Pietraszkiewicz in Warsaw, was remarkable for its detached thoughtfulness, its expressions of guilt, its sense of liberation, its self-centeredness:

> This event has no small impact on my future life. Mother was at once my greatest worry and greatest solace and greatest comfort! I couldn't help her in anything, but I comforted myself with the hope that maybe one day my good fortune would be a source of relief to her as well, and of happiness. Those dreams have gone up in smoke! I'm alone now. Nothing much ties me down anymore. I'll help my brothers a bit, otherwise I'm alone. That's why I've made a definite decision to abandon my teaching position and hook myself up to anything. Keep any eye out for anything that can be managed in Warsaw.

Not a word of remorse for not being present at her funeral, much less of anger for not having been told.[45]

On his way to Tuhanowicze, Mickiewicz visited what had been his childhood home in Nowogródek. As he described it to Czeczot:

> I arrived in a strange house, ran up to what had once been our courtyard. Grief kept me from noticing the desolation that was all about me; I found the little annex where I had once lived open but dark.... No one came out to meet me. I didn't hear "Adam, Adam!" I walked through all the nooks and crannies...; when suddenly from upstairs our old serving woman comes down.... This poor servant had spent her entire life with us, now she had nothing to survive on.... She had dwelled in this house for a long time, living off her work; now she still wanders around the desolateness. I would have given her my last penny, if I had had one then.

A few months later, the poet reimagined this scene in its entirety in *Forefathers' Eve*, part 4, but not without also introducing a faithful dog as well as robbers who hack at the floorboards of "the place where the bed of [the hero's] mother once stood" (Dz. 3:76).[46]

Mickiewicz's visit to Tuhanowicze did not begin propitiously. Just as he arrived, he "met a carriage right at the gate and immediately recognized, or rather felt, that M. was in it." "I didn't know what was happening to me," he recounted to Czeczot;, "We were passing each other, something in white flitted by, I didn't dare speak up, I don't at all know how I finally made it. I find out that I had run into M., which in my soul I knew." Maria returned a few days later, however, and several days after that, the two were standing as godparents for an acquaintance's child. They then traveled in the company of her brother Michał to the family's other estates, including one near Lake Świteź, where Mickiewicz wrote the ballad dedicated to Wereszczaka as well as what is otherwise a poetic trifle for Maria but for the epigraph from Dante: "Nessun maggior dolore che ricordarsi del tempo felice nella miseria!" [There is no greater pain than to recall the happy past in times of misery] (Dz. 1:172). There would indeed be misery, and it proved to be far more painful for Maria than for her lover.[47]

Near the end of the summer, Mickiewicz was informed by university authorities that the tsar had looked favorably on his request for a year's leave of absence from his teaching duties for reasons of health. (This was the Russian Empire, where even an inconsequential deviation from the bureaucratic norm required the autocrat's approval.) Before settling down in Vilnius, where he would spend the 1821–1822 academic year, Mickiewicz returned briefly to Kowno in order to "ostensibly get [his] things, ostensibly gather statistical and geographic observations [for a project conceived by the Philomaths], to rummage about in antiquities, but in truth just to go, and perhaps to see Ko. one more time."[48]

As Mickiewicz described it to Pietraszkiewicz, "it was a strange reception." "Adam," a hurt Kowalska huffed,

> shouldn't even have bothered showing himself, since he was abandoning Kowno. There's no other way of making up to her but to live all the while in Kowno; something impossible to effect. We therefore behave toward each other very coolly.

Cooler, rather, for the affair with Kowalska was far from over. As for Puttkamer, Mickiewicz's relationship with her was just beginning to heat up, and this, it would appear, in inverse proportion to their actual contact.[49]

Over the course of some eight months in Vilnius, the poet managed to see Puttkamer perhaps only a couple of times, although they did manage to exchange miniature portraits of each other. As for correspondence, it was rarely direct. Maria was, after all, the new wife of a relatively prominent member of society, and an affair, particularly with an impecunious schoolteacher, demanded discretion. Their incipient love was thus forced to blossom through intermediaries. In the beginning they corresponded through Mickiewicz's cousin, who happened to reside with the Wereszczakas in Tuhanowicze. When the cousin died in early 1822, the role of go-between devolved upon Zan, who, his genuine love for both Puttkamer and Mickiewicz notwithstanding, often found the task to be trying and even distasteful. "I prefer to be considered someone who cares less about the welfare and happiness of my friends than a go-between," he wrote at one point to Mickiewicz, "and just as you feel your pride abased whenever you have to ask something of us, so I feel my character degraded whenever you pin to it the name of go-between." Mickiewicz, for his part, was demanding and easily irritated, particularly when he felt that Zan (or any of his other friends who visited Puttkamer) was not providing him with sufficient detail about his beloved or when Zan dared question or moralize about the relationship:

> "One can forget anything!" Why do those words, which you said to me yesterday, this remedy for curing me, seem like a grain of poison? How could you, Tomasz, how could

you have dared to come up with such a thought. Will you always think so little of your friends' happiness?[50]

The first few letters Zan wrote to the lovers were, as much as this was possible under the circumstances, rather straightforward, conveying news of one party to the other and sometimes including verbatim excerpts from the letters of each to Zan. With time, however—and his role as intermediary lasted well into 1823—Zan began to present this information as "chapters" of a (never completed) novel he was writing entitled "Love and the World," in which the thoughts and adventures of the two lovers were stylized, often rather elliptically, into a sentimentalist tale. The affair between Mickiewicz and Puttkamer was thus in effect turned into a fiction, while the fiction at once narrated, interpolated, and determined the course of the real-life affair. Which was stranger is difficult to say.

But then at this very same time Mickiewicz himself was transforming his feelings for Puttkamer into his own poetic fiction, and the poetic fiction into a kind of hyperbolized simulacrum for genuine emotions, which it, in turn, stoked. After a few months in Vilnius, he was close to completing *Forefathers' Eve*, part 4, the first and arguably most powerful articulation of romantic love in Polish literature. In fact, so powerfully, so credibly did it deploy a desperate lover's discourse, that generations of readers assumed it to be nothing less than a versified chronicle of the poet's affair with Puttkamer. Indeed, with its evocation of the hero Gustaw's love for Maryla and her marriage to a man of means, but also of the young hero's schooldays and childhood home, *Forefathers' Eve*, part 4, came to constitute the first chapter of a romantic poet's symbolic autobiography.* Few in his audience, it seems, took to heart Gustaw's own condemnation of "those brigand books"—Goethe's, Madame Krüdener's, Rousseau's, Schiller's, and now, presumably, Mickiewicz's own—which could "warp" a young reader's mind with fantastic "delusions" (Dz. 3:49). Yet by the same token, it is significant that only here, in a poetic fiction—not in his or the Philomaths' correspondence nor even much later in his or his friends' reminiscences of the events—did Mickiewicz articulate a sense of the social dimensions inscribing his affair with Countess Wereszczaka-Puttkamer. A note of resentment toward wealth and status and inequality is palpable throughout *Forefathers' Eve*, part 4, and is aimed in no small part at Maryla.

Mickiewicz's affair with Puttkamer reached something of an appropriately melodramatic climax in the fall of 1822. Once again, the summer brought the two together, but this time as self-declared lovers. Parting was thus all the more difficult: for Puttkamer, since her predicament now seemed hopeless (in a literary sort of way); for Mickiewicz,

*I borrow the term from Grabowicz, "Symvolichna avtobiohrafiia."

because he knew that he was also having to return to detested Kowno. "You suffer, my friend," Maria wrote to Mickiewicz in French several days before his departure from Vilnius at the end of August:

> You're unhappy, you neglect yourself. . . . Forget me, my friend, if this is what's necessary for your happiness and peace of mind. If only my love were necessary for your happiness, you would be only too happy. But no. Instead of contributing to your happiness in any way, it is I who am the cause of all your sufferings. . . . If its necessary for your peace of mind not to see me anymore, I agree to that.
>
> In the name of God, burn this letter and show it to no one.

A month later, the countess Puttkamer took an overdose of laudanum.[51]

Not surprisingly, Maria survived the suicide attempt. As she wrote to Zan some days later:

> Heaven has not endowed everyone with the strength of character and tenacity to be able to sing, dance, and say "So it goes" in various adventures and misfortune. . . . What will you say of weak creatures who suffer without comfort and hope, unable to find anyone who would understand them. . . . My soul had already stopped animating my being, desiring to taste eternal life; it made a great voyage, saw much splendor, but unable to find free entry into the shrine of glory, it returned to sojourn in this world again.

A few weeks later, Mickiewicz managed to pass a note to her directly:

> Beloved Maria, I respect you and adore you as one respects and adores a heavenly being, my love is as innocent and divine as its object. But I cannot suppress violent emotions every time I remember that I have lost you forever, that I'll be only an observer of someone else's happiness, that you'll forget me. . . . My dearest, my only one, you don't see the abyss over which we're standing, what a frightful effect it can have on your health, on your peace of mind. I won't survive you for even a minute. Do you want to burden me with the terrible responsibility that I was the cause of your misfortune? If you want me to be calm, to be gay, to love you with a feeling of happiness, or at least without despair, give me an example, from now on I swear to imitate you.

His turns of phrase may have been more polished, but the emotions they articulated appear to have been little different from those of Maria. They were, after all, inspired by the same books, and then intensified by Mickiewicz's own fictionalizations. Indeed, as one story has it, it may have been about this time that an ostensibly distraught Mickiewicz traveled to Bolcieniki intent on dueling with Count Puttkamer. But then this is just a story, related many years after the events—and after the publication of *Forefathers' Eve*, part 4.[52]

Understandably, the lovers' sufferings disquieted their mutual friends. Czeczot, for one, suggested to Mickiewicz that he do his best to get a passport and go to the Sudetes where Puttkamer would meet him: "Have mercy on yourselves... let yourselves be saved, and I can say without hesitation that everything will turn out for the best." But not much did, and for the next year or so the lovers wallowed in their suffering—and inflicted it on their friends, particularly Zan, who with his uncomplaining goodness continued to serve as their at times much maligned intermediary. They met occasionally, in Vilnius, in Bolcieniki (once, in the countess's grove of funereal trees, "at 12 in the evening, where [she] had been wounded by a branch"). Puttkamer complained of "lethargic states"; Mickiewicz of "a dead soul." In the spring of 1823, Puttkamer gave Mickiewicz a mare called Beauty, which he took to riding in the countryside around Kowno. Czeczot laid out their friend's predicament at this time bluntly to Malewski:

> Adam took a certain mare from his lover; the other *donzella* [Kowalska] has to feed it.... I have no idea what will happen to him and his health. I'm losing all hope, and I'm running out of remedies.... What's going on with him? He's always in an abnormal state, his health is awful, he's killing himself with his pipe, his lack of sleep, and the hard labor of his duties, and he makes no effort to pull himself out of his lethargy, he won't dampen his imagination, because he's comfortable with this, but for a moment of divine rapture, for that brief transgression of earthly bounds, he suffers gravely on earth. And thither man isn't allowed to travel with impunity! Persuasions are useless, he once shot back beautifully in a letter that he doesn't need friends now but flatterers.

Puttkamer's horse to excite his imagination, Kowalska's body to comfort him, his friends' solicitude to baby him and gossip: Mickiewicz was ultimately happiest when worlds were spinning around his sun, and that sun was producing flames.[53]

Nonetheless, by the spring of 1823, the affair with Puttkamer was beginning to run its course. Not long after receiving Beauty, during a rendezvous in Vilnius, Mickiewicz wrote to his friends with cool resignation:

> I knew that [Maria's] feelings are not of the same nature as mine, that I've lost her, I know what will become of both her and me, and I don't consider her all that unhappy....
>
> I sincerely wish her all happiness, but not all of it can comfort me as it can her, and I therefore don't want to know about everything.
>
> I even wish that she should not hear about me anymore. I'll keep informed about her, but not through others.... I have no reproaches. Although she's suffering, she's had many happy moments; I never wanted to torment her, and I will not.

Puttkamer shared the same sense of end. Writing to Zan in early May 1823, she declared, "I have renounced the greatest joy that I had in my life, of seeing him."[54]

Although they would meet again before Mickiewicz's expulsion from Lithuania, both appear to have come to terms with the futility of their predicament. The drama was over, leaving them exhausted but strangely fulfilled, content, perhaps, with the knowledge that they had experienced a genuinely romantic love—and with memories they could now nourish just as romantically. In poems Mickiewicz would write during his exile in Russia and then as he traveled in the West, the figure of Maryla resurfaces insistently, not so much, perhaps, as a lost ideal lover, but rather as the loss of a loss, a symbol of what the poet never had, which soon enough came to be conflated with his native land, indeed, with nostalgia itself. After his death, his son Władysław found among his father's papers an envelope entitled "Letters from Lithuania." It contained a few notes from Puttkamer, her portrait, and a dried leaf, the material embodiments of words Mickiewicz wrote "to Maria" in late 1822:

> Thus in every place and at every time,
> Where I wept with you and where we played,
> Always and everywhere will I be with you,
> Because that's where I left a piece of my soul.
> (Dz. 1:156)[55]

7

For all of the heartache and consternation that his affair with Puttkamer caused Mickiewicz and his friends, the poet's year in Vilnius was at once productive, disappointing, and ominous.

In early 1822, just as he was feverishly communicating with Puttkamer through Zan, Mickiewicz informed Malewski:

> I'm living a truly literary life, I breathe only verse and nourish myself on it; I don't know how I'll get used to reading something decent again. After my Germanomania came Britainomania: with dictionary in hand I forced my way through Shakespeare. . . . As a result, Byron is now much easier going. I shall surely translate *The Giaour*. However, this perhaps greatest of poets will not chase Schiller from my pocket.

True, as far as *Forefathers' Eve*, part 4, is concerned, where Schiller is a constant presence. But from this point on, Byron came to occupy a singular place in the Polish poet's imagination, as he did for so many of his contemporaries on the Continent and in Russia. His impact on Mickiewicz's writing is undeniable, to judge only by the number of Byron's poems he translated. Yet more important, perhaps, it was the myth of the fiercely principled, rebelliously transgressive lord and, soon enough, "martyr" of Missolonghi, who insisted on enacting in life the ideals he expressed in his poetry, that captivated his younger contemporary in Lithuania. In this, Byron came to share the same space in Mickiewicz's pantheon as Napoleon, that other great "poet" of life.[56]

A good part of Mickiewicz's "literary life" in Vilnius during that sabbatical year was occupied with preparing *Poems*, volume 1, for print. This included changing the name of Johasia in one of the ballads to Maryla, which in any case appears in the volume often enough.* At the same time, he was hard at work on pieces for volume 2: besides *Grażyna*, on *Forefathers' Eve*, part 2, a dramatic "poem" depicting, purportedly, a pagan East Slavic ritual for the dead and in this respect related to the folkloric, otherworldly atmosphere of the ballads; on part 4, loosely connected to part 2 through the figure of Gustaw, whose existence between the living and the dead recalls the ghosts conjured by the shaman of part 2; and on part 1, never finished, which, it seems, was to limn the "prehistory" of Gustaw's affair with Maryla. (The numbering was a romantic mystification: part 3 would not be written until 1832, and would only be loosely connected with the preceding parts.**) Moreover, in January 1822, he wrote the poem to Joachim Lelewel celebrating "the commencement of [his] course on world history at the University of Vilnius" (Dz. 1:141). Its publication as a separate brochure only added to the aura that instantly surrounded the event in the eyes of Vilnius's student body.

Mickiewicz's poem to Lelewel was also an expression of his renewed involvement in Vilnius student life, but now as something of an elder. His appearance at a May 1821 fête organized by the Philareths in honor of Zan, during which he presented his friend with a ring, became an electrifying brush with celebrity for the younger students, "a sun... toward which everybody gravitated." The Philomaths themselves, however, had reached the conclusion that their *raison d'être* needed to be reexamined. In the fall of 1821, just before Malewski's departure for study in Germany, they decided to officially disband in order, it was hoped, to be able to reorganize all that much more effectively several months later. In the interim, the (non)society's members were charged with "(a) organizing the Order of Philareths more rigorously; (b) reforming the Association of Friends [that had grown out of Zan's May happenings]; (c) exerting influence on other secret organizations; (d) rewriting [the Philomath] bylaws."[57]

*Recounting a conversation he had with Maria during a visit to Bolcieniki in 1823, Odyniec has her remark jealously, "Mr. Mickiewicz is very fickle: in 'I Like It' he first had Johalka, then he changed the name." Odyniec to Czeczot, 29 July/10 August 1823, AF K 5:306.

**However, in a 20 April 1890 letter to Władysław Mickiewicz, Karolina Jaenisch-Pavlova, the woman Mickiewicz almost married in Russia, claims that when asked why he published only two parts of *Forefathers' Eve*, Mickiewicz reportedly responded that he found the other two parts "'so trivial and boring that [he] threw them in the fire'" (quoted in *Żywot* 1:271).

In their desire to expand their activities, the Philomaths were nonetheless preparing their own demise, albeit just as they had feared all along. Despite their efforts to exert maximum control over the proliferating fraternities and to enforce secrecy, it was only a matter of time before this commotion would draw the attention of the authorities, already spooked by events in the West—the assassination of a Prussian politician by a university student; revolutions in Spain, Naples, and Greece—and, closer to home, by rebellions in the Russian army. A scuffle between a group of Vilnius students and Russian officers in early 1822, two months before Tsar Alexander's visit to Vilnius, only exacerbated matters. In response, Prince Czartoryski, himself under pressure from an increasingly reactionary regime in St. Petersburg and fearful of any further scrutiny of his district, ordered the university authorities to oversee the burning of the Philareths' archive. At the same time, he initiated a secret investigation of student societies. In the course of this investigation the apartment in which Mickiewicz was staying in Vilnius was searched and he himself was interrogated by university authorities about his connections with the Philareths and Radiants as well as about the incident with the Russian officer. Although nothing came of the matter, at least for the moment, the prince ordered that Mickiewicz and some of his friends be closely watched.

This attention from university authorities was not the kind Mickiewicz was hoping to draw at this particular moment. For three years, his friends had been encouraging him to make every effort to leave Kowno, supposedly for reasons of health. The poet's success in securing the year's leave of absence for the 1821–1822 academic year would, they hoped, eventually translate into either a passport to go abroad, where Malewski would be waiting for him, or at least a transfer to a more hospitable educational climate. But despite his petitions to university authorities as well as to Czartoryski directly, despite the exertions of well-disposed doctors, of Lelewel, Malewski, Czeczot, and to a certain extent of the prince himself, what Mickiewicz obtained for all his efforts was 300 rubles from Czartoryski, whom the poet had impressed with both his poetic and scholarly talents. This ort was ostensibly meant as a stipend for travel abroad, but because the prince either could not or would not arrange for one, no passport was forthcoming. In the fall of 1822, after a productive but none-too-happy year in Vilnius, Mickiewicz had no choice but to return to Kowno.

In a letter from that November, Mickiewicz wrote to Malewski:

> Kowno is becoming home for me. I'm getting used to school, since I'm reading little, writing little, thinking and suffering often, and thus I need some dog's work. In the evenings I play boston for money, don't like any company, listen to music rarely, have no desire to play cards without money. I read only Byron, and cast aside books if written in a different spirit, since I don't like lies; if there's a description of happiness, family life,

> this rouses my indignation as much as the sight of married couples and children; this is my only aversion.

The games of boston were, of course, played at the Kowalskis, and this in spite of the fact that a month earlier Karolina had learned "about the existence of Peri" and as a consequence "ordered [Mickiewicz] to see her less often." But if in February 1823 their relationship was "complex and wretched," this did not prevent her from stabling Beauty nor, for that matter, inviting the poet on a trip to the Baltic seacoast. When Odyniec visited Mickiewicz in the spring of that year, the poet and Kowalska were, it would appear, on the best of terms. As Mickiewicz himself put it in a letter to Czeczot, "I have a friend here still, who brightens my otherwise unbearable existence; we've gotten accustomed to our conversations, [mutual] attentions, and shared entertainments." Indeed, it was precisely when the affair with Puttkamer was drawing to an end that Mickiewicz could say that only now did he "come to know [Kowalska] best."[58]

What did not, it seems, particularly "brighten his otherwise unbearable existence" was preparing the second volume of *Poems* for print. There was pressure, since subscribers to *Poems* were clamoring for the remaining two volumes they had been promised. By December 1822 *Grażyna* was finished. The next three months were spent editing it and *Forefathers' Eve*, parts 2 and 4, as well as writing the introductory poem "The Specter," which took the place of the jettisoned part 1. Once again, it was Czeczot, dogged and insistent—annoyingly so, as far as Mickiewicz was concerned—who forced his friend to deal with the details of the works that the poet had spilled onto paper in brief but concentrated bursts of inspiration. Having to carry out this labor via correspondence made it all the more frustrating. "As for the insufferable *vat*," he writes referring to a passage in *Forefathers' Eve*, part 2,

> you make the decision . . . ; I wash my hands of it and don't want to hear any more about any corrections. You have no idea how horribly, noxiously, most noxiously unbearable this is to me. Leave me alone!

Czeczot assumed, in effect, a role analogous to Zan's vis-à-vis Puttkamer and Malewski's vis-à-vis his father the rector: all seem to have been eager to play the intermediary in certain matters—literary, romantic, practical—that required maintenance on the part of the poet, but which he was more than willing to devolve onto others. Where there was no place for others was in the creative moment itself, when inspiration flowed, be it on paper or in love.[59]

Poems, volume 2, appeared in April 1823, less than one year after the first edition of volume 1. It contained *Grażyna*, "The Specter," a brief note on the ritual of Forefather's Eve, and *Forefathers' Eve*, parts 2 and 4. The latter required a few cuts with an eye toward the censor (and with his advice: the censor at this time happened to be Lelewel), most prominently a passage comparing a kiss to Holy Communion. Zawadzki published the volume in a run of 1,500, which for the time was quite extraordinary. But unlike volume 1, and despite the subscriptions, it did not sell out immediately. Mickiewicz was still complaining about unsold copies in 1826.[60]

On a visit to Vilnius a few days after its appearance, Mickiewicz gave a copy of the volume to Puttkamer. He inscribed it with a poem to "Maria, my sister," asking her to accept these "keepsakes of a lover" "from the hand of a brother" (Dz. 1:172). And what strange keepsakes they were. Here, in full public view now, was the reimagined story of their affair. But if this was disconcertingly obvious to Mickiewicz's friends or otherwise fodder for speculation in the small world of the region's society, Count Puttkamer, for his part, seemed either not to notice or care. As Zan reported to Mickiewicz, Maria's husband "was in raptures about the second part of *Forefathers' Eve* [i.e., part 4] and praised it so much that I was embarrassed; I couldn't help blushing."[61]

Like the first, the appearance of the second volume of *Poems* caused "quite a stir" in Warsaw:

> The classicists are very angry at *Forefathers' Eve*, and although they can't deny it uncommon imagination, they say there's too little order in it, etc., etc. The romantics, on the contrary, see in it creative genius, and women are crying over the beloved "Specter."

Much of the classicists' "anger" was simply malicious, expressed, moreover, in table talk or private correspondence—"dirty," "vulgar," "an impudent and presumptuous Lithuanian bear" were some of the choicer comments—as if thus refusing to dignify the provincial upstart by acknowledging him in print. The one review that appeared immediately after the publication of volume 2 did not emanate from their camp. Although it noted "shortcomings with regard to the rules of language," "in places a sloppiness incompatible with today's elegance of poetic diction," and "a certain coarseness of expression," there was something almost awed in its author's assessment of the young writer from Lithuania:

> Nature has gifted him with all the traits that are indispensably necessary for a poet, that is: he has a powerful, lively, and rich imagination, he is sensitive and tender . . . , and more often than not one can feel [in his works] ease, deftness, and variety in expressing thoughts and feelings. . . . Poland will soon recognize in him a genuine and original poet, something that it needs precisely at this time.

As for the classicists themselves, it was not until 1825 that they finally decided to react publicly to the revolution in sensibility that was challenging their hegemony over literary taste. By that time, however, the tears of sentimental ladies and the scribblings of epigones would effectively make the issue moot.[62]

8

On 3 May 1823, thirty-two years after the proclamation of a progressive constitution that was meant to rescue what then still remained of an independent Poland and bring it into the modern age, a few schoolboys at the Vilnius gymnasium wrote the words "*Vivat* the Constitution of the Third of May, oh, what a sweet memory for compatriots" on a blackboard, to which another added, "but there is no one to stand up for it." Thanks to the school's teacher of Russian, details of the incident soon made it to the governor of the province, who in turn reported it to Grand Duke Constantine, the viceroy of the Congress Kingdom and Alexander I's brother, as well as to the new rector of the university, Józef Twardowski, who in turn reported it to both Prince Czartoryski and the Russian minister of education. The university authorities decided to punish the students with brief incarceration and bad marks for behavior; the director of the school and a teacher were reprimanded. In what he thought would be the end of the matter, Twardowski tried to play the incident down in a report to the governor, acquitting it as "childish pranks." However, several days later, a graffito expressing the same sentiments in stronger terms but in suspiciously ungrammatical Polish appeared on Vilnius walls. The governor now charged the university authorities with creating a commission to investigate both incidents. Around the same time, a slightly unhinged student walked into the office of the Vilnius police chief insisting he had information which he could impart only to the grand duke himself. Although this turned out to be something of a hoax, coming as it did on top of the incidents in Vilnius it confirmed to the grand duke "that the spirit of the wards of the University of Vilnius has never ceased being restless and rebellious, and that the university administration is clearly sympathetic to it."[63]

Having disrupted the activities of secret patriotic organizations in the Congress Kingdom a year earlier, the grand duke was now eager "to undertake decisive measures in order to extirpate once and for all the slightest thought of such harmful and intolerable disorder" in Lithuania. To this end, he enjoined Senator Nikolai N. Novosiltsov, the emperor's plenipotentiary in Poland and point man for "reforming" the Polish educational system, to take charge of the entire investigation. On 7/19 July 1823, Novosiltsov arrived in Vilnius. By the end of the year, about a hundred young men were sitting in the city's many monasteries, the cells of which had been made over into so many holding pens.[64]

Thanks to Mickiewicz's portrayal of him in *Forefathers' Eve*, part 3 (1832), Novosiltsov looms in the Polish imagination as the embodiment of Russian maleficence, quite literally Biblical in its implications. Poetic license aside, the senator was, by all accounts, indeed despicable. "Debauched, licentious, bestial to the highest degree, shamelessly venal," he had "not a penny's worth of conscience, virtue, morality, or shame," and "to these virtues he added . . . an uncontrollable propensity for drink"; there was something almost obsessive about his distrust of Poles. Novosiltsov jumped on his new assignment, knowing full well that it would accrue for him even more favor with the tsar and more wealth for himself; it would also mean finishing off his rival and erstwhile friend, Czartoryski. In all of this he succeeded magnificently.[65]

Once in Vilnius, the senator set to rooting out any and every trace of unauthorized activity among the students of Lithuania, it being the most egregious manifestation of the spirit of "liberalism" infecting all of Polish education. He cast his net wide, cunningly, diligently connecting, and concocting, multifarious threads in order to uncover a massive "Polish" conspiracy among Vilnius's youth and its suspected protectors. Searches, arrests, and interrogations commenced in August 1823, bringing to the monastic detention centers of Vilnius schoolboys, students, and teachers from all parts of Lithuania. It was not long before Novosiltsov and his commission managed to link the incident at the Vilnius gymnasium with Zan's May fêtes and the Radiants, and from there with the Philareths. The threads finally led to the Philomaths.

Czeczot was the first to be arrested, on 10/22 October; two weeks later, on or about the night of 23 October/4 November, came the turn of Zan, Mickiewicz, and others. That same day, Czartoryski submitted his resignation as superintendent to Emperor Alexander. Malewski was detained in Germany a month later by Prussian authorities and forcibly returned to Vilnius (this was, after all, the Holy Alliance). Out of touch with his friends, he let a few things slip that confirmed suspicions about the Philomaths. Although interrogated several times, Pietraszkiewicz managed to avoid detention, which provided him with the opportunity to conceal the entire Philomath archive on his brother's estate.

Mickiewicz was arrested probably in Kowno, whither he had just returned from a trip to the Baltic with Kowalska. In May, he had been granted his second leave of absence, this time for two years and again with hopes of obtaining a passport for travel in the West. Now, instead, he was taken to Vilnius where, during an especially cold autumn, he was incarcerated in the Basilian cloister, just around the corner from the chapel housing the miracle-working icon of the Virgin Mary of Ostrabrama. It so happened that the first week of his detention coincided with the feast of Forefathers' Eve.

With the exception of Zan, who as the "Supremo" of Vilnius youth was imprisoned in the castle keep, the other Philomaths were scattered throughout the monasteries of Vilnius,

> which, numerous and spacious, provided several hundred cells for imprisonment. One person was held in each, and everywhere the windows were whited out with lime, boarded up on the outside, while the doors were put under lock and key. Sentries with carbines walked through the corridors, not allowing anyone to come near the prisons.

Those of the detainees' friends who were still at liberty,

> formed a committee to follow the course of the developing affair in order to save, as much as this was possible, themselves and their fraternity brothers. They thus immediately devised ways of communicating with the prisoners; and as far as the activities of the commission were concerned, although it worked in great secret..., they also found ways to obtain precise information [about them]... [thanks to] the venality of bureaucrats in Russia.

The prisoners employed methods common enough in such circumstances: drilling holes in cell walls and jimmying boards in the windows and floors; passing notes back and forth during deliveries of necessities; they even managed to leave their cells in the evenings and gather over wine, tea, talk, and music—all thanks to the penury but in many instances also the kindness of their guards. The townsfolk, but particularly women, including both Kowalska and Puttkamer, made every effort to aid their incarcerated brothers, friends, and lovers, be it with food, clothing, books, money, or simply their presence, glimpsed through the cracks in the cell windows or when the prisoners were being taken back and forth for interrogation. It was thus through them, these "messengers from heaven," that much of the information was passed.[66]

Most of the investigation took place in the governor's palace, where Novosiltsov made his living quarters. The commission, composed of tsarist functionaries and members of the university administration, both Russians and Poles, usually met in the evenings, by which time Novosiltsov was already drunk. Each interrogation followed a set routine:

> Prisoners were brought before the commission one by one and ordered to write an autobiography.... Answers to questions posed by the commission followed, also all in writing. In these, some, following the instructions set by our [i.e., the students'] committee, admitted everything they knew about the objectives and activities of the societies... for in truth they had no reason to conceal anything, not feeling guilty of any crime against the law or against the regime. Others, out of fear, did not want to admit that they belonged to any of these societies. These were persuaded with lists of colleagues and face-to-face confrontations.[67]

Since his name kept cropping up in the course of the interrogations, Zan very early on decided to assume as much of the responsibility for the whole affair as possible and in this connection was instrumental in mapping out the strategy to which those being questioned were to adhere. That the strategy succeeded as well as it did—there were, of course, inevitable, and hence damaging, lapses—says much about the sense of purpose and solidarity among the youths, testament to the power of the ideas and ideals promulgated by the Philomaths. It also says something about Zan's capacity for self-sacrifice, bordering on martyrdom, and almost messianic fervor. "Verily I say unto you," Mickiewicz would write to Czeczot some three years later, "that Tomasz's life during those few months is worth a great deal more than our current steadfastness. He stood the test of love!" Sadly, though, he did not quite stand the test of sanity: it was during his incarceration that winter that the gentle, unstable Zan began exhibiting signs of mental illness.[68]

Mickiewicz was interrogated three times, in mid-November 1823 and in late March and April 1824, shortly before his release on bail. The first session concerned his ostensible membership in the Rayants as well as the Philareths, which the poet could in all honesty disavow (with regard to the first: "I wasn't even in Vilnius at the time"; with regard to the second: "I was never a member, never made any vow, never had any obligations, never held any posts"), while at the same time concealing, per Zan's strategy, his collaboration on their bylaws and his authorship of their songs. At most, he admitted, he "had heard something about them." The second interrogation, as well as a face-to-face confrontation, concerned the advertising ditty for Polish sealing wax he had written four years earlier, particularly the line, "he who has not betrayed his country, a secret will not betray" (Dz. 1:452). Mickiewicz played this down, too, stating that "one rarely pays attention when writing such trivial verses." By the time he was brought in for what would be his final interrogation, on 20 April/2 May, the commission already knew about the Philomaths. Informed of this through the grapevine, Mickiewicz was circumspectly candid, admitting to membership, naming names already named, and insisting, in all honesty and as did all of the prisoners, on the lawfulness of the society's activities. Indeed, he assured his interrogators,

> as far as boundaries of duty and decency were concerned . . . we never transgressed them; we felt and we feel the sincerest gratitude toward the monarch for the boons extended to our nation and never violated the respect and obedience owed to the government.[69]

Between interrogations, Mickiewicz spent the time in his cell, which was actually a rather large—and hence very cold—hall. Fourteen others were incarcerated in the same Basilian monastery, among them Ignacy Domeyko, who recalled about those days:

> Midnight was sunset for us; we would gather in Adam's cell and until dawn spend the nights in quiet but not sad conversation. [One of the prisoners] would brew tea and make us laugh. Whoever had been summoned for interrogation earlier in the day would bring us news that he had gathered in the [interrogation] hall and on the street. . . . It was in that cell, on New Year's, that Adam read for us the beautiful poem "The old year has passed away, etc." ["New Year's" (Dz. 1:157–58)], and at matins on Christmas Eve there could be heard to the accompaniment of an organ a muffled [Christmas hymn]. . . . With the

> exception of the above-mentioned poem, Adam wrote nothing during his entire time in prison, but he read a great deal and was very friendly with us, pleasant in conversation; at times he would fall to musing and be silent, but he was calm.

Domeyko wrote these words in 1870, almost fifty years after the events and almost forty after the publication of *Forefathers' Eve*, part 3, in which Mickiewicz himself dramatically reimagined his time spent in the Basilian monastery lock-up. Retrospective projection notwithstanding, Domeyko's description of his friend's behavior in detention rings true. The conditions of his incarceration, the feeling of camaraderie with his fellow detainees, the thought that the whole experience in effect tested the Philomaths' mettle and the strength of their ideals seemed to alleviate the spleens of Kowno and the (melo)drama with Puttkamer. As the poet would write to Czeczot three years later, "I began to be happy at the Basilians."[70]

9

Mickiewicz was released on or about 21 April/3 May 1824, thanks to bail put up by Lelewel. Before leaving detention, the poet, like all the detainees upon release, had to sign a (pro forma) document vowing to appear before the commission should this be required, to remain silent about his interrogation, to never again belong to any society without the permission of the authorities, and "to inform" the authorities about the existence of such. Greeted at the monastery gate by Odyniec, the two headed straight for the apartment of Kowalska's sister in Vilnius, where Karolina was waiting and where Mickiewicz subsequently moved in.[71]

For the next six months Mickiewicz divided his time between Vilnius and Kowno, not certain yet of how the Philomath affair would finally play out. In contrast to his usual custom, he spent that summer in Kowno with Kowalska, going with her on what would be their final trip to the Baltic shore. Despite his protestations—she is not, he wrote to Malewski in July 1824, fresh from reading Kant, "my absolute"—he counted on her to offer him comforts that at this point would have been simply too disturbing to expect from Puttkamer. But it was, perhaps, precisely this comforting habitude that made his relationship with Kowalska—"that *feindliches Gestirn*" [hostile heavenly body] as he called her—so neurotically ambivalent. As he wrote in a poem addressed to her, which by way of explanation he included in that same July letter to Malewski:

> Eternal exiles from this ordinary world,
> Is it to their advantage or their harm
> That what conjoins them is, again, repugnance
> And that through *hatred* they must *love*? (Dz. 1:173)[72]

In Vilnius, Mickiewicz spent most of his time visiting his friends and frequenting the salons of some of the city's society, many of whom participated in bringing aid to the young detainees. They were eager to host a recognized poet whose aura was now enhanced by his imprisonment "for the cause." He, in turn, reciprocated by inscribing poems in the albums of his hosts and on occasion even improvising. This gift, with which he had entertained the Philomaths during the name-day fêtes, seemed, however, to acquire greater significance as the fate of those arrested was about to be decided. Several days before Zan was to be deported to Russia, a group of his closest friends gathered in his cell to say good-bye. After Czeczot sang a doleful farewell song in Belarusian,

> Mickiewicz stood in the middle [of the room], pale and emotional as never before, asked Freyend to play his favorite [tune] on the flute, and began to improvise an incidental song. At first he crooned calmly, but then his voice acquired ever greater strength, his visage kept changing, the final stanzas transfixed everyone listening into silent, awed amazement.

The description of this evening, too, comes from a memoir written some sixty years after the event, and thirty after the publication of *Forefathers' Eve*, part 3, in which the hero improvises to a flute played by a character named Frejend. The power of Mickiewicz's symbolic autobiography to elicit "memories" in others should never be underestimated.[73]

On 14/26 August 1824, Tsar Alexander I signed off on Novosiltsov's recommendations regarding his investigation of Vilnius student societies. Out of 108 persons "proven" to have taken part in Philomath and Philareth activities, twenty were singled out as instigators. Their transgression: "seeking to spread ill-advised Polish nationalism by means of teaching." Their punishment: assignment to "provinces remote from Poland." Term: not specified. In addition, Zan was sentenced to a year of confinement in prison and Czeczot to six months, both in western Siberia. They were the first to be deported. Lelewel, together with several other employees of the university, was fired. As for Mickiewicz, Novosiltsov noted that he could "teach Latin in German, French, Latin, and Russian, but because of weak health he wishes to enter the civil service, such that would require less mental effort than the teaching profession." Like the others, he was to be at the disposition of the imperial minister of education upon arrival in St. Petersburg.[74]

Mickiewicz was handed his deportation papers late on the night of 22 October/3 November, which, according to Odyniec, "he accepted calmly." He was ordered to leave "without delay." For the journey, the chief of police allotted him 130 rubles. Lelewel later slipped him another 100, and probably also letters of introduction to both Russian and Polish acquaintances in St. Petersburg.[75]

Mickiewicz spent his final two days in Vilnius, wrapping up business with his publisher—both made sure that there would be copies of *Poems* (four hundred of them!) to take to St. Petersburg—settling property matters with his brothers, and, of course, bidding adieu to friends. On the eve of his and the others' departure from the city, an acquaintance organized a farewell fête, which, as Ignacy Domeyko remembered it, "almost all the Philomaths and many Philareths" attended.

> That night everyone was more happy than sad, no one was allowed to bemoan or even mention what everyone had suffered.... We sang all our songs, the sad and happy ones, the Philareth and the May ones, beginning with "Hey, let's live life to the fullest" and "Toasts."
>
> Near the end, we urged Adam to improvise something. At first he didn't want to, but after a moment Freyend played his favorite [tune] on the flute, and to this tune he improvised a ballad.... We dispersed in silence, quietly, when the bells were already ringing for the first mass... and people were kneeling in the street.[76]

Accompanied for a short distance by well-wishers, Mickiewicz left Vilnius on 25 October/6 November, sharing his britzka with fellow Philomath Jan Sobolewski. Mickiewicz carried with him an album, probably a present from Puttkamer, that contained the poem "To Maria" as well as the text of an improvisation later entitled "The Renegade," an orientalist poem about constancy. On the road north, the poet and his companion caught up with Malewski and Jeżowski. In Kowno, they were joined by Pietraszkiewicz. After two days in the town that Mickiewicz had come to at once love and loathe, the group of friends set off "over the snow, toward an increasingly wilder land..., a land empty, white, and open" (Dz. 3:265–66). If this land was not quite the one Mickiewicz had over the years been seeking permission to see, it would, nonetheless, prove to be a vital detour for reaching his destination, both literally and figuratively. To his homeland, however, he would return only in the imagination.

CHAPTER THREE

EXILE (1824–1829)

After a journey of two weeks, Mickiewicz, Malewski, Jeżowski, Sobolewski, and Pietraszkiewicz arrived in St. Petersburg on 9/21 November 1824, two days after the Neva had inundated the city. The devastation of the flood notwithstanding—thousands were killed and hundreds of buildings damaged—the city filled the young men with awe:

> One can't compare it with anything. The magnificence of the various buildings, their number and beauty surpasses the imagination, the wide streets, the sidewalks covered with dressed stone, the granite lining the canals and banks of the Neva astonish with their size. I who, I think, know how to walk, tire rather quickly after traversing a street or two, because they are immeasurably longer than ours.

Having finally found a place to stay in a city notorious for its dearth of lodging even in the best of times and for commensurate prices, the young men set out to gawk like the provincials they were at the architectural, commercial, and cultural wonders of "Peter's creation," the capital of the Russian empire.[1]

I

The streets all ran toward the river:
Wide and long like ravines in the mountains.
Enormous houses of brick and of stone,
Clay on marble and marble on clay;
And all of them even, their roofs and their walls,
Like a corps in an army outfitted anew.

The houses are plastered with plaques and with signs;
Amid writing so varied and in so many tongues
Eye and ear wander as if in the tower of Babel.
("Petersburg"; Dz. 3:275)

St. Petersburg of the 1820s was a metropolis with a population of over 400,000. It was not only the hub of an expanding empire, with a massive bureaucracy revolving slavishly around the all-powerful tsar, but the seat now of a triumphant European power, whose military and political might was expressed in its features. Alexander I had set about rebuilding the city to reflect its imperial pretensions, quite literally: the heart of St. Petersburg was turned into a gigantic parade ground; its most prominent edifices—the Senate, the Admiralty, the Kazan Cathedral, the Ministry of War, the theaters—were all meant to evoke imperial Rome. Like its model, the city teemed with diplomats and artists, craftsmen and condotieri, petitioners, proselytizers, and mountebanks from all corners of the empire and beyond. It was this cosmopolitanism, epitomized by brilliant salons and an opera and theaters that hosted some of the most illustrious stars of the day, that in the teens and twenties attracted arguably the most talented generation of Russian writers, although St. Petersburg still had to share them with Russia's old capital, Moscow. As Pietraszkiewicz noted, there were bookstores aplenty, selling the latest in European literature, in both the original and in translation, and to a lesser extent the domestic product, which in any case was amply showcased in some dozen journals and numerous almanacs.[2]

St. Petersburg's cultural vibrancy was, however, a symptom of a society undergoing a profound sociopolitical transition, with its attendant hopes, tensions, disappointments, and crises. And in this regard, as Mickiewicz and his Russian contemporary Aleksandr Pushkin both came to understand in retrospect, the flood of 1824 could be read as something of an unsettling omen. Like Poles, progressive elements of Russian society had been buoyed by certain gestures on the part of the monarch in the years immediately following Napoleon's defeat. Flush with the victory over France and Russia's ostensible entry into Europe, but at the same time "infected" by French republican ideas, they saw in Alexander a ruler who, it seemed, shared many of their notions about reforming a backward empire. But the hopes of Russian progressives for the abolition of serfdom or even a constitution proved to be as unwarranted as the Poles' for the restoration of their state. Alexander's increasingly reactionary policies after 1820 revealed the face of a true Russian autocrat, fueling expressions of disillusionment proportional to expectations raised.

2

Within days of their arrival, Mickiewicz and his fellow exiles reported to the minister of education Aleksandr S. Shishkov, who also happened to be one of the most fossilized of Russia's literary classicists. Perhaps because of his antipathy toward Novosiltsov—and in this he was far from an exception among Russian officials—Shishkov proved unusually solicitous toward the young men. That he was planning to marry a Polish woman may also have been a factor. The minister at first proposed disposing of the exiles "according to their wishes and abilities" in any location other than the Polish provinces, but then, on the tsar's personal intervention, other than St. Petersburg as well. Pietraszkiewicz opted for Moscow. Factoring in the weather, Malewski requested to serve in Odessa with Count Mikhail S. Vorontsov, the governor-general of the southern province of Novorossiia. Jeżowski, writing for himself and Mickiewicz, expressed a desire that the two be sent "to either Kharkiv or Odessa and there to take service that would be suitable to [their] abilities." Mickiewicz was more specific, adding to this in his none too literate Russian a preference for the Richelieu Lycée in Odessa. Their requests were granted, and in the middle of December Shishkov informed General Jan Witt, commander of the army in Novorossiia and, in a peculiarly Russian twist, also the curator of its schools, to expect them. He also asked the finance ministry to allocate "Jeżowski and Mickiewicz two hundred rubles each" plus travel expenses for the long journey south, "on account of [their] penury."[3]

There exists, however, a curious note in the same dossier. At one point in this process, both Mickiewicz and Jeżowski expressed a desire "to devote themselves exclusively to the study of oriental languages." Three of their exiled colleagues had indeed opted for this route and enrolled in the University of Kazan, a center for training the expanding empire's corps of Orientalists. The interests of all of them in this direction were not only a reflection of romantic fashion. They were an outgrowth of their education at the University of Vilnius, which, thanks to Groddeck and Lelewel, had, in fact, already produced a true star in this field in the person of Józef Sękowski (Osip I. Senkovskii).[4]

Sękowski had settled in St. Petersburg in 1821, where he became the youngest professor ever appointed at the university. Cynical, conceited, and overbearingly contentious, he was disliked as much by Russians, for whom he was "foreign"—"a Russified Pole... with no respect for anything"—as he was by his fellow Poles, in whose eyes he was a self-loathing renegade. For all this, he was brilliant. Few knew the Near East as well as he, who had both studied it with the leading European Orientalists of the day and traveled it extensively. Mickiewicz's contacts with him in these early weeks of exile proved stimulating—he began studying oriental languages and the poem he wrote in the album of Sękowski's wife, entitled "North and East" (Dz. 1:181–82), was themed appropriately—but he was under no illusions as to the man's character. As he wrote later to Odyniec, "I advise you to watch him and keep an eye on him. I know him very, very, very, very, very well."[5]

Mickiewicz probably met Sękowski through Józef Przecławski, a Vilnius classmate who, like a growing number of Poles in search of a career, had settled in the imperial capital. Przecławski acted as the poet's first guide around the city and acquainted him with some of its Polonia: Konstanty Rdułtowski, a wealthy dilettante from the Nowogródek region, whose interests included English literature and Emanuel Swedenborg; Kasper Żelwietr, plenipotentiary of Polish aristocrats and a notorious bon vivant; and the painters Walenty Wańkowicz, Józef Oleszkiewicz, and Alexander Orłowski (who, as Mickiewicz would recall in *Pan Tadeusz*, "lived at the court, almost by the side of the emperor, as if in paradise," but "longed for his country" [Dz. 4:95]). These were, for now, just brief acquaintances, but ones that Mickiewicz would renew and deepen during his second sojourn in the city three years later. In the case of Oleszkiewicz, an eccentric mystic and one of St. Petersburg's most prominent Freemasons, the impact on the poet would prove to be profound.[6]

Of consequence too, albeit for very different reasons, was Mickiewicz's introduction to Tadeusz Bułharyn (Faddei V. Bulgarin). A veteran of the Napoleonic campaigns (first against the French and then alongside them) and a product of Vilnius's enlightened liberal circles, Bułharyn settled for good in St. Petersburg in 1819. By 1825, he was already a critic and editor of imposing influence—and soon enough a valuable asset of the tsarist secret police. However unsavory his reputation became among Russians—"a sloven and scoundrel," as Pushkin later called him, "doubly dangerous" as spy and critic, and in any case a "carpetbagger"—his credentials among his countrymen, at least at this point in his career, were unexceptionable, particularly in his role as an enthusiastic purveyor of Polish culture for the Russian market. "No one surpasses him in love of country and liberalism," a friend of the Philomaths reported to Jeżowski from St. Petersburg in 1820, "an indefatigable defender of everything that is Polish." Bułharyn's affection for Mickiewicz was genuine, as was his antipathy toward Novosiltsov, who targeted him too—a "liberal Pole," after all—for investigation. It was in part thanks to his (questionable) connections that the poet managed to avoid much unpleasantness during his years in Russia. Writing to Bułharyn from Berlin in 1829, Mickiewicz would remark: "I have inscribed the proofs of your friendship deep in my heart, convinced as I am of your noble-mindedness." There is no reason to doubt the sincerity of these words.[7]

It may, in fact, have been through Bułharyn, or at least through someone in his circle, that during this first brief stay in St. Petersburg Mickiewicz came to know Aleksandr A. Bestuzhev (Marlinskii) and Kondraty F. Ryleev, Russian writers not much older than he who, as leaders of a circle of St. Petersburg conspirators, would within a year initiate a republicanist revolt against the tsar. It was with Mickiewicz, Malewski, and Jeżowski that the future Decembrists chose to usher in that fateful year.

3

"They knew each other briefly, but intensely" ("The Monument of Peter the Great"; Dz. 3:281), Mickiewicz would recall of his relationship with Ryleev and his immediate circle, whom in an 1842 lecture at the Collège de France devoted in part to the Decembrists he would describe as being "the noblest, strongest, most ardent, [and] purest... of Russian youth" (Dz. 9:364/LS 3:292). They were, for the most part, his coevals, noblemen of both aristocratic and more modest origins, with literary ambitions and sensibilities similar to his own, inspirited by the same Enlightenment notions of civic duty, patriotism, friendship, and self-improvement. For them too, romanticism opened a window to their nation's past and folk and at the same time offered visions of liberty for the individual as well as a people. That both Bestuzhev and Ryleev knew Polish (Ryleev had translated several works from Polish, including some of Mickiewicz's ballads) helped ease their acquaintance, since Mickiewicz's Russian was still poor and his French not quite yet fluent. Although short-lived and surely magnified in his own mind retrospectively by the Decembrists' fates, Mickiewicz's friendship with Ryleev and Bestuzhev not only left a deep personal impression on the poet, but contributed significantly to shaping his views on Russia. For the first time he came to understand that a shared sensibility—literary, generational, philosophical, personal—could transcend national resentment and the political agendas informing it, that the Russian people were not to be equated with those who ruled them. The "foreign faces" of his "Russian friends" would always have "the right of citizenship in [his] dreams" ("To My Russian Friends"; Dz. 3:307).*

As editors of a literary almanac, Bestuzhev and Ryleev attracted a group of like-minded intellectuals, many of whom were also involved in the conspiracy. The line, however, between the initiated and the profane in this matter was rather fluid. Ryleev's apartment, which he shared with Bestuzhev in a building also housing the playwright Aleksandr S. Griboedov and the poet Aleksandr I. Odoevskii, was a focal point of literary discussions that simultaneously served as a vehicle for political discontent. As Mickiewicz recalled years later:

> They conspired openly. . . . Officers [and] bureaucrats gathered in Petersburg, in apartments whose windows opened out onto the street, and no one ever revealed the aim of their meetings. Public opinion was mightier than the authorities' threats. (Dz. 9:361/LS 3:289)

To Mickiewicz and his Philomath friends, veterans of clandestine activity (however innocent) and all too aware of its potential repercussions, this ingenuousness was troubling. More disturbing, the Russians' conversations—often over pickled cabbage, rye bread, and plenty of alcohol, punctuated by the singing of Bestuzhev's and Ryleev's "agitatory" songs—would drift from imaginings about reforming the political system to actual plans for deposing and even killing the tsar. Mickiewicz once recounted to an acquaintance how during one of these gatherings he refused to join in the toast, "Death to the tsar!"

*Until somebody walked off with it in 1836, Mickiewicz kept an album with pages "inscribed by Ryleev, Bestuzhev, and other victims of Nicholas from 1825" (*Żywot* 1:195 n. 2).

To the Russians' accusations of "cowardice and even treason," the Polish poet reportedly responded that "toasts such as these are always powerless and fruitless cheek; that those who drink them think they have accomplished a great deed, reassure themselves with this, and go to sleep." He added, nonetheless, that if they were being sincere, they should "arm themselves immediately and proceed to the tsar's palace, in which case he would go with them." Fortunately for Mickiewicz it never came to this. But "considering his close acquaintance with the Decembrists and his discussions with them about their projects for a future constitution, it was truly a miracle that he was not implicated in the uprising," which cost Ryleev his life on the gallows and Bestuzhev five years of exile in Siberia and, eventually, death in the Caucasus.[8]

Just before Mickiewicz's departure from St. Petersburg, Ryleev and Bestuzhev penned a brief note to their acquaintance Vasilii Tumanskii, a poet in Odessa, recommending the Pole as "a friend . . . and, in addition, a poet—the darling of his people." In the course of his journey and throughout his stay in the south, Mickiewicz would often come into contact with people close to the conspiracy. But for all the wishful speculation in this regard, there is no evidence that Mickiewicz or his friends were themselves in any way involved. Their own lesson was fresh, and in any case, they knew that someone was always watching.[9]

4

While the cogs of the imperial machine were set in motion, Mickiewicz and his friends spent the two months in St. Petersburg sightseeing, attending the opera and concerts, visiting (circumspectly) the homes of expatriates or their recent Russian acquaintances, and making the personal, informal contacts so crucial in a culture defined by bureaucratic formalism. It was not until 26 January/7 February 1825, in the middle of a Russian winter, that Mickiewicz, Jeżowski, and Malewski set off for Odessa. In preparation for "Mr le Fevrier," Malewski visited St. Petersburg's central bazaar, where he "called upon the services of all the provinces" to furnish him with a hat (from Arkhangelsk), stockings (from Yaroslavl), and boots (from Nizhny Novgorod).[10]

The road south led through Vitebsk (Vicebsk), Mogilev (Mahilaŭ), Gomel (Homel), Chernigov (Chernihiv), Kiev, and Elizavetgrad (Kirovohrad), where Mickiewicz and Jeżowski were to report to General Witt for instructions on where exactly they were to proceed. But already as the travelers were passing through Belarus, an order came down from the tsar rescinding the Poles' appointments to Odessa and, for that matter, to any of the southern provinces, where the nobility was still overwhelmingly Polish. The bureaucratic cogs began to grind once again. Although the exiles learned of the decision shortly after their arrival in Odessa, it would not be until November that Mickiewicz would finally leave that city. At the moment, however, the friends were unaware of these developments as they journeyed through the snows of Belarus and right-bank Ukraine, headed for "a land where oranges bloom, where the silkworm hangs his web, beneath a clear sky, on the shore of the sea, where the language of beloved arias is spoken everywhere."[11]

The travelers stopped in Kiev just as the annual fair of the local Ukrainian-Polish nobility was under way. Here they quickly made the acquaintance of several landowners from the region, on whose part the plight of the young Lithuanians inspired respect as well as sympathy. That one of the travelers was also Poland's most fashionable poet made them all the more welcome, particularly in the eyes of the women. As there was no special hurry and a few days at a manor were preferable to a night in a lousy inn, Mickiewicz and his friends were happy to accept the invitations that were invariably proffered.

The first visit they paid was to Pustowarówka (Pustovarivka), the estate of Bonawentura and Joanna Zaleski, some ninety kilometers southwest of Kiev. Zaleski was a landowning businessman, engaged in supplying goods—not always honestly or successfully—to the Russian government; his wife, a pretty, intelligent young woman, poetically inclined, patriotic, and unhappy in her marriage. The visit of this romantic exile shook her world. She fell in love. The fact that, like many of their neighbors, the Zaleskis owned a house in Odessa would only deepen her affections in the coming months; the fact that they subsequently visited Moscow would sustain them. On this account, however, Zaleska would find herself no less frustrated than several other women with whom she would be forced to share Mickiewicz's attentions over the next few years.

After a few days in Pustowarówka, Mickiewicz and Malewski traveled to Stebłów (Stebliv), the residence of Herman and Emilia Hołowiński, some hundred kilometers southeast of the Zaleski estate. Their stay there was brief as well, but "very pleasant," and the poet quitted it with a bit of (masterful) album verse for the lady of the manor:

> To those who wander 'midst the space of our days
> A narrow path is our life between oceans.—
> From a misty abyss we all fly into one that is dim.
> Some tumble straightwith, all the quicker to rest,
> While others are drawn by illusory vistas:
> By fruits or by gardens or the bedrock of glory. (Dz. 1:182)

Stebłów also served as something of an appetizer for things to come, affording Mickiewicz his first experience of dramatic nature. The manor's setting above the banks of the river Ros, where "gloomy . . . ravines" made their way through "huge cascades of granite" and then "again out into the great plain," excited his imagination. So too, apparently, did an ancient linden, which he would later feature in *Pan Tadeusz* among Poland's arboreal "monuments" (Dz. 4:104).[12]

Jeżowski and Mickiewicz finally arrived in Elizavetgrad sometime in mid-February, where they reported to Witt for further instructions. It turned out that there were no vacancies for teachers of Latin, Greek, or classical rhetoric at the Richelieu Lycée. But the general sent the candidates on anyway, ordering the school to furnish them with food, lodging as well as a salary ("in the beginning... between 600 and 750 rubles... annually") until appropriate slots became available. No one was aware that the issue was by now moot. Yet even after it was learned that the Poles were to be expelled from the south, the lycée would remain Mickiewicz's and Jeżowski's home and primary source of income for the duration of their stay in Odessa. As Mickiewicz put it, "They're paying us to eat oranges."[13]

The man who would be their "guardian angel" during their time in the southern port greeted the exiles graciously. Years later, Mickiewicz described Jan Witt as "the son of a Polish general, from a Greek mother, himself unaware of what nationality he belonged to or what religion he professed" (Dz. 9:362/LS 3:291). But Witt did in fact consider himself a Pole, and this may in part explain the solicitude he extended toward Mickiewicz and his friends. That his lover, Karolina Sobańska, would in time become Mickiewicz's lover as well probably explains the rest: "The general refused the beautiful Sobańska nothing." Yet for all of his hospitality, Witt never for a moment ceased exercising his duties as Alexander's chief spy in the south, which included tracing the threads of what, it was now becoming apparent, was an antigovernment plot of dangerous proportions. The possibility that the group of political undesirables from Vilnius could in some way also be involved was something he clearly had to consider.[14]

5

The travelers arrived in Odessa in the middle of an unusually cold, windy, and muddy February, aware that in the late spring they should expect more mud—the city's streets were unpaved—as well as the notorious episodes of blowing limestone dust in the summer. It was said, however, that "the streets were to be paved with filberts," and in any case the oranges were cheap, and "raisins, figs, almonds, and dates a dime a dozen"; the water, or so Mickiewicz claimed, was "so healthy that [his] teeth began to grow back." For the unemployed threesome there was now also plenty of free time.[15]

Founded only thirty years earlier, Odessa was in the midst of a remarkable boom. Under the administration of Count Mikhail A. Vorontsov, its population nearly doubled to about 40,000, while the city itself developed commensurately into an urban showcase. As the empire's premier Black Sea port, serving the vast agricultural lands of the Ukrainian steppe, Odessa was even more cosmopolitan than St. Petersburg. Here "the Russian jostle[d] against a Turk, a German against a Greek, an Englishman against an Armenian, a Frenchman against an Arab, an Italian against a Persian or a Bucharestian." Most conspicuous, however, were Poles, primarily grain-producing landowners from southwestern

Ukraine who owed their wealth to the port and who would descend on it in the spring and summer to watch over their affairs and relax by the sea. They built themselves sumptuous villas for the purpose and made sure that there was enough entertainment to fend off boredom. For devotees of music—and Mickiewicz and Malewski happened to be insatiable in this regard—the so-called Italian theater staged the newest Italian operas, but also French vaudevilles and Russian dramas. German and French shops carried the latest fashions and merchandise from Europe, while Greek and Jewish merchants purveyed an abundance of goods from the Near East.[16]

With time on his hands, Mickiewicz spent his idle hours learning Italian, at the opera, and above all socializing. As he would later write, "I led an oriental life in Odessa, or, to put it simply, an indolent one," "like a pasha"—courted and spoiled and in some cases seduced by a harem of women, "the Danaidae" (Dz. 1:231) who presided over the city's salons. Here was, after all, a handsome young man in his virile prime, charismatic but moody and somewhat eccentric, marked, moreover, by the dual misfortune of an ill-starred love and unjust persecution. Above all, he was a poet who had already demonstrated his power to immortalize in verse an object of his affections. Zaleska made sure he should be a regular guest at her home; but so too did Eugenia Szemiot, albeit more with motherly than erotic intentions; and, by some accounts, Avdotia P. Gur'eva, the young wife of Odessa's mayor, the first of several Russian women with whom Mickiewicz had affairs during his four and a half years in exile.[17]

Although he had mingled with provincial wealth in Lithuania, in Odessa the poet was for the first time exposed to a cosmopolitan aristocracy, Russian as well as Polish, which was as much at home in St. Petersburg, Moscow, or even the capitals of Europe as on a rural estate. His initial awkwardness in this new environment seems to have disappeared rather quickly as he learned the codes governing the social visit: the ability to make small talk about where people "are waltzing that day" and where "they are giving a dinner," about the price of grain, the weather, or "highway robbery in Greece" ("To Those Paying Visits"; Dz. 1:229); the capacity for witty as well as sentimental conversation; the rituals of flirting and the proprieties of an affair. He came to understand that his status as an exiled poet was good social capital, guaranteeing entrée into the homes of the city's elite (meals included), but also a form of erotic capital, in high demand among Odessa's ladies. His French improved proportionately.

In the contest for Mickiewicz's attentions—which, it seems, led to some nasty rivalries and underhanded tactics—no one was as successful as Karolina Sobańska, the mistress of General Witt. Like her Lithuanian namesake, she was older than the poet, by some four years, and no less stunning than Kowalska: "What grace, what a voice, and what bearing!" Née Rzewuska, she came from one of Poland's most distinguished—and as far as Russia was concerned, loyalist—families. Her brother Henryk was an accomplished storyteller and soon author of arguably the best Polish prose of the period; her sister Ewelina

(Hańska) eventually became the wife of Balzac. After receiving a brilliant upbringing in Vienna, Karolina married Hieronim Sobański, a rich landowner and Odessa businessman, from whom she separated quickly but did not immediately divorce. Witt's marital status was analogous. Nonetheless, the two insisted on flaunting their socially exceptionable liaison, which did not preclude (mutually acceptable) infidelities. Despite ostracism by the city's ladies, Sobańska's salon, or, rather, the mistress herself, proved impossible to resist, as Pushkin had learned some two years earlier.[18]

Mickiewicz was just as taken. Twenty years later, he confided to Margaret Fuller:

> She was [then] in the full radiance of her beauty. I was young then and in spirit in a mood similar to yours. . . . I began to become attached to that lady, but I was too romantic and too exclusive. She wanted to count me among *the others*. For a long time I was angry with her. Finally I understood that she was right and that she had behaved correctly.

He paid for Sobańska's affections with a series of erotic poems: it is probably she who is concealed behind the cryptonym "D. D." (Donna Dż[Gi]ovanna) that figures in a number of them. It would be a mistake, however, to read them as the chronicle of this or any particular affair. They constitute, rather, a highly conventionalized reflection of the atmosphere of Odessa's salons and boudoirs, with their rococo eroticism and aristocratic sybaritism, in which conventionalized affect was enacted daily and the elegant phrase and the well-turned *pointe* were at a premium. In this respect, the elegies and love sonnets of Mickiewicz's Odessa period could just as well have been addressed to Zaleska (Joanna = Giovanna)—and some probably were—to Gur'eva, or, for that matter, in a peculiar gesture of retrospective projection, to "Mary ja" ("From Petrarch"; *Dz.* 1:217). (Many of them were in fact recorded in the album Puttkamer had given the poet in Vilnius.) However this may be, the poems are evidence of an eroticism that is at once passionate and playful, physical and intellectual, confident but also readily indulged because insatiable: "I shut [the chattering] mouth, no longer willing to listen, / Just wanting to kiss and to kiss and to kiss" ("To D. D."; *Dz.* 1:199).[19]

Yet Mickiewicz soon realized that the price he was paying for these blandishments—"the weight of his soul" and his "peace of mind" ("A Farewell. To D. D."; *Dz.* 1:230)—was "dear," that "the bard" was in fact pandering to his "listener" ("Excuse"; *Dz.* 1:232). Several of his poems express distaste for the kind of exchanges that informed the economy of the salon: song for gold, hand for heart, wealth for poetry ("The Danaidae"; *Dz.* 1:231), metaphors that mask deeper resentments inscribed by social status. No less troubling, then, was the ease with which his poetry, and body, succeeded in securing *la dolce vita*, transforming what was supposed to be punitive exile into a life worthy of, well, "a pasha." As the censorious Jeżowski no doubt reminded Mickiewicz time and again, others of his cohort—Zan, Czeczot—were not so lucky. Is it the voice of his Odessa roommate that "whispers" about the poet in the sonnet "Excuse," "'Did the gods give him the voice of a bard / To sing only of himself in every sad verse?'" (Dz. 1:232)? The fact that it was probably in Odessa that Mickiewicz began writing *Konrad Wallenrod*, a poetic tale about the sacrifice of personal happiness for the collective good, seems to indicate that the "whisper" may have hit the cause.

For all this, in a gesture reminiscent of his affair with Kowalska, Mickiewicz was not about to renounce Sobańska and the pleasures she afforded. What he did not know at the time was that this enticing woman was also Witt's "secretary," who wrote "this . . . intelligent but illiterate man's . . . secret denunciations"; that her salon constituted something of an ongoing dragnet for taking the measure of political moods and opinions, and of the people who expressed them. To be sure, Mickiewicz was under no illusion about Witt himself—that he was "the Emperor's spy" was common knowledge—nor about the fact that he and his friends were under constant surveillance. When an acquaintance from Vilnius ran into Mickiewicz and Malewski at a performance of *Norma*, the three chose to meet "secretly, afraid as they were to do each other any harm." One could never be too careful.[20]

In honor of Malewski's sister's name-day, Jeżowski sent her a fanciful map of "the Black Sea kingdom" of which she was playfully dubbed the monarch. The drawing was intercepted by the tsarist post in Lithuania, which turned it over to Novosiltsov. In the eyes of someone obsessed with Poles' ostensible capacity for patriotic fractiousness, the drawing became prima facie evidence to this effect. "Beneath this insignificant drawing," wrote the Philomaths' nemesis to Grand Duke Constantine, "there is hidden a secret meaning" having to do, or so Novosiltsov construed it, with the Poles' desire to recover their historical territories. The upshot was a series of directives to Count Vorontsov, to Odessa's chief of police, to its postmaster, and, finally, to the director of the Richelieu Lycée to report any suspicious activity on the part of the Polish exiles. All the director could report in this regard, however, was that Jeżowski

> often went out alone or with his friend Mr. Mickiewicz; during the day he often returned to his apartment, on some days after 10:00 in the evening, also either alone or with his friend. They often received visits in their apartment from Mr. Malewski. . . . In addition, they received visits from two Poles unknown to [the director]. [The latter] noticed no acquaintance or ties on the part of Jeżowski with employees of the lycée except that . . . occasionally he came to eat dinner or supper with the lycée's housekeeper . . . , but usually . . . eats dinner and supper in a hotel, at a so-called club, together with his abovementioned friends Mickiewicz and Malewski.

Witt, for his part, reported in a letter to Emperor Alexander that because "a great number of inhabitants from the Polish provinces have gathered in Odessa, . . . [he] was compelled to watch [the Vilnius professors] with particular strictness, but here their behavior has proven to be entirely irreproachable."[21]

It was in this atmosphere of simultaneously oppressive restriction and sensual freedom that in August Mickiewicz traveled with Sobańska, her husband Hieronim, her brother Henryk, General Witt, and several others to the Crimea. This was not the first time that the poet had taken a trip beyond the confines of Odessa. The previous month, he had managed to sneak out of the closed city in order to visit the estate of one of his Odessa acquaintances, which was located in the steppe west of the city "amidst waves of throbbing meadows, amidst a flood of flowers" and "coral-red islands of bent" ("The Steppes of Akkerman"; Dz. 1:235). The journey to the Crimea, however, enjoyed the protection of Witt, who was making preparations for the emperor's trip that fall to Taganrog and at the same time tying together the last threads of his investigation into the antitsarist conspiracy in the south.

Among their traveling companions was a certain Aleksandr K. Boshniak, "a traitor [and] spy," as Mickiewicz described him in his Parisian lectures, "far more cunning than . . . even Cooper's Spy" (Dz. 9:363). For cover, Boshniak played

> an entomologist, a very modest and inconspicuous person, sloppily dressed, with glasses, to whom nobody paid any attention; as he conversed about his special area of studies, about insects, but particularly about shells, which he would collect everywhere, he would casually inquire about a person's place of birth, his occupation, his connections in the homeland, etc.

When upon his return to Odessa Mickiewicz ran into Boshniak at General Witt's, the disheveled entomologist had metamorphosed into an elegantly dressed officer. Taken aback, the poet is supposed to have remarked to Witt, "I thought that he was only interested in catching flies." "Oh," the general laughed, "he helps us by catching all sorts of flies."[22]

And indeed, on 13 August, Witt had informed Alexander that he had uncovered "an important and serious affair, which could have the direst of consequences, since it concerns the security" of the sovereign. According to Mickiewicz, "it was . . . Boshniak who provided Witt with secret information about the conspiracy" (Dz. 9:363/LS 3:291). Eleven years after the events, in his French-language drama *Les Confédérés de Bar* (1836), Mickiewicz would reimagine this trio—Sobańska, Witt, and Boshniak—against the backdrop of Poland's war against Russia in 1772. The character of the Doctor-spy is chilling; the General is portrayed as a ruthlessly efficient bureaucrat who is at the same time in the thrall of his lover; the countess Karolina is drawn with almost tragic sympathy.[23]

After riding out a storm on the Black Sea, "admiring the magnificent sight of the riotous waters" while his shipmates "lay half-alive in their cabins," Mickiewicz arrived in Eupatoria, a town in the northwest Crimea known for its therapeutic muds. With Eupatoria as a base, the poet spent the next two months sightseeing the western half of the peninsula. The Crimean khanate had by now been a part of the Russian Empire for a little over forty years. Although it was well on its way toward being absorbed into the Slavic world, the Tatar way of life was still much in evidence. Auls, with their porticoed wooden dwellings, mosques, veiled women, and Asiatic-looking men on sturdy ponies were set amid breathtaking vistas of sea, mountain, and steppe, all nurtured by a gentle and generous Mediterranean climate. A two-thousand year history was spelled out in the ruins of ancient Greek temples, Byzantine monasteries, Karaim strongholds, Genoese fortresses, and the palaces of Tatar khans.[24]

Mickiewicz's travels took him over the steppe of Kozlov to Simferopol. From there he traveled to Bahçesaray and then Çufut Kale: the former, the abandoned capital of what was once the Crimean khanate, "the Giray's now empty realm" ("Bakczysaraj"; Dz. 1:240), and which had earlier inspired Pushkin's *Fountain of Bakhchisarai* (1822); the latter, an old Karaim settlement carved into a sheer, towering cliff. Mickiewicz journeyed to, up, and down Çatyrdah, the "padishah" of Crimea's mountains ("Czatyrdah"; Dz. 1:247), its snow-covered peak visible from the steppe of Kozlov. He proceeded along the Black Sea coast from Aluşta, as it "murmured with the morning *namaz*" ("Ałuszta in the Daytime"; Dz. 1:245), west to Kuçuk Koy, then up through the Baydar Valley to Balaklava and Sebastopol, where "castles, shattered in disordered ruins," once "graced and guarded" "the thankless Crimea" and now sheltered "men baser than reptiles" ("Ruins of the Castle in Balaklava"; Dz. 1:251).

"I saw the Crimea!" Mickiewicz informed Lelewel in 1827.

> I survived a powerful storm on the sea and was one of the few who were well, who maintained enough strength and lucidity to observe fully an interesting sight. I trod the clouds on Çatyrdah (supposedly ancient Trapizond). I slept on the sofas of the Girays and played chess in a laurel grove with the steward of the late khan. I saw the orient in miniature.

What he does not mention is that here, amid the waves of a raging sea, atop snow-covered peaks, and along dizzying gorges (for someone from the flatlands of Lithuania, altitude was a relative thing), he came to experience something that he had heretofore known only from poetry and treatises on aesthetics: the power of nature to elicit the fascinating terror of the sublime. As his cycle of sonnets devoted to the Crimean voyage evinces, the Tatar peninsula proved to be a perfectly acceptable substitute for the Transcaucasian Orient Mickiewicz had dreamed of seeing.[25]

Halfway between Aluşta and Yalta, Mickiewicz paid a visit to Gustaw Olizar, a minor Polish poet soon to be implicated in the Decembrist conspiracy. Olizar lived at the foot of a magnificent promontory called Ajudah, where, as a consequence of an ill-fated love for a Russian woman, he had secluded himself on an estate he named "Cardiatricon." In

Fig. 5 Mickiewicz on Ajudah. Oil painting by Walenty Wańkowicz, 1828. Courtesy of the Adam Mickiewicz Museum of Literature, Warsaw.

his memoirs he claimed that this love "had won [him] the sympathy of Russia's leading poet [Pushkin happened to have fallen for the same woman] and the friendship of our poet laureate, Adam. . . . His Crimean sonnet entitled 'Ajudah' was dedicated to me and my lovelorn exile." However this may be, this particular sonnet inspired perhaps the most famous depiction of the young Mickiewicz, an 1828 painting by Wańkowicz subsequently lithographed in thousands of copies: dressed in stylish striped trousers, white Byronic shirt, red scarf, and fur burka, the poet "leans on Judah's crag" (Dz. 1:252) staring meditatively into the ethereal, oriental distance with one hand tucked under his chin, the other into his shirt à la Napoleon—the quintessential romantic.[26]

When Mickiewicz returned to Odessa at the end of October, Malewski and Jeżowski had already left. Per the directive of the tsar, both had received new postings in Moscow. Mickiewicz, for his part, had requested a position with the Archive of the Collegium of Foreign Affairs, also in Moscow. He was aware that the archive had become the employer of choice for some of Moscow's leading young intellectuals. Informed that there were no vacancies, Mickiewicz applied to the offices of the Moscow governor-general Dmitrii V. Golitsyn, where Malewski had already secured a posting. The attestation he requested from the University of Vilnius for the purpose included a newly minted diploma that declared Mickiewicz a candidate in philosophy (ABD) in the faculty of physical-mathematical sciences. This earned him the civil rank of district secretary, 12 on the Russian Table of Ranks (14 was the lowest), equivalent to a lieutenant in the army, with the right to be addressed "Your Nobleness."[27]

It was not until the middle of September that Golitsyn finally agreed to accept Mickiewicz, with the proviso that he would receive no salary "until he demonstrates in actual fact his abilities and zeal for service." It took another two months to approve the appointment and to appropriate the funds for the trip. On 12 November, the poet set out for Moscow, where yet another sinecure awaited him.[28]

Despite his ambivalence about the spiritual costs incurred, he was sad to leave a city that had at once spoiled and schooled him, socially, sexually, and as a poet. Moreover, the thought of exile in the heartland of Russia elicited a feeling of dread, as if "a grave were closing [on him] forever." The nine months in Odessa, he now realized, had been just a sweet delay of the inevitable. But then too, Mickiewicz was taking with him the fruits of what had turned out to be an extraordinarily productive year: some three dozen poems—album verse, elegies, fables, translations from Petrarch, erotic and Orientalist sonnets—as well as the first drafts of *Konrad Wallenrod*. He was determined to "fly and henceforth never to lower [his] flight" ("Meditations on the Day of Departure"; Dz. 1:207–8).

6

Mickiewicz had wanted to return north the way he had come, hoping thus to drop in on the Hołowińskis yet again. "Circumstances," however, "ordained it otherwise," and he returned instead through left-bank Ukraine, "traveling through . . . unknown regions to regions far more unknown." Along the way, he probably heard, if only as rumor, of the death of Emperor Alexander in Taganrog on 19 November/1 December.[29]

Like Malewski before him, Mickiewicz stopped for about a week in Kharkov (Kharkiv), the provincial capital of Sloboda Ukraine, some 550 kilometers northeast of Odessa, in order to pay a visit to Ignacy Daniłowicz, a scholar of law whom they both knew during his tenure at the University of Vilnius and who as a consequence of his suspected involvement with the Philomath-Philareth affair was now a professor at the university in this Ukrainian city. A friend of Lelewel, he was in constant contact with Warsaw, and Mickiewicz soon found himself "devouring" recent Polish journals in Daniłowicz's apartment. It so happened that one of them contained an unauthorized transcript of an improvisation he had delivered in Vilnius before his departure ("To Aleksander Chodźko"; Dz. 1:474–76), which, as Daniłowicz informed Lelewel, Mickiewicz insisted on "sending to his female admirers god knows where." (Two months later, however, the poet was berating Odyniec for publishing "those scribbles": "I can't believe that even after some wine I could make such crappy poetry."). The poet also got to meet Daniłowicz's colleague Petro Hulak-Artemovs'kyi, lecturer of Polish language at the university and at the same time a champion of a literature in what was then considered but a dialect of Russian. Over the next four years, Hulak and several of his former students translated a number of Mickiewicz's works into Ukrainian, in this way fixing, if not exactly directly, the name of the Polish poet in their efforts to extend the possibilities of this fledgling literary language.[30]

7

Mickiewicz arrived in Moscow sometime in the second week of December, moving into a boarding house (owned, coincidentally, by Novosiltsov) together with Malewski, Jeżowski, and another exiled Philomath. A few days later, they learned of the uprising in St. Petersburg's Senate Square and its suppression by Nicholas, Alexander's brother and somewhat reluctant successor to the throne. A wave of arrests followed, including those of Ryleev, Bestuzhev, and most of their circle. Dozens of sympathizers were seized in Moscow and taken to the imperial capital for interrogation. Although Russian society on the whole understood that justice was being done, the arrests nonetheless came as a shock, particularly as it became clear that some of the country's best and brightest were involved. In view of their contacts in St. Petersburg, as well as their already suspect situation as political exiles, the young men from Lithuania had reason for concern. Malewski recalled the scare they all received when someone, as a (rather misguided) joke, left a calling card for Mickiewicz purportedly from Ryleev and another conspirator. Nothing came of this, but the next few months were tense.[31]

The city in which Mickiewicz was now settling, the old capital of Russia where the new tsar would soon be invested, had by now almost fully recovered from Napoleon's devastating fires of 1812. Although not as populous as St. Petersburg, it was no less prosperous, "full of commercial activity, full of life." Its medieval origins conditioned a space very different from the new capital in the north. Churches stood on practically every street, "all of them beautiful [and] grand... with five towers." The streets were irregular, with narrow and dirty ones zigzagging among elegant boulevards, where small wooden houses abutted huge palaces. There were fewer foreigners. Rather, the presence of some of Russia's oldest families as well as of wealthy merchants still dressed in oriental fashion and sporting traditional beards contributed to an atmosphere that, in Pietraszkiewicz's words, "nurtured a national spirit." At the same time, it was a city of the "disgraced and disappointed," resentful of the "Germans" who had ostensibly come to control the imperial government. Yet what Moscow lacked in political heft and cosmopolitan glitter, it compensated for with intellectual vibrancy, which radiated largely from a university increasingly manned by native Russian scholars. Their interests were supported by a lively publication industry, including houses printing works in Polish, as well as by stimulating salons.[32]

After three months of Moscow cold, "absolutely the worst food," and no wine or coffee, Mickiewicz and his friends moved out of the boarding house into an apartment not far away. Malewski paid the rent up front while Jeżowski bought the pots and pans and assumed the role of "*maggiordomo*," responsible for "the keys, the bills, and pouring tea." Malewski had even borrowed a piano, with which he could satisfy his own as well as Mickiewicz's melomania. In September, however, Jeżowski was hired to teach Greek at the university, lodgings included, and his two friends were forced to move once again. They found an apartment even closer to the center, where they would live until the following May.[33]

In what appears to be his first letter to Zan since the arrests in Vilnius, Mickiewicz informed his friend in Orenburg that he and the others were "vegetating." "Rarely is there a book in hand; more often chess, almost always conversation. We have no acquaintances and no company beside our own." The poet was being only partly (carefully) disingenuous: with the investigation into the Decembrist affair going full tilt, the Polish exiles were keeping their heads down, and to themselves. Although they were "considered employees in the offices of the governor-general," Mickiewicz and Malewski "receive[d] no pay, but also [were] not forced to fulfill any duties of service." For the time being, the latter was living off his father's allowances and the former off his residuals as well as the 300 rubles Czartoryski had given him in Vilnius. It was enough, in any case, for him to offer to send Zan a few rubles.[34]

On 13/25 July 1826, Ryleev, together with four other Decembrist conspirators, was hanged in St. Petersburg. News of the executions horrified Moscow society, exacerbating what was already an anxious atmosphere in a city that the authorities considered a hotbed of "Jacobinism." The celebrations accompanying Nicholas's coronation in Moscow the following month could thus only be perceived as a cynical effort on the part of the new autocrat to erase the memories of the preceding year. Processions, parades, illuminations, fireworks, throngs drowning in "fountains gushing with wine" and "vats flowing with vodka"—unable to "trust his pen" on such an occasion, Mickiewicz "dare[ed] not describe... these events, so important for history," directing his addressee instead "to the newspapers, which will describe everything more accurately and honestly." He preferred "to observe and (as can only be expected) to rejoice along with others."[35]

All sarcasm aside, there was, nonetheless, if not necessarily joy, then at least some hope, insofar as occasions such as these usually called also for acts of mercy. Malewski and Mickiewicz decided to take advantage of the accession of the new tsar in order to petition for permission to visit Lithuania. Despite the intervention of their benefactor, Prince Golitsyn, their hopes were quickly dashed. The decision, after all, depended on a recommendation from Novosiltsov, who concluded that the pair's presence in Vilnius "could provide reason for unwarranted conclusions and revive emotions that are just beginning to be consigned to oblivion." The refusal was more a blow to Malewski than to Mickiewicz. The latter had no father or mother waiting for him on a comfortable estate in Lithuania. And in any case, Moscow was proving to be even more hospitable and invigorating than Odessa—indeed, more than even Poland itself.[36]

Mickiewicz had come from Odessa with a notebook of new poems, "sonnets, short elegies, etc. etc." In March, he was still working on his southern sonnets, on *Konrad Wallenrod*, and also on a "prologue" to *Forefathers' Eve*. Money, however, was running short, and royalties from the two volumes of *Poems* were now going only so far; he had, moreover, promised his subscribers three. But writing to Zan in June, he was still unable to finish *Wallenrod*, with which he hoped to "round out the third volume." "I don't know how much glory I'll gain [with it], but what's more important, I'll improve my finances." As it turned out, it would be over two years before this project came to fruition, and then quite differently than it was at first envisioned. He was forced to improve his finances by other means.[37]

Mickiewicz had just read a Russian translation of an overview of recent Polish literature by Franciszek Salezy Dmochowski, one of Warsaw's more moderate classicists, who praised the poet for his "gift of invention and description, deep emotion, boldness and loftiness of thought, magnificence and beauty of style." Mickiewicz grasped that the review was at once a reflection of and bound to generate demand. With his funds shrinking, and with the third volume of *Poems* still little more than a promise, he decided to publish the two cycles of sonnets he had brought with him from Odessa in a separate edition—not in Warsaw, though, or in Vilnius, but in Moscow.[38]

As the poet explained to Czeczot and Zan in early 1827, "I have no one to send them to in Vilnius. . . . Communications with Warsaw are difficult and full of delays." There was, however, something more at stake in this decision: the awareness of a Russian—or, rather, imperial—audience, more sophisticated, more *au courant*, than the one back in Poland. In Warsaw, after all, they were still paraphrasing the *Georgics*, "translating Legouvé, Delille, and, what's worse, Millevoye," while in Moscow "every new poem by Goethe arouse[d] universal enthusiasm, [was] translated right away, and commentated. Every novel by Walter Scott [was] immediately in circulation, every new work of philosophy [was] already in the bookstores." When Mickiewicz declared to Odyniec that "the *Crimean Sonnets* will be more to the liking of foreigners," what he meant, in effect, was not so much that a Russian audience might constitute a new market—how many Russians could read Polish anyhow?—but that their appearance in Moscow would imbue his work with the cachet of imperial fashion, a sure guarantee of increased sales.[39]

8

Mickiewicz's calculations in this regard were shaped in large part by a set of acquaintances whom he did not mention to Zan at this time. Already in December 1825, the poet had been briefly introduced to Nikolai A. Polevoi, a historian and literary critic who, together with his brother Ksenofont, was the publisher of *Moskovskii telegraf*, the first Russian "encyclopedic" journal and programmatically oriented toward the West. As Mickiewicz knew little Russian, their conversation in French initially seemed to go nowhere. Their acquaintance was renewed, however, in the spring of the following year, when Iurii I. Poznanskii showed Polevoi some translations he had made of Mickiewicz's early works. Although they were less than adequate, the critic was impressed, enough to pay a visit to the poet and enough to publish one of Poznanskii's translations ("Maryla's Grave Mound") in a May issue of the journal. A few issues later, Polevoi published the translation of Dmochowski's overview of Polish poetry, together with his own extensive notes, which were almost embarrassing in their praise of the Polish poet ("Russian literature has nothing that can compare to the fourth part of *Forefathers' Eve*"). That this liberal plebeian was also a great admirer of Napoleon surely helped nourish what soon became a genuine friendship. By the fall of 1826, Mickiewicz had become "like a member of the family in [the Polevoi] home," thrilled to find himself surrounded by a group of like-minded and appreciative Russians.[40]

The Polevois' home was a magnet for Moscow's intellectual and creative elite, mainly young men of Mickiewicz's generation, for whom romanticism—"Byron, Walter Scott, Goethe, Thomas Moore"—constituted the appropriate expression of the age and "Schylling," as Pietraszkiewicz wrote somewhat ironically, "oben ist." It was at the Polevois' that Mickiewicz first met Schelling's most ardent Russian admirers, the so-called Lovers of Wisdom—the poet Dmitrii V. Venevitinov, the prose writer Vladimir F. Odoevskii, the critic Ivan V. Kireevskii and his brother Petr—all employed by the Archives of the Ministry of Foreign Affairs, whither, not coincidentally, Mickiewicz had himself applied for a position while still in Odessa. But there were others: Evgenii A. Baratynskii and Nikolai M. Iazykov, two of the most talented poets of Pushkin's generation; Stepan P. Shevyrev, who, like the Kireevskiis, was already beginning to formulate notions about the importance of Russia's Slavic inheritance; Kapitolina Krasovskaia, the wife of one of Polevoi's contributors with whom, it appears, Mickiewicz "fell fatally in love" (and who died a short time later, reportedly on account of that love); and, most notably, Prince Petr A. Viazemskii, Polevoi's cash cow as far as the success of *Moskovskii telegraf* was concerned.[41]

Six years older than Mickiewicz, Viazemskii, along with Pushkin, had been a member of Arzamas, a St. Petersburg literary group in revolt against their classicist elders and, like the Philomaths, with a commitment to progressive ideals of education, brotherhood, and human liberties, but unlike their Vilnius coevals, aristocrats all with a propensity for wine rather than milk and actresses rather than schoolgirls. Viazemskii had served for several years under Novosiltsov in Warsaw, where he came to know a number of Polish political and literary figures and to sympathize, to some extent, with their national aspirations. His liberalism in matters both Polish and Russian eventually landed him among the "disgraced and disappointed" of Moscow, where he became *Moskovskii telegraf*'s most influential collaborator. Mickiewicz had in fact brought a letter of introduction to Viazemskii from Odessa, in which he was recommended as "endowed with great genius and a profoundly sensible mind." He was soon a frequent guest at both the prince's home in Moscow as well as his Ostaf'evo country estate. Among his papers, Mickiewicz kept a letter from Viazemskii's wife "as a memento of [their] hospitality." In a note he wrote on the letter, the poet explained:

> Once, I praised the coffee at the Viazemskiis. The next day they sent me a sack containing over a dozen measures of coffee. We refused to accept it by remarking that we had no desire to sit so long in exile so as to drink the contents of that sack (Dz. 17:537).

The proof, as always for Mickiewicz, was in the coffee.[42]

It was through Viazemskii that the poet's circle of Russian, but also Polish, acquaintances began to expand rapidly. But then Mickiewicz appears to have made Viazemskii's task in this regard an easy one. As the prince recalled many years later:

> Moscow gave Mickiewicz a hearty welcome. . . . Everything about Mickiewicz elicited and drew sympathy for him. He was very intelligent, well mannered, animated in conversation, with manners that were politely delicate. He behaved simply, that is, nobly and prudently; he did not play the political martyr; there was not a drop in him of that arrogance or ritual disparagement that one encounters . . . in some Poles. The touch of melancholy on his face notwithstanding, he was of a gay disposition, witty, quick with the appropriate and apt turn of phrase. . . . He felt comfortable everywhere: be it in the study of a scholar or writer, in the salon of an intelligent woman, or at a merry table with friends.[43]

To be sure, Mickiewicz's capacity to "feel comfortable" in a variety of social settings and by the same token to cross ideological as well as class distinctions was the usual privilege of an outsider. Yet it appears that this was a trait common to his Muscovite friends, too. A shared generational and aesthetic sensibility as well as the sheer joy of intellectual contact often transcended, at least at this time, such distinctions and even journalistic rivalries. When Mikhail P. Pogodin, the leading Russian historian of the generation and nascent Slavophile, set about founding *Moskovskii vestnik* as a commercial but also ideological alternative to *Moskovskii telegraf*, it was with the collaboration of many who were also regulars at the Polevois'. Pogodin's guests at the "fraternal dinner" he threw to celebrate the birth of his journal on 24 October/5 November 1826 included Baratynskii, Venevitinov, the Kireevskiis, Shevyrev, and, of course, Mickiewicz. As a pugnacious romantic and at the same time a Polish poet ensconced now amicably, it seemed, in the Russian "capital of Slavdom," he appealed to everyone.[44]

Present at Pogodin's dinner that day was also Aleksandr Pushkin. His arrival in Moscow a month earlier provoked a stir that practically rivaled the excitement of Nicholas's coronation. "Oh, what a bustle friendship albums and lorgnettes now find themselves in," Malewski informed his sisters about the Russian poet's return from six years of exile:

> He had previously been *confiné à la campagne* for his poems, the Emperor gave him permission to return now to Moscow. It's said that he had a long conversation with [Pushkin], promised him that he himself would be the Censor of his poetry, and in front of everyone dubbed him the first among Russian poets. The public cannot praise the Emperor's mercy enough.[45]

Pushkin's name was by no means unfamiliar to the Philomaths. They had heard of him back in Lithuania as early as 1820 (ostensibly "exiled [for his poetry] to the border with Persia so that [his Muse] could gad about a bit"), and then again in greater detail from his Decembrist friends in St. Petersburg as well as from Tumanskii in Odessa. He was the subject of gossip in that city's salons, where he himself had spent a year not long before their own arrival there. Surely Sobańska whispered a word or two about her Russian admirer to her Polish lover, and Olizar surely reminisced plaintively about his famous friend and rival. In one of his Crimean sonnets, "The Grave of Potocka," Mickiewicz acknowledged Pushkin's *Fountain of Bakhchiserai* (1822), in which the Russian happened to connect his own projection of the Crimean Orient with Poland. The two poets, both "darlings of their people," had much in common.[46]

They had been introduced sometime shortly before the dinner at Pogodin's thanks probably to the services of Sergei A. Sobolevskii. One of Pushkin's closest friends, a bibliophile, sometime poet, and at times outrageous bon vivant, yet another of the "archival youths," *Demon*, as Mickiewicz had nicknamed Sobolevskii, had met the Polish poet at the Polevois'. The two struck up a friendship that would be one of Mickiewicz's closest, weathering the Polish uprising of 1830 and Mickiewicz's sectarianism of the 1840s. But then Moscow was full of mutual friends—Viazemskii and Baratynskii and Venevitinov, to name just a few—and in any case, there were plenty of occasions for contact as Pushkin threw himself headlong into Moscow's social and literary life after two years of quiet in the countryside. Pushkin at this time also committed himself to Pogodin's *Moskovskii vestnik*, becoming, in Mickiewicz's words, the journal's "strongest prop," and earning, in the process, Polevoi's undying enmity. That the Polish poet belonged, in effect, to the latter's stable at *Moskovskii telegraf*—he published several articles there anonymously in the first months of 1827—seems to have made little difference. As he wrote to Odyniec that spring:

> I should now add that I know [Pushkin] and we see each other often. Pushkin is practically my age (two months younger), very witty and irresistible in conversation; he's read a great deal and knows modern literature well; he has a pure and lofty conception of poetry. He's recently written a tragedy, *Boris Godunov*; I know a few scenes from it, it's in the historical genre, well conceived and beautiful in its details.[47]

Fig. 6 Drawing of Mickiewicz (?) by Aleksandr Pushkin. Courtesy of the Adam Mickiewicz Museum of Literature, Warsaw.

For all this, however, Mickiewicz's account lacks warmth. Pushkin's "cold but sharp mind" (Dz. 9:360/LS 3:288), his flightiness, love of the good life, and aristocratism, but above all his penchant for vulgarity, may all have contributed to drawing a certain distance between him and the rather modest petty gentryman from Lithuania. At Pogodin's once, Pushkin was apparently acting so "horribly, vilely, disgustingly" that Mickiewicz "was obliged to say twice: 'Gentlemen, decent people don't speak of such things even when they're alone by themselves.'" Whatever the reason, there seems to have been little of the intimacy which from the very beginning marked Mickiewicz's friendships with Polevoi, Viazemskii, and Sobolevskii. For Pushkin's part, it appears that he was somewhat awed by the Polish poet, "waiting for him to speak, rather than speaking himself, and turning to him with his opinions as if seeking his approval." As the two grew closer over the next two years and Pushkin came to appreciate Mickiewicz as a poet, this sense of asymmetry, and incompatibility, intensified.[48]

But in these first months of their acquaintance, what did—or, rather, could—Pushkin really know of Mickiewicz the poet? Indeed, as Viazemskii observed, what could any of Mickiewicz's Russian friends know of "the degree and power of his gifts"? Although "all appreciated and came to love Mickiewicz the man, people could for the time being only take others' word for [those gifts] or believe in them by hearsay; only those very few who were acquainted with the Polish language could appreciate Mickiewicz the poet. . . . In the meantime, he quietly continued his poetic pursuits."[49]

These pursuits included *Konrad Wallenrod*, the tale of a disaffected foreigner living among his despised oppressors, which Mickiewicz was having such difficulty completing. But they also included the two cycles of sonnets that he had brought from Odessa and now decided to publish in Moscow. This decision seemed all the more appropriate considering that the first was devoted, ostensibly, to the fine ladies of Russia's finest southern city and the second to a Polish poet's impressions of a new jewel in the imperial Russian crown.

9

The first problem was finding a censor with a good knowledge of Polish. This responsibility devolved on Mikhail T. Kachenovskii, a professor of history at the University of Moscow and editor of the conservative journal *Vestnik Evropy*. He proved to be unexpectedly liberal. After deleting a sonnet for being insufficiently deferential to the tsar—"I know of only three salaams that cannot debase a man: / Before God, before parents, and before one's beloved" (Dz. 1:543)—Kachenovskii approved the manuscript for print on 28 October 1826. It was Malewski's turn now to grapple with the task, always so odious to Mickiewicz, of correcting the proofs, although this time the poet was at least in the next room to answer questions.

The volume, entitled simply *Sonnets*, appeared at the end of December 1826. Produced by the university printing office, it was "an attractive edition, nice print, nice paper," in a relatively large format. As he inscribed in the copy that he gave to her, its "beautiful garb" the author owed "to his best friend Joanna Zaleska" (*Dz.* 17:487), the inspiration, perhaps, for some of the sonnets themselves and now also their patron. But then Kowalska too rated a personally inscribed copy, hot off the presses, "as proof of respect, a memento of friendship" (*Dz.* 17:482), as did, but only a week later (2 January 1827), Puttkamer. In her case, unmistakable allusions in some of the sonnets made dedicatory niceties superfluous.[50]

The title page of *Sonnets* sported, appropriately enough, a motto from Petrarch ("Quand'era in parte altr'uom da quel, ch'io sono" [When I was, in part, a different man from the one I am today]). The Crimean cycle carried a separate motto, no less appropriate, from Goethe's *West-östlicher Diwan* ("Wer den Dichter will verstehen, / Muss in Dichters Lande gehen" [Who wants to understand the poet must visit the poet's land]). Prudently enough, it was dedicated, "to [Mickiewicz's] companions on the Crimean voyage." And then Mickiewicz made a novel gesture. As if endeavoring to authenticate his, a Slavic poet's, depiction of the Crimean Orient, he used his acquaintance with Sękowski to persuade Cafar Topçi-Başa, the adjunct professor of Persian language and literature at the University of St. Petersburg, to translate one of the sonnets into Persian. The latter obliged with what was, according to him, the first translation of a Western work into Persian. He prefaced his rendition of "View from the Steppes of Kozlov" with an almost mockingly "Orientalist" paean to his "beloved friend," "an excellent, educated, sagacious, scholarly, wise . . . young man . . . , a Pole who in the art of writing poetry has transcended his contemporaries." However, "on account of the lithographers and [Mickiewicz's] agents in St. Petersburg," the translation "came out too late," and it, together with Topçi-Başa's preface, was inserted into only a few copies of *Sonnets*.[51]

The copies of *Sonnets* that were intended for the Russian market sold out in the space of four months. (They sold particularly briskly in Kiev and St. Petersburg.) Sales in the Congress Kingdom, however, were somewhat slower, perhaps because the price was relatively high; perhaps because the ladies were unaccustomed to the large format; or perhaps, as Lelewel wrote to Mickiewicz, readers simply "gave up, not having the strength to understand what they were about." But Odyniec too was partially to blame. His incompetence in the business side of literary production, which Mickiewicz took very seriously, came to a head when only four months after their publication in Moscow a bootleg edition of *Sonnets* appeared in Lwów. The poet was beside himself. "You informed me," he berated his "ambassador,"

> that Piątkiewcz [the entrepreneur who forged Mickiewicz's permission for the bootleg printing] wanted to publish *Sonnets* and that you would do your best to stop this from

> occurring. How was I supposed to respond, not knowing the laws regulating book publishing in Poland nor the means by which to prevent abuses. Naturally, I relied on you and I could never have foreseen that you would trust the first printer that comes along and wait until I wrote that I do not give him my permission.... You're too timid an ambassador and don't want to act without instructions, which often I can't give you.

Mickiewicz's anger had only something to do with principle; more to the point was his need of money "to pay the local Vankas and their cabs and the delivery men of strawberries and wild strawberries." Henceforth, Mickiewicz would be exacting in matters concerning author's rights and the profits accruing from them.[52]

Shortly after the publication of the new volume, Mickiewicz wrote Lelewel, "If the *Sonnets* are received well, I intend to compose something more extensive in the oriental style; if, on the other hand, those minarets, namazes, izans, and other such barbaric sounds do not find favor in the classicists' delicate ears, if..., then... I'll be chagrined, but I'll keep writing." Sękowski,for one, would have discouraged him, deeming that Mickiewicz "made a bad mistake when he wanted to use eastern metaphors, expressions, etc. in his poems without knowing at all either Asian languages or the literatures of these peoples." As for the Warsaw classicists, the poet had no illusions about what to expect. Having chosen to effectively ignore Mickiewicz's first two volumes, they could no longer remain silent in the face of what was, quite clearly, a provocative challenge to literary taste and thus, in their eyes, a pernicious assault on "that dearest of our ancestors' legacies," the Polish language itself. If the erotic sonnets "grate[d] by their comical lack of decorum... [and] considered as sonnets [did] not withstand scrutiny," the Crimean ones offended with their unapologetic Orientalism: "Instead of expressing his impressions in the language he commands so well, he preferred to fill his verses with a parody of eastern expressions and concepts." In other, much harsher, words, "an abomination... everything [there] is ignominious, sordid, dirty, obscure; it all may be Crimean, Turkish, Tatar, but it is not Polish.... Mickiewicz is convinced, with conceit and pride, that madness is poetry, garbage color, darkness light, incomprehensibility perfection."[53]

This time, though, the fulminations of the classicists were met with an aggressive response from a new generation of critics, for whom romanticism was already an inalienable articulation of their sensibility and German aesthetics a given. Linguistic "transgressions" were no longer the issue: it was clear that the classicists' critique of *Sonnets* was nothing less than a belated pretext to discredit romanticism as such. What was at stake, therefore, was a profoundly new way of apperceiving the world, a poetics of "creative" imagination, as Maurycy Mochnacki, the most articulate representative of the "romantic school," put it, that broke rules in order to combine "the daring and exuberance of the eastern imagination with the melancholic enthusiasm of the northern romantics... [and] fuse into a single mysterious whole the spirit of the philosophy of the forgotten masters of modern civilization with its inspired idealism." For the next two years, polemics over *Sonnets* came to serve as proxies in the Polish "battle of the romantics with the classicists." It was, nonetheless, evident from the start that the classicists' cause, however earnest, was an exercise in futility.[54]

In this respect, Mickiewicz's suspicion that *Sonnets* "will be more to the liking of foreigners" was well-founded. It was not long before translations began appearing in the Russian press. His friend Viazemskii led the way (soon to be followed by the likes of Ivan I. Dmitriev, Ivan I. Kozlov, and then for the next two centuries by a host of other major and minor Russian literati), and Polevoi helped pave it. In a June issue of *Moskovskii telegraf*, Viazemskii prefaced his prose translation of the entire Crimean cycle with a lengthy, glowing appreciation, situating "this elegant work" firmly in its romantic context, beside Byron, Scott, and Moore, but no less saliently in the context of Polish-Russian relations. Lamenting the "familial misunderstanding" that had alienated these "fellow tribes," he praised Mickiewicz for his decision to publish *Sonnets* in Moscow and in this way to "promote the union" of the two Slavic "brothers." A romantically Orientalist depiction of a recently acquired Muslim land, intended, ostensibly, for an imperial audience, by someone whose own homeland had been annexed by the empire not so long ago seemed to have special resonance among the Polish poet's Russian friends.[55]

Not surprisingly, Mickiewicz's decision to publish *Sonnets* in Moscow was perceived somewhat differently by Poles. The classicists reacted with bemused envy upon hearing that "in Moscow Viazemskii, in Petersburg some illustrious littérateur and senator [i.e., Dmitriev] . . . have learned Polish in order to impart to their countrymen the fruits of this great poet." Most of Mickiewicz's friends, including Zan, were genuinely thrilled by his "success and glory." Not so the self-righteous Czeczot. The letter he sent Mickiewicz in this connection from his Siberian exile is not extant; the poet's response to it indicates that the depth of its censoriousness both surprised and hurt him. To his friend's accusations that he had betrayed one "lover" (that is, Poland) for the sybaritic blandishments of another, Mickiewicz replied:

> How can one link and connect meaningless gestures to this elevated and noble affect [i.e., love of the fatherland]? How in the world can dinners, dancing, and singing offend this divine lover? . . . By everything that is holy! You demean yourself, Janek, with genuine pedantry and cite the Moabites. How's that? You'd like to extract vengeance in an Old Testament way on the first-born, on dogs even. . . . Now I'll cite some more of the Bible for you: I'll tell you honestly that when I'm hungry, not only am I willing to eat the Moabites' tref steak, but even meat from the altar of Dagon and Baal—and will still remain the good Christian that I've always been.

To underscore how misguided Czeczot's imputations were in fact, Mickiewicz added in the next breath that he was "reading Schiller's *Fiesco* and Machiavelli's *History*," two of the most important ideological sources for *Konrad Wallenrod*. By the same token, he had no intention of changing his behavior. Quite the contrary, the poet's life in Moscow was soon enriched immeasurably by new social obligations as well as by new female acquaintances, both Russian and Polish.[56]

10

Sonnets appeared as Mickiewicz turned twenty-eight, already with "gray hairs among his dark ones." The success of the volume, at least in Russia, catapulted him into the ranks of the empire's literary celebrities. In Moscow, it helped open the doors to the city's leading salons. One was that of Avdot'ia P. Elagina, the Kireevskiis' mother, whose Sunday gatherings tended toward the Slavophilic but nonetheless attracted "everything in Moscow that was intelligent, educated, and talented," a fitting reflection of the hostess herself. On Wednesdays, these same intelligent, educated, and talented individuals, as well as "representatives of the beau monde, dignitaries and beauties," gathered in the dazzling salon of Princess Zinaida A. Volkonskaia, "the Corinne of the polar north."[57]

The daughter of an ambassador and scion of an illustrious Russian family, Volkonskaia was some eight years older than Mickiewicz. As a lady-in-waiting at the court of Alexander I and a romantic confidante of the tsar himself, she belonged to the highest strata of Russian society and was acquainted with practically all of the great names of Europe. Through her husband, one of Alexander's aides-de-camp, she was also close to several of the most prominent Decembrists, with whom she sympathized. But what attracted people to her salon in Moscow was not so much her social connections or wealth as her passion for beauty:

> Everything in this home carried the imprint of service to the arts and the mind. There would be readings, concerts, and Italian operas staged by dilettantes and amateurs. Among the artists and at their head stood the hostess herself. It is impossible for those who heard her to forget the impression made by her full, sonorous contralto and her spirited performance in the role of Tancredi in Rossini's opera.

Fig. 7 Zenaida Volkonskaia in the role of Tancredi. Oil painting by Feodor Bruni, 1820–22.

One of these performances surpassed all of Malewski's expectations, and he "had seen the opera more than once": "It [was] a role made especially for her; for a woman neither beautiful nor young, in *Tancredi* she was both beautiful and young." But neither Malewski nor Mickiewicz were able to visit as frequently as they would have liked. Evenings at Volkonskaia's did not come cheap: "One has to hire a sleigh, pay for better laundering of one's linen, etc. etc." This notwithstanding, by late spring of 1827 Mickiewicz was a welcome guest, one of the princess's favorite performers and soon enough an intimate.[58]

A measure of his relationship with Volkonskaia was the appropriately classicist poem he wrote that fall celebrating her "Greek room," which, "illuminated with an Etruscan lamp, was full of statues, statuettes, and all manner of ancient knick-knacks":

> Led through the darkness by her celestial gaze,
> In pursuit of her robe over ebony tiles,
> I entered.—Is this the land beyond Lethe's stream?
> That great mummy of cities, the corpse of Herculanum?
> No! At the beauty's command here, the world of the ancients
> Has been rebuilt....
>
> What shall I say upon my return to this, the world of us mortals?
> O, I shall say I was to paradise half-way,
> With a soul half-sad, half-joyous,
> That I had heard that blissful murmur—half-whispered
> And saw that blissful half-light and half-shadow,
> And experienced salvation—but only by half. (Dz. 1:266–68)*

The poem hints at an interest on Mickiewicz's part beyond bonds of friendship. Volkonskaia, though, resisted. This did not mean that she was unattracted to him, albeit her attraction, at once romantic in its pathos and aristocratic in its sympathy, was the kind one reserves for the exotic:

> Who is this man whose brow seems crowned with regrets, even amidst festivities and entertainments?... Is he tired of life?... Like a heavy chain round the hands of captives, does not remorse weigh down his thoughts? But no, his spirit is free and pure.... Noble in action, generous in sacrifice, everything that is true, everything that is beautiful warms and exalts him. His sadness is due to his exile and the fate of his tragic country.... A word is uttered and his joy is extinguished.
>
> Someone just mentioned in front of him a foreign land... *foreign* to us... sacred to him. It is where his mother wiped his first tear; it is where his heart loved for the first time, where thought for the fatherland made him a poet.... The young savage, transported to

*Mickiewicz personally translated the poem into French for Volkonskaia (*DzW* 1.2:256–57).

> Europe, notices a plant from his island; he hurls himself on it crying: O, Tahiti! . . . Thus the soul of a foreigner repeats the name of his native land.

Over the years, particularly when the two found themselves together in Rome, their affection for each other grew even deeper, developing into what was probably one of the poet's most cherished friendships. Volkonskaia would always "consider meeting [Mickiewicz] the most fortunate event in [her] life."[59]

Elagina's and Volkonskaia's salons provided yet another venue for what in any case were Mickiewicz's increasingly extensive contacts with Moscow's artistic and intellectual elite. He spent much of his free time—of which there was a great deal—in their company: breakfasts at Pogodin's; jaunts to the Russian countryside with the likes of Polevoi, Sobolevskii, Kireevskii, and Pushkin; evenings at Pogodin's, the Polevois', the Viazemskiis', and Sobolevskii's, arguing over philosophy, listening, on occasion, to Pushkin reading from his newest works, and joining them at the funeral of the poet Venevitinov, dead at the age of twenty-two of what everyone agreed was his unrequited love for Volkonskaia. He would on occasion visit with the old poet Dmitriev, who "did [Mickiewicz] the honor of translating one of the sonnets himself," and joined Pushkin's many friends at Sobolevskii's farewell party for the Russian poet on the eve of his departure to St. Petersburg. In the summer, Mickiewicz, together with the inseparable Malewski, spent some leisure time at Viazemskii's country estate of Ostaf'evo, and "practically every week [they] had to decline two invitations to dinner" at Volkonskaia's residence outside of Moscow and "accept only the third." Mickiewicz was eating voraciously "at the altar of Dagon and Baal" and on the surface, at least, enjoying it.[60]

In May of 1827, Mickiewicz and Malewski themselves moved out to the periphery of Moscow, this time leaving Jeżowski to fend for himself. If rent for the out-building of an old palace was higher than in town (sales of *Sonnets* were going well), it was also more spacious and quieter, set as it was amid "an English garden cut in half by the river Iauza." Aside from the "beau monde" and "monde barbare" that would descend on the park on weekends, this was "the countryside, and a beautiful countryside at that: no quacking of ducks, no squealing of piglets, no yelling of housekeepers." For Mickiewicz, the atmosphere proved conducive to work on *Konrad Wallenrod*, although the need to continually anticipate the censor's objections necessitated constant revisions. In mid-July, Malewski complained to Lelewel that he "was unable to squeeze the few dozen lines" out of Mickiewicz on which "hinged the almost completed, magnificent *Wallenrod*." By August, however, the poem was more or less finished.[61]

That September, Cyprian Daszkiewicz, another former Vilnius student and now a banker in Moscow who also served as Mickiewicz's plenipotentiary there, held a name-day party. The gathering was intimate, with only Poles present. In this it was reminiscent of the name-day fêtes in Vilnius, although on this occasion much more alcohol was consumed. Having recently finished his poetic tale, Mickiewicz was tired but nonetheless agreed to improvise a few lines in honor of the name-day boy. What came out showed a very different side of the Polish poet celebrated by his Russian friends as a "brother and countryman":

> If I remember correctly, he [i.e., Daszkiewicz] told me
> That I will gain fame for my rhymes,
> But he will be known in posterior times
> For his abacus only and hand.
> To exhaust one's hand on the Russians' machine,
> Pity him, please, every one,
> But he will avenge himself on all of those rogues,
> He will avenge himself on the jaws of the Russians. . . .
> Tiaras he'll tear off the heads of their priests—
> And will drown their women in streams,
> He'll demolish the towers of the Kremlin,
> And other miraculous feats he'll perform. . . .
> His only reward here is that now and again
> I'll pour out some rhymes in his praise,
> His only reward now is continual yearning
> That all of Moscow be burning! (*Dz.* 1:479–80)

Not the best poetry, to be sure, and the sentiments expressed were ostensibly those of Daszkiewicz. But as *Konrad Wallenrod* would soon make all too clear, they were sentiments that were certainly not alien to Mickiewicz himself. Indeed, he soon confided to Odyniec that he was working on still another poetic tale, "a pretty bizarre one, on a vast scale, and [didn't] know whether it'll ever be published." There is good reason to believe that the work in question was a first draft of what would later become the "Digression" to *Forefathers' Eve*, part 3, Mickiewicz's in part satirical, in part visionary, but in any case uncompromisingly negative depiction of the tsarist system.[62]

But such overt eruptions of anti-Russian sentiment were, it seems, rare, even among those with whom Mickiewicz felt most at ease. The new poem he was writing he was, in fact, "writing for [him]self." The poet had learned to be careful, to "slither stealthily like a snake" ("To My Russian Friends"; *Dz.* 3:308), knowing full well that his predicament was a precarious one and that his comportment was always under scrutiny, despite the good will of his Russian friends. Aside from his writing, then, his daily life was neither exceptionable nor exceptional. When his brother Aleksander came for a few-week visit to Moscow, he could report to Lelewel that

> Adam and Malewski are counted among those serving in the office of the governor-general, earn no salary, but also are not forced to perform any duties of service. The two

> dispose of their time as they please.... Adam and Malewski are heartily received by both their superior, Governor-General Golitsyn, and other illustrious homes, and there are streams of invitations. I found Adam working harder than I had expected.[63]

The autumn of 1827 proved unusually cold, while the cost of wood was prohibitive. Malewski and Mickiewicz were forced to move yet again. They found an apartment over the Medical Academy's print shop, within walking distance of everything, where they occupied separate rooms "so as not to get in each other's way." But as the weather grew even colder, the new accommodations, too, offered insufficient protection. "What of it," writes Malewski to his sisters,

> if I can see a hundred and fifty towers from my window, if I can do my usual rounds on foot... when it's cold, so cold. Adam's poetry is chattering its teeth and my prose is doing no better. I'm sitting like a Lapp covered with furs, and it's so cold, so cold.

But with the rent paid up front, vacating the new premises proved impossible. In any case, there was always a standing invitation at Volkonskaia's, where "it [was] warmer on the steps than by [Malewski's] stove." Too bad that one "couldn't visit her without a white ascot, without white gloves, and—oh, if only!—with a two-day beard!"[64]

As luck would have it, though, yet another temporary shelter materialized that fall in the person of Maria Szymanowska, who arrived in Moscow in November together with her blind sister and two teenage daughters, Helena and Celina. Nine years older than Mickiewicz, Szymanowska (née Wołowska) was the daughter of a Warsaw brewer and a member of a prominent Frankist clan. By the time she decided to settle in Russia, she was already one of Europe's most renowned pianists—Goethe adored her; Alexander I had appointed her first pianist of the court; Novosiltsov was among her most ardent admirers—and that rare woman of the time who, after a divorce, chose for herself an independent career as a professional. She was a person of "engaging urbanity, openness, naturalness, constantly sparkling wit, learning, uncommon musical talent and beautiful looks," who "would still... have stood out from the mass of civilized women even were she not to have had her priceless talent."[65]

Again, it was through Viazemskii, who knew Szymanowska from his Warsaw days, that Mickiewicz came to be acquainted with the pianist. Two days after they were first introduced, her sixteen-year-old daughter Helena noted in her diary on 24 November:

> Mr. Mickiewicz visited us. I had long wished to meet this famous poet, the creator of those beautiful ballads and sonnets that are so widely known and admired. He promised to visit us often and lend us certain Polish books.... Mr. Mickiewicz is as pleasant in company as he is in expressing his ideas and feelings.[66]

Fig. 8 Maria Szymanowska. Oil painting by Aleksander Kokular, 1825. Courtesy of the Adam Mickiewicz Museum of Literature, Warsaw.

Mickiewicz kept his promise, and then some. Together with Malewski, he was soon an almost daily guest in the home of "the queen of tones" ("To M.S."; Dz. 1:184). It became something of a Polish haven for him away from Moscow's Russian sea and, soon enough, from that of St. Petersburg. Indeed, nowhere during his years in Russia did he feel as at ease as in Szymanowska's family circle, which somehow managed to balance an openness to the aristocratic cosmopolitanism of the pianist's Russian admirers with unforced Polish hospitality. Her unaffected graciousness; her sense of play, which entertained as much as her play on the piano; the chatter and fuss of the teenage girls; the intimate circle of countrymen that would gather for Polish holidays; the banter between "His Romantic Highness" and "Her Archmusical Highness," founded on a shared love of music and poetry; and no less important, the Polish dishes her sister prepared so exquisitely—all of this created an atmosphere of domesticity that Mickiewicz had not experienced since his days in Kowno or, perhaps more aptly, Nowogródek. In Szymanowska, Mickiewicz found a maternal figure who, it seems, did not require the kind of erotic commitment demanded by the others.[67]

12

Although he had considered publishing *Wallenrod* in Poland, the success of *Sonnets* as well as apprehension about the Warsaw censor convinced Mickiewicz to publish his new poem in Russia as well. "Warsaw is far," he wrote to Odyniec, "and contacts are difficult, and the sales are not great." But because there was no longer anyone in the Moscow censor's office who could handle the Polish, he decided this time on St. Petersburg, where getting the work through a censor would in any case be easier. Malewski, for his part, had his eyes set on a career in the imperial capital. Both were waiting for an opportunity to accompany their superior, Prince Golitsyn, who was planning a trip there sometime that winter.[68]

Mickiewicz was also hoping that his presence in St. Petersburg would facilitate another project he had conceived that fall. Impressed by the relative (to Poland) modernism of Russian culture and at the same time depressed by Poles' ignorance of it, he had petitioned the Moscow censor for permission to publish with Malewski a Polish-language journal that would at the same time acquaint its readers with "the ever more numerous riches of Russian literature, the development of the sciences, arts, and crafts, the changes which the continual progress of civilization effects in a state as powerful as this." The journal was to be entitled *Iris*, "a periodical devoted to learning and literature." But despite assurances that the project's aim was to encourage mutual understanding, the sins of the Philomaths proved indefeasible; even the well-intentioned Shishkov refused to sign off on it. In light of this episode, the fate of *Konrad Wallenrod* is rather astonishing.[69]

Mickiewicz and Malewski left Moscow in the company of their superior on 1/13 December 1827, Malewski with plans for a permanent position in St. Petersburg, Mickiewicz for a short stay for now, to see *Wallenrod* through, but already considering eventually settling in the northern capital as well. They took up lodging with their old friend from Vilnius, Marian Piasecki, whom Mickiewicz had appointed his plenipotentiary in St. Petersburg, with a salary of "thanks and obeisances." Piasecki's immediate task was to urge the censor, Vasilii G. Anastasevich, to read the manuscript of *Wallenrod* as quickly as possible. In this he proved to be unusually effective, and the censor surprisingly compliant: Anastasevich signed off on the work on 9/21 of that month, insisting that only one line ("You are a slave, and a slave's only weapon is deceit" [*Dz.* 2:290]) be deleted.[70]

Malewski set about knocking on doors of the capital's bureaucracy. Mickiewicz, for his part, now had to tend to the publication of his new poem, but also to his brother Jerzy, now a doctor in the Russian navy, whom upon his arrival in St. Petersburg he had found "in a bacchanal mood" and "whose bad behavior caused [him] much grief." In any case, Mickiewicz and Malewski found plenty of time to renew old acquaintances and make new ones.[71]

Three years had passed since their first stay in St. Petersburg. Under Tsar Nicholas the city had been transformed into something resembling a military camp. The omnipresence of his secret police, the Third Department, was palpable everywhere. To his friends Mickiewicz too had changed, but in his case for the better. No longer the youthful, somewhat sickly, somewhat timid political exile from Lithuania,

> Mickiewicz had changed a bit in appearance; he had grown sideburns, which ma[de] him more distinguished, His complexion [was] healthier, he had become more virile. . . . In company, he [was] not eccentric, as he had been before, and indeed, [was] very loose and engaging. . . . His talent had matured, his conversation, enriched by both what he had read and what he had seen, [was], in addition, marked by a rich imagination. He now like[d] to talk a lot, often only his voice alone [was] to be heard in company, and everyone gladly [grew] silent in order to listen to him.

"His arrival in St. Petersburg created an unheard of sensation," and this among Russians as well as Poles, who "outvied each other in showing him their respect." Mickiewicz quite literally had to choose among the invitations that poured in daily.[72]

Shortly after the poet's arrival, Pushkin organized a festive breakfast for his Polish acquaintance from Moscow; Mickiewicz soon returned the honor in kind with a dinner. The two poets grew closer that winter, and Pushkin even introduced Mickiewicz to his father. Their relationship was lubricated by evenings at Anton A. Del'vig's, a friend of Pushkin from their school days, where the two poets would engage in "long and obstinate discussions . . . sometimes in Russian, sometimes in French. [Pushkin] spoke with ardor, often wittily, but not smoothly; [Mickiewicz], quietly, fluently, and always very logically."[73]

The symbolic import of an ostensible friendship between two poets, both "beloved of their people," was not lost on their contemporaries. To celebrate their presence together in St. Petersburg, Walenty Wańkowicz decided to paint portraits of them both: of Mickiewicz on the crag of Ajudah; of Pushkin (not extant), draped in a Byronic cape as well, "standing in thought and contemplation beneath a shade tree." They stood side by side on display in the artist's atelier, but on separate canvases. The ideological exigencies of succeeding decades would force them together into a single frame.[74]

It was about this time too that Pushkin, with the help of a literal translation, undertook to translate *Wallenrod* into Russian verse, which clearly tickled Mickiewicz's ego. The Russian poet gave up, however, after thirty-eight lines, realizing "that he [did] not know how to translate, that is, [did] not know how to submit himself to the hard work of a translator." More submissive in this respect was the blind Petersburg poet Kozlov, perhaps Byron's most enduring Russian admirer, who set to translating the *Crimean Sonnets*. Touched by this "poor blind man," Mickiewicz took to visiting Kozlov and, "sitting at the sickbed of the blind poet, would himself point out passages [in the translations] that did not reflect his thoughts faithfully." Perhaps it was out of sympathy that he declared to Odyniec that of all the Russian renditions of the work, Kozlov's were "the best."[75]

Even Vasilii Zhukovskii, one of the fathers of modern Russian literature, let on at one point that "were he to pick up his pen again, he'd devote it to translating [Mickiewicz's] poems." The Polish poet had not forgotten Zhukovskii's notice of his first volumes of poetry, and he was eager to meet the writer who was also tutor to the emperor's children. Armed with letters of introduction from both Viazemskii and Elagina, who assured Zhukovskii that he "would come to love this enchanting creature," Mickiewicz made a positive impression. The feeling, apparently, was mutual. He left Zhukovskii with a sense of genuine respect, albeit more for his stature as "a human being than a poet," whose "works were good insofar as they were written by a superlative human being who had infused them with his soul." Their brief acquaintance proved mutually beneficial. Zhukovskii tried pulling strings on Mickiewicz's behalf when the Polish poet was searching for a position in St. Petersburg. For his part, Mickiewicz wrote a lengthy note for the Russian poet characterizing the major personalities on the Polish literary scene shortly before the latter's trip to Warsaw in 1829 (Dz. 14:554–57) and recommended him to Lelewel as "a man of uncommon character, uncommon honesty, and a dear friend of mine." His disappointment was therefore great when in 1831, Zhukovskii, together with Pushkin, "shamed by his positions and by medals" ("To My Russian Friends"; Dz. 3:307), produced a pamphlet of triumphalist poems condemning the Polish uprising; but to say that he was surprised by their display of loyalty would be an overstatement.[76]

For all of the good will Mickiewicz encountered among the Russian literati of St. Petersburg, it was the Polish expatriate community that was the first to greet him like the celebrity he was, full of pride at the success of a countryman. Besides the acquaintances Mickiewicz had made in 1824—Bułharyn, Sękowski, Przecławski, Wańkowicz, Orłowski, Oleszkiewicz—the capital was also now home to a number of his old friends from Vilnius.

It was in their company, mostly male, mostly single, that Mickiewicz preferred to spend his evenings, "reminding" him as they did "of the amusements of his younger days." As Orłowski drew pictures of the assembled guests on napkins and scraps of paper and with Malewski tickling the keys of a piano, much food and alcohol was consumed and many anecdotes exchanged. Conversations ranged from free speech and literature to etymology and religion. Bułharyn would sometimes read from his newest (Russian-language) novel, while Sękowski managed to infuriate everyone with his cynical sarcasms. Mickiewicz, for his part, declaimed excerpts from his soon-to-be-published poem. And if the atmosphere was conducive he would improvise.[77]

The poet's Vilnius friends remembered well his talent for improvisation when at the Philomaths' name-day celebrations or during their incarceration, he had amused them with his impromptu verse. It was in a similar context, and in a similar vein (the subject matter notwithstanding) that he had improvised in Moscow for Daszkiewicz. Now, in St. Petersburg, his improvisations crossed into a different dimension.

Mickiewicz would ask the guests for a topic—"the beginning of the world and the miracles of creation" (Oleszkiewicz); the Polish legions (Bułharyn); Parry's expedition to the North Pole (Sękowski)—and then, always to the accompaniment of music, proceeded to develop the topic in rhyme, sometimes two topics a night, interspersing these longer "odes" with shorter improvisations about the guests or poetry or the immediate circumstances. The poet forbade his listeners to write his efforts down (for good reason, perhaps, as the improvisation at Daszkiewicz's would indicate). Even for those who were familiar with performances of Italian *improvisatori*, there was something extraordinary about Mickiewicz's displays of poetic prowess. These were not so much performances, exhibitions of the poet's facility with meter and rhyme and invention, as they were manifestations of some uncontrollable inner force, as if "the inspiration he had called forth was no longer obeying him, but had taken possession of his being." As he himself recalled years later, "God would give me special favors, I sometimes had extraordinary emotions, I would ascend into a state of ecstasy."[78]

The most remarkable of these improvisations occurred on 24 December, which also happened to be Mickiewicz's name-day. One of the poet's acquaintances organized a traditional Polish Christmas Eve supper. After the meal, and after many glasses of wine, Prince Leon Sapieha, scion of an ancient and illustrious Polish family, asked Mickiewicz to improvise. The poet told Malewski to play his favorite aria from *The Marriage of Figaro* and proceeded to improvise on events from sixteenth-century Polish history relating to the Sapiehas. As one participant of the evening noted down in his diary a few days later:

> He declaimed in one breath, as it were, an ode so grand that at the most beautiful passages everyone, thrilled as they were with admiration and seized with a kind of fervor, involuntarily let out cries and as if by some previous agreement repeated entire stanzas along with him. . . . A strange scene it was, as everyone strained keenly to hear the poet;

> for his part, he sat in a chair and attuned his voice to the music. Whoever wanted to see the expression on the poet's face or see his eyes would get up on a chair... and everyone remained silent, as if solemnly bringing an offering to the gods.

This, however, was just an appetizer. When some of the guests decided to call Mickiewicz on his claim that "he could easily improvise a tragedy," "the poet repaired to another room and after a quarter of an hour, while everyone was sitting in impatient expectation on chairs arranged in a semicircle, he came out and began improvising." He improvised several entire scenes to the enthusiastic applause of everyone present. But just as it seemed that he was done for the evening, Mickiewicz acceded to the demands of his audience and, again after a few minutes of solitude, added yet another scene to the tragedy. He had improvised, in all, "some two thousand lines."[79]

During the break, Mickiewicz remarked that "such an effort cost him nothing," adding, "When it comes to quickness of invention or improvisation I leave [Shakespeare] far behind. More than that, I know of no one who is my equal." None too modest, but Mickiewicz now grasped that he was capable of producing poetry on demand and could satisfy that demand completely. He could see this with his own eyes, after all, hear it in the enthusiastic shouts of his listeners, feel it in their embraces. The belief that this was a function not so much of a God-given talent, but rather of divine grace and divine choice would come with time. For now, his improvisations confirmed for him that his poetry had the power to move, even if, or perhaps because, it was produced at the behest of his Polish listeners. In its own way, *Konrad Wallenrod* was Mickiewicz's manifesto of this new-found relationship.[80]

13

The proofs were ready by the first week of January. Bułharyn had offered to pay for the printing out of his own pocket in return for a cut of the sales. Although Malewski helped in the editing, Mickiewicz complained that "the work was going slowly because everyone has slacked off and [he] had to run around and do the corrections [him]self." But once the proofs were completed, the poet did not wait for the book to come off the presses. He hurried back to Moscow on 27 January/8 February, leaving all the remaining arrangements, including the subscription, to Malewski and their Polish friends in St. Petersburg.[81]

Konrad Wallenrod, a Historical Tale from Lithuanian and Prussian History, appeared on 21 February/4 March 1828, in the print shop of Karol Kray. It contained three lithographs of scenes from the poem,* and "errors so numerous that entire lines [were] missing." Bułharyn gave

*While still in Moscow, Mickiewicz had planned an elaborate frontispiece, which, however, was never realized. "The scene is as follows," he wrote to the artist: "When holed up in a cell, [the hero], the grand master [of the Teutonic Knights], likes to drink to excess; at times like these he falls into a kind of violent fit, grabs a lute, and sings, and when the knights find him in this situation, he stops singing, gets angry, makes

the new work "of the most renowned Polish poet Adam Mickiewicz" plenty of publicity by announcing its appearance in his journal *Severnaia pchela*, one of the most widely read periodicals of the time. Szymanowska set three lyrical passages to song. In Vilnius, some one hundred copies disappeared from the shelves immediately. In Cracow, a scarcity of copies impelled well-meaning students to produce their own edition (which cost Mickiewicz 100 ducats from what was to have been an authorized Galician reprint).[82]

For all of its antiquarian dissimulation, Byronic opaqueness, and Scottian mystery, what is remarkable is that this historical tale of conspiracy and treason against a rapacious foreign foe, with its motto—"*Dovete adunque sapere, come sono due generazioni da combattere . . . bisogna essere volpe e leone*" [It should be understood that there are two types of fighting . . . it is necessary to be a fox and a lion] (Dz. 2:67)—taken from Machiavelli, was published in Russia at all.

Based, supposedly, on an episode from fourteenth-century Lithuanian history, the poem recounts the story of Konrad Wallenrod, a dark, brooding figure straight out of Byron who is elected grand master of the Teutonic Knights as they are about to conduct yet another campaign against the Lithuanians. As it turns out, Wallenrod is himself a Lithuanian who had been kidnapped by the Teutonic Knights together with a Lithuanian bard named Halban. The two had eventually made their way back to their native Lithuania, where Konrad, his national identity kept alive for all these years by Halban, married his old Lithuanian flame Aldona. But while battling the Germans he came to realize that in open combat the Lithuanians were no match for the much stronger foe. "Unable to find happiness at home, because there was none in his land" (Dz. 2:109), he had decided to abandon his wife and assume the identity of a Teutonic Knight in a treacherous scheme to destroy the order from within, "With one jolt of a column, to tear down the walls, / And like Samson, to perish beneath them" (Dz. 2:136). In this he now succeeds. As their grand master, he leads the Knights in a winter campaign against the Lithuanians that proves disastrous for the order. All this, however, comes at the cost of his love, his conscience, and, ultimately, his life. Discovered for what he is, Wallenrod commits suicide, broken, tragically, by a life of guile and deceit. "I cannot go on any longer," he says at one point,

> I am a human, after all!
> In ignoble duplicity my youth have I spent,
> In bloodshed and plunder—now stooping with age,

threats, and curses sacrilegiously. In moments like these [his mentor], the pagan [Lithuanian] priest, sits across from him and, fixing his glance on Wallenrod's face, disarms his anger. Just at that moment a pair of knights open the door. Wallenrod casts his lute to the ground and, standing at a table, stares angrily; the priest sits across from him, with his arms folded on his chest, and stares patiently into the eyes of the grand master" (Mickiewicz to Gotard Sobański, [10/22 August 1827], Dz. 14:420).

> Treacheries bore me, I'm unable to fight,
> Enough of revenge—even Germans are humans. (*Dz.* 2:128–29)

But Halban, who had disguised himself as Wallenrod's minstrel, survives his pupil in order to preserve the memory of his deed in song, the "ark of the covenant / Between ages gone by and the present," guarding "the nation's cathedral of memories, / With an archangel's wings and an archangel's voice— / Wielding at times an archangel's sword" (*Dz.* 2:101).

For once, Novosiltsov's paranoia was fully justified, proving that suspicion makes for perceptive criticism. In a lengthy report *cum* review to Grand Duke Constantine, Mickiewicz's nemesis saw right through the work's "historicism," claiming that in the guise of "the alluring beauty of poetry" the work "instructs how to nurse a concealed enmity, a sham loyalty, and how to prepare people living among us, who are considered foreigners because they are not of the same ethnicity, for treason most insidious." Citing Bułharyn's advertisement, Novosiltsov broadened his denunciation (part of its aim was, after all, to destroy Bułharyn as well):

> Why all these emphatic pronouncements about a mediocre work, which, to be sure, contains in places some very good verses, but also many weak ones and ones without meaning, and consists of pied rags, as it were, of uneven sections, which should have no place in a work that is being praised so. . . . So-called patriots see in Mickiewicz a representative of their concealed thoughts and by praising . . . his works propagate their own sentiments among others.

What Novosiltsov did not know at the time was that Bułharyn (whose tactics were in fact no different than his) was working for the Third Department. Thanks largely to his intervention, Mickiewicz was spared any unpleasantness. The tsar decided "to let the matter pass without any serious repercussions."[83]

Nonetheless, as a consequence of Novosiltsov's critique, the Warsaw press was for a time forbidden to mention Mickiewicz's name.* This did not, of course, prevent Poles from expressing their views on *Wallenrod* in other fora—and express them they did, in correspondence, conversation, and, ultimately, behavior. That the work happened to appear just as the Polish Diet was holding a highly visible, and potentially explosive, trial

*The ban was lifted in 1829, with the proviso, however, that only negative opinions of the poet could appear in print.

of the conspiratorial Patriotic Society on charges of treason served only to hasten the transformation of Mickiewicz's poetics into politics.

It was, then, not so much the language or style of *Wallenrod* that elicited the disapproval of Warsaw's neoclassicists. On this score they were, in fact, surprisingly indulgent. To be sure, they criticized the poem's logic, its narrative ellipses and vagueness, its patchy composition (Mickiewicz would concur with them on this). But they also found that "Mickiewicz is more comprehensible in this freakish work than he was in *Ballads* and *Sonnets*"; "that his Polish is purer, that the author has improved his grammar a bit." Yet this, as Novosiltsov had remarked, was precisely what made *Wallenrod* all the more insidious. No. In the eyes of the Polish classicists, all of them raised on the republican virtues of Old Polish gentry culture, it was the work's moral trajectory that offended. That Mickiewicz should choose for a hero—and thus an ideal for emulation—someone who was "a traitor, a madman, and a drunk" was inexcusable. In doing so, he offended not only, or not so much even, good taste, but the good name of the Polish people, with its reputation, ostensibly, for integrity and probity. As Kajetan Koźmian, the most implacable of Mickiewicz's neoclassicist adversaries, insisted, "I do not want a Poland obtained at the price of honor!"[84]

For a generation raised in bondage, however, the work proved electrifying. If the illegal reprint of *Wallenrod* constituted an eloquent, albeit misguided, tribute to its impact among Cracow's students, the work's reception in the Congress Kingdom was commensurate with the degree of its citizenry's radicalization. "Every class," wrote a German chronicler of the November Uprising in 1830, "women and youths, the army and civilians drank in this great and patriotic poem with boundless enthusiasm." And here too, aesthetic criteria were not much more of an issue than they were for the loyalist neoclassicists. Although early reactions among romantic readers noted "all of the beauties in this masterpiece," while at the same time questioning some of the poet's aesthetic decisions, what they were responding to first and foremost were the political implications of Mickiewicz's work. As the student who was instrumental in reprinting *Wallenrod* in Cracow recalled some sixty years later:

> As I read [the poem], the ardor of my listeners increased . . . until it finally exploded in such frenzied ecstasy that some almost began going crazy. I remember that when I was declaiming the lines . . . :
>
> Happiness he could not find at home,
> Because there was none in his land [Dz. 2:109]—
>
> there resounded a moan so keen that it reverberates in my ears to this day.[85]

In his chronicle of the 1830–1831 uprising, the romantic critic and politician Maurycy Mochnacki observed:

> Every . . . people wanting to regain its existence . . . needs enthusiasm and poetry. . . . Everything that spoke to the imagination *appeared* to be concerned with the fatherland oppressed by its enemies. In this way, literature in Poland, like the people, began to conspire. We are thus able to grasp why it is precisely at this time . . . that a person such as Adam Mickiewicz emerged in this literature.

The operative word here is, of course, "appeared." The fact that Mickiewicz's treasonous hero is ultimately a tragic figure who breaks down in the face of the moral implications of his actions and dies a lonely, self-inflicted death appears to have gone unremarked by those intent on reading the work as a call to arms rather than something approaching a cry of despair. For generations, his countrymen would be moved solely by *Konrad Wallenrod's* tyrtean dimension: "We understood this solemn, this great, this terrible challenge to our oppressors. We threw down our books and the sword of the Archangel flashed in our hand."[86]

Indeed, the poem would come to be perceived not only as a blueprint for conspiracy and resistance, but, more egregiously, as legitimating the belief that patriotic ends could justify even the most despicable means. With time, the term "Wallenrodism," denoting a strategy of dissimulation by the weak in their struggle against a stronger oppressor—or even dissimulation, pure and simple—would be used to characterize a specific mode of Polish behavior, praised by some, reviled by others, and exploited by patriot and scoundrel alike.

In view of this, the enthusiastic reaction to *Wallenrod* by Mickiewicz's Russian contemporaries is, at first glance, as puzzling as the censor's permission. Within two months of its appearance, Shevyrev produced a prose translation of the poem that, in subsequent years, was followed by a slew of translations of various excerpts. Actually, translation even proved to be unnecessary. "The circle of the poet's numerous Russian admirers knew the poem without knowing the Polish language, that is, knew its contents and pored over its minutiae and beauties." After *Sonnets*, *Wallenrod* became Mickiewicz's most popular work among Russians until it was finally banned, together with any mention of his name, in 1834.[87]

In an anonymous review of the Polish original, the editor of *Moskovskii telegraf*, remarked that Mickiewicz's new poem,

> as both the Polish classicists and romantics admit, sets him above all contemporary Polish poets. . . . It's sad to think that we Russians, we, for whom the Polish language is closer than that of any other people, on account of our ignorance of this rich, beautiful,

and kindred language, are deprived of the enjoyment of reading this new, outstanding work of Polish poetry.

To this, Polevoi added a characteristic note, "With a joyful feeling of pride, we are tracking the majestic flight of a genius, our fellow countryman!" There is no reason to believe that he wrote these words in anything but good faith. Indeed, Polevoi and other sympathetic Russian readers had every right to claim Mickiewicz as their own. It is they, after all, who nurtured him, who reinforced his talent with encouragement and adulation; it is they who legitimated him in the eyes of his fellow Poles. By the same token, the subtext of *Wallenrod* was all too transparent and, in fact, equally legible against the background of the Decembrist conspiracy. One did not, of course, write of such things in Nicholas's Russia, and to even suggest them would have been tantamount to denouncing Mickiewicz. Polevoi, it seems, was not averse to playing his own version of Wallenrod.[88]

And what of Mickiewicz himself? He was "not particularly pleased with *Wallenrod*; there [were] beautiful passages, but not everything [was] to [his] liking." The poet was particularly dissatisfied with the compositional adjustments he was forced to make with an eye toward the censor. The fact that Russians greeted his work with enthusiasm and poets of the caliber of Pushkin were eager to translate it was "enough to arouse jealousy." As for its reception back home, for the moment he only had inklings, and in any case the magnitude of *Wallenrod's* impact would not be felt fully until the outbreak of the uprising. With time, however, Mickiewicz came to view the poem critically, as little more than "a political pamphlet... important for its time." At one point, he even went so far as to express a desire to "buy up all editions of *Wallenrod* and burn them on one pyre..., since by extolling treason in it, [he] had promoted that repulsive idea among [his] people."[89]

This, however, was years later, when the work had acquired a turbulent life of its own. At the time it was written, though, it marked a radical metamorphosis in Mickiewicz's conception of himself as a poet. Until now, his had been largely the voice of a militant romantic bent on transforming the aesthetic horizon of Polish literature. Hence the ballads and stylizations of folk ritual, hence the tales from the Lithuanian Middle Ages, the apotheoses of romantic love, and the Oriental sonnets—all constitutive elements of the European romantic repertoire that he almost single-handedly made Polish, but also intensely personal—self-indulgent, even, as the poet himself suggested in the erotic sonnets. But by this very same token, this was a repertoire that was, at least for those who shared his sensibility, universally understood; it was precisely this poetry that earned Mickiewicz the international recognition he so craved for both himself and his literature. In depicting a hero who sacrifices personal happiness for the good of his collective, Mickiewicz was in a sense telling of his own willingness to sacrifice himself as an artist for the sake of his nation's political struggle. If this gesture was to no small degree the function of a conscience troubled by his charmed life in Russia, it was no less a function of the self-confidence that came with fame.

But the very behavior of *Wallenrod's* eponymous hero also articulated the complexity of his creator's predicament. For Mickiewicz, the threat Russia posed to Poland's existence was obvious; so too was its asymmetrical nature, necessitating precisely a strategy of resistance by other means. Yet many enlightened citizens of that same imperial colossus had proven to be not just hospitable, and sympathetic, hosts, but had become an intimate part of the poet's life. Would not treason against their state for the sake of one's own nation also not be understood as a betrayal of genuine friendships? The choices were painful, with, ultimately, profound repercussions on Mickiewicz's own behavior in 1830, when news of the Polish insurgents' attack on Grand Duke Constantine's residence in Warsaw prompted one insurgent to exclaim, "The word became flesh, and Wallenrod—the Belvedere Palace."[90]

14

In an April 1828 letter to Zan that accompanied two copies of *Wallenrod* as well as 100 rubles to be divided between him and Czeczot, Mickiewicz reported from Moscow:

> My life flows uneventfully and, for all intents and purposes, happily; so happily that I worry whether envious Nemesis is not preparing some new vexations for me. Calmness, freedom of thought (at least privately). Pleasant diversions every now and again, never any violently passionate emotions (private ones, it goes without saying).... I'm pretty lazy now, although I'm always reading and thinking a great deal. My every day goes by uniformly. In the morning, I read, sometimes—rarely—I write, at two or three I eat dinner or get dressed for dinner; I go to concerts in the evening or to some other entertainment and often return late. I am also teaching some ladies Polish.

Mickiewicz's serenity came with the knowledge of a job well done and hence a sense of confidence in his abilities to guarantee a no less serene future, understandable fears for tomorrow notwithstanding. Yet Mickiewicz, as was his wont in letters to Zan, was also being somewhat disingenuous. His private, emotional, life was a bit more tumultuous than he let on.[91]

In the same letter, Mickiewicz writes that "despite Petersburg's many pleasures, [he] tore himself away to Moscow" in order "to catch the Zaleski family before their departure" back to Ukraine. The poet's benefactress and sometime lover had arrived in Moscow together with her husband in July of 1827, ostensibly to see the city but above all to see Mickiewicz again. He and Malewski acted as their *ciceroni*, in return for which they "ate the Zaleskis out of house and home." Since her husband was absent for much of the time, Zaleska felt less constrained to lavish her attentions on the poet, which included translating the Crimean sonnets as well as *Wallenrod* into French. But the lavisher received less in return than she had hoped.[92]

To be sure, Mickiewicz enjoyed Zaleska's company immensely but, it would seem, only as a "friend" (she was, after all, married), "a patron of [his] sad fate," a comfort in a foreign land, someone to whom he "owed" his capacity to "endure suffering" and "pain" ("To a Friend"; Dz. 1:269). For Zaleska, however, the poet's presence made "holy" a city she had heretofore found unattractive. Upon her return to Odessa in early 1828, the thought that she might never see him again made "death frightening"; his silence, despite her pleas "for one word from him," made her desperate. Jettisoning all sense of propriety, she dared open herself up to him directly, at the same time relinquishing, it seems, all hope of reciprocity:

> I fear that my frequent letters spare you, at the very sight of the address, from a reflex of impatience. They must surely importune you, overwhelm you; I feel this, I know this, and yet I do not have the courage to throw my pen away when an excess of suffering leads me to my desk in order to seek consolation next to you. . . . It is dark, so dark in my soul that only loneliness like that of the grave will be able to cure it.—Have mercy, tell me what your travel plans are and if I shall see you . . . , for it is only this hope that keeps me here.—Adieu, adieu, there are feelings that belong more in heaven than on earth, and such are the ones I harbor for you.

Relieved by the seeming finality of her adieus, Mickiewicz finally—after many months—succumbed to her entreaties "for a word," but certainly not for any kind of commitment. Disabusing her of hope for a rendezvous, he offered little more than a few kind pieces of advice concerning her health.[93]

Zaleska would never get to see her "dear Adam" again. What she did see, and what was surely a sign of abiding affection on the part of the poet, was the dedication to her, as well as her husband, of *Konrad Wallenrod*, a work that Mickiewicz had begun while still in Odessa but which now constituted "a memento of the year 1827" (Dz. 2:68).

But the pressure Zaleska exerted on Mickiewicz paled in comparison to the predicament he found himself in with Karolina Jaenisch, one of the "young ladies" the poet was tutoring in Polish. The daughter of a Russified German professor, this third in a series of Karolinas was some seven years younger than Mickiewicz but certainly a match for him intellectually. Thanks to her father, Jaenisch was well versed in the natural sciences (always of interest to Mickiewicz) as well as in painting, music, and aesthetics and, according to the poet Nikolai M. Iazykov, knew "an extraordinary number of languages: Russian, French, German, . . . Spanish, Italian, Swedish, and Dutch," which "she constantly flashed and showed off." She was no less annoyingly generous with her gift for poetry, "loudly declaiming her verses and monopolizing conversation." Later, as Karolina Pavlova, this "dark-eyed, thick-haired, but skinny" young woman would become one of Russia's most notable female poets.[94]

Fig. 9 Karolina Jaenisch. Portrait by K. Moldawski, 1841. Courtesy of the Adam Mickiewicz Museum of Literature, Warsaw.

Like other Russians whose "eyes were opened to Polish literature" by the appearance of *Sonnets*, Jaenisch too expressed a desire to learn Polish. Having been introduced to Mickiewicz at Volkonskaia's salon in the winter of 1826, she convinced her father that only their author himself would do as a tutor. She soon made such progress that, as her teacher remarked, "it amazed everyone except those who kn[e]w her unusual talent for every kind of subject." Within a year Jaenisch was already translating *Wallenrod* into German, although Mickiewicz admonished her for not "making better use of her time." The comment captures eloquently the nature of their relationship. Jaenisch's study of Polish, the translations of her tutor's poetry, her portraits of him, all were at once gifts to her beloved and attempts at making his most intimate possessions hers. Mickiewicz's response was at first dismissive, just as his pet name for her, "the Painter," was more condescending than affectionate. His only extant letter to Jaenisch, a humorous description of a game of chess couched in military terminology, set the tone for their relationship, figuring it, somewhat puerilely, as one of conquest and defense.[95]

By the fall of the following year, however, their relationship had taken a turn for the serious. On 10/22 November 1827, Mickiewicz apparently declared his love for Jaenisch, which this "young" woman with "an overly active imagination, whose common sense had been stifled by an enormous amount of reading" understood as a proposal. To his friends, as well as to himself, the poet would insist on denying that this was ever his intent, and in any case, when Jaenisch's uncle, the benefactor of her family, "declared that he would disinherit [her] father were their union to be contracted," it appeared that the whole question would become moot. Yet neither Jaenisch nor Mickiewicz found the strength to break things off. She was too infatuated and always held out the hope that minds could be changed; he, it seems, maintained the relationship out of a pity masking as much his fear of commitment as an inability to make sense of his own desires. Mickiewicz's second, and this time final, departure to St. Petersburg in the spring of 1828 may in part be viewed as an attempt to create facts on the ground. Absence certainly did not make his heart grow fonder, but then neither did it make it any more decisive.[96]

Social convention precluded direct correspondence between the two, hence, as he had done once before in such circumstances, Mickiewicz enlisted a go-between. This time the lot fell to Daszkiewicz. That the latter happened to himself be in love with Jaenisch—hopelessly, of course—made Mickiewicz's vacillations doubly cruel. In a letter written shortly after his arrival in St. Petersburg in April 1828, the poet inquired, again in military terms, how Daszkiewicz's "campaigns [were] going," then immediately warned him to stay away from the Jaenisch "fortress," since his own "siege has not yet been lifted and who knows if [he] would not storm it again." But some three months later, denying that he ever proposed to her, Mickiewicz informed Daszkiewicz that he "likes the Painter, but [is] certainly not so in love as to be jealous or to be unable to live without her." Indeed, he suggested that she should feel free to look for "other candidates for marriage." Then again, after counseling Daszkiewicz how he should deal with Jaenisch and, at the same time, insinuating that the two would simply never be happy, the poet proceeded to castigate his friend for his jealousy, maintaining that he himself "has no claims on the Painter," although "were [he] to return to Moscow or stay in Russia . . . [he] might then think about her."[97]

As Daszkiewicz's predicament was becoming increasingly untenable and Jaenisch's behavior increasingly hysterical, Mickiewicz's own conduct was becoming increasingly neurotic. He continued to delay, equivocate, and, indeed, to manipulate. Finally, although still insisting that he was never in love, that he never promised anything, that there were numerous obstacles on both his end and hers, he seemed to relent, reluctantly. In early 1829, the poet instructed Daszkiewicz to tell Jaenisch that he would go to Moscow "and marry her or get engaged and arrange a *rendez-vous* in Dresden." Positing an alternative here was symptomatic, particularly in view of the fact that Mickiewicz still had no idea whether he would receive permission to travel abroad. And then there were the conditions: "If Karolina keeps behaving erratically and getting sick, tell her that she'll never hear from me [again]." In any case, he warned Daszkiewicz that once he passed this proposal on to Jaenisch, he was "to henceforth consider her [Mickiewicz's] wife."[98]

In the face of these conditions and hesitations, Jaenisch could no longer restrain herself. She wrote Mickiewicz a letter directly, begging him to come back to Moscow "to decide her fate one way or another," unable as she was "to bear the uncertainty any longer, the continual expectation, the incessant agitation":

> I see now that I'm unable to live without thinking of you; . . . that my entire existence is but a continuous memory. Mickiewicz! whatever happens, my soul is yours. If I can't live for you, my life is finished. . . . Was I not a thousand times happier when I could not hope? I met you, I got to know you, I understood you . . . , through the power of my love I understood your soul! You fell in love with me—what misfortune can be as great as that good fortune? . . . I now know that were I to abandon this hope, so inexpressibly beautiful, that you gave me, I would never again find happiness. . . . Farewell, my beloved!

As happened so often in the poet's relationships with women—and would happen again and again—Mickiewicz let external circumstances decide for him. Jaenisch's apparent resignation certainly made matters easier; his departure for the West solved them.[99]

15

Mickiewicz's initial indecision with regard to Jaenisch may indeed be explained, but only in part, by a genuine sense of uncertainty about his own future. For now, proceeds from his publications kept him in money; his various acquaintances kept him fed and entertained. Tending to the sales of his books as well as preparing a new edition of his works occupied some of his time, while reading, writing letters, visits of and to friends, and social obligations helped pass it. He was, nonetheless, still unemployed, and he was not the kind of writer to sit at a desk according to a daily routine. He was getting restless. The brief stay in St. Petersburg in 1827–1828, with its Polish community as well as cosmopolitan sophistication, had convinced him that it was time to at least leave Moscow and rejoin Malewski.

By the same token, the poet never ceased dreaming about other destinations. Like his fellow exiles, he grasped at any opportunity to seek permission to return to Poland, to which end—ostensibly on account of Mickiewicz's "family circumstances"—Pushkin wrote a supporting letter to the secret police. But as long as Novosiltsov continued to be obsessed with the Philomaths' peripeties, this prospect seemed unlikely; in any case, he considered other, and truth be told, more exciting possibilities. "The Caucasus or Crimea?" he wrote to Zan, "Sometimes even Orenburg sounds tempting, sometimes I dream of Italy." His influential Russian friends—Golitsyn, Volkonskaia, Viazemskii, Zhukovskii—as well as Bułharyn were well aware of these dreams and made every effort to help. For now, though, Mickiewicz's immediate task was to gain permission to settle in the northern capital. In April, he petitioned Golitsyn for a two-month leave of absence "in the hope of finding a position in St. Petersburg." Golitsyn granted the request, just as he would end up granting another three.[100]

Mickiewicz's return to Moscow in early 1828 was thus a brief one. He was particularly heartened by the fact that Szymanowska had also decided on St. Petersburg. Several days before Zaleska's departure, for Fat Tuesday, the poet, Szymanowska, Viazemskii, Daszkiewicz, and several others descended on their friend from Ukraine, all dressed in an assortment of costumes ("Mickiewicz, half Spaniard, half Spanish lady"). It was there, among the Polish expatriates of Moscow, that Viazemskii first heard Mickiewicz improvise:

> He improvised many verses to the accompaniment of piano music with amazing skill, from what I could understand and from the delight of his listeners. He improvised a few very touching couplets in my honor, and then I gave him a subject—the battle of Navarino—and there were many truly poetic surges. He finished with a fantasia to Szymanowska's [composition] "Murmure," and his poetry then became a murmur and harmonized amazingly with the music.

With his knowledge of Polish, Viazemskii was one of the few Russians who could appreciate Mickiewicz's extraordinary gift. Soon enough, however, other Russians got an opportunity to marvel at his improvisations—in French.[101]

Near the end of April 1828, just as Mickiewicz was preparing to depart for St. Petersburg, Sobolevskii threw a surprise farewell dinner for his Polish friend. Most of Mickiewicz's Russian acquaintances in Moscow were present: Baratynskii, the Kireevskiis, Nikolai Polevoi, and Shevyrev (Viazemskii happened to be in St. Petersburg at the time). As a keepsake of the occasion, and of the friendships Mickiewicz had made in Moscow over the previous two years, they had ordered a large silver goblet to be made, inscribed with their names. Ivan Kireevskii presented it to Mickiewicz with a poem, describing it as containing a talisman whose "living power

> Will instill your dream with living wings
> And lo, those whose names the goblet circle
> Will embrace that dream of yours....
> And beckoned by your reminiscences
> Will echo from afar your thoughts.

Baratynskii followed with a poem that chided his Polish friend for being too beholden to Byron:

> Whenever I find you, inspired Mickiewicz,
> Before Lord Byron on bended knee,
> I think: o humbled worshipper!
> Arise, arise and mind that you yourself are god!

"Powerfully moved," Mickiewicz quitted their display of affection and admiration with an improvisation in French, in which he riffed on the theme of Kireevskii's poem. As he later reported to Odyniec, "It was greeted with a mighty ovation—I was bidden farewell with tears." Mickiewicz did not mention to his friend that at one point Baratynskii fell to his knees, exclaiming, "My God, why aren't you a Russian!"[102]

16

Arriving in St. Petersburg on 22 April/4 May, Mickiewicz once again settled in with Malewski. The building where they rented an apartment, on Bol'shaia Meshchanskaia in what was then a working class neighborhood of the city, happened to be also the home of Nikolai V. Gogol'-Janovskii, an ambitious fledgling writer from Ukraine. Mickiewicz surely must have noticed the young dandy with a prominent nose making his way up the staircase. The two would cross paths again, but not until 1837, and under very different circumstances.

Mickiewicz had come to St. Petersburg ostensibly to find himself a position. He applied to the Ministry of Internal Affairs, then to the Post, the governor-general's, and finally the Collegium of Foreign Affairs. Yet he did so perfunctorily. "I could have gotten a position paying several thousand rubles," he wrote to Daszkiewicz in May, "but I don't want to work, because I have no talent for it." He was, in fact, determined more than ever to secure permission to travel abroad. In this, however, even Viazemskii was convinced that Mickiewicz "would be refused," and he, like others, "advised him not even to think about it."[103]

But Mickiewicz had also come to St. Petersburg with plans for a new publication. What he had projected in 1826 as the third volume of *Poems*, which would consist of *Wallenrod* as well as works not included in the first two, had over the subsequent two years metamorphosed into a kind of collected works that would comprise most everything he had hitherto written. On 28 April/10 May, only days after the poet's arrival in St. Petersburg, the censor Anastasevich gave his initial approval, and without retracting his earlier decision concerning *Konrad Wallenrod*. But instead of facilitating matters, this delayed the appearance of the edition for close to a year. The upshot was that someone else beat the author to the punch.

In early May 1828, Mickiewicz received two unexpected letters from Paris. The first was from Leonard Chodźko, a schoolmate of his from Vilnius and now a self-appointed ambassador of Polish culture in France; the second, from Countess Klementyna Ostrowska, a wealthy Polish aristocrat living in Paris. Chodźko informed the poet that thanks to the generosity of the countess, he had had a set of type characters specially made to print Polish books as part of a project "to refresh the Polish past and defend its present before the world." He had decided that the first publication in the series would be a two-volume edition of Mickiewicz's poetry, "since [the poet] had been chased out of Vilnius and must now be in straitened circumstances." All proceeds would thus go to the author. One thousand copies of *Poems*, which consisted of *Ballads and Romances*, *Forefathers' Eve*, *Grażyna*, *Sonnets*, and miscellaneous poems, were printed by the shop of Barbezat and Delarue. On excellent paper, with a wide variety of type faces, the publication was truly "a monument to the Polish language erected on foreign soil." Lelewel provided a portrait of the poet for the frontispiece and, as his plenipotentiary, also gave permission for the edition to proceed in the first place. It was Lelewel too who turned over the 3,200 florins that Ostrowska advanced Mickiewicz from projected sales in Poland.[104]

Chodźko's letter was the first Mickiewicz had heard of the venture. Upon receiving copies, but particularly Ostrowska's promissory note, he was "unpleasantly surprised, seeing that people unknown to [him] [were] giving [him] presents." He then went on to complain that the publishers made a mess of the distribution and pricing. Mickiewicz's displeasure, it seems, was as much a function of pride as it was of a sense that he had once again lost control over the fate of his works. That he was in the process of himself producing an authorized edition made the appearance of what was, in effect, a competing edition all the more irritating. After all, this was a poet who had already suffered financially on account of two unauthorized editions; who complained that the likes of Bułharyn and Pushkin were making far more from their works than he was for *Wallenrod*; whose correspondence with Odyniec and Lelewel evinced constant concern for how his works were disseminated, for potential costs and proceeds; and whose first reaction on hearing of the Paris edition was to wonder whether it "would be harmful or profitable." Mickiewicz finally did get around to thanking Ostrowska, albeit somewhat coolly and a year later, and Chodźko several months after that, but he never forgave them for the "unpleasant surprise." In the meantime, a third volume, which included *Konrad Wallenrod* and other poems, was added to the edition. There was, nonetheless, a touch of irony here: after Mickiewicz's emigration to Paris, it is precisely this edition of *Poems* that would become the authorized one, with a total of eight volumes by 1836 and a combined seven editions during the poet's lifetime.[105]

The Paris edition of his collected poems was not, however, the only one to compete with Mickiewicz's own. At almost the same time that Chodźko was setting his version in Paris, Lelewel had convinced a colleague in the Grand Duchy of Poznań, where "only three copies [of Mickiewicz's works] could be found," to also print something approaching an authorized edition. As with the Paris edition, the Poznań publication was, more than anything, a work of love on the part of a small group of enlightened Poles eager to honor the poet, and remunerate him "on very favorable" terms. Indeed, the publisher, Józef Muczkowski, made every effort to secure Mickiewicz's permission as well as protect his copyright: prominently displayed on the title page were the words "Property of the Author."[106]

A subscription drive in the grand duchy proved surprisingly successful, drawing some five hundred takers; money for "the unfortunate writer" poured in. But despite the best efforts of Muczkowski to beat out his rivals in Paris and, no less important, to see *Wallenrod* in print before the Prussian censor changed his mind, all four volumes of the Poznań edition did not appear until the fall of 1828. The haste showed. The books were sloppily printed on bad paper and in a weird format, the poems themselves appearing in no recognizable order and with works by other writers inserted to fill out the third volume. Mickiewicz expressed his gratitude for the good intentions, praising in particular the publisher for his conscientiousness with regard to copyright at a time "when an author's property is respected so little." He even suggested a fifth volume to include new poems that were soon to appear in the Petersburg edition. Behind Muczkowski's back, however, the poet apparently referred to his achievement as "a very poor edition."[107]

With little else to do, then, but tend to the publication of *Poems*, write letters, and perform favors for those not in the capital, Mickiewicz spent most of his time in St. Petersburg visiting and being visited.

While Viazemskii was still in town for the spring and early summer of 1828, there were numerous occasions to breakfast or dine or even indulge in "meretricious visits" together with Russian literati—with Pushkin, Zhukovskii, Griboedov, with the fable writer Ivan A. Krylov, and A. N. Olenin, the director of the emperor's library. It was around this time too that Mickiewicz produced what would be, tellingly enough, his only translation from Russian, of Pushkin's "Reminiscence" (Dz. 1:289–90). But perhaps a more precious expression of Mickiewicz's affection for his friends were his improvisations. Now Russian writers in St. Petersburg could for themselves experience that "face illuminated by the fire of inspiration," full of "something disquieting and prophetic," even though the poet, improvising in French prose, himself compared his efforts "with those of a child dead in the arms of his mother, with magma burning beneath the earth without a volcano's knowledge to erupt." Whether Pushkin really did once "jump up from his seat and, with his hands in his hair and practically running about the room, exclaim, 'Quel génie! quel feu sacré! qui suis-je auprès de lui?'" is another matter, but in 1835 the Russian poet did begin writing a novella entitled "Egyptian Nights," in which he attempted to grasp the phenomenon of improvisation.[108]

But then St. Petersburg's salons were galvanized by Mickiewicz's very presence. "An incomparable creature!" recalled Pushkin's beloved Anna P. Kern, "so gentle, good-humored, accommodating himself to everyone so tenderly that everyone went into raptures over him." This came as no surprise to Sobańska, who happened to be in St. Petersburg in the spring of 1828 and who, it seems, tried to restart their relationship. This time, however, Mickiewicz was "not up to it" (Pushkin, though, was), and in any case, he had found a new object for his affections.[109]

He had met Avdot'ia M. Bakunina, the daughter of the governor-general of St. Petersburg, in the salon of her cousin, Admiral Shishkov, the same Shishkov who four years earlier had treated the newly exiled schoolteacher from Kowno with such dignity. She "was an intelligent young lady, educated and very poetically attuned," and certainly no amateur as a painter. If, as Mickiewicz informed Daszkiewicz—to what was most certainly his friend's consternation—"she was not at all pretty," Bakunina had "more character and sense" than her prettier rival in Moscow. Although he claimed to his friend that he was in love with neither, matters went even further with Bakunina than they had with Jaenisch (which may in part explain Mickiewicz's vacillations with regard to the latter). The poet, it seems, was ready to ask for her hand—"were it not," as he explained to his daughter many years later, "for the fact that she was a Russian" (or was this just convenient rationalization?). Bakunina was *herem*, cursed, in the orientalizing terminology of the Philomaths, something that the poet's Polish friends, especially Malewski, took very seriously. "What would Poles say," Przecławski recalls Mickiewicz as confessing,

> if I married a Russian, a senator's daughter, cousin of the great Kutuzov and of one of the ministers? Every Pole would assume that I was motivated by low and ignoble impulses. I have no right to debase myself in this way, for I would cause harm to my people.

Nothing came of what would have certainly been a mésalliance of scandalous proportions and, truth be said, an inconceivable union for either party. After her death, Bakunina's family even burnt the poet's letters to her. In 1845, though, Mickiewicz would meet her nephew Mikhail. The poet's relationship with him would in its own way prove to be no less intriguing than his affair with the anarchist's aunt.[110]

For all of the sincerity that informed the hospitality and, indeed, adulation showered on Mickiewicz by St. Petersburg's salons and its cultural elite, his status in a city obsessed with fashion was essentially that of a fashionable celebrity, perhaps not quite the exotic creature Volkonskaia's portrait suggests, but certainly someone extraordinary, a romantic outsider. This is not to say that the poet shied away from the attention. He rarely turned down an invitation to a Sunday at the Shishkov's, an all-night dinner at some restaurant with Pushkin *et alia*, or an evening at the opera (a social and, for some, sexual must). But after Odessa and Moscow, such attention was no longer a novelty; that it came from strangers, in foreign tongues, made it taxing and somehow unsatisfying. What Mickiewicz craved was family.

He found brothers aplenty in the colony of Polish expatriates residing in the capital, old acquaintances from Lithuania as well as newer ones whom he met in Russia. Aside from Malewski, of course, he drew particularly close to Aleksander Chodźko, a Philareth several years his junior, who had come to St. Petersburg of his own volition to study Eastern languages. Over the course of that year, the three were practically inseparable and usually could be found in the company of other Philareths who for whatever reason had settled in St. Petersburg. As for the Poles with whom he had become acquainted upon his arrival in Russia four years earlier—Bułharyn, Orłowski, Żelwietr, Wańkowicz—none fascinated him as much as Józef Oleszkiewicz. It was a fascination that ultimately changed Mickiewicz's life.

Born in 1777, Oleszkiewicz had studied painting in Vilnius and then with Jacques-Louis David in Paris. It was there that he absorbed the teachings of the French mystic Louis-Claude de Saint-Martin, whose ideas had become particularly fashionable also among Russian Freemasons. Upon settling in St. Petersburg in 1810, Oleszkiewicz became active in the movement and by the 1820s attained a high degree in the Masonic hierarchy. Inordinately "gentle, understanding, and kind," the painter was one of those rare individuals who truly practiced what he preached, believing as he did "in the living presence of God always and everywhere." A strict vegetarian who quite literally would not kill a fly, he collected stray cats, which then would lounge by the dozens in every room of his apartment—and infesting it with fleas whose lives, of course, were every bit as sacrosanct as those of their hosts. Although his painting guaranteed him a decent income, "he was always penniless, since he gave everything to the poor, who constantly kept his apartment under siege." In the eyes of most, he was simply an annoying eccentric, a mystic preoccupied by all manner of paranormal phenomena—"animal magnetism, somnambulism, ecstasy, lunatism, clairvoyance, the secrets of premonition, spiritual attraction and repulsion, foreseeing the future, and many other mysteries"—who never passed up an opportunity to expound on his mystical ideas. As Mickiewicz would write of Oleszkiewicz several years later in an eponymously titled poem:

> No one understood what his mutterings meant;
> Some were amazed, and others just laughed,
> Everyone cried, "Our wizard is again acting strange"

—except one:

> Although peer he did not into the face of the painter,
> Although he didn't quite catch what the others said of him,
> But the sound of his voice, his mysterious words
> Shook him so! (Dz. 3:302)[111]

Mickiewicz "took a fancy to his speeches, which, though they often wander[ed] off the topic, nonetheless sometimes manifest[ed] both a soul full of ardor and a capacity for thought." On top of their discussions, Oleszkiewicz supplied the poet with all manner of literature on spiritual topics—by Saint-Martin, Swedenborg, Jacob Boehme, Johann Arndt, Philip Jacob Spener, and perhaps his own (not extant) theosophical writings—and most probably introduced him to like-minded adepts, of whom (post-) Masonic St. Petersburg certainly had its fill. For a personality inclined toward superstition and fascinated by the irrational, all this not so much opened up a new dimension, but rather reinforced his own presentiments, his own questions about the limits of reason.[112]

Oleszkiewicz, for his part, was fascinated by Mickiewicz's talent for poetic improvisation. Through the prism of Saint-Martin's meditations on the connection between poetry, divine inspiration, and prophecy, he recognized in his friend a poet inspired from above. As he supposedly confided to Odyniec shortly before Mickiewicz left Russia: "He fends off the spirit like Jacob, but that won't do much good. He's a chosen vessel, and sooner or later Grace will fill him, and through him it will flow onto others." How much this was a case of retrospective projection on Odyniec's part is difficult to determine, just as it is difficult to determine what immediate effect Oleszkiewicz's assessment of him had on the poet. It would not be long, however, before Mickiewicz came to realize how much of the mystic's teachings he had, in fact, internalized.[113]

The remainder of the poet's surrogate family in St. Petersburg was of a more mundane variety, consisting as it did of the Szymanowskas, a mother and her two daughters. Practically a day did not go by without Mickiewicz dropping in for a visit, be it for a midday meal, an evening at the pianist's popular salon, or just to loll about while Malewski and Chodźko tutored Helena and Celina. Indeed, the unemployed Mickiewicz would sometimes spend entire days with the Szymanowskas, reading, listening to Szymanowska play and the girls sing, going on excursions together around St. Petersburg, to the theater, to the bazaar, to Orłowski's or Wańkowicz's studios, horsing around with mother and daughters alike, and "arguing with Ms. Celina." Helena, for her part, was falling in love with Malewski, thanks in part to the poetry of "Franciszek's friend," which, as she noted in her diary, taught her "that *love* was not an empty word and... that [her] turn too will come." The two would be married four years later. Mickiewicz, of course, had no idea that the same fate awaited him with "the gorgeous black-eyed" Celina, but he did have a peculiar series of dreams at the time:

> Someone knocked at the door. In walks a well-dressed man and hands me a visiting card. Not seeing a name on it, I ask: Who's it from? "Why don't you look closer." . . . There's no name, but all around the edges . . . is a drawing of every imaginable instrument of torture. . . .
>
> It was a while before I fell asleep again. I imagined I was approaching a church. . . . On the church porch the wind blows off my hat, I chase it, pick it up, and am standing in front of three ladies dressed for a wedding. . . . The eldest, apparently the mother of the bride, spoke up: "How's this, Mr. Mickiewicz, that you're late for your wedding?" "What do you mean, my wedding?" "Don't deny it; after all you accepted the card and have it with you." I take out . . . the card, and lifting up the hem of the bride's . . . dress, she fit the card into the spot out of which it had been cut out. "So you see?" . . . We go to the altar and stand there. I look at my intended, who is covered with a veil. Show yourself, I yelled, and again woke up. . . . I fell asleep again. . . .
>
> Approaching the church, . . . my hat, blown off by the wind, rolled on the porch. I bend down after it, chase it down, pick it up. Whereupon Mrs. Szymanowska speaks up: "So, Mr. Mickiewicz, you're taking Celina away from me."[114]

17

Anastasevich's provisional permission for the publication of *Poems* turned out to be precisely that, provisional. As Mickiewicz began turning his manuscript in to the printer (Karol Kray again), he ran up against another, more exacting censor. The biggest obstacle, not surprisingly, was *Konrad Wallenrod*. Intent on seeing the poem reprinted, Mickiewicz agreed to write an addendum to his original preface in which he now characterized "the MONARCH" as "a Father" who "guarantees everyone free possession of property and, what is even dearer, moral and intellectual property," who "preserves his subjects' . . . faith, customs, and language. . . . May the name of this Father be praised by all generations and in all tongues as well!" (*Dz.* 2:317–18). Mickiewicz was under no illusions with regard to the price a poet—a Polish poet, to boot, and one with a record—had to pay for the privilege of practicing his craft in Nicholas's realm (and was not Pushkin's predicament even more humiliating?). If this was what it took to republish *Wallenrod*, a work that was as profitable as it was pregnant, so be it.

The delay in publication—there were, in addition, problems with the type—also meant that Mickiewicz could continue supplementing the edition with new poems. For all the hours he idled away at Szymanowska's, the poet had not been unproductive. Besides new bits of album verse and two ballads ("The Watch" and "Three Budryses," both of which

Pushkin translated several years later), Mickiewicz included two takes on Arabic verse, an articulation of his abiding interest in the world he encountered in the Crimea as well as the yield of his many conversations about things Oriental with Chodźko, Topçi-Başa, and, above all, the invidious Sękowski (aesthetics, in this instance, trumping ethics). One, "Szanfary," was a paraphrase of a qasida based on a French translation by Silvestre de Sacy; the other, "The Faris," an imitation of a qasida, dedicated to Kozlov and written "in honor of Emir Tadż-ul-Fechra," a.k.a. Wacław Rzewuski, a Polish adventurer who had converted to Islam. Inspired, supposedly, by the "rush, rattle, [and] whistle of the wind" on a Petersburg sleighride, this first-person poem about an Arab horseman battling the elements, "piercing the heavens first with thought then with soul" (Dz. 1:314), became one of Mickiewicz's most enduring, resonating as it did with Orientalist fashion and by the same token distilling its romantic quintessence: transgressive, individualistic, omnipotent freedom.[115]

The Petersburg edition of *Poems* finally appeared in March 1829, in some two thousand copies, at a price of 4 rubles silver or 15 in paper. Potential pirates were warned that they would "be subject to legal prosecution." With the exception of Philomath juvenilia, some occasional verse, and, it goes without saying, "Ode to Youth," its two volumes contained practically everything Mickiewicz had written to date. Polevoi was ecstatic:

> Now that Goethe has grown silent and Byron is no more, Mickiewicz—and of this we should be proud—is not only Poland's premier poet, but is, perhaps, the first of all poets living today. *Wallenrod, Forefathers' Eve, Sonnets,* "Faris" are the works of a creative imagination that not a single living poet in England, Germany, France, and Italy can match.

The reaction in Poland, however, to what was, after all, a collection of works that for the most part had been already thoroughly digested, focused on Mickiewicz's preface.[116]

With title and attitude meant to evoke Byron's "English Bards and Scotch Reviewers," "On Warsaw Critics and Reviewers" was intended as a "satirical" answer to Mickiewicz's neoclassicist detractors. In this, it was certainly on the mark in calling attention to "Warsaw's *Kleinstädterei.*" But it was also surprisingly immature in its provocative condescension, as if Mickiewicz's successes in the cosmopolitan capitals of Russia gave him license to belittle a literary milieu about which he in fact knew very little. (Kajetan Koźmian went so far as to imply that Mickiewicz was in the pay of the Russians.) What irked the Warsaw critics, then, was precisely the piece's presumptuous dismissal of the capital's literary culture. Franciszek Dmochowski wrote an entire booklet in response in which he defended "the contributions" of Warsaw's "literati, both those already dead and those still living," from an attack that, arrogance aside, was in essence ill-informed. Even the poet's staunchest defenders in Warsaw—Mochnacki, Lelewel—found the essay somewhat outré. "He yells at a plague-stricken, barricaded Warsaw, while that is where multitudes of his readers live, to say nothing of his admirers." And although never remorseful, Mickiewicz himself quickly came to understand that there was indeed something unnecessarily malicious in the tone of his remarks. "I can't understand why you are so angry at Dmochowski," he wrote to his acolyte Odyniec, "a person who is attacked has to defend himself; there's nothing mean in his response." In what was, perhaps, a form of compensation, Mickiewicz in fact went on to treat these same critics with remarkable equanimity as poets in his 1829 note to Zhukovskii outlining the current state of Polish literature. He never wrote, as he had threatened, a rebuttal to his critics; but then too, he surely realized that he would only be beating a dead horse.[117]

18

While Malewski was put in charge of the sales, Mickiewicz did not remain idle, remitting packages of books to sellers in Warsaw, Lithuania, and Kiev. This sudden concern with distribution, and what he hoped would be a quick turnaround, was necessitated by the fact that the poet had paid for the publication out of his own pocket. And now, more than ever, he needed money.*

In the fall of 1828, Malewski had gotten permission for a brief visit to Lithuania. What had seemed impossible two years earlier was now at least in the realm of possibility. Prodded, no doubt, by Bułharyn, Mickiewicz sent off a letter to the former's "friend," Count Aleksandr Kh. Benkendorf, the head of the Third Department. Arguing that he "did not deserve [his] verdict, since [he] was never put on trial, did not deserve [his] sentence, since [he] was never condemned," the poet requested to be allowed to settle in St. Petersburg on account of "the state of [his] personal and family matters"; but "the state of [his] health require[d] making a trip to German spas." Thanks to Bułharyn, and perhaps also Zhukovskii, the matter moved surprisingly quickly, and favorably. With the tsar's own approval, Benkendorf interceded on Mickiewicz's behalf with Grand Duke Constantine, asking the viceroy to permit the poet "to travel abroad in order to take a cure for his disease . . . , which in the opinion of local doctors will soon cut his life short." Propitiously self-induced or not (echoes of Kowno), an illness had indeed felled Mickiewicz that winter, and there were well-meaning doctors who were willing to attest to its seriousness. Constantine had nothing against the request, as long as his brother the tsar was amenable, and in early March gave his approval. A passport was issued in the name of "Adam Mickiewicz, the well-known Polish poet."[118]

Uncertain of the outcome of his petition, Mickiewicz had in the meantime decided to try yet another approach. He applied to the Collegium of Foreign Affairs for a position with "one of our embassies or consulates in Italy, France, or Spain," even if it were to be unpaid,

*Mickiewicz would eventually make 2,250 paper rubles on the edition, which was only a bit less than Malewski's annual salary in 1829.

and, if this proved impossible, to be allowed to take an exam for potential translators. Not surprisingly, things moved much slower here than in the Third Department. By the time the collegium was ready to offer him a position, Mickiewicz was already abroad.[119]

On 13 March, Malewski informed his father about changes in his life. "The greatest and most painful change for me," he wrote, "is Mickiewicz's departure. The emperor has permitted him to go abroad to take the waters.... In him I'm losing my only, my time-tested friend, someone who for many reasons has claims to my gratitude." One must assume that Mickiewicz's feelings in this regard were mutual, though repressed somewhat by the bustle of preparing for his voyage. His first concern was another, now final, trip to Moscow, to tidy up matters and bid farewell to those friends who still remained there. Volkonskaia had left earlier that year for Rome, in the company of Shevyrev. Viazemskii was away. Daszkiewicz was in St. Petersburg. But there were others whom Mickiewicz would soon be leaving behind forever.[120]

First and foremost among them was Jeżowski, then his Russian friends, the brothers Polevoi as well as Pogodin. Since the latter had been unable to attend the first send-off for the poet a year earlier, he now himself arranged a farewell breakfast for Mickiewicz, to which he invited many of Moscow's literati. Among the guests was Pushkin, who was setting off on a voyage of his own, albeit in the opposite direction, to the Caucasus. All Pogodin could say of the conversation between the two poets was, "Prejudice is cold, and faith is ardent." In any case, shortly before Mickiewicz's return to St. Petersburg, Pushkin gave his Polish acquaintance a copy of his newest work, the poem *Poltava*. Mickiewicz, in turn, gave the Russian poet an edition of Byron's works, in which he wrote, in Polish, "Byron for Pushkin, from an admirer of both" (Dz. 17:508).[121]

"He lived among us," wrote Pushkin several years later, in an effort to put his recollections of his encounters with Mickiewicz into verse,

> Amidst, for him, a foreign tribe, no malice
> In his soul did harbor he toward us, and we,
> We loved him. Peaceable he was and gracious,
> He frequented our gatherings. With him
> We shared both candid thoughts
> And songs (he was inspired from up above
> And gazed on life from there). He'd often speak
> Of ages that were yet to come
> When nations, their contentions all forgotten,
> Would in one great family unite.
> We listened to him avidly. He left
> Us for the West—and with a blessing
> We saw him off.

Pushkin never finished the poem, unable, as its numerous enjambments would indicate, to make sense of his conflicted feelings about the man, the poet, and the Pole. By 1834, after all, events had belied any notions of a united Slavic family. Pushkin himself had teamed up with Zhukovskii in 1831 to rhetorically crush the Polish uprising, and a year later Mickiewicz accused him of "having sold his soul forever for the favors of the tsar" and of "gloating at the martyrdom of friends" ("To My Russian Friends"; Dz. 3:307). Pushkin, for his part, now considered his once "peaceable guest" "an enemy," "a spiteful poet." More nuanced, in this respect, would be *The Bronze Horseman* (1833), the Russian poet's ambivalent projection of St. Petersburg, which was written, in part, with a view toward Mickiewicz's indictment of the city in the "Digression" to *Forefathers' Eve*, part 3, as the capital of an evil empire. More nuanced too would be Mickiewicz's French-language obituary he wrote of Pushkin in 1837 for *Le Globe*:

> No country has ever managed to produce more than one person who could to such a degree combine abilities so variegated and seemingly incompatible. . . . I knew this Russian poet rather well and for a rather long period of time; I noticed in him a nature too susceptible to first impressions and at times flighty, but always sincere, noble-minded, and capable of expressing his feelings. His shortcomings appeared to be a function of the circumstances amidst which he was raised; and what was good in him sprung from his heart. (Dz. 5:291)

The obituary, whose gist Mickiewicz would repeat several years later in his lectures at the Collège de France, was signed simply "A Friend of Pushkin."[122]

There was, however, one other matter that Mickiewicz had to see to in Moscow, perhaps the most pressing and at the same time potentially the most troublesome—Karolina Jaenisch.

The tsar's permission to travel as well as Jaenisch's letter had effectively decided matters for him. In so many words, Jaenisch had given up on extracting any kind of commitment, and now that Mickiewicz would actually be going—fleeing—to Dresden, he ceased vacillating. It was with relief that he could say good-bye. As he wrote to Malewski from the road back to St. Petersburg, "The trip didn't go badly, I wrapped up matters, [and] managed to avoid what I feared would be unpleasant"—laconic, business-like, a sigh. Jaenisch, however, would not let it end on this note. She insisted on having the final word. This time she wrote in her native German, not in the language of poets and lovers:

> Farewell, my friend! Once more I thank you for everything—for your friendship—for your love. I swore to you that I would earn this love, that I would be exactly like you wished me to be. Never believe that I'm capable of breaking this vow, this is my only plea to you. These words are probably the last I'll be able to say to you—believe them, and when you have forgotten them, reread this letter and consider that the promise that I made to

> you is sacred and that I must keep it because I love you. . . . I shall often take out of my heart the treasure of my memories and examine them with joy; for each one of them is a pure diamond.

She kept her promise well: in the 1840s, Karolina Jaenisch-Pavlova wrote five poems inspired by her love for Mickiewicz. Two of them commemorated "November 10," that "cherished date" when, "with childish faith," she "doomed [her]self to [him] forever without fear." And in 1890, at the age of eighty-two, she could still write to the poet's son:

> For me, he's not stopped living. I love him now as I loved him over all of these years of absence. He is mine as he once was.[123]

And Mickiewicz? In 1830, when he was already in Rome and with Daszkiewicz recently deceased of tuberculosis, the poet still could not decide—in this case, whether he should write to Jaenisch. He never did, insisting to the end that he "never promised her anything." Daszkiewicz's death, however, which everyone at the time believed to have been hastened by his unrequited love for Jaenisch, occasioned much remorse. The poet dedicated *Forefathers' Eve*, part 3, to him, among others, although as so much else in the work, his friend's death would now be made to serve a higher purpose.[124]

19

Upon his return to St. Petersburg, Mickiewicz informed Odyniec of his immediate plans. Because of his finances, he decided to travel by sea to Lübeck, and then to Dresden (instead of to Berlin via Riga and Klaipeda). "If you have the means to travel now," he went on,

> run to Dresden and wait for me there. You can imagine, dear Edward, how happy this thought makes me. Oh, would that we could see Italy together.

A week later, and somewhat to the surprise of Mickiewicz and his roommates, Odyniec appeared in St. Petersburg. He had come there on a lark, bringing with him some proceeds from Warsaw from the sale of the poet's books, but also to plan their tour of Europe together. Mickiewicz would set off alone, and Odyniec would return to Poland and then meet up with him in Dresden as originally planned.[125]

Mickiewicz was hoping to board a ship to Lübeck—or, to be more accurate, Travemünde—at the end of May. Announcements of his impending departure were placed in the Petersburg papers. Together with his friends, he set about collecting as much money as possible. Thanks to a loan from Piasecki, there was now enough for him to be "well supplied for an entire year"; he could also count on a steady income as more of his books were sold. As for "all matters concerning [him] and [his] assets, consisting of works published by [him] and a house... in the town of Nowogródek," Mickiewicz entrusted them legally to Malewski. Amid his preparations, he found the time to introduce Odyniec to those closest to him in St. Petersburg, to Oleszkiewicz, Żelwietr, Orłowski, the ladies Szymanowska, of course, as well as to the blind poet Kozlov (neither Zhukovskii nor Viazemskii was in town). He also showed his friend the manuscript of a "history of the future" "in French," which he had been working on of late. It was about Europe in the twenty-first century, recalled Odyniec years later, in which there appeared, among other things, "entire fleets of flying balloons" and "acoustic devices with the help of which one could, while sitting by the fireplace in hotels, listen to concerts being given in town or public lectures." Odyniec fabricated much in his memoirs, but his imagination was not up to this.[126]

What had begun as leisurely preparations for the journey suddenly acquired urgency on 13/25 May. Late that evening, Mickiewicz and Odyniec returned home from the theater to find "candles lit in every corner [of the apartment], and in the middle of the room Adam's travel trunk surrounded by piles of clothing and underwear, which Franciszek Malewski was bringing in and Marian [Piasecki] was packing." Piasecki had just learned of the unexpected arrival of the steamer that was to take Mickiewicz to Lübeck. There was no time for good-byes. Mickiewicz raced down to the Neva and at eight that morning boarded a packet-boat to Kronshtadt together with Chodźko and Olenin. Just before his departure for Lübeck on the steamer *George IV*, Volkonskaia's husband arrived with a packet from Szymanowska. It included bills of exchange, introductory letters to a number of her acquaintances in Germany and Italy, a barcarole and a polonaise she had recently composed, as well as notes of farewell from her, Odyniec, Helena, Celina, and Malewski. "In vain," his best friend wrote,

> did I argue that it's not Christian to cry so for those who are leaving, that it's a sign of unbelief in immortality, but nothing helps, the tears can't be assuaged. It seems to me that this is your family crying for you. God bless you!

Mickiewicz left Russia on 15/27 May 1829, three days after Nicholas I was crowned king of Poland. He would never see Malewski nor his friend's future wife Helena again; nor Szymanowska, who died two years later of cholera.[127]

20

Shortly before the poet's departure, Nikolai Polevoi informed his readers:

> Mickiewicz is now leaving Russia and going to Italy. New inspirations await him amidst the ruins of Rome and the tombs of immortals. We, his [now] distant fellow countrymen,

> his distant friends, will await new poetry from him, and we hope that he will bring forth for us new masterpieces.

"We shall be tracking the flight [of this young eagle]," he added, "rejoicing that he is *ours*."[128]

For all of his misunderstanding of Mickiewicz's predicament in Russia, or, perhaps more accurately, in spite of it, the poet had found in Polevoi, and indeed in all of his Russian friends, enthusiastic hosts who recognized his talents and, misunderstandings notwithstanding, were eager to create an atmosphere that encouraged them to flourish. Theirs was, after all, also a struggle for a new sensibility, and in Mickiewicz they had met an articulate ally. That he was a Pole made this all the more salient. It was "Russian writers," observed another contributor to *Moskovskii telegraf* in a review of Kozlov's translation of the Crimean sonnets, who

> greeted Mickiewicz as a new light on the horizon of universal literature. Our journals rendered him the praise he deserved; [and now] our writers are trying to transplant to his native soil the delightful flowers of his poetry.

By giving him the imprimatur of the imperial center, Russians in effect validated Mickiewicz in his own eyes and, willy-nilly, in the eyes of his fellow Poles. "You gave him to us strong," Kozlov supposedly remarked to Odyniec, "and we return him to you powerful." As Mickiewicz reminded his friends time and again, his road to fame lay not through Warsaw, much less through Vilnius or Poznań, but through the capitals of Russia.[129]

By the same token, as Malewski himself was forced to admit, the "unreserved praise" of "Russian literati and women" went to Mickiewicz's head, often to the detriment of his relationships with Poles. "I've seen people," he wrote to Lelewel, who would "walk away indignant that Mickiewicz would continue smoking his pipe" while they praised some Polish classicist author;

> whose blood would run cold . . . when Adam did not want to improvise after dinner, when he didn't walk across the room and make an effort to present himself to *a Polish count!* [when] he didn't write a poem in an album, didn't present someone with a copy of his poems, [when] he clearly demonstrated that he was not poor, didn't need their favors, sneered a bit at their patronage, at suggestions they gave him for writing on a given subject.[130]

Try as Malewski might to explain away this arrogance as an expression of Mickiewicz's independence—which in its own way it certainly was—the fact remains that the poet's behavior was a function of the cosmopolitanism of the imperial capitals. Driven by the acclamation of its *Kulturträgers*, Russian society demonstrated its sophistication by opening the door of its salons to this talented petty gentryman from Poland, transforming him into a celebrity. This is something that the arbiters of taste in Warsaw, for whatever reason, seemed unwilling to countenance. For Mickiewicz, their denial was simply a mark as much of ignorance as it was of provincialism. He taunted them with this in the preface to the St. Petersburg edition of *Poems*, and he extended his condescension, misguidedly perhaps, even to his many admirers from Poland.

Mickiewicz's contacts with Russians did not cease with his departure. On the contrary, he sought them out abroad, and they him; and whether new acquaintances or old, they greeted him warmly, often serving as his entrée into the world of European society and culture. Yet as Viazemskii observed some forty-five years later, Mickiewicz may "have felt sympathy for Russians, but as a Pole he did not like Russia, which had destroyed Poland." This is something that perhaps only his Polish friends in Moscow and St. Petersburg could fully grasp. *Konrad Wallenrod* was, in this respect, written for them.[131]

On the steamer heading for Lübeck, Mickiewicz recalled many years later, "I almost instinctively hid beneath the deck. But on the high seas, when I was sure that no one would detain me, I went up on deck and tossed coins with the image of the Russian eagle into the sea." He held on to his Russian passport, however.[132]

CHAPTER FOUR

THE GRAND TOUR (1829–1831)

The first two letters Mickiewicz sent from the West were to Malewski and Szymanowska. The one to Malewski avoided sentimentality. It boasted, rather, of the poet's ability to fend for himself: to get a carriage to Lübeck; to haggle when necessary; to exchange currency "with all the cold-bloodedness of a banker" (ducats, it appears, were at a premium). Everything Mickiewicz reported seeing or doing was new and interesting and exciting—"in a word, a real tourist." The letter to Szymanowska was demonstratively nostalgic, full of longing for the familiar: "I myself wanted this trip and I'm not lamenting my fate . . . , but it's sad to travel knowing that wherever I arrive, no one will greet me, no one will be happy at my arrival." In this, however, Mickiewicz was quite mistaken.[1]

I

It was a Saturday, 30 May 1829, when the *George IV* steamed into Travemünde. The four-day voyage was uneventful, but unexpectedly expensive: 30 ducats (72 paper rubles) for first class, since, as the poet explained to Malewski, "it was impossible to travel second class because of the bad food and discomfort." Once in port, Mickiewicz, never one to "to exert" himself, nonetheless managed to deposit his bills of exchange, arrange a ride to Lübeck, and from there to Hamburg, where he stayed for several days. The weather, however, turned, and, as he wrote to Lelewel, he "was unable to see much because of the incessant rain." As to where he should travel next, Mickiewicz had no set plan, "maybe to Berlin, maybe past Berlin directly to Dresden." He opted for the former, in part because he knew Zhukovskii would be in the Prussian capital accompanying Nicholas on his visit to meet with Frederick William III.[2]

The poet arrived in Berlin around 7 June, "amidst rain, chill, fog, dew, over mud worse than in Lithuania." His mood was foul, made all the fouler by food poisoning from oysters he had eaten on the way and difficulty finding a room. But once the weather cleared and he had had a chance to "view beautiful paintings," Mickiewicz cheered up. Seeing old friends from Russia also contributed to lifting his spirits, particularly since through them he could send letters and packages back east as well as remind them, as he had Bułharyn, to intervene on behalf of Zan, Czeczot, and others of his friends less fortunate than he.[3]

With Szymanowska's letters in hand, Mickiewicz paid a visit to Karl Friedrich Zelter, a composer and friend of Goethe, through whom he hoped to announce his impending arrival in Weimar. Obliging, Zelter wrote ahead to Goethe that their mutual friend "warmly" recommended to him, "'the prince of poets,' her talented fellow countryman and poet." Szymanowska's other letter gained Mickiewicz entry to the home of Abraham Mendelssohn-Bartholdy, a converted Jewish banker and patron of the arts, whose twenty-year-old son Felix had already made a name for himself as a pianist and composer. The poet missed the latter on this occasion, but the two would become acquainted soon enough in Rome.[4]

It was only by accident, however, when one of the many Polish students studying at the university recognized Mickiewicz strolling down Unter den Linden, that the Polish community in Berlin learned of the poet's presence in the city. "'Twas You, Mickiewicz!" wrote the student that day, memorializing the moment in a poem he later presented to his idol,

> I'm sure I'm not mistaken,
> I recognized You by the sign You pressed into my soul;
> I was unknown to You, but knew You well enough
> Ere now, before I saw You!

Mickiewicz's arrival came at a particularly auspicious time, since in addition to the students, Berlin was now also full of Polish landowners descending on the city from the Grand Duchy of Poznań for the annual wool fair. Berlin's Poles were electrified by the news and immediately began organizing activities to make the poet feel welcome, "scrambling to show their admiration for Mickiewicz or offer their services. Every day there were either private gatherings or dinners."[5]

As a special treat, they insisted on taking Mickiewicz to one of Hegel's lectures, which happened to be "on the difference between *Vernunft* and *Verstand*." The poet was not impressed. He remarked afterwards "that anyone who speaks so abstrusely and agonizes for an entire hour in order to explain the meaning of two concepts surely must not understand himself." The Polish Berliners' "infatuation with Hegel displeased him," which, in turn, did not go over well with "the local metaphysicians," for whom Hegel constituted something of a litmus test. They apparently decided that "Adam's not for [them]!"[6]

This dissonant note was soon enough muffled amid the general excitement of the moment. Nevertheless, the negative impression Hegel left on Mickiewicz would with time turn into animus. Whether it was on account of the lecture itself or, what is more likely, the poet's inherent antirationalism, combined with an "uncivilized Lithuanian's" mistrust for abstraction and a hostility toward things German, the philosopher came to embody for him a danger in some ways even more nefarious than Russian might. "Moscow fights us with ignorance," the poet once told one of the students he met in Berlin, "but it has not subdued us and will not! The Prussians have blinded you with a false light, and herein lies the difference between Russian and Prussian enslavement." None of the philosophers that Mickiewicz would discuss in his Parisian lectures of 1843 came in for greater opprobrium than Hegel and his "scholastic" followers, who, in his opinion, "lacked . . . all sense of reality" (Dz. 10:222/LS 4:350).[7]

But a very different experience awaited Mickiewicz at a lecture of Eduard Gans, the renowned professor of jurisprudence, whose course on revolutionary France was no less popular than Hegel's. Speaking of Napoleon's "hundred days," Gans remarked that this moment could well serve as

> the most magnificent material for a modern epic. . . . I know . . . of no other living poet who could celebrate in verse this great subject except for the one who extended me the honor of being present at my lecture as a member of a people fighting to the last at the side of this hero. He has demonstrated unheard of talents in his . . . works and that is why I believe he is the only one worthy of celebrating material so sublime.

How Gans could assess Mickiewicz's talents is unclear, since only bits and pieces of his work had appeared in German, but at the conclusion of the lecture the professor "took [the poet] by the shoulder and left the auditorium with him." News of this gesture spread quickly. Within a few days the *Allgemeine Preussische Staats-Zeitung* announced that "the most famous of Poland's living poets, Adam Mickiewicz" was passing through the city "on his way from St. Petersburg to Rome."[8]

The Polish community was, of course, more qualified to judge in this respect. And here Mickiewicz did not disappoint. On at least three occasions, the poet improvised for them at receptions organized for him in restaurants and in private homes. To judge by reminiscences, these were moments as extraordinary as those in St. Petersburg and, for those who were present, as unforgettable:

> Mickiewicz's entire person appeared to be transformed into a superterrestrial being. What an enchanting sound to his voice! What an inconceivable power in his words! The *wieszcz*, the Master, the Messenger of God struck with his voice the hearts of his listeners as if with the rod of Aaron, and tears came to their eyes! . . .

The enthusiasm reached its highest peak when the poet..., in a moment of general elation,... uttered with all the pride of inner conviction words that we have faithfully preserved in our memory:

> Have you, Goethe, Schiller,
> Seen a poet who's my peer...

"No, no!" voices answered, "You're the *wieszcz* of *wieszczes*! You're a *wieszcz* on behalf of God! A *wieszcz*... clutching the sword of the Archangel. You're Polish, you're our spirit! You're Polish, our Guardian Archangel! You will make the nation happy, just as you have made us happy."

Another eyewitness, the Polish philosopher Karol Libelt, also writing many years later, described Mickiewicz's voice as being "weak, almost shrill," but in any case he too recalled the poet's "magical power... over the hearts and minds of his listeners." How much greater, then, the elation among the Poles of Prussia when at yet another fête Mickiewicz proclaimed:

> Be it Poznań or Lithuania,
> Though different weapons we all bear,
> Nothing, brothers, does forbid us
> To hold our hands together. (Dz. 1:484)[9]

On 30 June, the eve of Mickiewicz's departure, his Polish hosts organized a farewell dinner in one of Berlin's best restaurants to which they also invited German guests from the university. The poet again improvised a few verses, whereupon everyone joined together in singing the refrain, "Now that you're leaving, farewell, / Speak of our friendship well." It was all "a bit puerile [*burschikos*]," as Mickiewicz put it to Malewski, but "the students fêted me and accompanied me to the carriage that night, and I grew to respect the Poznań landowners." What the poet had originally intended to be a brief visit had extended to three weeks.[10]

For those who remained behind, Mickiewicz's presence appears to have had a singular effect. "Henceforth, harmony, love, brotherhood, enthusiasm for studies, moral conduct in life and relationships, and on top of this a kind of exaltation, a sense of presentiment and expectation, hope, and a belief in the future inspirited all minds and hearts." As for Mickiewicz, he left with ambivalent feelings. He "didn't like the city, but the people affected [him] greatly." To be sure, there was the friction over Hegel. More than just an intellectual misunderstanding, worship of the Prussian philosopher seemed to him just another, ominous, expression of "the adoption of foreign customs" on the part of Berlin's

Poles. Nonetheless, the genuineness of their respect and affection touched Mickiewicz. He opened up, bonded. That he deigned to improvise for them is perhaps the most palpable indication of the comfort he felt in their company. Indeed, their reaction to his improvisations, awed, adoring, almost hysterical in its surrender to the poet's words and person, served to further validate Oleszkiewicz's observations about the special nature of his gift.[11]

2

From Berlin Mickiewicz set out for Dresden, where he was supposed to meet up with Odyniec. His eventual destination, as he wrote to friends, was Munich, and then Italy. There was no mention of either Weimar or Goethe; in fact, he hadn't even bothered to pick up a personal letter of introduction to the German poet he had requested from Zelter. In any case, the trip to Munich would allow him to take the waters in Karlsbad (Karlovy Vary).

Dresden made a better impression on Mickiewicz than Berlin. Although "cramped and dark, [it was] much more pleasant." There were, it seemed, almost as many Poles as Germans in the city that had once been the home of two Polish kings, and the women "were all beautiful." Szymanowska's letters again proved useful in making acquaintances, but this, what would turn out to be just his first, stay in the Saxon capital was brief. It was, nonetheless, clearly enjoyable:

> Fifty steps away we have the Elbe and beautiful strolls. There are so many things for me to see! My day usually goes by something like this: at six (if the weather's good), swimming lessons;* after eight I go with a catalogue in my pocket to the picture gallery and sit there, or rather walk, till twelve or two; then somewhere to dinner with the dear General—or a chat or social visits.

The general was Karol Kniaziewicz, participant in the Kościuszko uprising, one of the commanders of the Polish Legions in Italy, veteran of 1812—and a storehouse of anecdotes about those heroic times. Five years later, Mickiewicz will depict him in *Pan Tadeusz* as a master swordsman among the Polish generals who in 1812 rode into Lithuania with the Napoleonic armies.[12]

But not all Poles in Dresden rated equally in the poet's affections. Upon meeting Mickiewicz, a young Polish aristocrat from Galicia remembered him as being "conceited and sullen," "spoiled by tributes from his countrymen," and "constantly posing." "When the daughter of the house... served him a cup of tea, he accepted it completely indifferently

*Henceforth, swimming, be it in rivers, lakes, or seas, would become one of Mickiewicz's passions.

and, after tasting it, gave it back to her…, saying, 'Too strong.'" As Malewski reminded Lelewel à propos the frictions in Berlin, Mickiewicz "never had any luck with first acquaintances, but profited rather from attachments that grew more intimate with time." Yet his initial reserve with those who could not immediately impress him or offer something to spark his interest, or whom he perceived as lacking in sincerity, was often read as arrogance and even disrespect—and perhaps it was.[13]

Without waiting for Odyniec, Mickiewicz left Dresden in the middle of July for Karlsbad, where he was expecting his friend to join him. The road to the spa led south along the Elbe through the Saxon Alps and then west through Bohemia and Prague.* Seven years earlier, Malewski had taken the same route and in Prague had met some of the intellectuals driving the Czech revival—the philologist and romantic forger Václav Hanka, the poets František Ladislav Čelakovský, Josef Krasoslav Chmelenský, Antonín Marek, the lexicographer Josef Jungmann, the historian František Palacký. Thanks in part to these contacts, the Czechs knew about "one of the most illustrious of the newer Polish poets" (Chmelenský had translated some of his works), and he about them (Mickiewicz had written a review of Pavel Šafárik's *History of Slavic Language and Literature in All Their Dialects* [1826] for *Moskovskii telegraf* [Dz. 5:168–70]). Now the poet had an opportunity to meet for himself yet another group of Slavic romantics with interests similar to his own: Slavic history and antiquities, Slavic folklore and language, and the revival of a Slavic people.[14]

For all this, Mickiewicz devoted only a few days to Prague. He visited Hanka, to whom he gave a copy of his Petersburg *Poems*, and "before his departure… spent a pleasant evening" with Čelakovský at U Hroznu, one of the few Czech cafés in this thoroughly Germanified city. Who, besides Čelakovský, toasted the Polish poet that evening remains uncertain, but it seems that someone there encouraged the author of *Konrad Wallenrod* to write a poem about the Czech national hero Jan Žižka, the fifteenth-century leader of the Hussite struggle against the Hapsburgs. Mickiewicz apparently never did—or if he did, never finished—explaining, years later, that "a hero who projects himself from the single perspective of hate and revenge appeared to [him] as but an episode, not a finished whole." This notwithstanding, and as disappointed as the Czechs were "that his stay in Prague was so short," it nonetheless established ties that would serve Mickiewicz well. Hanka in particular became a source of books and bibliographical information on the Slavs, especially valuable when Mickiewicz was preparing his lectures at the Collège de France, several of which were devoted to the Czechs. His opinion, however, of his brother Slavs would prove to be ambivalent at best: "modest, indigent, hardworking scholars… who love their nation," but whose concern with language and history and "Austrian legalism" would never win them independence (Dz. 10:39, 48/LS 4:52, 67–68).[15]

*Mickiewicz never did pass through Pardubice.

Karlsbad presented something of a contrast to the Bohemian capital. A thoroughly cosmopolitan locale, its curative waters had long made it one of the most popular destinations for royalty, aristocrats, and not quite aristocrats from all over Europe. Mickiewicz, for his part, and despite what was written in his passport, registered modestly, as "kaiser. russ. Beamter." The Poles there—and there were many—like those in Berlin eagerly sought out their celebrity. Mickiewicz found them irksome, either poetasters hoping for

Fig. 10 Antoni Edward Odyniec. After a painting by Antoni Brodowski, ca. 1829. Courtesy of the Adam Mickiewicz Museum of Literature, Warsaw.

his blessing or "fools, gentry, ostensibly, who bring shame" to Poles. He shied away from them; on the street he would "bow coldly or at least without changing the features on his face and without a word go further on his way." The waters, though, as the poet recalled near the end of his life, "served him very well," and "were beneficial to [his] health." The constant attention from people he had no interest in was, nonetheless, annoying. It was with a sense of relief, then, that he greeted the arrival of Odyniec, with whom he finally left the spa on 13 August. For the next fourteen months, through Bohemia, Germany, Switzerland, Italy, and then Switzerland again, the two would be practically inseparable.[16]

Mickiewicz's relationship with the younger Odyniec had never been an intimate one, akin, rather, to that of master and star-struck pupil. Months of daily proximity strained even that. Their personalities were, as Mickiewicz explained to Jeżowski, "worlds apart." An extrovert open to everyone and everything, Odyniec was a decent person, kind, and, when necessary, pragmatic, which proved invaluable during their travels. But he was also immature, flighty, and not particularly complex, "circling," as his friend put it, "around the edges of life, never hitching [himself] to anything and never penetrating anything deeply." Mickiewicz indulged him, but generally treated him with a condescension that often enough shaded into annoyed impatience. As the poet confided to Malewski, his closest friend in every respect, Odyniec "is too different from me in age, in his way of thinking, and in his entire mode of being." For his part, Odyniec behaved like an eager puppy, capable of at once entertaining and irking the poet, and at the same time genuinely devoted to him, always ready to please and tend to his idol's needs and whims. And this, ultimately, proved to be Odyniec's ticket to fame. One of the admittedly perverse charms of *Letters from a Journey*, the epistolary travelogue that Odyniec composed some forty years later as a record of his travels with the poet, is predicated precisely on the asymmetrical nature of the relationship, with Mickiewicz projected as a charismatic sage—albeit distinctly human—and the author his not always comprehending, not always sufferable, but always grateful acolyte. Odyniec's credibility in his role as Mickiewicz's amanuensis is another matter.[17]

3

Their destination now was indeed Weimar: Goethe was about to celebrate his eightieth birthday, and the two travelers wanted to make the great man's acquaintance before the crowds descended on the capital of Saxe-Weimar. From Karlsbad they made the short trip to Marienbad (Mariánské Lázně), where they ran into Salomea Bécu, their favorite hostess from Vilnius, and then northwest through Eger (Cheb) to meditate briefly at the site of Wallenstein's murder. In Franzensbad (Františkovy Lázně) (Mickiewicz was, after all, supposedly traveling for reasons of health) they met Adolf Januszkiewicz, a mutual friend from Vilnius who would soon join them in Rome and whose dignified behavior at the hands of the Russians during the November Uprising would earn him a prominent place in *Forefathers' Eve*, part 3. But keen on making it to Weimar, they hurried through Hof, Schleiz, and even Jena, vowing, however, to return to the scene of one of Napoleon's greatest victories as soon as events permitted.

On the evening of 17 August, Mickiewicz and Odyniec checked into the Hotel Elephant in Weimar, just a few steps away from *his* house. Like all who would want to pay their respects to Europe's most eminent poet and sage, the two Poles had to undergo something of a screening process, which was entrusted to Goethe's daughter-in-law Ottilie. Szymanowska's name worked magic: first a dinner with Ottilie and the next day a personal invitation from Goethe himself. Two days after their arrival in Weimar, Mickiewicz and Odyniec were standing in his graciously condescending presence. A few words about Szymanowska, a few words about Polish literature—about which, he admitted, he knew very little ("but then there's so much a man has to do in this life")—were enough to earn them an invitation to dinner that evening at the table of his daughter-in-law. Although the fact that Szymanowska recommended him as warmly as she did raised his profile, to Goethe Mickiewicz was, ultimately, yet one more of the many, many admiring strangers whose attentions were the price of his fame—an unpleasant necessity, as the Prince of Poets confided to Zelter.[18]

Ottilie Goethe, however, was clearly charmed by the older of the two Poles. As she assured Mickiewicz some months later in a letter that for all of its conventional niceties at the same time breathes with genuine emotion, he had gained "not only the respect of [their] home, but also its affection." Over the course of the next two weeks—Ottilie convinced Mickiewicz and Odyniec to stay for birthday festivities—she invited the two for several dinners and evenings, some of which were attended by the old man himself. During one of the soirées, when Goethe had already left the room, Mickiewicz thought to entertain the remaining guests with a trick—or was it? He asked each lady in attendance to deposit a ring on a tray, but only one that "she had worn for many years without removing." After they had dropped them in a pile,

> Mickiewicz went to a corner, examined them keenly, and then handed them out one by one to their owners, who were completely unknown to him, and guessed the name . . . and also the age of each. Through all this he had become deathly pale and his forehead broke out in cold beads of sweat.

The author of this reminiscence, the writer and actor Karl von Holtei, adds that years later, "each time [he] saw [Mickiewicz's] name in the French papers in connection with the most unbelievable tales, this pale seeker of rings from Weimar would appear before [his] eyes."[19]

In the days immediately preceding Goethe's birthday, well-wishers and curiosity seekers began arriving from all over Europe. Many of them registered at the Hotel Elephant, among them the sculptor Pierre-Jean David d'Angers, together with his own Odyniec, the writer Victor Pavie. David d'Angers, who had come to Weimar to make a bust of Goethe, was aware of Mickiewicz, thanks to a French-language notice about Chodźko's edition in the *Revue Encyclopédique*. He took an immediate liking to the Polish poet and proposed then and there to fashion a medallion of him. As Mickiewicz was posing, the sculptor asked him to recite something of his poetry. Mickiewicz obliged with an extemporaneous French translation of "The Faris." David d'Angers's image of the thirty-one-year-old poet's profile—thick hair and fashionable mutton-chops, a rather prominent, pointed nose, full lips caught between sneer and smile, and somewhat sleepy eyes—would eventually become one of the most reproduced. (A bust would come later.) But Mickiewicz must have clearly made an impression on Goethe as well, for he too asked the Polish poet to sit for his "court" painter, Johann Joseph Schmeller, so that he could add "such an interesting guest to his collection of famous people he knew."[20]

On 28 August, the day of Goethe's birthday, Mickiewicz and Odyniec joined the citizens of Weimar and other visitors in extending their own best wishes. While Goethe retired for a dinner with ladies only, the men of Weimar gathered in a restaurant for a cash banquet. As foreigners, Mickiewicz and Odyniec were treated as guests, but as foreigners with unreproducible names they were directed to seats marked simply "Pole 1, Pole 2," to the great amusement of those assembled. The following day, "die beiden Polen," as everyone, including Goethe, referred to them, accompanied the poet to the stage premier of *Faust*. Mickiewicz, it seems, was not particularly impressed by the whole (a somewhat liberal adaptation), but in any case impressed enough to "translate the prologue . . . there in Weimar."[21]

This was the first (in this case, not even extant) of what would be only a meager handful of verses that Mickiewicz wrote over the course of the next two years. To be sure, there were, if one is to believe Odyniec, projects and plans—a poem about Twardowski, Poland's equivalent of Faust; a tragedy about Prometheus; an opera about the Polish Legions—but if such in fact did exist, nothing came of them. Mickiewicz tried justifying his barrenness by joking at one point that his "muse, like everything dear to [him], is by birth from northern climes." Yet he was clearly suffering from some sort of block. Perhaps this was just a function of constant movement and sensual overload, of the glut of churches, galleries, and ruins as well as a spate of new acquaintances. For the moment, and during the remainder of his journey, the poet submitted, allowing himself to be distracted by this thought. Once he settled in Rome, however, this inability to produce began to loom increasingly large, at once symptom and cause of a deepening depression.[22]

On 31 August, the last full day of their pilgrimage to Weimar, Mickiewicz and Odyniec, in the company of David d'Angers and Pavie, took the short trip to Jena, where they all reflected on Napoleon's greatness. They paid one final visit to Goethe, who honored Mickiewicz, as he did so many others (including Odyniec), with a gift of one of his quills and an autographed off-print of a poem ("Am acht und zwanzigsten August 1826"). Although this time Mickiewicz did not, as he did in 1827, "practically kneel at the sight of [Goethe's] hand," he now certainly "felt himself the most fortunate of people."[23]

4

"Like the Wandering Jew, making practically no stops," Mickiewicz and Odyniec hurried across Thuringia and Hesse to Frankfurt, where they cashed in a bill of exchange for a pile of gold coins and took in Beethoven's *Fidelio*. They booked a steamer to Mainz, and then down the Rhine to Koblentz and finally Bonn. What was to be a trip freighted with romantic nostalgia, with forests and medieval castles, turned out to be a disappointment. "This . . . river has become bourgeoisified," Mickiewicz later complained to Ottilie Goethe,

> The ax of civilization has not left a single forest on the hills, not a single tree worthy of the name. Everywhere vineyards and vineyards without end. . . . Here and there amid these fields one can still see an ancient castle; they stand there like prisoners of war condemned to humiliating work in the fields, while at the same time modern cottages, squat, smooth, well-whitewashed, akin to good-natured Flemish burghers, multiply happily amid cabbages and carrots.

Mickiewicz's visit in Bonn to August Wilhelm Schlegel, another idol of his youth, heartened him a bit, particularly when the conversation turned to Schlegel's interest in Hindu culture. This notwithstanding, in a travel diary he supposedly began at the behest of Odyniec, Mickiewicz pithily summed up his impressions of Germany: "Hamburg—steak; Weimar—Goethe; Bonn—potatoes." Or, as he put it later to Jeżowski, "Aside from seeing Saxon Switzerland, Goethe, and Schlegel, I got nothing out of Germany."[24]

The travelers sailed back upriver to Mainz, then journeyed overland through Darmstadt, Heidelberg, and Karlsruhe. On the road they ran into David d'Angers and Pavie again, with whom they made a brief trip to Strasbourg to marvel at the cathedral. On parting, Mickiewicz gave the sculptor his French translation of "The Faris," which he had polished for him "as a token of friendship." "Mickiewicz is gentle, calm, kind," David d'Angers noted down shortly after their encounter,

> but proud beyond measure. He prefers to go without something rather than being refused, particularly by a boor, or to be forced to negotiate with all these boors. He's always pensive; always striding ahead without looking about, he sometimes doesn't know where he's going. . . . He's very modest and completely disorganized. If his friend were not there to take care of his accounts, he'd be at a loss, for he is not in the least capable of doing

> numbers. . . . He smokes a lot and drinks a lot. He doesn't like to, but it's a way of feeding his life and perhaps forgetting his soul. . . . He loves liberty a great deal, and all of this thoughts are directed toward his country's independence.

Throughout Mickiewicz's years in Paris, David d'Angers would himself serve as something of his protector and an entrée into the salons of the city's artistic elite, always afraid that his impractical Polish friend might not manage on his own.[25]

Eager now to get to Italy, Mickiewicz and Odyniec hurried along the Rhine, passing through Freiburg just as the weather began to turn. For the next two weeks it rained almost continuously. Aside from making the ride—and often the walk—miserable, the weather deprived them of sights they had set their hearts on, and served only to hasten their journey. Fog and rain spoiled the play of light off the Rhine Falls at Schuffhausen. They obscured their first views of the Alps, shrouded Zurich and its lake, on both ends, and made travel in the mountains treacherous. Years later, Mickiewicz recalled how he had "seen a bull on a mountainous crag fighting with the sand that was sliding out from under him and taking him down into the precipice. The struggle lasted some two hours, and the bull made it out." The sight left a powerful impression, serving him, perhaps, as an allegory of his own fate. Somewhere above Chur, the sun broke through long enough for the two tourists to see the sources of the Rhine.[26]

As they were crossing the Alps at Splügen, Mickiewicz wrote his second poem since leaving Russia. It was addressed to Maria Puttkamer:

> So it seems as if never, never with you can I part!
> You sail the ocean with me and then you follow on land,
> I see your footsteps glistening on the mountain ice
> And hear your voice amidst the roar of the Alpine falls,
> And my hair stands on end when I turn 'round to look,
> At once dreading to see you and thirsting to.
> (To *** In the Alps in Splügen 1829; Dz. 1:329)

Like the Crimean landscapes, the Alpine sublime elicited nostalgia for both a land and a woman the poet realized were irretrievably lost and that could now only be possessed—and, like the nature around him, reimagined—in the subjunctive space of poetry. A year later, in Rome, after having sent Puttkamer and her mother two rosaries blessed by the pope, Mickiewicz received a letter from Maria. "Your image," she wrote in French,

> is always present in my soul, each word I heard from your mouth still resonates in my heart. Often I think I see you, hear you, but these are just figments of my imagina-

> tion.... Perhaps upon your return you will no longer find me among the living;... have me buried with my rosary, which I always carry with me.

"The sight of Her hand," the poet later wrote to her cousin Ignacy Domeyko,

> intoxicated me so much that I cried like a child.... We'll never ever see each other again. But tell Her that she always has a place in my heart, from which no one will ever dislodge Her, and where no one will ever replace Her.

Mickiewicz subsequently noted on Puttkamer's letter that it was her last.[27]

5

On the descent down the Italian side of the Alps to Chiavenna it rained so hard that the road became impassable to vehicles. Mickiewicz and Odyniec were forced to slog and slip several miles through mud and landslides and fractious streams. Como was largely under water when they reached it from Riva. But they had finally made it to Italy, and the rains began tapering off.

On 27 September 1829, the companions were already in Milan, the capital of Hapsburg Italy. They spent a week visiting churches and galleries, attending the opera and ballet at La Scala, and eating ice cream in the cafés. On 3 October, ensconced more or less comfortably in a *vetura*, they set out across Lombardy toward Venice. The journey lasted all but four days, with stops in Brescia, Verona, Vicenza, and Padua. Mickiewicz, however, was not up for sightseeing, "ill" as he "was continually from Milan to Venice."[28]

The two travelers arrived in Venice on 7 October with letters of recommendation to a local musician from both Szymanowska and Volkonskaia. They stayed for two weeks, exploring what Odyniec's *Guide du voyageur* suggested they explore, at the same time eager to view the city through the eyes of Childe Harold. Perhaps it was this that made Venice appear even more spellbinding to Mickiewicz than it already was. But then too, its appeal was conditioned by his acquaintance with a certain Rachel ("an actress") with whom he shared the carriage from Milan to Venice and then the city itself, and most probably a bed. Little wonder that the pearl of the Adriatic "made a greater impression on Adam than did Milan."[29]

With Byron still in hand, the two left Venice on 20 October, traveling back to Padua, then south, across the border of the Papal States, through Ferrara and Bologna. There they were joined in their *vetura* by the Scottish painter William Allan, who ended up accompanying them all the way to Rome. As someone who had traveled throughout the Russian Empire and lived for a time on Polish estates, he shared with them stories about familiar people and places; as a friend of Walter Scott, he entertained them with anecdotes about one of their literary heroes. Together they crossed the Apennines to Florence, where Allan helped guide them through its treasures.

Florence too had its share of Szymanowska's admirers. On her recommendation Mickiewicz introduced himself to the Russian chargé d'affaires to the Tuscan court, Prince Aleksandr M. Gorchakov, one of "the small number of honest people in this world," as Szymanowska assured the poet. But it was thanks to Lelewel that he met Sebastiano Ciampi, a classical philologist who had taught in Warsaw for several years, and then Michał Ogiński, a veteran of Poland's wars for independence and composer of some of the best known Polish polonaises. When not playing chess with Ogiński or "discussing the past," Mickiewicz spent his evenings at the theater with Odyniec, enthralled by the acting of Luigi Vestri. Days, of course, were devoted to art. It is here that the poet developed his life-long attraction to Raphael; the Baptisterium of St. John and the Church of Santa Croce would draw him back to Florence repeatedly. His "senses," as he wrote to Jeżowski, were "slowly awakening to the arts, which [he was] now beginning to appreciate and comprehend."[30]

After close to three weeks of churches and galleries, statues and canvases, tombs, domes, and towers, "of artistic riches that are simply inconceivable," the Polish travelers and their Scottish friend finally made their way to Rome, with brief visits to Siena and Viterbo. On 18 November, "at ten minutes past three in the afternoon [they] saw Rome, that is, the dome of St. Peter's, and at four [they] were on the Piazza del Popolo." Volkonskaia had promised them that the view there would be "magnificent."[31]

6

Like so many grand tourists before them—aristocrats, artists, and nouveaux riches from all corners of Europe—Mickiewicz and Odyniec arrived in a city that was the fundamental fantasy of a classical education. As the poet wrote to his daughter many years later as she embarked on her own grand tour: "You have no idea how [in Nowogródek] we longed for [Rome] when reading Livy, Suetonius, and Tacitus. We were still taught then according to the precepts of the old Polish Commonwealth; we lived in it and in Rome"—religiously, of course, as the navel of the Catholic universe, but politically too, as the cradle of the republican myth. Rome was where Christian culture absorbed and reinterpreted and was nourished by a classical heritage that was eternally present in and as a past in ruins. For someone as well versed in the classics as Mickiewicz, every landmark, every edifice, and every name elicited countless associations, except that now they were tangible.[32]

But the See of St. Peter also ruled over a modern secular realm that, like the other regions of the fragmented Italian peninsula, was experiencing the social and political tensions of a disintegrating post-Napoleonic order. The hills were full of vagabonds and brigands. Grain riots broke out with increasing frequency in the impoverished countryside, and only Catholic charity helped ease poverty in the city. Cells of Carbonari, intent on creating a unified republican Italy, were plotting everywhere (a lodge had recently been discovered in Rome). After the six-year rule of the authoritarian Leo XII, marked by grim repression and a resurgence of reactionary Catholicism, the recent election of Pius VIII offered a glimmer of hope only insofar as his frail health augured a short reign. His subjects, though, to whom Carnival had been denied the previous year on account of his predecessor's death, prayed that he hold on at least until the beginning of Lent.

Volkonskaia had prepared rooms for the poet in her palazzo on Monte di Branzo, hoping that he would lodge with her throughout his stay in Rome. For all of his affection for the princess, the thought of living in a home that he knew would be receiving a constant stream of visitors, that would be hosting almost daily soirées and frequent balls, and whose lady could at times be too doting was not appealing. His "nurse" and "quartermaster" Odyniec found instead a room for themselves in a hotel on the Corso. The autumn and winter, however, proved unusually wet and cold that year—"as cold as in Moscow," Mickiewicz assured Sobolevskii, with a rare snowfall to boot—and the room they had taken offered little protection. They soon moved out, renting an apartment not far from Volkonskaia, on Via del Orso. It too proved to be cold and damp, and the two Poles once almost asphyxiated themselves trying to heat it. Thankfully, they found themselves spending little time there.[33]

Mickiewicz called on Volkonskaia on the very day following his arrival. The princess had returned to Italy in part for health, in part for love, and in part for her son's education, taking Shevyrev along as his tutor. But Rome beckoned also for another reason. She had been considering converting to Catholicism, and for someone of her standing, as well as with her sense of the dramatic, such a gesture could only be effected amid appropriately portentous surroundings. Volkonskaia's social connections and aesthetic predilections being what they were, she had immediately established a salon in Rome that was even more brilliant and more cosmopolitan than the one in Moscow. Her Polish friend became a regular, practically daily, guest there too, and not only at her soirées, with their inevitable musical or theatrical entertainments, but in the more intimate company of her household, be it for breakfast or dinner or just to chat with the charming hostess. For her part, Volkonskaia picked up where she had left off in Russia, smothering Mickiewicz with her generosity, doing everything in her power—out of what she assured him was "a friendship as immortal as [their] souls"—to make his stay in Rome interesting, enlightening, comfortable, and free of care.[34]

To this end, Volkonskaia hurried to acquaint Mickiewicz with her friend Prince Grigorii I. Gagarin, Emperor Nicholas's envoy in Rome and hence the representative of the king of Poland at the Vatican—an important contact for anyone traveling on a Russian passport. Before long, the poet was dropping in regularly to play chess and discuss politics with the Russian diplomat. He also took advantage of the prince's library to borrow a copy of Livy, whose history now held "a strange attraction" for him, "since in the evening one could go look at eventful places about which one had read that morning."[35]

Mickiewicz and Odyniec had arrived in Rome at the beginning of winter season, as Europe's beau monde descended on the city to play until spring, when heat and the threat of disease would chase them out. Thanks initially to Volkonskaia and Gagarin, at balls, routs, soirées as well as more intimate dinners, Mickiewicz came to know an international gallery of aristocrats, beauties, diplomats, opera stars, ecclesiastics, scholars, and artists, among them Bartolomeo Cardinal Pacca, Pope Pius's frequent surrogate at ceremonial occasions; the Papal secretary of state Giuseppi Cardinal Albani; and the pope's personal doctor, Domenico Morichini; the archeologists Antonio Nibby and Filippo Visconti; Byron's erstwhile lover Teresa Guiccioli; the painters Horace Vernet, director of the Académie de France in Rome, Vincenzo Camuccini, who reorganized the Vatican museum for Pius VIII, and Johann Friedrich Overbeck, one of the founders of the anticlassicist Nazerene school; as well as the Danish sculptor Bertel Thorvaldsen, creator of some of Warsaw's most prominent monuments, to whom Szymanowska recommended Mickiewicz as "one of our best poets . . . a man of superior personal merits [and] an enthusiast of the arts." These encounters led, in turn, to private visits to the artists' studios, a tour of the Vatican's vaults and gardens by torchlight, seats at the installation ceremonies for two new cardinals, and invitations to more visits and balls and dinners and soirées.[36]

Of these, particularly stirring for Mickiewicz was his visit to Hortense de Beauharnais Bonaparte, wife of Napoleon's brother Louis, ex-queen of Holland and mother of Louis Napoleon, who invited the poet and Odyniec to her Tuesday soirée. There he met ex-King Jérôme Bonaparte, the same Jérôme whose dashing figure Mickiewicz had glimpsed as a child in Nowogródek and with whom he now struck up an acquaintance that would last until the poet's death. During his initial visit, Mickiewicz apparently assured Hortense, to her gratification, "that the star in which Napoleon had believed has not been extinguished forever." Her twenty-one-year-old son exhibited little interest in that star in the winter of 1829. As Emperor Napoleon III, he would be the addressee of Mickiewicz's last poem.[37]

7

A week after his arrival in Rome, Mickiewicz was introduced to Count Stanisław Ankwicz, a wealthy Galician landowner of burgher origins who had come to Rome on account of his nineteen-year-old daughter's health. Ankwicz immediately extended the poet an invitation to a ball he was hosting for Rome's Polonia, for the most part an assortment of Sanguszkos, Czartoryskis, Radziwiłłs, Potockis, and Dunins, representatives of some of Poland's most illustrious families. A toothache prevented the poet from attending, but he did keep his promise to visit Ankwicz and his family at their residence on via Mercede. The count's daughter, Henryka Ewa, known to everyone as Henrietta, would not have had it otherwise. Having heard that Mickiewicz was in Italy, she "was thrilled with joy at the thought that she might be seeing him soon." This none too pretty, sickly, but intelligent and

Fig. 11 Henrietta Ewa Ankwicz. Engraving after a portrait by Giuseppe Craffonara, 1830. Courtesy of the Adam Mickiewicz Museum of Literature, Warsaw.

well-educated young lady was not, it seems, disappointed. The poet, for his part, found himself drawn to this "sensitive soul and lofty mind," whose entire world consisted of family, illustrious and interesting friends, and conversations about music, poetry, and art; whose time was spent absorbing the history and beauty of Italy as she waited for romance—and her doting parents for an appropriate match.[38]

Mickiewicz and Odyniec were soon daily guests at the Ankwiczes. It was with them that they celebrated a traditional Polish Christmas Eve that year, which coincided with Mickiewicz's birthday as well as his and Ewa's name days, and then in April a traditional Polish Easter. Together with her cousin Marcelina Łempicka, Henrietta took it upon herself to act as Odyniec's and Mickiewicz's cicerone. Armed with guidebooks, Livy, Gibbon, and Niebuhr, and often in the company of Visconti, Allen, and other enthusiasts of the Eternal City's wonders, the foursome combed "Rome's gates, tombs, and temples" ("To My Cicerone"; *Dz.* 1:323) and, when it was too cold or wet, its churches and museums. The artistic and architectural riches of Rome had Mickiewicz's "head reeling." "If one were to gather all the statues and casts of Dresden, Venice, and even Florence," he wrote to Malewski,

> one could hide them in a corner of the Vatican. The Museum here is a veritable city of statues. . . . After Rome, one will forever lose the desire to view sculptures and paintings, and what one once viewed with enthusiasm, one now remembers with a kind of embarrassment.

When the weather warmed up some in March and April, Ankwicz hired out carriages for day-trips to Fiumicino, Frascati, Albano, Palestrina, Genazzano, Ostia, Tivoli, and Subiaco. On foot and on donkey, the merry company visited ruins, villas, and monasteries, an evocative juxtaposition of the pagan imperial and the Christian, of transience, vanity, and the fastness of faith.[39]

This almost daily contact with a young woman of Henrietta's intelligence and sensitivity, of marriageable age and with a generous dowry, seems to have prompted notions of something more serious, commitment even, on the part of the thirty-one-year-old bachelor. "The time when people marry on their own has passed," Mickiewicz wrote to Malewski, "and a new epoch has begun, when they are married by others. I fear living to an age when, as they say, the devil himself makes the match." The poet was undoubtedly referring to Odyniec here, who in his naïve way was indeed trying to play the matchmaker. Henrietta, for her part, did nothing to discourage either Mickiewicz's advances or Odyniec's intrigues, thrilled as she was by the poet's attentions. He was, as she noted in her journal, her "*beloved*, honneur de son siècle et gloire de la Pologne." That the author of *Wallenrod* wrote a poem in her album that spring, addressing her as his "guiding angel," capable of "seeing through to the heart of even a rock" and of "guessing the past from a single expression" ("To My Cicerone"; *Dz.* 1:323), was the fulfillment of a cherished dream—and one Henrietta wanted to share with the entire world. In a letter she sent (anonymously) to a Lwów newspaper, she described Mickiewicz as someone

> with the spark of genius, all the more worthy of respect for his simplicity and modesty, since he never speaks about his own works. . . . He would rather converse in the company of four, and although he is usually melancholy, in a smaller group his conversation is lively, full of various interesting facts, informed by broad erudition. . . . He loves [music] as much as poetry . . . and knows [it] so well, one would think that he had spent his entire life studying it. . . . I like him even more on strolls amid the ruins of ancient Rome. . . . Discoursing on these shards and the transience of human works, his poetic genius metamorphoses into simple and ordinary remarks, but suddenly fascinated by something, he becomes so great and original that I always want to write down everything he says so as not to forget it.[40]

Henrietta was unquestionably captivated by Mickiewicz, just as she was eager to parade that captivation before those less fortunate than she. But did she "also know the *pilgrim's* future?" ("To My Cicerone"; *Dz.* 1:323)—that question neither she nor Mickiewicz was able or even willing to confront. There was something not altogether real in their mutual attraction, hovering between platonic and erotic. But then, as someone who saw them together often recalled years later, Henrietta seemed "to have prized not the man, but the poet; she was in love with his celebrity not his person." Her parents, flattered by the interest Poland's most celebrated living poet was taking in their beloved daughter, for the time being chose to indulge their star-struck child.[41]

Henrietta was not, however, alone in wanting to escort Mickiewicz around the ruins and museums of Rome. She was forced to share this pleasure with another young lady, one whose expectations were somewhat different, but no less high. The poet had met Anastaziia S. Khliustin at Volkonskaia's shortly after his arrival. The twenty-one-year-old Russian was in Rome together with her younger brother Semen and their mother Vera Ivanovna, née Tolstoi, who had brought them to the city for the sake of their health and education. Vera Khliustin "had provided [her daughter] with everything that was advantageous: wealth, a command of languages, connections with Italian, German, Swiss, French, and English aristocracy; she gave her everything except the virtues of her heart." Anastaziia was beautiful, vain, and by all accounts brilliant, yet another of Russia's so-called Corinnes, "du Tanaïs" *vel* "Borysthénide." Her upbringing effectively prepared her for a role as mistress of a salon, which she in fact would play with spectacular success once she settled in Paris in the late 1830s. Khliustin's life was, in this respect, devoted to collecting not so much the rich and the distinguished, but rather anyone who could satisfy her craving for intellectual and aesthetic stimulation—and by the same token reflect her own brilliance. In "the Polish Byron," whose poems "swept [her] away, transported" her, she immediately found someone who could "enchant [her] with his wit." And it was precisely wit, understood as at once "bon mots, . . . witticisms and . . . repartees," discussions of ideas that mattered to them both, and playful flirting, that became the basis for a mutually stimulating friendship that was nourished by almost daily contact in Rome and then in Naples and Geneva.[42]

But intense as it was, this friendship never inspired "the ode in [her] honor" that Anastaziia had been expecting, and it did not stand the test of time. The same cannot be said of the relationship that developed between Mickiewicz and Anastaziia's mother. That years later, in a political atmosphere inimical to manifestations of Polish-Russian amity, the poet should ask this Russian aristocrat to be the godmother of his first son is proof enough of his regard. "Sweet, gentle," and of "unusual modesty," Vera Ivanovna embraced her godson's entire family, and this during some of its most difficult years, when many of their fellow Poles would distance themselves from it. Her genuinely disinterested solicitude for the Mickiewiczes ended only with her death in 1880.[43]

It goes without saying that the Khliustins' circle of acquaintances was no less exquisite than Volkonskaia's or, for that matter, Gagarin's and the Ankwiczes', and in any case, these circles overlapped. But it was thanks specifically to the Khliustins that Mickiewicz met James Fenimore Cooper, who with his family was on his own grand tour of the Continent. At a soirée Vera Ivanovna organized for the American writer in early March, the Polish poet and the creator of *The Leatherstocking Tales* struck up an immediate friendship. After all, both had an interest in the psychology of spies and traitors,* and Mickiewicz had long been fascinated by America. A few weeks later, a Polish newspaper was already reporting that "Mickiewicz . . . could often be seen on walks with the famous American novelist Cooper and with the Russian woman of letters Khliustin."[44]

"There was none, perhaps," observed Cooper's daughter, "whose society gave the [American] author more pleasure than that of the distinguished Polish poet . . . , a man whose appearance, manner and conversation were full of originality and genius." On their walks through Rome as well as on jaunts in the Roman Campagna, Cooper learned much about Poland from Mickiewicz, which subsequently informed the American writer's efforts on behalf of the Polish uprising and that "much injured and gallant people . . . , willing to sacrifice all for liberty . . . [and] their own redemption." Mickiewicz, for his part, even contemplated a trip to America. This was, perhaps, now no more than a whim, but Sobolevskii took it seriously enough and warned his Polish friend that "by going overseas, he would be slicing his fame in half." It was not, however, the last time the idea would cross Mickiewicz's mind.[45]

*Many years later, a critic hostile to Mickiewicz noted comfortingly that "the original idea for [Wallenrod's] skewed heroism did not emerge in Poland. . . . Mickiewicz was to a certain degree only reproducing Cooper's *Spy*" (J. Koźmian, "Dwa ideały" [1851], in *Pisma*, 4).

8

In a note declining an invitation from Khliustin because he "was having dinner at Princess Volkonskaia's and [had] to be at her place at 2:00," Mickiewicz at the same time assured her that he had not "forgotten about their date at the Vatican" that evening to see a display of lights and fireworks. The poet must have dispatched many such notes, and not only to Khliustin. The first few months he spent in Rome were an almost continual round of sightseeing and social functions, in company that was generous, well-meaning, stimulating, but by the same token demanding. For all of his unaffectedness, Mickiewicz was playing, and was expected to play, a role or, rather, several of them: Pole; intellectual authority in matters of art and politics; witty flirt; sensitive suitor; but above all, romantic poet. He would sometimes grow impatient, mocking his Polish aristocratic admirers for their mangling of the language, berating them for their unwillingness to support the arts; but then this too was a role he was expected to play.[46]

Nonetheless, all this took its toll, and the weather that winter did not help. Not since his days in Kowno did Mickiewicz fall ill as frequently as he did in Rome—teeth and gums mostly, as well as varieties of fever and sore throat. The Russian women around him did their maternal best, "sending enough jars of jam to last [him] a couple of months," but which in his capricious pride he refused. Mickiewicz's body was expressing what he could articulate in so many words only to those he most trusted.[47]

"If you only knew," he wrote to Sobolevskii in January, "what a miserable life we lead here, that is, I lead here, since I'm vegetating like a veritable Kamchadal, almost always muffled up and stitched into a quilted coat." To Lelewel a few weeks later, he complained that he had been "rotting... for three months already, since the constant rains prevent[ed] [him] from seeing anything besides churches and galleries. The sheer number of these, in turn, [was] beginning to exhaust despite the novelty and variety of artefacts...." Odyniec, moreover, was getting tiresome. "Without a common language," the two "shut [themselves] off in [their] shells; except for living together, [they] were... far apart." On top of this, news reached Mickiewicz of the death in Arkhangelsk of Jan Sobolewski, his "comrade at the Basilians and in the kibitka," and then two months later, that of Daszkiewicz. Malewski's observation that these were their cohort's "first departed" lodged deeply in his soul, not only reminding him of his own mortality, but making him anxious for those he had left behind in Russia. Mickiewicz was depressed, his "muse had fallen asleep." His friend Aleksander Potocki, scion of one of Poland's wealthiest families, was urging the poet to accompany him to Naples. The Near East also beckoned, but only if the state of his finances permitted.[48]

As he had in Vilnius and then again in St. Petersburg, Mickiewicz responded by seeking refuge of a sort among a small group of male friends. All were Poles and petty gentrymen like himself whom he had encountered at various social affairs in Rome. It was an intimate, comfortable haven, away from the often taxing conventions governing high society and, for that matter, relations with women. Conversation was less forced, the humor more uninhibited, he "breathed more easily" among them. The group included Antoni Strzelecki, the tutor of a young Polish aristocrat, whose extensive knowledge of antiquities the poet put to good use on his strolls through the city; Father Stanisław Parczewski, a budding novelist whose manuscript Mickiewicz held in high regard; and Wojciech Stattler, a painter from Cracow whose "views [on art] much impress[ed] and enrich[ed]" the poet. It was Stattler who portrayed him that year as a prematurely aged man, "sitting bent over and in thought, . . . silent, . . . a loner locked in a cell who was having frightening visions."[49]

They usually met in Strzelecki's room, off the Spanish Steps, where, as Stattler recalled years later, Mickiewicz

> would occupy a small couch, extending his hand along his long-stemmed amber pipe in order to delight in the best brands of tobacco and blow thick wreathes of smoke, creating clouds above his head out of which he would skillfully braid various scrolls.
>
> He would while away entire evenings in this way, inspiring the most interesting conversations. Strzelecki . . . would provide him with material from the most recent finds in Rome. . . . Stanisław Parczewski . . . recounted sketches of ancient customs. Odyniec would sustain and enliven the conversation, larding it with his rhymes. However, most enjoyable for Adam was to chat with his friends about Poland of old. Anecdotes [about those times] would provoke bouts of gleeful laughter, which he was unable to control. . . . He would bounce on the couch, running his hand through his hair.

Discussions became impassioned, however, when the subject of Hegel was raised, this thanks to the presence of Stefan Garczyński. Seven years his junior, Mickiewicz had met this "young, beautiful, melancholy, romantic soul" during his stay in Berlin, where Garczyński was among the most implacable defenders of German philosophy. Mickiewicz had made a "deep impression" on this partially Germanified student from Great Poland, since he had come to Rome expressly to see more of the poet. In the heat of their arguments, aimed "not so much as weapons but as so many presents for a lover," a friendship was forged, one that became as intimate and as selfless as any the poet had nourished. Their paths would diverge and then meet again several times over the next three years, the remainder of Garczyński's brief life.[50]

The arrival of spring that year, with its change in the weather and hence opportunities to explore more of Rome and its surrounding countryside in the company of Henrietta, lifted the poet's spirits. Even his "muse," which he was increasingly associating with the figure of his "cicerone," came to life. But the poem he wrote for her raised more questions than it answered about their uncertain relationship. The poem he wrote around this same time for—or rather about—Henrietta's cousin Marcelina, a pious young lady whom Mickiewicz and Odyniec had jokingly nicknamed "the cardinal," suggests a yearning, however tentative, for resolution of a different kind.[51]

"When it came to religion," Przecławski recalled about his friend in St. Petersburg, Mickiewicz "was like nearly all young people of that time. He was far from being an atheist or an encyclopedist, but he was influenced by an indifference prevalent in that period." The poet's attitude toward religion was of a prescriptive nature. Catholicism was an integral part of Polish custom and culture, whose practice he took for granted and thus could comfortably coexist with an acknowledgment of Enlightenment ideals and a taste for Voltaire and then Byron. Neither arrest nor exile seemed to alter this equation. He found Russian Orthodoxy somewhat repugnant, but so too, it seems, Pushkin's cynicism in this regard. To be sure, the mystics to whom Oleszkiewicz introduced the poet fascinated him, but in the way one is fascinated, as Mickiewicz certainly was, by varieties of arational experience, and by those who, like Oleszkiewicz, appeared to have access to it. The sight of Marcelina's holy communion seems to have rekindled this fascination, but now in the context of Catholic practice:

> Christ hosted you at his table today,
> And even some angels were jealous;
> You lower your eyes, which burn with the Deity!
> Modest and holy, how with your humility
> You terrify me!—Heartless sinners,
> When we lay our sleepy brow to rest,
> Your praying lips the dawn shuts gently
> As before the Lamb of God you kneel.
> It is then that your guardian Angel alights,
> As silent and pure as the light of the moon . . .
>   I'd not care for the pleasures of all of my days
>   If I could dream through one night just like you.
> ("To M. Ł. On the Day of Her Holy Communion";
> Dz. 1:322)

These are the words of someone trying to fathom the mystery of faith—all the more powerful because of its simplicity and innocence, unmediated, unreflective, arational—to which be it reflexivity, reason, pride, or fear deny full access. The village girl communing with her dead lover in the ballad "Romanticism" had metamorphosed into a religiously devout young lady communing with God, and folk belief in the supernatural into a question of faith. It is with this question that Mickiewicz began to wrestle in Rome. He would wrestle with it, "like Jacob," for the remainder of his life.[52]

9

With summer approaching, Rome began to empty. The Ankwiczes left for Paris in early May. As a token of farewell, Mickiewicz gave Henrietta a copy of *Poems*, admonishing her in his dedication "not [to] cry, during neither day nor night, and [to] stay in good health" (*Dz.* 17:492). He too was eager to leave, his sense of dislocation now deepened by the sudden death of his friend Father Parczewski, which left him "saddened and crushed."[53]

Mickiewicz finally decided to take Aleksander Potocki up on his invitation to join him in Naples. Not long after the Ankwiczes' departure, he set out for the south, still in the company of Odyniec. Potocki was there to greet them on their arrival on 10 May, his company and carriage always at their disposal, as they had been in Rome. The Khliustins—mother, daughter, and son—arrived a few days later. But after a week of sightseeing the capital of the Kingdom of Two Sicilies and its environs, Mickiewicz found himself "not all too thrilled by [his] stay in Naples." Writing to Henrietta's mother, he blamed his indifference on his "bad mood and ill health." Apparently the news of Sobolewski's and Daszkiewicz's deaths had "affected him greatly," Odyniec explained to Malewski, "and disposed him to the blackest of forebodings, particularly with regard to you." The frustrating absence of letters from Russia exacerbated the poet's anxiety, and this not only about his friends but also about his finances, since those letters contained the means for replenishing them. Mickiewicz booked passage on a steamer and sailed off to Sicily, alone.[54]

The trip took him around the coast of the island. In Messina he "slept through one earthquake, unaware of it; a second time, bouncing on a horse in the countryside, [he] didn't notice at all that the earth was shaking." To his disappointment, windblown sand from North Africa obscured his view of Mount Etna. But solitude—he was alone, effectively, for the first time since his departure from Karlsbad—proved revivifying. After ten days he was ready to return to Potocki, the Khliustins, and even to Odyniec. In his bag was a branch of a pepper tree, proof for those in Lithuania who might ask that he had been in the land where pepper grows.[55]

The remainder of Mickiewicz's stay in Naples was devoted to sightseeing and "enjoying and reveling in the beauties of nature" in the company of Potocki and the Khliustins. Thanks to their excursions together over the course of the next month, the poet came to know Anastaziia's brother better. Jaded somewhat and enamored of Byron, Semen was no less intelligent and well-educated than his sister, but without her focus and also without her pretensions. It was with him that Mickiewicz and Odyniec clambered up Vesuvius, where they stood over the crater's "very maw... lighting a walking stick and a cigar in its flames," and it was with him that they repeatedly visited Pompeii. The ruined-preserved city dazzled Mickiewicz:

> It's impossible to imagine, without seeing them for oneself, the taste and elegance of the ancients; it seems that every item, from an altar to a set of common scales to pails and pots, was painted by decorators for a theater, for a performance of some opera or ballet.... Few masterpieces of modern art can stand up to these marvelous frescos.... No gallery has made such a great impression on me.

But just as impressive were the preternaturally stark temples of Paestum, "in comparison to which the Colosseum loses much and the façade of St. Peter's looks even paler than it did at first glance." Never since his trip to the Crimea had Mickiewicz been so effusive about the sights he had seen.[56]

There were, of course, also the occasional social visits, without which Anastaziia would not have been able to breathe, particularly since she was eager to show off her Polish poet. Mickiewicz took a special liking to the eighty-six-year-old archbishop of Tarentum, Giuseppe Capecelatro, formerly minister to Joseph Bonaparte and Murat and now, in his dotage, devoted to his beloved cats. But politics, at least as a subject of table-talk, still remained the old Bonapartist's passion. On this point, apparently, Mickiewicz pleasantly surprised the archbishop and his guests by insisting, with what one of the latter called his "political perspicacity," that the days of the Bourbons in France were numbered.[57]

By the middle of June, Mickiewicz, Odyniec, and the Khliustins had largely exhausted the sightseeing suggestions of both their cultural memory and the *Guide de voyageur.* Potocki had left earlier, but not without first opening a line of credit for the poet with his personal banker in Naples. This eased Mickiewicz's anxieties somewhat, as did the arrival, finally, of a packet of letters from Russia. Naples had now grown on him, and so too, thanks to Potocki, a way of life that he compared to that of "the independent princes wandering around there in such numbers,"

> smoking our pipes, trying to decide whether to spend Carnival in Naples or in Rome, whether to go to Paris or to London for the winter.... In addition, I have the fortunate capacity of not thinking about the future and no one can convince me that I'm not some great lord, as long as I have napoleons in my pocket. Unfortunately, one could live as one pleased only if one were able to be a traveler or a poet! But all of our faults and caprices also travel with us.[58]

For the immediate future, Mickiewicz and Odyniec decided on Geneva, where the Khliustins would be spending the remainder of the summer. More compellingly, the poet was also hoping that the Ankwiczes might pass through there on their return from

Paris. He missed Henrietta. Her absence, it seems, in a "land / Where the lemon tree blooms, . . . Where ivy like a wreathe / Decks the ancient ruins," made what might otherwise have been "paradise" incomplete ("To H***. An Invitation to Naples (An Imitation of Goethe)"; *Dz.* 1:324).

Mickiewicz and Odyniec settled on a plan to travel by coach from Rome to Milan via Florence and Genoa, and then from Milan on foot over the Alps to Switzerland. On 20 June, the two travelers returned to a stifling, shuttered, and practically empty summertime Rome in perpetual fear of malaria. They stayed only a few days, long enough to attend Stattler's wedding to an Italian girl and to enjoy the St. Peter's Day festivities. After a final, moonlit evening amid the ruins of the Colosseum, Mickiewicz and Odyniec set out on the morning of 1 July for Switzerland, the latter with plans to journey on to France and England, the former not quite certain when or even whether he would return to the city that had transformed him into an international celebrity.

10

If his years in Russia had proved decisive in establishing Mickiewicz's stature as a romantic poet of extraordinary talent, they proved to be no less decisive in maturing a personal style that allowed this impoverished petty gentryman and schoolteacher from Lithuania to navigate an entire range of social situations with seductive ease. After all, how many in the salons of Rome had heard of the poet, much less read him? To be sure, the recommendations of his old friend Volkonskaia, and then those of Gagarin and the Khliustins, who were familiar with his poetry if only in translation, counted for much, as did word of mouth. But to a Vernet or a Cooper or a Bonaparte, that this Pole wrote poetry mattered only insofar as this was part of his image, as was the fact that this poetry was, as they were made to understand, romantic and in the language of what was perceived to be an unjustly beleaguered people (the Parisian *Journal des débats*, for one, had "Mickiewietz" "singing the lost freedom of his country with the passion and tears of an Italian"). Rather, it was thanks to a capacity for, as Odyniec put it, "never trying, but simply being *himself*"—what Italians since the time of Castiglione recognized as *sprezzatura*—that in Rome Mickiewicz secured his status as a star.[59]

Comely, presentable, self-confidently modest, but also capricious and somewhat eccentric, his French fluent enough to impress those around him with erudition and discernment, to sparkle with wit as well as irony, and to charm with unaffected earnestness—Mickiewicz captivated nearly everyone he encountered. Odyniec was at loss to explain this appeal:

> How could a young man, without a great name or fortune, without connections and influence, indeed, in the least propitious of circumstances, all by himself, and in such a

> relatively short time, gain such favor and popularity.... There is... in people some mysterious power, which one can't see with the eye nor define precisely with the mind, but which one feels clearly and either succumbs to it with love or flees from it with either apprehension or abhorrence.

Today, one might say Mickiewicz had charisma, but that would only be to disappoint his amanuensis' optimism that "one day, perhaps, magnetism will explain" it all.[60]

And whether by coincidence or not, it was just as Mickiewicz was delighting Roman society that spring that two translations of *Konrad Wallenrod*, one of which also included *The Crimean Sonnets* and the poet's own rendition of "The Faris," appeared in Paris.* There had, of course, been earlier translations, French as well as German, but these were bits and pieces—individual ballads, "Ode to Youth," *The Crimean Sonnets*, fragments from *Wallenrod*—and for the most part in peripheral periodicals. Now, however, the works that had established his star in Russian were being made available in the lingua franca of Europe's cultured elites, eliciting, in turn, the inevitable interest in the figure of their author.

The verdict was roundly flattering: "Europe notches another great poet." French reviewers immediately situated Mickiewicz alongside Goethe, Schiller, Byron, Lamartine, and Hugo, without, however, denying him originality, which they derived first and foremost from his predicament as a Pole, a phenomenon at once exotic, politically salient, and lamentable: "If he were permitted to sing an independent and free fatherland, what immortal sounds would we be hearing from someone whose heart, rent by the misfortunes of his country, has not succumbed in exile." But in this, their well-intentioned liberalism, they unwittingly caused the poet grief.[61]

It was not so much biographical inaccuracies—"exiled for a time in Tartary, imprisoned in a dungeon without heat during the long Russian winters"—but rather how in their naïveté Western critics projected the Philomath affair to their international audience, right down to the indiscreet naming of names. Mickiewicz vented his displeasure on Leonard Chodźko, who the poet knew, without saying as much, was the source of these potentially damaging indiscretions. The French reviewers, after all,

> trumpeted the Society of Rayants as political and important, which is what our enemies have tried to prove and continue to do so, but which we have until now denied.... These articles arm our persecutors with swords and will serve as proof, because they seem to have been written by our friends.... Remember that except for me all of my friends are still in exile and that to depict them as dangerous people is to forever bar their return.

Konrad Wallenrod. Romans historique traduit du polonais d'Adam Mickiewicz, trans. Jean-Henri Burgaud des Marat (Gagnard, 1830); and *Konrad Wallenrod. Récit historique. Tiré des annales de Lithuanie et de Prussie. Le Faris. Sonnets de Crimée*, trans. M. M. Félix Miaskowski and G. Fulgence (Librarire Sédillot, 1830).

Otherwise, though, the articles, particularly Alphonse d'Herbelot's extensive appreciation in *Revue encyclopédique*, "afforded [Mickiewicz] great pleasure...." "It is always flattering," he wrote to Chodźko, "for an author to draw the attention of such [an outstanding writer]," particularly when that writer happened to remark that "Mickiewicz is not only a masterful and lofty artist, he is an inspired one."[62]

Mickiewicz was setting out from Rome as one of romantic Europe's most exciting new talents, a poet with the potential for international stardom. Within a year, the uprising in Poland, the country whose sufferings and aspirations to a large degree conditioned his celebrity in the eyes of the West, would effectively derail that potential.

II

The road Mickiewicz and Odyniec took to Florence, through Terni, Assisi, and Peruggia, happened to be the same one that the Ankwiczes had taken two months earlier. For all of the intrinsic allure that the artificial waterfall in Terni, "the capital of the Franciscans," and Peruggia may have had for the poet, he experienced them all through the traces ostensibly left by Henrietta: "Were it not for Henrietta, I would not have had the courage to go to Terni in the terrible heat"; "I have no doubt that [she and her mother] had visited [Assisi]." (For her part, Henrietta had written in her diary that in a chapel in Peruggia she had "offered [herself] and Adam up to the care of the Mother of God.") One of the few visits Mickiewicz paid in Florence was to Henrietta's doctor (who assured him of improvements in her health). The poet wrote to the Ankwiczes urging them to stop in Geneva on their way back from Paris. He informed them that he himself had decided "to visit Rome again and devote a few months more to familiarizing [himself] with it in greater depth," but he would, of course, "prefer to be [there] at the same time" as the Ankwiczes. As in Naples, Henrietta's absence was eliciting associations and nourishing plans that were as nebulous as their object.[63]

After three days in a fondly familiar Florence, the two travelers journeyed on to Pisa and thence to Genoa. It was "on the road to Genoa" that sometime in the middle of July 1830 Mickiewicz wrote an extraordinary—and to some extent completely unexpected—poem. With its devastatingly bleak vision of the Polish national struggle as one of conspiracy, self-destruction, and martyrdom, "To a Polish Mother" derives from the same sense of hopeless inevitability as *Konrad Wallenrod*:

> Your son will be called to a war without glory
> And to a martyrdom... without resurrection. [...]
> There he will learn [...]
> To quietly poison with words stinking of rot,
> To be unassuming like a snake when it's cold.
> [...]

Once he is vanquished, the dry wood of a scaffold
Will remain as his grave's only marker,
All his glory will be but a woman's brief sobs
And the converse of kinsmen long into the night.
(Dz. 1:320–21)

Mickiewicz was drawing on his own experiences in Russia, convinced as he was of the futility of armed struggle against the empire's might—"unequal, unimaginable, leading to inevitable defeat"—but fearful of the moral and psychological consequences of struggle by other means. At the same time, the poem seemed to apprehend the sense of anxiety pervading Europe in July 1830, on the eve of the revolution in France, the outbreak of the Polish uprising four months later, and the eruption of revolutionary unrest in Italy in 1831. But it also effectively adumbrated, in the darkest of colors, what several generations of Poles would experience *after* the defeat of the November uprising and then again in the wake of the uprising of 1863. Some would later accuse Mickiewicz of defeatism, but the poem's uncanny prescience is impossible to deny, as is its significance for understanding the poet's own reluctance when confronted with the fruits of his presentiments.[64]

During their brief stay in Genoa, Mickiewicz and Odyniec ran into Ottilie's husband August Goethe, whom they knew from Weimar and with whom they now spent two days sightseeing the city, but largely in an alcoholic haze thanks to August's fondness for wine. They also met the director of the Genoa opera, a Pole, who, according to Odyniec, tried to induce Mickiewicz to write a libretto for him. Nothing came of this project. Nonetheless, as the poet was writing the third part of *Forefathers' Eve* two years later, it was the structural devices of opera—arias, duets, and choruses—that in large part determined the drama's shape.[65]

The two travelers arrived in Milan on 20 July, happy that they would be seeing the Khliustins there on their own way to Geneva. But beyond meeting Semen on the street unexpectedly, what made Mickiewicz's and Odyniec's visit to the city special this time was a letter of introduction to the director of Milan's hospital, through whom the two Poles got a tour of the city's ateliers, a home-cooked meal, and an invitation to visit Alessandro Manzoni, at that time arguably Italy's most prominent writer, whose poem "Il Cinque maggio" on Napoleon's death was already a classic. Mickiewicz, though, passed up this opportunity to meet its author, preferring instead to spend the evening with the Khliustins before their departure.

After a brief ride from Milan to Sesto Calende and then a passage up Lago Maggiore to Fariolo, Mickiewicz and Odyniec set out over the Alps on foot (but also by carriage when the occasion presented itself), dressed in the requisite garb of Alpine pilgrims:

"an outer shirt of gray linen... down to the knees, girded by a black lacquered belt, and with a short cape from the neck,... a straw hat with a rather large brim and an oil-skin backpack... with a tin mess kit attached to it." After deliberating whether they should take umbrellas or walking sticks, they finally decided on both. The walking sticks came to serve as a sign of comity with the many other romantic tourists making the obligatory eight-day pilgrimage through the Alpine sublime: the Simplon Pass, Martigny, Col de Balme, Chamonix, "the eternal snows" of Mont Blanc (but only from Flégère), and the delightfully terrifying Mer de Glace.[66]

Awaiting the tired, but clearly exhilarated, Polish pilgrims in Geneva was a dinner at the Khliustins—and news of the July Revolution in Paris, which, by all accounts, "Adam had predicted."[67]

12

"You cannot imagine," wrote Mickiewicz to Semen Khliustin describing the atmosphere in Geneva in the early days of August 1830,

> the excitement of the Genevans with the arrival of each courier; they run, they ask, they argue.... We're not far behind. We go to the park often to listen to the political conversations of groups of strollers, because one must keep up with the times.

Among the liberal Swiss intellectual elite that gathered in the Khliustins' salon—the writer Charles-Victor de Bonstetten, the historian and economist Léonard de Sismondi, the botanist Auguste de Candolle—the implications of the revolution in France were practically the sole topic of conversation. And with the spread of revolutionary sentiment to Belgium, Mickiewicz was now regarded as something of a political sage in Anastaziia's circle, his presentiments about changes in post-Congress Europe seemingly confirmed with every new issue of the *Journal de Genève*.[68]

Yet for all of the political hopes that the July events engendered, they were also the source of much personal anxiety for Mickiewicz. The Ankwiczes were to have left Paris in the beginning of August, and the poet was hoping to see them before setting off for the Oberland. Now, however, the French capital was in the midst of upheaval, and he had not heard from them for several weeks. "Don't you think we read newspapers here," he berated Henrietta's mother,

> and thus can't guess what is going on in my heart while reading them? If I at least knew what street you lived on and thus could coordinate this with news of those [street] battles, I might be calmer.... After all of your other griefs [i.e., the death of Mrs. Ankwicz's father], getting yourself caught up in this wrangle was the last thing you needed.

Mickiewicz felt he could not wait any longer. The Ankwiczes arrived in Geneva on 15 August, a few hours after his departure for the Bernese Alps.[69]

This time Odyniec was not Mickiewicz's only companion on this no less obligatory trip for romantic seekers of the sublime. In Geneva the two had run into the eighteen-year-old Zygmunt Krasiński, an acquaintance of Odyniec from Warsaw, whose father presided over that city's most prominent neoclassicist salon, the headquarters, as it were, for Mickiewicz's literary antagonists. The highly strung young count and literary prodigy, who was already the author of several prose tales *à la frénétique* as well as a recent overview of Polish literature for Bonstetten's *Bibliothèque universelle*, was himself taking the grand tour in the company of his tutor. When it became apparent that their travel plans coincided, he eagerly agreed to join Mickiewicz and Odyniec for the excursion through the Oberland. Krasiński was as awestruck by the poet as he was by the magnificent sublime of a raging storm on Lake Thun, the waterfalls of the Lauterbrunnen Valley, the Jungfrau, the rapids of the Aar at Handeck, the Teufelsbrücke Bridge at night, and a three-day stay atop Rigi. "Oh, how wrong were the opinions about [Mickiewicz] in Warsaw," he gushed to his father, anticipating his prejudice against Warsaw's romantic nemesis:

> He has a broad range of knowledge, knows Polish, French, Italian, German, English, Latin, and Greek. He has a superb grasp of European politics, history, philosophy, mathematics, chemistry, and physics. Perhaps no one in Poland is as conversant about literature as he is. Speaking with him one might think that there's not a book he hasn't read. He has very reasonable, serious opinions about things. He's usually sad and pensive; misfortune has already carved furrows on his thirty-year-old brow. He's always calm, quiet, but one can see from his eyes that any given spark can ignite a flame in his breast. To me he seemed the very ideal of a learned man and a genius in the full sense of the word.[70]

As for Mickiewicz, his sadness and pensiveness as well as spells of bad weather notwithstanding, he could barely contain his wonder at the sights, sounds, and vistas of the Bernese Alps and his "joy" at seeing "northern vegetation, green grass, and fir trees." Despite his declaration to Czeczot that he was not about to describe the journey, he was unable to restrain himself:

> I was amidst glaciers where the Rhine, Rhône, and all the great rivers of Europe begin. I was on mountains from which one can see twelve lakes and several countries. I heard a cascading avalanche (from quite a distance, admittedly). I saw so many waterfalls that a list of them would fill the rest of this page.

Yet the excursion also cemented a new friendship for the poet in the person of Krasiński, one that over the many years the two writers knew each other would be filled with mutual admiration but also, as Krasiński matured into both an artistic and ideological rival for the hearts and minds of Poles, with the kind of venomous conflict that informs a younger man's relationship with a mentor whom he feels ostensibly betrayed his ideals. In this respect, the mark Mickiewicz left on Krasiński during those few weeks spent together in Switzerland proved indelible. "I learned from him," the young writer presciently assured his father, "to look at the things of this world in a colder, more beautiful, and more impartial light; I rid myself of many prejudices and false perceptions, and this will surely have an impact on the remainder of my life, an impact both good and noble."[71]

The company returned to Geneva on 4 September. Having learned during his trip that the Ankwiczes had finally arrived safely, albeit "trembling with fear... convinced that [in Paris they] were watching the end of the world," his mood became all the brighter. Thanks to the Khliustins, he could now even boast a new wardrobe. For the next few weeks, their Italian routine—daily visits, long walks with the young ladies, excursions to the environs of Geneva, organized and funded, as before, by the count—was temporarily restored. Mickiewicz decided to join the Ankwiczes in Rome for the winter. But all this simply served to disguise a relationship that at least as far as the poet was concerned was stalled and one that as far as Henrietta's parents were concerned was never meant to advance beyond friendship. Henrietta, it seems, was caught in the middle, too weak, too submissive, and too indecisive to try making a difference.[72]

What change did occur in old routines occurred in the Khliustin household. During Mickiewicz's absence, Anastaziia had become engaged to Count Adolphe de Circourt, the secretary of the recently deposed prime minister of France, hence now a monarchist exile in Switzerland. Although he was considered one of the most informed men of the day ("he knows seven languages," wrote Mickiewicz, not without some sarcasm), and in this respect an ideal match for a young lady perpetually in need of intellectual stimulation, his political views as well as his station could not but transform the nature of at least the political discussion in the Khliustins' salon. The sudden appearance of this "foreign speculator," as Mickiewicz jokingly called him, disrupted the special relationship the poet had developed with Anastaziia, "lowering" the price of his "affects and sighs" "to such a degree that they now [had] only a nominal value." Mickiewicz's visits to the Khliustins became less frequent, and rather to see Vera Ivanovna and Semen.[73]

Mickiewicz spent another month in Geneva, mostly in the company of the Ankwiczes, the Khliustins, and Krasiński and his English friend Henry Reeve,* hiking, picnicking, sailing the lake, reading newspapers, discussing literature and current events, and shooting fireworks. Krasiński's review in *Bibliothèque universelle* of the recent French translation of Mickiewicz's works, with its insistence that "truth is the salient feature of his imagery,"

*Reeve would shortly go on to translate several of Mickiewicz's poems into English, including "The Faris," one of the Crimean sonnets, and fragments of *Konrad Wallenrod*, all published in 1831.

must have surely pleased the older writer as the work of an extraordinarily talented pupil pleases a teacher. On the surface, at least, and for the moment, the poet felt content in Geneva, and it was no less "difficult to tear [him]self away from it all" than it had been a month earlier.[74]

On 5 October the Ankwiczes left Geneva heading back to Italy. Mickiewicz and Henrietta exchanged gifts, certain they would be seeing each other soon but uncertain to what end. Five days later, Mickiewicz set out in the same direction, this time, however, by himself. After fourteen months of nearly continual companionship, he was parting with Odyniec. "It was sad and touching," Krasiński wrote his father,

> to see him saying good-bye to Odyniec. The thought that they may never see each other again tinted the moment with pain. They hugged each other for a long time, Odyniec with tears in his eyes, Mickiewicz with steelier comportment, but with a face on which the deepest sadness was evident. Thus they parted, and Odyniec moaned for him as if for a lover.

The two would in fact see each other again in less than two years, but not before their world had been turned upside down. For the moment, though, the poet was returning to Rome, "once again all by [him]self like a lonesome pine."[75]

13

Mickiewicz traveled back to Italy along the same route he had taken with Odyniec two months earlier. It made him "sad," he confessed to his erstwhile companion, "to stop in the places and rooms where, traveling on foot, we once rested for the night, because of all of our trips, that one was the most pleasant." But if Mickiewicz had always been prone to varieties of *Weltschmerz*, it appears now that his disaffection was becoming debilitating, enough to emerge as its own object: "How often a person who is unhappy with himself is wont to change his likes and desires. In the north I longed for the south, and here [in Italy] I long for snows and forests." Mickiewicz felt adrift. He was returning to Rome largely for the sake of Ankwicz, but beyond this he had no definite plans. The uncertainty marking their relationship served only to intensify his sense of dislocation.[76]

He caught up with the Ankwiczes in Milan. What exactly transpired there between the poet and the Ankwiczes is unclear. Years later, Henrietta recalled how they spent those two weeks sightseeing the city, this time with the poet in the role of cicerone. The count, though, had finally seen enough. Against the objections of Henrietta's mother, who all along had been rather sympathetic to Mickiewicz, Ankwicz took his family and left Milan without so much as a word of farewell, letting Mickiewicz know none too subtly that he should harbor no illusions regarding his daughter. A few days later, Mickiewicz too "left Milan, sick and careworn" and apparently "resigned to his fate." "*Mon parti est pris*," he confided to Odyniec. In any case, Mickiewicz added, Henrietta's "health is very bad, and I foresee a sad future for her. Stupid parents, they'll finish her off, he with a strange sort of reserve, she with a surfeit of solicitude." They would see each other in Rome over the course of the next few months, but the hope, if their indeed ever had been any, of something more than an inspired friendship would no longer be a factor. The anatomy of his predicament would continue to haunt Mickiewicz for years to come.[77]

The poet returned to Rome at the end of October. For the first time since Kowno he had an apartment to himself. Despite the bankruptcy of his Paris publisher, on which he "lost," or so he claimed, "6,000 francs," his financial situation was "secure until May" and, it would seem, until well after, as long as Malewski and his agents in Warsaw remembered to send residuals. "After the chaos of travel, there came a whirlwind of intense reading, wherein Dante, the Winckelmannites, Niebuhr, newspapers, and chronicles [were] jumbled as much on the table as they [were] in [his] head." Yet as Krasiński remarked upon seeing Mickiewicz in late November, "He had grown terribly sad and gaunt. Suffering has so lined his face that one can't but feel pity looking at him." His social life became more subdued, confined as it was largely to Volkonskaia and the now purely ritual visits to the Ankwiczes. He spent "most of his time" in a small circle of Polish friends, some old, some new. Garczyński was still there and still single-mindedly devoted to his studies, as was Garczyński's cousin, along with Father Stanisław Chołoniewski, whom Mickiewicz had known in passing earlier but to whom only now he "drew very close." They were shortly joined by Count Henryk Rzewuski, Karolina Sobańska's brother, the same Rzewuski who in 1825 had accompanied Mickiewicz on his travels through the Crimea.[78]

Seven years older than the poet, Rzewuski was a consummate story-teller, a talent that for Mickiewicz was as preciously peculiar to the Polish gentry ethos as oriental costumes, anarchic spontaneity, and patriarchalism, all of which he felt was being driven to extinction by Gallic modernity. "He gave me new life," Mickiewicz wrote of Rzewuski, "with his [knowledge of] traditions, his anecdotes, and his gentry style, drawn fresh from country life." At the same time, "listening to his Polish," the poet realized "how much [he was] missing because of a lack of books and, what's worse, of Polish conversation for so many years." Mickiewicz, it seems, beseeched Rzewuski to write it all down, which the latter finally did: his tales of eighteenth-century provincial gentry life, published in 1839–1841 under the title *The Memoirs of Mr. Seweryn Soplica*, are now a classic of Polish romantic prose.[79]

With their nostalgic evocation of a vanishing way of life, their salty humor, and their delight in the textures of the spoken word, Rzewuski's stories provided Mickiewicz with "great comfort" and with material that would soon enough make its way into *Pan Tadeusz*, his own evocation of old Poland. Father Chołoniewski offered Mickiewicz a different form of solace. The same age as Rzewuski and of lineage almost as good, Chołoniewski had given up on a career at the tsar's court in order to become a priest. His was a conservative, postrevolutionary Catholicism, influenced by personal friendships with the French philosopher Joseph de Maistre and the German romantic playwright Zacharias Werner, hence inimical to the entire Enlightenment enterprise and informed by an uncompromising belief in the infallibility of the papal Church. His arguments to this effect and, no less important, his patient solicitude appear to have impelled Mickiewicz to look at his own faith anew, as a potential source of both justification and reassurance. "I owe him much," the poet admitted in hindsight, "[he afforded me] much consolation, many happy moments, and a new perspective on the world, on people, and on learning."[80]

Mickiewicz was at this time also "reading much" and above all "meditating on the works of l'abbé [Félicité-Robert] Lamennais," whom he advised Odyniec to "read with close attention." The French theologian's *Essay on Indifference in Matters of Religion* (1817–1824), an ultramontane critique of individual reason and a curiously argued defense of Catholicism as a bulwark against the ravages of revolutionary rationalism, reinforced the poet's conversations with Chołoniewski. What seems to have resonated most, however, was Lamennais's efforts to seek a reconciliation between religion and liberalism, whereby a reformed Catholic Church would position itself as a guarantor of social stability, which by itself would ensure the progress of liberty. Lamennais, in other words, offered Mickiewicz a vision of Catholicism that refused to cede to individual reason, and thus to secular governments, monopoly over what was, after all, an article of immutable divine law. That as editor of the journal *L'Avenir*, with its motto "God and Liberty," the French cleric extended this principle to a vociferous defense of the Polish cause made his vision of the Church as a repository of progressive values all the more appealing. But beyond doctrine, what was no less compelling was the figure of the dissident theologian himself, whose steadfast insistence on the correctness of his way in the face of hostility from both the Church hierarchy and the July Monarchy Mickiewicz would come to appreciate and, indeed, emulate in his own conflicts with those same authorities.[81]

The poet's discussions with Chołoniewski and his discovery of Lamennais combined to stir spiritual longings which to some extent had been planted by the recently deceased Oleszkiewicz (he died on 5 October) and which the poet had begun articulating ever so tentatively in his poem to Łempicka. It is no coincidence that in an early draft of *The Books of the Polish Nation and the Polish Pilgrimage*, Mickiewicz acknowledged "the teachings of a Pole named Oleszkiewicz, who died not long ago, and the teachings of Father Stanisław, who is still alive, . . . and the books of a priest called Lamennais" (Dz. 5:335), thus linking the three in a personal pantheon of spiritual mentors.

But this was later, in 1832, when those stirrings had crystallized into an unambiguous declaration of faith. In the fall of 1830, Mickiewicz was still only capable of expressing them in comfortably familiar—aesthetic—categories:

> Earthly artist! what mean your paintings,
> What mean your sculptures and your words?

And you complain that someone from the crowd
Can't grasp your thoughts, your speech, your works?
Gaze at the Master, O child of God, and suffer,
Unknown to the crowd or held in contempt.
("Master of Masters"; *Dz.* 1:327)

Indeed, to judge by Semen Khliustin's reaction, Mickiewicz's growing attraction to religion—to Catholicism, no less—came as something of a shock to someone who had known the poet well during his months in Italy and Switzerland:

> Certainly some sort of reinforcement is necessary in this world, until one finds a more agreeable way of leaving it. But I had thought that like myself you would find this foothold in hatred for might and not in some imaginary, capricious, emollient love, good only for concealing the intrigues of an infernal caste, which, as far as I'm concerned, is the cause of all of our political ills, good only for the despicable and sordid interests of this caste, but apt to seduce only weak souls or, rather, people without a soul. I had known you as someone who holds these opinions. Could you have changed?[82]

What Khliustin did not seem to have grasped was the depth of Mickiewicz's depression. Now that his illusions about Ankwicz had been dispelled, the poet had no concrete plans for the future; his depression fraught any decision in this regard with anxiety. The outbreak of an uprising in the Congress Kingdom of Poland on 29 November forced additional decisions, making his paralysis all the more agonizing. At least faith held out the promise of solace as well as purpose.

On 8 December, after many years of indifference, Mickiewicz went to confession. Chołoniewski commemorated the occasion, and the ostensible success of his ministrations, with a gift of St. Thomas à Kempis's *Imitation of Christ*, assuring his friend in the dedication that "nothing will be able to erase the memory [of this event] from [the poet's] heart." The act of contrition may have eased Mickiewicz's conscience; it did not, however, make him any more decisive, nor, for that matter, any happier.[83]

14

On the night of 29 November 1830, a cohort of young conspirators led by cadets in the Polish army attacked the Belvedere Palace in Warsaw with the intention of subduing the tsar's viceroy, Grand Duke Constantine. Constantine, however, managed to flee, while rebellious officers of the Polish army initially failed to mobilize their units against Russian forces; in any case, not all in the Polish military supported the uprising. The course of the revolt that night was ultimately decided by the people of Warsaw, who attacked the arsenal and, together with the rebellious units, quickly gained control of the city. Caught by surprise and convinced that the uprising would end in disaster, an administrative council made up of the Congress Kingdom's leading conservatives, with Prince Adam Czartoryski at its head, hoped at first to come to some sort of compromise with Constantine and his brother, the tsar. Their plans were opposed by a revolutionary club led by the romantic literary critic Maurycy Mochnacki, who soon forced the council to constitute a provisional government, which besides Czartoryski and Mochnacki himself now also included Mickiewicz's protector and former professor Joachim Lelewel. On 13 December, the Polish Diet in Warsaw declared a national uprising that was to encompass all of partitioned Poland.

News of the uprising reached Rome in the first half of December, competing with speculation about the outcome of the conclave assembled to choose the successor to Pius VIII, who had died on 1 December. Poles in Rome mobilized immediately, either setting out to join the uprising or fundraising for the cause. Rzewuski was ready to do both; Garczyński left as soon as he heard the news, Mickiewicz having apparently "given him all the [money] he had" for the trip. The poet, for his part, remained in Rome.[84]

On 30 December, Mickiewicz wrote Semen Khliustin to now ask for some money for himself, informing him that he too was "in all likelihood leaving in a few days for the other side of the Alps," "although," he added, "the date of [his] departure was not yet set." Writing the next day to Semen's sister, now Madame de Circourt, the poet was even vaguer: "I'm probably leaving Italy, perhaps very soon." In both letters he described his state in Rome as miserable. "For some time," he complained to the newlywed, "I'm in no shape to stitch two thoughts together. . . . I do nothing now but run around aimlessly during the day and pray at night." "Every wet sheet of a dirty German newspaper" now fascinated him more "than all the Da Vincis and Raphaels" in Rome; "the newspaper reading room [was] now [his] museum." But January passed; Nicholas was dethroned as the king of Poland; a full-scale war had broken out between Poland and Russia—and the poet was still in Rome.[85]

It was 20 February 1831 when, after months of silence, Mickiewicz wrote to Szymanowska. The spirit of revolution had now gripped Italy as well, engulfing Modena, Parma, and the Papal States; "Rome [was] full of fear." "I'm living here in a very nasty predicament," the poet informed his friend(s) in St. Petersburg,

> a few weeks ago I was just about to travel over the Alps, when after clearing up various obstacles standing in the way of my departure, new ones emerged. . . . Everyone is afraid of the masses and the Transtiberians, who assume that instigators and foreigners are one and the same thing. . . . We walk the streets here with pistols in our pockets, always fearful of a knife in the back, and in the evening we lock ourselves up in our homes. . . . I'd love to get out of here as fast as possible and am waiting for a steamer, since it's becoming increasingly difficult to travel by land.

Some two weeks later he was writing to Garczyński that he was "still sitting in Rome, and fretting, and feeling bored." "Various circumstances have delayed my departure," he explained to his friend, who by now was already fighting in the ranks of the Polish insurgents. "There are disturbances in Romagna and the roads are not particularly safe. Nevertheless, I'm thinking of heading out, particularly since I now have the means."[86]

But March was already coming to an end. The new pope, Gregory XVI, asked for Austrian intervention to quell the revolutions in Italy. In Poland, the insurgent army won several important battles against Russian forces. The poet, however, continued to tarry. On 4 April, after a long silence, a worried Mickiewicz informed his brother Franciszek about "the unforeseen circumstances that perforce detained" him, although now he "once again ha[d] to think about leaving." By the time the hunchbacked Franciszek received his brother's letter, he himself was already the veteran of several engagements.[87]

The young Mendelssohn, on his own grand tour of Italy, found the poet's apathy, melancholy, and equivocating at this juncture simply "tiresome":

> If he looks at St. Peter's, he deplores the times of the hierarchy; if the sky is blue and beautiful, he wishes it were dull and gloomy; it if is gloomy, he is freezing; if he sees the Colosseum, he wishes he had lived during that period. I wonder what sort of a figure he would have made in the days of Titus!

To Sobolevskii, who had arrived in Rome at the beginning of February, Mickiewicz "appeared to be satisfied with his lot, although he was worn down by some kind of sorrow or, rather, by intense worry." "He told me," recalled Sobolevskii many years later, "that it was because he was not in Poland; . . . [that] as a national poet he felt obligated to be part of the movement." "Then why don't you go?" Sobolevskii asked. Upon hearing that it was, ostensibly, a matter of money, he immediately took charge of Mickiewicz's finances—they may have been in disarray but certainly not depleted—and began making arrangements for them to travel north together. Nonetheless, it was not until the middle of April that the poet finally declared that he was "now leaving without fail." Visas on his Russian passport permitting him to travel are dated 16 and 17 April.[88]

Mickiewicz had been assuring his correspondents for several months now about his intention to leave Rome, but somehow various "obstacles," "circumstances," "difficulties"—he never explained what they were—seemed to continually thwart it. He was dissembling when he told Sobolevskii that he had given everything he had to Garczyński. To be sure, revolutionary disorder in Italy made travel hazardous, and neither Austria nor Prussia were about to facilitate the passage of potential Polish insurgents through their territories. Yet the fact remains that Garczyński and any number of Polish men who found themselves in similar predicaments left to join the uprising almost as soon as they had heard of its outbreak and then succeeded, by hook or by crook, in making their way to the Congress Kingdom. Mickiewicz did neither. In fact, as the poet confessed later to Count Ankwicz, he even "made fun of his countrymen taking other roads [to Poland] and arrogated to [him]self a greater degree of foresight." This "foresight," for which he felt God later punished him, meant that it took Mickiewicz over four months to leave Rome, and by the time he finally did attempt to cross into the Congress Kingdom another four months later, the uprising had run its course.[89]

But then too, Mickiewicz was not optimistic about the outcome of a Polish-Russian conflict. Now that the forebodings he had articulated some five months earlier in "To a Polish Mother" had to some extent materialized, the poet "was convinced that [the uprising] [could] not succeed and that its consequences would be disastrous . . . , and even were it to be successful, he did not believe in its durability or the good it might bring." No admirer of the tsarist regime, Sobolevskii may, for his part, have encouraged Mickiewicz in this belief, and in his delay as well, hoping perhaps in this way to preserve his remarkable friend.[90]

It is difficult to say what finally moved the poet. Maybe indeed it was news of the spread of the uprising to his homeland in Lithuania, where even his hunchbacked brother had joined the fight. By April, though, Mickiewicz had probably heard how deeply he was already implicated, willy-nilly, in the whole mess. The cadets storming the Belvedere Palace in Warsaw did so in the name of his Wallenrod; "practically every wall [in the city]" featured, "written in large letters," lines from his "Ode to Youth"—"Welcome, O morning star of liberty,/What comes now is salvation's sun!"—as did the first issue of one of the insurgent newspapers. In Mickiewicz, recalled Kajetan Koźmian, "the revolution had found its minstrel or pagan Lithuanian bard, or, rather, its Tyrteus." Although written while the poet was already well on his way, Maurycy Gosławski's poem addressed "To Mickiewicz Idling in Rome during the National War," with its epigraph from *Konrad Wallenrod*, best expressed the ineluctable pressure that effectively forced a reluctant, skeptical Mickiewicz to fulfill a role he himself had created and now others demanded he play:

> O worshipped bard! who with ardent words
> Knew how to strike the hearts of his brothers . . . ,
> The world of your thoughts, like a thunderbolt's flash,
> Shines bright now in front of your eyes.
> Why are you not, then, amidst it? . . .
> Hurry—abandon distant Rome,
> Hurry—for if we prove victorious,
> To breathe Polish air having not served its cause will be a lasting disgrace.
> If we perish in the rubble,

> Then hear, O bard, in those days of sorrow
> To share a grave with us unworthy will he be
> Who has not shared our blood and honor!

The remaining years of Mickiewicz's life, everything that he would write and preach and do, would to a greater or lesser extent be conditioned by the need to prove that he too deserved a place in that grave.[91]

CHAPTER FIVE

CRISIS AND REBIRTH (1831–1832)

Mickiewicz left Rome on 19 April 1831 in the company of Sobolevskii, a Russian prince, his Polish wife, their son, their painter, and another Russian. He was "sad" to leave a city that he had come to "love like a second fatherland." The poet's immediate destination was Geneva; but beyond that, he was still uncertain. On the eve of his departure, Mickiewicz had said good-bye to Henrietta with a gift of Byron, in which he underlined the poem "Farewell! If Ever Fondest Prayer":

> My soul nor deigns nor dares complain
> Though Grief and Passion there rebel:
> I only know we loved in vain—
> I only feel—Farewell!—Farewell!

He also went to confession. On emerging, the poet was apparently so moved that he left Rome with a vague "desire to enter the priesthood."[1]

I

The Italian countryside must have been tranquil by now, and Mickiewicz and company were certainly in no hurry. This was not a man rushing off to join his embattled brethren, but rather a tourist revisiting favorite places—the ravines around Civita Castellane, the waterfall in Terni, the unfinished Raphael in Folignio, Lake Trasimeno. The journey was punctuated by arguments (usually between Russian husband and Polish wife) about the sense and odds of the uprising; Mickiewicz, for his part, continued to insist on the unsoundness of the former and the slimness of the latter.

After spending a full three days in Florence, Mickiewicz and Sobolevskii continued on alone to Bologna, where Sobolevskii "found paradise or, at least, one of its houris, in the person of a Miss della Antoni." Whether his Polish friend, too, found his bit of paradise there, Sobolevskii does not say. On 3 May, some three weeks after having left Rome, the two friends parted in Fiorenzuola, Sobolevskii heading for London and Mickiewicz to Geneva via Turin. That same day in Warsaw, at an assembly marking Polish Constitution Day, the Society of Friends of Learning, the most prestigious scholarly institution in the Congress Kingdom and repository of Poland's Enlightenment values, chose Mickiewicz as a member. His symbolic presence in an embattled Warsaw made his physical absence all the more salient.[2]

The Khliustins were still in Geneva. So too was Krasiński, who, having chosen obedience to his loyalist father over his desire to join the uprising, was undergoing his own crisis of conscience. Mickiewicz spent about a week in the Swiss city, making travel arrangements but also tarrying—he was still "undecided." At one point, while still in Rome, he had planned on going north through Bavaria. His plans changed, it seems, upon hearing that a ship "with a heavy load" (i.e., arms) intended for the insurgents in Lithuania was to set sail for Palanga from London. On 21 May, the poet headed for Paris, with the idea of continuing on from there to England and then, perhaps, to Lithuania.[3]

2

It was already June—again, a rather leisurely pace—when Mickiewicz arrived in Paris, his first visit to the city where he would eventually settle for the remainder of his life. The capital of France had become an arena for Polish irredentist activity since even before the July Revolution and the November Uprising. The uprising, however, imbued the hopes of the small group of émigrés there with a sense of tangible purpose. Paris was now the node for diplomatic efforts on the part of the Polish insurgent government as well as for propaganda and fundraising on its behalf. Directing these activities was the Polish Legation, headed by Mickiewicz's acquaintance from Dresden, General Kniaziewicz, which exploited the network already established by, among others, Leonard Chodźko. The poet did not need any letters of introduction.

But what, exactly, he hoped to accomplish in Paris remained unclear. As he informed Krasiński at the end of June, "he was still undecided" about the trip to London. For the moment, though, there was enough in the city to distract him. David (still at work on a bust of his Polish friend) took him to meet Charles Nodier, now head librarian of the Bibliothèque de l'Arsenal, where he regularly hosted Victor Hugo, Charles Sainte-Beuve, and Alfred de Vigny, the nucleus of the French romantic movement. Chodźko, for his part, introduced Mickiewicz to the circle around *L'Avenir*—Alphonse d'Herbelot; Charles de Montalembert, one of Lamennais's closest collaborators and the youngest member of the House of Peers, and perhaps even Lamennais himself—which, in contrast to the July Monarchy's feckless stance toward the Polish uprising, was consistent and unequivocal in its support for the Polish cause. As Mickiewicz wrote to Lelewel a year later, Lamennais was "the only Frenchman who sincerely cried for us; his tears were the only ones I saw in Paris." An exaggeration, to be sure—from Lafayette's Comité Central Français en Faveur des Polonais to donations of money from veterans, merchants, workers, and schoolchildren, the Polish cause galvanized every stratum of French society, with the exception, however, of those that mattered.[4]

Mickiewicz was disgusted by the attitudes of French politicians. King Louis Philippe mouthed sympathies but had no compelling political reason to aid a people that, for what it was worth, had once been France's staunchest ally and now believed it was defending—sacrificing itself for—a progressive Europe against imperial reaction and even possible aggression. As for the French Republicans, they were, in the poet's view, no different; both they and the party of power represented the same "financial liberalism." "Ever since I left Lithuania," he wrote to Count Ankwicz shortly after leaving Paris,

> I've become convinced more than ever... that the world and people are not the way we imagine them to be, but I have never been so disappointed as I am now with France.... Egotism, the purest, driest, coldest egotism. They love us terribly, they adore us, hug us, but that costs nothing. At first I observed this with calm contempt, but soon I lost patience, I told my acquaintances the truth and fled from them.[5]

The poet's aversion to French politics and, by emotional extension, toward the French in general—"cold, egotistical, vanity and lust for money," even worse, willing, in their rationalist "wisdom," "to tip the cup of their pride at God's funeral" ("The Sages"; Dz. 1:329)—was in part a function of his own indecisiveness and confusion in the face of what was by now a looming disaster. News from Poland, but particularly from Lithuania, was increasingly grim. "Every newspaper," he wrote to Semen Khliustin on 16 July,

> brings me news of the death of some relative, some acquaintance. Places where I spent my youth are so many piles of ashes soaked with blood.... Suffice it to say that Russian units in Lithuania consist largely of Circassians, Kirghiz, and Kalmuks, commanded by Germans or other foreign mercenaries. You yourself know better whether these peoples have the slightest sense of pity or humaneness. It would be very regrettable should one of these Germans or Frenchmen fall into my hands if heaven ever permits me to rejoin my compatriots.

For over a month Mickiewicz had "lived in constant readiness, leaving daily but continually held back by some obstacles." Again, what these obstacles were remains not altogether clear. What is clear is that the ship bearing arms for the Lithuanian insurgents sailed from London without him. He now regretted his decision to travel through Paris, aware that others who had been in his position were already "there, in place," without him. His "only goal now and only plea to heaven [was]—to make it."[6]

It was not until mid-July that an opportunity finally presented itself. Mickiewicz decided to accompany his Vilnius acquaintance (and father of his future son-in-law), the poet Antoni Gorecki, on a mission to Warsaw entrusted to them by the Polish Legation in Paris, which also lent them a generous sum for the trip. The two left the French capital on 21 July. By this time the uprising in Lithuania was collapsing, and the Polish-Russian war was entering its denouement.

3

Their route led through Châlons, Nancy, Würzburg, and Leipzig to Dresden. Both were traveling on German passports and under false names—Mickiewicz's was "Adam Mühl." On the road to Nancy, Gorecki wrote a poem dedicated "To Adam Mickiewicz, My Companion on the Journey of 1831" in which he captured at once the poet's enduring reluctance, his sense of guilt, and his self-indulgent inclination to wrap it all in his newly-found faith:

> Too bad—you sigh now, Adam, always doubting heaven's mercy?
> 'Twould you behoove to have far fewer sins on you,
> Beware! you with your sins will make it through all right...

The trip was not a happy one. As Gorecki informed Leonard Chodźko from Würzburg, Mickiewicz was "worried about Lithuania, ... constantly lost in thought and smok[ing] cigars." In Leipzig, the Polish emissaries paid a visit to Richard Otto Spazier, a young German journalist who had just published the first book-length account of the Polish uprising and whom Mickiewicz now promised to provide with information he could include in a second, expanded version. Not only did Spazier do so, acknowledging the poet's help in his *History of the Uprising of the Polish People in the years 1830 and 1831* (1832), but five years later he would again outstrip his countrymen in enthusiasm for the Polish cause by being the first to translate *Pan Tadeusz* into German.[7]

Mickiewicz and Gorecki arrived in Dresden on 6 August. The city was familiar to the poet from his brief stay there two years earlier, as were many of its Polish residents. Their number, however, was beginning to swell as Poles sought refuge from the unrest in Poland or fled before the cholera epidemic that over the past year had spread rapidly throughout the Russian Empire and was now knocking on western doors. Among the new arrivals was Julian Ursyn Niemcewicz, the seventy-year-old dean of Polish politics and literature, one of the authors of the Constitution of the Third of May, a veteran of the Kościuszko uprising, and now, as a member of the insurrectionary government in Warsaw, on a diplomatic mission to England. Ever since he had sent him a copy of the first volume of *Poems*, Mickiewicz had sought the approval of the poet whose patriotic ballads were recited and sung in every literate Polish household. Thanks to Viazemskii, he had managed to get in touch with Niemcewicz from Russia. Now, just as they were about to set out in opposite directions, he finally got to meet the man considered to be the living embodiment of recent Polish history. Although their contact in Dresden was brief, their paths would cross often enough when both soon found themselves sharing the fate of émigrés in France.

For the moment, Niemcewicz proved useful in helping Mickiewicz map out his route to Poland. The advance of the cholera epidemic had complicated matters. The city of Poznań, through which the poet intended to travel east, was under quarantine, while another *cordon sanitaire*—doubly prophylactic, of course—had been established along the Grand Duchy of Poznań's border with the Congress Kingdom. It was this obstacle that probably convinced Gorecki to abandon his own plans and remain in Dresden. Mickiewicz, for his part, decided to continue, not at all sure what to expect, still beset by old doubts, but at the same time impelled by a desire to finally join his own—if not in this world, then in the next, where, he felt, he "would be greeted better than anywhere on earth."[8]

4

Traveling "strictly incognito," Mickiewicz crossed the Silesian border into the Grand Duchy of Poznań sometime in the middle of August, his immediate aim to make his way to the border. The Prussian authorities were not, it seems, particularly interested in "Adam Mühl." After a few days in the neighborhood of Kopaszewo, "Adam—[once known as] Mickiewicz, then Mühl, finally as Niegolewski"—was driven east to Śmiełów, the estate of Hieronim Gorzeński, situated not far from the border with the Congress Kingdom, near the confluence of the Warta and Prosna Rivers. Potential crossing points were relatively well patrolled, both on the Prussian and Russian sides, but Gorzeński had experience with facilitating illegal passage between the two states. He had Mickiewicz taken somewhere northeast of Śmiełów where, according to the poet, "with the help of some peasant, he crossed . . . into the lands of Congress Poland." For whatever reason, though, "he tarried there very briefly" and returned to Śmiełów, hoping, perhaps, to try again some other day. That day would never come. Around 12 September, Mickiewicz and his hosts learned of the surrender of Warsaw to Russian forces five days earlier.[9]

Many years later, the poet would recall these weeks in late August and September as perhaps his most desperate. He was initially overcome by "a desire to commit suicide; only considerations for the trouble this would cause the master of the house where he lived restrained him"; he then began to mull about "entering the priesthood." Despite his doubts as to the entire enterprise, he was unable now to forgive himself for "not having managed to be if only for a minute" with those of his friends who took part in the uprising; he felt condemned to "envy them forever." But he could also try to forget or at least suppress what from this moment would be a growing, ever more insidious sense of guilt.[10]

As he waited, ostensibly, in Śmiełów to attempt yet another crossing, Mickiewicz found time to pay visits to nearby estates and even go hunting. And he also found time to get himself entangled in yet another messy affair with yet another highly strung married woman.

Konstancja Łubieńska, née Bojanowska, was about the same age as Mickiewicz, from a well-to-do, and on occasion roisterous, Poznań family. When the poet met her in Śmiełów, the home of her younger sister Antonina Gorzeńska, she had been married for twelve years and had four children. Well educated in Dresden and, like Karolina Jaenisch, with a penchant for parading her erudition, this by all accounts beautiful, intelligent, and unconventional woman was also known among her neighbors as something of a poet. Mickiewicz's unexpected appearance in Łubieńska's provincial world stirred her imagination. She was, after all, "a woman whom anyone writing poetry could turn this way and that." The poet, for his part, in need of comfort and pity, was not at all averse to her affections. Theirs would be a long, tortuous relationship, marked by moments of self-indulgent melodrama, "grief and trouble," but also by emotional accommodation and spiritual affection as the two matured and changed. It would last until Mickiewicz's last days, and even beyond his death.[11]

Fig. 12 Konstancja Łubieńska-Wodopolowa. After a portrait by an unknown artist. Courtesy of the Adam Mickiewicz Museum of Literature, Warsaw.

When news of the collapse of the uprising reached Śmiełów, Mickiewicz saw no reason to tarry any longer. He decided "to return," for the moment, to Dresden, but unsure of where he would go next—back to Italy? perhaps to America? The trip to the Silesian border, in the company now of Łubieńska, was, however, leisurely, with visits to a series of Poznań landowners eager to host the man now universally recognized as Poland's bard, an international literary celebrity whose poetry, after all, the grand duchy's Poles had been consuming enthusiastically and with pride since they had subscribed to Muczkowski's edition of his works. During his visit to the estate of Krzyżanowo, the hosts "erected triumphal gates and carpeted the paths where Adam was to walk with roses." And when he finally did arrive, recalled one of the guests years later, she saw a man

> of medium height, with a slim build; the complexion of his face was slightly pale, all the more so in contrast to his black whiskers and locks. His features were regular, well-defined, his forehead tall, beautiful. . . . In general, the expression on his face at that moment was half tender, half cold. . . . I don't know whether a flash of lightening would have moved me more—the bard's glance acted on me with some kind of magnetic power.

He was, as always, happy to play a game of chess, but when asked, he refused to improvise and showed displeasure when Łubieńska sat down at the piano to sing one of his poems.[12]

Similar scenes repeated themselves at other nearby estates in September, October, and November of that year. More often, though, families such as the Morawskis, Mycielskis, Taczanowskis, Zakrzewskis, Skórzewskis, Turnos, and Grabowskis contented themselves with hosting the poet in more intimate circumstances. Some stays were shorter, some longer, with walks in a park or nearby forest, visits to neighbors, hunts, repasts, conversations in the salon, political arguments, flirtations, and games of chess or checkers. Occasionally Mickiewicz would mark his presence with a few lines in a lady's album; and only exceptionally did he agree to improvise, as he did for the ladies at the Taczanowskis' Choryń estate, where he apparently "depicted the future of Poland in the darkest of colors." But as a rule, "he did not like being given albums to sign or reciting poetry." What he did not mind, it seems, was standing in as an honorary godfather in a kind of second baptism of grown children, a common practice among gentry hoping to "enhance" their lineage through kinship with a famous figure. Not surprisingly, one of the fortunate in this regard was the youngest daughter of Łubieńska, for whose sake the poet made a lengthy detour to Konstancja's estate north of Poznań at the end of September.[13]

These christenings were the most overt manifestations of the esteem in which the gentry of the grand duchy held the poet. In private, they hoped for even more. As one of his hostesses informed him the following year:

> There are families here that would be proud if you belonged to them, and although, perhaps, they may not be all too alluring, they are nonetheless pleasant, sensible, and loving,

albeit not wealthy. Our daughters would like to share your fate—and this would in no way cause you any embarrassment.

Dealing with Łubieńska was difficult enough. But he was not ungrateful, and memories of these visits, gatherings, and displays of affection would later surface in letters to some of his hosts in the region, and then eventually make their way into *Pan Tadeusz*. Yet at the same time—and something that his hosts either did not or preferred not to notice—the poet was profoundly unhappy, as if, as he later wrote to Volkonskaia, "in the forests of Poznań" he was leading "an animal or, rather, vegetal existence."[14]

At the end of November, Mickiewicz and Łubieńska reached Konarzewo, the estate of her brother Ksawery, not far from the Silesian border. Yet instead of returning directly to Dresden, the poet once again allowed himself to be drawn into the social life of the neighborhood, unable, in what he later described as his "torpor," to decide on some definitive course. Exacerbating his predicament were encounters with veterans of the uprising, who were now filtering into the grand duchy in ever increasing numbers, some to wait out, in hiding, the course of events, others already on their way to emigration in the West. Their very presence constituted a rebuke not only to his failure as the author of *Wallenrod*, but even more so to his way of life precisely in the wake of this failure. After all, gossip about his "iniquitous life . . . with a disreputable woman," and this "while everyone was fighting," was spreading from estate to estate. It was at this time too that Mickiewicz received a response to a letter he had sent at the beginning of November to Malewski in which his friend implored him to be strong in his new-found faith and to give hope to others with his words. "Like a Phoenix . . . on the smoldering ruins of the last . . . European revolution, intone the song of the future religious life that God has instilled in you, his chosen one." But all Mickiewicz could manage now was a paraphrase of Gottfried August Bürger's "Lenore," the hit ballad about a young woman whose lover returns from war as a ghoul to take her with him to his grave (*Dz.* 1:335–39). Mickiewicz called his version "Flight"—as in escape.[15]

In these circumstances, it was as much a godsend as it was a relief to learn about the fate of his older brother. Despite his condition and age, Franciszek had fought valiantly in the uprising in both Lithuania and the Congress Kingdom and, like so many of his fellow fighters, was now interned in East Prussia. The news presented the poet with an opportunity to at once confront and compensate, however inadequately, for his own nonfeasance.

After several unsuccessful attempts at making contact, Mickiewicz decided to take his leave of Łubieńska and travel to Poznań in order to seek the help of Józef Grabowski, the director of the local gentry credit union who also headed a committee in charge of providing support for the Polish insurrection and now of aiding its defeated veterans. The two brothers finally connected sometime in early December. Franciszek begged his brother to come to East Prussia, and Mickiewicz, it seems, immediately headed out to meet him but, "on account of great difficulties," soon turned back. He "beseeched" Franciszek to come to Konarzewo instead, particularly in view of the fact that the tsar had declared a partial amnesty, which thus freed the Prussian authorities to either force the Polish internees back to the Congress Kingdom or into emigration to France. The poet sent his brother detailed instructions on what routes to take as well as a hundred thalers, assuring him that he should have no trouble making his way to the grand duchy. Grabowski, for his part, promised to take Franciszek under his wing as soon as he arrived. Shortly before Christmas, Franciszek settled in at Grabowski's estate of Łukowo, north of Poznań, where he would end up living for the next seventeen years.[16]

As his brother was making his way to Łukowo, Mickiewicz himself traveled north again, this time to Objezierze, the estate of Wincenty Turno, not far from the Grabowskis. He had been drawn there by news that Garczyński, demobilized since October, was now staying with the Turnos. Their days spent together at Objezierze cemented a friendship already thickened in Rome, despite their disagreements over German philosophy. As the author of several poems published in insurrectionary periodicals, Garczyński could no longer conceal his own literary ambitions from the man who had inspired in him "the unshakeable desire to write." He had brought with him a case full of manuscripts that he was eager for his friend to read. Mickiewicz was impressed, recognizing in Garczyński "a great talent" that "will go far," indeed, one that was "already at a stage" at which his own "most recent works had arrived." But Mickiewicz was also entranced by his friend's stories of the uprising—so much so that he would later publish "Ordon's Redoubt," his own poem about a Polish artillery officer who blows himself up together with his battery in order to prevent it from falling into the hands of the Russians, in a volume of Garczyński's poetry, claiming that it was "written under the influence [of his friend's] stories" and hence was their "common property."[17]

On news of Franciszek's imminent arrival in Łukowo, the two friends hurried over the river to the Grabowskis for the Christmas holidays. Mickiewicz had not seen his brother for over seven years. It was perhaps his presence, with all of the associations and memories it evoked of Christmases spent in Nowogródek, that made the poet nostalgic. He insisted, "to the point of being almost comical," that the Christmas Eve supper in Łukowo be conducted according to strict Polish, or, rather, Polish-Lithuanian, custom, with a meal of "national dishes" to "be eaten on straw . . . with a star hanging on a hair [over the table]." His new-found piety, too, was on display, as he "crossed himself at the table and frequently went to mass." More often than not, however, he was simply "pensive, rarely gay."[18]

Garczyński returned to Objezierze shortly after the holidays; Mickiewicz stayed on with his brother for a few days longer, hoping to make arrangements regarding his sibling's future. As for himself, he had made plans with Garczyński to settle in Dresden for the time being. Now, though, he set off for Poznań, having received a tempting offer some weeks earlier from the publishers of the first Poznań edition of his works. They were planning a series devoted to contemporary Polish poets under the title *The New Polish Parnassus*, which they were hoping to inaugurate with a volume of Mickiewicz's poetry. To this end, they proposed to reprint, in the new format, all of the poet's works that had appeared in Muczkowski's 1828–1829 edition as well as "some heretofore unknown to the public." Not only did Mickiewicz agree—for which agreement he received 100 thalers—but he also made suggestions as to whom else they should include in the series. Not surprisingly, his list was weighted heavily toward Lithuanian poets (and friends): Odyniec, Gorecki, Aleksander Chodźko, and Julian Korsak. As for the previously unpublished works that the editors promised, when the volume appeared in early March, only the ballad "Flight" was added. In any case, and despite the seemingly enthusiastic welcome Mickiewicz received there, the new edition did not sell well in the grand duchy. In Warsaw, on the other hand, where it was published by the firm of S. H. Merzbach, it sold out within a year.[19]

At the end of January, as the volume was being readied for print, Mickiewicz accepted an invitation to Choryń, the estate of Józef Taczanowski, south of Poznań. He ended up staying there some six weeks, dragging his visit out so that he could spend some more time with his brother, who arrived in Choryń from Łukowo at the beginning of February. The three weeks they spent at the Taczanowskis' turned out to be their last together. Mickiewicz would nonetheless remain in contact with Franciszek to the end of his life, and Franciszek, with his nephews and nieces till the end of his. The poet never ceased urging his brother to settle with him in Paris, but to no avail; Franciszek preferred to salve his intense homesickness among the grand duchy's gentry, not quite his own, perhaps, but at least among Poles. He would be visited there in 1847–1848 by Mickiewicz's eldest daughter Maria and in 1860 by her brother Władysław. His last hours in 1862 were spent with yet another of his brother's children, Aleksander, who traveled especially from Paris to be at his dying uncle's bedside.

It was already the beginning of March 1832 when Mickiewicz finally set out for Dresden. To the local gentry who had hosted him with such warmth and enthusiasm during the preceding seven months he bid farewell at a reception held in his honor in Poznań. How he then made it back across Silesia to Saxony remains unclear—he was, after all, no longer traveling on a Russian passport. Rumor had it, though, that it was in the company of Łubieńska, who had disguised the poet "in her servant's livery."[20]

5

In a letter to Henryk Rzewuski's wife Julia sent shortly after his arrival in Dresden, Mickiewicz wrote:

> This entire year from my departure from Italy was so horrible that I'm afraid to think about it, just as one fears thinking about an illness or a bad deed, but then you wouldn't understand the pungency of that last comparison. I prefer, then, to remain silent about the past, and the future is more uncertain than ever.

His passport no longer valid, the poet appeared to be "confined [to Dresden] for a long time," "without any way of moving on." Both Garczyński and Odyniec were already waiting for him there, but even they could barely console him. On the contrary, the bustle in the Saxon capital in the months following the collapse of the uprising served only to intensify the poet's feelings of remorse.[21]

With the end of the Polish-Russian war, Dresden—the seat, after all, of the last Saxon duke of Warsaw—had become a natural transit point for those Polish fighters who had chosen to emigrate to France. Most were convinced that, as in the years following the last partition, new Polish formations would be—were already being—organized "on the banks of the Rhine and the Seine" to continue the struggle "for our freedom and yours." And in any case, in a gesture meant to placate a citizenry angry with its unwillingness to intervene in any way in the Polish-Russian conflict, the French government had invited Polish refugees to settle in France and had offered them subsidies to boot. As the Polish soldiers made their way west from Prussia and Galicia, the German populace greeted them everywhere with enthusiasm, caring for them along the way and enshrining the deeds of the "bootless but courageous men of pluck, the fleeing heroes and exiles" in songs, poems, and lithographs. In Dresden, the city's Polish community, too, quickly organized a relief committee on behalf of the emigrating veterans. Its leading citizens opened their homes to them, supplied them with funds and necessities, and often personally tended to the wounded and sick.[22]

For Mickiewicz, though, "the sight of [Polish] soldiers and officers" passing through the Saxon capital, "trekking to France in poverty and need," was but a constant reminder of his own failure. To make matters worse, waiting for him in Dresden was a four-month-old letter from Semen Khliustin, in which his Russian friend, of all people, jabbed a finger into the poet's open wound:

> Sobolevskii . . . informed me that you are in Dresden. . . . I feel sorry for you. Death [in Poland] would have been a fate befitting you. Life for us others can be but a choice of death. You had a beautiful death within reach, without having to wait for it. How sad.[23]

The thought that he must somehow atone for what he understood to be at once "an illness" and "a bad deed" now consumed Mickiewicz. As he wrote to Lelewel, who himself had already emigrated to Paris:

> God did not allow me to be a participant of any kind in a great and, for the future, fecund work. I live only with the hope that in my coffin I will not lay my hand idly on my breast.

Before his mentor and one of the leaders of the insurrectionary government, Mickiewicz could not permit himself the luxury of indulging in self-pity. Yet the inadvertent image of a living death belies his ostensible forthrightness. Indeed, so debilitating was his condition that the poet, by some accounts, sought the help of Johann Christian Heinroth, medical counselor to the Saxon court and professor of psychology in Leipzig, whose theories about the psychopathology of guilt and sin seemed to address directly the poet's inner turmoil. Perhaps this is the mysterious "Heinre<i>ch," whom in a draft of *The Books of the Polish Nation and the Polish Pilgrimage* (Dz. 5:335) Mickiewicz acknowledges, together with Oleszkiewicz, Chołoniewski, and Lamennais, for providing a form of spiritual wisdom that helped him weather "the period of the greatest mortification in [his] life."[24]

Oppressed by "extreme . . . melancholy," by "pain and inner tension," incapable of socializing, the poet confined himself once again to the company of a small group of friends, the same, in part, that he had known in Rome two seemingly very long years earlier: Garczyński, who was working intensely on his poetry to the accompaniment of a telltale cough; Odyniec, his once annoying perkiness now somehow palliative, who was translating Byron and Moore as he waited to join up with his betrothed in Königsberg; but also Ignacy Domeyko (a.k.a Żegota), Mickiewicz's good-natured friend and cellmate from Vilnius, now a veteran of the uprising in Lithuania. Mickiewicz too was now writing again, if only by returning to a translation of Byron's *Giaour* he had begun when still in Kowno. As he wrote to Rzewuski's wife about what he termed their little "monastery," only her husband was missing, but more keenly so was Father Chołoniewski, his source of "solace" during those dark days in Rome. With apartments within earshot of each other on Dresden's Altmarket, the friends passed the evenings and nights "bound in thought and soul," arguing with Garczyński over Hegel, reading each other's poetry, recounting anecdotes about the recent war, offering advice on Mickiewicz's predicament with Łubieńska, and, most intently, discussing what went wrong and what was to be done.[25]

For Mickiewicz, there was now no question that the Polish "movement" needed to be imbued with "a morally religious fiber," founded "on the bedrock of Catholicism." "Perhaps," as he wrote to Lelewel, "our nation is called to proclaim to peoples the gospel of nationality, morality, and religion." For all of their earnestness, however, the poet's remedies were, as he himself admitted, nebulous, formulated with relatively scant knowledge of the debates, disagreements, and factionalism that, having to a large extent helped doom the uprising, were now already beginning to rive the emigration (thanks in no small part to Lelewel himself). Rather, they seemed to reflect, more than anything, not only, or not so much even, the positions of Chołoniewski and Lamennais, but Mickiewicz's own inner struggles and a sense of their resolution. As he expressed in a poem he wrote at the time:

> When a child of the world calls me calm,
> I hide my stormy soul from its sight,
> And listless pride, like a robe of mist,
> Gilds my inner thunder with a cloud;

And only at night—when it's quiet—I vent
On Your [God's] bosom a storm solved in tears.
("An Evening Conversation"; Dz. 1:328)[26]

6

On 23 March, shortly after seeing a performance of *The Magic Flute*, Mickiewicz had a dream, "obscure and incomprehensible." "After getting up, I wrote it down in verse... on the spur of the moment and without corrections" (Dz. 1:332–34), he noted while recopying the poem eight years later—a gesture that in itself seals the significance of that night.

It was a dream of winter. Mickiewicz is running after a procession to the River Jordan. The procession is divided into two rows: those on the right are dressed in white and carry candles pointing downward; those on the left are in mourning and carry flowers. Suddenly, a woman from the right approaches him, as does a little boy begging alms for his father. Mickiewicz gives the boy a coin, the woman, two; Mickiewicz gives six, the woman twelve, and so on until both have nothing more to give.

"Give it back," the crowd scolded the boy, "they're just joking!"
"If they begrudge it," the boy answered, "I will."
But I no longer felt like taking it back.
With her white hand the figure [the woman*] gave me a blessing.

Now it is summer—a warm sun, blue sky, "the smells of Italy, of roses and jasmine." Mickiewicz espies Henrietta in a white dress on the shores of Lake Albano, seemingly floating amidst butterflies, her "face as beautiful as Our Lord's Transfiguration."

I wanted to greet her, but I lost all my strength....
But my bliss, oh, that nocturnal bliss,
Who could describe it? more powerful than anything diurnal....
At last I took her by the hand like a sister....

Henrietta informs Mickiewicz that her parents have promised her to someone else, but she wants to fly like a swallow to Lithuania. "I know about all of your friends," she tells him,

I'll find them: they're lying in graves and in churches.
And vanish I'll have to in forests and lakes,
And question the trees and talk to the herbs,

*Mickiewicz's own note of explanation.

> They know strange things about you, they'll tell
> Me everything, where you have been and what you've been doing.

He wants to fly with her, but then grows frightened, realizing that "she wants to ask the trees and the bushes about" him:

> And at once I remembered all of my misdeeds,
> My moments of foolishness, outbursts of madness,
> And I felt how my heart was so powerfully sundered,
> So unworthy of her and of heaven and gladness.
> Then I noticed the swallow, already returning;
> And following, as if an army in black:
> Lindens and pine trees, wormwood and savory,
> All bearing witness against me.

The poet awakes, his "face to the heavens," his hands crossed, "as if prepared for a funeral." Tears flow down his cheeks, while all around him he can still sense the fresh scents of "Italy and jasmine and the Albano Mountains, and the roses of the Palatine" (Dz. 1:332–34).

It is a remarkable dream, a *songe* rather than a *rêve*, as Jean-Charles Gille-Maisani would have it.* Intimations of guilt and atonement, of disappointed love and nostalgia at once intersect with and seemingly resolve in symbols of ordeal and passage, death and rebirth—themes that the dream shares with Mozart's opera of Masonic initiation. Shortly after that night, while "praying in church," Mickiewicz, according to Odyniec, "felt as if suddenly a sphere of poetry burst above him." "For three days," the poet recalled some years later,

> he could not tear himself away from writing. The table was covered with blank paper, and all day he practically lay on the table and wrote; he would tear himself away from work just barely enough to eat something when the need arose, after which he would immediately return to his room and continue with his work.

Within a week, he had written over 1,500 lines, the core scenes of *Forefathers' Eve*, part 3.[27]

These scenes, five, perhaps seven, in all, constitute a metanoia; they not so much chronicle a profoundly transformative experience as they are the very process in and through which this experience occurred—quite literally, an improvisation. This, after all, is how Mickiewicz himself designated the central scene of the drama, which he "wrote in a single night" and, as Odyniec would have it, "even recopied, for fear that he might die on the

*Gille-Maisani, *Adam Mickiewicz*, 370 n. 21.

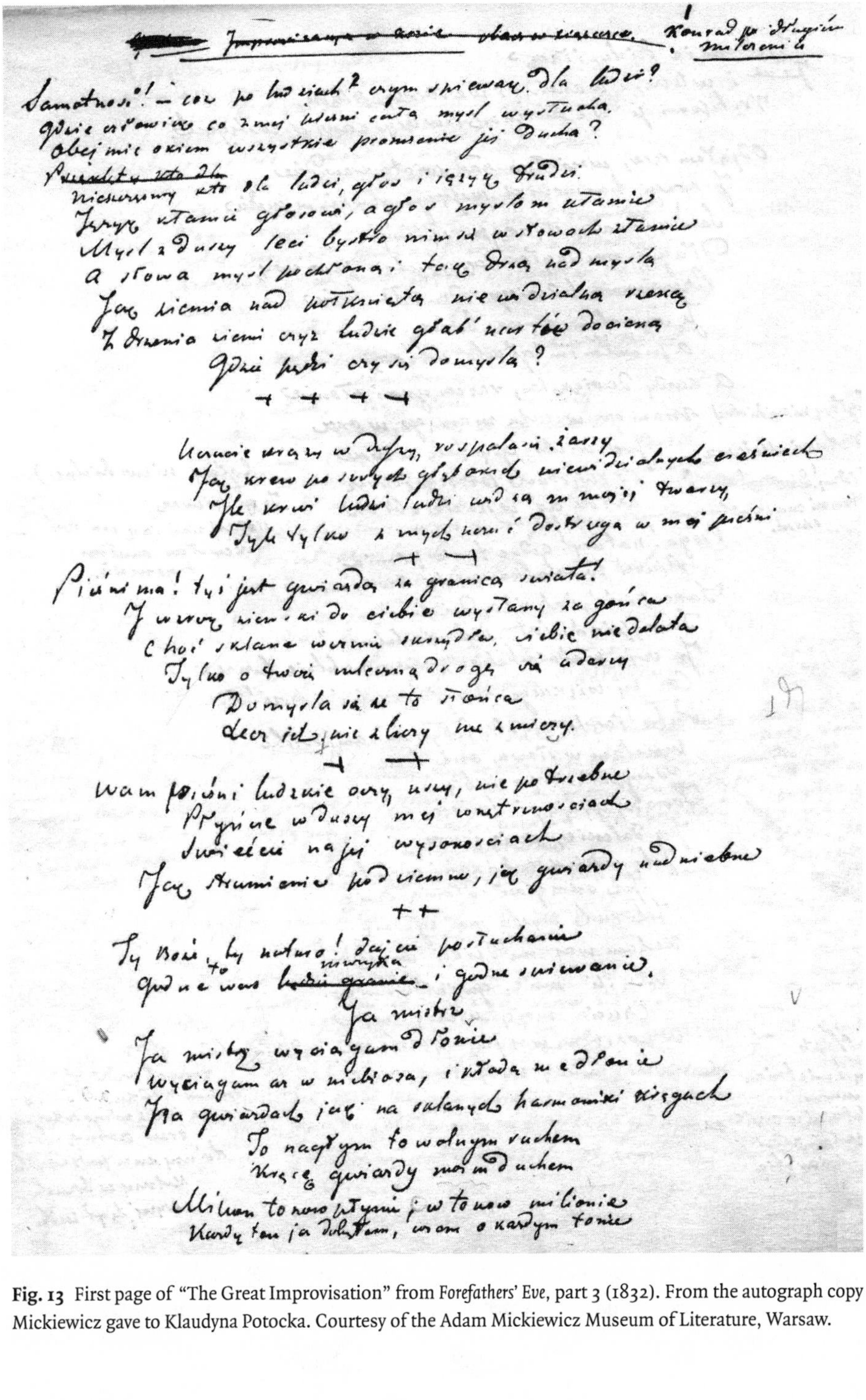

~~[illegible]~~ ~~Improwizacya [illegible] [illegible]~~. Konrad po długiem milczeniu

Samotność! — cóż po ludziach? czym śpiewak dla ludzi?
Gdzie człowiek co z mej pieśni całą myśl wysłucha,
Obejmie okiem wszystkie promienie jej ducha?
~~[illegible] kto dla~~
Nieszczęsny kto dla ludzi, głos i język trudzi.
Język kłamie głosowi, a głos myślom kłamie
Myśl z duszy leci bystro nim się w słowach złamie
A słowa myśl pochłoną i tak drżą nad myślą
Jak ziemia nad połkniętą niewidzialną rzeką
Z drżenia ziemi czyż ludzie głąb' nurtu docieką
Gdzie pędzi czy się domyślą?

+ + + +

Uczucie krąży w duszy, rozpala się, żarzy
Jak krew po swoich głębokich niewidzialnych ciałach
Ile krwi ludzi ludzie widzą w mojej twarzy,
Tyle tylko z myśli mojej dostrzegą w mej pieśni

+ +

Pieśni ma! tyś jest gwiazdą za granicą świata!
I wzrok ziemski do ciebie wysłany za gońca
Choć szklane weźmie skrzydła, ciebie nie dolata
Tylko o twoją mleczną drogę się uderzy
Domyśla się że to słońca
Lecz ich nie zliczy nie zmierzy.

+ +

Wam pieśni ludzkie oczy, uszy, nie potrzebne
Płyńcie w duszy mej wnętrznościach
Świećcie na jej wysokościach
Jak strumienie podziemne, jak gwiazdy nadniebne

+ +

Ty Boże, ty naturo! dajcie posłuchanie
Godne was to ~~ludzi granie~~ muzyka i godne śpiewanie.
Ja mistrz
Ja mistrz wyciągam dłonie
Wyciągam aż w niebiosa, i kładę me dłonie
Na gwiazdach jak na szklanych harmoniki kręgach
To nagłym to wolnym ruchem
Kręcę gwiazdy moim duchem
Milion tonów płynie; w tonów milionie
Każdy ton ja dobyłem, wiem o każdym tonie

Fig. 13 First page of "The Great Improvisation" from *Forefathers' Eve*, part 3 (1832). From the autograph copy Mickiewicz gave to Klaudyna Potocka. Courtesy of the Adam Mickiewicz Museum of Literature, Warsaw.

following day." But then this designation may well describe the remaining scenes as well, all produced in this initial burst of "extraordinary inspiration."[28]

It begins as an ecstatic monologue by a persona identified as Konrad, a poet whose name, on top of his emergence in the drama in place of a symbolically deceased Gustaw ("GUSTAVUS OBIIT M. D. CCC. XXIII CALENDIS NOVEMBRIS . . . HIC NATUS CONRADUS M. D. CCC. XXIII CALENDIS NOVEMBRIS" [Dz. 3:131]), leaves little doubt as to his identity. In a flood of synesthetic imagery replete with "ribbons of lightening" and "the spheres of a glass harmonica," with cosmic "tones" "weaving themselves into rainbows and chords and stanzas," the poet casts himself as a supreme creator, his "singing worthy of God and of nature." The "song" he sings

> is a great one, a song-creation;
> Such a song is power, prowess,
> Such a song is immortality!
> Immortality I feel, and immortality I create,
> What more, O God, could You accomplish? (Dz. 3:157–58)

This feeling of creative omnipotence impels the poet to challenge God, but on the strength of affect, an all-encompassing love for his nation with which he embraces its "past and future generations" "like a friend, a lover, a husband, like a father" (Dz. 3:159), and which ultimately assumes it:

> Now my soul is my nation incarnate
> My body has swallowed its soul,
> My nation and I are one.
> My name is Million—for in the name of millions
> I love and I undergo torments. (Dz. 3:164)

In the face of God's ostensible indifference to his collective's fate, the poet demands that he himself be given "the power to govern souls" so that he can "create" of his nation "a living song," a song that, unlike God's, will be a song of happiness (Dz. 3:161). But God, whom the poet accuses now of being nothing but cold, unfeeling reason, remains silent. In a gesture of at once Promethean pride and Oedipal desperation, he challenges God one last time:

> Answer me, or against Your essence I shall fire; . . .
> I'll shake Your entire dominion's expanse;
> Because I'll fire my voice at the very boundaries of creation,

That voice which will resound across the generations:
I'll shout that You are not our father but...
A Tsar! (Dz. 3:165–66)

This final imprecation—and in 1832, none could be more blasphemous in the mouth of a Pole—is uttered not by Konrad but by a devil. From this point on, like a shaman undergoing a chain of spirit actualizations, the poet's voice incarnates a series of personae. At first it speaks as if possessed by an evil spirit, a distillate of defiant pride and satanic logic, who commands the evil eye. This spirit is subsequently exorcised by a monk, Father Piotr, who in turn now himself begins to "channel" the poet's voice. And it is in the person of this humble Bernardine, prostrating himself before God "like dust" (Dz. 3:188), that Mickiewicz finally experiences what he had demanded all along, a prophetic "vision."

As a generation of youths is being driven across a snowy wasteland into exile in the north, the entire Polish nation is about to be crucified by Russia, Prussia, and Austria, with the help of France:

All of Europe is dragging it, mocking it—...
"Gaul, Gaul will judge it!" they scream.
Gaul found no fault and—washes his hands,
And the kings scream,...
"Crucify it—or we'll say you're the emperor's enemy."
And Gaul handed it over....
Oh, Lord, I see the cross already—oh, for how long, for how long
Must it bear it....
The cross has arms as long as all Europe,
Forged of three effete peoples like of three hardened woods.
They're dragging it now; my Nation's on the throne of atonement—
"I thirst," it said—and Rakus gives vinegar, Borus some bile,
And mother Freedom stands at its feet all in tears.
Look—now the Muscovite thug sprang to with a spear
And shed my nation's innocent blood....
He alone will reform, and God will forgive him. (Dz. 3:189–90)

From among the youths driven into exile, one manages to make his way back to the West, and it will be he who will "resurrect" the nation. "A terrible man" with "three faces" and "three brows," this "viceroy of freedom"

Stands on three crowns, but himself is without one;
And his life is the labor of labors,
And his title is the people of peoples;
From a foreign mother, his blood is of heroes of old.
And his name is forty-four. (Dz. 3:189–91)

Father Piotr falls asleep and is now himself reincarnated in the person of Henrietta-Ewa.* While praying for the Lithuanian youths exiled to Russia, including "the one who published those songs, . . . some of them beautiful" (Dz. 3:184), she experiences the final vision in the sequence, of a mystic rose that comes alive and asks to be laid on the girl's heart, "like a holy apostle, the Lord's lover, on the divine bosom of Christ" (Dz. 3:187).

This sequence of visionary scenes, the essence of Mickiewicz's metanoia, is itself generated by a scene that takes the poet—and thus his transformation from Gustaw into Konrad—back to 1823. Here, characters named Zan, Frejend, Suzin, Feliks Kołakowski, Jan Sobolewski, Adolf (Januszkiewicz), and Żegota (Ignacy Domeyko) join the poet not so much in recreating the cell in the Dominican monastery in Vilnius but in creating the portrait of a martyred generation as it undergoes its own ordeal of passage. Atonement thus occurs retrospectively, as if Konrad's detention—then—with all of its ostensible suffering and putative analogies to the persecution of the infants at the hands of Herod, somehow compensated—now—for what Mickiewicz considered his failure. As he remarked some years later, in *Forefathers' Eve*, part 3, he "vomited out the pride and foulness that had been collecting [in him] for ten years."[29]

When asked, as he invariably was over the years, whom exactly he had envisioned as that "viceroy of freedom," that savior of Poland with the cabbalistically cryptic name, Mickiewicz answered variously. In his last lecture at the Collège de France in 1844, he would insist that the man "with three faces and three tones" was none other than Andrzej Towiański (Dz. 11:188/LS 5:295–96), the Lithuanian mystic whom the poet had accepted as his spiritual guide three years earlier. In other, more lucid moments he conceded, "When I was writing, I knew, but now I no longer do." On still another occasion, however, although maintaining that "he sketched the features of that man unconsciously, without any reflection" and that the number forty-four "appeared by itself in a moment of inspiration," Mickiewicz admitted "that that man would be himself." This was his most truthful answer, one that only confirmed what the names Gustaw and Konrad, the prison cell in Vilnius, and the reference to the one who managed to get away all suggested in their own no uncertain terms. Mickiewicz had come to believe that his "improvisation" was nothing less than a genuine call, that he had indeed become that "chosen vessel" whom

*In the final, published version of *Forefathers' Eve*, Mickiewicz transposed Father Piotr's and Ewa's visions.

Oleszkiewicz had foretold in St. Petersburg, "through whom [Grace] would flow onto others." As the poet told a friend years later, at that moment "he felt the entire magnitude of the sacrifice reposited on such a man." It was a burden that for the remainder of his life Mickiewicz would at once bear and nurse and brandish, all in an effort to compensate for what he perceived as his breach against the expectations of the national collective. That it would also destroy him as a poet was a sacrifice he was ultimately willing to make.[30]

7

The bursting sphere released a flood. Mickiewicz became, in his own words, "a *Schreibsmachine*." In the course of some two months he not only completed the third part of *Forefathers' Eve* (over 3,700 lines), but also the translation of *The Giaour* (another 1,300) and a half dozen shorter poems.[31]

"Ordon's Redoubt," "Death of a Colonel" (like "Grażyna," a poem about a woman-warrior), and "A Soldier's Song" were all based on anecdotes from the November uprising the poet had heard told by his friends. "If I had been as fortunate as you," he once reportedly told them, "and had fought against the Russians, I would write an epic about those memorable battles of yours." But although in the case of "Ordon's Redoubt" he was more than willing to give credit where credit was due, in writing these poems Mickiewicz was also appropriating his friends' experiences for his own artistic—and psychological—purposes. As a veteran general is purported to have silenced the poet as he was criticizing the Polish army's performance during the uprising, "Mr. Mickiewicz is right, we did not meet our mandate; we should have all died, so that only Mr. Mickiewicz could remain and describe everything in verse."[32]

The remaining poems—"Sages"* and "Reason and Faith"—were, as Mickiewicz put it to Lelewel, "less appropriate to the circumstances." Together with the earlier "Master of Masters" and "An Evening Conversation," they trace the poet's "conversion" over the course of the preceding year, a process marked by a tension between, precisely, "reason and faith"—or, if you will, between pride and humility—that peculiar dialectic that inscribes the very nature of a prophetic call:

> When like a cloud before the sun I bowed
> My wise and thunderous brow before the Lord,
> He raised it up to heaven like a rainbow's arc
> And painted it with a myriad of rays....
>
> Lord! the breath of humility has fired my pride;
> Although I burn sublimely in the blue of heaven,

* "Sages," as Mickiewicz noted, "was conceived in Paris, written in Dresden" (Dz. 1:572).

Lord! 'twas not my own brilliance that set them ablaze,
My flame is but a pale reflection of your fires!
("Reason and Faith"; *Dz.* 1:330)[33]

As for *Forefathers' Eve* itself, Mickiewicz continued to add scenes that essentially thickened the putatively historical context of his personal narrative, underscored its prophetic, prefigurative thrust, and at the same time bound part three, albeit not all too convincingly, with the parts he had written in Lithuania. In a scene set in a Warsaw salon, he dredges up his old battles with the capital's literati, accusing them now—not entirely fairly, to be sure—of ignoring the suffering of Poland as they insist on clinging to classicist dicta about art or to some half-baked notions about the idyllic nature of the Slavic soul. But it is above all onto the figure of Novosiltsov that the poet "vomits" his bile and frustration and guilt. He casts his nemesis as at once a vulgar, insecure opportunist and a stupid instrument of pure evil, intent on "the destruction of the Polish nationality," for which he harbored "an instinctual and bestial hatred" (*Dz.* 3:121). Surrounding the senator are henchmen and lackeys, Poles and Russians alike, all bearing the actual names of ostensible participants in the events of 1823, who, as Mickiewicz would now have it, contributed to "the martyrdom" of Lithuania's "children and youths" (*Dz.* 3:122).*

On 29 April 1832, "on Low Sunday..., ten years after writing part four," Mickiewicz "finished copying" *Forefathers' Eve*, part three (*Dz.* 3:535). He would continue to edit it and to add bits and pieces for the next six months, but the drama itself was complete. However, to the nine dramatic scenes proper the poet now decided to append what he would later call "The Digression," six short epic poems that chronicle a "pilgrim's" (presumably Konrad's) journey into the heart of Russian whiteness. As Mickiewicz later explained in the preface to the French translation of *Forefathers' Eve*, these poems constitute "a kind of travelogue... [which], it seems,... serves to create a transition to the... parts of this drama that are supposed to follow" (*Dz.* 5:272). It is quite possible that this devastatingly satiric yet dispassionate depiction of kibitkas rushing across Russia's snow-covered expanses to St. Petersburg and then of the northern capital itself, with its grotesquely syncretic imperial architecture, brutal displays of military might, triumphalist monuments (Falconet's statue of Peter I), sympathetic Russian bards (Ryleev *vel* Pushkin), Polish exiles, and ominously rising waters, was in large part a re-creation from memory of that "rather bizarre" poem Mickiewicz had been writing while still in Russia and which he now reshaped for a different set of circumstances and imbued with a different artistic function. However this may be, the continuation of Konrad's saga that it seemed to promise never materialized.[34]

* Among Novosiltsov's henchmen, Mickiewicz depicted the figure of "The Doctor" August Bécu, the second husband of his friend Salomea and the stepfather of Juliusz Słowacki. Bécu was only marginally implicated in the entire affair, but the fact that he was killed by lightening several months later was perhaps reason enough to include him in a drama inscribed by mystical correspondences. Although Słowacki was dissuaded from challenging Mickiewicz to a duel after *Forefathers' Eve* was published later that year, the drama's depiction of his stepfather was a humiliation that Mickiewicz's poetic rival would never live down.

8

The release of creative energy was cathartic, loosening as it did the knots of remorse and depression that had been effectively paralyzing Mickiewicz since Rome. Work itself, as the poet wrote his brother, the very process of writing, made him "gay and, under the circumstances, happy." He "resumed feeling, thinking, living." But he was doing so by compensating his own failure through the failure of his collective. He had convinced himself that *Forefathers' Eve* was nothing less than "a continuation of the war, which, now that swords have been put away, one must wage with the pen." The defeat of the uprising had become the object-cause of his own revitalization.[35]

Mickiewicz would "recall those few months in Dresden fondly." Surrounded by a circle of indulgent friends (augmented now by the person of Gorecki) who hung on to every word he was producing, he gradually emerged from his depression. As Domeyko recalled years later:

> Sometimes Adam would read excerpts from what he was writing; he'd occasionally intone [a Polish song] or some passage from Mozart. He smoked his pipe constantly and frequently fell to musing. We'd often go to the Italian opera and for walks. . . . We also spent quite a bit of time in the picture gallery in front of Raphael's divine *Madonna*, Correggio's *Night*, and Titian's *Christ*. But we found our main source of joy and stimulation above all at Sunday masses in the cathedral, with its superb devotional music.

When the weather turned warmer, the friends set out on a week-long excursion to the Saxon Alps, joined, this time, by Wincenty Pol, another veteran of the uprising and soon its most popular bard.[36]

Mickiewicz was now also awaiting Volkonskaia. The princess had been trying to track him down for close to a year, and after finally receiving an answer from the poet in March, she announced her intention to visit him in Dresden. Her letters contained effusive greetings from his acquaintances in Rome, from the Rzewuskis, Shevyrev, the Ankwiczes, and Chołoniewski. But it was another of these acquaintances who actually appeared in Dresden that spring. After taking part in the uprising, Aleksander Potocki had chosen emigration—and hence a substantially more modest existence—despite the tsar's offer of amnesty and the promise to return his confiscated estates. Not even Karolina Sobańska, who too happened to appear in Dresden at this time, was able to convince Potocki otherwise. Of course, neither he nor Mickiewicz was aware that Sobańska's visit to the Saxon capital had been arranged by Witt, charging his beloved now to spy on her émigré countrymen in order to glean information about potential "conspiracies," the "secret contacts they were maintaining with Russia," and "the Machiavellian system they were hoping to spread." That her activities in Dresden would soon lead to her fall from grace with the Russian monarch is another story.[37]

Sobańska, however, was a chapter that for Mickiewicz had been closed long ago. He had other concerns now, and other emotional investments. Discreetly, the poet was still corresponding with Łubieńska, who, it seems, was at this time seriously contemplating a divorce. In Dresden, though, he found yet another source of succor, not erotic, to be sure, yet no less deeply felt.

Sometime in May, the poet was asked to join the Polish committee for refugees in Dresden, which entrusted him with, "among other things, tracking down prominent officers and, in general, Poles of outstanding character who might need funds for travel to France but who . . . were unwilling to apply for them." The guiding force of the committee was Klaudyna Potocka, wife of Bernard, another wealthy Potocki, and by all accounts one of the more remarkable personalities of her time. After serving as a volunteer nurse during the uprising, she joined the fleeing fighters in their trek west, where she resumed her ministrations in Dresden. Having donated to the relief committee a considerable sum from the sale of her valuables, she ignored her own progressing illness and took to personally caring for the refugees, on occasion even sewing shirts and bandages for them. "Tall, thin, . . . pale, . . . , with dignity and moral strength in her eyes," Potocka had the aura "of something unearthly, funereal about her," although "when her mind was energized by some sweet hope for Poland, her eyes shone with the demonic light of inspiration." With her "terrifying humility" and "utter selflessness," she exerted a "mysterious influence on others," one "so powerful that the highest minds (e.g., Mickiewicz) succumbed to it no less than a simple foot soldier." Powerful indeed, for before his departure from Dresden, Mickiewicz presented Potocka with his own clean copy of *Forefathers' Eve*, part 3.[38]

This extraordinary gift may have also been, in part, a token of the poet's gratitude for the care Potocka began lavishing on an increasingly weaker Garczyński. His friend's condition—tuberculosis, of course—had taken a turn for the worse not long after his arrival in Dresden; the regimen of mineral waters that both Mickiewicz and Odyniec had prescribed for him apparently did more harm than good. But the unmistakable intimations of mortality impelled Garczyński to write even more frantically. By July he had finished *Wacław*, a poem only slightly shorter than *Forefathers' Eve*, which grew increasingly on Mickiewicz the nearer his friend approached his inevitable end.

9

Russia had never been pleased by the presence, to say nothing of the activities, of the Polish émigrés in Dresden. By May 1832, with the Congress Kingdom now effectively pacified, it was growing increasingly impatient with Saxony's indulgence toward the "traitors." Pope Gregory XVI's condemnation that June of the Polish "revolt against the legitimate authority of princes" served only to strengthen the empire's case. The Russian chargé d'affaires began exerting none too subtle pressure on the Saxon authorities to finally force the departure of any veterans who refused to accept the tsar's offer of amnesty.[39]

As someone who had not participated in the uprising, Mickiewicz was, in effect, free to stay or leave as he chose. But as he wrote to Volkonskaia in the middle of April, although his "persistent thought, [his] fondest intention" was "to return to Italy," he refused to apply for the necessary Russian passport—he had assured his brother that he would "never ever revert to Russian rule." "I'll remain, then, in Saxony," he informed the princess, "until, until... for eight years I've been unable to finish this sentence with regard to my comings and goings." By the end of May, however, Mickiewicz, unforeseeably, finally did. He decided to follow the Polish veterans to France, since, as he wrote to Grabowski, he "could not trust his caretakers [i.e., the Russians], knowing full well the extent of their reach." More pressing, however, were "literary matters." The poet now had "ready for print one epic poem [i.e., *Forefathers' Eve*] and a few minor fragments, all more or less concerning [the Polish] cause." As much as he may have shuddered at the thought of returning to a city he "loathed like hell itself," he understood that his work could appear only in Paris.[40]

Odyniec left Dresden sometime in the beginning of June, heading for Königsberg to marry his fiancée; Domeyko, like other veterans of the uprising, was being forced out of Saxony. Mickiewicz saw no reason to stay any longer. He had "finished almost everything he had intended to" in Dresden, and Volkonskaia would not be passing through after all; she had fallen ill in the Tyrol, where, as she put it melodramatically, "eternity was now beginning for" her. As for Garczyński, the poet assured himself that he was leaving his ailing friend in the care of someone he could trust absolutely. He decided to accompany Domeyko to Paris, hoping, at the same time, to "tarry some here and there in Germany." With a passport from the French mission in hand, Mickiewicz joined his friend and nine others, all Polish officers or former officials of the insurrectionary government, in a carriage that set off from Dresden on 23 June in the direction of Strasbourg.[41]

The three and a half months Mickiewicz spent in Dresden together with Garczyński, Domeyko, Odyniec, Gorecki, and Potocka were, as he himself would later recall, "times that will remain... unequaled." "Like someone who is magnetized draws strength from the eyes of his friends," he wrote to Odyniec in 1833, "so I drew fire and desire from you." Over the course of some eight weeks he had produced "a third or even half as much of what [he] had heretofore published." But it was not how much, but what he had written that mattered. The poet was convinced that *Forefathers' Eve*, part 3, would become "the one work of [his] worth reading." In effecting his own transformation, he believed the work, or, rather, the vision his poetry made manifest, contained the germ, the template, for what he hoped would be the transformation of Poland and, by extension, Europe itself, a promise of collective rebirth and salvation. It was a vision Mickiewicz was now eager to reveal to the entire Polish emigration. "Important matters... [were] impelling [him] to" Paris.[42]

CHAPTER SIX ❧

EMIGRATION (1832–1834)

Although they were all traveling as private citizens, Mickiewicz and his companions were greeted no less effusively by the natives of Saxony, Bavaria, and Baden than the thousands of emigrating veterans who had preceded them over the previous ten months. "At every stop," recalled Aleksander Jełowicki, one of the young officers accompanying the poet,

> committees organized by friends of Poland . . . would greet us. A Pole could make his way from the first German town to France without a penny; in every town his needs were seen to and the [Polish national anthem] was sung to see him off.

Mickiewicz squared accounts some months later, when he dedicated the German translation of *The Books of the Polish Nation and the Polish Pilgrimage* to "the German people, as a sign of his sincerest respect and gratitude for the fraternal reception accorded him and his unfortunate compatriots during their Pilgrimage" (Dz. 17:549).[1]

Confronted with the Germans' generosity, the travelers had to repeatedly insist on paying their own way, for unlike most Polish émigrés heading for France, they had chosen to decline the meager subsidy earmarked for them by the French government. To do otherwise would have obliged them to proceed to one of the so-called *dépôts* that had been established for veterans of the uprising all over France—in Avignon, Besançon, Châteauroux, and eventually elsewhere. As of April, these fighters—bedraggled but still flush, the darlings of a restive European left—were confined under the supervision of the police instead of the Ministry of War, displaced persons now rather than potential legionnaires. They were, of course, also barred from settling in Paris, while those already there were being encouraged to leave. That a number of émigrés were involved in antigovernment disturbances in the beginning of June certainly did not endear them to Louis Philippe's insecure regime.

I

From Dresden the road led through Leipzig, Bayreuth, and Nuremberg, where Mickiewicz sought permission, unsuccessfully, to make a detour from his mandated itinerary to Bolzano to see the ailing Volkonskaia. After two days in Nuremberg, the group set out for Karlsruhe. "The journey," Domeyko recalled, "was not boring for Mickiewicz." Among his companions was an old veteran, who regaled the travelers with stories of the Kościuszko uprising, the Polish Legions, and Grand Duke Constantine's prisons; another had been a captain in Napoleon's entourage who accompanied the emperor to Elba and then from Borodino to Waterloo; still others described their participation in the latest uprising. However—and understandably, considering that three of the travelers had served as representatives to the insurrectionary Diet—"the main topic of conversation was the course of recent events." Mickiewicz's opinions on the subject were, as another of his companions, Henryk Nakwaski, put it, "most peculiar":

> He reckoned everything in a patriarchally poetic way. Although he is a very modest man, sensible and not conceited, he is, nonetheless, ever the poet. Speaking once of the devastations of war, I related how [a certain] colonel, the commander of an escort assigned to [protect] the government [as it was fleeing], told his soldiers to behave decently when he spent the night at my place.... "I would have burnt the home down," Mickiewicz piped up, "so that the Russians could not desecrate it with their presence, and would not have tried to spare the village." What a poetic thought!... Let poets write, but God forbid they should rule.

Although God mercifully heeded Nakwaski's plea, Mickiewicz, for his part, would never cease preaching his "peculiarly" "poetic" brand of politics, often breathtaking in its aesthetic effect, and in this sense strangely compelling—precisely for its utter lack, more often than not, of practical sense.[2]

After a few days in Karlsruhe, where the prince of Baden sent them tickets to his theater and opened up his park and palace to them, Mickiewicz and Domeyko continued on to Strasbourg, arriving at the bridge over the Rhine on 11 July. The German customs agent refused to take the usual fee from them upon learning they were Poles; on the French side sentries greeted them with a hearty "Vivent les Polonais!" "We drove into France," remembered Domeyko, "as if after some great victory, as if entering our own country."[3]

The companions' first order of business was to obtain passports for Metz, whence they intended to make their way to Paris. But not only did the local prefect refuse, he also forbade them to stay in Strasbourg, urging them instead to go to one of the *dépôts*. He had enough trouble with the Polish veterans already settled in the city, who could be "seen on the streets in bedraggled uniforms . . . looking, as they say, for an opportunity. Many of them also proved to be swindlers, who, pretending to be officers, swindled the inhabitants and exploited their goodwill." This notwithstanding, Mickiewicz received a pleasant welcome from the city's Polish community, which "attended to him with particular effort." The poet, in turn, proved to be "polite and appeared calm throughout his stay."[4]

Faced with the prefect's refusal of their first request, Mickiewicz and Domeyko decided to apply for a passport to Châlons-sur-Marne so as to be at least closer to Paris. In his application, the poet stressed that he "does not find [him]self in a situation of having to ask for any help from the French government." After a few days, during which time the two had an opportunity to marvel once again at the Strasbourg cathedral, they received permission for the journey to Châlons but only according to a strict itinerary and, of course, with the express prohibition of "entering Paris under any pretext whatsoever." On the passport, Mickiewicz was described as having "a height of 1 m. 69 cm.; hair and eyebrows—black; forehead—sloped; eyes—blue-gray; nose—medium; mouth—idem; beard—black; chin—round; face—oval; skin—healthy, without any particular markings."[5]

Their stay in Châlons-sur-Marne proved to be longer than they expected, as they waited for permission to travel to Paris. Upon their arrival in the capital of Champagne on 19 July, they "encountered cholera and a frightened populace." The death there of a Polish veteran who had managed to make it through the entire uprising without a scratch and through cholera epidemics in Poland and Germany, only to succumb to the disease in Châlons for some reason, had a profound effect on Mickiewicz. "Until late at night he thought and spoke of nothing else but the deceased, and only at dawn did he shut his eyes. . . . The next day he was also very melancholy, didn't eat, and spoke little."[6]

To distract themselves, the companions visited points of interest in the surrounding countryside and then took a tour of the Jackson Champagne cellars, each named after the European capital for which cases of "the satanic, ersatz, fashionable wine" (Dz. 4:339) were destined (St. Petersburg's were the longest). But as the second anniversary of *les Trois Glorieuses* (27, 28, 29 July), approached, the two Poles, eager to celebrate the July Revolution together with the locals, received yet another taste of the new regime's true colors. On account, ostensibly, of the cholera, the authorities of Châlons banned all large gatherings in the town. Not to be deterred, Mickiewicz and Domeyko accepted the invitation of a local national guardsman and traveled to celebrate the second anniversary of the July revolution in nearby Suippes. The parades, dancing, greased pole climbing, and illuminations organized by the French "middle class" did not disappoint.[7]

On their return to Châlons, Mickiewicz and Domeyko learned that no definite decision had yet been made regarding their request to go to Paris. By now they were bored and frustrated and began inquiring whether there might not be some other, less official way of entering the capital. "There's only one way to do it," they were told by a certain functionary:

> "And what's that?" Adam asked him, sure that he'd facilitate a secret journey for us. "To go by mail-coach," he answered. How's that? By courier? . . . In a government carriage? No more, no less. "But who'll let us into the city? And as soon as they see the passports, they'll arrest us!" "No one will dare stop the courier either on the road or on its entry into the city."

A day later, on 31 July at three o'clock in the morning, Mickiewicz and Domeyko were roused from their sleep by "the stench of Paris, the stench of coal gas mixed, it seemed, with all of the stenches of the entire world." The two travelers alit in front of the Hôtel du Metz on rue de Richelieu, where Lelewel was already waiting for them.[8]

2

It had been a little over a year since Mickiewicz first visited the city he had so quickly come to detest. For him, as for many of his contemporaries, "the capital of the civilized world" emblematized the very worst of the new bourgeois order, wherein money defined class and class, an increasingly fractured society. Grand boulevards lined with fashionable stores, theaters, cafés, and entertainments were fed by the narrow streets of fetid, overcrowded old *quartiers*, their residents often on the verge of starvation and rebellion. "There is the greatest luxury here, the greatest wretchedness," wrote Fryderyk Chopin, who had preceded Mickiewicz to Paris by a year, "the greatest virtue, the greatest crime . . . more yelling, noise, rattling, and mud than one can imagine." For its part, the July Monarchy, its legitimacy continually tested by an aggressive press that fostered the country's "weakness for politics, . . . without regard for gender, age, or class," sought to consolidate its hold on power by carefully negotiating between republican radicalism and restorationist reaction. Liberal in some respects, authoritarian in others, the *juste-milieu* proved acceptable, perhaps, only to those who profited from it.[9]

But then too, it was precisely the money, the contrasts, and noise, the loose morals and relative political freedoms, the revolutionary heritage as well as the persistent expectations of a revolutionary tomorrow that made Louis Philippe's Paris so alluring. Intellectuals, artists, and activists of every stripe descended on the city from all corners of Europe and beyond. Over the course of his twenty or so years in Paris, Mickiewicz gazed at the same wonders and horrors, pleasures and novelties as other émigrés and visitors to the city—Rossini, Heine, Liszt, Princess Belgiojoso, Cavour, Marx, Gogol, Herzen, Bakunin, Wagner, Margaret Fuller, and Mustafa Reshid Pasha. Some of these figures he would meet and even come to know closely, others he would pass anonymously in the throngs strolling the sidewalks of Paris, gaping at the shop windows and other attractions.

If in 1831 there were only some 150 Poles living in the Department of the Seine, by 1832 their number had swelled to close to 2,000 (by the 1840s that number doubled). Although by no means the largest of the city's émigré communities—there were about 37,000 foreigners living in Paris at the time—politically it was the most conspicuous but in other ways also the most insular. From the earliest days of the uprising, its cause—that of a freedom-loving people willing to resist despotic power to the death—was embraced enthusiastically by French republicans and guaranteed to bring out the city's poor and working classes whenever an appropriate occasion arose. Opposition newspapers kept the Polish cause in the public eye, while performances of such melodramas as *Les Polonais en 1831*, *La Révolution polonaise*, and especially the "mélodrame-monstre" *Les Polonais* at the Cirque Olimpique played to sold out houses—and then like other fashions quickly faded into obscurity.[10]

The hub of pro-Polish sentiment in Paris was Lafayette's Franco-Polish Committee, in existence since January 1831 to lend material as well as spiritual support to Poland's struggle. With the collapse of the uprising, it took upon itself the task of providing financial sustenance to émigrés who had chosen to settle in Paris, while at the same time continuing to inform the French public of Poland's plight and urging Louis Philippe to take some sort of substantive action on its behalf. The government's refusal to do so (not without pressure from Russia) soon made the Polish cause a touchstone for opposition to the July Monarchy itself, and of the Polish exiles willy-nilly allies of the French left. When "the streets would periodically rush to the barricades, . . . Poles would applaud with pleasure, hoping wars and then their triumphant return to Poland would follow, and though these republican attempts usually came to naught, [the émigrés'] knightly fervor cooled not a wit."[11]

At the time of Mickiewicz's arrival, the Polish community in Paris was composed primarily of insurrectionary politicians, generals, publicists, and a few artists—overwhelmingly male, of course, and mostly without families—who, upon fleeing west as the uprising collapsed, had declined the French government's offers of assistance for the privilege of living, and agitating, in the capital. Like their less privileged brethren in the provincial *dépôts*, they too viewed their exile as temporary. The November Uprising was for them but the next chapter in Poland's struggle for liberation, and their work in the emigration "a continuation of the war." Most of them believed—vainly, as it soon turned out—that the Napoleonic as well as republican traditions of their hosts would somehow guarantee their transience as exiles, that before long the formation of legions, or if not legions, then revolution, or if not revolution, then diplomacy would pave their return to an independent homeland. These alternative strategies for the eventual liberation of Poland were, in fact, to a large extent conditioned by the ideological differences that had emerged during the course of the uprising and which the émigrés now lugged to France along with their archives and uniforms. There, in an unfamiliar environment, amid a growing sense of dislocation nourished by impotence, hindsight, and homesickness, those differences festered, making any attempt to bring the emigration together under a single umbrella impossible.[12]

The first victim of what was to become a phenomenon painfully common among the exiles was the Polish National Committee, founded in Paris in the last weeks of 1831 "to look out for the good of the nation" and to continue the struggle for liberation in solidarity with revolutionary forces throughout Europe. Headquartered on the Left Bank at a hotel on rue Taranne, it was constituted under the presidency of Lelewel, who had represented the Polish left in the insurrectionary government and at the same time headed the radical opposition to it. Although claiming to speak for the entire emigration (which now numbered well over 4,500, albeit settled primarily in the provinces), the original eighty-one members of Lelewel's committee spoke for few beyond themselves. Moreover, despite his leftist credentials and contacts with French, German, and Italian revolutionaries, the ascetic scholar was nonetheless viewed by some as too moderate, and in any case, his political ambitions were incommensurate with his abilities as a leader. Soon enough, in March 1832, the most radical members of the committee seceded to form the Polish Democratic Society. Those who remained were tagged as middle-of-the-roaders and struggled now to maintain their legitimacy in the face of growing dissatisfaction with the committee's activities. By October 1832 its functions were effectively usurped by yet another committee of "national unity."

For its part, the Polish Democratic Society would undergo protracted, often shrilly tempestuous, growing pains before finally emerging in the mid-1830s as a disciplined and viable mass party, particularly among the denizens of the *dépôts*. In any case, both the Democrats and Lelewel's committee were made up of leftists committed in one degree or another to social reform in some future independent Poland, with hopes of bringing it about on a tide of European revolutions, political as well as social. But then the uprising of 1830—and this was one of the causes of its collapse—was no less the work of conservative, in some cases less-than-willing, aristocrats, whose desire for the liberation of their country by no means implied any eagerness for change in—or, for that matter, regret about—its social order. Centered around the figure of Prince Czartoryski, the ex-president of the insurrectionary government, the conservative wing of the emigration sought to advance Poland's cause through French-language propaganda, high-level diplomacy, and personal contacts among Europe's elites, although it too was not averse to dabbling in conspiratorial activity. Eventually headquartered in the Hôtel Lambert on the Île St. Louis, Czartoryski's party worked hard to win over the emigration to its republican, and in the end royalist, program. It sponsored scholarships, a welfare organization, a library, and the Polish Literary Society, which, its innocuous name notwithstanding, constituted the propaganda arm of the faction.

The Polish Democratic Society and Czartoryski's Hôtel Lambert were, however, but the most prominent, and ultimately most resilient, players in a rather sad game of increasingly diminishing returns. In the wake of countless meetings, arguments, lofty declarations, and rancor, other committees and factions came into and went out of existence. Some developed ties to European revolutionary movements—the Carbonari, Young Europe—and prepared to send secret emissaries to Poland; others encouraged veterans to serve in various armies in Europe, North Africa, and the Near East; still others put their faith in the Catholic Church. Efforts to reconstitute the insurrectionary Diet in exile miscarried on several occasions amid procedural disagreements driven not so much by intractable ideological differences as by personal considerations. And on top of the ideological divides, there remained a not always subtle rift between émigrés from the Congress Kingdom and those from the old grand duchy, stemming, it seems, from a belief on the part of the latter that Poles from the kingdom were somehow too Western, too willing to abandon certain Old Polish "shortcomings," which, ostensibly, were "just as necessary for Poland's rebirth as national virtues."[13]

In this olio of competing camps, personalities, programs, and institutions, the name of Poland's most illustrious bard, author of "Ode to Youth" and *Konrad Wallenrod*, was at a premium. Indeed, while still in Dresden, Mickiewicz had been tapped as a corresponding member by Czartoryski's Literary Society. More portentously, however, some émigrés in the *dépôts*, largely lower ranking officers and foot soldiers, were already looking to the poet as something of a savior, come to France "to gild hearts longing for the Fatherland with the star of hope," who, "God willing, will before long strike the heavens with a hymn of thanksgiving for the good fortunes of peoples." Expectations in the emigration were running high.[14]

3

No sooner had he alit in Paris, Mickiewicz was whisked off by Lelewel to see Józef Bohdan Zaleski, a thirty-year-old poet from the Ukrainian provinces and a left-leaning veteran of the uprising and its government. Mickiewicz had taken note of Zaleski's folk-inspired, somewhat sentimentalist poetry while still in Russia and had come to consider him the best poet of his generation (besides himself, of course). Emigration, however, had not been kind to Zaleski's imagination. Steeped in regional nature and with an essentially optimistic vision of man's place in it, it had grown atrophied amid the dislocation of exile and the din of urban life. Unable to write, Zaleski immersed himself instead in émigré politics, deftly balancing leftist reflexes with a growing attraction to Catholicism. Mickiewicz "immediately found [himself] on a friendly footing" with this gentle, sensitive man he called "the Cossack." That first evening, "until late into the night," in the strictest of confidence, he read him *Forefathers' Eve*, part 3. For the next ten years, the two would live, "one might say, inseparably, in a communion of spirits," as if they "as a twosome had only one spirit," even when they found themselves living many kilometers apart.[15]

Fig. 14 Józef Bohdan Zaleski. Lithograph, ca. 1844. Courtesy of the Adam Mickiewicz Museum of Literature, Warsaw.

It was, however, the émigrés from Lithuania who first took it upon themselves to welcome Mickiewicz to Paris officially. At a dinner in honor of his arrival, attended by, among others, Lelewel and Mickiewicz's old friend Gorecki, with champagne flowing, the poet felt comfortable enough to improvise "three times, for some two hours" on a theme suggested by his former professor. Several days later, Mickiewicz was again invited to an affair, this time, though, together with much of the Parisian émigré community to greet General Józef Dwernicki, a dubious hero of the uprising in whom the emigration nonetheless saw a potential alternative to the feckless Lelewel. Amid toasts, speeches, and laudatory odes, Mickiewicz too paid his due to the occasionally victorious general by improvising some verses in his honor. "The entire world flocked to" the poet.[16]

In the boisterous crowd that day was Juliusz Słowacki, who in a letter to his mother Salomea Bécu pronounced Mickiewicz's improvisation "pretty feeble." Słowacki had been living in Paris for a year already and had just published his first two volumes of poetry ("an architecturally beautiful edifice," according to Mickiewicz, "like a lofty church—but a church in which there is no God"). Like his fellow émigrés, he had been looking forward to meeting the poet he at once idolized and conceived to be, with something bordering on obsession, his only serious rival. But neither, it seems, had been willing to take the first step. Now, though, in the throng of émigrés strolling after dinner in a spacious park on the Champs d'Elysée, it was Mickiewicz who approached the younger poet. The two exchanged flatteries, and Mickiewicz recalled meeting Słowacki, then still a precocious young lad, in his mother's salon in Vilnius. A few hours later, they found themselves together again at a soirée for Polish artists, "drinking much champagne" and "declaiming . . . poems" as Chopin played the piano. The evening was pleasant enough. Słowacki, however, could not resist informing his mother that some drunken Pole kept insisting he "was being way too modest" with regard to Mickiewicz. Modesty was something Słowacki could never be accused of.[17]

The two poets encountered each other occasionally over the course of the next few months—before the publication of *Forefathers' Eve* forced an embarrassed and livid Słowacki to flee Paris—at public events, soirées, but most often at meetings of the Society of Lithuanian and Ruthenian Lands, of which both became members. Founded in December 1831, the society sought to inform the public about the lands and people of "occupied" Poland—that is, Lithuania—and to "disseminate the Lithuanian nationality" by gathering materials and publishing works about the uprising in Lithuania and about the region itself.[18]

Mickiewicz quickly warmed up to the society's activities, and for the remainder of the year it served as his most prominent public arena. What appears to have caught the former Philomath's imagination was not only the society's desire to highlight the contribution of Lithuania and Ruthenia to the recent struggle, but also the means by which this contribution was to be acknowledged. Having spent evenings listening to Garczyński's, Domeyko's, and Pol's accounts of the uprising, Mickiewicz proposed that the society focus its energy on "encouraging the writing of memoirs":

> In the history of the war we are less concerned about general tactical and strategic regulations, which we can find in books.... More important for us are detailed observations and comments of a local nature.... In general, the history of each detachment will be best if it is told like the history of a single man, like one's own,... interpolating details and anecdotes whenever appropriate. (Dz. 6:215–16)

These memoirs were to constitute not so much a strategic handbook for some future insurrection nor even, perhaps, a history of the uprising in these regions per se, but rather something akin to a collection of local lore, a potential repository of information about mores and behavior and a way of life that the poet sensed he might never see again and that might, in fact, be verging on extinction. He had already begun writing *Pan Tadeusz.*

Tired of traveling but uncomfortable in Paris, Mickiewicz felt at home among the familiar accents and focused activities of the society. He took part in its work with energy and dedication. Lelewel, however, wished to harness this energy for his own purposes, particularly as by the end of August his committee was in turmoil, riven by petty disputes and personal ambitions, under pressure from dissatisfied exiles in the provinces, and threatened with more defections—all of which Mickiewicz was observing now "from a gloomy point of view." Hoping to draw the poet into the work of his committee, Lelewel asked his former student and a survivor, as it were, of the Decembrist uprising to draw up a proclamation addressed to Russian liberals on the upcoming anniversary of the failed rebellion. Although little of Mickiewicz's original draft made it into the published version (which, thanks to a protest from the Russian ambassador, resulted in Lelewel's expulsion from Paris), the request itself was timely.[19]

Mickiewicz had recently happened on a pamphlet published shortly after the fall of Warsaw in which Zhukovskii and Pushkin, in a series of triumphalist odes, celebrated Russia's imperial might and the "crushing" of the Polish "mutiny."* Now, as he was preparing Lelewel's proclamation, declaring that "it is not in the interests of nations to destroy

**Na vziatie Varshavy. Tri stikhotvoreniia V. Zhukovskogo i A. Pushkina* (1831).

each other," that "the day despots fall will be the first day of harmony and peace among nations" (Dz. 6:306), Mickiewicz found a fitting coda to *Forefathers' Eve*, part 3. Addressing his "Russian friends," he wrote:

> If to you from afar, from a people that's free,
> These pitiable songs make their way to the north
> And resound from on high o'er a land trapped in ice,
> May they liberty auger, like cranes in the spring.
>
> By my voice you shall know me; while I was enchained,
> Like a snake I crawled noiseless, deceiving the despot. . . .
>
> Now I spill this chalice of poison before all of the world. . . .
>
> And whoever of you should complain, his complaint
> Will to me be akin to the bark of a dog who has so
> Gotten used to a collar so long and so patiently worn
> That it's ready to snap at the hand that tugs on it. (Dz. 3:307–8)

4

Mickiewicz appended his epistle to Russian friends to *Forefathers' Eve*, part 3, at the very last moment, just as the final sheets were being printed sometime in late October. During these first weeks in Paris, the publication of the new work was Mickiewicz's biggest concern, the reason, after all, he had so reluctantly decided to come to the city in the first place. But now that his French publisher had gone bankrupt, the poet was forced to publish the work himself. He nonetheless decided on maintaining continuity with Barbezat's edition of *Poems*, hence *Forefathers' Eve*, part 3, was to come out as its fourth volume. With Domeyko reading the proofs, Mickiewicz set about editing the text he had brought with him from Dresden, shifting the order of scenes, adding notes as well as a foreword, which limned the historical context of the drama on the basis of recent accounts of events by Leonard Chodźko and Lelewel. He also added a dedication: "To the memory of Jan Sobolewski, Cyprian Daszkiewicz, Feliks Kółakowski, fellow students, fellow prisoners, fellow exiles; persecuted for love of the fatherland, died of longing for the fatherland, in Arkhangelsk, on the Moscow River, in Petersburg, martyrs for the national cause" (Dz. 3:119). All were indeed Mickiewicz's friends and cellmates, and all indeed had been persecuted and died in exile in Russia. But to elevate them to the status of martyrs was a brazen gesture, intended, ultimately, to compensate for—or, to put it less kindly, obscure—the conditions of the poet's own exile. As Mickiewicz began making enemies in the émigré community, the *facts* would inevitably be mobilized against him.

To be sure, Mickiewicz genuinely "considered [his] work a continuation of the war," an act of at once assertion and atonement on the part of a poet now dedicated unequivocally to the national cause. But it was also a way of earning badly needed money. Ever since Barbezat had gone out of business in 1828, taking Mickiewicz's royalties down with him, the poet's finances were precarious. Aside from the advance he received for the most recent Poznań edition of his poems, he had been living largely off a loan of 200 thalers from Grabowski. Now this too was depleted, and although he lived modestly—Słowacki described him as dressed "in *liederlich* fashion, with a wrinkled shirt collar and in a grimy frock coat," and this at a reception at Prince Czartoryski's—Mickiewicz's situation was becoming so dire that he was finally forced to pawn his watch. When Aleksander Jełowicki, his erstwhile traveling companion from Dresden who by now had set himself up as a publisher in exile, offered to buy out the entire run of volume four (2,000 copies) for 2,000 francs, Mickiewicz, understandably, jumped. By mid-September, "he had something to live on" and was even ready to pay Grabowski back.[20]

Poems, volume four, was ready sometime in the beginning of November, printed, like almost all Polish-language works in Paris, in the shop of the Pinard sisters on the quai Voltaire. With the exception of a few trusted people, however, no one in Paris would have access to it for another two months. While still in Dresden, Mickiewicz had insisted on secrecy, with the hope, it seems, of getting the work to readers in Poland before the partitioning authorities could catch on. To this end, "the publishers conceal[ed] its existence as conscientiously as possible, until it [made] it to the homeland, since Pozzo di Borgo [the Russian ambassador in Paris] might [have] prevented it from going into circulation." After a lengthy "quarantine," during which time Jełowicki and others indeed managed to smuggle copies of the volume into Poland,* *Forefathers' Eve*, part 3, finally went on sale in Paris at the beginning of January 1833.[21]

"With [*Forefathers' Eve*, part 3]," declared Zaleski, "a new poetic epoch begins for Mickiewicz."

> *Forefathers' Eve* will be a gigantic, original, and national poem, something akin to our *Divina Comedia*. An enormous edifice that will embrace the death throes of the Polish nation and all the worlds of poetry and philosophy. . . . The heroes of the poem are God and the poet himself. I read . . . the poem on my knees.

Another early émigré reader was perhaps more to the point when she noted that "with this fourth volume Mickiewicz has fully taken his place beside the prophets of Israel."

*Copies of *Forefathers' Eve* were confiscated in the Austrian partition as early as February 1833, incurring arrest and hefty fines. So too in the Russian partition, where the censor officially placed volume four of *Poems* on the index in December 1833. Shortly thereafter, not only all of the poet's works but the very mention of his name in print were banned.

For indeed, *Forefathers' Eve* was nothing less than a "prophetic manifesto,"* a vision of Poland's past, present, and future inscribed by and in its own particularist way itself inscribing the struggle between cosmic good and evil. And it was the vision of a poet, an aggressively, even hypertrophically romantic poet, "inspired by God's spirit," whose power of imagination—his genius—in effect sanctioned his presumption to intercede on behalf of his people before God, "a kind of Messiah for that poor nation." Over the course of the ensuing decades, when Poland did not exist as a state, this power ostensibly guaranteed that it would continue to exist as a nation and that even in the face of defeat and dislocation, persecution and indifference, it would one day bring about Poland's resurrection.[22]

Yet shortly after its publication, Mickiewicz complained to Odyniec that "in the emigration *Forefathers' Eve* seems to have made little impression." Only one review of the work appeared at the time—not at all surprising, though, in view of the paucity of émigré periodicals in 1833. (That no reviews appeared in partitioned Poland or Russia goes without saying.) Describing the work as a "rich and powerful" mixture of history and satire, *Pielgrzym Polski* singled out the Improvisation for demonstrating "the full might of [the poet's] imagination, the full resplendence of his inspiration." But it also called attention to the dispassionate nature of "The Digression," which despite the sharpness of its satire, was intended "but to open the eyes of a blinded nation [i.e., Russia]."[23]

Mickiewicz's complaint to Odyniec was, however, a bit disingenuous, dictated, in part, by his unquenchable need for sympathy and attention. In private he was only too well aware of what he had created. As he wrote in a travesty of Horace's Ode 3.30 ("Exegi monumentum aere perennius"):

> Young people read me in Nowogródek and Minsk
> And are quick to make copies many times over.
> I'm in the good graces of housekeepers' daughters,
> And even the masters'll read me for lack of anything better!
> That's why despite threats from the tsar, and despite every guard on the border,
> Jews smuggle tomes of my works into Lithuania. (*Dz.* 1:375)

For his as well as succeeding generations of Poles, be it in the homeland or in the emigration, the name Konrad would henceforth be synonymous with struggle against oppression and tyranny of any kind. No less fatefully, however, the figure of Konrad, that is, of Mickiewicz himself, established a new—ineluctable, as it turned out, and in its own way tyrannical—paradigm of a Polish poet, at once artist and prophet and national tribune—the *wieszcz*—whose willingness to sacrifice personal happiness for a Promethean mission

*The term is Wiktor Weintraub's, *Poeta i prorok*, 149.

on his collective's behalf implied an inextricable jointure between the dictates of literature and the exigencies of the national cause.

Over the course of the following year, even as he was immersed in work on a radically different poetic undertaking, Mickiewicz's "spirit" continued to be "torn away... to subsequent parts of *Forefathers' Eve*." He was intent on "making it the only work of [his] worth reading." In an emotional letter thanking Niemcewicz effusively for his no less effusive praise of the drama, Mickiewicz informed "the Patriarch" of Polish letters that indeed "the Vilnius scenes are a preamble to *Petersburg prisons, forced labor, and exile in Siberia*" and that in what would thus constitute the continuation of *Forefathers' Eve*, part 3, he planned on "encompassing the entire history of the persecution and martyrdom of our Fatherland." "A broad undertaking and rich in subjects" to be sure, but one that Mickiewicz would in fact struggle to realize for the remainder of his life, without success. "Bits and pieces" on "loose sheets of paper" were all he could produce, and those he burned before his final journey to Istanbul. But then, what he had produced in Dresden would suffice for generations.[24]

5

Shortly after his arrival in Paris, Mickiewicz received an unwanted and troublesome visitor. In a gesture as courageous as it was histrionic, Łubieńska, it appears, was ready to sue for a divorce, leave her four children, and move in with the man she loved. Mickiewicz managed to talk the "poor creature" out of her "strange thoughts," and she returned home via Dresden "suffering terribly." To make matters worse, someone in the family had intercepted their correspondence and was blustering to defend the Łubieńskis' honor. In the end, no one ventured to Paris with a challenge, but the entire experience left Mickiewicz "morally exhausted," and, as had happened so often in the past under similar circumstances, he literally fell ill "on Łubieńska's account." Yet just as he thought matters had finally been settled, that "disgusting coquette," as Garczyński now called her, "who was not worth [Mickiewicz's] little finger," again tried "to entangle" him, importuning the poet with insistent letters. This time Mickiewicz "decided never to respond to anything of hers again." But Łubieńska refused to give up her desire. Although it would take another ten years and momentous changes in both of their lives, she nonetheless succeeded in reestablishing contact with her beloved, her affection sublimated by this point in a barely veiled autobiographical novella, not-always-appreciated patronage, and, ultimately, a "spiritual friendship" that would last until the poet's death.[25]

The "difficulties and griefs" caused by Łubieńska gnawed at Mickiewicz, working their way into the epic poem he had begun writing shortly after his arrival in Paris but also compounding the frustration he was beginning to experience on account of his growing involvement with émigré politics. As "variously colored factions... [were] hissing and spitting venom at each other . . . , the Democrats at Lelewel, Czartoryski and the aristocrats at Lelewel and the Democrats, the military at everyone, everyone at the military," when, "in a word, the entire emigration appeared to the world as a multitongued serpent," all of the factions "insistently called upon [Mickiewicz] to join this, as it was then called, movement." "Émigré affairs [began to] consume [his] time and often ruin [his] humor."[26]

To a certain extent the poet sympathized with positions espoused by Lelewel and the left in general, above all that Poland's social order needed to be reformed and that the country's fate was tied to a revolutionary transformation of Europe, to a struggle against all despotisms stifling the right of nations to self-determination and their fraternal coexistence. But it was precisely on the left that the noise and quarreling were loudest. The doctrinairism of its more radical members, at times needlessly provocative and laced with ad hominem insults and finger-pointing, vexed the poet. Like much of the emigration, he was particularly upset by the Democrats' willingness to air Poland's historical dirty laundry—the plight of its peasantry, the social egotism of the aristocracy—in front of anyone who they thought should listen. Although Lelewel invited him to meetings on rue Taranne, Mickiewicz shied away from active participation—and soon distanced himself from the left altogether. By the time his mentor was expelled from Paris in December, their relationship had cooled. His feud with the Democrats, however, would smolder for years.

Repelled as he may have been by the fractiousness of émigré politics, Mickiewicz was nonetheless determined to play an active role in the emigration. Involvement with the largely apolitical Lithuanian-Ruthenian Society became one outlet for his energy. Another was the Polish Literary Society, where the poet was made a collaborating member and delegated to the section dealing with history, geography, and statistics. There was, finally, the Society for Scholarly Aid, also a vehicle for the Czartoryski camp, founded to provide educational opportunities for émigrés. Upon its inception, Mickiewicz donated 200 francs out of the 2,000 he received from Jełowicki and was soon appointed to the society's governing board. The poet attended the societies' meetings with punctilious regularity and was often called upon to prepare "various . . . papers, articles, and projects." Yet if his work for them resulted in tangibles—be it in the form of collecting and publishing memoirs, informing the French public about Poland, or granting scholarships—it also brought the poet into the orbit of Czartoryski's coterie, with whom in matters of ideology and political strategy "he differed strongly." This notwithstanding, he had never forgotten the prince's solicitude toward the students of Vilnius, and he had genuine respect for this unselfish patriot, himself a victim of Novosiltsov's animus and Nicholas's retribution, who now, at the age of sixty-two, proved indefatigable in his efforts on behalf of the Polish cause. Although mistrusted by the more conservative members of Czartoryski's circle, Mickiewicz developed a rather close relationship with the prince during these early years of emigration and was a frequent guest in his salon. But just as he refused to sign declarations issued by Lelewel, so too he demurred from affixing his name to petitions in support of the prince.[27]

For on the question of what should be done, Mickiewicz's was in all respects a "third way," incompatible with either the left or the right. This does not mean that there were no points of convergence between his views and those of Lelewel or the Democrats, on the one hand, or those of the circle around Czartoryski, on the other—which, of course, neither side could fully tolerate. More decisive in this respect was the fact that Mickiewicz's growing conflicts with émigré factions were informed by what in essence was a disjuncture between two irreconcilable modes of cognition, one conditioned by reason, the other by affect. To be sure, the poet's views at this time still reflected the influence of Lamennais's "Avenirism," with its programmatic linkage of the pope and the people, of Catholicism and the cause of liberty. It was, in fact, in the fall of 1832 that Mickiewicz renewed his ties with Montalembert, and through him with Lamennais himself, who was now living in La Chânais. Yet what drew the Polish poet to the Avenirists in the first place was precisely their romantic conception of Catholicism, their willingness to let affect, the imagination, and idealistic maximalism serve as guides in matters of doctrine. Although with time Mickiewicz found even Lamennais's reformism too "intellectualizing," his writings had an undeniable impact on shaping the poet's own relations to the church and, by the same token, his vision of the emigration's, and Poland's, predicament. And it was the absence of religious conviction—a lived, activist, affective faith that makes inspired vision possible—that he now felt to lie at the root of the emigration's paralyzing discontents. In a scheme as infinite and as certain as God's providence, notions of left, right, democrat, republican, or royalist were inconsequential.[28]

6

Mickiewicz had arrived in Paris with a vision of Poland's place in the providential order of things. It was a vision of a crucified nation that held out the promise of, or rather, like the crucifixion of Christ, that *guaranteed* its eventual resurrection. Now, with the defeat of the uprising an irrevocable fact and with those who had suffered it dislocated and in disarray, Mickiewicz set about expounding the ideological, as it were, ramifications of this vision. Naïvely, but, like every prophet, with the certainty that comes from revelation, he believed that only through it could the emigration transcend its fractures and thus effect God's plan. As such, it would no longer be an "emigration," made up of "wanderers" or "exiles," but a "pilgrimage," for "the Pole... hath made a vow to journey to the holy land, the free Fatherland... until he shall find it" (Dz. 5:21).[29]

Conceiving it initially as a "catechism of the Polish pilgrimage" (Dz. 512), Mickiewicz subsequently renamed his vision *The Books of the Polish Nation and the Polish Pilgrimage.* In cadences borrowed from the Old Testament prophets and old Polish sermons, the first part of the work tells the history of human freedom. Inscribed by the dialectic of religious faith and idolatrous oppression, of *communitas* and structure,* it traces a series of falls and rebirths, with each moment in the series prefiguring, biblically, successive ones. After a golden age in the distant past, when "there were no laws, only the will of God" (Dz. 5:9), mankind succumbed to idolatry, which led to its enslavement by the Roman emperor. Christ's death and resurrection redeemed mankind, destroying the empire and ushering in an age of liberty and brotherhood founded on a renewed faith in God. The second fall occurred when this medieval Christian order was corrupted by egotistical kings worshipping a new pantheon of idols—Profit, Honor, Commerce, Balance of Power, Well-being, Realpolitik, Self-interest—which turned nation against nation and once again subjected them to the rule of tyranny. As the corruption of Europe reached its apogee in the emergence of a "Satanic trinity" (Dz. 5:15)—Catherine II, Frederick II, and Maria Theresa—only one Christian nation remained—Poland. Its faith was ardent; its love of liberty unconditional; its defense of Christian Europe selfless, which God rewarded by "marrying" Poland and Lithuania in what was to be a prefiguration of the future comity of nations. But when Poland's rulers and gentry were about "to make all Poles brothers, at first the burghers and later the peasants" (Dz. 5:18), the three tyrants grew frightened and resolved to destroy it. Like the executioners of Christ, Russia, Prussia, and Austria murdered Poland, with France in the role of Pilate. Their triumph, however, would be short-lived:

> For the Polish Nation did not die, its body lieth in the grave, and its soul had descended from the earth, that is, from public life, into the abyss, that is, among the private lives of people suffering bondage in their country and outside of their country, that it may see their sufferings.

Two "days" had already passed: the first with the massacre of Warsaw residents by Russian troops in 1794; the second with the taking of Warsaw in 1831. "But on the third day soul shall return to body, and the nation shall arise and free all the peoples of Europe from bondage" (Dz. 5:19–20). Poland will emerge as a new Christ, not, however, the Christ of individual salvation, but the Christ of nations.

This was not, of course, history, but a millenarian dream, a compensatory construct that in times of crisis and transition has been the common inheritance of the oppressed the world over. In this scheme, humiliation, defeat, and dislocation are the guarantors, indeed, a condition, for eventual triumph, wherein the last shall be first, and the first last—the last, messianically, redeeming the first. And so too, only the few shall be chosen, the true believers, the instruments of salvation, who will usher in the new age. For Mickiewicz, this vanguard was the Polish emigration.

*The terms are Victor Turner's, *The Ritual Process*, 94–130.

The second part of the work consequently shifts focus to the "pilgrimage," "the soul of the Polish Nation" (*Dz.* 5:21). The rhetoric of the work shifts as well to resemble that of the New Testament—appropriately enough, since Mickiewicz projected the émigrés as nothing less than apostles militant. In twenty-four short chapters, most of which are structured like parables, the poet depicted the emigration as beset on all sides by the corrupt and the foreign, by French and English "politicians and know-it-alls," "merchants and businessmen" (*Dz.* 5:58–59). Its task amid the temptations of "civilization"—materialism, a false sense of honor, distinction and rank, commerce, "liberalism"—was to reject everything foreign and turn inward, to accept its ordeal and become pure and unified and holy in order to make itself worthy of the sacred mission entrusted to it. To this end, it had to transform itself into something akin to a military monastic order—and here Mickiewicz was peculiarly specific. He admonished émigrés to commemorate holidays in a prescribed manner, to deliberate appropriately, to be humble, pious, obedient, modest, charitable, willing to take up arms as soon as the occasion arose, and even to adopt a uniform garment, the old-fashioned Polish traveler's overcoat. There was something unnervingly authoritarian, and paranoid, to all this, reminiscent, in fact, of the behavior of many a sect or, for that matter, of militant religious movements—which, ultimately, was what Mickiewicz would have the Polish pilgrimage become.

It goes without saying that for a pilgrimage organized along the lines of a religious confraternity there was no room for political parties:

> There are some of You who say: Let Poland rather lie in slavery than awake as an aristocracy; and others: Let her rather lie than awake as a democracy; and others: Let her rather lie than have such and such boundaries, and others, no, such and such. . . .
>
> Verily I say unto You: Inquire not as to what shall be the government of Poland; it sufficeth You to know that it shall be better than all Ye knew of. . . .
>
> And each of You hath in his soul the seed of the future laws and the measure of the future boundaries.
>
> So far as Ye enlarge and better your spirit, so far shall Ye better Your laws and enlarge Your boundaries. (*Dz.* 5:55)

Just as *The Book of the Polish Nation* was not history, *The Book of the Polish Pilgrimage* was by no means a prescription for any kind of political or social program. What Mickiewicz juxtaposes here, as he does throughout the *Books*, is ideology and faith or, more precisely, reason and affect. And affect made politics irrelevant.

The *Books* conclude with a "litany" in which the pilgrim asks to be delivered through the blood of Polish martyrs, past, present, and future, and then beseeches the Lord "for a universal war for the Freedom of peoples" (*Dz.* 5:62). But again, Mickiewicz was far from espousing some sort of concrete revolutionary program; rather, his was an arational, millenarian revolutionism, a vision of an imminent, "universal," and total upheaval, washed by necessity—mystically—in blood. For it was only through an act of sacrificial cleansing that "the independence, integrity, and freedom of the Fatherland" (Dz. 5:62) would at last be attained.

As befitted a work "not imagined, but gathered together from Polish histories and writings, and from the tales and the teachings of Poles" and, in part, revealed "through the grace of God," Mickiewicz published the *Books* anonymously—he was, after all, serving only as God's chosen vessel. Formatted to resemble a portable prayer book, it was addressed explicitly to the "Brothers-Confederates-Soldiers" settled in the *dépôts*, whose "elders" Mickiewicz charged with "explaining and commentating on" the *Books* (Dz. 5:59). To this end, the poet published his "little brochure" "at [his] own expense," distributing it "for the most part free of charge." Like all prophets, he was eager to project, even to force, his personal metanoia as a template for the transformation, and salvation, of his entire collective. The problem, as with so many prophets, was that few took him seriously, or, rather, as Krasiński was quick to grasp, "few underst[ood] his aims, aims that are most pure and sacred. He alone speaks sincerely, he alone knows what sacrifice is, which is why... it is difficult for him among people who have their own interests in mind."[30]

To be sure, Mickiewicz's prescription for what he felt ailed both Poland and the emigration did not entirely lack for resonance. In the eyes of an anonymous émigré emissary to Poland, the poet "had put himself at the head of the Polish pilgrims," "he had embraced the great calling of leading the chosen people in the wilderness and accepted the duty of seeking the shortest and surest paths to salvation." A pamphlet published in Paris went so far as to actually call for the creation of "an order of Polish exiles." And when, a year later, it came time to vote for representatives to yet another committee claiming to speak for the emigration, Mickiewicz received 1,160 votes, more than twice as many as the leading candidate from the Democrats and more than three times as many as Prince Czartoryski.[31]

Nonetheless, in the eyes of the emigration's leaders—those "men of reason," as the poet derisively referred to them (Dz. 6: 270)—be it on the right or the left, Mickiewicz's politics were, at best, "poetic, fantastic ideas"; at worst, the ravings of a fanatical Catholic, "a prophet of the past," who "seeks... to discourage... the emigration from all discussions about and inquiries into the future state of... Poland, and invites it only to pious meditation." But then even the pope, upon reading the French translation of *The Books*, found the work objectionable, characterizing it as "full of temerity and badness." Others simply couldn't believe that "Mickiewicz really does pray." As the poet complained to Odyniec, "The democrats hate me, the aristocrats look at me askance, the doctrinaires... think I'm a madman."[32]

Yet ideology notwithstanding, everyone read what came to be known as Mickiewicz's Gospel. A second edition of the *Books* appeared only days after the publication of the first in early December 1832; a third came out in March 1833—in all, an astonishing 10,000 copies. Demand was such that by 1834 still another edition had to be printed. And almost simultaneously, in the spring of 1833, two editions of the work appeared in Lwów, printed—clandestinely—by the Ossolineum National Institute. From there, copies were distributed throughout all three partitions, where over the course of the following decades the *Books* became required reading for patriots and conspirators. But even among them the poet's millennial politics found few takers.[33]

As one émigré critic summed it up from a distance of some seven years, although readers were captivated by "the simplicity of expression" and the "biblical solemnity" of the *Books*, by "the invigorating and fresh patriotism they exuded," the work "was not a triumph for Mickiewicz's political thought."

> The political prospects of the book met with the fate of all noble... ideas that, founded as they are on absolute *truth*, do not want to negotiate with passions nor heed worldly matters....
>
> Mickiewicz proffered the word of love to us, but we played with it as with a word of beauty. The parable did not extinguish the war, because it did not overcome its causes in the real world.

"Everyone," concluded the critic, "learned the catechism by heart, but no one was converted."[34]

However, the story of the *Books'* reception had an unexpected coda. Translated almost immediately into German, English, and, most important, French, the work quickly achieved a measure of international renown. Somehow its fervent, biblically inflected melding of religion, nationalism, and liberation politics succeeded in mitigating its xenophobic nativism and spoke to the peculiar spirituality of romantic Catholics. Not surprisingly, it was Montalembert who initiated the best known French translation of a work he felt "corresponded exactly to [Lamennais's] views on God and liberty." Provided with a word for word rendering by one of Mickiewicz's friends, the count proceeded to "correct and rewrite" it (he was learning Polish at the time precisely for this purpose), and then prefaced the translation with a fiery plea on behalf of the Polish cause; Lamennais himself appended a "hymn to Poland."[35]

Le Livre des Pèlerins Polonais fixed Mickiewicz's name on the intellectual map of Europe. Sainte-Beuve called it "a unique work; a profoundly national and religious belief dictated it to an ardent poet." Giuseppe Mazzini, in turn, called their author "the premier poet of the age," while Pierre Ballanche likened him "to the fervent and believing priests of the Middle Ages, to those monks who one day leave their monastery after having knelt and prayed at the altar..., who leave it to preach a crusade." Even Thomas Carlyle called the work "wonderful," despite the "fire, slaughter, Polish patriotism, Jesus Christ and Robespierre." Lamennais, for his part, who had followed Montalembert's enterprise closely, encouraging it at every step, declared, "Such a pure expression of Faith and of Liberty is altogether a miracle in our age of servitude and unbelief." "This little work," he went on, "will be of immense benefit not only for Poles, but also for the French and all people into whose languages it will be translated." And indeed, in the space of a decade, the work was translated or paraphrased into Italian, Lithuanian, Croatian, Romanian, Hungarian, and Ukrainian—all "little" peoples of Europe, struggling like Poland, *mutatis mutandis*, for their own rightful place in the community of nations.[36]

7

In imagining a faith-based alternative to the increasingly polarized ideological debates within the emigration, Mickiewicz was not entirely isolated. Faced with defeat and dislocation, a small group of émigrés, lapsed Catholics, mostly, some with a history of leftist sympathies, began seeking at least consolation in their traditional faith, if not necessarily the catalytic role Mickiewicz envisioned for it. They found in the poet someone who not only shared their beliefs, but to a certain extent also their path to those beliefs, and someone whose force of character and eloquent sagacity helped sustain them. In the late fall of 1832, they began gathering at Mickiewicz's new lodgings on rue Louis le Grand, where, as Domeyko recalled,

> the spirit of Catholicism would manifest itself in his conversation, and he knew how to transport us vividly and ardently to our chapels, church fairs, holidays, and processions. We liked to listen to him, and gradually piety became the most prominent feature and subject of conversation among us, that is, those who belonged to our circle.[37]

Aside from Domeyko and Bohdan Zaleski, this circle included Zaleski's distant kinsman, Józef; Mickiewicz's old friend Gorecki; his publisher Aleksander Jełowicki; Cezary Plater, the president of the Society of Lithuanian and Ruthenian Lands; and the musician Stefan Zan, the youngest brother of Mickiewicz's beloved Tomasz. Chopin too was a frequent visitor for a while, as was Hieronim Kajsiewicz, an impoverished young radical poet in the early throes of a spiritual crisis. But of all of them, it was the poet Stefan Witwicki, a friend of Zaleski and Odyniec from Warsaw, who found a special place in Mickiewicz's affections. A dark, handsome dandy three years Mickiewicz's junior, he had debuted with poems so derivative of *Ballads and Romances* as to be almost parodies, which guaranteed their popularity among composers. During the uprising he had made a name for himself as the author of patriotic verse. Like Zaleski, Witwicki had become a devout Catholic in emigration, and he and Mickiewicz soon "began seeing each other often." Woven in the course of "frequent conversations and strolls," it was a mutually invigorating relationship, "heartfelt and intimate," built, it seems, as much on emotional camaraderie as on the depth of shared religious convictions and the kind of nativist notions that were making their way into

Mickiewicz's writing. The bitterness of their break some ten years later, largely a function of Witwicki's rigid Catholicism, would be a measure of the intensity of their friendship.[38]

Yet another member of the circle was Bogdan Jański, a gifted graduate of the University of Warsaw who had been studying law and economics in Paris since before the uprising. Nearly ten years Mickiewicz's junior, this selfless, ascetic man was a perpetual seeker, introspective, drawn to spiritualism, but also genuinely committed to social justice. For a time he had been an active member of the Saint-Simonist community in Paris, which he tried to engage in the Polish cause, and vice versa. The collapse of the uprising, however, on top of the fractures among Saint-Simon's followers, precipitated a spiritual crisis for Jański. It was at this point in his life that Mickiewicz "noticed him, looked him over, and came to like him." Before long they were sharing the apartment on rue Louis le Grande, as well as a Christian sensibility informed as much by personal quest as by a suspicion of dogma. In part under the poet's guidance, Jański managed a none too surprising transition from neo-Christian socialism to Catholic nationalism. Their relationship, thickened in hours of long, at times painfully intimate conversation, soon became the basis for close collaboration. It was Jański who produced the literal translation of the *Books* for Montalembert. And it was Jański who now provided Mickiewicz with a platform for disseminating his vision of a new world order.[39]

After his experiences with Lelewel's committee and then the publication of the *Books*, Mickiewicz was not especially eager to engage in everyday émigré politics—that "wound," as he described it, "festering with maggots." He had anticipated the Democrats' reaction to his "gospel," although its vitriol took him aback. The reception of his vision by Czartoryski's camp was no less disheartening. In October, the poet had sent some "thoughts" to the prince on the reconvocation of the Diet in exile, in which he imagined Poland's traditional legislative body not only as "the legal authority of the Polish nation," but as "the moral authority of Europe." Invoking the names of "Lamennais, Schelling, Lamartine, Chateaubriand"—programmatic Catholics all, who understood "which way the wind was blowing"—he would have the Diet condemn "as godless all wars over borders, commerce, ports, etc.," "recognize all people as children of a single family," and proclaim "that just as Christ put an end to all bloody sacrifices with his death, so too Poland will put an end to wars" (Dz. 6:307–9). It goes without saying that these "thoughts" were dismissed with condescending bemusement: "du sublime au ridicule," as Czartoryski's secretary put it.[40]

In the face of indifference and derision, the poet admitted to Niemcewicz in mid-March that he now would "watch [the emigration's machinations] from a distance . . . , since among the drunk the best approach is to wait until they sober up." Yet like all who are convinced that theirs is the absolute truth, Mickiewicz could not resist. That very same month, he was presented with an opportunity "to exert influence on the emigration," thanks to "an organ familiar to the emigration for four months." He seized the opportunity immediately.[41]

In November 1832, Eustachy Januszkiewicz, an enterprising publisher and himself a habitué of the poet's circle of Catholics, had founded one of the emigration's first periodicals. Inspired, surely, by Mickiewicz, he called it *Pielgrzym Polski*—the Polish pilgrim. Primarily informational, with no particular factional affiliation, the four-page biweekly "devoted to politics and national literature" nonetheless soon managed a subscription of five hundred, more than twice the number than its superbly edited democratic competition. Mickiewicz was a contributor from the very first issue, with a review of the kind of memoir that as a member of the Lithuanian-Ruthenian Society he had encouraged veterans to publish. *Pielgrzym*, for its part, printed a favorable review of *Forefathers' Eve* as well as a prepublication excerpt from the *Books* (together with an editorial comment claiming that "literature has heretofore never had a book so beneficial"). On 1 April the poet took over the reins of the paper—without any remuneration—together with Jański.[42]

According to its new editors, the aim of *Pielgrzym Polski* would now be to serve as a "moral" "intermediary between the homeland and the emigration, on the one hand providing information about the nation . . . ; on the other drawing readers' attention to everything taking place in the emigration" (*Dz.* 6:223–24). Its main mission, however, its "fundamental conception, its kernel"—and here the messianic tones grew clear—was

> to serve Europe and mankind . . . by serving our fatherland, Poland; . . . that just as all the quandaries of foreign politics will not be resolved until justice is dispensed toward Poland, so too only a free and independent Poland can effectively resolve all quandaries of a politically theoretical nature, toward the resolution of which Western European thought vainly struggles and for which it sheds the blood of its people. (*Dz.* 6:224)

For the next three months, until the end of June 1833, *Pielgrzym Polski* became Mickiewicz's pulpit—fifteen issues filled almost exclusively, albeit anonymously, with the poet's peculiar semiotics of current events.

On subjects ranging from French laws concerning the émigrés to émigré factionalism, from events in the Near East to systems of taxation, from the Constitution of 3 May and how Poles celebrate Holy Week to the traits of a future national leader, Mickiewicz provided analyses and prescriptions that were as consistent as they were insistent—and, often enough, as naïve as they were morally principled. Europe, in his view, was seeing the emergence of two absolutely inimical "parties": on the one hand the "Muscovite," nefarious and despotic, which had already infiltrated and co-opted *every* ideological faction and regime in Europe, from the English Tories and French Carlists to the Jacobins and the *juste-milieu*; and, on the other, the "Polish," whose very name evoked freedom and equality because of its willingness to sacrifice itself for the freedom and equality of all the peoples of Europe—"for *your* freedom and *ours*," not, "contrary to all the old logic of diplomacy," for *our* freedom and *yours* ("About the Polish Party"; Dz. 6:228). Between these two intractable forces there could be "no negotiations, pacts, compacts, armistices, exchanges of letters" ("About a Meeting of the Society of Lithuania and the Ruthenian Lands and about the Insurrectionaries' Constitution"; Dz. 6:232). There could be none because this was an unmediatable struggle between absolute evil and absolute good informed, ultimately, by the no less unmediatable opposition between reason and affect: between constitutions on paper and constitutions inscribed "in the hearts of the people" (Dz. 6:232); between taxes and a "*subsidium charitativum*" ("About the Desire of Peoples for a New System of Taxation"; Dz. 6:288); between all manners of governments, parliaments, laws, and political philosophies and the people—between "men of reason and madmen." "In times when minds sick with sophistry allow themselves to debate about everything on the right and the left," Mickiewicz declared, "the mind of mankind, expelled from books and deliberations, seeks refuge in the last bunker, in the hearts of *people of feeling*" ("About Men of Reason and Madmen"; Dz. 6:272).

Perhaps nowhere were Mickiewicz's politics of affect—and of poetic imagination—more in evidence than in a series of articles he devoted to two of the emigration's less "reasonable" undertakings. Both were hatched in response to what the poet too, like the denizens of "German taverns, French faubourgs, and even Italian huts," (mis)recognized as "symptoms" "of great transformations in the European order" (My Thoughts about the Polish Diet; Dz. 6:307). On news that a revolution was being planned in Frankfurt, several hundred Polish fighters left their *dépôt* in Besançon on 7 April in order to aid their German brothers. As they were crossing Switzerland, they learned that the "revolution" had fizzled. Unable to return now to France, the "Holy Legion," as the would-be revolutionaries styled themselves, found themselves stranded in the canton of Bern. At nearly the same time, several dozen émigré emissaries under the leadership of the blustering but incompetent colonel Józef Zaliwski crossed into the Congress Kingdom from Galicia as an ostensible guerrilla vanguard of what was hoped would be a new insurrection. Concocted by Lelewel in concert with Polish and French Carbonari (and perhaps with the knowledge of Mickiewicz himself), the action was a fiasco. After a few days of wandering, with no support from locals, Zaliwski managed to slip back into Galicia unharmed. Many of his comrades, however, were captured and their leaders hanged.

Both events came as something of a rude awakening for the émigrés, who were eagerly awaiting any turn of events that even remotely offered a chance to liberate Poland and pave their way back home. But to those who now sought to distance themselves from these undertakings, Mickiewicz was as unsparing as he was implacable:

> We often hear: "There has already been enough blood shed for Poland." Oh, were it so!... Let us recall that several tens of thousands of armed men bore their blood out of the country before the enemy, that that blood was trothed to the Fatherland; does anyone

> think it can be stolen! The longer one waits with payment, the higher the interest that will have to be paid. ("About the Apoliticals and the Politics of *Pielgrzym*"; *Dz.* 6:269)

More disturbing, perhaps, than this demand for sacrificial blood as the necessary price for national salvation was the poet's disconnect with the reality of blood. It was the same disconnect that compelled Mickiewicz to criticize in Dresden the Polish army's performance during the uprising, the same that called for burning down the homes of those who quartered Russians, the same that inspired him to urge the Lithuanian-Ruthenian Society "to gather materials for biographies of all Poles who . . . have been martyred for the national cause" (*Dz.* 6:189).* Poetic, to be sure, perhaps even noble, but, like crucified Poland and "The Pilgrim's Litany," these were masochistic fantasies structured around a profound sense of guilt. Mickiewicz's opponents, on both right and left, were quick to pick this scab: "We'd suggest to the Pilgrim," "so generous a dispenser of Polish blood," "that instead of sitting in Paris like some Peter the Hermit, he [strap on] a knapsack and with cross and sword in hand lead the emigration to Poland." After all, "during the last revolution (and could he not have participated?) he did not solve matters there, at the appropriate time and place . . . , did not endeavor to steer the national ship to calmer shores."[43]

Mickiewicz admitted at one point "that [he] would be taken for a madman" (*Dz.* 6:309)—which he was, of course, and much to his delight. The company he imagined himself keeping was in this respect unexceptionable:

> Only *deeds* or *words* and *thoughts* that engender deeds are what we call politics, action. Such deeds are struggle, victory, or martyrdom; such words were, for example, first the words of the Gospels, then of those that emulated them: the words of the Koran, the words of Wycliffe, Hus, Luther, Saint-Simon— . . . the deliberations of the Convention, . . . the daily orders of Napoleon. (*Dz.* 6:266)

But these were different times, unamenable, it seems, to prophets and seers even if, or rather especially when, the prophet was a poet. "The trouble is," concluded one of Czartoryski's agents about the articles in *Pielgrzym*, "that a genius can at the same time be a fool." To the overwhelming majority of the emigration, concerned now increasingly with routinizing, for better or worse, ideological positions that might sustain it in exile, Mickiewicz's uncompromising stance was as deluded as it was incomprehensible. As the organ of the Czartoryski faction put it in response to the poet's article on "men of reason and madmen":

> It is *reasonable* to avoid all exaggeration, that is, to honor God, but not in Jesuit fashion . . . ; to honor what is national, albeit the virtues not the prejudices of our ancestors. We submit

*During his first days in Dresden, Mickiewicz had in fact suggested "the creation of an alphabetized catalogue of national martyrs" (Mickiewicz to Lelewel, 23 March 1832, *Dz.* 15:140).

> that if it is *madness* to import to the country from abroad godlessness and disdain for what is national, it would be *unreasonable* also *to wait* with idle hands instead of studying and taking advantage of the rest; *unreasonable* to return to the fatherland without considering what is worthy of imitating abroad, even *more unreasonable* to hold useful reforms in contempt.

On at least this one issue the Democrats concurred with Czartoryski.[44]

Mickiewicz's last article for *Pielgrzym Polski* appeared on 28 June. It was a curious piece, purporting to be an excerpt from a Polish newspaper dated 1899 (the poet-prophet had been tinkering with a French-language "History of the Future" since the fall of 1832), in which the emigration's "wounds" were refigured as foibles in a gently satiric, self-mocking light. "We became convinced," recounts an old émigré, "that talking is proof of an incapacity to act, for if man were omnipotent, he would never talk, and the most powerful would be the least garrulous" ("Excerpts from a Letter to One of the Editors"; Dz. 6:300). In the face of the "unpleasantness" he experienced in his self-ordained role as the emigration's conscience, the poet began to distance himself, to "laugh at everything that concerned" him, be it his "fame" or his "works." Over the preceding few months, he in fact tried to put it all in perspective in a series of (unpublished) satirical poems and paraphrases of La Fontaine that made bitter, sometimes ad hominem, fun of the emigration's ostensible shortcomings. In any event, by June he had had enough. As he wrote to Niemcewicz with a feeling of increasing resignation:

> To respond to one's countrymen every now and again, to do what one can, and, besides, not get involved in the events of the day, in the debates and dietines, to wait for the future, this, it seems to me, should be the strategy of people of integrity. One should give everyone the freedom to seek out their own ways—be it with arms or conspiracies, since in truth it's impossible to foresee where our terrestrial salvation lies, or the fate of our nation.[45]

8

Eleven months by the Seine had not lessened Mickiewicz's "aversion to Paris." His efforts to reach the emigration seemed to have come up against a wall of intractable ideological as well as personal differences. His own uncompromising stance aside, he was unable to fully grasp that the turmoil of the uprising had conditioned those differences, which by this very same token diminished his authority in the eyes of those who had actually participated in it. That in censuring Lamennais in 1834 for his *Words of a Believer*, the pope himself condemned the ideas informing Mickiewicz's initiatives only weakened it further. Łubieńska, for her part, did her best to exacerbate his "worries." She continued to be a persistent thorn, the cause of "deep sorrow," until well into the spring of 1833, despite Garczyński's assurances that his friend should have no "pangs of conscience about a thing that is not even worth remembering." No less persistent, however, was the concern for daily bread.[46]

A year's expenses in Paris came to about 1,200 francs, and Mickiewicz had gone through the 2,000 he had received for the fourth volume of *Poems*. He had, after all, initially published *The Books* at his own expense and had most copies distributed gratis. The donation he made to the Society for Scholarly Aid was not an isolated gesture. He had sent money to a cousin interned in Prussia and probably to others as well—he had always been generous to those close to him. Odyniec occasionally sent him the residuals from the Poznań edition, but this was an irregular and at any rate none-too-substantial source of income. What Mickiewicz counted on for the moment was his translation of *The Giaour*, to which he had returned in Dresden solely for a quick profit but which he still had not finished. Nonetheless, when in the fall of 1832 the poet tried to sell it to the Lwów publisher Jan Milikowski for 100 thalers, the latter balked. At one point, Mickiewicz was even willing to release "the rights to [his] poetry for a life-long pension, small, to be sure, but certain." Yet nothing came of this either. He was forced to pawn a tie pin. Hoping "to finish and sell" *The Giaour*, he worked away at the translation until the spring of 1833 amid constant interruptions, without much enthusiasm; it "bored and wearied [him] terribly." More frustratingly, though, translating that "rogue and bore" interrupted work on what since at least September was becoming Mickiewicz's "beloved child."[47]

Some six months earlier, in early December 1832, Mickiewicz had informed Odyniec that he was "feeling a poetic rush," that despite "all [his] vexations [i.e., Łubieńska], all the troubles with proof-reading [i.e., *Forefathers' Eve*, *The Books*], and on top of this, various scribblings, papers, articles, and projects," he had already "dashed off a thousand lines" of "a gentry poem à la [Goethe's] *Herman and Dorothea*." "The insurrectionary gentry," he added, "likes it very much." To Niemcewicz he described it as "a country poem,"

> in which [he was] trying to preserve a memento of old [Polish] customs and sketch as best [he could] a depiction of [Polish] country life, hunts, entertainments, battles, forays, etc. It is set in Lithuania around 1812, when old traditions were still alive and one could still see the remnants of old country life.[48]

Perhaps it began germinating as early as the fall and winter of 1831, amid the forests, fields, and manors near Poznań, with their hunts, coffee, and expeditions for mushrooms. But it was on "the Paris pavement" that it began to take shape, amid "the oaths and the lies, the untimely schemes, / The belated regrets, the horrible quarrels" of the emigration (*Dz.* 4:383)—or, to be more precise, in the apartment on Louis le Grand, where the "insurrectionary gentry," that small group of like-minded émigrés who by and large had their roots in Lithuania and Ruthenia, would gather and there "help [him] in [his] conversation,"

> Adding word upon word to [his] song,
> Like the fairy-tale cranes above that wild island,
> Flying over the charmed castle in spring
> And hearing the enchanted boy's loud-sounding cries,
> Each bird dropped a single feather for him,
> He made himself wings and returned to his home. (Dz. 4:386)

Never before had Mickiewicz been as eager to share his work with others. Indeed, much like those memoirs he was encouraging veterans of the uprising to write, the poet's friends—Gorecki, Domeyko, Jański, Zan, Zaleski, Witwicki—served as living repositories of lore, of anecdotes, names, traditions, and sentiments, that refreshed his own extraordinary memory of a place and time for which they all, collectively, were pining:

> the only country
> Where a Pole can a tad of happiness still find:
> The country of one's childhood. (Dz. 4:385)

The poem—called "Żegota" at first, in honor of Domeyko, then "Tadeusz"—grew slowly over the course of that winter and spring, in stretches and spurts and with frequent interruptions. It was a time when letters from the Ankwiczes had reopened old wounds and resentments. Their "correspondence was like their earlier behavior: each time that [Mickiewicz] would slip away, [they] would entice with hints and promises, and when [he] would respond more affectionately, [they] would retreat and only talk pleasantries." "I had no idea," Mickiewicz tartly responded to them, "that my letters might be more interesting than those of any of your other acquaintances." He left their subsequent letters unanswered, maintaining that "even if they searched [him] out, [he] would not have the heart to approach them [again]." Despite Henrietta's imploring rebukes, castigating him for ostensibly "wanting to worry [her family] with a silence so long and so cruel," the poet remained unmoved. It was clear that after recognizing herself in *Forefathers' Eve*, part 3, the young lady—together, of course, with her parents—seemed more concerned than ever, and equally content, with occupying a place in the *imagination* of Poland's national bard, and through it in posterity. She need not have worried. Just as he had done ten years earlier, Mickiewicz was again putting paid in verse to a complex romantic entanglement, refiguring it as the love of the intrepid but unmoneyed gentryman Jacek Soplica for Ewa, the daughter of the proud magnate Horeszko, who refuses to countenance a mésalliance. Jacek ends up killing Horeszko, but he does not get Ewa.[49]

By January 1833, Mickiewicz had completed "almost two huge cantos." It was "with great regret," then, that he "had to shelve it" in order to finish translating *The Giaour*. He finally managed to "return to his *Gentryman*" in the beginning of April (and all the while still bent on continuing *Forefathers' Eve*). By May he had "completed the third canto," aware now that "it was likely to be a lengthy shindy." All he needed was some quiet.[50]

The previous March, Mickiewicz had moved out of the city center to Domeyko's apartment on Carrefour de l'Observatoire, "a few dozen steps from" the Jardin du Luxembourg, hoping to be closer to nature and further away from importunate countrymen. But even here he got little peace. The poet was "consumed by current events," which "often shattered [his] soul into pieces, whereupon [he] had to patch it up and glue it together in solitude." He "often complained... that 'they were strangling his little Tadeusz in diapers'"—but then too, they were beginning to insinuate themselves into the poem. The meetings at rue Taranne, feckless and susceptible to demagogic manipulation, the recriminations over the misguided missions of emissaries, the largely unspoken tensions between émigrés from the Congress Kingdom and those from Lithuania and Ruthenia, all grist for Mickiewicz's mill on the pages of *Pielgrzym*, were gradually reconfiguring the drift of the "idyll," thickening the story of the luckless lovers with figures of emissaries, internecine strife, and the coalescence of a riven collective in the face of an external foe.[51]

Yet life near the gardens started to pall as well, and Mickiewicz's health began to suffer. Every so often he made trips outside the metropolis, to Sèvres, where Zaleski had settled for a time, or to Nogent-sur-Marne to visit Kajsiewicz. In early May, the poet's friends found him an apartment in the city again, "fairly spacious, albeit over a stable," on rue Saint-Nicolas d'Antin; Mickiewicz "liked it immediately." That it was "the narrowest and dirtiest street in Paris" seemed to make little difference. He began to withdraw, and *Pan Tadeusz* provided the haven. "I live [now]," he wrote to Odyniec in late May, "in Lithuania, in forests and taverns, with the gentry, the Jews, etc." He was again experiencing the flow, "writing some hundred, hundred and fifty verses a day in one sitting, which he would then read [to his friends] in the evening." On occasion, he would "encourage [them] to bring bits of [their own] gentry rhapsodies," but, like Witwicki's description of the Lithuanian forest primeval, they became unrecognizable once he incorporated them into his tale. By the end of May, Mickiewicz had completed yet another canto, "although there still remained a great deal of work." News that Garczyński was now seriously ill interrupted it all.[52]

9

Mickiewicz had known since the previous November that his friend's health had taken a turn for the worse. In the letter informing his friend of his state, Garczyński had written that he wanted to "send [Mickiewicz] all of [his] poetry," with the hope that he "would not refuse to help publish it" and even "act on [his] behalf with a few thalers." The message was clear. Garczyński was ill enough to have begun tending to his legacy in earnest. Two months later, in January 1833, he was urging Mickiewicz "to begin printing as soon as possible, since spring [was] a ways off, and it is only in the spring that doctors [were] promising an improvement in [his] health."[53]

Mickiewicz did not hesitate. Having received the manuscript in mid-January, he set about preparing it for print. Both Witwicki and Domeyko lent a hand, but it was Mickiewicz who took much of the burden upon himself. "You should know," he wrote to Garczyński in May, "that I did all the proofs myself, something I would have been incapable of undertaking with my own poetry." He suggested changes here, excisions there, but always with delicacy—and under the assumption, perhaps, that in his state Garczyński would not object. When his friend did, however feebly, Mickiewicz assured him that he was but "conversing with [Garczyński's] soul, at times arguing, quarreling, but always, as in [their] life together, parting in agreement." Editing became, in effect, collaboration. Mickiewicz removed entire poems, (re)wrote passages, and then went so far as to add his own "Ordon's Redoubt" as his and Garczyński's "common property."[54]

At the beginning of May, after several weeks of intense work on the part of Mickiewicz and friends, the first volume of Garczyński's *Poems*, consisting entirely of the poetic tale *Wacław*, appeared in Paris. Mickiewicz was unable to contain his enthusiasm for his friend's poem—but what he also felt, either by right of friendship or inspiration or hours of arguing about German philosophy, was just as much his own:

> I... read some parts to one of my friends..., they made a greater impression on him than my new *Forefathers' Eve*.... I was never capable of feeling poetic envy, but it seems to me that were *Wacław* not your work, I would be envious of the author. Now I love it as if it were [our] common child.

Mickiewicz was far more restrained about Garczyński's remaining poems, which were to be included in the second volume; and although he promised his friend a review of the whole in *Pielgrzym*, one never appeared. It was only on the tenth anniversary of Garczyński's death, in the course of his second year of lectures on Slavic literatures at the Collège de France, that Mickiewicz finally kept his promise. He devoted an entire three lectures to *Wacław*.[55]

By January, Garczyński's cough had become persistent. His doctors counseled him to travel south, to Switzerland, Italy, but not until spring or summer. Potocka, that "angelic, priceless soul," was at his side almost constantly. Spring in Dresden made the cough even worse. In May, Garczyński decided to finally head out to Bex for a few months of sheep's whey cure, and then, he hoped, to Italy. He suggested a rendezvous with Mickiewicz in

Fig. 15 Stefan Garczyński. Engraving after a portrait by an unknown artist, ca. 1830. Courtesy of the Adam Mickiewicz Museum of Literature, Warsaw.

Strasbourg, but his friend, unaware, perhaps, of how much Garczyński's health had deteriorated, "undid everything," citing "a complete lack of funds and passport difficulties" (although two weeks earlier he had informed Garczyński that he was contemplating a trip to the Near East). He now assured his friend that he would make every effort to meet up with him. What he needed was a passport and money.[56]

Thanks to the intervention of Lafayette, Dwernicki, and his old acquaintance from Rome Fenimore Cooper, Mickiewicz was able to obtain a passport to Switzerland and Italy. In doing so, he had had no compunction about again turning his failure to participate in the uprising to his advantage. As he wrote to the minister of foreign affairs, "Since I took no part in the recent political events that had occurred in Poland, I do not belong to the category of refugees." At the same time, he set about putting his financial house in order.[57]

Milikowski, the publisher from Lwów, was now in Paris and "would not let [the poet] alone, either at home or on the street, trying to make a deal for a poem [*Pan Tadeusz*] that [was] not even half-written, . . . offering 2,000 francs for it." Mickiewicz refused, hoping that another, "very profitable" offer from a publisher in Cracow would materialize. But the poet needed money immediately. Without waiting for an answer from Cracow, he turned instead to Aleksander Jełowicki, co-owner of the Polish Bookstore and Print Shop in Paris, who was willing, "with joy and with pride, to give him 4,000 francs." There was, however, more to the deal. In a contract dated 3 July, Mickiewicz agreed: (1) to sell all the rights to his translation of *The Giaour*; (2) to authorize Jełowicki to reprint the fourth volume of *Poems* (in 2,000 copies); (3) to sell *Pan Tadeusz* once it was finished to Jełowicki, who would print 3,000 copies and retain exclusive rights to it for three years; (4) to empower Jełowicki with publishing an authorized edition of his complete works (in 3,000 copies), to which the publisher would have exclusive rights again for three years. In return, Mickiewicz was to get a total of 6,500 francs, 2,000 upon signing and 4,500 upon submitting all the manuscripts for the new edition. The sum was substantial, but so too were the poet's future concessions. A week later, he informed his brother that, thanks to the deal, he "managed to pay off his debts . . . and again had capital for a year." No less important, he "could now pay for the trip" to Bex and beyond.[58]

Leaving Domeyko in charge of seeing the second volume of Garczyński's poetry through to print, Mickiewicz got into a *coupé* around 5 July. "Bypassing Geneva, [he] headed straight for Lausanne," and then across the lake to Bex. On the boat he ran into Potocka, who herself was hurrying to Garczyński's side despite her own weakened state. "That woman," Mickiewicz wrote to Domeyko, "reconciles mankind and can again inspire faith in virtue and goodness on earth." It was raining hard upon their arrival in Bex; dense fog hid the mountains. The sight of Garczyński, his "face so pale and sad," "tore" Mickiewicz's "soul apart." Potocka returned to Geneva after a few days, leaving the poet to care for Garczyński alone. There, amid the gradually clearing Alps, with his friend slowly fading at an inn, Mickiewicz briefly imagined a different world. He would fetch Odyniec and his wife and together they "would remain [in Switzerland] until something new happened in the world. [They] would buy a pair of Swiss cows and a rooster, who would crow beneath the window, reminding them of Lithuania; [they] would also buy geese and turkeys etc." Some part of Mickiewicz continued to abide in the idyllic nostalgia of *Pan Tadeusz*. He was "in no humor," though, to do any writing.[59]

For the remaining three weeks in Bex, he watched Garczyński drink ewe's whey, and then "lose all [his] strength." There was nothing to do but go to Geneva, where the presence of doctors could offer at least an illusion of treatment, albeit little hope; indeed, as far as Mickiewicz was concerned, there was none. In Geneva, Garczyński's state worsened. "Over three days, convulsions with coughing, fever, and pain in the lungs." These were "terrible days," followed, as so often happened in the course of the illness, by deceptive signs of improvement, and euphoria. Garczyński "thought incessantly" about the fate of his book, "despairing over every erratum." Mickiewicz often lost patience, "barely able to control [himself] from saying something nasty or in angry silence rebuking eccentricities of illness [he] should have been forgiving." He pleaded with Domeyko to send something, anything, from the printer to set Garczyński's mind at ease.[60]

After three weeks in Geneva, with Mickiewicz himself "indisposed"—the usual: no appetite, trouble with his teeth, "a nervous . . . cough"—"*all* the doctors [were] dispatching [Garczyński south] as quickly as possible, because in such illnesses every doctor is eager to dispatch a patient further away." They decided on Avignon. Traveling through Lyons, then down the Rhône "extremely slowly," they reached the old papal see sometime in the beginning of September. "You can just imagine," Mickiewicz wrote to Domeyko, "the trouble of traveling with someone who is ill, whom one has to lug in one's arms from carriage to room, in a country where innkeepers, having gazed into our eyes and seeing little life, do not want to take us!" To make matters worse, Mickiewicz was running out of money, but he refused to take advantage of Potocka's generosity: "As long as I have my own [money], I don't want anyone else's." Just as his strength was beginning to wane, an acquaintance of Garczyński, one Tadeusz Pągowski, appeared in Avignon to help tend the dying man. Mickiewicz took advantage of his presence to make a trip to Marseilles, ostensibly to obtain passports for Italy, but really for a much needed respite. Within a few days he was summoned back, only to find his "friend greatly changed." A day later, on 20 September 1833, Garczyński passed away:

> He stopped breathing in the night, at 6:00; so gently that one can't call this short moment of passage from misery to a better world decease. . . . Potocka . . . arrived a few days before his death and brightened his final minutes on earth. The night he died I was with him until late; then, exhausted by insomnia and the road, I went to sleep. Pągowski stood watch by his bed; alarmed by the quietness of the sick man's sleep, he drew close and found him lifeless.

Garczyński had lived long enough, though, to see the second volume of his works in print.[61]

They buried Garczyński in the cemetery at Avignon. Mickiewicz himself wrote the epitaph for the slab they had affixed to the cemetery wall over the grave of a Polish "soldier," "*wieszcz*," and "exile" (Dz. 17:529).

Mickiewicz had done all he could. He was exhausted, "like a Frenchman returning from 1812, demoralized, weak, an out and out ragamuffin, practically without shoes." To Potocka, however, he was more akin to a saint: "I sensed his soul in his genius, and I gazed at him with admiration, with tears. He is superior to us all: in heart, virtue, soul, just as he is a genius superior to the chosen."[62]

To distract himself, Mickiewicz decided to do some sightseeing before returning to Paris. With Pągowski in tow, the poet visited Petrarch's waterfall in Vaucluse, the Roman aqueduct over the Gard, and Nîmes, with its coliseum, temple ruins, and Jardins de la Fontaine. The route north led again through Lyons, but now he could take some time to see the city. He paid a call on Victor Pavie, the writer he had met with David d'Angers in Weimar, and then completely by chance ran into Zaleski, who had been trying to find the poet for the previous several days. The two returned to Paris together in the middle of October, Mickiewicz "with an illness that had been nagging [him] for the past few months." He had written to his brother that he had to be "in Paris for the winter in order to attend to many affairs." But there was really only one "affair" that truly concerned him, the manuscript of *Pan Tadeusz*, four entire books already, which he had entrusted to Domeyko before leaving for Bex.[63]

10

Mickiewicz's decision to travel to Garczyński's side was perhaps taken as much out of a desire to "flee Paris" as it was out of genuine devotion to his dying friend. By the same token, though, and as much as the poet may have wished otherwise, "it was out of the question to think about writing to the sound of coughing and while constantly gazing at Stefan's suffering." Indeed, Garczyński's ordeal served to bring into relief old knots of guilt, resentment, and self-pity. And, as had happened to Mickiewicz so often in the past, those knots expressed themselves as "illness," "moving from teeth to head to chest." Upon his return to rue Saint-Nicolas d'Antin in mid-October, the poet "shut [him]self in, and after three days of cure expelled all evil," freeing a burst of creative energy no less extraordinary than the one in Dresden. "I am healthy and fresh again," he informed Odyniec, "I go out rarely, I write and I write."[64]

Mickiewicz produced the remaining eight books of *Pan Tadeusz*—over six thousand lines!—in four months, and revised what he had written earlier. By 11 November, he had finished canto five (comparing the poem now, however "immodestly," to Walter Scott); in the second half of that month he was on canto six; a few weeks later he was "finishing a . . . poem, which [he] now lov[ed] most as one loves a youngest child."[65]

Over the course of those four months, the poet had few distractions. He had withdrawn into a small circle of friends, effectively shutting out the émigré whirl as well as the Parisian cesspool. Days were spent writing, evenings most often "with Stefan [Witwicki], Antoni [Gorecki] . . . , playing chess with Zan, arguing at times with Bohdan [Zaleski]." "Gaunt, wan, with an expressive face and lively eyes," he was "always at work," despite a winter suffering from various maladies, and with an almost empty pocketbook. To be sure, civic demands were still made of him, and he tried to meet them conscientiously. The upshot, however, was predictable. "There's a Society here of Civilization of some sort," Mickiewicz informed Kajsiewicz,

> that conceived of a plan to found a library for Poles . . . ; I dash off a note, trudge with it in the mud, and return home for tea. The next day there's a commotion among our Parisian brethren . . . ; various people are accusing various others of trying to co-opt and exploit the library, which doesn't exist yet and God knows whether it will ever exist.

As far as Mickiewicz was concerned, the emigration, as he said on more than one occasion, was "drunk." To emissaries from Galicia seeking advice from the author of the émigré gospel, the poet tried to explain that they should not count on their compatriots in France, occupied as they now were "with fathoming social theories, organizing a future Poland . . . [and] arguing over aristocracy and democracy" (*Dz.* 6:314). The realities of the emigration had, at least for the moment, put Mickiewicz's millennial hopes for the Pilgrimage in abeyance. He compensated by losing himself in "descriptions of [Lithuanian] domestic life, hunts, legal schemes . . . etc." "Writing about these things," he reported to his brother, "entertained me beyond measure, transporting me back to our native realm."[66]

In the middle of February 1834, recalled Zaleski forty years later, Mickiewicz "got up from his writing table with a beaming face and cried out [to his friends], 'Thank God! I just signed off on *Pan Tadeusz* with a big finis.' " "Twelve huge cantos!" the poet informed Odyniec on 14 February, "a lot that's mediocre, but also a lot that's good." He was now eager to have it printed as quickly as possible, if for no other reason than to replenish his finances—or so he hoped, since he had already gone through the advance Jełowicki had proffered for the poem.[67]

The next five months were spent preparing the work for print and reading proofs, chores that Mickiewicz always dreaded. The most immediate task was revising the manuscript, and as befit, perhaps, a narrative about the transformation of a national collective, the poet insisted that the work of revision too be a collective effort. He enjoined his friends "to point out serious errors for correction, be it transgressions of spirit, of content, of form, or, finally, of vocabulary and turns of phrase." Some suggestions he accepted, others not, but in the end it was he who made the emendations. These, in turn, he tried out in readings for the emigration's elite, at evenings attended by Prince Czartoryski, Generals Kniaziewicz and Pac, Czartoryski's nephew Władysław Zamoyski, and the wife of General Małachowski. "We all listened with delight to his depiction of scenes," noted Niemcewicz about one such reading where the aromas of pea soup and Polish sausage at the table helped intensify the nostalgia, "they transported us, not without emotion and often with laughter, back to our native realm."[68]

If the chore of revision was to some extent eased by the participation of friends, proofreading was another matter. In order "to supervise the printing and proofs more sedulously," Mickiewicz moved temporarily to a hotel on rue de Seine, closer to the print shop on quai Voltaire. He had asked Jełowicki to hire Jański to help with the proofs, but the whole process still proved to be inordinately tedious. At one point, the poet, like some medieval monk, noted in the margin of a printer's sheet, "I'm copying these verses, a sleepy A. M., and it's late to boot, after handing the proofs in tomorrow, maybe I'll die soon, these perhaps are the last" (*Dz.* 17:541). Mickiewicz survived, though, and by mid-June 1834 the poem, printed in two volumes, was ready. As he had done with *Forefathers' Eve*, part 3, Jełowicki held off with sales in Paris "until copies made their way to Poland." Finally, on 10 August 1834, close to two years after it began germinating, *Pan Tadeusz, or The Last Foray in Lithuania: A Gentry Tale from 1811 and 1812, in Twelve Books*, published by Aleksander Jełowicki, with a frontispiece depicting David d'Anger's bust of the author, went on sale at the book shop of A. Pinard.[69]

II

Nearly two years earlier, in early November 1832, Mickiewicz had delivered a lecture at a meeting of the Lithuanian and Ruthenian Society entitled "Where and How One Should Seek the National Spirit." Although it contained many of the ideas he was developing at the time in *The Books of the Polish Nation and Pilgrimage*, the poet also turned inward for a moment, to what he felt at once constituted and preserved "the soul of the Nation," be it in its pilgrimage or at home:

> The principal and only national school for us were the notions and affects of old Poland, alive still in the memories of parents, relatives, and friends, manifested in their conversations, gathered together in various moral and political maxims that guided the common folk's assessments of people and events, that meted out praise to some and rebuke to others. This internal, domestic tradition consists of the remains of notions and affects that vivified our ancestors, and after the decline, disruption, and suppression of public discourse, this tradition took refuge in the homes of the gentry and the common folk. As in an ailing body blood and vital powers gather around the heart—that is where one should seek it, that is where one should reanimate it, that is whence one should convey

it throughout the entire body. It is from these traditions that both the country's independence and the future form of its government must evolve. (Dz. 6:191–92)

If these musings were indeed reminiscent of the *Books*, they at the same time reconfigured the terms informing the revelation Mickiewicz had brought with him from Dresden. The nation's "soul," which "hath descended from the earth, that is, from public life, into the abyss, that is, to the private life of people who suffer bondage in their country and outside of their country" (Dz. 5:19–20), existed now also in another hypostasis, as native tradition, a force capable of revitalizing Poland from within at a moment when the nation and its institutions were in a state of suspension.

Pan Tadeusz was, in this sense, a narrative about the possibility of internal revitalization. To be sure, the figure of Napoleon, poised to liberate Lithuania on his way to Moscow, frames the entire tale. But when the transformative tide of history finally sweeps through the provincial Lithuanian estate of Soplicowo in book eleven, it does so in the uniforms of Polish Legionnaires, commanded by Prince Józef Poniatowski, "Dąbrowski, Kniaziewicz, Małachowski, Giedrojć, and Grabowski" (Dz. 4:310). As such, it serves only to consummate a transformation that had already occurred within, from an anarchic, Old Polish gentry society, with its laminated social, personal, and regional conflicts, to a unified, nationally conscious—modern—collective. In the course of an escalating feud with the Soplicas over the ownership of a ruined castle, the Horeszkos and their allies the Dobrzyńskis, an impoverished, fractious clan originally from lands now part of the Congress Kingdom, resort to a traditional remedy in such circumstances, an armed foray. Intervention by a Russian garrison, however, forces the Soplicas and the Horeszkos, Mazovians and Lithuanians, to transcend their differences and stand as one in the face of the imperial interloper. Played out as a "social drama"* of breach, crisis, redress, and reintegration, the collective's underlying tensions are brought into relief by the feud, compelling it to reassess its most fundamental values as a matter of survival. Change occurs, but only as a function of tradition, which thus guarantees the persistence of tradition and, ultimately, its capacity for revitalization.

However, the social drama enacted in *Pan Tadeusz* is itself informed by the personal drama of a single individual, the hot-headed gentryman Jacek Soplica, whose conflict with the magnate Horeszko over the hand of the latter's daughter constitutes the drama's originary moment. Egged on by "the Satan of pride" (Dz. 4:295), Jacek shoots Horeszko, but does so just as a Russian army is besieging the magnate's castle, thus overdetermining his personal as well as social transgression by (the appearance of) national apostasy.

*The notion of social drama is Victor Turner's, developed in, among others of his studies devoted to it, "Social Dramas and Ritual Metaphors," in his *Dramas, Fields, and Metaphors*, 23–59.

To atone for his crime(s), Jacek dons a habit and assumes the monastic name of Father Robak ("worm"), initiating a transformation that serves as a template for the transformation of the collective. His subsequent engagement as a warrior-monk in the Napoleonic wars, then as an emissary to Prussia, Austria, and his native Lithuania to prepare the ground for the arrival of the Grande Armée, and, finally, his fatal lunge to save the last living heir of the Horeszkos from the bullet of a Russian soldier are all gestures that adumbrate the collective's new ethos, one founded on self-abnegation and sacrifice for the national cause. Through Robak's deathbed confession, in which the monk reveals his true identity as Jacek Soplica and narrates the vicissitudes of his transformation, Mickiewicz effectively conflates his hero's personal ordeal with the ordeal of the collective. Robak's life comes to embody, and simultaneously make sense of, the drama of his collective and, ultimately, of postpartition Poland itself.

Jacek/Robak thus emerges as yet another in a series of Mickiewicz's heroes, from Grażyna/Litawor and Alf/Wallenrod to Gustaw/Konrad/Father Piotr, whose change of identity inscribes a process of personal metamorphosis and hence a new chapter in the poet's symbolic autobiography. In the figure of the proud gentryman turned humble but heroic monk, the poet once again replays and refigures the cycle of guilt and atonement, pride and humility that was set in motion by *Konrad Wallenrod*. "Who knows," confesses Robak about his activity as an emissary,

> perhaps now I sinned once again!
> Too eager, perhaps, to follow commands, I hastened the uprising!
> The thought that the house of Soplica'd be the first to answer the call [...]!
> That thought... it was pure, so it seems... (Dz. 4:302)

Yet if in *Forefathers' Eve*, part 3, Mickiewicz literally exorcised the guilt, "vomiting out the pride and foulness that had been collecting [in him] for ten years," he also compensated by assuming the role of a prophet and thus effectively internalized the very pride he wanted to purge. Now, in *Pan Tadeusz*, the poet seems to call this role into question. It is, after all, as a self-effacing emissary, a "worm" aerating, turning, and nourishing the soil, preparing old ground for the appearance of the new, that Mickiewicz has Jacek/Robak atone for his pride, his doubts, and the remorse over "untimely intentions" (Dz. 4:383) and unmet expectations:

> Jacek in Rome did not die (as was rumored),
> He just changed his old life, his position, and name;
> And all of his trespasses against God and the Fatherland
> He expunged through great deeds and the life of a saint.
> (Dz. 4:315)

It is only in death, then, through his sacrificial self-effacement, that Jacek/Robak is finally reconciled with the collective he had fractured and subsequently sought to redeem.[70]

In 1838, after several years spent in virtual isolation on the Isle of Jersey, Stanisław Worcell, a close acquaintance of Mickiewicz during their first months of emigration in Paris, finally got a chance to read *Pan Tadeusz*. Deeply moved by the experience, he wrote the poet a letter in which he described the work as "a gravestone placed on old Poland by the hand of a genius" but one that at the same time "bonds the past with the future and brings forth from the grave the nucleus of our future life." Worcell recognized in the poem at once an epitaph for an irrevocably vanishing world and a guarantee, if only in the subjunctive, of its eventual revitalization. Słowacki too seemed to have grasped the significance of Mickiewicz's achievement, when in an unfinished canto of his poem *Beniowski* he wrote:

> Before this poem somehow
> Some enormous throne of darkness collapses;
> Something falls . . . and we heard—and we listened:
> That was Time retreating—turning its face
> To look back just once more . . . at the beauty afar,
> Which entrances like rainbows . . .
> Which sets with such rose-tinted clouds . . .
> Let's move on . . . the God of time . . . took a step.[71]

Yet few other of Mickiewicz's contemporaries were as percipient, or as prescient. If the print run of 2,000 of the fourth volume of *Poems* (containing *Forefathers' Eve*, part 3) sold out within a year, copies of the first printing of *Pan Tadeusz* were still to be had as late as the 1850s. And when in 1844 a second printing did appear, it was as part of a new edition of Mickiewicz's collected works. The poet's readers were, after all, of a generation that imagined itself already spoken for by the hyperromantic heroes of *Konrad Wallenrod* and *Forefathers' Eve*, but at the same time also one that had been brought up on classicist poetics. As far as it was concerned, *Pan Tadeusz* met neither expectation. Some chided Mickiewicz for missing an opportunity to create a genuine epic, with national heroes appropriate for the time. Witwicki went so far as to fault the poet for invoking Lithuania rather than Poland in its opening line. But what ultimately confused readers of *Pan Tadeusz* was Mickiewicz's gently ironic evocation of the everyday sights, smells, and sounds of a provincial, backward world on the verge of extinction, with its bear hunts and tribunals, repasts and vegetable patches, gentry estates and Jewish taverns, petty quarrels and forays. The work was dismissed as being too mundane, even vulgar—"porcine," as Słowacki described it in another mood—in a word, too "realistic" and, by this very same token, as trivializing the national past and its traditions. As the second-generation romantic

Cyprian Norwid concluded sarcastically, "An exceedingly national poem indeed, in which [everyone] eats, drinks, gathers mushrooms, and waits for the French to make a Fatherland for them."[72]

It would, in fact, take a new generation of readers, one with a sensibility nurtured on European realism, for whom modernity was erasing all traces of the world Mickiewicz had depicted, to recognize in *Pan Tadeusz* a genuine national epic. As the consequences of yet another failed uprising made the existence of Poland seem even more tenuous and hope for its restoration seemingly all the more remote, it was these readers who sought comfort in the poem's seamless, "noumenal" tapestry,* wherein nature constitutes the woof to society's warp and where amid the humor and pathos of everyday life there is no room for winter. It is they, and then every subsequent generation of Poles, who bore out Niemcewicz's contention that in *Pan Tadeusz* "the Polish nation would never die."[73]

Curiously, though, Mickiewicz himself expressed ambivalence toward his own creation, even echoing, to some extent, the objections of his contemporaries. To be sure, the work afforded him "immeasurable pleasure," salving his intense longing for home and at the same time allowing him to block out the realities of émigré life. And in the unfinished epilogue to *Pan Tadeusz*, written when the poem was already at the printers, he even expressed the hope that "these simple books" would "one day find their way beneath thatched roofs," where

> A steward dozing at the table
> Or the manager or even the master himself
> Would not forbid them to be read
> And would himself deign to listen, explaining
> The more difficult lines to those who are younger,
> Praising their beauty and excusing their faults.
> (Dz. 4:386–87)

Yet if Zaleski is to be believed, the poet agreed with his friends' misgivings that, among other things, the "provincial gentry's quarrels" "lowered the atmosphere of a serious epic somewhat." "Ha!" Mickiewicz supposedly replied, "I should raise the mood of the entire poem by a half tone or so." As he wrote to Odyniec upon completing *Pan Tadeusz:*

> It seems to me that never again will I use my pen for such trifles. Only that work is worth anything which can improve man and from which he can learn wisdom. Maybe I would have even neglected *Tadeusz*, but I was closing in on the end.

*The term is Alina Witkowska's, *Mickiewicz*, 186.

"I almost didn't finish it," the poet added, "because my spirit was being drawn elsewhere, to new parts of *Forefathers' Eve*." Indeed, it was *Forefather's Eve* that he "wanted to make the only work of [his] worth reading, if only God would allow [him] to complete it." He did not, nor, for that matter, did he allow Mickiewicz to "rectify" the ostensible shortcomings of his gentry tale in some "son of *Tadeusz*." *Pan Tadeusz* was in fact the last major work of poetry Mickiewicz would write.[74]

Mickiewicz had always produced in bursts, with periods of intense creative activity followed by lulls. But neither the three years in Kowno that resulted in the first two volumes of *Poems* nor the explosion of poetry and improvisation in Russia can compare with the extraordinary eruption that began in Dresden in April 1832. Within the space of little more than two years, Mickiewicz wrote—was writing almost simultaneously—*Forefathers' Eve*, part 3, *The Books of the Polish Nation and Pilgrimage*, and *Pan Tadeusz*, to say nothing of the unfinished "History of the Future," over a dozen shorter poems and fables, as well as a slew of articles for *Pielgrzym Polski*. Yet the lull that followed, commensurate, perhaps, with the intensity of the eruption, would be not so much longer, as qualitatively different. A series of wrenching transformations—from Gustaw to Konrad to Robak—marked by an increasingly more radical effacement of the poet *qua* poet for the sake of his collective, had, it seems, run its course. There would be more metamorphoses, no less dramatic and no less consequential, but they would no longer be enacted symbolically, in and as poetry.

12

Sometime at the beginning of May 1834, Zaleski moved out again to outlying Sèvres. Unable to bear the thought of spending the summer in Paris, Mickiewicz decided to join him, even though the second volume of *Pan Tadeusz* was not yet ready. Taking the proofs with him, the poet rented an apartment in Bellevue not far from Zaleski. The spring that year was "unusually beautiful, almost continually fair, warm, aromatic." Mickiewicz "would make trips beyond Sèvres every day" in the company of his friend, "wandering through the forests . . . all the way to Saint-Germain," his pockets crammed with proofs, which he liked to correct "lying on the grass with pencil in hand." Yet despite his distaste for the task, correcting proofs now became "a kind of *contre-coup* against violent attacks of spleen."[75]

As Mickiewicz wrote to Kajsiewicz a few weeks later, those "spring months went by very sadly for me. I often suffered from the spleen and had my fill of various personal misfortunes." Surely completing *Pan Tadeusz*—his child, as he so often referred to it, one he had borne for over two years—had something to do with his depression, but so too did frustration with his inability to restart *Forefathers' Eve*. The flow that had kept the poet energized since Dresden had dissipated, leaving him enervated and apathetic. Not surprisingly, a meeting and then dinner with Balzac had left him unimpressed. "A great man once," he confided to Jełowicki, "an author on whom for a time great hopes were

Fig. 16 Bust of Mickiewicz by David d'Angers, 1834. Courtesy of the Adam Mickiewicz Museum of Literature, Warsaw.

pinned, . . . a pretty clever writer, but a weak mind, without a great idea, without new conceptions," and certainly far inferior to both Hugo and Sainte-Beuve. Whether he had actually read anything by this "small, dark, well-fed man," and the lover of Sobańska's sister, is another matter.[76]

That Mickiewicz found himself without an immediate source of income that spring only compounded a growing sense of resentment. Somehow he had managed to go through both the advance and the payment he had received from Jełowicki for *Pan Tadeusz* and had become, as Zaleski euphemistically put it, "something of [the publisher's] ward." When his cousin Łucjan Stypułkowski settled in Havre after internment in Prussia, the poet was forced to "move heaven and earth in order to get him 100 francs." By June, Jełowicki was refusing to extend any further credit, and Mickiewicz found himself "in great poverty," although even now he managed to scrape up another 30 francs for his cousin. One last hope was money that Odyniec had been collecting for him in Dresden, residuals from the 1832 Poznań and Warsaw editions, now some several thousand francs. As it would happen, however, the person entrusted with the sum apparently gambled it all away on his way to Paris, leaving Mickiewicz with nothing.[77]

For the moment, the poet could rely on the generosity of his friends. During the two months in Bellevue, he boarded regularly at Zaleski's hotel and was, in any case, always a welcome guest among the Polonia living in the suburbs. In early June, Niemcewicz invited him to Montmorency, where the elderly writer had made a home for himself after two years in England. The four-day visit, spent over traditional Polish food, afternoon tea with other veterans of the liberation struggle, games of whist, and long conversations, was a pleasant distraction. But it was also an opportunity for Mickiewicz to come to know a man whom he respected immensely for his long, selfless service to the Polish cause, and whose experiences in the service of that cause were a source of innumerable anecdotes. Solicitous, generous, with a genuine appreciation for the talent of a writer some forty years his junior, Niemcewicz was gradually coming to assume the role of a kindly father figure, replacing, as such, the ascetic, demanding, and often inconsiderate Lelewel.

But there was in Bellevue yet another welcoming home, where Mickiewicz appears to have found a different form of distraction. He had settled that summer not far from Princess Karolina Giedroyć, an aristocrat from Lithuania who was living in Bellevue with her two daughters, Karolina Białopiotrowicz and Łucja Rautenstrauch. Of the same age as Mickiewicz, Princess Łucja had a rather remarkable past. As a child, she had been introduced to Napoleon and together with her sister had for a time been attached to the court of Empress Josephine. The first woman to attend courses on literature at the University of Warsaw, Rautenstrauch soon began writing herself, mostly romances, and thanks in part to her translation of Madame de Staël's *Corinne*, was soon herself tagged with the moniker—the third in a series of "Corinnes" in Mickiewicz's ambit. Upon separating from her physically as well as politically loathsome husband, she settled for a time in

Paris, intent on continuing her literary career. Whatever the nature of their bond—and Rautenstrauch was said to have nurtured "a closer, more powerful relationship with Mickiewicz, in which people even recognized the kernel of feelings more ardent than those of friendship"—the two saw much of each other that summer. His eyes haunted her:

> It is sometimes impossible to walk past his gaze indifferently; when he let's that glance fall on you with all its sharpness, you can be sure that you'll feel pierced to the quick. Sometimes it wanders mistily... you then see in him the entire depth of Beethoven's unbounded compositions... the melody of Chopin's fantastic improvisations... at other times it seems to rend the celestial vaults, foretell the ages, fathom the future, comprehend it. One sees then in those eyes that the earth has disappeared from before them.

Some years later, after settling for a time in Dresden and then Cracow, she asked Mickiewicz for at least a simulacrum of those eyes in the person of any one of the poet's children, whom she repeatedly offered to take under her wing.[78]

In the middle of June, Mickiewicz set out for Paris to pay his regards to Klaudyna Potocka, who had come to the city for a brief visit. Waiting for him there too was a letter from Odyniec informing the poet that Celina Szymanowska had just passed through Dresden on her way to Paris. A few days later, a "badly dressed" Celina alit from her carriage in Paris, "breathless, covered with dust from the voyage"—and eager to renew her acquaintance with the man she had come to France to marry.[79]

CHAPTER SEVEN

DOMESTICITY (1834–1839)

In the late fall of 1833, Mickiewicz received a visit from his old Petersburg acquaintance Dr. Stanisław Morawski. Besides precious news of mutual friends in Russia—Malewski settling in with his new wife Helena Szymanowska; Pietraszkiewicz exiled to Tobolsk; Zan still in Orenburg; Czeczot languishing in poverty in Tver—Morawski brought Mickiewicz a proposition, hatched, it seems, together with Helena Szymanowska. The proposition was simple: would Mickiewicz consider marrying her sister Celina. As far as the poet was concerned at the time, or so he assured Odyniec, the whole thing was less than serious and he responded in kind, with "a few words said in jest." Morawski, however, appears to have understood those words in earnest, hence on his part as an opportunity to "join two inseparable friends from school even more closely through bonds of kinship." On his return to St. Petersburg at the beginning of March, he set to matchmaking. In a diary entry of 7/19 March 1834, Helena recorded that Celina "assented" to the proposition. But her observation that she did so "with joy" was something of a misunderstanding.[1]

I

With the unexpected death of Maria Szymanowska in 1831, that special world of artistic celebrity in which Celina and Helena had been reared, with its postconcert receptions, daily visits from eminent admirers, brilliant salons, and entertainments, soon evaporated, together with the income. To be sure, the home away from Polish hearth that their mother had managed to establish in St. Petersburg continued to draw the city's expatriates, but even this began to dissipate. Helena adjusted quickly, finding comfort and stability in her relationship with Malewski. Her younger sister was not as fortunate. Shortly after Maria's death, and just as Helena was settling into her role as a happy new wife, the twenty-year-old

Fig. 17 Celina Mickiewicz née Szymanowska. Daguerreotype, ca. 1840. Courtesy of the Adam Mickiewicz Museum of Literature, Warsaw.

Celina was dealt another blow: the young man to whom she had been engaged for over a year had a change of heart. For the introverted, mercurial, and headstrong young woman, the rejection simply hastened a slide from mourning into melancholia.

Abandoned by the three people she loved most, Celina decided to return to Warsaw, to her father. Józef Szymanowski had remarried, and relations between stepmother and stepdaughter were immediately strained, which served only to exacerbate what Celina described as her "darkness." "I am unable to get used to the happiness of so many people," she wrote to her sister in the spring of 1832. "Everyone appears to love me and is very kind, but even this bothers me; I [always] think they're making fun of me, since I no longer believe anyone." Rather than live with her father's family, she chose to stay with a relative, where she had "a room upstairs and permission not to ever have to go downstairs." As she confessed to Helena, "I am indifferent to everything, I'd like this lethargy to last as long as possible . . . I'm like a clock which people wind regularly." But just as she was getting accustomed to life in the new environment that summer, her father died.[2]

Orphaned, without resources, and with the prospect of old maidenhood looming, Celina moved in with her maternal grandparents, feeling as if she "were a weight to *[her]self* and to others." "I'd be better off with our Parents," she confided ominously to her sister in October, "even if this means being in the other world." Plans to return to St. Petersburg, which in any case would have meant the unbearable sight of more family happiness and more well-meaning but ineffectual solicitude, came to naught. For the next year and a half, Celina vegetated, living off the kindness of her grandparents and tending her younger half-siblings, for whom, as children, she showed little affection. When Helena and Dr. Morawski laid out their plan in March 1834, she acquiesced without giving it much thought, unable to grasp in her apathy, or simply incapable of appreciating, all of the implications of tying her fate to Poland's beloved, but also a penniless émigré. What she imagined was not, perhaps, so much the celebrity that the match might promise, but rather a return to a prelapsarian world defined by celebrity.[3]

Celina had had no particular attachment to Mickiewicz. Their relationship, such as there could have been between a fractious teenager and a man twice her age but unfolding over the course of some two years of almost daily contact and with the awareness that

Mickiewicz was one of her mother's dearest friends, had been marked by playful tension, by arguments and admonitions. It was in one of her snits, when, despite everyone's cajoling, Celina refused to go to the theater with her mother's St. Petersburg crowd on the eve of Mickiewicz's departure, that she last saw the poet. And as much as she made a show of despair at the news of his unexpected embarkation, "wailing until blood came gushing out her nose," her farewell note was detached and somewhat recherché: she thanked Mickiewicz for his "good advice," wished him happy trails, and then dropped a "*larme d'une repente*" on the paper for her tantrum the night before. A few months later, she was engaged to the man who would eventually jilt her.[4]

For Mickiewicz, Celina had been little more than a child, "a beautiful" one, to be sure, but something of an "oddball"—beautiful in a dark "Hispanic" sort of way, odd in her moodiness, willfulness, and propensity for melancholy. If in St. Petersburg he at times played the role of substitute father, always trying to talk sense into the girl—"the truth," as her mother put it—the poet nonetheless showed little patience with the girl's behavior. It was he who, on the night of her refusal to go to the theater, finally put a stop to the game: "Fine, better that you don't go if you're going to put up such a fuss." How telling, in this respect, that the only poem Mickiewicz ever addressed to Celina, a clever bit of album verse written, perhaps, in 1827, is constructed around a military conceit:

> The recruitment begins, I see in the distance
> A huge throng of uhlans, hussars, and soldiers;
> Bearing their names like banners unfurled,
> Hoping to lay down an entire camp of various arms in this album.
> So it will come to pass—by then a graying hero I'll be
> And reflecting on the prime of my life with regret,
> I'll recount to my friends that there on the army's right flank
> I was the first grenadier. (Dz. 1:184)

As he traveled in Europe, the poet would occasionally inquire about the "little girl" in letters to Maria, pleased to "hear that she was being less erratic," curious whether "she was already married," and even "reserving for [himself] [the right] to stand as godfather to her son." But these inquiries were little more than addenda to a correspondence concerned above all with the well-being of the mother. With his friend's death, they ceased, uprising and emigration notwithstanding.[5]

What, then, could have impelled Mickiewicz to marry Celina Szymanowska? Answering this question is far more difficult than assessing the consequences of the decision, which proved fateful in ways that neither of them could even have begun to imagine. "Love," of course, had little to do with it; Mickiewicz, as one acquaintance observed, simply "allowed himself, as was his wont, to be led to the altar." He himself was not altogether able to articulate his reasoning, much less the chain of events, behind his decision. To his brother he explained that Celina

> was the daughter of an artist who had died in Petersburg. I knew her when she was a child in her mother's home. She grew up, lost her parents, and summoned by me, she came to share my uncertain fate. I was sad this entire last year; illness, then some sort of nostalgia and spleen constantly preyed on me. I was looking for comfort in domestic bliss.

To which he added, inscrutably, "for as long as one can live at home." A few days earlier, Mickiewicz spelled it out somewhat differently—and disingenuously—to Kajsiewicz:

> Celina Szymanowska is the daughter of a famous artist. I liked her once as a kind, lively, and happy child. We parted, not foreseeing or intuiting that we will meet again one day. Celina lost her parents, my marriage to another person [i.e., Ankwicz] did not come to pass. We recalled our old, long acquaintance—she came to me and we immediately went to the altar.

The letters to Franciszek and Kajsiewicz were both written several days after the wedding. Both read as attempts to create, *post facto*, a coherent narrative of the events leading up to his decision, and as all such narratives go, as much for one's own sake as for that of others. It is telling, then, that in both instances Mickiewicz insisted on introducing Celina as Maria's daughter.[6]

Two weeks before the wedding, however—that is, four days after Celina's arrival in Paris—writing to a person with whom he could often be open, if not necessarily frank, Mickiewicz had not yet had an opportunity to take full stock of his predicament. "I'm marrying Celina," the poet informed Odyniec on 2 July, still "amazed," though, at what he called her "scatter-brained arrival." "I wanted to send her away with nothing," he went on,

> but Celina confused me with her good comportment, declaring that she'll take her stuff and return, with no ill will toward me. The thought of putting her through all this trouble made me feel bad. In any case, I like her. And I could go on about how melancholy I've been these days and how the weight of life has been suffocating me.

If what stopped Mickiewicz from sending Celina away was indeed a sense of at once reproach and compassion, the poet's gesture was, by its very nature, narcissistically cruel, allowing him as it did to displace his own "melancholy" onto someone ostensibly more miserable—and weaker—than he. Years later, he confided "that he married Celina because, . . . having been jilted . . . , she was an unfortunate orphan, and that he had known her to be happy when she was with her mother." But then this was long after Celina's mental breakdown, when compassion was about the only emotion that Mickiewicz was capable of extending.[7]

2

The courtship was brief. Although their first moments together were awkward, Mickiewicz began spending his evenings at the Wołowskis, Franciszek and Tekla, relatives of Celina with whom she had been staying since her arrival in Paris. Some three days after the poet's first visit, Celina informed her sister that "within three or at most four weeks she would be Adam's wife." Shortly thereafter, she received legal permission from her grandparents in Warsaw to "contract matrimony according to [her] own choice," together with their blessing. As the day of their wedding approached, Mickiewicz decided to make "a sincere confession of [his] entire life to [Celina] and appealed to her for similar frankness." What this may have consisted of remains a mystery.[8]

The wedding was set for 22 July, which also happened to be Celina's twenty-second birthday. Family and friends were to meet first at Mickiewicz's new apartment on rue de la Pépinière, whence they would all repair to the Wołowskis on rue de Richelieu and then to the Church of St. Louis d'Antin, near the Opera, for the ceremony. Mickiewicz had left his house early that morning; by the time he returned home to get dressed for the wedding, everyone had already left, and there was no one to answer the door. In a panic, the poet ran to the apartment of his friend Eustachy Januszkiewicz, who himself was getting dressed for the wedding, borrowed his "tuxedo, vest, and white ascot and drove off to the Wołowskis." Mickiewicz had forgotten that he had had the key to his apartment all along.[9]

The ceremony was modest, conducted by a Polish priest and witnessed by the Wołowskis, Julian Ursyn Niemcewicz, Aleksander Jełowicki, and Ignacy Domeyko. As Mickiewicz gazed at his bride covered "from head to foot in a long white veil" and holding "a beautiful bouquet of white orange blossoms," he was suddenly reminded of his dream in St. Petersburg, instruments of torture and all. Unnerved by the uncanny, he asked Celina to immediately uncover herself.[10]

The newlyweds, together with a small group of acquaintances, were treated to "a truly Polish dinner at the Wołowskis." The bride was "beautiful, tall, with marvelous eyes"; the groom seemed happy and content. "What joins them together," wrote Jełowicki a few days later, "is true love, a love that is constant and strong. Neither is wealthy, but they will be happy!" At the reception, the two shared "a ducat each, some bread, and sugar," traditional symbols of future good fortune.[11]

Yet amid the good cheer there was whispering. Celina was, after all, "of Israelite origins, and Mickiewicz, a Lithuanian from across the Niemen River," which, as Niemcewicz somewhat spitefully noted, immediately inspired an appropriate epigram at the dinner:

> "By some miracle unheard of
> The Niemen met the river Jordan"

That Celina was Jewish certainly did not endear her to the Polish émigré community. Few were as blunt as Krasiński, who a month after the wedding complained to one of his correspondents that "those Jews always have to appropriate everything for themselves in Poland." Most were content with using code, which, in any case, was no less malicious. As "befit her kind," Celina was "a sly one, cheeky, . . . pushing her way in everywhere and insinuating herself everywhere." And though neither she nor Mickiewicz had anything to live on, she at least had "the protection of her class, which, content that it had come into possession of the poet, will not let him languish in poverty and will support him."[12]

None of this, of course, would have mattered had Celina Szymanowska married just any poet. Her husband, though, happened to be Poland's greatest living voice, a spiritual leader of the nation in exile, its *common* good. In this respect, Celina's Jewishness only exacerbated the perception that she had "appropriated"—"as befit her kind"—this common good for herself. As one émigré expressed it succinctly, "Public opinion . . . disapproves of Mickiewicz's idea of entering into matrimony."[13]

Indeed, less than a month into the marriage, Klementyna Tańska-Hoffmanowa, one of the more percipient chroniclers of Polish émigré life, observed:

> This is not the wife for Mickiewicz. . . . There is something unnatural about her. . . . I don't augur them much happiness. . . . That there's reason to worry that poor Mickiewicz might, besides a laurel wreath, be wearing a wreath of a different kind is evident from the fact that . . . in the morning one can find her at home dirty, unkempt—but as soon as she goes out in public, out come the ribbons, gewgaws, and countless ringlets. Besides all this, there's sure to be poverty; she's the purser, he doesn't inquire about anything and says that he got married so as to not have to worry about anything.

Even a lark—at Mickiewicz's urging, Celina put on a man's hat (à la George Sand) to match her black dress—"upset the emigration . . . finishing off [the newlywed pair] in the opinion of the public." Celina was in a no-win situation.[14]

But "the big question, an issue national in scope, concern[ed] the impact that this marriage would have on the great poet's writing." No one was more eager for an answer than the man who posed it. After all, Jełowicki's livelihood as a publisher in good part depended on a happily productive Mickiewicz. It was, nonetheless, a question that haunted everyone. As another observer remarked, "By assuming the narrow chores associated with the responsibilities of a father of a family, [the poet] puts a stop to his vivid imagination, the world of dreams comes to an end, *il faudra descendre à la réalité qui tue la poésie.*" Of course, the longer Mickiewicz remained silent, the more his marriage to Celina was charged.[15]

Whatever the verdict—and not all of the gossip was negative—Adam Mickiewicz's decision to take Celina Szymanowska for his wife became one of the most talked about events in the émigré community, "interrupting," as Mickiewicz himself noted wryly, "the political discussions in Paris for a few days."[16]

3

Mickiewicz did not, it seems, take too much to heart the ado his decision occasioned. A few weeks after the wedding, he could write to his brother that "Celina [was] the wife [he'd] been looking for, brave in the face of all privations, with modest demands, always gay." To Odyniec he confided that during that time "not once had [he] been in a sour mood and often felt gay and frivolous," something he "had not been for a long time." And as far as he could tell, Celina too was "completely happy and glad like a child." Indeed, as she herself informed her sister, "I can now assure you . . . that I have at last found the happiness that I dreamed of, Adam means the world to me, I care about nothing else."[17]

The apartment Mickiewicz had rented for them (with the Wołowskis' help) on rue de la Pépinière was, in 1834, "practically on the outskirts" of Paris and hence affordable. It was on the first floor, "with a garden," "three rooms and their own furniture" (although visitors did not fail to notice that the poet did "not have a room of his own"), and, of course, a piano, if only a borrowed one. Celina, however, immediately came to "regret" never having learned the basics of homemaking from her blind aunt and, at least in the beginning, found the task difficult, particularly in the kitchen—Mickiewicz apparently did not like French cooking. The poet joked that, after making coffee in the morning, Celina "pretends to do housework, putters around, chirps, and laughs till evening." Tańska-Hoffmanowa was a bit more caustic:

> She's so ignorant of housekeeping that when her husband once told her that he'd like to eat kasha—she bought Tartarian buckwheat, told the cook to boil it in a pot, and vigorously to boot—and was mightily surprised that what resulted was not kasha.

Celina, for her part, complained of "not being satisfied with the help" as well as the high cost of everything.[18]

Yet despite initial missteps and perhaps none too eagerly, Celina nevertheless seemed willing to at least make an effort at building a home for the man who "meant the world" to her. Not so her new husband, who appeared in no hurry to change his old ways and habits. "In the evenings," Mickiewicz wrote to Odyniec some three weeks into the marriage,

> the same old crew, Domeyko, Zan, and a few others. . . . But my acquaintances have not completely gotten used to my new piece of furniture and are a bit embarrassed. Slowly, however, I'll return to my old way of life and begin doing something.

But if Mickiewicz expected Celina to play the role of a traditional wife, a mute ornament ready to please with a bowl of hot Polish food for himself and his pals, he miscalculated. Celina, after all, had been brought up spoiled by celebrity and was accustomed to getting her way. And she certainly remembered that Mickiewicz himself had once been a satellite of her mother's—and, by extension, her own—special world. In the end, as Tańska-Hoffmanowa observed,

> both parties lack delicacy, he talks to her as if to a servant and she, it sometimes seems, deems it a personal victory that such a genius should serve her—Take off my shoes! Get out! What business is it of yours! which one can hear her saying to her husband on visits—whereas at home he shouts: Fill my pipe! bring in the wood, and so forth.

Potentially more troublesome, however, was Celina's labile sense of self, which made her at once capricious and defensive, bound to resent any patronizing exertion of authority on the part of her mate, much less expressions of condescension. There was some truth to the opinion "that she was not at all made for him, and that he will not be happy with her."[19]

And indeed, all was not sweetness and light, particularly when it came to money. After the fellow had run off with Mickiewicz's residuals, the poet was effectively penniless. Celina was not much better off—some jewels, a trousseau as well as part ownership of a townhouse in Warsaw—but unlike her husband, she was accustomed to certain luxuries, which she now realized, reluctantly, that she would have to forgo. For the first year or so they managed somehow, living "as modestly and frugally as possible," "very rarely going out," and depending on the generosity of others to go to the theater. There was the occasional ruble from the sale of Celina's things in St. Petersburg and then some money after her grandmother's death in Warsaw. But by the spring of 1835, they were forced to let their servant go, and Celina had to "take care of both the house and kitchen by herself." Yet neither seemed overly concerned. When at one point Januszkiewicz asked about the state of their affairs, Mickiewicz

> answered . . . that Plato . . . maintained that nothing kills the soul more than thinking about tomorrow, then, in the words of the Gospel, told me to consider the birds of the air, etc. His venerable Celina is another Adam, pretty but, like him, pretty disorganized, caring little about what will happen in two, three months.

With the birth of their first child, the Mickiewiczes' financial situation grew markedly worse, even desperate.[20]

Maria (named after Celina's mother, although some could not resist making other connections) was born without any difficulties on 7 September 1835. Mickiewicz was overjoyed, marveling at "the collection of charms, virtues, qualities, and merits in the child" (soon, however, he was complaining that Maria, or Marynia or Misia, as she was called, was "good-humored" but "with few brains"). Celina, for her part, complained that "her nose didn't come out too well, although perhaps its outlines indicate that it'll be charming one day." For both, however, the child was an expense that was becoming increasingly more difficult to bear, and they "did not have a penny of steady income nor [did they] expect any." Unable to afford a nursemaid, Celina was forced to breast-feed Misia herself and often depended on neighbors and friends for help with the child. She had, by then, "sold many of her things"; a few months after Maria's birth she pawned most of her jewelry. Mickiewicz trawled acquaintances for outstanding debts, not always, of course, successfully. Although that winter his brother Aleksander, now a professor in Kiev, sent him—at great risk to himself—1,000 złotys, even the apartment on rue de la Pépinière finally proved unaffordable. Taking advantage of David d'Anger's offer, they moved into his temporarily vacated house in Domont, some sixteen kilometers north of Paris. As Niemcewicz noted after a visit from Celina, "The poor woman eats her heart out about her husband's predicament—one of our leading poets, and now in utter indigence."[21]

As Maria's godfather, Niemcewicz felt he had a particular responsibility toward the Mickiewiczes and, despite his own limited resources, did as much as he could to secure aid for the poet's family. In this, however, he was not alone. Prince Czartoryski importuned two successive French ministers of the interior for over a year until in the summer of 1837 the government finally agreed to dole out to the poet "a monthly stipend of 80 francs and a one-time payment of 1,000"—not, however, "as an émigré, but out of a fund for the support of *gens des lettres*."[22]

The efforts of Mickiewicz's friends in this regard were no less energetic, albeit always discreet and always behind his back so as not to ruffle his pride. As Jełowicki explained it to an addressee in Poland:

> Our poet is in a very difficult situation and it would be a desirable thing if wealthier people gave some thought to a way they could come to his aid, but you must realize . . . that he is extremely proud and that one has to be as delicate as possible with him. One would have to, for instance, offer him a certain sum for his works or manuscripts, and this could best be done through me [as his publisher].

But to Jełowicki's somewhat indignant disappointment, the landowners of Volhynia were unforthcoming. Mickiewicz's other publisher, however, Januszkiewicz, had better luck. His almost identical appeal to the conscience of fellow Poles succeeded not only in collecting over 500 francs (which he turned over to the poet under the pretext that the sum "was what was left over from publishing *Pielgrzym*"), but also in finding a "buyer," at 3,000 francs, for the manuscript of *Pan Tadeusz* (which actually remained in the hands of Stefan Zan, who was to return it to Mickiewicz at some later date). For his part, Bohdan Zaleski managed to pass on a bit of money from an anonymous donor in Poland. Amid this outpouring of generosity, all of it, as it happened, from ladies, it was perhaps inevitable that Łubieńska too should try to help the man she loved. But her efforts at discretion were, perhaps intentionally, inept. As Mickiewicz informed Odyniec:

> Mrs. Ł. wrote to me about some sort of remittance. A while back I received 250 fr. from a banker, together with a note signed *Adam* and a declaration that it is an old debt. . . . Without looking at the handwriting, I thought that [someone else] had sent it. Imagine my surprise when I now see from Mrs. Ł.'s card where this sum came from. If I get more remittances of this kind, I will not accept them. Please explain to Mrs. Ł. what an awkward situation she puts me in.

Łubieńska was chastened, but only briefly.[23]

4

What made matters worse, one, as it were, knotting the other, was Mickiewicz's inability—or, more accurately, lack of desire—to write. As he complained to Odyniec a few weeks after the wedding, "I idled all this time away and just made the most of life." His assurance, however, that he would "return to [his] old way of life and begin doing something" proved frustratingly difficult to live up to. Producing even an article for an émigré newspaper became a chore, dragged out over several months. "It's hard going," Mickiewicz conceded to the editor in September 1834, "I'm not in the mood for writing. . . . You'll have to wait." The editor was still waiting in January—for a piece that ultimately remained unwritten. With time, his friends began to despair, lamenting that "besides his poetic talent, he has such a varied store of knowledge, which he could put to use as a writer for the great and much desired benefit of his countrymen; but alas, to remind him of this is like talking to a wall." As one observer put it sanguinely shortly after Maria's birth, "Mickiewicz produced a work—his daughter."[24]

Invariably, the poet blamed the noise and bustle of Paris, where, "as in a roadside inn, it is difficult to find a quiet corner and every day some new racket distracts one's thoughts." Celina, however, saw it differently. Shortly before they were forced to abandon their apartment in the city, she confided to Januszkiewicz that it was their financial situation "that worried Adam, made him anxious, incapable of getting down to work," that "he didn't finish works that he'd started. . . ." Yet when an admiring countryman from Poznań naïvely offered the poet 1,000 francs to compose a ballad on a subject he himself suggested, Mickiewicz indignantly refused. This "was not a poetic time for" him.[25]

To be sure, the poet continued—tried—to write. He attempted to resuscitate something he had begun in 1832, a French-language piece in prose entitled "A History of the Future"—new revolutions in France, the capture of Berlin by republican armies from Ukraine, the execution of the Prussian king, the proclamation of a European commonwealth—which Januszkiewicz was already planning to publish in the summer of 1835. For a second time, though, Mickiewicz abandoned this exercise in futurology and turned, instead, to refiguring the past. Since at least 1833, the Literary Society had been encouraging him to write a history of Poland. He now set about this project with his usual—Philomath—energy, doing extensive research and managing even to produce sizable chunks of text, although he remained stuck in the earliest period. But he realized, soon enough, that he was "in over his head," "sure," as he put it, "that I will once again publish something unfinished, as I've been doing all of my life." He "slogged on," however, laboring over the history for several years, despite "constantly . . . encountering new difficulties, in which it was [getting] harder to get at the truth."[26]

That Mickiewicz never did complete his history was to some degree conditioned by his growing realization of what it meant to be an émigré writer, that "his talent," as Jełowicki explained, "although colossal, [could] not be profitable until there [was] freedom of the press in our country." It began dawning on the poet that if any money were to be made, it would have to be in the French-language market, and not only through translations of his works. He waded in reluctantly, however, prodded, at first, by Spazier, who in 1835 managed to convince him to write a piece on modern religious painting in Germany (*Dz.* 5:274–82), which he published in his *Revue du Nord*. That same year, and in the same *Revue du Nord*, Mickiewicz published yet another piece, a short story of the 1830 uprising entitled "A Draftee's Honeymoon: A Fragment from the Memoirs of a Polish Sergeant (*Dz.* 5:248–58/*MP* 1:133–47). In both instances Mickiewicz had asked for anonymity, but as Spazier went ahead and printed the poet's name anyhow, Mickiewicz broke off his collaboration. Jański too sought to help his friend by having him commissioned to write entries for the *Encyclopédie Catholique*. After producing one article, though, on St. Adalbert (*Dz.* 7:149–59), he gave up here as well.[27]

In the fall of 1836, thanks to Chopin and his friend Franz Liszt, Mickiewicz received an invitation to the salon of Marie d'Agoult. The countess had just left her husband and two children for the Hungarian composer and moved into the Hôtel de France, where she shared a parlor with George Sand, that other notoriously liberated woman of the day who was herself about to become the lover of an East European composer. Both Sand and the hostess immediately took a liking to Poland's incarnation of Byron. Shortly afterward, this time at an evening at Chopin's, Sand suggested to Mickiewicz that he might try his hand at writing a drama in French. Whether it was the suggestion itself, the woman making it, or simply to "satisfy [his] basic needs," the idea energized the poet. For the first time in months he "found the desire to [write] again." By the end of the year, a clearly buoyed

Mickiewicz informed Odyniec, "I'm writing a work in French now; if it succeeds and the public likes it (it's already finished), it may improve our finances; I have another similar little piece on the burner if the first one does well."[28]

That first work was indeed a drama, entitled *The Confederates of Bar* (Dz. 3:347–416/ MP 1: 17–85).* Hoping (somewhat belatedly now) to tap into the French vogue for things Polish, Mickiewicz based it on events leading up to the first partition of Poland in 1772, larding it liberally with expressions of Franco-Polish amity and attempting to cater to the theatrical tastes of a Parisian audience by playing up the stage effects as well as the Slavic exotica. For all this, however, the play is imbued with Mickiewicz's romantic self: the Ukrainian setting brought back memories of the southern steppe, and with them of Sobańska, Witt, and Boshniak, whom the poet now refigured in the play's principle characters. Mickiewicz was now ready to "see whether [he] could make more off of French literature than off of [Polish]."[29]

The reaction to the play among its first French readers was lukewarm. "Apart from a worthy study of character and the historical color," one of them reportedly observed, "there was a certain lack of dramatic energy," a sentiment echoed by Félicien Mallefille, the tutor of Sand's children, who "found in it beautiful emotions and thoughts, but completely lacking in action, interest, and dramatic edge, as the French understand it." But Sand seemed to gush over what d'Agoult called "the precious manuscript." Her compliments, however, were subtly left-handed:

> In those sections where style dominates action, it seemed to me as beautiful as that of the best old writers in our language. In those sections where, of necessity, action dominates style . . . the style seemed to me what it should be, but somewhat choppy. . . . Perhaps . . . the characters should be shown with less hesitation and reticence. The spirit of our language does not put up with such abstemiousness to so great a degree, and although our modern playwrights are unstinting in this regard, our old and illustrious masters, who are the ancestors *through kinship* of your genius, are very frugal with it. . . . I can only say that if the beautiful, the great, and the powerful must be crowned, your work will be so.

Whether, as Mallefille believed, it was "out of politeness, rather, than sincerity," or whether she genuinely sensed something inaccessible to others, or, for that matter, whether it was because she was all too aware that the well-being of the Polish poet and his family in part depended on it, Sand nevertheless felt that the play was worth promoting. No less subtly, though, she also prepared Mickiewicz for disappointment. "The French public," she warned, "is so basely ignorant these days . . . that . . . it is capable of booing even a play by Shakespeare were it to be presented under another name."[30]

*Only the first two acts of *Les Confédérés de Bar* are extant.

Mickiewicz, for his part, was almost obsequiously grateful—a sentiment he would have never indulged had the praise come from one of his own—and inordinately flattered (somehow the letter of this "most exceptionally talented of women writers" even managed to make it into a Poznań periodical). "My work," he wrote to Sand upon receiving the manuscript with her corrections "has now become precious to me thanks to your notes." But then too, these "honorary tracks of adorable talons" could be potentially precious in other ways. However qualified, the imprimatur of France's most popular writer was a powerful recommendation.[31]

At the urging of David d'Angers, Mickiewicz had turned earlier to Alfred de Vigny, fresh off his success with the play *Chatterton*, asking the French writer whether he thought *Confederates* was "viable." But beyond offering "some serious observations" and vague promises, de Vigny had done nothing. Sand's reaction, however, forced de Vigny to reconsider, and he now approached the director of the Théâtre de la Porte Saint-Martin with the Polish poet's play as well as with a letter from Sand. D'Agoult, for her part, took it upon herself to intercede on Mickiewicz's behalf with Pierre Bocage, Hugo's favorite actor. Neither initiative succeeded. D'Agoult was met with an uncomprehending "Miss quoi?" And although de Vigny managed to get Mickiewicz an interview at Porte Saint-Martin, "it produced no result." The director, the poet informed de Vigny,

> had no time to listen to my reading, he asked me for the manuscript so that he could read it at his leisure. M. de Vigny's recommendation, he said, is of imm-im-mense importance!...He added...that Mme. Sand's approbation is of great weight!...great weight!...In order, then, to appreciate a work so highly and deeply recommended, [he] has to collect himself, meditate in solitude, in the silence of the night, far from visitors, from intruders, etc., etc.

The Confederates of Bar ended up being rejected, its manuscript left to languish—and partially vanish—in some Parisian director's office. It was with no great regrets, though, that Mickiewicz abandoned his in any case half-hearted foray on the French stage—he never even bothered finishing the other "little piece" he had mentioned to Odyniec, a play also drawn from the history of Polish uprisings entitled *Jakub Jasiński, or the Two Polands* (Dz. 3:417–37/*MP* 1:88–108*).[32]

For all their frustrations and disappointments, Mickiewicz's adventures in the world of French letters nonetheless served only to magnify the affection as well as solicitude of his French friends. Sand, for one, always quick to recognize talent when she saw it, had grown increasingly fascinated with this Polish "genius," whom she considered "equal to

*Only the first four scenes of *Jacques Jasinski ou les deux Polognes*, based on events connected with the Kościuszko uprising in Vilnius, are extant.

Byron," at the least. Indeed, in an essay she began writing in September 1837 entitled "Sur le drame fantastique," it was precisely with Byron, and with Goethe as well, that she chose to compare Mickiewicz—and she did so most favorably. Despite the "Catholic form" of *Forefathers' Eve*, part 3, which in any case she seemed to indulge on account of the poet's Polish origins as well as patriotism, Sand insisted that "there was quite a distance between [its hero Konrad's] generous and burning fervor and evangelical resignation." "Konrad," she concluded,

> is truly a man of his age and, in contrast to Faust, does not construct a pantheistic nature whose order and cold beauty console him in the absence of God. He does not consume himself like Manfred in the expectation of a mysterious revelation from God and his own being, which only death can fulfill. Konrad is no longer a man of doubt, no longer a man of despair; he is a man of life.

Sand's "huge screed on Goethe, Byron et Mickiewicz" finally appeared in *Revue des Deux Mondes* almost two years later. Among her countrymen, however, few shared her enthusiasm, much less the personal investment that engendered it.[33]

For Poles, however, Mickiewicz's foray into French literature raised other issues altogether. The news that he was "writing a *French* drama . . . for profit" aroused consternation. That poverty should "force our only literary genius" "to write in French" and thus ostensibly disrupt his work on the history of Poland was, for Tańska-Hoffmanowa, nothing short of a national disgrace. Maybe such fears were justified; but it would appear, rather, that working on the history became a convenient excuse on Mickiewicz's own part for his inability to produce anything else. When in the fall of 1835 Januszkiewicz decided to prepare an eighth volume of *Poems* (more, perhaps, out of a desire to put some change into the poet's pocket than line his own), he hoped it would consist not only of previously uncollected works, but also of something new to fill it out. Mickiewicz, however, responded, "When do I have time for poetry now; just as you have problems with formats, so now I'm sweating . . . over hordes of Pechenegs and Magyars." Yet as the publication deadline dragged out (Januszkiewicz's printers were apparently unhappy with their working conditions) and no more appropriate older works were to be found, and as Mickiewicz remained "stuck on the first chapters" of his history, the poet finally succumbed to his publisher's request for something new—or, at least, something that had not yet seen the light of day.[34]

Over the years, as Mickiewicz explored his faith, his struggle to navigate between it and "reason" had been continually guided by a kind of *lectio divina*. Not all of the masters he communed with were orthodox Catholics by any means, but all of them were spiritual seekers, in pursuit, through self-surrender and contemplation, of truths inaccessible to the rational mind. And of all of them—Pythagoras, St. Thomas à Kempis, Joseph de Maistre, Franz Baader, sundry visionaries—none "furnished" the poet with the kind of "store for extended meditation" as did Saint-Martin, Angelus Silesius, and Jakob Böhme, "that greatest of modern mystics." In the course of his readings, Mickiewicz had extracted dozens of aphorisms as indices for further contemplation. Now, in yet another effort to share his own path with a readership he felt was in sore need of spiritual guidance, the poet set about rephrasing the mystics' gnomes—often quite loosely—into a collection of 120 distichs that he entitled simply *Apothegms and Sayings from the Works of Jakob Boehme, Angelus Silesius, and Saint-Martin.*[35]

Ranging in subject from "The Purpose of Creation," "Whence Evil?" and "Egotism" to "Joy and Suffering," "History and Prophecy," "Apostleship and Philosophy," and "The Desire for Immortality," Mickiewicz's carefully considered selection had little to say about strictly theological matters or even mystical experience per se. Rather, it mapped a spiritual quest for inner strength and harmony, the attainment of which is continually threatened by the temptations of Satan, human vanity, and reason. As such, its focus was, throughout, on man's personal relationship with a God that dwells within every being:

> You look up toward the heavens but won't look into yourself;
> He who seeks in Heaven only will never find God.
> ("Where is Heaven"; *Dz.* 1:382)

But the collection also contained a number of gnomes that may be construed as a figure—or is it a justification?—for Mickiewicz's own predicament when Januszkiewicz asked the poet to produce something new for the projected volume. These addressed the virtues of silence and the relationship between locution and conduct, between, as one of them would have it, "Word and Deed":

> In words we see only intentions; in action, power;
> To pass a day well is harder than writing a tome. (*Dz.* 1:380)

Indeed, as the poet observed to Kajsiewicz shortly after completing *Pan Tadeusz:*

> We have written too much for entertainment or for ends that were too trivial. Remember, please, these words of Saint-Martin: "On ne devrait écrire des vers qu'après avoir fait un miracle." It appears to me that those times will yet return when one will have to be a saint in order to be a poet... so as to awaken in people a respect for art, which for too long has been an actress, a harlot, or a political newspaper.[36]

Apothegms and Sayings was published in the fall of 1836, together with "The Faris," two ballads written in Russia, and a few other previously uncollected poems and translations.

They appeared as the eighth volume of the Paris edition of *Poems*—the eighth and the last. Willy-nilly, Mickiewicz had made—and rationalized—his choice.

5

For that same small group of seekers who had been gathering around Mickiewicz since 1832, the publication of *Apothegms and Sayings* only affirmed the poet's spiritual authority, no less compelling, in this respect, than the masters he invoked in the title of his collection. To Mickiewicz, however, himself caught in a seemingly intractable struggle with pride, striving, as so many of the maxims in the collection would indicate, for self-effacement, the role of teacher was "frightening"—precisely because it stoked his pride. He cautioned those who would be his acolytes "not to believe blindly in any person and to judge every one of [his] words," yet at the same time he insisted on mentoring. "All outward strength depends on inner struggle and victory," he counseled Kajsiewicz and his friend Leonard Rettel in response to their (nonextant) plea for guidance,

> Like a helmsman amidst a storm, people that look inward often leap to the rudder. They gaze at the sky, move little, sometimes barely move their arm, but the fate of the vessel is in their hands.... Only do not think that in writing this I have myself in mind; I write of people whom we need, whom if we had, our vessel would not sink.

The ambivalence of the injunction notwithstanding, Mickiewicz was indeed hoping that someone else might take his place at the helm, particularly now, when the mundane concerns of money and home were proving to be a burden and his own effort at self-perfection such a struggle. For the moment, he found such a person in Bogdan Jański.[37]

On a late autumn day in 1834, when "the Catholic party," as they were commonly, and derisively, referred to, was meeting at Mickiewicz's for its weekly Bible study, the poet at one point suggested that they transform their quest for personal salvation into work for the "salvation of Poland." What was needed, he argued, was "a new order," whose mission would be "to pray daily for [them]selves, the Fatherland, and [their] neighbors, for friends as well as enemies; to fulfill the Lord's commandments through word and deed, and by example encourage [their] countrymen to do likewise." Joining Mickiewicz in founding what they provisionally called the Society of United Brethren were Gorecki, Witwicki, Cezary Plater, the two Zaleskis, Bohdan and Józef, and then Domeyko and Jański. The society was a loosely organized affair and, in any case, short-lived, but it lay the groundwork for a more consequential endeavor thanks to the fervor of the recently born-again Jański. Neither an "aristocrat," as Mickiewicz put it, of Plater's ilk, nor a "democrat" of Bohdan Zaleski's, nor "too haughty" like the poet himself, it was the introspective ex-Saint-Simonist who, with Mickiewicz's encouragement, set out—in conscious emulation of the apostles—to proselytize among the émigrés with the aim of organizing a community of brethren along more formal lines, one that in time would in fact evolve into a genuine religious order.[38]

By the end of 1835, Jański had succeeded in ministering to a number of émigrés, as a result of which several decided to enter the priesthood.* Kajsiewicz was the first, guided, like Jański before him, by Mickiewicz's spiritual mentoring. He was soon joined by Piotr Semenenko, then by Edward Duński and Józef Hube, all veterans of the uprising and disaffected democrats. Others held off with making a commitment, but were no less drawn to Jański's vision of a Polish Catholic religious order dedicated to prayer for themselves and, through prayer, to "service to the national cause" and to social justice. In early 1836, Jański felt it was time to gather this "brotherhood of national ministry" into a cloister-like commune. Thanks in part to Mickiewicz's fundraising efforts—Cezary Plater, Montalembert, and Czartoryski all contributed—Jański rented an apartment to this end on rue Notre-Dame-des-Champs, not far from the Collège Stanislas and its seminary. The poet, together with other members of the erstwhile Society of United Brethren who for various reasons could not pursue the communal life, served as a kind of board of overseers for what came to be known simply as Jański's "little home."[39]

What its earliest inhabitants sought in the home was an alternative to a shiftless émigré existence, with its internecine party strife and uncertain future. What they found was a haven ordered around a daily routine of "praying together, studying together; helping each other, serving each other by turn; reading the lives of the saints during dinner" (but also, in their spare time, *Erotika biblion*, Honoré-Gabriel de Riqueti's exploration of sex in the Bible). Mickiewicz visited occasionally, sometimes for the holidays, sometimes to pray with the brethren at nearby St. Suplice, sometimes to give advice and admonishment—vicariously experiencing a way of life that was effectively barred to him. He was not always pleased with Jański's efforts, whose apostolic zeal was matched, perhaps, only by his fiscal improvidence. Yet when all he "saw and heard everywhere" was "poverty," when so "many [émigrés] had taken their own lives," and only the strong seemed able to survive, the poet was glad that "the home [was] proving to be beneficial by its very existence, by the example it [was] setting, by the fact that it [was] a thorn in the side of the emigration, that people were talking about it and hence had to talk about religion."[40]

If Czartoryski's people were, for their own reasons, willing to lend a discrete hand to Jański's enterprise, the Democrats, not surprisingly, had a field day:

> We've been receiving... amusing details about a Jesuit congregation [in] Paris.... It recognizes papal authority and would have us pray in order to save Poland. We'd laugh at a

*Because he was still married, Jański himself was unable to set out on a path that he desperately desired, so desperately that he tried to convince his wife in Poland to enter a convent, which would have freed him to follow his calling (see Micewski, *Bogdan Jański*, 383).

> few bigots or respect the faith of a few madmen, were it not for the fact that this association has influenced weak minds and . . . exerted a harmful influence on our country.

It was clear to them that "the teacher, leader, guardian, and prophet" of what they referred to sarcastically as The Society of the Lamb of God was none other than Mickiewicz—behind whom, of course, stood aristocrats, Moscow, the pope, and Metternich.[41]

Despite these attacks, and despite being hounded by the French police, which, for its part, believed that it had uncovered a cell of Polish revolutionaries, Jański's home flourished. By the end of 1838, "the Founder" had managed to establish a network of homes around Paris and even beyond, as an increasing number of émigrés chose—or occasionally pretended to choose—the religious life. And despite the "deficits and financial chaos" plaguing the community, despite the inevitable bickering, gossip, and magnified petty feuds endemic to all such arrangements, Jański could nonetheless claim some accomplishments. Not the least of these, certainly, was an outpost in Rome. In the summer of 1837, Kajsiewicz and Semenenko decided to go to the Eternal City, encouraged by Mickiewicz to study theology with a view toward eventually founding a monastic order dedicated to serving God, church, and Poland. With the poet's tearful blessing, the two acolytes left Paris in September 1838, together with a loan of 300 francs and a letter to Princess Volkonskaia, the pious protectress now of all religious Poles in Rome; they would be joined there shortly by Duński and Hube. Five years later, they would return to France as the Congregation of the Resurrection of the Lord—but this time as sworn enemies of their spiritual mentor.[42]

6

The home the Mickiewiczes occupied in Domont during the spring, summer, and fall of 1836 was "spacious and beautiful," in a village with "nice surroundings." Witwicki lived in nearby Montmorency, as did Niemcewicz, whose goddaughter's constant "bum! bum! gu! bum! dum!" even elicited a playful ode. There was never a shortage of visitors from Paris. In October, however, as winter approached and "communications with Paris [grew] more difficult with every day," Mickiewicz decided to move his family back to the city.[43]

For the next six months, the Mickiewiczes resided on rue des Marais-Saint-Germain in the Latin Quarter, across the street from Januszkiewicz's and Jełowicki's Polish Bookstore and Print Shop and about a twenty-minute walk from Jański's "home"—in the very heart, in other words, of the émigré stew. The apartment was cramped, and Maria had just begun walking. Mickiewicz's cousin Łucjan Stypułkowski, whom the poet had been helping ever since his emigration to France, lived nearby and now became a regular dinner guest as well as something of a confidant for Celina and a dependable source of help. Mickiewicz divided his time mostly between his few French acquaintances and Jański's commune. His work on the history of Poland was barely budging. It was around this time too that he renewed some old Russian friendships, made new ones, and found himself mourning another.

In early 1837, the Circourts, together with Anastaziia's mother, had finally decided to settle in Paris. Anastaziia had been to the city several times over the past two years, making sure on each visit to get in touch with the man whose intellect and originality never ceased to dazzle her. Once ensconced in Paris, the energetic *savante* wasted little time in establishing her indispensable salon, to which Mickiewicz had a standing invitation. But it was really the presence of Vera Ivanovna Khliustin, Anastaziia's fifty-some-year-old mother, that drew the poet to the Circourts. He became a regular dinner guest at Khliustin's on Thursdays, usually with Celina and, in time, their brood in tow to bask in the affections the Russian grand dame extended to his entire family.

But if the Circourts' move to Paris had only been a matter of time, Sergei Sobolevskii's visit in the fall of 1836 came as a surprise. Sobolevskii had not seen Mickiewicz since they parted in Fiorenzuola in 1831, although over the intervening years he had been receiving news of his Polish friend from countrymen who had encountered the poet in Paris. What Sobolevskii found now took him aback. "This period," he recalled some thirty years later, "was the most difficult of all of the times that I had seen M., for he had not a shred of hope and many worries." Their meeting was awkward at first, "but little by little the intimacy and trust returned." On his way back from England the following spring, Sobolevskii dropped by again, and "Monsieur et Madame Mickiewicz" took the occasion to invite him to a modest Slavic dinner at their place: "*borchetztz*, *khren* (horseradish), and all the bread [he] could eat."[44]

It was during Sobolevskii's stay in Paris that winter, and probably thanks to him, that Mickiewicz came to finally meet Nikolai Gogol', the eccentric young man in flamboyant waistcoats whom he had passed years ago in St. Petersburg when the two lived briefly in the same building on Staraia Meshchanskaia. Since that time Gogol' had emerged as Russia's most celebrated new talent, the author of several collections of short stories and a comedy that amused even a tsar notorious for his lack of a sense of humor. He was traveling in Europe now, hard at work on a novel but also undergoing the beginnings of a spiritual crisis. The two writers' acquaintance, however, was brief. In late February, they learned of Pushkin's death in a senseless duel. The news unnerved Gogol'. He fled, hysterically, to Rome, where he soon found himself a haven at Volkonskaia's—and surrounded by Mickiewicz's spiritual protégés, all pressuring him to convert to Catholicism. As for Mickiewicz, he did not, as rumor then had it, try to avenge Pushkin by challenging his killer; he did, however, immediately compose an obituary of the man he had "known quite closely and for a pretty long period of time." "The bullet that struck Pushkin," he wrote in *Le Globe*,

> was a terrible blow to intellectual Russia. . . . It is not given to a country to produce more than once a man who brings together to such a degree the most varied of talents that at

> the same time seem to be mutually exclusive. Pushkin . . . astounded his listeners with his liveliness, subtlety, and lucidity of his mind. He was gifted with a prodigeous memory, a sureness of judgment, and delicate and refined taste. . . . I found him to have a nature that was a bit too impressionable and sometimes flighty, but always frank, noble, and effusive. (Dz. 5:291/MP 1:305).

As Mickiewicz modestly informed Viazemskii two years later, he did not "attach any literary significance to" the obituary; what he hoped it would convey was "proof of the feelings [he] had for some of [his] dear enemies." Pushkin's peculiar combination of brilliance, frivolousness, and sincerity at once fascinated, troubled, and puzzled him. The Russian poet would appear again three years later, in Mickiewicz's lectures on Slavic literature, as elusive and as inscrutable as ever.[45]

In April 1837, the Mickiewiczes moved once again, to a larger apartment on rue Val-de-Grâce near the Observatory. It was "quite far away" ("*at the gates of hell*" for old Niemcewicz) and therefore cheaper, but with "a large yard with a garden and a lawn" for little Maria. For the summer, though, they decamped to St. Germain-en-Lay, with its magnificent view of Paris below—and at a distance. The state of their finances had begun to improve, thanks to the efforts of Czartoryski as well as the generous ladies enlisted by Zaleski and Januszkiewicz. By the time the Mickiewiczes returned to the city in the fall, Celina could afford to order "a sable boa, as beautiful as possible," from her sister in St. Petersburg; "everyone here wears them," she wrote, before adding that it would "come in very handy for the winter." Mickiewicz, for his part, finally bought her a piano of their own, a "*carré* Erard, the best craftsman" in Paris.[46]

Mickiewicz himself spent only part of that summer in St. Germain. Shopping *Les Confédérés*, dealing with Jański's home, and preparing for Kajsiewicz's and Semenenko's departure for Rome all kept him in Paris for much of the time, but so too did tending to yet another friend dying of consumption. Like the ordeal at the bedside of Garczyński, the experience exhausted Mickiewicz and reminded him of his own mortality. He felt a need to take stock. In September, together with Jański, Cezary Plater, and two wavering émigrés they were hoping to convert, the poet made a pilgrimage to a Jesuit monastery in St. Acheul, near Amiens. "I sit in a cell," the poet reported to Celina, "get up at six, don't smoke my pipe as much, and drink less wine than usual," all of which he hoped would make her glad. He returned from the trip satisfied (the two waverers had been successfully converted); indeed, as he wrote to Domeyko, "revived."[47]

That fall and winter, however, proved bittersweet for Mickiewicz. Just as Kajsiewicz, his spiritual son for the past four years, was finally setting out on his own, Odyniec, a son of an entirely different sort, informed him from Dresden that in order to save his estate from confiscation he had no choice now but to return to Lithuania. Mickiewicz reacted to the news with equanimity. Emigration, he concluded, "augured nothing propitious for the future"; by returning, Odyniec would at least be "in a more tolerable and even more serviceable situation." Yet at the same time, the poet was effectively losing a friend and confidant. "We lived far from each other," he wrote to the man who so often annoyed him, but whom over the years he had, on a certain level, come to love and trust, "and although we rarely corresponded, it nonetheless seems that we were somewhere in the same country, on the same shore; now you are sailing across the ocean!"[48]

Indeed, that metaphorical ocean would prove far more impassable than the real one across which Mickiewicz's other close friend had now decided to sail. Having received a degree in engineering from the École des Mines, Domeyko was unexpectedly offered a lucrative position as a professor of chemistry and mineralogy in Coquimbo, Chile, "on the opposite side of the earth's globe" from Lithuania. Mickiewicz encouraged him to accept, for the same ambivalent reasons he had made no effort to dissuade Odyniec from his decision. For the next several years Domeyko proved to be a faithful correspondent, a sounding board for the poet's thoughts and troubles, but also a generous source of information about a world that had captivated Mickiewicz ever since he was a child. Odyniec, for his part, had warned Mickiewicz before his departure back across the border of the Russian Empire that the two "would even have to forgo contact by mail." This did not, however, apply to their children, whom they used, on occasion, as proxies.[49]

But then Mickiewicz was soon himself forced to consider leaving Paris in search of a better life. His hopes for success in French theater, encouraged by well-meaning French admirers, had proved to be something of a delusion. The funds he received from the outpouring of charity on his behalf only went so far, as did the sentiment that impelled it. Januszkiewicz tried his best to replenish his friend's—and his own—coffers by publishing a new edition of the eight-volume *Poems* in 1838. Everyone, however, saw through the ruse immediately: only the first three volumes were actually new (including the first authorized edition of "Ode to Youth"), while the remaining five were simply rebound versions of unsold copies of the original run. With another child on the way—and Jański's home and the needs of the novices in Rome and still another tubercular friend in need of nursing—it was becoming impossible to survive on the eighty-franc stipend the poet was collecting from the French government. By June 1838, Jański was once again pawning Celina's jewelry—just in time for the birth of Mickiewicz's son on 27 June.

They named the boy Władysław, "since according to the Polish calendar the patron of that day is our saint of the north." The "new citizen" of France was, at least at first, "healthy, very quiet, and suck[ed] enthusiastically and with energy"—a foretaste, perhaps, of how he would approach his father's legacy. For a godfather, Mickiewicz chose Czartoryski, a gesture more of gratitude and respect than of political allegiance, but one that in the polarized atmosphere of the émigré hothouse was immediately scanned for political implications. More egregious, under the circumstances, was the poet's choice of godmother, the Russian aristocrat Vera Khliustin, "an old acquaintance of my husband," as Celina delicately put it to her sister without naming names. As Władysław recalled many years later in his memoirs, "The democrats were surprised by the choice of the prince, whom the conservatives recognized as their leader; the aristocrats, for their part, did not like the fact that Mrs. Khliustin was a Russian"—but then neither did the democrats.[50]

In the beginning of October, Mickiewicz got wind of an opening for a professor of Latin literature at the Academy of Lausanne. By the middle of the month he was on his way to Switzerland, his first extended absence from home since marrying Celina. The speed with which he made his decision says as much about his desire to leave Paris as it does about the state of his finances. Whether he could have foreseen the consequences is impossible to say.

7

The road to Lausanne took Mickiewicz through Geneva, where he "spent the entire day" with Aleksander Potocki, his friend from happier times in Italy, then to Vevey and Henryk Nakwaski, one of his companions on the trip west from Dresden in 1832 and to whom he now turned as someone with connections in the canton. But it was purely by chance, in a hotel café in Lausanne, that he met the person who took it upon himself to open the appropriate doors for the poet. Having heard that "some Pole" was staying at the Lion d'Or, Giovanni Scovazzi, a Piedmontese revolutionary and himself an émigré who was now a professor of Italian language and literature at the academy, "hurried to the hotel to become acquainted with him." Mickiewicz explained that he was in Lausanne hoping to apply for the position in Latin literature. As Scovazzi recalled years later,

> Since I had a close relationship with the rector [Charles] Monnard, I proposed to introduce him.... He greeted us warmly. Mickiewicz began to inquire about the conditions and deadlines of the competition.... I was surprised at the deference [Monnard] showed him, and when Adam insisted on being told the day of the competition, Monnard said: "The examination is over. It's honor enough for us that we shall have Adam Mickiewicz for a professor in our academy."

Mickiewicz was impressed—by the warmth and sincerity of the people he met in Lausanne, by "the free air he breathed" there, no less than by Monnard's flattering respect.[51]

The rector's was not, however, the last word, and Mickiewicz would need more than just a name and reputation to sway others in his favor. Nonetheless, to Celina he wrote as if the job was his, and he was eager to make the sell to his skeptical wife:

> There are only six or seven hours of lectures a week, and the salary is about 2,800 francs.... For that kind of money we'd live well. The country's as beautiful as a picture.

> Geneva's a few hours away, easier to get to than from our place to the Wołowskis. We'd go to Italy for vacation. In short, we'd have it very good here.

He asked her to go to confession for his intention.[52]

In the same breath, though, Mickiewicz informed Celina that yet another position, that of "a professor *des littératures comparées*," had opened up in Geneva itself, something he would, in fact, have preferred. The poet mobilized both Circourts to this end, but his bid was unrealistic. Despite Anastaziia's "guarantee" that "Mickiewicz is recognized as the greatest living poet" among Slavs; that his French is fluent "in an original way, expressive and very eloquent, without ever degenerating into neological barbarity"; and knows Latin "like a palatine from the days of Sobieski," his status as a Polish émigré and, more egregiously, his demonstrative Catholicism were viewed as serious liabilities in staid, Protestant Geneva. Lausanne, nevertheless, remained in play, and here Mickiewicz turned to Czartoryski (as his superior in Lithuania) as well as to Sismondi for letters of recommendation, while at the same time asking friends in Paris to send the search committee translations of his works as well as copies of what he had written in French. But it was another chance acquaintance, this time with Juste Olivier, professor of Swiss history at the academy and, like his wife Caroline, also a poet and critic, that proved to be especially salutary. Olivier persuaded Charles Sainte-Beuve, himself fresh from a visiting professorship in Lausanne, to write a letter on Mickiewicz's behalf. The prominent French critic responded immediately, and with flattering enthusiasm: "A poet of the first order . . . , the Byron of his country, but a moral and Christian Byron, he has, in his own fate and that of his country, something that merits all possible sympathy, and I have admired him greatly for a long time."[53]

On his countrymen in Switzerland, however, "Miciek," as he was called with a wink, made a somewhat different impression. The poet came across as conceited and close-minded, stuck in a "Polish gentry shell" that made him "impatient" with the "democratism" of the Swiss, who treated him "not like the bard of Lithuania, but simply as a candidate for the chair, and ask[ed] each other, what does he *know*?"

> They want titles, but he says he's not an dentist. Nonetheless, he is collecting [attestations of his] qualifications and sending various translations of his works to them—even geniuses have to submit to necessity.

And indeed, despite the assurances of Mickiewicz's influential friends, the academy's search committee was not immediately convinced. As far as his qualifications were concerned, Sainte-Beuve's letter seems to have put their questions to rest, as did the sample of Mickiewicz's writing. More troubling, though, was the poet's status as an émigré as well as "the role he may have played in events of a political nature." On this point, it was

Sismondi's intervention that proved decisive, albeit in tandem with a background check by the appropriate functionaries. On 23 November, the academy "unanimously accepted the services of Mr. Mickiewicz." By that time, however, the poet was no longer in Switzerland. Celina, he learned, had had a breakdown.[54]

8

Her behavior had often struck the émigré community as "mannered," somehow unnatural, and she had always dressed eccentrically. No one, however, seems to have put much stock into this—or if they did, it was chalked up to her pampered upbringing or, more discreetly, to her race. Once, however, on an outing together with Stefan Zan, as Celina was walking on ahead, Mickiewicz himself "happened to glance at her and was struck by his wife's outfit and proud carriage." "'Look,' he turned to Zan, 'she looks like a veritable madwoman!'"

> And indeed, it was impossible to mistake her for anything else. She had on a satin dress. She had behung herself with earrings, chains, bracelets, and all the jewelry she had, in a word, she was dressed as if for a ball and not for a visit to the country.

The source of this anecdote, Alojzy Niewiarowicz's "reminiscences," is notoriously unreliable; yet it captures, in hindsight, that moment in the first days of November when those who knew Celina suddenly grasped the significance of the odd attire, the posturing, the faux pas, the disorganized household, and her propensity for "melancholy."[55]

On 1 November, Niemcewicz ran into an obviously manic Celina at Czartoryski's as she was collecting money for a hospital for indigent émigrés. "She was unusually lively and talkative," he noted in his diary, "so much so, that I began to fear for her." The next day she was "babbling what she had on her heart and what she wouldn't dare say if she were well." A week later, Januszkiewicz reported to a friend that Mickiewicz's "comely spouse had come down with something akin to brain fever, . . . in a word, . . . she is, to a certain degree, mad—she seems inspired; she'll redeem mankind, Poland, and will summon all unbelievers to faith"—in a word, monomania, as the French psychiatric profession then classified it.[56]

The breakdown was in all likelihood triggered by a sudden collapse of defense mechanisms, never particularly robust in the first place, in the face of a confluence of mounting anxieties. The persistent poverty, constant worry about the well-being of a growing family, a mistrustful émigré community, unmet demands for attention from a none-too-attentive husband (and flattering but nonetheless disconcerting attention from Jański)—all this was now exacerbated by what seems to have been postpartum depression. And it was precisely at this critical moment, when the "darkness" that had haunted Celina for years suddenly began enveloping her once again, that Mickiewicz happened not to be there for her.

The family and friends who rushed to tend to her were not quite sure what to make of the illness, "whether its cause," as Januszkiewicz put it, "was moral or physical." Since Celina was nursing Władysław at the time, the general consensus was that "the breast-milk had gone to her head," although Januszkiewicz, for one, surmised that, besides her "enthusiasm for things religious," "she ha[d] a rather strong personality, and the absence of her husband redouble[d] her blood pressure." But others were quick to point out too—and not without subtext—that "the entire Szymanowski family had always been prone to this illness." And indeed, while in her delirium, in which Celina believed that "she [was] called upon to resurrect Poland," she was at the same time obsessed with the idea of "redeeming the Jews." It was as if her breakdown precipitated an irruption of existential ambiguity, articulating her unresolved predicament betwixt and between her Jewishness, always and continually suppressed, and her Polishness, its Catholic component now more salient than ever—and embodied, inevitably, in the figure of her husband. "She is . . . Our Lady of Częstochowa," wrote Januszkiewicz of her ravings, "and her coronation will take place in Poland, and her Adam, who had never betrayed Poland . . ., will be the Polish king."[57]

Jański wrote immediately to Mickiewicz informing him of the crisis and urging him to return at once. In the meantime, he, the Wołowskis, Januszkiewicz, and many others spent "day and night" at Celina's side; Zaleski and Niemcewicz contributed money; her cousin, Aleksandra Wołowska-Faucher, took in three-year-old Maria, while baby Władysław, who himself was ill, was put in the care of the Ludwik Platers. Doctors, both Polish and French, were consulted but could do little. "There were moments of sublime inspiration," wrote Januszkiewicz, fascinated, it seems, by the living poetry of madness, "and during them she spoke of religion, man's relationship with God, of our obligations, and in language that was powerful, full of luster, Biblical almost." There were also moments of passing calm, but when Celina sat down to the piano to sing one of her mother's compositions to Mickiewicz's verse, "what a terrifying performance it was! She had tears in her eyes and such fire in her soul that it seemed that that breast would shatter and burst upon issuing the final note."[58]

Jański's letter did not find Mickiewicz until mid-November. On 13 November the poet informed the Lausanne Board of Public Education that "his wife's dangerous illness compelled him to return to Paris." By the 18th he was back at the apartment on Val-de-Grâce, where he found his "wife in the most horrible of illnesses, practically abandoned by doctors, [his] child, [his] son dying, Misia in a stranger's home, everything in ruins." The poet, Januszkiewicz recounted,

> was struck dumb on the staircase upon hearing those cries, those terrifying screams. For two hours he was incapable of saying a word to us. Tears came to his aid, he cried for a long time, then he fortified himself with courage and went to [Celina]. She recognized him, calmed down, talked with him sensibly for three hours, and then . . . relapsed into her earlier state.[59]

For the next month, Mickiewicz tried to deal with Celina at home.

> Everyone who knew him offer[ed] to help him with everything. Two people [were] needed to keep an eye out [on her] during the night, and every day there came fifteen or twenty volunteers. Our ladies s[a]t and sle[pt] with the ill woman.

At one point, it was decided that a change of locale might help, and Mickiewicz rented a place on Allé des Vanves, again on the city's outskirts, this time on the western Left Bank near the Seine. Sainte-Beuve arrived just as they were moving. Mickiewicz, he wrote to Caroline Olivier, "was in a trance," exhausted from the effort of "persuading [his wife] to dress and put on her shoes." Over the next few weeks, there were moments of lucidity and calm, so that even little Maria was allowed an occasional visit. But there were also moments when Celina would act out, focusing her energies with peculiar glee on hurtfully provoking those around her. "For six weeks," Januszkiewicz reported,

> Adam was the object of this behavior. [At one point] she brought him to such a state of despair that he wanted to beat her, but having reflected a bit, he hid himself in the cook's room. But she found him there, and Adam wanted to jump from the fourth floor in order to put an end to his torture.

Mickiewicz understood that he had no other option but to hospitalize Celina. A few days before Christmas, he placed her in a *maison de santé* in Vanves, just south of Paris.[60]

The asylum was run by Jean-Pierre Falret and Félix Voisin and was considered one of the most progressive.* Theirs was a humane approach, combining medical treatment with religious ministration. Their new patient was encouraged to engage in arts and crafts, to sew, read, to play the piano. But she was also not allowed any visits from family, and this weighed on her terribly. Her only contact with those closest to her was by mail and, at least initially, exclusively in French so that the doctors could follow the correspondence and learn more about her and her family situation. Unfortunately, Celina's letters are not extant. Mickiewicz's, however, are, and they constitute a chronicle of patience, tenderness, forced hope, brave face, but also obtuse rationalization, always, however, with an eye toward doctors' orders to avoid anything that might upset the patient. For three months he wrote at least once a week, sometimes more, urging Celina to be calm—as if he believed his words could make it so—her good behavior a condition for reunion with husband and children. "I will repeat in every letter," the poet wrote at the beginning of her confinement,

*Falret is in fact now considered a pioneer in the study of bipolar disorder.

> that you need only be calm and obedient if you want to return home. Can't you wait calmly for a few days? . . . Does the sacrifice of a few days cost so much? There are, after all, mothers who live apart from their children for years. Your own mother undertook long trips, she left you in order to ensure your welfare, and you don't want to endure our absence when it concerns our happiness!

He encouraged her to take up embroidery, to play the piano; he sent books (although not Polish ones), pieces of her mother's jewelry, and new shoes. In early February, writing now in Polish, he begged Celina to persevere, to get better, to be patient, reminding her that he too knew what it meant to be in "prison":

> In my youth I also sat in a clink, worse than yours; I remember that at that time prison cured me of an onset of melancholy. It looks as if you too were destined to taste this bitter medicine.

He assured her that he "fel[t] and underst[oo]d everything she [was] going through": "After all, whenever my teeth hurt, despite all of your sympathy, I had to finally go to the dentist."[61]

All anachronism aside, Mickiewicz's insensitivity to certain manifestations of Celina's condition gives pause, given, especially, that he himself had experienced moments of seemingly debilitating depression. Hers, however, was a qualitatively different form of darkness, and his preaching, exemplifying, and trivializing were perhaps the only weapons, and only defenses, he could muster against what was, at bottom, an incomprehensible phenomenon, one that had transformed his wife while destroying the little there was of family happiness. He struggled against the illness tenaciously, fighting, as it were, for Celina's, as well as his family's, soul. That struggle at once constituted and articulated the closest thing to love for her. As Tańska-Hoffmanowa observed:

> I never would have thought that he was so strongly attached to her; such manifestations of love as he has displayed and continues to display have never been depicted *in any novel*. This is a man worthy of admiration—his soul measures up to his mind and his talent.

But then this was not the first time that others marveled at his capacity for selfless compassion when circumstances demanded.[62]

With Celina a gnawing, exhausting source of concern, Mickiewicz could hardly think about the position awaiting him in Lausanne. The offer was a good one, but the semester there began on 8 January, and he still had not officially accepted, much less prepared a course of study that the Board of Public Education was now repeatedly demanding.

"His distress is such," wrote Sainte-Beuve, who had made Mickiewicz's installation in Lausanne into something of a personal mission,

> that he can't cope: poor man, he always says *tomorrow*, hoping that *tomorrow* she'll be better. He doesn't even know the exact state of his wife. . . . I sympathize with this most miserable of men.

Mickiewicz was distracted, "in no state to engage in anything, unable to read anything through the whole time, even newspapers." "I myself am amazed," he wrote to Domeyko, "that I survived everything up till now, but I've aged in my soul!" He moved back to an apartment on Saint-Nicolas d'Antin in order to be closer to the children. And, as Celina began to show signs of improvement, it was inevitable that he should start complaining of various ailments of his own, "a stubborn cold and . . . severe weakness and torpor." The Academy of Lausanne, for its part, thrilled by the prospect of having "a scholar as distinguished as Mickiewicz," was, in view of the circumstances, willing to forbear.[63]

Throughout January and February and then March of 1839, Mickiewicz tried his best to console Celina, assuring her that her doctors felt her condition was improving and that she would be coming home shortly but that there were sound medical reasons for her continued confinement: first it was on account of her period, which she must "see through in peace," otherwise "at home she might fret and become irritated"; then, because March was approaching, and "the doctors consider[ed] the month of March dangerous for all illnesses." It was thus only as that ominous month was drawing to a close that Celina was finally deemed fit enough to go home.[64]

Most everyone agreed that she had "recuperated fully." Hoffmanowa even claimed that "she had become strangely more beautiful . . . , very melancholy, she herself speaks to those closest to her about the illness she had suffered . . . and this in itself is proof of the full recovery of her senses." Writing to her sister for the first time since the breakdown, Celina insisted that she was "now better, just as before the illness." Witwicki, however, was not so sure—and in this respect probably echoed Mickiewicz's own apprehensions. "This is a big secret," he confided to Zaleski, "but I'll tell you that her health is not yet completely guaranteed in everything." An ostensibly new life in Lausanne, with its "independence and beautiful location," but above all far away from Paris and all the things it signified, was something for which everyone involved now yearned.[65]

On 4 June, Mikhail Pogodin and Stepan Shevyrev, Mickiewicz's old friends from Moscow, paid the poet an unexpected visit. From Volkonskaia and Gogol' in Rome they had heard he was despondent, that life in emigration had taken its toll. And indeed, they found a man who "had grown thin, had grayed, and had aged." "People blossom here quickly," he explained to them, "and quickly wilt." A week later, on 11 June, Mickiewicz set out with his family for Switzerland.[66]

CHAPTER EIGHT

ACADEME (1839–1841)

The trip to Lausanne was leisurely, taking the Mickiewiczes through Dijon, Besançon, and Geneva. This was Celina's first excursion outside of the Department of the Seine since her arrival in Paris five years earlier; that she "had not a spot of the trouble with the children that [she]'d been expecting" seems to have made it all the more enjoyable. For Mickiewicz, the journey was an opportunity to relax and take stock. Like the group of émigrés that had organized an ambivalently heartfelt farewell for him on the eve of his departure, he understood that his decision to go to Lausanne—or, rather, leave Paris—was, under the circumstances, a salutary one. But it was those same circumstances that had prevented Mickiewicz from tending to his prospects in Lausanne, and these were not as propitious as they had appeared seven months earlier.[1]

I

The poet, it seems, assumed that the matter of his appointment was settled and that the position would be there for his taking. Upon his arrival, though, he learned that this was not the case. Mickiewicz's silence over the past year, particularly in the face of repeated requests to provide a program of study, appears to have irked some members of the Council of Public Education, which, in addition, had just experienced a change in presidency. The poet, for his part, blamed the uncertainties on what he misconstrued to have been "a revolution" in the canton's government, and, as he reminded Zaleski by way of justification, revolutions, together with the Russian embassy, "always had a way of impacting" him. He nonetheless expressed confidence that he "would regain [his] position" soon enough. But the authorities in Lausanne seemed intent on drawing the

Fig. 18 Mickiewicz in 1839. Daguerreotype. Courtesy of the Adam Mickiewicz Museum of Literature, Warsaw.

process out, "interminably and seemingly without end," and the Vaudois bureaucracy proved no less efficient in this respect than any other.[2]

The delays and confusion surrounding Mickiewicz's appointment were in some measure a function of the political configurations obtaining at the time in Lausanne, the capital of Vaud Canton since 1803, where, after its constitutional revolution in 1830, tensions between the canton's liberals and conservatives were most palpable. The political rift had also come to reflect the transformation of the town from an idyllic eighteenth-century haven for the likes of Gibbon and Rousseau into a relatively modern, if still dazzlingly picturesque, urban center, spreading rapidly around the old center down to the shores of Lake Geneva. With a population of well over 15,000 and a diversifying economy, Lausanne was now perceived by the surrounding countryside to be a bastion of liberalism. And predictably enough, it was the academy that came to serve as a lightening rod in this respect. The institution was, after all, already providing employment for one radical émigré, Scovazzi; now it was preparing to appoint his even more radical countryman Luigi Melegari (aka Thomas Emery), a friend of Mazzini and one of the cofounders of Young Italy, at the same time as it was considering the candidacy of yet another émigré from a no less fractious nation, and a devout Catholic to boot. That thought, as Juste Olivier put it to his wife, made some on the Council of Public Education "quite prickly, above all against Mickiewicz." It was not until the very end of July that the academy finally suggested to the council that it would be "advisable" to ask the poet to assume his teaching duties.[3]

As the authorities dithered—and as Scovazzi and the Oliviers as well as a visiting Sainte-Beuve pulled whatever strings they could for their Polish acquaintance—the Mickiewiczes settled in, first in a hotel then, in the beginning of July, in a furnished apartment on rue Saint-Pierre. The apartment was somewhat expensive (eighty Swiss francs, plus an additional four for a monthly supply of wine), "without a garden" and in a dirty and noisy neighborhood; the windows, though, "looked out on Lake Geneva and the Alps." Yet to Mickiewicz, their beauty seemed "a distant, sham brilliance, which tricks the eyes like a camera obscura," serving only to remind him of "Lithuanian landscapes, in which one can lie down and immediately fall asleep." The town itself he found "rather boring," which in any case he relieved by excursions to Geneva, Echichens, Annecy, and Chamonix. And despite what he described as the "friendliness" of Lausanne's inhabitants, the Mickiewiczes had a difficult time adjusting at first, still and always feeling "like Gypsies, guests wherever [they] went." They never did get fully used to their new environment—even after several months in Switzerland, Mickiewicz "asserted that he d[id]n't know it at all." Nonetheless, the solicitude and warmth extended him and his family by the town's intelligentsia—by the Oliviers, Scovazzi, Melegari, Monnard, but also by Alexandre Vinet, a philosopher and literary critic at the academy, and especially the Polish émigré Wiktor Jundziłł—went a long way in palliating an existence among a people the poet described as "cold and ponderous," "forged [...] out of the granite of the Alpine crags." Of these friendships, none were as heartfelt as that with Caroline Olivier, who would henceforth become a regular presence in Mickiewicz's life.[4]

With his appointment, finally, to the academy in late September, the poet soon found himself with little time on his hands for moping. "Who informed you that I'm bored in Lausanne?" he wrote to Kajsiewicz and Semenenko six months after his arrival. "As if I had time to be bored! Lessons six hours a week and entire volumes that need to be perused."[5]

2

Mickiewicz's appointment was as "assistant professor." It required him to teach the "history of Latin literature and explicate authors" three or four hours a week at the academy and, in addition, four hours a week of the same at the town's *gymnase*. Compensation for two semesters was a generous 1,800 Swiss francs (2,700 French). In accepting the offer to teach for two semesters, Mickiewicz promised "to zealously fulfill the duties" required of him but at the same time petitioned the Council of State—presumptuously, perhaps—to reduce his hours, arguing that "during his first year a foreign professor must... come to know his audience" and be ready "to accommodate the demands of his public," which entails "putting together not only a course, but each individual lesson" and even having to "change the original plan." The council agreed, but only with respect to his hours at the academy, which were reduced to twice weekly.[6]

Mickiewicz's petition proved prescient. The poet, it seems, had been ready to give an overview of the Late Antique, including early Christian, writers, whereas the academy assumed that he would begin, as tradition dictated, with the Augustan classics. As a consequence, Mickiewicz was indeed forced to change his original plan. For two months he prepared for the course, scouring the cantonal library for appropriate material, importuning acquaintances for books he could not obtain in Lausanne, but above all drawing upon his prodigious memory. Yet amid the bibliographies and histories of Latin literature, amid the textbooks of poetics and rhetoric and critical editions of Plautus, Cato and Terence, as his eyes glazed over reading "*de re metrica, de asse romano, de siglis* etc. etc.," he "would sometimes get all sentimental... as [he] called up before [his] eyes old memories of university days."[7]

On 12 November 1839, a Tuesday, at four o'clock, Mickiewicz delivered his first lecture at the Academy of Lausanne. He was terrified. "I feel as if I'm walking onto a scaffold," he confided to Juste Olivier before the class began, and once it did, he was forced to take off his coat in front of the expectant audience thronging the amphitheater. The poet had prepared a written lecture, "but when he saw the audience, he got fired up and instead of reading began to talk, and he talked for the entire lecture." Despite "a slightly foreign accent" and a somewhat "unkempt" appearance, the academy's new professor of Latin literature made an immediate impression on both his students and those of Lausanne's intelligentsia who had come to hear him that day. As he reported to Domeyko a few weeks later, "[My] first public lecture caused me anxiety enough, but it went well and after it the students serenaded me." With a wink, Mickiewicz reminded himself of Groddeck. The Vilnius philologist had trained him well.[8]

Over the course of the two semesters, from mid-November to the beginning of July, Mickiewicz worked "like a convict at hard labor," two hours a week at the academy, four hours a week in the highest grade of the collegium, and, of course, many hours at home and in the library. It had been over fifteen years since he had had to prepare weekly lessons and stand in front of a roomful of students, and he was forced to apply himself, something he "had grown unaccustomed to." In his conscientiousness, he was not content to rely solely on memory and intellect. "I don't get up from my table for entire days," he informed Zaleski in late November, "and often I'll parse some difficult Latin meter until one at night. On teaching days I have to be on my feet by seven. I then devour Latin and spit French." He was often compelled to decline invitations to social affairs, "all covered as [he was] with Latin mud and smelling too much... of the classicist," and even had to pass up a traditional Christmas Eve, since "in this philosophico-democratic country... there are few holidays and work can be neither missed nor put off."[9]

His labors, however, did not go unappreciated, and neither did his erudition, his grasp of the subject, the originality of his views, and his enthusiasm. Indeed, as Mickiewicz grew more comfortable in front of his classes, he gradually jettisoned written lectures in favor of improvisation, with names, dates, and quotations scribbled on pieces of paper as *aides de memoir*, but more often than not taken directly from memory.* Guiding his listeners through the history of Latin literature, from its significance in relation to the literatures of ancient Greece, Asia, and the Germanic peoples, its periodization, and its beginnings, to individual authors, from Andronicus to Cicero, and then, in the second semester, from Virgil to Livy, Mickiewicz strove for historical synthesis through wide-ranging comparison. At this, he dazzled. As one report put it:

> From the very first lectures... his listeners recognized in him a great talent for literary criticism.... His knowledge of the personal life of the Roman people in connection with their art and literature, his knowledge of the spirit of the Latin language and that of the poets and orators for whom it served as an instrument, the astonishing insight with which he plumbs their individual natures combined with an examination of their writings, his apt comparisons of the ancient literature of Rome with various modern literatures,... finally, the sense of freshness with which he imbues material that seemed to have been exhausted and the inspiration of the mind of a poet that enlivens his natural gifts and the fruits of his labor—these... are the reasons for the increasing success of a course that captivates the youth, attracts more listeners with every day, and delights those who are in a better position to evaluate it.

*Only the contents of most of the first-semester lectures are extant, partly in Mickiewicz's own hand, partly on the basis of students' notes, published first in their entirety, together with the poet's preparatory notes and bibliographies for his lectures, in Polish translation, by Józef Kowalski in *Pisma prozaiczne francuskie*, volume 7 of *Dzieła wszystkie* (Wydanie Sejmowe), 245–336, 417–526. Cf. *Dz.* 7:165–252.

The report, moreover—and it was by no means an isolated one, nor was it a product of one of Mickiewicz's admiring acquaintances—drew particular attention to what is perhaps most remarkable about the poet's performance, that it was in a language foreign to him. To be sure, he committed errors, stumbled occasionally, and when he found himself at a loss for words, "he would... make do by simply creating a new word." But according to yet another report, this time by Monnard himself:

> His language renders his thoughts so clearly,... so ardently that infelicitous particulars disappear with the appropriate usage of words and the energy with which they are employed. And when it comes to translating an author, M. Mickiewicz does so with a precision that bespeaks a rare understanding of French,... a most natural knowledge of our language.

In short, "We are speaking of genius."[10]

By the end of the first semester, it was clear to everyone that Mickiewicz had more than just earned his keep. His "presence... adds genuine luster to [Lausanne's] institutions of higher learning, since he seems to offer all of the qualities of a scholar and a skilled professor." On 26 February, the academy unanimously proposed to the Council of Public Education that "for the honor of the Canton of Vaud and in the interest of higher education" Mickiewicz be promoted to full professor, "a position... worthy of his merits and fame." And in an unprecedented gesture, the academy's proposal, which was followed, in turn, by that of the Council of Public Education to the Council of State, was joined by a petition of twenty students. They praised Mickiewicz for the "clarity" and "rare precision" of his lectures, the "sharpness and salience" of his thought, and a "vast knowledge of literature, philology, and history, knowledge acquired and honed by a mind that is rigorous, original, with taste that is sure and judgment that is sound." But above all, it was what they learned that really mattered:

> Latin literature... seems to us now like an organism that is born and develops amidst events extrinsic to it; none of the influences on it are now unknown to us, each author has a specific character and is well-defined; all of the great literary and historical issues are tackled, the small details of trivial erudition are neatly dealt with.[11]

There were, by all accounts, no dissenting voices, no objections to the promotion, which, moreover, was being effected without the usual competition and despite the brevity of Mickiewicz's tenure. On 13 March, the chairman of Vaud's Council of State informed the poet of his appointment to full professor, with a salary of 3,000 Swiss francs (4,000 French). A week later, Mickiewicz accepted—with the mistaken impression that his teaching load would be reduced—grateful for "a salary higher than usual"

("1,500 francs more than other professors," the poet liked to boast in his letters, and occasionally even inflated the figure).[12]

3

In comparison to Paris, Lausanne was markedly less expensive. Celina was finally able to afford a maid again, and even while Mickiewicz was still on an assistant professor's salary, they felt secure enough to look for more comfortable lodgings, all the more necessary since Celina was pregnant yet again. In December 1839, during a "mild and utterly Italian winter," they moved into one of the more luxurious dwellings in Lausanne, a mansion called Beau-Séjour (Napoleon had apparently slept there) located below the old town center toward the lake. They shared the first floor with its owner; the second was occupied by Wiktor Jundziłł, together with his wife and ten children; and the third by some relatives of Benjamin Constant. It was a "beautiful house," with a "gorgeous living room, huge mirrors, and huge windows with a view onto a garden and the lake." The Jundziłłs, "a respectable family, albeit a bit assimilated," proved to be ideal neighbors—Wiktor, an expropriated landowner from Lithuania and eight years the poet's senior, quickly became a trusted friend, while his numerous brood either played with Maria or helped sit baby Władysław.[13]

The Mickiewicz's spent the next nine months in Beau-Séjour, the most tranquil, perhaps, of their life as a family. For once, material survival was no longer a concern. The children had nice clothes and good shoes, and Mickiewicz himself felt as if he were "living like a prince!" Four-year-old Maria would run down in the morning to find her father "sitting at a table piled high with papers" as he prepared for classes. They would go for walks in the garden "to examine the bushes, flowers, and insects," which, more than the flora of Lausanne, held an almost mystical fascination for Mickiewicz: in a fragment of verse he wrote at the time he dreamed of "fleeing... onto a leaf and like a butterfly searching / There for a home and a nest" ("To Flee with One's Soul onto a Leaf..."; Dz. 1:414). Both parents helped with their daughter's ABCs, although she preferred her more forgiving and playful father. At dusk, with Celina at the piano (which they had had transported for them from Paris), they would sing Polish folksongs, often together with the children from upstairs, whom Mickiewicz spoiled as much as he did his own. Besides the Jundziłłs, Scovazzi and Melegari—to whom Mickiewicz was growing particularly attached—were regular guests. For Maria, Lausanne was, in retrospect, "like the epitome of childhood, warmed by the blue sky and by marvelous nature, as well as by the caresses of [her] father, who spent more time with [her] there than he was able to later." Only little Władysław seems to have been a constant source of anxiety, "delicate as a girl," as his father put it, and often ill. But then Celina began obsessing about the danger of goiter—her way of signaling that despite their ostensible good fortune she was unhappy.

Mickiewicz had hoped that "in Lausanne Celina would find some company, that in a small town it would be easier for her to make acquaintances." He was forced to admit now that on this score he had been mistaken. "Celina," he fretted in March, "is lonelier than in Paris and . . . would be very glad to return."[14]

Mickiewicz himself, though, seemed less than content. "To be honest," he confessed to Domeyko in February, the "apartment is perhaps my biggest and only joy." To be sure, for the first time in his life his future seemed predictably secure. By dint of both hard work and talent, he had succeeded in carving out a place for himself in Lausanne and, as a consequence, found himself surrounded by an appreciative, even doting public, uninterested, for once, in his contrarian politics and piety, which in any case it could not understand. But then this, perhaps, was precisely the cause of his discontent. The circle of his regular correspondents had effectively narrowed to Witwicki, Bohdan Zaleski, and Domeyko. As for the emigration in Paris, Jański's mission, or the novices in Rome, they all seemed increasingly distant. It was not until the middle of March, after over two years of silence, that the poet finally responded to by all accounts numerous letters from Kajsiewicz and Semenenko. Only then did he learn that Jański had joined them in Rome and that he was, in fact, "very ill . . . and there [was] little hope for his recovery." (He died three months later, at the age of thirty-three, yet another of the poet's friends to succumb to consumption.)[15]

And as Mickiewicz saw his world contracting, as he reluctantly began growing inured to the possibility of spending the remainder of his life in what he later characterized to his daughter as the "leaden and stifling . . . atmosphere of the quiet town . . . , where everyone was perfectly satisfied by the material well-being of the country," for a brief moment the urge to write poetry returned. It had come earlier, in August, before the move to Beau-Séjour, and was, as on earlier occasions, impelled by an effort to resume *Forefathers' Eve*, although rather than trying to continue the narrative, he set to rewriting part 1, left unfinished some fifteen years before. But yet again, he was unable to recover the thread. "Inspiration abandoned me," he informed Zaleski a few months later, "and I stopped writing." What he did manage to produce, though, in the days or months that followed was a handful of pithy lyrics, most of them unfinished, none polished, none published during his lifetime—and, like the first epigraph to this biography, almost all self-epitaphs for a dead man walking:

> When my corpse sits down here among you,
> Looks into your eyes, and speaks,
> My soul at that moment is ever so distant,
> It wanders and keens, how it keens.
>
> ("When My Corpse . . ."; *Dz.* 1:412)

The verses are suffused with a sense of fatalistic resignation, of distance and detachment, as if the poet were stepping outside of his body to make an accounting—full of guilt and remorse—of a life that was, ostensibly, finished. All that remained for him now in the face of challenges, of threatening "cliffs" and "storm clouds" and "lightning," was "to flow, to flow, and to flow" ("Above the Great and Crystalline Waters..."; Dz. 1:414). The contrast with the romantically intrepid Faris defying the elements could not be more striking.[16]

4

On 26 June 1840, Mickiewicz delivered his inaugural lecture as full professor of Latin literature at the Academy of Lausanne. It had been originally scheduled for May, but had to be postponed "on account of family matters": on the 26th of that month Celina gave birth to a daughter, "a robust and in [Mickiewicz's] opinion very pretty child," indeed, "a pure Slav," as he later put it, "of a different race than the [other] two." They called her Helena, in honor of her aunt. Jundziłł and his daughter, also Helena, were asked to stand as godparents. "Fortunately," noted a reporter for the recently founded *Courrier suisse*, "the delay in the ceremony neither set back nor aborted... the scholar's lecture."[17]

At eleven o'clock on the appointed day the hall was full, "the number and attentiveness of the audience a testimony to its interest in the professor and the importance attached to his appointment." A week earlier, Mickiewicz had announced to the faculty of sciences and letters that in the 1840/1841 academic year he would take his students from Livy to Suetonius in the first semester, and in the second he would "analyze the poets of the decline, above all the Christian poets," the subject he had wanted to teach in Lausanne from the outset. For his inaugural he apparently prepared a lecture on the Augustan age. But once he found himself before his audience, the poet decided, instead, to speak ex promptu on Christian poetry, focusing on the fourth-century Spanish poet Prudentius. "M. Mickiewicz," reported *Le Courrier suisse*,

> far from immuring himself in the narrow confines of academic discourse for the occasion, provided, in an improvisation full of life and originality, an admirable example of his teaching.... His choice of passages, his comparisons, his skill in bringing out their significance demonstrated in all of its learning and charm the exceptionally pure and delightful literary talent of the professor.[18]

Mickiewicz's lecture was preceded by a speech from the president of the Council of Public Education Emmanuel de la Harpe, who welcomed the poet as a future "son of the fatherland" and "the man who will initiate a new generation into a knowledge of the beauties of the literature of a great ancient nation." La Harpe was followed by Monnard, the rector of the academy, who turned to the poet and asked him "to accept in exchange for everything [he] brings to" the people of Vaud "that which [they] possess: a free country and loving hearts." "Pitch your wayfaring tent, battered by storms, beneath our sun, fortunate in its liberty, so that your family may find peace and prosperity beneath the sky of the Canton of Vaud," Monnard concluded, "be our brother."[19]

Like practically everyone else in Lausanne, however, Monnard was by now aware that keeping Mickiewicz under that free Vaudois sun might not, in fact, be possible. A chair of Slavic literatures was about to be created at the Collège de France in Paris, and it was obvious that Mickiewicz would be a candidate.

The idea of the chair in fact first coalesced around the figure of the poet. It originated with the liberal French economist Léon Faucher, who in 1837 married Celina's cousin and companion Aleksandra Wołowska, and who also happened to be the well-connected editor of the influential *Courrier français*. As Faucher came to know his in-law, he recognized in him not only a brilliant mind, but someone who, thanks in part to his years in Russia as well as contacts with the Czechs, had an informed and acutely original view of the Slavic world, to say nothing of the knowledge he had absorbed working on his (stalled) history of Poland. There were already chairs in Turkic, Sanskrit, and Chinese at the Collège; why not, then, a chair to give voice to "nearly sixty million people" "in the north and east of Europe," and this at a time when Russia, an empire of Slavs, was asserting itself on the Continent. Faucher began promoting the idea to, among others, Montalembert and Czartoryski, who immediately grasped the potential of such a chair—in the hands of a Pole, of course—for furthering the Polish cause. At the same time, Faucher broached the project to his friend Victor Cousin, the director of the École Normale and France's most renowned educator, who, by all accounts, stood a good chance of becoming the next minister of education. Soon the idea of a new chair at the Collège began percolating among decisionmakers in Paris, usually in tandem with Mickiewicz's name. By December 1839, just as the poet was expressing some confidence about his appointment to a full professorship in Lausanne, he was also able to inform Domeyko that "there [were] some hopes that [he] might get a position in Paris."[20]

On 1 March 1840, Louis Philippe once again tapped Adolphe Thiers, the right-wing liberal historian and also a friend of Faucher, to head the government; Thiers, as had been predicted, gave Cousin the portfolio of education. Faucher's idea now seemed all the nearer to realization. With the possibility of a conflict with Russia in the Near East looming, it was certainly timely. A few days after the new government was installed, Czartoryski prepared a memorandum for Cousin outlining the rationale for a Slavic chair. Faucher, for his part, wrote to Mickiewicz informing him that he "had spoken to M. Cousin . . . about the need to create a chair of Slavic languages and literatures at the Collège de France and had presented [Mickiewicz] as the only man capable of filling it." The salary would not be extraordinary, only 5,000 francs, but classes lasted a mere seven months and met only twice a week; there was also the possibility of earning additional income by working in one of the libraries. More important, wrote Faucher, appealing as much to Mickiewicz's messianic vanity as to his sense of patriotic duty,

> The creation of a chair of Slavic languages will be important for another reason: it will provide a center for Polish exiles. For want of a political fatherland, it will give them a literary one; it would be nice for it to become the instrument of such a mission.

All he needed now was the poet's authorization to press his case. To encourage him, Faucher let his wife append a few strategic words to her cousin Celina:

> Not Paris itself, but your friends living in Paris, . . . should draw you here and have primacy over Lausanne. But above all, it appears to us that Adam's vocation would fit better with the position here, despite the triumphs he's already achieved.

A few days later, Faucher pulled out the stops to get an answer from Mickiewicz: "I ask this in the name of your wife, your children, our little Maria, and all those who have a Polish heart."[21]

Mickiewicz's reply was curious. He informed Faucher that the Swiss had just offered him a position with a salary "equivalent to 5,000" French francs (an exaggeration); that he "will have six lessons a week" (what he had been teaching all along, and in any case a much lighter load than other professors); that his future was uncertain, since "the next best revolution is likely to sweep away the entire . . . academy" (another exaggeration); and that this "political danger [was] nothing in comparison to the danger" of coming down with goiter (something of which he had not been aware, "but almost all the women [of Vaud] have goiter"). Although Faucher could have taken the first two points for a signal that Mickiewicz might want to bargain, the letter *in toto* reads like a checklist of reasons why the poet should not remain in Lausanne, addressed more to himself, though, than his in-law. "I have decided," the poet concluded, "to accept the chair in Paris, if Mr. Cousin decides to create it." Yet at almost the same time, he informed the Vaudois Council of State of his willingness to accept the nomination for a full professorship at the Academy of Lausanne. Mickiewicz, it seems, was not yet ready to entrust his future to the new French government, which, as Sainte-Beuve reminded him, might in any case not "be around in three days."[22]

The Collège de France was, after all, a public institution. Creating a new chair required not only approval of the king and the new Council of Ministers, but also the appropriation of public monies, hence of the Parliament as well. This, of course, could be a slow and deliberate process, conditioned, as always, by considerations other than strictly budgetary ones. In this particular instance, there were also delicate foreign policy implications to consider—for all of Thiers's bluster over Russia's pretensions in the Near East, he was unwilling to antagonize it unnecessarily on the issue of Poland, and neither were most members of Parliament. Nonetheless, in mid-April, after persistent pressure from Faucher, Czartoryski, Montalembert, and others, Cousin himself wrote to Mickiewicz informing the poet about the plan to create the chair and his intention to invite him to fill it. "Your presence in a public chair in Paris," wrote the minister of education, "will by itself be an event of great enough political significance." He made sure, however, to let Mickiewicz know in no uncertain terms that the position was to be "an undertaking of a literary nature and nothing more." Indeed, if in his letter to the poet Cousin spoke of "a course on Slavic languages and literatures," in his official proposal the minister spoke of "a new chair... to teach Slavic language and literature"—emphatically in the singular. Polish, in this respect, ostensibly constituted, "after Russian," "the most widely spoken of Slavic dialects."[23]

Thanks in part to Faucher's personal intervention with Thiers, Cousin managed to push his proposal through a somewhat resistant Council of Ministers and gain the approval of the king. On 20 April, Cousin took the project to Parliament. From the budget committee, which recommended appropriation, the proposal moved on to the Chamber of Deputies, where after some debate the recommendation was approved against relatively minimal opposition, and then to the Chamber of Peers, which on 9 July voted to create a Chair of Slavic Language and Literature at the Collège de France, one of the most prestigious institutions of higher learning in Europe.

Mickiewicz, however, remained circumspectly noncommittal. As he had explained to Cousin at the very beginning of the process, "I think... I should hold on to my present position until the establishment of the chair... and the possibility of having a position in France analogous to one I occupy here allows me to make a definite decision." The chair may have been established, but it had not yet been officially offered to Mickiewicz. Cousin, for his part, reflecting perhaps Louis Philippe's own anxieties, continued to express concern about how the Russian or Austrian ambassador might react to the appointment of a Polish émigré to a position with the potential to affect not just French public opinion.[24]

As Faucher and Czartoryski sought to reassure the minister on this matter, they at the same time kept assuring Mickiewicz that his nomination was only a matter of time. Naturalization, without which the poet could not be appointed to full professor, was, they insisted, a mere formality.* They pleaded with Mickiewicz, in the name of everything patriotic, to finally give Cousin a definite reply. "In my opinion," Czartoryski practically commanded his "beloved groomsman," "it is your duty to accept this position without fail, not for the sake of the emigration alone, but for the sake of all Poland, I would even say for the sake of all Slavdom."[25]

There was in all this a bit of a misunderstanding. As Mickiewicz wrote repeatedly to his friends, he felt obliged to accept the chair if only to prevent "some German from barging

*Mickiewicz never did become a naturalized citizen of France, despite this promise and, subsequently, his own repeated efforts.

in and slandering us from it." At the same time, though, Lausanne, for all of its drawbacks, meant security. After years of émigré penury and uncertainty, this was something the poet, with a wife and three children, was loath to abandon for what could yet turn out to be an empty promise. Nonetheless, he maintained to Faucher that he was "determined to forego all advantages in order to return to his old activities and to see his friends again." Celina, moreover—and under the circumstances this was a consideration that Mickiewicz could not ignore—"yearn[ed] for Paris, her family, and ha[d] a horrible fear of goiter." The poet was waiting for a guarantee in writing. In the middle of August, Cousin informed him that he was finally ready to forward Mickiewicz's name to Louis Phillipe for approval. On 16 August, the poet accepted the offer, adding:

> Writers of the North consider [a Slavic chair in Paris] to be very important for their countries.... Despite the diversity of opinions and interests that divide our races, your creation..., thanks to its purely literary nature, suits the enlightened inclinations of Poles as well as those of the Czechs and Russians. All Slavs unite on this occasion... in a common expression of gratitude to the government of His Majesty.[26]

The king approved the nomination on 8 September. In addition to his appointment to the chair "à titre provisoir," with its salary of 5,000 francs, Mickiewicz was also charged with "compiling a catalogue of Slavic manuscripts, in various dialects, which reside in the Royal Library." He was joining a faculty that during his four-year tenure at the Collège de France would include the philologist Jean-Jacques Ampère, the philosopher Jules Barthélemy-Saint-Hilaire, the Hellenist Jean François Boissonade de Fontarabie, the physiologist Claude Bernard, the orientalist Stanislas Julien, and the physicist Henri Victor Regnault. To the great French historian Jules Michelet, however, and his colleague Edgar Quinet, Mickiewicz proved to be more than a colleague; he became a close friend and an abiding inspiration.[27]

5

With classes at the academy finished in mid-July, and as he awaited a definite decision about his appointment in Paris, Mickiewicz took every advantage he could of the free time he now finally had. Near the end of July, Bohdan and Józef Zaleski paid him a visit, and "for almost a month" the three "rambled all over Switzerland." Some two weeks later, Mickiewicz again set out on a hike, but this time alone. "It's very good for my health," he informed Zaleski from Interlaken, "and I feel so energetic I even have the urge to write poetry." Fresh Alpine air aside, it would appear that Mickiewicz needed to get away from his family. Indeed, after several weeks of carefree wandering, he returned to an entire series of domestic calamities.[28]

The least of them was Maria's disappointment at her father's failure to be back home in time for the "ball *grandiose*" her mother had arranged for her birthday. More serious, however, was Władysław's illness. "Always miserable and weak," the two-year-old had come down with a potentially fatal "inflammation of the brain." And now, to add to Mickiewicz's grief, Celina suffered a relapse. "My wife," he informed Zaleski a week after his return, "was gravely ill, my little son barely escaped death.... Once again we were broken apart, me with my wife in the country, one child at home, the other with the Jundziłłs." To her sister, Celina explained her illness as an "inflammation of the intestines." Sainte-Beuve, for one, knew better, adding that Celina's condition "always has the effect of demoralizing [Mickiewicz] and rendering him incapable of resolve and any manner of thinking." In this instance, however, her relapse may in fact have had the opposite effect. It underscored for the poet that patriotic duty was not the only reason for accepting the position in Paris.[29]

On 23 September, Mickiewicz informed the Council of State of Vaud of his decision to resign as a professor of the Academy of Lausanne. "The French government," he explained,

> is going to establish... a chair of Slavic literatures; it offered it to me; very serious considerations compel me to accept it. Slavs consider this chair to be a position of great importance in the current circumstances.... Poles fear... that should I turn down the offer..., a foreigner might be appointed... and bring to bear an attitude hostile to our people. I thus feel obliged to accept this position..., which in the opinion of my countrymen has been entrusted to me in the interests of our national cause.

At the same time, he asked the Council for permission to retain the title of full professor, without, however, the salary that went with it for the previous six months. The title, he concluded, "will be a treasured souvenir of my stay in Vaud, where I experienced so many expressions of kindness and goodwill on the part of the government and the public."[30]

The news of Mickiewicz's resignation was not unexpected. Yet if the citizens of Lausanne were deeply disappointed, they displayed no rancor. On the contrary, their respect for Mickiewicz's decision was perhaps the most palpable token of their respect for the man. Not only did the Council reject Mickiewicz's request to forego his full professor's salary, and not only did it allow him to retain his title, but it recommended that he be made an honorary professor of the academy. "This act... will not be simply a piece of paper for you," they assured Mickiewicz,

> it will remind you of a small corner of the earth that was thrilled to have you for a few days, where your noble nature was appreciated, where your teaching, at once eloquent and profound, left a trace that will not be easily erased. Our affection and admiration will accompany you... in your new career.[31]

Classes at the Collège were not to begin until late December, but Mickiewicz was ready to set out for Paris immediately after handing in his resignation. The last week of his stay was filled with a series of farewell receptions, "all [of which] warmed his heart greatly." "As much as he may have come down on the Swiss and the Vaudoises during his first stay [here] and upon his arrival... last year," remarked Henryk Nakwaski, "he now praised them in equal measure." As the poet himself had predicted to Czartoryski a few months earlier, he was "leaving Lausanne not without some regret." Several months later, he was "recalling [it] as a paradise."[32]

On 5 October, at eight o'clock in the morning, "the Family of Mickiewicz, the great genius, got into a modest hired wagon. Only émigrés were there to bid him farewell: Jundziłł and his children, an Italian from Genoa [Scovazzi], [Nakwaski], and one Swiss, a professor, Olivier"—all people Mickiewicz had grown close to during his sixteen months in Lausanne and with whom he would remain in contact in the years ahead. That same day, noted Nakwaski in his diary, he witnessed another departure. Some Russian aristocrats were leaving the Hotel Gibbon in two huge carriages: "No one offered them a friendly hand, not a tear was shed—but boy, there was sure a lot of onlookers!!"[33]

Mickiewicz's leave-taking did not, of course, go unnoticed. *Le Courrier suisse*, perhaps his most ardent fan, reported his departure with what was, in effect, a heartfelt, and provincially self-effacing, eulogy:

> M. Mickiewicz is leaving us; but if the services of this outstanding man are no longer able to belong to us, his name, nonetheless, remains.... However swift M. Mickiewicz's passage may have been among us, far be it that his name should be the only gift he made us, and it would be somewhat ungrateful to say: *Ostenderunt nobis hunc tantum fata....* M. Mickiewicz leaves... a mark that will never be erased.[34]

6

From Lausanne to Bern, and then through Fribourg, the Mickiewiczes "did not take... the most direct route" to Paris: "poets," after all, "are permitted not to know the laws of geometry." Besides their household goods, Celina had also taken along the two servants she had employed in Lausanne. "You wouldn't believe," she explained to her sister, "how difficult it is to have a good and faithful servant"; but then too, they were Swiss, hence cheaper. Mickiewicz, for his part, had to borrow some 2,000 francs for the journey.[35]

"The roving family" arrived in Strasbourg on 8 October, "with difficulty, but without any incidents." "Little Władysław's health [was] still very delicate"; "Helena cried more often than usual, perhaps because her little body was tired by being constantly cooped up in a wagon and rocked by the rumble-tumble." The weather, though, was "nice, the customs officers pleasant, but the innkeepers [were] the same as always." This was Mickiewicz's fifth time in the capital of Alsace, and he was still able to "take it in with new wonder," which he tried to impress on his daughter. After several days of rest "in a beautiful apartment with a view of the Rhine" and visits to local Poles, the Mickiewiczes made their way back to Paris. They were met there, on 13 October, by the poet's cousin Łucjan Stypułkowski, whom Mickiewicz had asked to arrange temporary lodgings ("three rooms [or four] and five beds, but at the very least four"), but above all to "be there at their arrival," what with "three children, two servants, and tons of luggage."[36]

The family took rooms in a furnished hotel on Chausée d'Antin, "not far from the Wołowskis, hence good for the wife and children," while Mickiewicz and Stypułkowski searched out something more permanent. A week later, the Mickiewiczes moved into a second-floor apartment on Rue d'Amsterdam, today a corner of the Gare St. Lazare, in 1840 just barely on a map of Paris. It was not cheap (1,100 francs per annum), but Mickiewicz at least "had a separate room, set off by a salon from [Celina's]," where, ostensibly, he "wouldn't hear the children screaming and [where] he'd be able to work in peace." It took some time, as well as the sale of their Erard, to furnish it. And as if on cue, Celina again briefly "lost it."[37]

Little had changed in the emigration during Mickiewicz's absence; it was "a bit older," but still "active and seething." If anything, ideological differences among the émigrés had hardened into predictability: "the same stupidity," as Mickiewicz put it, "and even livelier quarrels." In this respect, the poet's appointment provided an ideal opportunity to reiterate calcified positions. The right, predictably, expressed "joy . . . as Poles upon learning whom the government had chosen"; the left, no less predictably, deplored the choice of "a man least qualified for [the chair]," who, it maintained, accepted it only "with a view toward himself" and, moreover, used family connections (Faucher) as well as political protection (Czartoryski) to secure it.[38]

As annoying as all this may have been to Mickiewicz, it was, in its own way, rejuvenescent. He found himself a center of attention once again, not for something as ostensibly banal as his genius—this he knew he possessed—but for his capacity to stir, to have an impact on the emigration, to flow *against* the grain. With its guarantee of material comfort in recognition of his hard work and talents, with its disinterested plaudits and genuine affection, perhaps Lausanne had offered the poet what he needed; émigré Paris was what he desired.

Mickiewicz wasted little time plunging back into a routine that he had, in effect, simply interrupted for sixteen months. Some friends had died, others had joined the priesthood, but most of the familiar faces were still there. Witwicki, Cezary Plater, Januszkiewicz, Gorecki, Stefan Zan—the circle of, for the most part, Lithuanians and devout Catholics welcomed the poet back into its ambit, thrilled that one of theirs was about to step onto an extraordinary stage, but at the same time somewhat bitter that he had obtained the chair "in a manner ... unworthy of either [him] or" the Collège. Within days of his arrival, he joined the Polish Club on rue Godot-le-Mauroy, an exclusive establishment that offered a reading room as well as billiards, chess, cards, checkers, and dinners, with which, apparently, "he was very satisfied"—as "a government employee and salaried," he could finally afford it. Before long, the Mickiewiczes were themselves holding regular soirées, on Saturdays, with music—besides Chopin and Celina herself on a new piano, Mickiewicz was particularly keen on the Polish guitarist Stanisław Szczepanowski—discussion, arguments, and the requisite games of cards and chess.[39]

With George Sand back in Paris, Mickiewicz now also had an opportunity to renew his most precious French acquaintance. He saw her often, at her place on rue Pigalle that she shared with Chopin, at Madame d'Agoult's, or at the salon of the most celebrated singer of the day (and Chopin's pupil), Pauline Viardot-Garcia—so often, in fact, that soon rumors were circulating to the effect that that Sand woman was trying to seduce the Polish poet as well. Sainte-Beuve, though, moved quickly to assure a concerned Caroline Olivier that "she loves Mickiewicz much, but without paying court to him, nor with any malicious intent. ... They're good together, and that's about all."[40]

For all of the socializing, the joy of seeing old friends and rediscovering familiar places, Mickiewicz was at the same time faced with a daunting task. His inaugural lecture at the Collège was scheduled for 22 December; he had two months to prepare for a lecture on a subject about which he could hardly claim much expertise. Like all Slavic intellectuals of the day, he had, of course, kept up with the newest developments in what was, in any case, a field in its infancy; many basic texts—including grammars and dictionaries—were only now being published for the first time, and there was still relatively little in the way of secondary literature. But despite this, and notwithstanding his extensive work on Polish history, Mickiewicz was an amateur, brilliant, to be sure, perceptive, often profound, always original, with an unusually capacious mind, but an amateur nonetheless. There was, in this respect, a good deal of truth to the Democrats' assertion that Mickiewicz was far less qualified than any number of ostensible candidates for the position, "Hanka, Šafárik, Jungmann, Kollár, and, finally Joachim Lelewel, to name a few." If the systematic, meticulous way with which he approached his courses in Lausanne was a reflection precisely of his intimate knowledge of Latin philology, the somewhat haphazard nature of his preparations for the course on Slavic literature indicated, if anything, a none too certain grasp of the material he was about to present. But then the Collège was not an institution of higher learning in the normal sense of the word. The courses it offered were, as he assured his brother, "for a nonprofessional public only," and in order to draw listeners, "professors must compensate with their eloquence." This arrangement, in other words, suited Mickiewicz's genius well. As Šafárik himself remarked upon hearing of the poet's appointment, "In all honesty, I don't expect much from this for scholarship."[41]

To make matters worse, the libraries and bookstores of Paris were not as rich in materials as Mickiewicz would have liked. The newly appointed professor found himself having to depend, often enough, on private collections. Zaleski, with his abiding interest in all things Slavic, was especially helpful, not only by lending books, but, more important, by providing bibliographic guidance. No less forthcoming in this regard were Mickiewicz's Russian acquaintances in Paris—the historian Pavel A. Mukhanov; the journalist Aleksandr I. Turgenev, an intimate of Viazemskii, Zhukovskii, and Pushkin; and, of course, Madame de Circourt—who, in turn, on occasion importuned friends in Russia on her friend's behalf. Their willingness to help Mickiewicz was certainly a measure of their admiration, yet it was also, perhaps, guided by ulterior motives. After all, with its potential to affect public opinion, Russians were no less concerned about the professor's performance than Poles. In this, their instincts proved sound: Mickiewicz in effect organized his entire course around what he already in his articles for *Pielgrzym Polski* projected as an age-old tug of two Slavic "ideas," the Polish and the Russian.

7

In contrast to his first lecture in Lausanne, Mickiewicz approached his Parisian debut "without the least bit of fear, but also without enthusiasm." A month earlier, as he was preoccupied with preparing for the course, Celina had what appears to have been a particularly trying relapse. The poet was "awfully glum and falling off his feet," with "increasingly less energy to bear" his "domestic grief"; "the children were squealing and wasting away." "Melancholy," he confessed to Zaleski, "has gradually found its way into the depths of my soul, whence it is difficult to chase away, particularly since I often have little time or freedom to work." His was indeed "a horrible cross to bear." But this too somehow passed, at least for the moment, and on 22 December, at 1:45 in the afternoon, Mickiewicz walked into an amphitheater at the Collège de France to inaugurate what would be a four-year course devoted, ostensibly, to Slavic languages and literatures.[42]

The room had begun filling an hour before the lecture; by the time it was about to commence, the auditorium was packed. Up front in the well, separated by a barrier from the professor's chair, sat "Czartoryski, Niemcewicz, [the former minister of education, Narcisse-Achille de] Salvandy, Montalembert, Michelet... and others," including, of course, Faucher and his wife. Cousin, however, was not present; as everyone had predicted, Thiers's cabinet had collapsed at the end of October. As for the rest of the audience, "There were some twenty women, Poles, and of the men most were also Poles, but there were also Frenchmen and others"—two Russians, including Aleksandr Turgenev, a few Germans, and "even subjects of the poor pasha of Egypt, recognizable by their caps." Practically all of the poet's Parisian friends were present. Mickiewicz entered wearing "a coat, dressed as for every day, with only a new hat in his hand, his hair tousled, his face unperturbed,... he walked in naturally, without bowing, . . . applause broke out." He was also a bit redder than usual, having "put down about half a bottle of Champagne just before the lecture for additional courage."[43]

The poet lectured for just about the entire allotted hour. Although he placed "a few squares of paper and small cards in front of him, he glanced at them only once or twice during the whole time." He spoke about the difficulty of his task, a foreigner lecturing in a language foreign to him about a literature foreign to the audience. But for all the modesty, this was, if anything, little more than an artful attempt to cover for what he himself must have felt was his lack of qualifications (and preparation) and hence to mold his listeners' expectations:

> In a course such as this, one cannot take the road specified by a familiar and preordained scholarly method. . . . Having already transcended the compass of grammar and philology, I will have to present to you, offer up to your assessment, monuments of literature, fruits of art. . . . Can preparatory research, even were we to have the time for it, provide us with the power to bring to the light of day the hidden life of a masterpiece . . . ? No; in order for life to erupt from a word created by an artist, it is necessary to pronounce a creative word on it, but such a word is impossible to pronounce when one does not command all the secrets of a language. (Dz. 8:14/LS 1:2*)[44]

The remainder of the lecture—which Czartoryski, for one, found "full of ideas, but by no means always clear"—Mickiewicz devoted to arguing how the Slavic world had always striven to be part of the West and how France now created an opportunity, here, in this most cosmopolitan of all cities, for "European peoples to learn about each other and even . . . to learn about themselves" (Dz. 8:15/LS 1:3–4). He spoke of how little the West was aware of this portion of Europe and of its civilizatory, literary, and scientific achievements; he spoke of the Slavs' "many dialects"—how (after Kollár) Russian is the language of "law and commands," Polish "the language of literature and conversation," Czech "the language of scholarship," South Slavic still a primitive "language of poetry

*The history of the "text" known as *Les Slaves* or *Littérature Slave* is complex. Excerpts and summaries of the lectures in Polish translation appeared more or less regularly in émigré as well as Poznań periodicals, most notably in the Parisian *Dziennik Narodowy*, which subsequently published each course in separate editions (1842, 1843, 1844, 1845), the first three years on the basis of notes and stenograms, the fourth on the basis of its French edition (1845). Since the lectures exist only as notes and (not always complete) stenograms that were translated immediately into Polish and in some cases back into French, with little or no editorial input from Mickiewicz, establishing a definitive version has proven almost impossible. There is still no critical edition of the lectures in the original French (published in full for the first time in 1849). Whereas Leon Płoszewski's Polish text in *Dzieła*, vols. 8–11, constitutes an attempt to bring together all existing witnesses (including a published German version), it too contains many inaccuracies; it is, nonetheless, the most comprehensive version available. In my quotations from the lectures, the first reference is to Płoszewski's version in *Dzieła*, the second is to the French stenogram as it appears in *Littérature slave* (LS). The two, however, do not always correspond.

and music" (*Dz.* 8:18/*LS* 1:7–8); and he insisted, in the end, that "almost all Slavic peoples" had been "implicated" in the struggle between "the eagle of Russia" and "the eagle of Poland" (*Dz.* 8:21/*LS* 1:11). As the lecture was drawing to a close, some mason began hammering outside the window. "The professor winced; immediately someone from the audience . . . drove the mason away." There was applause when Mickiewicz finished, "but briefer than at the beginning," and none during the lecture itself. Niemcewicz walked up to the poet and gave him a paternal kiss on the forehead.[45]

Witwicki considered Mickiewicz's performance "a complete success," albeit the professor's "manner of speaking was clipped, a bit acerbic, . . . by which . . . one could recognize a foreigner's timidity and lack of confidence." Turgenev could not but remark on "the strong Polish accent." Januszkiewicz agreed, but noted that even the Russians "admitt[ed] that Mickiewicz was worth listening to." Predictably, the right-wing Polish press enthused; the left simply ignored. French newspapers gave good reviews, noting, of course, "the light accent," but also the poet's ease with the language and his "unusual felicity of expression." As *Le Siècle* put it:

> This first lecture fulfilled with dignity the hopes that the talent and lofty reputation of the professor had raised. His language, strewn with daring images yet marked by a great and noble simplicity, his superb sense of beauty, combined with a profound and varied knowledge, produced a most vivid impression.[46]

As for Mickiewicz, "he was unhappy . . . with the lecture, and it seemed to him that it was a lot worse than it was." Upon reflection, however, he felt that "it was given . . . decently, clearly, and cleanly with regard to style," that "even though he was in a bad mood, [it] was successful enough, not brilliant, but decent." He seemed happy with the French reaction, but considered the whole thing little more than "un succès d'estime."[47]

Mickiewicz's debut before the civilized world transformed that year's Christmas Eve, together with the celebration of the poet's name-day, into an unusually joyous occasion. Some sixty people gathered at the Polish Club to drink toasts to the new professor. Celina was there, as was Maria, in a Swiss outfit. Niemcewicz "spoke at length about Mickiewicz, who answered just as lengthily." After the traditional meal, many of the guests, "mostly from Lithuania," repaired to the Mickiewiczes to listen to Stanisław Szczepanowski play the guitar. That evening, however, served only as an appetizer for what was to come.[48]

8

To celebrate Mickiewicz's name-day in proper fashion as well as the professor's debut at the Collège, Januszkiewicz invited some forty guests to his place on Christmas Day, mostly people from their circle, "poets, musicians, and everything that holds a pen be it badly or well," including Juliusz Słowacki, who had returned to Paris in 1838 after a six-year self-imposed exile. During supper, the guests raised toast after toast to the guest of honor, until finally Słowacki was asked to say a few words:

> [He] improvised . . . beautifully, but great pride shone through his verses. He threw himself at Mickiewicz's feet, albeit not out of respect, but as if vanquished. He then spoke again, but this time with more generous emotion.

After some hesitation, Mickiewicz stood up to reply:

> His entire face assumed a kind of angelic mien and a strange, ineffable brightness ringed his temples. Everyone stood up as if at the appearance of a deity come to pay mortals a visit. And he let flow from his mouth a river of words, the most wondrous thoughts and rhymes, with such force, such fury and power and at the same time with such grace that nothing could equal them. . . . We stood transfixed, the silence was deathly.

In the space of about 150 lines, the poet first spoke of his memories of and affection for Słowacki. He then turned to rebuke his friends for not having faith in his ability to lecture in a foreign tongue: "But I knew I would be able to speak, since be it in French or in German or in any other language, I feel that I have something to reveal to the world." Finally, he returned to the subject of poetry, "spoke of the poet's mission and concluded that there is only one road for him, hence (pointing to his heart) through love, thither (pointing to heaven) to God!"[49]

The reaction of those present approached hysteria. One guest got an attack "of spasms that lasted all night"; another took to bed "and ailed for two days"; "Słowacki wept," but then so did those around him:

> A kind of feeling of collective love swept over everyone. Near strangers embraced like old friends and swore mutual friendship. . . . The sick said they were healed, and artists felt imbued with a new creative force, which the genius had imparted to them at that moment.

The reception lasted well into the morning. The impression the poet made was apparently so powerful that "even the next day . . . those who described the evening left [an impression] equally as powerful on others." This was, by all accounts (and there were many of them), Mickiewicz's most affecting improvisation.[50]

After the poet had departed, Januszkiewicz suggested to those remaining that they surprise him with a cup commemorating the extraordinary evening and present it to him on New Years Day. The preparations for this occasion were more considered. Januszkiewicz decked his apartment out with "national coats of arms, . . . [David d'Angers's] bust of Adam . . . , a garland; Szczepanowski, whose playing ha[d] a great effect on Adam, [was] invited to play."[51]

It was largely the same group that had gathered at Januszkiewicz's on Christmas Day. Słowacki was chosen to present the cup, a rather garish thing, inscribed "To Adam Mickiewicz in commemoration of 25 December 1840," with little escutcheons containing the titles of the poet's works embossed all around, together with a slightly altered quote from his poem to Lelewel: "My name has run out ahead of King Bolesław's ranks, / Among Germanic judges and the sagacious Franks" (*Dz.* 1:142–43). Mickiewicz drank a toast of gratitude, and the cup was passed around to the accompaniment of Philareth songs, for years now an integral part of Polish intellectual folklore. After dinner, Mickiewicz took a place by the piano, filled the cup with wine, and again began improvising. After a while he launched into "a prophecy, that Poland will have a king, and its high priests and hetmans and knights." As he uttered the word "king," however, he was interrupted by a shout of "not so fast" from an unappreciative democrat, who felt the poet was referring to Czartoryski. The flow was broken; Mickiewicz could not (or would not) go on.[52]

It was after three in the morning when the guests began leaving, and they did so "with mixed impressions." The poet, for his part, was pleased with his cup, which he placed next to the one he had received from his Russian friends at the farewell dinner in Moscow some thirteen years earlier.[53]

News of the two improvisations spread quickly and widely, and not without some interesting repercussions. When Sand learned of them, she immediately recognized in Mickiewicz that trait which in part fed her fascination with Chopin. "Mickiewicz," she gushed in her *Journal intime*, "is the only great ecstatic I know . . . he is touched by that *grand intellectual disease* that makes him akin to the famous ascetics, to Socrates, to Jesus, to St. John, Dante, and Jeanne d'Arc."[54]

In describing the December improvisation for the purposes of her own near ecstatic musings, Sand referred to Słowacki as "a certain fairly mediocre poet." Her knowledge of the events came second-hand, and so too, most likely, did her opinion of Słowacki. But then something analogous soon appeared in an article published two months after the evening in a Poznań newspaper. The anonymous author, clearly no admirer of the younger poet (quite possibly the host himself), claimed that Mickiewicz had responded to Słowacki's improvisation by telling him "that he was not a poet . . . because [he] lacked love and faith." Mickiewicz may indeed have uttered something to that effect, but having it aired in print, and thus once again being humiliated, ostensibly, by his imagined rival, mortified an already humbled Słowacki. He immediately submitted a bitterly sarcastic response to one of the émigré newspapers, blaming his abasement on a Catholic, Lithuanian cabal. A month later, in May, he published the first five cantos of his Byronic masterpiece *Beniowski*. It concludes with a grandiose reimagining of a relationship that, it goes without saying, Słowacki experienced far more anxiously than the poet he had set up as his inexorable superego:

> You will always find me before you,
> Unbroken, haughty, and awesome . . . [. . .]
> Although today you repulse me?—the future is mine!—
> And beyond the grave will my triumph be! . . . [. . .]
> And the verdict I'll leave to the ages.—My bard, fare thee well!
> With you, God of the past, this canto concludes. [. . .]
> Fare thee well!—thus bid adieu not two foes,
> But two Gods, each on his confrontive sun.[55]

Mickiewicz's circle read both responses as a slap in the face to their regional and religious émigré collective. After deliberations, to which Mickiewicz was a party, it was decided that one of them should challenge Słowacki to a duel—a real one. Thanks to the intervention of Cezary Plater, the affair ended on a reconciliatory breakfast. But neither it nor the closure that the poem itself seemed to suggest succeeded in laying to rest what had become an abiding obsession on the part of the younger "God," one that would come back to haunt Mickiewicz soon.

But then too, the improvisations seemed to startle Mickiewicz himself. As he reported to Zaleski a few days after the first:

> I responded [to Słowacki] with inspiration that I have not experienced since I was writing *Forefathers' Eve*. This was good, because everyone from various parties broke down in tears and felt great affection toward us, and for a moment everyone was filled with love. At that moment, the spirit of poetry was with me.

The second improvisation only confirmed that the "gift from above" had returned, that as his "spirit soared" he felt himself to once again be a "vessel" through which God chose to speak. As he grew more confident on the daïs at the Collège, as the notes he would place before him became little more than props, the lectures assumed the flow of improvisation, wherein the discourse of scholarship (such as it was) alternately vied and fused with the voice of prophecy. Romantic form found its content.[56]

9

For the next six months, until the end of June 1841, Mickiewicz lectured twice a week, on Tuesdays and Fridays, for one hour in the afternoon—forty-one lectures in all (he missed only two). "When it came time to prepare," his daughter recalled years later, "he would more often than not pace around the living room the evening before, and [Celina] would play Mozart for him for hours on end. He never made any notes, and the next day he would leave in the morning with the lecture ready." If not, then, an improvisation in the strict sense of the word, each lecture was nonetheless ostensibly conceived and delivered as such, "demanding," as one of the émigré newspapers observed, "inspiration at every moment." And in this respect, Mickiewicz did not disappoint. There were times enough when his audience would "listen with inexpressible delight" as "he brought to light ever new vistas"; at one lecture (25 June)—devoted, not coincidentally, to prophecy—"some cried." As one French paper put it, "To try and reproduce the poet's inspiration, which animates his words, that elevated and religious diction which gives them something of greatness, would be to do so in vain."[57]

But if Mickiewicz's performance—enthusiastic, emotional, "never ever boring"—often riveted his listeners, it also came at a price. He was, after all, "a great improviser," as a correspondent from Paris explained to his Polish readers in Poznań, "following the impulse of his own whim" but at the same time "not submitting himself to the laws that are and must be indispensable for... scholarship." And indeed, from the very beginning the course was prone to all the dangers inherent in improvisation. Mickiewicz would jump from topic to topic, go off on tangents and digressions, and then not return to what was, supposedly, the main theme of a given lecture. He would repeat himself, discuss topics in one lecture that he had already covered in a previous one or, conversely, forget to deal with something he had announced he would treat later. As Witwicki reported to Zaleski, "there is at times disorder in the discussion, he goes on now about this and then again about that, just as it comes to him."[58]

For a scholar at home with his discipline all this might ostensibly pass. Mickiewicz's grasp of his subject, however, was not particularly sure, the state of Slavic studies at the time notwithstanding. For one, much of his information was second hand, drawn, moreover, from relatively few sources, and this usually uncritically and without attribution. But even here he often let his imagination get the better of facts, which in any case he would sometimes simply get wrong. He jumbled quotations, contradicted himself in the course of single lectures, and, as if incapable of braking his rhetorical momentum, embellished or even distorted for the purposes of the moment. Above all, he generalized and asserted categorically, leaving little room for nuance: "all," "none," "every," "always," "never," "everyone," "as everyone knows"—or, better yet, "as some have noted," although who, exactly, he rarely bothered to enumerate. "A little more methodological rigor wouldn't harm," remarked one French observer, "and sometimes one begins to deplore those broad vistas and synthetic overviews."[59]

Already the first lecture raised suspicions as to the professor's credibility, on the part, no less, of his colleague Michelet. But if in this instance it was the French historian who showed his ignorance (*guzla* is indeed a Balkan instrument and was not, as he believed, a product of Mérimée's imagination), Mickiewicz was, nonetheless, forced at one point to defend his "method" in public, having received what he said were "letters from Slavic scholars who either criticize[d] the outline of his lectures or objected to some of the details." His response, though, was as sweeping and as categorical—and as effectively evasive—as the lectures themselves. "I mention this correspondence," he proclaimed in his fifth lecture (12 January),

> because it is in every way typical; it is characteristic of the literary situation of the Slavs. . . . Literature is not practiced there for entertainment, art is not practiced for art's sake. . . . It is enough sometimes to launch into a critique of some poet to set into motion all the religious and political issues dividing the Slavic peoples. . . . It's impossible for me to embark upon a polemic to which I'm being challenged; above all, such a polemic would be interesting exclusively to the Slavic portion of my audience, and this at best only to a few people who have devoted themselves especially to Slavic studies. (Dz. 8:53/*LS*, 1:51–52)[60]

Amid this flood of facts and factoids, impressionistic ideas and rhetorically driven pronouncements, sometimes breath-taking insights but no less breath-takingly embarrassing gaffes and contradictions, to try and trace a coherent plan or conception would be as futile as it would be thankless, and, indeed, wrong-headed. Rather, as the poet conducted his occasionally rapt audience from the prehistory of the Slavs to the end of the sixteenth century, classifying, along the way, the Slavic dialects, discussing old legends and Slavic chronicles, explicating the *Lay of Prince Igor's Campaign* and Serbian epics, describing the rise of Muscovy and the Czech and Polish Middle Ages, and examining the Polish Golden Age, what emerged was a cluster of seemingly disconnected insights: that the absence of revelation among the Slavs was at once a blessing, a curse, and a promise; that the Slavic world is essentially bipolar, reflecting two antagonistic "ideas," the Polish and the Russian; that charismatic leadership, even when despotic, is necessary to impel history; and that prophecy is the highest measure of literature. During this first year of lectures, these insights were barely signaled, cropping up here and there in moments of inspiration with little elaboration or consistency in the course of what was largely a chronological exposition of history, larded heavily with extensive quotations (he "read poetry very nicely and pleasantly") and analyses of texts. Over the next three years, however, these same insights would begin to coalesce into nothing less than a renewed articulation of messianism, an extension of the vision informing *Forefathers' Eve*, part 3, *The Books of the Polish Nation and Polish Pilgrimage*, and the articles in *Pielgrzym*, but at the same time transformed and augmented by a new revelation.[61]

Reactions to all this were for the most part muted, and not all too frequent. The French press remained well-disposed, if only because Faucher and Adolphe Lèbre, yet another fan whom the poet had met in Lausanne and who was now the editor of the Catholic weekly *Le Semeur*, were still willing to write the occasional article about the course when others had moved on. As for his fellow émigrés, Mickiewicz himself thought he put his finger on it when he wrote to his brother that "they attend . . . in order to sniff out what party I belong to, aristocrat? democrat?" To be sure, but opinions on that matter had gelled long ago. What most roiled the émigrés now—and in this instance, "everyone," on both the right and the left—was the poet's ostensible fascination with Russia, and this, to their mind, not only at the expense of Poland, but in terms so admiring that, as one democrat put it, "Moscow itself could not complain about the course." In a particularly egregious flight of inspiration, Mickiewicz apparently claimed in one lecture (5 January) that it was Russia that was ordained to civilize the Slavs since by repelling the Mongols it had exhibited energy and a will to act. Scandalous words indeed—one Democratic paper went so far as to accuse the professor of apostasy—but then even Mickiewicz realized, in retrospect, that he had gone too far: when it came time to publish the Polish translation of this, his third lecture later that year, the poet insisted on "editing this entire passage . . . himself," since the stenogram, supposedly, "had not fully conveyed his thoughts." As could be expected, the decision to publish what was a version of the lecture revised *ex post facto* did not help matters.[62]

For the first three months the lectures appear to have been well attended, by the curious and the serious, the duty-bound and the fashion-conscious alike. In this respect, the publication that winter of the first substantive (but not necessarily always accurate) biography of the poet in French proved to be an effective piece of advertising. Its author, the prominent French literary critic Louis Loménie, was generally quite complimentary, although he warned his readers that "despite their beauty," the "purely national nature" of Mickiewicz's poetry as well as "a fantastic that draws more from the domain of faith than reason" made it "incomprehensible [to the French] and sometimes naïve to the point of puerility." Mickiewicz, for his part, was not altogether displeased. "The biographer's opinion about my poetry," he wrote to a young Pole hard at work translating it into French, "is very sensible and agrees with mine. The Frenchman knows his public's taste."[63]

Indeed, despite Loménie's enthusiastic approval of Cousin's choice for the chair of Slavic Literature, Mickiewicz's course inevitably began to suffer the same fate as that of any fad in Paris: from standing room only in the first few weeks to at most a few dozen listeners by April, and in any case overwhelmingly Poles. "The French," complained the professor to Domeyko, "care little about Slavdom"; and only the Polish press continued to publish abstracts of each lecture. Nonetheless, even a few French—Lèbre and Michelet's son-in-law Alfred Dumesnil among them—became regulars. Michelet himself came often as did Madames d'Agoult and Sand, usually in the company of Chopin. For his part, Aleksandr Turgenev hardly missed a lecture and regularly sent largely enthusiastic synopses to his friends in Russia, with the naïve hope that they might even get published. And then too, for visitors to Paris—Germans, Englishmen, Italians, various Slavs—an hour or two spent listening to this somewhat exotic, charismatic professor from the "North," with his "deep gaze" and "sad and dreamy physiognomy," his "angular face" and "prominent mouth creased at both corners," and "that harshly accented voice," became one of the city's attractions of the season.[64]

As the summer approached, the audience began to "disperse" and to "yawn." But the final lecture of the year, the forty-first, was well attended, drawing as it did those "who had not listened to the entire course and wanted, as it were, to figure everything out on the basis of the last lecture." In the previous lecture, some listeners cried as Mickiewicz practically channeled the voice of a sixteenth-century Polish Jesuit preacher. On 29 June, with the amphitheater again full of eager listeners, he was no less inspired. Returning to the notion of a bipolar Slavic world, caught between Russia and Poland, and its implications for the future of Europe, Mickiewicz spoke "as if he were not himself. His thought flowed in cascades, but words could barely keep up with it." When the professor concluded, he was greeted with "lively applause" (Dz. 8:597/LS, 2:295).[65]

10

A month after the final lecture, Mickiewicz was compelled to readmit Celina to the hospital in Vanves. As before, the poet's decision was a last resort. His wife had been suffering increasingly more frequent relapses ever since they had returned to Paris, exhausting Mickiewicz and disrupting the lives of the children. As he informed Jundziłł in February, "We're often deeply sad, and whenever I have to prepare for my course, when there's trouble at home, my mental health then suffers much and I age greatly." These spells, peculiar in their almost monthly regularity, would usually pass within a week, and Celina would return to family life, taking care of the children—Władysław's health was still delicate—humoring her husband, and playing the good hostess to his friends at their Saturday soirées. Indeed, in moments of calm, she could be "fantastically beautiful," "white like a pure dawn, with fathomless eyes, dark and large" and "hair the same color as her eyes."[66]

Mickiewicz tried to manage as best as he had already learned how. Each successive breakdown would nonetheless "knock the poor fellow off his feet," and Witwicki, for one, could "not understand how he could give his lecture[s]." Yet the course provided something of a distraction, as did the social obligations that went with it: a few hours spent with Witwicki after a lecture; dinner at the Polish Club; visits to Khliustin, Viardot, Sand; recitals by Chopin; a brief visit to the Zaleskis in Fontainebleau. Mickiewicz even decided to finally seek the French citizenship Cousin had promised in hopes of improving his position at the Collège, aware, though, that despite assurances the process could be a long one. That May his beloved Niemcewicz, age eighty-three, passed away, which required Mickiewicz's presence at the requisite rituals and input about how best to honor this most honored of Polish patriots. By the end of June, however, with the course finished and forced to spend more time at home, the poet no longer had the strength to tend to Celina and at the same time take care of the children. "I persevered for many months in great sadness," he informed Jundziłł in September. "With my wife constantly ailing, I finally had to shelter her in a home."[67]

On 30 July, shortly after he had left Celina once again in the care of Drs. Voisin and Falret, Mickiewicz returned home "with his soul in the clutches of affliction." As he was sitting in his study feeling "hopeless and near despair," the doorbell rang. The poet soon found himself face to face with "a man of medium build," about his age, slim but firm, with "closely cropped gray hair, neatly combed, covering a tall, full forehead." His "grayish blue eyes," "pleasant but sharp," gazed at him from behind blue-tinted wire-rimmed glasses. The man introduced himself as Andrzej Towiański and reminded Mickiewicz that they had met in Vilnius some twenty years earlier. I "bear good tidings," he announced and then proceeded to "tell [the poet] things about [him] which only God and [he himself] could know." What, exactly, it was that his visitor imparted, Mickiewicz never revealed, but, as he confided to Scovazzi some years later, "I spent a frightful night! It was Jacob wrestling. I finally believed in the power of the mercy of the Lord." From this moment on, Mickiewicz's "aim in life would be determined, and [his] path foreordained."[68]

CHAPTER NINE

SECTARIANISM (1841–1846)

On 15 December 1840, close to a million people gathered on a route from the Arc de Triomphe to the Invalides, stamping their feet in the fourteen-degree cold, to witness the arrival of Napoleon's remains from St. Helena. Like most of his fellow émigrés, Mickiewicz watched entranced as the towering catafalque drawn by sixteen magnificent horses carried the remains of the emperor past plaster statues of French heroes and kings, smoking braziers, and escutcheons inscribed with the names and dates of his victories. And right then and there, "in broad daylight," the poet had a vision (or so he later maintained when such premonitions were at a premium): "I saw a man driving a one-horse carriage from the depths of [Lithuania], in poverty, through mud and mist, and I sensed that this man was bearing *greatness! great things!*" Unbeknownst to Mickiewicz, that man was somewhere there in the enormous crowd, having come to Paris expressly to commune with the spirit of the victor at Austerlitz.[1]

I

Andrzej Towiański experienced his first call on 11 May 1828, while praying in the Bernardine church in Vilnius. On a date that would subsequently be marked in red on the Towianist calendar, he "saw in his spirit for the first time the entire Cause for the realization of which he had been sent to earth." The son of a relatively well-to-do landowner, he was at the time a twenty-nine-year-old magistrate at the city court with a law degree from the University of Vilnius—a former classmate, in fact, of Mickiewicz, although never part of his circle. He had been a sickly child, intensely introspective and deeply religious. As a young man with a taste for romantic poetry, the occult, and, quite possibly, Jewish mysticism, he had already sensed that he "bore within him God's thought." Now, as a magistrate, he had an opportunity to observe the workings of human nature, while at the same time already exercising an uncompromising moral focus in meting out justice. The experience in the Bernardine church simply confirmed his vocation. He felt destined to "move the earth from pole to pole."[2]

Before long, in the persons of his schoolmate Ferdynand Gutt, a bright, sensitive graduate of Vilnius's medical school with a deeply felt social conscience, and Walenty Wańkowicz,

Fig. 19 Andrzej Towiański. Daguerreotype, ca. 1850. Courtesy of the Adam Mickiewicz Museum of Literature, Warsaw.

the "dim-witted" painter known for his portrait of Mickiewicz on the Crimean crag, Towiański found two acolytes. He began speaking to them of a ladder of spiritual perfection, of Christ and Napoleon, and of the interdependence of this world and the world of spirits; of the need "to work in faith on the moral perfection of oneself and others who are pure, to lay away moral and physical strength" so as to be ready for the imminent arrival on earth of a "new man" of God, "a Christ from among our own people," who will lead mankind in a great spiritual rebirth. "Pure, simple, and uninfected . . . by worldly wisdom," Gutt had no doubt that this "man of providence" was already standing before him, the very same man, in fact, whom "[Mickiewicz] would later see in Father Piotr's Vision [in *Forefathers' Eve*, part 3]."[3]

Two years after his life-altering experience, Towiański married Karolina Max, the beautiful, and spiritually evolved, daughter of a polonized German wainwright. Gossip had it that the two spent their wedding night "in a cemetery, calling up spirits so as to consummate their *marriage* not only physically, but also *spiritually*." However this may be, Karolina quickly grasped her role as Towiański's helpmate, the female half of a "holy family" in which she embodied St. Philomena and St. Margaret combined. For the moment, though, she remained in the background, nurturing a family while her husband made his first attempts to spread his message. Unaffected by the uprising, which in any case he deemed misbegotten, Towiański resigned from his position at the municipal court and in 1832 traveled to St. Petersburg, for decades a magnet for spiritualists of various stripes. After a year and a half of ambitious, but unsuccessful, proselytizing—apparently two of the tsar's ministers, Sergei G. Stroganov and Mikhail M. Speranskii, refused to bite—he took his mission to the spas of Central Europe and the Polish émigrés of Dresden. There too, however, his gospel met with skepticism, although Mickiewicz's friend Odyniec, who ran into Towiański in Dresden in 1835–1836, found "a great deal of benefit" in his contacts with him, "particularly with respect to his psychological analysis of the phenomena of inner life."[4]

By 1837, Towiański was back in Lithuania, heir now to the family estate in Antoszwińcie. Chastened somewhat by his failure to win any converts in his travels, albeit all the wiser, he turned his attention to administering his property, a fifteen-chimney village with some ninety souls. He approached the task with the same inner focus he had exercised in the courtroom. Each of his actions, each decision constituted a form of spiritual labor, wherein even the most minor chore provided an occasion for considering its spiritual significance and every undertaking, right down to dancing the polonaise, demanded an appropriate spiritual posture—what Towiański called "tone." "There were times," Mickiewicz recalled him saying, "when I would meditate for an entire day on how shoes should be cobbled, I would contemplate for several hours in prayer what kind of nails to buy . . . for shingles, so that everything would be in truth." Needless to say, "despite his deep grasp of things, he underst[oo]d not a single joke or pun."[5]

Not an easy master to serve, by any means, for a proper spiritual posture implied an exacting moral code, together with incessant sermonizing to this effect. But if all of this assumed acceptance on the part of his peasants of their lot in life, Towiański was, by the same token, a master more sensitive than most to the miseries a serf endured in neofeudal Lithuania. He was a strict but loving father who cared almost as much for the physical as for the moral well-being of his subjects. With time, and with a good dose of romantic populism, that sensitivity metastasized into idolization. "In us the tone of the peasant, of the Slav," he taught—or at least as Mickiewicz explained it—"is fouled, contaminated as it is by doctrines, irony, the conventions of the salon. The peasant's tone: child-like love, simplicity, openness."[6]

Not surprisingly, Towiański's efforts to "speak spiritually to [peasants] as brethren" were not particularly appreciated by his spiritually less enlightened neighbors, who at one point had him investigated for symptoms of insanity. And then too, there was the matter of the chapel *vel* "temple" he had built on the estate and rumors of the "masses he performed" there, with "a woman standing on the altar dressed as Truth, like St. Philomena." In any case, all that the tsarist police found objectionable was the statue of Napoleon Towiański had erected on his property; they probably assumed that this was a political statement.[7]

Exactly eleven years later, on 11 May 1839, Towiański had his second revelation. "He sensed God's Cause" and immediately took this to be a summons "to build new structures on a new foundation." He obtained a passport, cashed in for an extended voyage, arranged for the care of five of his six children—and patiently awaited further signs. Finally, on 23 July 1840, "there appeared in a bright light over Antoszwińcie a white cross in the sky"; "that same day the Most Blessed Mother appeared with her arm outstretched toward France." All was clear now: the "new foundation" would be the Polish emigration. Towiański gathered his peasants in the chapel, bequeathed to them a set of "directives and admonitions," and with their blessing and that of the parish priest set off west with his wife and eldest son Jan. Gutt, together with his wife Anna, Karolina's older, uglier, and, as it would turn out, even more powerful sister, whom the Towiańskis had managed to foist on their friend, followed a year later. So too did Wańkowicz.[8]

After extended stays in Poznań and Saxony, the Towiańskis came to Paris only long enough to witness Napoleon's funeral. From there they traveled on to Brussels, where in the person of General Jan Skrzynecki, a veteran of the Napoleonic campaigns and a hero of the uprising whom Towiański had met earlier at Czech spas, he hoped to gain his first prominent émigré convert. In the course of a seventeen-day retreat at the inn where Napoleon stayed before the battle of Waterloo, Towiański laid out his vision.

Memorialized in a screed entitled *Symposium*,* it was a typically syncretic one, combining elements of Christian adventist theology—Towiański always did insist that he was a

*Written on 17 January 1841, *Biesiada* was first published in a lithographed edition in 1842 by Towiański's Catholic adversaries as a way of compromising him.

faithful son of the Church—with not-so-Christian notions of palingenesy and spiritualism, of a kind with much of the illuminism of the day. "Columns" of good and evil spirits circled around the globe, reincarnating themselves in various (not necessarily only human) earthly forms and "impelling" them either "upward" toward good or "nether" toward evil; souls "groaned" for total spiritual transformation in God; mankind "worked" and "stirred" and "effected sacrifices" in order to draw progressively closer to divinity; and all this across seven epochs, the first of which had been initiated by the appearance of Christ, the remainder to be so by "men of providence." Of course the first of these providentials was none other than Towiański himself, forerun by the "pure spirit" of Napoleon and now called to realize the second epoch of God's Cause. There was not a word here about Poland as such.[9]

All of this was—and by its nature cannot but remain—very obscure, expressed, moreover, in an appropriately eccentric language that wove the rhetoric of personal revelation and Biblical discourse with dialectisms, neologisms, anachronisms, and legalese, comprehensible, if one may use this word, only to the initiated.* But then it was not so much *what* Towiański said, whether it actually made any sense, but rather *how* he spoke, how he gazed, how he modulated his voice, how he smiled and frowned, how, with his right hand tucked à la Napoleon into his high-buttoned frock-coat and his eyes peering through blue-tinted spectacles, he exuded absolute conviction and confidence in his truth. In Skrzynecki's case, this only went so far: the magic of the moment, when despite his gout the general fell on his knees in the mud of Waterloo, dissipated soon enough upon more reasoned, orthodox reflection. For Mickiewicz, the resonance of both the message and the messenger would be profound and lasting, "as if something had been set aseething and aboiling in [his] heart."[10]

2

For some eight years now Mickiewicz had been adrift. His inability—or, rather, his lack of desire—to write had effectively discomposed his image as a romantic poet. His failure to move the emigration on his terms had alienated him even further from a collective whose increasingly hopeless predicament, with its concomitant sense of homesickness and dislocation, he was nonetheless forced to share. Marriage had become more a source of grief than comfort. When for a moment it appeared as if he might find a vocation and, as he himself publicly admitted, a place that offered him "everything that could tie an exile to a foreign land" (*Dz.* 8:8/*LS* 1:1), his unassuageable conscience impelled him to abandon that prospect for yet another opportunity to atone through deed. For all of its potential,

*If my translations of Towiański's texts as well as those of his disciples may at times read like gibberish, it is because that is how they read in the original. For a historical analogy in English, one might look to the *Book of Mormon* (1829), albeit without the Old Testament "realism"; or, for that matter, just google the word "spiritual."

however, the appointment at the Collège was fraught with anxiety, the pressure of continual public scrutiny and high expectations made all the more vexing by a realization that he might not be up to the task. To be sure, his faith continued to sustain him. Yet short of complete submission to the Church, which, unlike so many of his friends, he was neither able nor willing to countenance, its power to revitalize was, it seems, exhausted. Mickiewicz felt spiritually unfulfilled and restless. As he confided to Witwicki at one point, "I was not born for happiness."[11]

Celina's reinstitutionalization that July served only to bring all the frustrations and regrets, the sense of instability, lack of compass, and émigré listlessness to a chaotic surface. Poetry, emigration, family, the church, even the course at the Collège—just so many dead ends. And now, precisely as his self-pity was at its most intense, there appeared a man, confident, focused, and accepting, who claimed that "everything would be simple, clear, comprehensible..., one need only prostrate oneself and surrender to Christ the Lord." Towiański brought Mickiewicz a promise of multiple reliefs: "this would be [Celina's] final illness"; the emigration was coming to an end; "artistic rapture" was, in fact, "a misfortune sent as punishment for the sinner." "God," he assured the poet, "has called upon me to give you an inner fatherland and an external one as well." There was, truly, a purpose after all. Mickiewicz surrendered, and for perhaps the first time in his adult life he finally felt "at peace"; there were "flowers and spring both in [his] heart and in [his] soul." As he recalled several years later to one of his own disciples:

> As far as I remember, from my earliest youth I was always seeking something, first from every book, then in every person, in every country. After looking around, after coming to know, I would realize that it was not that same *something*. But now God has... shown to me that *something* through [Towiański], that essence, which is it alone, beside which everything else is an illusion.

Mickiewicz had found his "haven of last resort."[12]

Suddenly everything made sense—the previous year's improvisation at Januszkiewicz's, the "vision" during Napoleon's funeral, in fact a lifetime of dreams and prophecies, omens and premonitions. Hopes that he had cherished now felt "nearer," notions he had always nourished "were explained and buttressed by categorical proofs." The world of spirits, Towiański assured him, did indeed exist; "the influence of the invisible, incorporeal world on the sphere of human thoughts and actions" was an irrefutable fact. The Catholic faith, "one of the vital elements of [Poland's] independence and future existence," could indeed be roused from its routinized torpor through spiritual renewal. Napoleon was indeed the great "name of the age," whose mission to save a world "corrupted by the eighteenth century" was guided by his "constant contact with the invisible world." And Towiański himself: was he not himself, perhaps, that "great man of the future, the hoped-for national Messiah [whom] Poland... awaited and presaged in the future"? As Mickiewicz explained to Skrzynecki some months later,

> My faith in Andrzej is the upshot of my entire life, of my whole nature, and of all my spiritual labors. Whoever reads my works should be convinced of this. I won't mention minor poems sent out into the world in my youth ("Romanticism," "Ode to Youth"); my later works, namely, *The Books of the Pilgrimage* and *Forefathers' Eve*, part 4 [i.e., 3], attest to the fact that I intuited and foretold what is happening.

Most crucially, what Towiański seemed to be offering Mickiewicz was a way, finally, of transforming words and thoughts into a deed of ostensibly immense spiritual—and, hence, practical—consequence. It would take some five years for the poet to realize that in this his faith in Towiański may have been founded on a misunderstanding.[13]

For the moment, though, what tipped the scale was this "artless Lithuanian's" way with the sick Celina. "On the strength of Andrzej's promise" and "against the advice of her doctors," "in the heat and in the midst of a storm," Mickiewicz checked his still "completely deranged" wife out of the sanitarium and brought her to Towiański's apartment in Nanterre. There, thanks to his "*prayers and advice*," together with a ritual laying on of hands and the gift of an amulet, "she miraculously came to her senses." Never mind that this was a protracted ordeal; that Celina remained sequestered for days, while Towiański by turns cajoled and browbeat and comforted the woman, reminding her of the great spiritual powers she possessed on account of being Jewish; never mind that even Towiański wondered whether she had fully recovered—to Mickiewicz this was nothing short of a miracle, and the man who had wrought it "a prophet,... a storehouse of wondrous divine mysteries," in possession of much power. Even Celina muttered on being healed, "Moses walked on the mountain and spoke."[14]

Celina's recovery, though, was just one of many "unimpeachable signs and proofs" that Towiański had ostensibly vouchsafed Mickiewicz. A few weeks after their initial encounter, Brother Andrzej had a remarkable vision in which, through a past-life regression, he divined for the poet nothing less than his purpose on earth, or, rather, that of his wandering spirit:

> It had been a stony-hearted knight famous for his valor, constancy, and ascetic life. It had been a monk famous for his asceticism and martyrdom. It had been the Maid of Orléans. It had been a prophet before Jesus Christ. It is a prophet today and will be one before the third [of the seven men of God]. It is suffering its most recent lives because of its failure to fulfill the Lord's admonition.

Towiański concluded that Mickiewicz was none other than "great Israel," descended from that most ancient clan of spirits which was destined to save the world. But was this all that the appellation suggested? Had Mickiewicz, perhaps, confided to his spiritual advisor what he had once ostensibly confided to Jaenisch and would later repeat to Ksawery Branicki, and what his Jewish contemporaries apparently had on good authority, that "as a Frankist, the greatest poet that Poland ever had... belong[ed] to [their] nation"?[15]

As Odyniec had recognized from his own conversations with Towiański, the mystic was deft at negotiating not so much the journeys of spirits as the labyrinths of human souls. He had come to Paris well acquainted with Mickiewicz's works and even knew a thing or two about the man himself. Now, with the poet standing—or, more likely, kneeling—before him, prepared, in his despair and hope, to surrender unconditionally, Brother Andrzej grasped quickly enough the knot of anxieties, complexes, doubts, and desires that at once nourished and tormented the author of *Forefathers' Eve*. Of course in the process of working them through, Towiański was not beyond manipulating them for his own purposes. But by this very same token, he was also confirming—flattering—Mickiewicz's aspirations. In a note written to the poet some three months after his conversion, Towiański recorded a vision he supposedly experienced in which Mickiewicz recited to him "*with great force, fervor, and joy*":

> I was a prophet and will remain one,
> I'll pay my bygone debts.
> And this new path of contrition,
> Ever closer to my God,
> Will arouse my torpid fervor
> For singing praises to the Word.
> And I'll let forth a song in wisdom,
> Which I sang out of vanity before.

The Man of God needed the Poet-Prophet as much as the seeker needed journey's end.[16]

Proofs of Towiański's mission were not, however, vouchsafed Mickiewicz alone. At about the same time as Towiański was revealing his "teachings about creation, about the destinies of peoples and nations, about their generations, their natures, and the relationship of human spirits with the visible and invisible world" to the poet, he was also "confiding his mysteries" to two other prominent émigrés. One was Mickiewicz's old friend Antoni Gorecki, known for his piety; the other was Izydor Sobański, a veteran of the uprising and a popular figure among the exiles, albeit with a weakness for things arcane. It was to this trio of "the chosen" that on Saturday, 7 August 1841, at 10:00 A.M., "the brother... from Lithuania" announced the inception of what he called "God's Cause" and with it the creation of "a sacred Contingent under the leadership of Jesus Christ devoted to the impending cause of the people." He sent his three "ministers" forth into the émigré community to bear witness to "the imminent arrival of... days of joy"—while he himself went into seclusion in Nanterre to await a sign indicating the appropriate moment to reveal his message in person.[17]

And bear witness Mickiewicz did, in letters and conversations overflowing with the indescribable rapture of rebirth and the certainty of faith. "Great events are imminent," he proclaimed to anyone who would listen; "God is taking [the emigration] under his wing"; signs that its "misfortunes are about to end" and that "a new redemption of the world would soon ensue" were already nigh. "Fall on your knees and thank the Lord," he enjoined Zaleski, for "great things" were happening. "Hurry, hurry, hurry to [Paris] immediately to comfort, to gladden your heart, to adorn it with blossoms and greenery," upon which in a burst of inspiration Mickiewicz broke into ecstatic, and none too coherent, verse:

> My nightingale! Take wing and sing!
> Sing and bid farewell
> To dreams fulfilled and the tears you've spilled,
> To your perfected song. . . .
> For a voice was heard and the die was cast.
> And the mysterious weight of years
> Brought forth a fruit and wonders wrought!
> And it will lift the world. (Dz. 1:414)[18]

Yet when pressed about the nature and implications of these miracles and signs, Mickiewicz proved defensive and frustratingly unforthcoming: "To write more," he declared, "is impermissible." Like others who visited him during those first weeks of ecstasy, Ludwik Plater "found him with a radiant face, his spirit soaring, and unusually agitated." But after hearing him go on about the miracle that God was revealing to the emigration, about its imminent return home and the need to "wait patiently for the event that was soon to occur," Plater could only shrug. "What all this is founded on," he admitted to Czartoryski, "I don't know." To Mickiewicz, however, nothing could have been clearer:

> This is what God had decided . . . by means of extraordinary events that are nigh, that will occur without fail. It is this that is being revealed at the moment, what is about to be fulfilled, but one must believe that this is so.[19]

And indeed, Towiański's injunctions about discretion notwithstanding, no *rational* explanation *could* be forthcoming. This was ultimately a matter of faith, as ineffable as it was irrefutable. Under the circumstances, perhaps the fullest response to those who would assay it was the resigned silence of a believer. "I cannot write at length about this," Mickiewicz quit his brother, "I only repeat that time will soon manifest to all what we know and what every one of you can feel with your spirit... if you trust in God more than you do in the wisdom and power of the world."[20]

Rumors quickly spread throughout the émigré community, where minds were "in a constant state of paroxysm": "Within six months Poland [was to] be as it once was, and the emigration [would] return to the homeland," "not in the course of current events," moreover, "but through an extraordinary occurrence"; more prosaically but no less fantastically, it was bruited that "the sultan had died, Russia [was] threatening Constantinople, a new arrangement of the countries of Europe [was] about to take place." And all this because of the appearance of a mysterious "guest" from Lithuania, "a mystical figure... who effected a great revolution in Mickiewicz and awakened in him a conviction of a return to Poland that was certain and nigh." Some took the rumors to heart, with one émigré going so far as to "sell [his] furniture and move to an auberge... in order to be less... tied down." Others sought explanations from the poet only to walk away bemused. Still others surmised that perhaps "out of grief" Mickiewicz too had finally lost it. But no, to everyone attempting to "detect... any gesture that... might indicate a man... suffering from a loss of sanity," the poet appeared "healthy in body and mind, natural, garrulous, calmer than ever."[21]

"Many thought I'd gone mad," Mickiewicz conceded to Domeyko, "but now that they're convinced that I'm saner than ever, it goes without saying that now I'm simply *a mystic!*" To Jundziłł, however, the poet insisted on his sanity in more ominous terms. "How could other people, known for their common sense and enlightenment, have gone crazy together with me," he wrote, pointing to Gorecki and Sobański "as evidence of the truth of [his] words." Mickiewicz, it seems, was already beginning to measure the world with the circumscription of a sectarian, wherein there were only us and them, those who made the leap, "unconcerned about the gossip of people and their faith or lack thereof," and those who did not. And if, as he assured Zaleski, he "had not the slightest intention of converting" the latter, neither was he likely to take kindly to those who would question his beliefs or, worse, try to sway him.[22]

But no less ominous was the fullness with which Mickiewicz surrendered. Within weeks the poet was addressing Brother Andrzej as *Mistrz* (Master). "In everything I've learned from... this Lithuanian unschooled even in worldly wisdom," he explained to Jundziłł, "I see a master! a master in history and philosophy and poetry and politics"—a man perfect in every respect, but by the same token one who at once terrified and captivated him like a protective, accepting, omnipotent father. It was only a matter of time before he began addressing his *Mistrz* as *Pan*, that is, "Lord and Master."[23]

3

Thanks to the carelessness of the bishop of Paris, Towiański succeeded in ordering a mass in Notre-Dame for the morning of 27 September, yet another day subsequently marked in red on the Towianist calendar. Two days earlier, Mickiewicz had his publisher Januszkiewicz send out invitations "to every émigré living in Paris" asking his "brethren to take part in a mass... for the intention of accepting and giving thanks for the grace poured down by the Lord." Some two hundred did, together with Celina, Karolina Towiańska (with son), Gorecki, and Sobański, as well as a handful of sympathizers whom the threesome of "ministers" had already managed to incline to the Cause. For the duration of the mass Towiański and Mickiewicz knelt before the altar, then "took communion very contritely." (Sobański, for his part, "sat among the rest and had a tired and unnatural cast, seemingly embarrassed.") The service concluded, Towiański rose to speak ("something forbidden to absolutely everyone in the world" under the rules of the church); his moment had finally come. The "man of Providence" spoke for forty minutes, informing those gathered in the cathedral that he had been "sent by the Lord" to minister to the emigration and to proclaim "that the... end of its and the Fatherland's sufferings [was] approaching, that the work of mankind's renewal had already been inaugurated and completed in heaven, that it [was] descending to earth and would be entrusted to people whom Providence chooses as its instrument, that the times [were] fast approaching when the Gospel would become the law binding mankind." Falling to his knees, he declared "in a solemn and raised voice" that God's Cause and the reign of Christ had already begun. He promised to explain everything in writing soon. "The émigrés cried, Mickiewicz and his wife cried, and everyone felt sorry for Mickiewicz."[24]

Towiański's debut "caused a huge commotion among the Poles in Paris." "Some ma[d]e him out to be a madman, others a con man, others f[ou]nd him to be none too pure in his practices." Opinion, in other words, was not all that divided. As could be expected, the Democrats saw in the whole affair a plot by Catholic royalists, or maybe even Russian agents, meant to distract the emigration "from resolute action"—and in any case, they had given up on Mickiewicz long ago. The Czartoryski camp, for its part, was as embarrassed as it was concerned. If in public it reacted to Towiański's coming out with reserve, privately the prince's people expressed alarm at the notion that, as one of them put it directly to Mickiewicz, the emigration's "future efforts should rest on mystical, and thus ephemeral, vague, impermanent, exultation and not on national virtues." Its reputation with a host already feeling importuned by its presence was at stake, and with it that of the Polish cause.[25]

It was, however, among "the Catholic party" that Towiański's appearance and Mickiewicz's conversion caused the greatest consternation. After all, Witwicki reminded his friend, many of them "owed [the poet] the greatest service a man can render fellow man, when not so long ago [he] [him]self... turned them toward God, toward Christ the Lord and His Holy Church." Now, it seemed to some, he was betraying the very teachings he had impressed so lovingly on others. Smelling the telltale odors of heterodoxy, a few of the more concerned—among them Cezary Plater, Witwicki, and Aleksander Jełowicki—met immediately after the service in Notre-Dame in order to draw up an orthodox response. "Catholics," they declared, "are forbidden to believe in what does not come from the Church through normal channels, regardless of whether the matter comes from God or not; that no miracles, no occurrences should deviate us from this rule, since Satan too works miracles."[26]

Few noses proved more sensitive in this regard than Jełowicki's, Mickiewicz's erstwhile publisher, ardent admirer, and acolyte. In his new vocation as a warrior of the church, he seems to have found in the specter of Towianism his own cause, which effectively served to (at)test his faith. Recently returned from theological studies in Rome and with his ordination only weeks away, he set about investigating and interviewing and mobilizing, all the while keeping his cohort in Rome—Fathers Kajsiewicz, Semenenko, Hube, and Duński—informed of the latest developments. Ever since their days at Jański's Little Home, and with Mickiewicz's encouragement, this coterie of pious patriots had been contemplating the creation of a Polish monastic order. That they now chose to forge their Fraternity of the Resurrection in a struggle against what they deemed to be heresy and possibly even national apostasy says much about their conflicted relationship with the man they "loved like son[s]." For Jełowicki in particular, this struggle turned into an obsession.[27]

But then too, among this "little flock" were also some of Mickiewicz's closest friends. It was to them that he turned first with the joyous news of his conversion, hoping that they might share in the miracle. Zaleski, for one, was taken aback initially, fearing, like so many others, "whether betimes in the presence of his mentally ill wife [Mickiewicz] himself had not gone crazy." He nonetheless tried to indulge him with assurances that he too was "constantly awaiting some miracle or sign that would move [him] profoundly, transform [him] and impel [him] to action on behalf of a great cause." As a devout Catholic, though, Zaleski was frightened, for his friend, certainly, whom he implored to at least go to confession, but even more for himself: all the talk about spirits and the seven ages and men of providence bordered dangerously on the heterodox. He never did get to experience any miracles or signs, and never could bring himself to share in his friend's new life. By the same token, though, he also declined to condemn it. Like Mickiewicz, he was always mindful that theirs was a relationship built on the mutual "respect for . . . the freedom of [the other's] spirit, . . . leaving the entire matter between [themselves] and the truth to [their] spirit and the Lord."[28]

The same could not be said for Witwicki, a very different personality than the softhearted, solicitous Zaleski. No less stubborn than Mickiewicz, it was now becoming evident that he was also no less doctrinaire than Jełowicki. From the very beginning, Witwicki had expressed more than just skepticism of what he called his friend's "ecstasies." He felt that they were, in fact, dangerous, that in his moment of despair Mickiewicz may have "added to *what is there* something *that is not*." As for Towiański, Witwicki's confessor assured him he was a man "in heresy," which assurance sufficed. His appearance constituted, in this respect, "a great temptation for [Mickiewicz]—all the more frightening in that many... might follow." Whether it was Witwicki's unforbearing tone, his insistence that Mickiewicz submit to "an immediate and *satisfactory* confession," or his doubts about the miraculous nature of Celina's recovery, or whether it was his disingenuous attempt to implicate Zaleski in his efforts to lead their mutual friend away from temptation, Mickiewicz was deeply hurt by his reaction to his transformation. "Between us," he told Witwicki after a visit to his sunny apartment in Paris, "the sun of the soul is no longer as bright as it was earlier." What was once an intensely intimate relationship cooled markedly. When "in the old days," Witwicki complained to Zaleski, "not a day would go by that we wouldn't see each other,... now [Mickiewicz] doesn't come see me for a month, doesn't even drop in, though he passes my entryway." The rift would only grow wider as Witwicki drew increasingly, and publicly, closer to the Catholics militant while Mickiewicz, in turn, "envelop[ed] himself more and more in Towianism, like a fly in a spider-web." For all of his genuine love for the poet, Witwicki could never "forget that [he himself was] first and foremost a defender and servant of the Church."[29]

Witwicki's fears, though, were all too justified. In the weeks following Towiański's appearance in Paris, some from Mickiewicz's circle soon found themselves, too, attracted to the Master's teachings, if only thanks to the authority of his no less persuasive, no less charismatic "minister," whom over the years they had come to trust instinctively in matters of spirit. Eustachy Januszkiewicz succumbed almost immediately. After a three-hour conversation with the poet only days after the latter's conversion, the publisher was awestruck:

> Gazing at the bright faces of [Mickiewicz, Gorecki, and Sobański], in which a genuine conviction about the truth is reflected as in a mirror, since we take them to be sensible people, respectful of God and people, since it's impossible to assume that they would seduce others, one is left with no other choice but to believe or await a portent of events.

It was not long before a handful of others—Stefan Zan, Kajsiewicz's once inseparable companion Leonard Rettel, Aleksander Chodźko, the poet's, as well as Celina's, old friend from St. Petersburg, in the West now after ten years in the Near East working for the Russian diplomatic service—each with his own need for spiritual comfort, chose to follow their mentor. "From childhood," Chodźko confessed at one point to Mickiewicz, "you've been an exemplar for me in poetry and everything that is noble. That is why I came to believe in you so, that is why I place all my hopes in you, as you do in the Lord." (Chodźko also placed a bundle of securities in the poet's hands, hoping his friend could sell them for a higher profit in Paris while he himself took off for England.) Willy-nilly, Mickiewicz was nurturing yet another stable of disciples whose loyalty to him, in effect their gateway to the Master, would not waver, particularly in the face of rifts that inevitably began disrupting God's Cause.[30]

And indeed, there was trouble in Towiański's budding garden almost from the start. The first to have his doubts was also the first to have converted. After those initial moments of captivation by a man who was "good, humble and easy, and honest," General Skrzynecki sensed that something was amiss when Towiański wouldn't "openly admit the divinity of Christ," when he let on that "he had not been to confession for some twenty years," and then walked off in a huff when confronted on these issues. "I even suspect him of charlatanism," the general ventured to Mickiewicz. But so too, soon enough, did "minister" Gorecki, who realized that "the whole thing was a comedy or madness" upon learning that the sermon the Master had given in Notre-Dame, which was supposedly dictated directly by God, had been subsequently redacted with Mickiewicz's help. Although Towiański decided against publishing it, the damage was done. These turns of events now became just so much fodder for those arraying themselves against the self-proclaimed prophet and at the same time hoping to deprogram his most prominent disciple. After all, "if the simple but none-too-great mind of Gorecki was capable of grasping that clumsy Satan had appeared in our midst through the mouth of a Prophet, why could the mighty mind of Mickiewicz not admit this truth."[31]

But neither Mickiewicz nor Towiański viewed the defections as much of a setback. The company of believers was, in fact, slowly growing. On 8 December (the tsar's name-day, as one émigré newspaper thought it was noting ironically), a handful of them gathered at the ancient church of Saint-Séverin in the Latin Quarter for another public manifestation of faith. With all due solemnity, the Master proceeded to hang in one of the chapels a copy of the icon of Our Lady of Ostrobrama in Vilnius, painted especially for the occasion by Wańkowicz. In yet another appeal to his émigré brethren, "martyrs for freedom who long and feel," Towiański called upon them to come before the image and "examine [their] heart of hearts" in preparation for the "great hour of God in which God's Cause will appear before the world in its heavenly glory"; those who were "chosen first to serve the Cause" he enjoined to form "a contingent of the Lord . . . which that Lord . . . will use for active service in the Cause of his mercy." Henceforth, Saint-Séverin would serve as the Towianists' ecclesiastical camouflage in Paris.[32]

4

Mickiewicz spent most of the first few weeks of his new life in Nanterre, to be near Towiański as he worked his cure on Celina and to sit at the Master's feet or meditate on the notes he would send from an adjoining room. For Towiański the two ministrations were inseparable. The spiritual progress of his most important disciple was, as he conceived it, inextricably intertwined with that of his wife. Celina was, after all, of "Israel" and, as such, the reincarnation of an ancient and particularly powerful spirit whose destiny, together with that of her people, was inseparable from Mickiewicz's and his. Yet if by September Celina had recovered enough to have become pregnant again, she was, by the same token, proving to be less receptive now to the Master's teachings than during the cure. In a cryptic note, Towiański warned Mickiewicz that her spirit was "petrifying" because "her husband and children [were] satiating her with the earth." He was genuinely intent on saving Celina, for her own sake, certainly, but also for the successful realization of his mission, wherein Jews and women were to play a particularly prominent role. No less crucially, however, he was intent on tightening the bonds between himself and the poet. If this required meddling in and manipulating what in any case was a troubled marriage, so be it: the success of the Cause demanded it.[33]

Mickiewicz's life began to revolve now almost exclusively around the Master and his mission. As the poet's daughter recalled years later, it was as if "a cloud . . . had gathered above our home, which would cast its shadow on it for a long time to come. . . . Henceforth many unknown people began appearing at [the Mickiewiczes], the old circle slowly thinned out, and some kind of unusual atmosphere took over the home, which for . . . the children was difficult and heavy." Although in October the poet managed to find time to serve out his obligation with the National Guard ("gallantly" to boot), he resigned from his position at the Bibliothèque Royale. His duties as Niemcewicz's successor to the presidency of the Literary Society's History Section were, however, a different matter. Just as years earlier the Society of Lithuania and Ruthenia had become for him a platform for expounding his views on the emigration, chairmanship of the section presented him with an opportunity to spread the Master's word. If any of the society's members expressed apprehension in this regard, their fears were well-founded.[34]

When it came to the second year of his course, which Mickiewicz began in mid-December 1841, he nonetheless proved restrained—at least at the outset. His first lecture was not well received. He spoke vaguely about how "the progress of learning" can sometimes be outpaced by "an unknown man, a stranger to scholarship, working outside the confines of scholarly societies and academies" and even mentioned palingenesy (Dz. 9:15/LS 2:309–10), but in this regard no one in the "numerous," "motley" audience seemed to take particular note. Rather, what drew objections from a number of Poles was, as Czartoryski was compelled to complain directly to Mickiewicz, not only his "forays into the most extreme social politics with the intention of adapting them to Slavdom," but his ostensible "Slavo-Russian tendencies" and "magnification of Muscovy's might" at the expense of Poland. Yet in this regard, Mickiewicz's first lecture simply reiterated ideas informing the previous year's course, with its focus on the struggle between the Russian and Polish "ideas." The professor now promised to develop them (he had, for the moment, quit examining the rest of the Slavic world) through an analysis of texts much closer to his heart, those from "the end of the seventeenth century as well as the eighteenth century" to "the poetic and philosophical works of . . . contemporary literature" (Dz. 9:9/LS 2:301).

In any case, all seemed to agree that he "spoke... with the inspiration of a poet" and "had touched a prophetic string."[35]

By February, however, as Mickiewicz was about to launch into his account of the recent past, it was becoming increasingly apparent to some of his listeners that "Adam's ideas... often allude[d] to Towiański's teachings." When, with his usual penchant for unfounded assertion, Mickiewicz claimed that the Russian "idea" was powerful because it addressed "moral not material" concerns (*Dz.* 9:234/*LS* 3:136), Witwicki, for one, smelled "total Towianism." When the professor insisted that "among Poles" things "always flowed from political considerations, [but] among Russians, from religious ones" (*Dz.* 9:259/*LS* 3:167), even his Russian listeners took note. "Mickiewicz has become either reborn or revitalized," Aleksandr Turgenev informed his friends in Russia; although "he gets carried away by his imagination and by a mystical view of history... there is much *Wahrheit* in his *Dichtung*." But then too, for an audience incapable of viewing Poland's struggle with Russia ("ideas" notwithstanding) as anything but a political zero-sum game, Mickiewicz's notion of "expiation through suffering," with its awe of Russia's artlessly spiritual—genuinely Slavic—might and concomitant critique of Polish constitutionalism, proved disturbing because not fully comprehensible. As one observer noted, "Mickiewicz does not indicate clearly enough around which banner the Slavs should rally...—forced to make a necessary choice between the concepts of Eastern civilization and schism and Western notions of development and Catholicism, he does not explain that aspect of the subject and leaves everything in the air."[36]

If he could, Mickiewicz would have had it otherwise. "Full of Towiański's precepts, he... wanted to speak of them, but [could] not and—torn inside—he [would] often express his ideas vaguely, confusedly, and badly." As it was, the Master felt that the time—or perhaps the messenger—was not yet ripe, at least not in the arena that was the Collège. His disciple, however, could not restrain himself from "confirming publicly what had already been spreading quietly." All that he needed was an opportunity.[37]

Mickiewicz knew full well that by publicly accusing the "enlightened" authors of the Constitution of the Third of May of abandoning the "ancient historical wisdom of the folk" in favor of "foreign theories" (*Dz.* 9:225/*LS* 3:126), he would be touching a raw nerve among Czartoryski's supporters, the title of whose house organ, *3 Maj*, eponymized, after all, the revered document. When at a meeting, then, of the Literary Society commemorating the anniversary of the constitution the prince himself "publicly flogged" the professor for his lecture, Mickiewicz finally exploded. "With great vehemence and fire in his eyes," he proclaimed that the time for discussing and advising was over, that "new times have drawn nigh," that "it is necessary to strip off everything, to reveal and bare the naked soul, and there, within it, to find everything" (*Dz.* 13:303). "Don't call me a critic," he went on "in anger," "but a *wieszcz*; I admit to that role, since today it would be shirking responsibility, it would be a crime to deny it out of modesty, out of any considerations"

(Dz. 13:304). "I stand to bear witness among you that God's great mercy has come," he concluded,

> The Fatherland has risen from the dead and is amidst you. . . . It is the responsibility of *wieszczes* . . . to show the nation the way; but this isn't enough today. . . . The time has come when inspiration must become deed and deed inspiration, for in God's work, as in a clap of thunder, . . . the bolt and the strike are one. (Dz. 13:304–5)

With that Mickiewicz "struck his palm with his fist" (Dz. 13:307) and walked out, "leaving the gathering as if thunderstruck," unsure what to make of it all. In the room, weeping as he spoke, were Karolina Towiański, the Gutts, and Ksawera Deybel, another early convert to the Cause who had been living with the Mickiewiczes for the previous few months as Maria's governess.[38]

5

"Some said that he'd gone mad, since he spoke with great fervor and about nothing more than Towianism"; others read the outburst as an announcement "that the Towianists [were] planning an expedition to Poland"; still others, in all earnestness, understood "the fatherland amidst us to mean Mickiewicz's newly born son." Indeed, that very same morning, Celina had given birth to the couple's fourth child. They named him Aleksander Andrzej Stefan: Aleksander, in honor of the day's patron saint, and perhaps too for Mickiewicz's younger brother, but also for Aleksander Chodźko, whom the poet had recently converted to the Cause; then Andrzej; and finally Stefan, not in honor of Witwicki, of course, but Stefan Zan, yet another recent convert. Towiański was chosen to stand as godfather (Mickiewicz would reciprocate four months later by proxy) and Anna Gutt as godmother. To the spiritual bonds linking the expanding Towianist "family" were now added those of symbolic kinship, no less important for Poles from Lithuania.[39]

For the past month, Towiański had taken to using the Mickiewiczes' apartment on rue d'Amsterdam to hold a series of what he called conferences for his still small band of disciples as well as for those "with a sincere and pure desire" to hear him. (The Master had no patience with people intent on "debating" him: "Whoever seeks his advice will find it," Mickiewicz warned Jełowicki, "whoever wants to argue has no need of seeing him.") As one visitor recalled years later, it was customary for the poet on these occasions to greet his guests, potential converts all, and then line them up

> into two rows . . . so that there would be a space between them; after which he stepped into an adjoining room and returned shortly thereafter with a man of medium height

> and . . . build, in a long brown frock-coat buttoned to the top, with a white ascot high on his neck. . . . His figure and his head with graying hair gave the impression of . . . a serious and gentle priest. . . . He stood with his back to the window between the two rows and began speaking. He had a sonorous, affective voice and a talent for oratorical exposition; at times he would speak calmly and quietly, but from moment to moment would increasingly raise his volume, so that in the end he was almost shouting; his face turned red, and he gesticulated.

Mickiewicz, for his part, "stood erect with his hands clasped behind his back, his head raised high, sighing deeply and loudly."[40]

For those who might express a desire for more, the poet was glad to facilitate a private session with the Master, but not before putting the potential candidate through a preparatory ordeal:

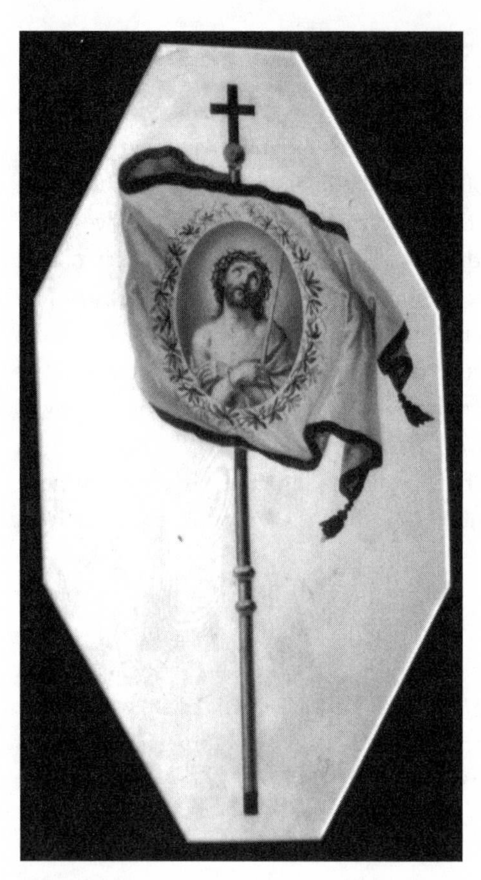

Fig. 20 Banner of the Circle of God's Cause. Courtesy of the Adam Mickiewicz Museum of Literature, Warsaw.

> With the erstwhile prestige of his name, the sternness of his professorial demeanor, finally by assuming a terrifying appearance deliberately concocted to this end, the poet attempted to . . . arouse and excite faith in the candidate in his absolute wisdom and omniscience. . . . Having seated the candidate [as if for hypnosis], Mickiewicz fixes him with his eyes . . . and beginning first with casual musings, he bombards him now with lofty dicta, now bears down on him with unexpected questions. . . . Sometimes . . . in order to distract the candidate's attention so as to ambush it, he discourses on chemistry, physics, botany, industrial inventions, but then immediately begins thundering at him with new maxims of the strange doctrine and bears down on the candidate with new questions. If in the course of this ordeal the candidate exhibits a capacity for mysticism and a bent for unconditional exaltation, if he vows that he is ready to believe blindly in everything that will be given him to believe, he is admitted to Towiański.[41]

By the end of April, Towiański—or, rather, Towiański with Mickiewicz—had in this way succeeded in attracting twenty-four followers, "the number," the Master apparently deemed, "needed to begin [his] work." On 4 May 1842, he assembled them all at his home in Nanterre to announce the creation of the Circle of God's Cause. He began the convocation with a review of his mission in France and then, to his sobbing and sighing disciples kneeling before him, the "Servant of God" unveiled the banner of the Cause, the now mortally ill Wańkowicz's rendering of Guido Reni's *Ecce Homo*. After explicating the image's significance, the Master proceeded to hand out medallions with a picture of the Virgin Mary, her hands emitting rays toward earth, to Mickiewicz and five other disciples. Everyone then joined in with hymn ("God is our refuge and strength") and prayer. By way of conclusion, Towiański offered another brief sermon, in which he exhorted the brethren to, among other things, "struggle with [Russia] . . . through the force of love" and "sacrifice [them]selves for the good of the nation oppressing [them]." This set the tone for the closing canticle:

> Accept, O Lord, our labors, our battles, and our life in sacrifice:
> May your love and your truth gladden our vale!
> May the enemy, in submission, come to know your holy laws!
> May he disseminate in fraternal union your Name throughout the ages![42]

Similar scenes were played out over the course of the next four weeks, both in Nanterre and at the Mickiewiczes', against the background of a flurry of proselytizing.* By 1 June 1842, when a group numbering some seventeen converts (with Celina among them) was presented with the medallions as well as with little notebooks for recording their special Towianist moments, Towiański could claim nearly fifty disciples for his Cause.

Who were these people?

There was, of course, the original inner circle, consisting of Towiański's wife Karolina and son Jan, as well as the Gutts, Ferdynand and Anna; Wańkowicz died in mid-May, but not before completing a series of Towianist-inspired images—of Napoleon, of various saints, and of the Man of God himself. As for the remaining disciples, they were overwhelmingly men, mostly bachelors or grass widowers, damaged in one way or another by years of émigré existence. Uprooted, disaffected, and languishing, they were all in search of direction and consolation, of the kind of stability that a family with a strong but loving father, a source of at once comfort and authority, could provide. Almost all were veterans of the uprising, mostly mid-level officers, always prepared—indeed hoping—for the next call to action, but also accustomed to obedience. Most were petty gentry, but a few belonged to

*At one point Towiański, abetted by Mickiewicz, even tried to crash a reception for professors of the Collège at the Tuileries in an effort to convert King Louis Philippe. The Master was escorted out, ostensibly "because he was not wearing a tuxedo" (Canonico, *André Towiański*, 28).

prominent families or had married into them, although they, too, often found themselves eking out a living in emigration. They came from various regions of partitioned Poland and as émigrés had belonged to various political orientations. Several—among them Rettel, Stefan Zan, Feliks Wrotnowski, Eustachy Januszkiewicz and his brother Romuald—had been part of the Catholic coterie that Mickiewicz had inspired and patronized. There was even one Gershon Ram, a Jew from Vilnius, whom Towiański counted on as a potential entrée into the world of "Israel." A few were literati, artists, and musicians, but there were also craftsmen and engineers. A number, curiously enough, had studied law. For the most part they were unremarkable, suddenly made to feel remarkable on the strength of their conversion and the Master's affections. One or two were probably mentally unbalanced—and some, as would later emerge, less than sincere. However this may be, Wrotnowski surely spoke for all of them when he maintained, "Never before had I tasted of such brotherhood, and neither earth nor sea nor years could dissolve such brotherhood... our sufferings, our worries, our strivings, pure cravings, desires left unsatisfied by anything, secret hopes—everything has been revealed, explained, made clear, fulfilled beyond measure!"[43]

By the same token, Towiański's charisma and his promise of salvation proved no less irresistible to individuals who were by any measure quite remarkable. Fifty-three-year-old Karol Różycki, a veteran of the Napoleonic wars, had distinguished himself as one of the most intrepid military leaders of the 1830 uprising (Mickiewicz thought highly of his memoir of the war); as a Towianist he would acquit himself just as intrepidly, particularly when loyalty to the Master was at a premium. Seweryn Goszczyński, one of the original instigators of the uprising as well as a hero of subsequent conspiracies, was, next to Zaleski, the most prominent of the so-called Ukrainian romantics, the author of a frenetic tale of the Cossack past, a romantic travelogue, but also of a peculiarly misguided nativist essay in which he had lambasted Mickiewicz for imitating Western poetry. After several years of radical politics as well as a period of Polish Slavophilism, he began gravitating toward religion, which he now finally embraced thanks to the man "who had shown [him] everything as it really was: the Church, God, Christianity, Mary, Prayer, the Sacraments, Heaven, hell, man, human existence, sin, Napoleon, Kościuszko, France, Poland."[44]

And then there was Słowacki. His conversion, like that of Goszczyński, took place after the formation of the original Circle, but it was no less intense, or typical, for that. "God's love and grace," he informed his mother on 2 August 1842, some three weeks after his first encounter with Towiański, "have revived many withered hopes within me.... I am surrounded by a circle of loving people... it seems as if God's blessing is upon me." Some three months later he felt loved and blessed enough to "approach Adam first, apologizing to him for ever having offended him in any way." This particular love-fest, though, would be short-lived; Słowacki had always been content only in a party of one.[45]

Within Towiański's community of believers, however, accomplishments in this world ultimately meant little: "No one among us is privileged before God." What mattered was each disciple's tone and the quality of spiritual feeling he or she "effused" for the Cause and for the Master. This, in the end, could be achieved only through what Towiański called "the threefold sacrifice," "in spirit, then in body, and finally in all of life, in all of man's affairs." The intuitions, dreams, and spiritual accomplishments of national bards and heroes were thus no more nor less portentous than those of the Master's disciples less gifted in this world. But then too, since powerful spirits, both good and evil, could emerge from among even the most unremarkable, rivalries and conflicts were inevitable. In any case, the faith of all the brethren was put to the test almost immediately.[46]

Although the Russian embassy had been keeping its eye on him at least since his appearance in the West and had even called him in for an interview (hence the rumors of Russian agency), it deemed Towiański's "mystical tone... to obviously be evidence of a distorted mind" and therefore not worth the worry. Nonetheless, when Towiański refused to heed the ambassador's advice to return to Lithuania, the Third Department finally decided to declare him an émigré and confiscate his property in the homeland. But it was the French who acted first (perhaps with a nudge from Russia). Sensitive as Louis Philippe's security organs were to *any* unusual activity among the Polish émigrés, they ordered Towiański to leave the country—just as he was hoping to "tear down the hitherto existing barrier with brother Frenchman." "Obedient to the Lord's beck and call" and "empowered to resist all evil only in accordance with [God's] wishes," the Man of Destiny bid farewell to the brethren at Saint-Séverin on 18 July, leaving Mickiewicz in charge of the flock (and Gutt to watch over him). For the next six years the Master would be directing the work of the Circle from abroad, first from Oostende and Brussels, then from Switzerland, in effect channeling himself through Mickiewicz, the Gutts, and other surrogates. And although "the Master's spirit was always present" among them, there would always be "great longing for [him] in the Circle."[47]

6

News of Towiański's impending departure probably reached Mickiewicz in Saint-Germain-en-Laye, where he was staying with his newly augmented family for the summer. He had just concluded the second year of his course with a series of lectures devoted to Polish and Russian literary developments in the very recent past. With the insight given only to someone with intimate knowledge of the personalities and events, the professor provided his listeners with a brief history of Russian mysticism during the reign of Alexander I as well as of the Decembrist movement. He returned once again to Pushkin, retelling his story as tragedy and asserting in the end that with him "Russian literature... had ceased" (Dz. 9:366/LS 3:295). He spoke—in superlatives, of course—of Viazemskii ("one of the most prominent..."; Dz. 9:369) and Zhukovskii ("incontestably..."; Dz. 9:413*); of

*This as well as the previous epithet is missing in LS.

Brodziński ("the first to recognize..."; *Dz.* 9:373/*LS* 3:303), Goszczyński, and Zaleski ("the greatest of Slavic poets"; *Dz.* 9:414/*LS* 3:349); Słowacki, though, he stubbornly ignored.

Then too, the professor made no mention of the one writer whose work articulated the romantic turn in Polish—if not Slavic—literature most programmatically. To be sure, he spoke about the so-called "Lithuanian School" and sneaked in at this point a reference to Sand's article about "fantastic drama," which Mickiewicz interpreted as asserting "that Lithuanian writers place the center of action in the world of spirits, and conceive the visible world and men as vessels" (*Dz.* 9:380–81/*LS* 3:311). Genuine reticence about discussing his own work kept him from elaborating. The facts, nonetheless, demanded it: how could a course on Slavic literature that proclaimed messianism to be "the hallmark of Polish national poetry" (*Dz.* 9:414/*LS* 3:348) not treat its most prominent exponent? The professor finessed. In what was at once a tribute to his friend on the tenth anniversary of his death and an appropriation of his legacy, he decided to examine Garczyński's *History of Wacław* as, in effect, a simulacrum for *Forefathers' Eve*, part 3.

Mickiewicz devoted nearly three lectures to *Wacław*. Declaring it "the most comprehensive and philosophical work that exists in the Slavic languages" (*Dz.* 9:388/*LS* 3:320), he claimed that its author was "the first of all the poets discussed so far... to proclaim that he was appearing with a mission," that "he [did] not write like an artist, like a poet, a man of letters: he [felt] that he must espouse a cause" (*Dz.* 9:412/*LS* 3:346). In a gesture of willful misprision on the part of his exegete, Garczyński now became "the most Polish... of all poets" because "all of [his] poems were imbued with messianism" (*Dz.* 9:414/*LS* 3:348–49)—and Polish messianism was to "decide the Slavic question," "solve the question of the Jewish people," and, finally, in view of Napoleon's role in the history of Poland, affect the destiny of France (*Dz.* 9:427–29/*LS* 365–66).

In this respect the conclusion of Mickiewicz's final lecture of the course was even more intriguing. Mustering a series of ostensibly prophetic excerpts from various Polish writers, Mickiewicz announced that "after the [appearance] of two men presiding over the epochs, one may expect and predict the appearance of a third who will combine their traits" (*Dz.* 9:429).* No specifics, of course, but the identities of this spiritual triad were self-evident: Christ—Napoleon—Towiański. The professor's "nearly eight hundred listeners... were stunned."[48]

As a form of "labor" for the Cause, prophesying and bearing witness to the uninitiated cost Mickiewicz relatively little. He always knew that his improvisatory powers could both inspirit and awe, and in any case, like his proselytizing or, for that matter, his daily life, they had been guided over the past year by his stern but loving Master. Towiański's unexpected withdrawal changed everything. Suddenly, Mickiewicz found himself if not completely abandoned—communication between the two remained constant—then at

*This passage is missing in *LS*.

least without the comforting, physical presence of the one human being who had made everything seem right. By appointing him custodian of the Circle, Towiański was putting his favorite disciple to the test, challenging him, as it were, to finally "bear fruit" for the Cause. The Master understood his pupil well.

Mickiewicz did his best to live up to expectations. Shortly after Towiański's departure, he organized an outing for several brethren to Malmaison in the hope of contacting Napoleon's spirit. He invited the entire circle to Saint-Germain-en-Laye—a twenty-eight minute train ride from Paris on France's first rail line—for a spiritual picnic in the woods (the Philomath in him seemed to reawaken), where "they spent the day under enormous walnut trees, on the grass, talking and singing with patriarchal simplicity." Nonetheless, Mickiewicz felt overwhelmed. "I crumble more than I ascend," he confessed to Towiański in early September.

> You gave me the groan for the Lord, but strength is not descending. It often seems to me that I'm already a spirit standing and atoning in immobility, so dark is my past and the old winding ways are carrying my spirit backward to self-communion. . . . In my dreams I have frequent and difficult struggles with contrary spirits. . . . I face them valiantly, but my powers fail me. The same thing is probably happening to me when I'm awake.

The Master's response, however, was appropriately opaque. "I put myself in your situation," Towiański wrote by way of fortifying his disciple,

> and feel the thorns of your life—and see how everything will turn out fine. You've liberated yourself significantly from the shackles of this vale—and ascend significantly toward a happier country. But, my most beloved Brother, you must complete this liberation, asserting your spirit in requisite freedom.

Mickiewicz, like the remaining brethren, was left to act on intuition, on the strength of his "tone." "The Lord," Towiański assured them, "[would] reveal his will."[49]

And so he did. In early October, Mickiewicz found himself "in a state of great excitement." He recalled how he "had experienced such states in the past but had completely forgotten about them, and only now, strangely enough, they returned." "But those," he informed Towiański, "had been feelings of freedom and power, without any thought, without direction, without desire. In the past I would have vented them on poetry, now I awaited direction." It came in the form of three successive visitations, from the Virgin Mary, Christ, and, finally, Napoleon. All three apparently intimated to Mickiewicz the true nature of the "office" with which he had been charged. He, in turn, faithfully recorded their words—in beautiful poetic prose.[50]

Mickiewicz now sensed his own powers waxing. Although he found presiding at the Towianist rituals "the most difficult of services," he mastered the Master's jargon with the same uncanny ease with which he had once appropriated Schiller and Byron and the Bible. And he could always count on the force of his own charisma, qualitatively different from that of the quietist Towiański but certainly no less compelling, anchored, as ever, in an intuitive grasp of things that faith only made more decisive. Most crucially, he learned to make sense of the Master's babble (he was, after all, a philologist, with a poet's way with words). Yet by this very same token, in making its nuances accessible to those less acute than he, Mickiewicz in effect retold, and in retelling he did to Towiański's directives what he had done to the writers he discussed in his lectures: he spoke through them, lucidly (under the circumstances) and forcefully. To be sure, Mickiewicz turned to his master constantly, seeking advice and approval for his and the Circle's every undertaking. In this, as in every aspect of his life, Towiański's word was sacred, its authority absolute and absolutely infallible. For all of its power, though, its presence in Paris in spirit only opened up a world of possibilities for his most trusted disciple—the same disciple who in *Forefathers' Eve* had dreamed of "governing the souls" of his countrymen and in *The Books of the Polish Pilgrimage* sought to prescribe how they should dress and celebrate and speak. Under Mickiewicz's guidance, what had been a rather loosely-knit assemblage of needy seekers orbiting around a charismatic teacher began to routinize into a cult.[51]

7

In the months immediately following Towiański's expulsion, the Circle of God's Cause had met occasionally and irregularly, usually in connection with the arrival of some new epistle from the Master, which Mickiewicz would proceed to interpret for the brethren. But aside from a petition that all forty-five of them signed protesting the government's decision to banish this "man of Providence," and tentative attempts to proselytize among the French, there was little of what they called "movement." "Some of the brethren are weakening or have weakened," Mickiewicz reported to Towiański in November, "Gerszon wants to luxuriate too much and is a spiritual lay-about; [Seweryn] Pilchowski is impatient and has difficulty surrendering himself to the Nap[oleonic] idea; [Mikołaj] Kamieński longs for conversation, craves spiritual partnership, but has difficulty with work."[52]

Meanwhile, all around them the emigration was in a roil. "Prince Czartoryski and his bloc [took them] for madmen, the democrats, for a Muscovite party... Witwicki persecute[d] [them] like heretics. Bohdan [Zaleski] avoid[ed] [them] out of fear." *Pszonka*, a satirical periodical published by the Democrats, hounded the "buffo-Prophet" and "serio-Poet" mercilessly, poking fun at every aspect of Towiański's doctrine, from metempsychosis ("every man was on earth innumerable times, be it in the form of sand, clay, gold, granite, be it as grass, a carrot, cabbage, parsnip, or an ass, a horse, an ox, a sparrow, a fish, a fly; he could even have appeared in the form of Moses or Christ, Alexander or Napoleon, Ptolemy or Copernicus...") to the eccentricities of his language ("tickling ones feelings"; "hunting for souls"), concluding with the observation that "where two asses are gathered, there is [Towiański's] Spirit in the midst of them."[53]

Most implacable, however, was agitation "within the walls of the church." Having determined that "Towiański... clearly deviated from the teachings of Christ" and that as such his doctrine "was particularly dangerous were it to spread to Poland," the fathers of the freshly minted Congregation of the Resurrection of the Lord descended on Paris from Rome, intent on exposing the heresy—and, at the same time, extricating their former friend and mentor from its clutches. Fathers Kajsiewicz and Duński ensconced themselves in the Church of St. Roch, where every Sunday they piqued curious émigrés with denunciations of "false prophets." Jełowicki, for his part, was hoping to compromise the sect by circulating copies of Towiański's *Symposium*, which he had managed to wheedle out of the repentant Skrzynecki. To all this the brethren responded with passive defiance, attending the services at St. Roch's regularly and en masse, demonstratively taking Holy Communion, but no less demonstratively "keeping to themselves off to the side," their anger at the "doctors and the Pharisees" sometimes barely in check. As for Jełowicki's plans to publish the *Symposium*, Mickiewicz was in fact thrilled at the prospect, hoping, as he wrote to Towiański, "to get hold of it and read it in the Circle for our uplift and edification." (Its author was somewhat less enthusiastic, playing the screed down as something

Fig. 21 The Resurrectionists (sitting: second from left, Piotr Semenenko; third from left, Hieronim Kajsiewicz; right, Aleksander Jełowicki). Photograph from the 1860s–1870s. Courtesy of the Adam Mickiewicz Museum of Literature, Warsaw.

he had slapped together "an hour before" his séance with Skrzynecki.) And in any case, all of this made it ever clearer that "God was on [their] side."[54]

Yet conversions to the Cause were becoming fewer and further between, and the Circle increasingly isolated. Mickiewicz's protestations that he and his brethren "want[ed] to live and die in the one and only Catholic Church of Christ," "that they [were] ready... to be martyred for the faith and the Church," and "consider[ed] Towiański solely a man sent to arouse more ardent Christian feelings and enforce the Gospels," were not, it seems, deemed sufficiently sincere by the Resurrectionists; nor, for that matter, was an interview they arranged for Mickiewicz with the archbishop of Paris. Duński went so far as to refuse to take Zan's confession unless "he renounced Master Andrzej." Aleksander Chodźko, recently returned from England to devote himself completely to Mickiewicz through the Cause,* was denied membership in the Polish Club—in response to which those of the sect who were members quit in solidarity. Willy-nilly, the brethren began cutting themselves off from those who would condemn them or, for that matter, even question the revelation of the "New Testament." "In order to maintain the full sanctity of [our actions]," Mickiewicz explained to the brethren about their participation in observances of the anniversary of the November Uprising, "we must forget that we are émigrés, even that we are Poles, and take to heart only what our service in God's Cause dictates." It was not long before they took to walking out, en masse, during the Resurrectionists' sermons, and then boycotting the services at St. Roch altogether. As the Master reminded them, "Whoever agitates against us in body and soul is an enemy of the Cause."[55]

By the end of 1842, however, the Circle itself was in a roil, stressed as it was more by a lack of direction within than by pressures from without. As his appointed stand-in, Mickiewicz remained in privileged contact with Towiański. But the Master also took to channeling himself through other surrogates, particularly those lucky enough to be permitted to visit him in Belgium. The confusion this inevitably created was by no means unintentional. Playing one disciple against another made the brethren only that much more dependent on their Master, and by the same token kept his vicar in constant check. It was not long before disagreements began erupting within the Circle, with one even ending in the violent misuse of umbrellas. Brethren were feeling increasingly empowered to act on the strength of their visions, dreams, or simply intuition, perhaps the most valuable commodity in the Towianist economy of exaltation. Brother Romuald Januszkiewicz's hysterical attempt, "on orders from the Lord," to convert Prince Czartoryski as he was leaving Christmas mass was but the most scandalous consequence of imaginations stoked by continual contact with spirits. His "inspired" baptism of Gerszon Ram, ostensibly *in extremis*, which "he conducted with singular solemnity and power," was almost as

*Becoming, in the process, something akin to an evangelist, assiduously noting down Mickiewicz's words of wisdom over the course of the next thirteen years.

egregious. Mickiewicz was finally forced to intervene, declaring that "every act of every one of [the brethren] must... be sanctioned and have the support of the Circle."[56]

To this end, and perhaps also as a precaution against an ever vigilant French police, Brother Adam resolved in January 1843 to organize the Circle into "septets." Mickiewicz would now be able to exercise greater control over the brethren—and at the same time create at least the illusion of meaningful activity. Towiański, for his part, was pleased, agreeing to "yield this more daring movement on the road of [their] ministry to [his disciple's] inspiration."[57]

Membership in a septet—there were eight in all, even when attrition reduced some to as few as two members—was determined by lot, with each then electing a "guardian" to preside over it. Aside from his office as the leader of the entire Circle, Mickiewicz was chosen to also lead the second septet, which had among its members Brothers Romuald Januszkiewicz (Eustachy's brother), Stefan Zan, and Seweryn Pilchowski, together with two "adjunct" sisters, Celina Mickiewicz and Ksawera Deybel—all, as would become clear soon enough, reincarnations of particularly powerful, and fractious, spirits. Henceforth the septets met separately (the Circle now gathered in its entirety only on special occasions), while the guardians of each would convene at Mickiewicz's to hear his allocutions and convey directives to their respective septets. But the ex-Philomath continued to fine-tune the structure. In April, he ordered the septets to meet "on the same day, at the same time, that is on Saturday evenings" in order to enable the "partnering" of spirits; and each septet was now to elect its guardian unanimously, by secret ballot, with solemnity and prayer—a template, Mickiewicz hoped, for "conducting elections in a future Poland." In addition, two brethren were to be designated every day to be "on call" at Brother Adam's side. The Cause had become a full-time concern.[58]

Sundays had already been reserved for fasting according to the "new testament," whereby the brethren were to "abstain from all moral and mental amusements, from all entertainment, from all forms of employment, and busy [themselves] solely with thoughts of God's and Poland's Cause according to the Master's ideas." Now Wednesdays were to be devoted to the Cause as well, for silent confession in the spirit. But this too soon called for fine-tuning. In July, Mickiewicz decided to institute a form of confession adapted specifically to the requirements of the Cause's tone, what he called "confession to the second degree." As the summoned brother stood before him, the brother doing the summoning would sit and "point out [the former's] sins to him, in tone, that is, with love." More ominously, though, "one [was] to take into account in this confession even [a brother's] private life, one's personal relationships with him, in which one had observed transgressions concerning the Cause." No one was exempted from this ritual self-criticism, least of all Mickiewicz, who as the Circle's leader made the rounds of all the septets to hear from individual brethren "what may have gone amiss in the Cause and what [he] in particular may have let slide." In the name, ostensibly, of sincerity, humility, and purity of faith, Mickiewicz was sowing the seeds of collective tyranny, and assuring mutual destruction.[59]

For the moment, though, like the Napoleonic general he at times imagined himself to be, Mickiewicz exhorted the septets to become soldiers of the Cause, toiling "so as to arrive at total forgetfulness of self." At weekly gatherings and in a stream of directives—which often did indeed employ the terse rhythms of a commanding officer's order of the day—he instructed the brethren to elevate their tone, "to listen to everyone... as if [they] were listening to Christ speaking through them," to "seize the morning from Satan," and to express the "progress of the Cause... on [their] faces." He enjoined them to fast and pray and go to mass on important occasions—which were becoming increasingly more frequent, in inverse proportion to their import. He assigned them topics to consider—"what each brother would do... if... the entire Circle [even Towiański himself] were to die and he remained alone"; "what still remains to be done, even though [they] have all made a sacrifice of this world"; what it means "to become a fool for Christ"—and, eventually, to "write everything down" in their little notebooks. These he would hand out, blessed by the Master, to deserving brethren at special ceremonies, where before the banner of the Sacred Cause they would pray and weep and kiss each others' hands and feet. To commemorate the Battle of Waterloo he shared with the guardians a loaf of bread baked in Waterloo while instructing them to ponder the significance of bullets collected on the battlefield as if they were so many relics. But above all, Mickiewicz demanded that "each brother... replicate in spirit all of the Master's deeds": he asked them to wait, to prepare themselves in spirit for a signal from on high.[60]

Mickiewicz understood only too well that for all of their ostensible efficacy in the realm of spirit, the fasts and confessions and meditations were just so much make-work, a simulacrum for the genuine "deeds" that they all craved and by the same token critical for warding off "sluggishness" and "lack of movement." "When there is production of the spirit in the Circle," he lectured the brethren, "the Cause is certainly progressing, even if on the outside there is a maximum of immobility, even if in Paris no one were to know about us." But of that, of course, there was hardly a chance, as every émigré periodical reminded its readers, with little benefit of a doubt now being extended to the sectarians. Indeed, any efforts on the part of the Circle to actually initiate some "action" in the émigré community were invariably deemed suspect. When Mickiewicz invited émigrés to sign on to an open letter he had drawn up condemning the decision of one of their own to convert to Russian Orthodoxy in order to receive amnesty, many refused, unwilling, ultimately, to be associated with anything smelling of Towianism. The poet was genuinely hurt by their reaction, and at a public gathering condemned the emigration, but above all the Resurrectionists, for "inciting minds not against Russia but against the Towianists."[61]

This experience with the letter burned the Circle. Any ideas the brethren may have harbored about influencing the course of the emigration were in effect dashed against what they considered a rock of misunderstanding, prejudice, and, as Mickiewicz himself put it in yet another fiery Third of May speech before the Polish Literary Society, "pride, hatred, and bondage." "Until [the emigration] itself experienced rebirth in the spirit," until it learned to act with "exaltation," its "efforts would bear no fruit." In view of this resistance, the Circle decided "to avoid embarking on any purely political activities." Their tone would remain "Christly-Napoleonic," just as the Master had always insisted.[62]

All this did not mean, however, that the Circle turned radically inward, away from any efforts to act in the outside world—except that it could "act against [it] and join issue with it only if the beginning of action or resistance [was] in the spirit." Others, not yet ready perhaps, would simply have to let that spirit work through them, would have to intuit the truth of the Cause on their own. Here the brethren could move matters along "by [their] work of the spirit and [their] deed through the Spirit." But there was little they could do against those in the thrall of "the potentate of darkness," "the material side," as Mickiewicz referred to them, "the Jesuits," who worked to stifle Towiański's truth for others. In the persons of the Resurrectionists, Witwicki, and the Platers, they seemed to have succeeded in "hardening" the Polish emigration against the Master. The French, however, were another matter entirely. They were, after all, at the very center of Towiański's cosmogony, "a nation striding at the forefront of human progress," pulsing with the spirit of Napoleon. And in this respect, encounters with this chosen people were proving themselves to be promising indeed.[63]

As early as the fall of 1842, a group of French sectarians gathered around one Pierre-Michel Vintras, a visionary from Bayeux notorious for producing bleeding communion wafers, had been seeking to establish a relationship with their (quite literally, perhaps) kindred spirits in the Circle of God's Cause.* That Vintras—or, as the founder of l'Œuvre de la Miséricorde styled himself, Sthrathanael—happened to be in jail now on charges of fraud probably contributed to his orphaned disciples' interest in the Polish mystic. From the outset, though, Towiański made it clear that if the Vintrasists were hoping to find a new home in the Polish circle, it would be on his terms—there was room in this world for only one Man of Providence. Although he encouraged Mickiewicz to remain in contact with Pierre-Michel's disciples and "sow the word" among them, he nonetheless counseled his surrogate "to keep the French brethren on the sharp leash of God's thought in idea and tone—force them to action." He was willing to bide his time until the French submitted to him accordingly, "with spiritual toil, hardship, labor, backbreaking work," until they "conceived of themselves an act of the spirit." By August 1843, some seven of them did, becoming in due course some of the Master's most ardent acolytes. As far as Mickiewicz was concerned, however, it was the Collège that offered the most promising avenue for proselytizing among God's other chosen people.[64]

*The idea of organizing the Circle into septets probably derived from the Vintrasists.

In May 1843, the historian Edgar Quinet, fresh from a brilliant two-year series of lectures at the University of Lyon that he had just published under the title *Le Génie des religions* and now appointed to the chair of Southern Literatures at the Collège, joined Michelet to co-teach a course whose fierce anticlericalism became the sensation of the Parisian season.* Their ultramontane opponents were quick to respond by staging noisy demonstrations at their lectures. At Michelet's and Quinet's request, Mickiewicz joined his colleagues at the Collège in a show of support, "the three together constituting the voice of France and prophets of a new Revolution." Assisting Brother Adam in his "service" were his Towianist brethren, who, like their leader, seized this opportunity to engage in a spiritual war against the official Church, as much their enemy now as the enemy of progressive France. That the French professors waged their battle from, as Mickiewicz put it, "semi-religious" positions was irrelevant for the moment: they might just eventually "grasp the vessel of Christ's grace placed on this earth." And if Michelet did not, in Mickiewicz's estimation, "possess tone" (too much the rationalist and decidedly no fan of Napoleon), Quinet was a different matter, "not reaching quite as far" as his colleague, perhaps, but capable of "maintaining himself better." Here was a potential convert, and Mickiewicz even delegated brethren to "minister" to him. For the moment these efforts met with no success, but Mickiewicz continued to hold on to the hope that if not now, then surely somewhere down the road the author of a poem glorifying Napoleon would eventually recognize the truth.[65]

Yet if the evolving relationship with the French was a sign that the Lord "appointed the spirit of" the Circle to bear "fruit in battles in spirit and in deed," the fruit it produced at the Saturday evening gatherings proved problematic. Brother Seweryn Pilchowski, for one, was disturbed by the Circle's "joint action" in support of the French professors at the Collège, which led to "an altercation of a personal nature" with another brother. This was not the first time that this "Satanic spirit" had erupted, and it was but a foretaste of things to come from someone who felt "superior to all the brethren in spiritual purity." For the moment, though, Mickiewicz managed to contain the damage. At the next gathering of his septet "Brother Pilchowski kissed [his] hand and showed emotion."[66]

More ominous, however, were the consequences of a dream Vintras communicated to Mickiewicz (aka Brother Ruthmael) in May 1843. Apparently the spirit of Tsar Alexander had informed the French mystic of his "ardent desire to serve the Polish cause," but only if the Circle assuaged his "horrible torments" on account of his sins against Poland. "In response, Brother Adam called on the entire Circle to perform an act of forgiveness," for which he ordered a special mass. The dream may have fit neatly with Towiański's (as well as Mickiewicz's?) notion that it was Poland's Christian duty, and part of her penance, to see Russia "become as great and as happy as God's judgment had ordained." It

*Published subsequently as *Des Jésuites* (1843).

did not go over well with Słowacki, who pronounced a "*veto*, in the Polish spirit, against the Russian tendency" and defected from the Circle. There were, to be sure, other reasons for his decision (an uncompromising sense of his autonomy chief among them), but he was not the only brother troubled by the "administration's" "Russian tendencies," which, after all, went against everything the emigration held dear. With time they would grow even more disturbing. But then so too would other tendencies that—and as cults inevitably go—were already beginning to eat away at the Circle's experiment in Christian living.[67]

8

Słowacki's defection in November 1843 occurred at a critical moment of Towiański's mission, and at a no less critical time for Mickiewicz. Sometime earlier that year, after much meditation, the Master received the appropriate sign from above—perhaps the mighty comet that appeared in the skies over Europe that March—telling him to take his Cause to God's vicar in Rome. "Politics, Fatherland," he pronounced, "these are the body of *the Word*, but Rome always was and will be bonded to *the Word* for the sake of this earth." By July he was ready (the brethren in Paris having collected sufficient funds for the journey), and he asked Mickiewicz to meet him in Brussels, whence he might accompany him as far as Switzerland. "I consider this imperative," Towiański let his disciple know, and reminded him that "it was almost the second anniversary of [their] fortunate union." Not that Mickiewicz needed encouragement. After all, other brethren had been granted permission to visit the Master since his expulsion. There were, nonetheless, more immediate, pressing concerns that made the pilgrimage to Brussels imperative.[68]

To outside observers, the Circle had all the appearance of a well-disciplined, mindless cult. As Mickiewicz's nemesis Jełowicki noted earlier that spring, "Adam sighs, everyone sighs, Adam twitches, everyone goes into convulsions—a flock of sheep, those Goszczyńskis, Słowackis, Bońkowskis, Wrotnowskis, Kołyskos, Pilchowskis, people who earlier were unchecked and unrestrained, all now become emotional on command or fly into a rage, cry or thunder, humble themselves or bristle." He had no idea, though, of the energy—organizational, psychological, emotional, and, of course, spiritual—that Mickiewicz was forced to expend in order to maintain this discipline. On top of this, the outreach to the French required a great deal of careful strategy, to say nothing of the efforts it took to control the damage it was wreaking within the Circle. And all along, from December 1842 until 27 June 1843, twice a week for an hour, Mickiewicz continued to lecture at the Collège, although he "often skipped lectures on Fridays." Even Towiański entreated the Brother *Wieszcz* "to nurse [him]self . . . , probing what inwardly and outwardly could nurse [him]." But if in his reports to the Master, Mickiewicz tried to remain upbeat, describing how "within the Circle there was much grace," how he had never seen so much "emotion," how "total" "the submission" was, the poet was exhausted, and the picture was certainly not as rosy. "My work is difficult," the poet admitted to Towiański.[69]

Of course, "sluggishness" and "lack of movement" were still a problem, despite—or, just as likely, because of—the brethren's "deeds in spirit." No less troubling, though, were the "frequent strains within the Circle," the constant "search for action, the anticipation of events of some sort, grasping at news from beyond the Circle." But when

Fig. 22 Ksawera Deybel. Daguerreotype. Courtesy of the Adam Mickiewicz Museum of Literature, Warsaw.

Mickiewicz ascribed these to "a lack of serenity" among the brethren, he could just as well have been speaking about his own life at home, which, he confided to Ferdynand Gutt, "consumes the greatest portion of my strength." This time, however, Celina was not the only source of discontent, nor was the discontent any longer a private family matter.[70]

Anna Ksawera (Xawera) Deybel arrived in Paris sometime at the end of 1841. The twenty-three-year-old daughter of the owners of the same pension for girls in Vilnius where some of the Philomaths used to tutor and flirt, Ksawera was an aspiring singer, who at one point gave voice lessons to the daughter of Maria Puttkamer. Her ambitions had taken her to St. Petersburg, and now to Paris. How she ended up at the Mickiewiczes'—via the Puttkamers? the Malewskis, whom she met in St. Petersburg? Towiański?—or when remains unclear. In any case, in June 1842, a month after the birth of her fourth child, Celina informed her aunt that "a young woman, Miss Deybel, [was] now living with [them], very kind and altogether well-bred, who [was] engaged in educating little Maria, but only out of friendship." "Little Miss Deybel," as Słowacki lampooned her, was a diminutive creature, not particularly beautiful, but, by all accounts, with eyes to die for. Towiański once remarked that "when [he] spoke with Ksawera, she kept her eyes *closed; [he] could not meet with her otherwise.*" That she had escaped the Lithuanian provinces for St. Petersburg and then the West in pursuit of a career was testimony enough to her strength and determination, but perhaps also of her desperation.[71]

Earlier that year, shortly before she moved in with the Mickiewiczes, Ksawera too had accepted Towiański as her master. And she did so with a fervor unusual even among the Towianists. As one observer noted, she "was, apparently, exceedingly powerful in inspiration." After all, the security and love all of the brethren craved in a good father resided for her, a sister, in a figure of the opposite sex. Indeed, Towiański was in this respect only one of several with whom she could pursue her desire, sublimated or otherwise. Demographics guaranteed that the "Israelite princess," as Master Andrzej dubbed her as much on account of those "magnetic" eyes as on the strength of her metempsychotic adventures, would be busy—and confused, and confusing, in turn, to those she happened to imprint upon. Desires of body and of spirit were, inevitably perhaps, becoming inextricably intertwined. In June, Mickiewicz warned the Circle that "a lustful gaze is a transgression, and if the power of lasciviousness takes in the spirit at which it was directed, it places us in contact with it and debits our account."[72]

Mickiewicz's admonition was directed at Ksawera as much as it was at the brethren, but it originated undoubtedly in his own predicament. The attraction between himself and the little woman from Vilnius was immediate and strong, forged as it was in the realm of the spirit. That night in early October 1842 when Napoleon had spoken through Mickiewicz to announce a miracle that would "éclaircir le globe," it was Ksawera who subsequently helped correct his French, inspiring him to replace *éclaircir* with *illuminer* on the basis of an experience with the emperor's spirit that she herself just happened to have had some days earlier. Mickiewicz realized right then, if not earlier, that they were kindred spirits, experiencing in sync that spiritual "stirring" so highly prized by their Master. And her miraculous cure notwithstanding, it was precisely that sensation that Celina, in her reticence with regard to the Cause, in her spiritual "torpor," had been unable or unwilling to achieve. Deybel quickly grasped the implications of her situation—and she was not shy about letting Celina know it. Shortly before his departure for Brussels, "at a very important moment for him," Deybel apparently "threw [Mickiewicz] into a welter." A new type of tumult was brewing in the Mickiewicz household.[73]

Having left the Circle in the care of Seweryn Goszczyński, with instructions on how to deal with individual brethren and with the French, as well as what days would be most propitious for holding meetings and at what time ("from 8:00 to 11:00 in the morning," when "a man is usually most spiritual; just as he is during a new moon and in the first quarter of every month, and is least spiritual, strongest in earth during a full moon and the last quarter"), Mickiewicz departed for Brussels in mid-July. Only there, upon seeing the perfect man in all his "meekness, fire, strength, and perspicacity," did he "realize how far [he himself] had sunk." Towiański observed immediately that all was not well with his disciple. In his own inimitable way, on a note sent to the poet from an adjoining room to which it was his wont to retire sometimes for days on end, he suggested that their upcoming journey together should be devoted to "finding ways appropriate for shielding oneself against every turmoil—of seeing everything that surrounds one in unity and light." This meant, first and foremost, a pilgrimage to Waterloo, where "the spirit of Napoleon braces a spirit free of turmoil in practice, in deeds."[74]

Before setting out with the Towiańskis for Switzerland, Mickiewicz paid a visit to his former professor, protector, and friend Joachim Lelewel, who had settled in Brussels after his expulsion from France some ten years earlier and where he now was barely surviving. The two had not separated on the best of terms; their communications since had been infrequent and limited to official business. The eminently rationalist historian and democrat had from its inception only contempt for the Catholic revival among the émigrés, spearheaded in large part by his former student. Towianism, however, was simply incomprehensible. When upon bidding farewell to Lelewel Mickiewicz mentioned something about "keeping one's soul at peace," the impoverished scholar answered that "the soul is at peace, it's just that the body is sometimes hungry." There was little left to add.[75]

The pilgrims' road took them through Aachen, Mainz, Frankfurt, Mannheim, Kehl, and Freiburg, then on to Lausanne and Martigny, where Mickiewicz was to see the Towiańskis off to Rome. The pope, however, was not the only mighty of this world to whom the Man of Providence needed to announce the Cause. In Frankfurt he paid a visit to Amschel Mayer Rothschild, son of the founder of the Rothschild banking empire and perhaps the richest man in Europe at the time, informing him "on orders from on high" that "God has decided to deliver Israel from misery and humiliation," that "God's thought has rested on [the banker's] tribe... for the sake of Israel," and that he was to "ready [his] spirit for the great hour in which the Lord calls [him] to serve." What Rothschild made of all this remains a mystery, but he proved somewhat more attentive than Louis Philippe—at least he did not have the prophet of the New Epoch escorted out the door.[76]

For Mickiewicz, the journey came to resemble something out of a biblical fairy tale, as if the Towiańskis were "a royal family traveling in disguise," whom everyone recognized but refused to let on. "There was not a single detail, from shoes to the Master's living quarters," he recalled for the Circle's edification upon his return to Paris,

> that was not calculated, not considered from the perspective of the Cause. He is mindful of everything and himself arranges everything. Traveling... with several people, he frequently walks all over a town in the rain with his things before finding quarters appropriate in every way. He arranges [everything] with the innkeeper, bears arguments, doesn't back down on anything, he maintains his tone in the smallest of matters.... He overcomes everything by the power of the Cause's tone and the blessing of heaven.

Would that he and Celina, Mickiewicz wrote to his wife in the course of the trek, be able to "live [so] cheaply and well," to accomplish "everything with such freedom of spirit and gaiety." Celina no doubt understood the hint, but a desire to experience the Towiańskis' familial bliss first hand was not quite the reason now for her own unexpected journey to Lausanne at the beginning of September.[77]

A month after Mickiewicz's departure, Celina had turned to Goszczyński in his role as the Circle's leader pro tem for a "long and important conversation," "a kind of confession," she called it. She admitted to Brother Seweryn that it was only recently that she had come to "feel and understand the Cause," but what she really wanted to discuss was "how until now she did not know the tone she should maintain as woman of the house. She did not conceal the lack of harmony that existed hitherto between herself and Sister Deybel, whose spiritual superiority she recognized." Although he sensed Celina's "humility and strong resolution to work on attaining complete spiritual purity," Goszczyński offered little in response, just as he proved largely ineffective in the face of sluggishness, backbiting, arguments over money (Pilchowski again), complaints about Ferdynand Gutt's imperiousness, and even defections among the brethren. With the situation at home becoming untenable, and Goszczyński not in a position or unwilling to become involved, Celina decided to take her complaint directly to the Master.[78]

Towiański appreciated Deybel's temperament—her fate concerned him, he still kept "knocking at [her] spirit"—but not at the expense of the Mickiewiczes' marriage, which was critical for the progress of the Cause as he conceived it. In any case, Sister Ksawera had recently overstepped the bounds by flirting with a certain Bérard, who, quick on the uptake, tried to entice her to join "a holy septet made up of women." The Master acceded to Celina's request for intervention. "The welfare of Sister Ksawera," he wrote, "depends now on her making a sacrifice to God, and this by keeping her spirit, which breaks loose to dominate at every step, on Christ's sharp leash." "She'll fulfill this," he added threateningly, "either now or after ages of misery." Manipulative as always, Towiański addressed his note to Mickiewicz, who, it seems, was supposed to pass it on to Deybel (and, one assumes, communicate its contents to Celina). But the poet appended a note of his own, in which he reassured Deybel that her transgressions only "served to elicit the obligatory stirring of God's spirit." It is unlikely that Celina was privy to this enclosure, for she left Lausanne feeling vindicated. Although chastened for the moment by the Master's admonition, Deybel, for her part, could nonetheless feel secure in the thought that her other master was willing to treat her transgressions with forbearance.[79]

Upon the arrival of Ferdynand Gutt in Lausanne in mid-September, Mickiewicz traveled with the Towiańskis as far as Martigny, whence the blessed company set off for Rome "to bind, through God's office, the heretofore divided tones of spirit and earth." For strength and inspiration, they would track Napoleon's victorious 1800 campaign against the Austrians. Mickiewicz, for his part, returned to Lausanne, and then at the end of the month left for Paris. During his nearly three weeks in the city that had treated him and his family with such extraordinary solicitude, the now honorary professor did not pass up an opportunity to visit old friends. He had remained in contact with many of them over the years, especially the Oliviers. When Caroline had come to Paris in the spring of 1842 with the manuscript of a novel she was hoping to publish there, Mickiewicz had made her feel at home in that "narrow-minded" city, shepherding her around to salons and theaters with extraordinary solicitude. But ever the apostle, and friendships notwithstanding, Brother Adam also paid his visits in Lausanne to proselytize. With most he was unsuccessful; in his friend Giovanni Scovazzi he managed to elicit the first stirrings of conversion among Italians, who in later years would prove to be the Master's most durable adepts.[80]

Mickiewicz returned to Paris revitalized. To his great joy but also disappointment, he found waiting for him a letter from Franciszek Malewski—joy at the unexpected news that his dearest friend and Celina's brother-in-law had been allowed a visit to the West, disappointment that in their travels they had missed each other and that to meet now would be impossible. The only recompense was a brief exchange of letters, the first since 1831, not as open and sincere as either would have wished, but enough for Mickiewicz to learn the latest about the fates of mutual friends—Tomasz Zan had returned to Lithuania; Onufry Pietraszkiewicz was aging; Teodor Łoziński had died in Vologda; Józef Kowalewski had married in Kazan, his health failing. Malewski soon returned to Russia, and once again the two friends were fated to communicate through their wives, with the usual, unsatisfying circumspection.[81]

Mickiewicz's personal disappointment was quickly overshadowed by disappointment of a more portentous nature. This was to be, after all, a time of especially focused spiritual labor, when the Master enjoined his disciples to "link" with him in "fraternal spiritual exertion" on behalf of his ministry in Rome. Yet exert as they might, the Vatican was obviously not on their wavelength—the Resurrectionists had made sure of that. The brethren soon learned that on 24 October Towiański had been sent packing without having been granted an audience with the pope; for their part, Cardinals Medici and Lambruschini "received him with the greatest of fury." But then all this meant little in the larger scheme of things. As Mickiewicz explained to the brethren,

> *The will of the Lord was fulfilled in spirit, not in human deed.* These words contain both the Master's victory and the purity with which he performed his ministry in spirit. The Apostolic See will come to recognize this sooner or later. The deed has been accomplished, and the See has been summoned to an accounting.[82]

Mickiewicz was nonetheless faced with the thankless task of restoring tone and confidence to a somewhat dispirited, and fracturing, Circle. Hoping to put a stop to the backbiting that had surfaced during his absence and the sense of aimlessness that had plagued it for months, he enjoined the brethren to refrain from visiting each other "without good reason, for entertainment's sake, to find out what's new," and act, rather, like soldiers, who never "go to their captain or comrades without a reason." Słowacki's defection had unnerved him, and he asked the entire Circle to reach inside itself to try and understand its cause. By early December, though, Mickiewicz himself seemed to be discouraged, lamenting that "the movement of the spirit within the Circle [had been] interrupted," its "overall life . . . halted." It was becoming clear that some new form of activity, and not just in the realm of spirit, was imperative in order to mobilize the brethren.[83]

In this regard, the fiasco in Rome was not without its brighter consequences. Not one to be discouraged, but at the same time running out of options, Towiański decided to hinge the progress of the Cause on the goodwill of his most articulate and prominent disciple. Soon after his expulsion from the Eternal City, as he passed through Marengo on his way back to Switzerland, he wrote to Mickiewicz suggesting that the fourth year of his lectures at the Collège be devoted to "examining a higher will," and "although the tone of the Cause [was] rendered but weakly and incompletely" in it, as his only "public writing" *The Symposium*, should now "serve as [the professor's] object of analysis from the podium." From Mickiewicz's perspective, this was a deed that could, he hoped, finally stir the Circle. On the eve of his first lecture, he announced to the brethren that they would now be putting their "youth in God's service" behind them and entering manhood. "We must," he concluded, "go out into the world like men, with the strength of a man." The brethren were "to pray that God strengthen [the professor] and bestow upon him the appropriate tone and stance"—and, it goes without saying, attend the lectures en masse in order to bear witness to the Cause. 1844 was bound to be a good year. By the Master's own numerological calculations, it was when the world would finally experience the descent of "the Gift of Grace and Mercy."[84]

9

Mickiewicz's willingness to devote the fourth year of his course at the Collège to *The Symposium* was in many ways a natural culmination of the lectures he had delivered during the 1842/1843 academic year.

In contrast to the first two years, in which the poet had guided his listeners on a chronologically organized tour from the Slavs' semilegendary beginnings up through modern times, with stops along the way to examine their history as well as their literature, the course he inaugurated in December 1842 proceeded instead along three interconnected tracks: the literary, the ethnographic, and the philosophical.

The first took up contemporary Slavic literature by looking at those writers who, Mickiewicz insisted, manifested their modernity through an "appeal to *genius*, to *inspiration*, what we have called *messianism*" (*Dz.* 10:60/*LS* 4:86). But although he considered, in this connection, Pushkin, the Czech Slavophile Ján Kollár, and the Serbian poet Simeon Milutinović, Mickiewicz made it clear from the start that only Polish writers had "managed to produce a literature that belongs to them alone, a truly original literature ... that [is] but an echo of the mighty voice of the folk, which is universally recognized as the voice of God" (*Dz.* 10:9–10/*LS* 4:5–7). And here Mickiewicz reserved the most space, nearly five lectures, to an analysis of *The Un-Divine Comedy*, a work published anonymously in 1835 but generally known to be by his precocious acquaintance from years back, Zygmunt Krasiński. Although not uncritical of certain of its aspects, the professor nonetheless proclaimed it a "national drama through and through" since, it goes without saying, it "touched upon all the issues of *Polish messianism*" (*Dz.* 10:138/*LS* 4:109). No less significantly, however, it evoked for Mickiewicz a vision of a new, specifically Slavic drama that would contain elements of folklore and the national, the supernatural, and the supranational—and which only the grandiose Cirque Olympique in Paris was suited to produce. As with Garczyński's *Wacław*, Mickiewicz had found in *The Un-Divine Comedy* yet another sympathetic vehicle for channeling himself.

The second track consisted of "*études*," as he characterized them—ostensibly learned disquisitions on the "primordial" history of the Slavs, their mythology and social organization, and the "architectonics" of their language (*Dz.* 10:9/*LS* 4:4) (which in any case he never got around to discussing); all this, though, by way of introducing his audience to what he called "Slavic philosophy" and its place in the philosophical discourse of Europe (*Dz.* 10:191/*LS* 4:300–301). But if on the one hand the *études* constituted an embarrassing olio of even by most scholarly standards of the time utterly fantastic etymological ruminations (Zeus derived from the Slavic word for "day," Rhea from the Slavic word for "river," Hades from the Slavic word for "hideous," while the Slavs themselves were said to be descended from the Assyrians),* they also served to drive home, often with passion and genuine inspiration, Mickiewicz's point about the momentous potential of the Slavs.

Unspoiled by complex mythographies mediated by priestly castes, the Slavs had developed a "natural" "folk" religion that left them uniquely situated to receive the revelation of Christ in all its simplicity and by the same token to create an original philosophy. Such a philosophy would at once challenge and transcend the systems of the day, the French no less than the German, but only as long as it was willing to jettison the old forms, the "religious" no less than the "syllogistic." "It is not enough to publish books and propagate systems," Mickiewicz proclaimed, "it is necessary to demonstrate the reality of these systems through strength, through life"—in other words, a philosophy of deed, as exemplified by Napoleon and soon to be realized by the French and Polish nations (Dz. 10:268–69/ LS 4:424–25). And if *The Un-Divine Comedy* was, in this respect, an intimation of these possibilities, so too were the writings of Polish romantic philosophers, of Bronisław Trentowski, August Cieszkowski, and Ludwik Królikowski. Nonetheless, they all remained precisely that, just intimations.

Not so, however, another philosopher, neither German, French, nor Polish, whose name began appearing in Mickiewicz's lectures with a regularity that ultimately compensated for its absence in the Continental discourse of the day. Somehow the Polish professor had managed to get hold of Thomas Carlyle's 1841 edition of Ralph Waldo Emerson's first volume of *Essays*. He was spellbound, so much so that he even tracked down an 1841 issue of *The Dial* in search of Emerson's lecture "Man the Reformer." In the author of "Prudence," "Spiritual Laws," and "The Over-Soul," Mickiewicz had at last found a kindred spirit, someone whose writings seemed to him "as if devoted to elucidating Polish philosophers and poets" (Dz. 10:119/LS 4:178–79) but in whom he quickly recognized "a sort of American Socrates" (Dz. 10:142/LS 4:217), a thinker already expounding a philosophy that Mickiewicz himself was only just adumbrating. Emerson now came to serve ever more frequently as something of a touchstone, an authority to be deployed—albeit in Mickiewicz's idiosyncratic way—in order to buttress his own views on the written word as deed, the primacy of the spirit, the relationship of man and nature and of man and the spiritual world. And despite his objections to what to his taste was the Transcendentalist's too radical abstraction of spiritual man from his age, his nation, and the world, Mickiewicz nonetheless found himself returning to Emerson repeatedly in the final year of the course,

*Although he cited a number of respectable scholars of the day (e.g., Šafárik, Hammer-Purgstall, Jacob Grimm, Schlegel, Niebuhr), Mickiewicz nonetheless preferred to draw largely on amateur sleuths (e.g., Francesco Appendini, Friedrich Nork [Korn], Gregor Dankovský), whose ramblings were even more fantastic than his own.

elated, it seems, to finally have come across independent confirmation of his own view on things.

Mickiewicz concluded the third year of his course on 27 June 1843. Over the preceding few months, his own brand of inspired scholarship, with its unmistakable intimations of heterodoxy, had come to be associated increasingly in the eyes of his audience with the anti-Jesuit lectures of Michelet and Quinet. To their Catholic opponents, the trio now constituted nothing less than "a society of *illuminati* at the Collège de France." And just as he had expressed solidarity with his French colleagues by demonstratively attending their lectures, so they returned the gesture with their presence at the Polish professor's final lecture of the course.[85]

It was, by all accounts, a remarkable improvisation on what Mickiewicz called the political history of the Slavic states. Reiterating themes he had been developing over the past three years, but now with a confidence and clarity born of his Towianist convictions, Mickiewicz again focused on the distinction between the Russian and Polish "ideas" (the Czechs and the South Slavs had "for some time now been checked in their development" [*Dz.* 10:314/*LS* 4:500]). Imbued with the spirit of Attila, Genghis Khan, and Tamerlane, "Russia [was] a land ruled *spiritually*," its might a function of the absolute power of its ruler (*Dz.* 10:306/*LS* 4:486); Poland was a land of institutions, its "moral focus" a function of the free will of its citizens and the inspiration of the Holy Spirit (*Dz.* 10:307–8/*LS* 4:488–87). And for all of its weaknesses, for all of its misguided attempts at "constitutionalism," it was, in the end, Poland that, on account of its sufferings and sacrifices, was destined to become "the cradle" of a new spirit. In fraternal concert with Napoleonic France, it would unite the nations of Europe.

"Mickiewicz," one Polish observer noted, spoke "with fervor," his lecture was "full of superb images and extraordinary volleys of thought." Michelet and Quinet "were moved to tears." The poet himself was pleased with his performance. "God blessed" the lecture, he boasted to Towiański. "Everyone was affected."[86]

Yet for all of its fireworks, the third year of Mickiewicz's course left some of his listeners and readers bemused, if not annoyed. The show, it seems, was getting tiresome: "purely *poetic* improvisation . . . too meager and empty *as scholarship*," as one Polish listener put it; to a Russian reader, in turn, "there was much that was to the point [albeit] with a touch not of falsehood but of inaccuracy." And although the Slovenian philologist Jernej Kopitar contented himself with personally communicating to Mickiewicz a list of fourteen pedantic correctives, Kollár, the embodiment of Czech Slavophilism in Mickiewicz's narrative, was incensed, accusing the Polish professor of "errors, exaggerations, biases, and even a complete lack of knowledge of [Czechs] and [their] circumstances." A certain "doctor at a Parisian insane asylum" simply came "to the conclusion that [Mickiewicz] was a madman." Over the entire auditorium, moreover, there now hovered the specter of Towianism, which haunted the course implicitly in the views that Mickiewicz espoused from the lectern, and, quite explicitly, in the persons of Master Andrzej's disciples, whose conspicuous presence at Brother Adam's lectures constituted a requisite form of "service" on behalf of the Cause.[87]

This notwithstanding, people continued to attend, if with less frequency and in smaller numbers; and some, particularly French youth, left impressed, even inspired. Both Quinet and Michelet were transfixed by "the fluency of [Mickiewicz's] delivery, the trajectory of his thoughts, and his deft choice of expressions," by his capacity to transform his lectures into a passionate declaration of faith. They took away with them that year nothing less than a lesson in romantic pedagogy, one that conflated research and improvisation, scholarship and prophecy, reason and affect, word and deed, which they strove to emulate in their own lectures at the Collège. "What characterized [this] new method of teaching," Michelet recalled years later, "was the strength of faith, the effort to educe from history not a doctrine, but a *principle for action* in order to condition not only minds, but the soul and the will. . . . It was an appeal to heroism, to great and lofty deeds, to unlimited sacrifice."[88]

George Sand, for her part, took away renewed "admiration and sympathy" for a man she characterized in an article devoted to the course as "the moral expression of Poland, a model of her essence in the sphere of emotions." Although she objected to the "conservatism" of Mickiewicz's revelation (she was writing, after all, for the progressive *Revue indépendante*), she nonetheless conceded that he "may have . . . discovered in the dogmatically religious idea that sustains him and [his race] the direct path to the social regeneration of the Slavic family." And like so many of Mickiewicz's French listeners, she took away a feeling of gratitude for what Quinet would later call the "filial emotion" with which the Polish professor spoke of the French, hoping that his enthusiasm for—if not necessarily conception of—his adopted country would somehow inspire "better days for French youth eager for a crusade in the name of principles that will yet be transformed in this age."[89]

Sand's review of the course, together with her publication a month later of the lectures on the *Un-Divine Comedy* in the same *Revue indépendante*, meant much to Mickiewicz. It could, he calculated (and he admitted as much to Brother Gutt), serve as a particularly effective medium for propagating the Cause. It was, then, with this in mind as well that he encouraged two of his Towianist brethren to translate the first two years of the course into German. Aware, however, that the first course and to a certain extent even the second did not yet fully reflect the entire depth and breadth of his revelation (to say nothing of the many factual errors that he admitted they contained), Mickiewicz felt it necessary to guide his readers to what they articulated *in posse*. "The final lectures," he wrote in a brief foreword,

> are the most important, we draw the readers' attention to them in particular, we tried to demonstrate in them how the idea of messianism, paved by the historical movements

> of the Slavic peoples, shaped in the moral heart of the Polish nation, is beginning to emerge into the light of day, and merging with the political interests of France and touching upon problems of German philosophy, is becoming a European idea. The works of poetry and philosophy that we analyzed in this course, and even the present work, should be taken as individual sparks of this idea, which is rapidly becoming a reality, cast from its heights onto the lower atmosphere—political, philosophical, and literary—in which we live today. (Dz. 8:8/LS 1:111)

But from this retrospective perspective even the third-year course barely hinted at the truths Mickiewicz was to reveal in his final year at the Collège or, for that matter, at the drama this entailed.[90]

On 22 December 1843, in an auditorium packed with the usual assortment of anxious émigrés, French listeners enthused by the lectures of Michelet and Quinet, the requisite "phalanx" of Towianists, and agents of the prefecture, Mickiewicz finally erupted. For some two years he had contained himself, suppressing the urge to articulate fully truths that he believed had "descended" to him "from an invisible and impalpable realm" (Dz. 11:183/LS 5:289). Now, at the command of the Master, before whose "portrait he had stood in rapture for hours in order to prepare himself," Mickiewicz could at last drop all pretense of scholarship. As he instructed his fellow Towianists, "he was no longer to be considered a professor" but "an organ of the Cause, an organ of the Circle, performing his service in and through the Cause." The past, with its inconvenient demands for dates and names, would no longer constrain him. He was here to reveal to the world the present and the future, "to pour forth all the fire, love, and power [he] had managed to collect in [his] soul" (Dz. 11:12/LS 5:10). "The time has come," he announced to his listeners, "to answer the summons coming from the Slavic countries, which commands me to put details aside and speak with the voice of the Slavic spirit to the genius of a GREAT NATION, to evoke that spirit and explain its mysteries" (Dz. 11:9/LS 5:5). The chair would thus no longer serve as "a symbolic arc of the future union of Slavic tribes" nor as "a tribune from which could be heard the historical truth," but as "a military outpost . . . , a bastion, which the genius of France entrusts to the Slavic spirit" (Dz. 11:13/LS 5:11). With this, and always mindful "of that verse of the Gospel [Lk 21.14] in which it is forbidden for one who wishes to speak of great truths . . . to come with premeditated phrases in one's head" (Dz. 11:177/LS 5:279), Mickiewicz launched into what was to become the greatest of his improvisations, sustained, astonishingly, over fourteen lectures. He himself "did not know what [he] was going to say," but he was intent on transforming his word, unmediated now by forethought or writing and impelled only by "intuition," into nothing less than the deed for which he so fervently thirsted. His performance would be the very proof of the truths he spoke. As an awed Michelet was overheard saying at one point, Mickiewicz "was no longer a poet but a prophet."[91]

And indeed, there was something of an Old Testament prophet's inspired thunder in the bursts of indignation and resentment that Mickiewicz now directed against "the official Church" and "people of official learning," the "*doctrinaires*" (Dz. 11:107/LS 5:165), as he called them, "men of the past" whose "desiccated souls [were] incapable of the fire of passion" (Dz. 11:28/LS 5:36). Themselves calcified by books and ritual, rationalism and fear, pride and egotism, they would "use every means to hinder those who stride ahead"—those whom Mickiewicz charged, drawing on Emerson again, with a capacity for "intuition," that "extraordinary movement of the spirit which elevates man above himself," enabling him to "lay within himself the cornerstone of the edifice of a free society" (Dz. 11:29, 31/LS 5:36, 40–41). And it was precisely this openness to intuition, this capacity "for understanding elevated things, for igniting a passion for them, and making them a reality" (Dz. 11:28/LS 5:36), that distinguished the two peoples, the Slavs and the French, linking their destinies like tinder and flint, from which would "burst a light that would illuminate the future" (Dz. 11:33).* The embodiment of this link, "the spouse of this unfortunate [Polish] nation" and at the same time "the most powerful of spirits" (Dz. 11:57/LS 5:82) was none other than Napoleon, whose own capacity to "peer deep inside himself and from there draw strength to ascend ever higher" (Dz. 11:21/LS 5:24) allowed him to "accomplish the most, toil the most, realize the most on earth" of any "Christian since the days of Jesus Christ. Every second of his life . . . was a deed" (Dz. 11:72/LS 5:107).

For three months Mickiewicz preached his word from the daïs at the Collège, now railing against the official Church and the *doctrinaires*, now pleading for "sympathy" from his French listeners, now testifying to the new revelation, and always with a view toward demonstrating "the mysterious ties that bound victorious France and suffering Poland" (Dz. 11:38/LS 5:52)—but ultimately, of course, toward finally witnessing the Master before his audience.

Yet if to some all this seemed "like the Sibyl, dark, revelatory, mad," or, as many more would have it, simply "nonsense," it was also treading on dangerous ground. Already upon sitting through the first lecture of the year Stefan Witwicki was compelled to wonder whether the authorities "wouldn't prohibit the course." And indeed, although Mickiewicz's attacks on all forms of "officialdom," be it ecclesiastical, philosophical, or political, together with his impassioned appeals to the French and the spirit of Bonapartism, may have induced "horror" among orthodox Catholics and derisive smirks from the Democrats and Czartoryski's people alike, for the French authorities they were crossing a line.[92]

By March, after the ninth lecture, in which Mickiewicz proclaimed that on account of its "ingenuity" and "holy fire" France was being called to action (Dz. 11:118/LS 5:183), it became clear to the Ministry of the Interior that "the professor was allowing himself to get carried away by the most reprehensible attacks against the social order, the government,

*This final sentence of lecture 3 (9 January 1844) does not appear in the French edition.

and the Catholic religion." Something needed to be done. Cousin's successor at the Ministry of Public Education, Abel-François Villemain, had no choice but to invite his troublesome employee for a talk. "He said that the government couldn't tolerate this, that [Mickiewicz] was coming out against it, that [he] was undermining its foundations, and he asked [him] whether [he] couldn't just leave these matters alone." Should he decide to "discontinue the course voluntarily," Villemain suggested, the ministry would let him "keep [his] pay and other significant perquisites." "I have to fulfill my duty," Mickiewicz replied. As he informed his brother two months later:

> I could already have been comfortably mired in mud, since . . . the ministry would have given me a substantial increase in salary [Mickiewicz was exaggerating here] and freed me from my duties were I to cease serving the cause that I serve. I could have already sold myself dearly. But the same conscience that did not permit me to seek a career in Russia or to grow fat in Lausanne does not permit me to stop in the middle of the road. And I'm sure that if I remain faithful to my inner voice, nothing bad will happen to me.[93]

Mickiewicz prepared for the next lecture as if it would be his last. He had asked Towiański "to give [him] official absolution in spirit at 11:00 [on the eve of the lecture], and on the following day, at 8:00 AM, . . . communion in spirit." This would be, after all, the moment to finally fulfill the promise he had made at the beginning of the course, to analyze Towiański's *Symposium** and thus reveal the Master to the world. Rumors of his showdown with Villemain, some maintaining that the professor had even been "ready to sacrifice himself" for the cause, guaranteed "a full auditorium."[94]

With "many standing outside," Mickiewicz opened his lecture of 19 March on a curious note: an explanation of intimations in the *Symposium*—and they were only intimations—that animals and plants have souls. But then, in a brilliantly executed rhetorical maneuver, he quoted Emerson in order to segue into a riff on the Word, whereupon, using the example of Jesus Christ as a bridge, he launched into a passage on inspired men of action—Alexander the Great, Julius Caesar, Napoleon—returned again to the theme of the Word, and finally concluded with a magnificent cadenza: "I am but a single spark flying from the torch, and whoever would want to trace whence it came will find . . . HIM, who is the path, the life, and the truth." "I stand in the face of heaven as a living witness to the new revelation," he continued with a shout "his arms upraised,"

> and I dare summon all from among the Poles and the French present here who know the revelation to answer me with a living word, to answer my question: Does it exist, yes or no?

*The Resurrectionists had, willy-nilly, again done Mickiewicz "a strangely great favor" by now publishing a French version of the *Symposium* (Mickiewicz to F. Gutt, 20 March [1844], Dz. 16:223).

(Those to whom the summons was directed rose and, raising their hands, answered: Yes.)

Those among the Poles and the French who have seen this revelation incarnate and have acknowledged that their Master exists, let them answer: Yes or no?

(Those to whom the summons was directed rose and answered: Yes.)

Fig. 23 Mickiewicz at the Collège de France, 19 March 1844. Contemporary caricature. Courtesy of the Adam Mickiewicz Museum of Literature, Warsaw.

One Russian even yelled, "We carry this in us as well." With this, the professor announced that his "service before God and [his listeners] [was] concluded" (Dz. 11:133–34/ LS 5:209).[95]

Mickiewicz was ecstatic. "God had given me so much strength," he gushed to Gutt in a letter the following day, "that after those . . . seventy-five minutes . . . I felt *no* bodily fatigue and could have given another lecture that evening." Among his listeners, however, his improvisation elicited a gamut of emotions. Indifference was certainly not one of them. "Many, not belonging to the Circle, were caught up in the ardor"; "a certain lady" even "collapsed in nervous convulsions." From among the Towianists, and particularly the "female adepts," "shouts mixed with sobbing could be heard. One of [them] remained for a while with her hands clasped, arms raised above her head, and outstretched toward the professor"; "another waited until the professor came down from the daïs and then threw herself at his feet, wanting to kiss them." The entire show, with its "clapping and foot stomping," may indeed have been "carefully staged," as one observer suspected, but to Goszczyński "all felt"—no simile here—"the descent of the Holy Spirit." And as was his and other Towianists' wont, he kissed the professor's hand after the lecture. As for "the rest," Poles and non-Poles alike, "they began leaving as if woken from a dream, some indignant, others saddened, still others laughing,"—or, as the satirical *Pszonka* observed, "with both hands covering their foreheads, red with shame."[96]

Not so Quinet, who the following day, during the first lecture of his own course at the Collège,* came out publicly, and unequivocally, in defense of Mickiewicz. "In the name of the Slavs," he announced to his listeners (trying hard to emulate his colleague's style),

> the premier poet of the Slavs, our dear, our heroic Mickiewicz is battling with his holy word for a cause that often coincides with ours. Who has ever heard words more sincere, more religious, more Christian, more extraordinary than those of this exile among the remnants of his people, like a prophet under the willow tree? Oh, if the soul of the martyrs and the saints of Poland is not with him, I don't know where it is.

"The deed of the 19th was confirmed by the deed of the 20th," crowed Mickiewicz in response. "He held me up as a prophet *dear to [the French]*," indisputable proof that "the Cause has already . . . made progress."[97]

This, however, was precisely what the functionaries at the Ministry of the Interior had feared, and more than they were willing to tolerate. After digesting the police reports, the undersecretary of interior affairs demanded that Villemain "put a quick end to these intolerable scandals." And, as if determined to demonstrate Mickiewicz's point about "men of the past," he warned that if the professor did "not take [the minister's] admonitions

*Published as *L'Ultramontanisme ou l'Église Romaine et la société moderne* (1844).

to heart," the ministry would "find it necessary to exercise against him measures that the law ha[d] at its disposal with regard to refugees whose conduct compromise[d] the public order."[98]

As luck would have it, the offending lecture just happened to be the last before the Easter break, giving everyone involved a month to consider options. Mickiewicz seemed resigned at one point, willing, as he told a Russian acquaintance, "to quit lecturing and make a living from private lessons." Michelet, however, certainly the more dynamic of the poet's two closest colleagues at the Collège, refused to leave it at this. As "denunciations against Mickiewicz poured in from all quarters," as Mickiewicz's old friend and translator Montalembert protested against the scandalous lecture on the floor of the Chamber of Peers, and as the Ministry of Public Education was now seriously considering "suspending Mickiewicz or forcing him to take a leave of absence," Michelet paid "a hundred visits a day" on behalf of his colleague; "to all those who . . . told him that Mickiewicz was a madman, he emphasized the greatness of the course, how much he found his teaching appropriate for everyone, albeit conducted in alternative ways." Mickiewicz was genuinely moved by this display of solicitude. "I am more concerned by your anxiety," he wrote to Michelet, "than by all the obstacles and all the ill will that I could ever encounter." He assured him that the minister of public education was very well disposed toward him, adding, however, that Emperor Nicholas had been as well. He need not have worried. The minister's sentiments proved unexpectedly less fickle than the tsar's.[99]

By the middle of April, as he was setting about editing the third and fourth years of the course for publication in the original French, Mickiewicz was ready to resume lecturing. But the relative conscientiousness with which he prepared for the upcoming lecture betrayed a sense on his part that his tenure at the Collège was indeed drawing to a close. He asked Towiański for permission to lithograph one of Wańkowicz's allegorical paintings of Napoleon for an upcoming lecture and also for advice on how to proceed with the course. The Master's counsel in this regard was more explicit than usual:

> Pause for a week, maybe two—after which renew the preceding tone—announce that you have fulfilled the obligations of a Christian—a brother—a friend—that communion in the most important interests of man today is your highest good—since in these true, Christian interests God's thought of saving man today may be fulfilled. . . . After which return to the strictures of the course itself, ease up on the tone—and depending on circumstances and events, raise your tone—using *The Symposium* as your text.

Mickiewicz fulfilled Towiański's directive to a tee.[100]

On 23 April, still a bit under the weather from a cold he had contracted a week earlier, the professor reconvened his course. In anticipation of a public whose curiosity had been whetted by Mickiewicz's last performance and the rumors it had spawned, a larger auditorium was assigned for the lecture, the same in which Michelet usually held his. Women were particularly in evidence, "eager," as one émigré newspaper put it, "for sensations that might exercise their nerves." The lecture, however, proved to be a disappointment. In providing his listeners with something of an overview of the course (with the requisite allusions, nonetheless, to "a single, total man," in whom "was concentrated the common strength of all higher spirits" [Dz. 11:146/LS 5:229]), Mickiewicz was "calm, reasonable, even dry in comparison to the ardor and emotion to which his listeners had grown accustomed from the beginning of the . . . academic year." But this was according to plan—as was the increasing heat of the subsequent lecture. Reaching out again to Emerson, his soul-mate across the Atlantic, the professor proclaimed "a holy war against people of books and systems, against this artificial world, spoiled and rotten" (Dz. 11:150/LS 5:236), going so far as to suggest at one point that although "no one is about to set fire to libraries," it would not be a bad idea if "people began visiting them less often" (Dz. 11:158/LS 5:249). After enthusing over the inherent "intuitiveness" of the French spirit, "constantly and doggedly aiming for *the immediate, the total, the universal,*" he concluded the lecture by insisting that "the happiness of peoples and families" of the future (Dz. 11:160/LS 5:252) could be attained only if women too were liberated from the suffocating philosophical and social systems of the past.[101]

Whether or not, as *Pszonka* had imagined it, Mickiewicz had really planned on becoming a "martyr" for the Cause, the lecture of 30 April seemed to have produced precisely that effect. "Mr. Mickiewicz," the prefect of police informed Villemain, "had completely transformed the chair into a tribune and made of the course in literature entrusted to him a purely political activity, all the more threatening in that the religious mysticism marking his lectures [was] addressed in particular to people with lively imaginations, whom he [was] pushing in the direction of fanaticism." No lecture was held the following Tuesday, nor the Tuesday after that. It appeared that the Ministry of the Interior had finally forced Villemain's hand—and that the poet had indeed achieved the "martyrdom" he craved. But for some reason the French authorities seemed content with simply elongating the proverbial rope.[102]

After a two-week hiatus, Mickiewicz stood again before a full auditorium, "tall, pale, skinny, dressed completely in black," his "face carrying traces of moral suffering soothed by fervent mysticism," his "gaze dimmed and sort of misty," "almost always hidden beneath long lashes," his "head tousled, tilted slightly back"—"clearly a man inspired." In a low, hollow voice that would soon become "so piercing that it was impossible to bear its momentousness," Mickiewicz again took up his denunciation of books and learning, which he contrasted with intuition and deed and inspired action. His "duty," he proclaimed, "was to outpace the course of time," "to make of [his listeners] witnesses in spirit to those mysterious workings to which Providence subjects people whom it destines to accept the new spirit." "Poland's destiny," he went on, "was to incarnate the new revelation, France's destiny [was] to be the first to accept it." With this, he announced, his "task as professor of Slavic [was] now consummated" (Dz. 11:170–71/LS 5:269–70). Yet the momentum of inspiration kept impelling him. "France," he continued, "can no longer return to a life *in and for itself*," it "cannot abandon [Christian nations] in the middle of a spiritual rout! [*Applause; commotion among the listeners*...]" (Dz. 11:171–72/LS 5:270–71). At this point, "a Frenchwoman... shot up and tried to make her way to the podium to kiss him, but unable to do so, she crumpled and for a long time screamed, '*Oui, c'est vrai!*'" Evoking the image of a "resurrected Christ, a Christ transfigured, armed with all the attributes of power, an avenging Christ and one who rewards, the Christ of the Last Judgment, of the Apocalypse and Michelangelo," he finally declared that this "lecture concluded [the] course"... but that there would be "one more meeting, the last" (Dz. 11:174/LS 5:274–75).[103]

"The excitement... was extraordinary," the policeman assigned to the lecture reported. "One simple woman, near the podium, fainted; another woman fell on her knees shouting, 'Long live Adam Mickiewicz!' The rest of the ladies (there were some thirty of them) expressed great emotion." The professor, for his part, "finished his lecture calmly, since the professor [was] used to similar scenes at the Towianists' private meetings." Mickiewicz had put in a performance as dramatically flawless as it was genuinely inspired. Everyone was left in suspense.[104]

On 28 May 1844, the auditorium filled quickly, "for the most part with French" eager to witness the sensation of the season. The Towianists, for their part, had "purified" themselves for the day with "a spiritual confession of [their] life in the Cause," and for good reason: "It had been announced... that that day would conclude once and for all both Brother Adam's service at the Collège and [theirs]." Applause was, as always, encouraged, since "applause rocks matter; produced at the appropriate word, it impresses that word into a spirit through structure set into motion"—or so, at least, Brother Adam had explained.[105]

Mickiewicz began his lecture with a reiteration of his mandate as professor of Slavic literature. He would speak of himself "for the first and last time," but only, ostensibly, in order to characterize his "professorial mission." This, it now turned out, was nothing less than "a *ministry of the word*," inspired directly by "the spirit of Him who dictated the Gospel" (Dz. 11:177/LS 277–79). Projecting himself as at once teacher and preacher, evangelist and prophet, he insisted that his mission as a Pole was to "help the French understand... the divine aspect of [their] own history" (Dz. 11:178/LS 5:281), embodied, as he asserted for the umpteenth time, in the person/spirit of Napoleon. Nevertheless, for all of the great leader's capacity to "fathom the mysterious hopes of his time" and "pave the way for their realization," this most profound, most inspired, most brilliant of men failed, succumbing as he did to the temptations of this world (Dz. 11:185–86/LS 5:293–95). But "when one genius called to serving [God's cause] falls, another appears to take his place" (Dz 11:187/LS 5:295). "It was vouchsafed me," Mickiewicz now proclaimed, "to have foreseen him." "*The man with three visages and three tones,*" he quoted himself, updating for the occasion Father Peter's vision from *Forefathers' Eve*, "had already revealed himself to the Israelites, to the French, and to the Slavs." "This man alone," Mickiewicz assured his listeners, was "capable of continuing the work of realizing the Napoleonic ideal" (*Dz.* 11:187–88/*LS* 5:296–97). And what that ideal was the professor now revealed for all to see by passing out copies of the lithograph, prepared a few weeks earlier, of Wańkowicz's allegory of Napoleon: eyes full of suffering turned upward, "imploring God"; under his outstretched hands "a map of Europe, which [was to be] transformed in the near future"; on his head, a wreath and a long, trailing veil—"the marriage wreath and veil of nations called to unite them like husband and wife in the spirit of the Cause under [his] direction." "Seek here that man!" Mickiewicz urged his listeners,

> evoke the spirit of your hero, the man of destiny. Only his spirit can lead you to the *man preordained*. This image is the sign by which you shall know him.... It will serve me as a witness that I have fulfilled my obligation. There will come a day that you will be called to account how you have fulfilled yours. (*Dz.* 11:190/*LS* 5:300)

"He looked like a man in ecstasy," one observer noted, "but an ecstasy that was unhealthy."[106]

"In my conscience," Mickiewicz informed Towiański the following day, "I have the sense that I fulfilled what I could." He had concluded the lecture by quoting two "toasts" with which Towiański had ended his *Symposium*—albeit without a word of commentary. The Master was pleased, claiming that "God was with Adam," that he himself "had achieved less in Paris... but was chased out anyhow." Mickiewicz's listeners, though—including even some of the Master's own disciples—were, by all accounts, disappointed. As the professor stepped down from the rostrum, many in the audience "still waited to hear something more," until, as one émigré newspaper reported, "Mr. S. Goszczyński asked what they were all waiting for. Upon which everyone moved out of the auditorium in silence, with faces on which one could read unsatiated curiosity." For Villemain, however, what Mickiewicz had uttered that afternoon was, regrettably, plenty. On 31 May, a month before the official end of the semester, the minister of education informed the prefect of the police that "Mr. Mickiewicz's lectures would not take place today or on any subsequent days."[107]

"What a truly lamentable thing," wrote one of the poet's countrymen, summing up emotions that Mickiewicz's performance at the Collège had stirred among Poles of every political persuasion, in country no less than in the emigration, "a genius of a man, a Pole, promoting publicly, to everyone's indignation, the nonsense of that nut or spy Towiański and giving a course in Slavic for the benefit of Moscow." Their poet-prophet, of all people, had squandered a unique opportunity to "explain, besides literature, the law, institutions, and entire life of Poland, . . . to not only elucidate many common misconceptions about Poland, but at the same time become a mouthpiece of its desires, hopes, and needs." What hurt most, perhaps, was that he had done so in a manner that had compromised the entire Polish community in the forum that was Paris, before a world upon whose sympathy their entire cause depended.[108]

The French viewed the affair from a somewhat different perspective. On 20 June, an enthused delegation of Quinet's listeners paid his suspended colleague a visit "in order to congratulate him on account of his doctrines" and inform him that a subscription was being taken up for a commemorative medallion depicting the Collège's three heterodox

Fig. 24 "That they all may be one": Mickiewicz, Jules Michelet, and Edgar Quinet. Medal by Maurice Borrel, 1845. Courtesy of the Adam Mickiewicz Museum of Literature, Warsaw.

professors.* To be sure, there were bemused expressions at what one French newspaper later described as Mickiewicz's descent into "the kind of mysticism... where the ridiculous borders on the sublime," to say nothing of outrage from the Catholic right at "Mr. Mickiewicz's... humanitarian fantasies." Yet when, two months after the suspension of the course, a conservative representative to the Chamber of Deputies questioned the outlay for the chair on account of its professor's "scandalous" attempts to propagate "a new religion," Villemain, together with much of the French press, framed his response not so much in terms of Mickiewicz's religious views but of his right to express them; the Collège, after all, was "an institution of higher and free learning," where "teaching... can and must enjoy almost complete freedom." In the end, and despite pressure from the Department of the Interior, Villemain could not bring himself to take the decisive step. After some negotiation, he suggested that for the moment the professor simply take a paid sabbatical until the beginning of the next academic year. Mickiewicz, for his part, had no intention of ever lecturing again. As he confided to Aleksander Chodźko a few weeks later, "I have completed my work in this arena."[109]

It was not until October that Mickiewicz and Villemain finally formalized the arrangement. After a conversation with the minister, the professor officially requested a sabbatical for the winter semester, ostensibly "in order to complete the publication of everything [he] had professed at the Collège de France." Nonetheless, he insisted in his letter that "in [his] lectures [he] had no other aim... but to educe [...] the *idea* of the Slavic race, which is all the more important for France to understand since in our time a true idea becomes a principle of force and an instrument of action to whom it is revealed." The sabbatical, with pay, would subsequently be renewed every year by Villemain and his successors, although in 1846 Mickiewicz himself asked that his salary be split with his replacement at the Collège, Cyprien Robert. This arrangement would last until 1852, when Napoleon III finally fired his uncle's ardent admirer.[110]

10

Eight months earlier, in February 1844, as Mickiewicz was fulminating against all forms of writing and book-learning from his podium at the Collège, a new, four-volume edition of his collected works, this time entitled *Writings*, appeared in Paris. The edition was a labor of love (if not of editorial competence) on the part of Aleksander Chodźko and Eustachy Januszkiewicz, two of the poet's most devoted acolytes. Aside from works published previously in the successive volumes of *Poems*, it included, for the first time, articles from *Pielgrzym* as well as *The Books of the Polish Nation and the Polish Pilgrimage*. More

*The medallion was finally presented to Mickiewicz in August of the following year. In 1884, an enlarged copy of it was hung in the hall of the Collège de France where the three professors had once lectured.

significantly, though, it contained a foreword in which Chodźko, channeling the voice of his mentor, laid out a credo that Mickiewicz had been formulating for nearly a decade. The opening sentence was simple and blunt: "Poetry as it has hitherto been understood has come to a close." The poetry collected in *Writings* was, in this respect, to "be considered completely finished," constituting as it did "an epoch apart in the life of the poet." "What had hitherto been latent therein as a premonition on the part their creator now stands before him in the entire colossal vastness of its visible reality, ever since *poetry as word* has incarnated itself in *poetry as deed*." "The highest poetry," Chodźko/Mickiewicz concluded, "is the highest truth; both come from the same source—inspiration." That this edition of Mickiewicz's poetry brought its author a 6,000 franc honorarium was an irony not lost on the leftist satirists of *Pszonka*.[111]

Deed, action, movement, all impelled by inspiration and intuition—these were themes that had surfaced insistently throughout and, in effect, *as* the fourth year of Mickiewicz's course. The very pathos and drama of improvisation were what had transformed each lecture into a performative utterance, a deed. But inasmuch as the course was Brother Adam's special "service" for the Cause, it was, at the same time, just the most tangible realization of Towiański's wish to see his word acknowledged by the French. For all their insights about the malaise enervating mid-nineteenth-century Europe, for all their prophetic power and at times incendiary invective, Mickiewicz's lectures were, in this respect, little more than revival meetings aimed at converting his French listeners.

Indeed, practically every convocation of the brethren was now devoted to devising means by which the Circle could "reveal God's Cause to France in a dramatic fashion." The Towianists were encouraged to provide Brother Adam with suggestions for his lectures (with the caveat that they should "stimulate him, not hold him back") and to assist him at the lectures themselves by "establishing with listeners outwith the same partnership that the Master had established within the Circle." Yet herein lay a rub. The nation that had produced "the saint for the present age" and "harbinger of the new Word" was, as such, inherently more spiritually evolved than those who would convert them. One just had to look at the "refined organism" of the French, Mickiewicz insisted in one of his lectures, "they practically don't have a body anymore, *they've shed matter*; spirit has already consumed body; . . . [they've] already attained the fruition of the spirit here on earth" (Dz. 11:118/LS 5:183). This notwithstanding, it was the Towianists alone who understood this "secret." All they could hope to accomplish, then, given this peculiar spiritual asymmetry, was to reveal their secret to the French and in this way move an already chosen people to action; they themselves were to "prepare to forget everything in order to ignite within themselves the flame of love for France." And it just so happened that there appeared among them a spirit that was willing to provide the tinder, "a living example."[112]

Marie Lemoine was a simple soul, but certainly with a flair for the dramatic. As Mickiewicz was leaving one of his lectures, "she had fallen at [his] feet in public . . . , crying out in tears that she is . . . a sister, that she has to be one." Lemoine's "deed" raised eyebrows even among the Towianists, testing, as it did, the intensity of their own fervor. But it was precisely on this account that Mickiewicz hoped to use her in order to nudge the Circle's conscience. "In Sister Marie," he admonished the Guardians, "we should recognize what a France mobilized by the spirit of the Cause will be." To think otherwise would be nothing short of pharisaism, a betrayal of the Master.[113]

Towiański himself was not altogether convinced of Lemoine's sincerity; with regard to her mores, though, he was certain. That the grisette was living out of wedlock with one of the brethren was wrong, morally, to be sure, but also as far as public relations were concerned. There were already rumors enough about real or imagined deviations among the Towianists. The Master suggested that Lemoine "find a Christian shelter in [Mickiewicz's] home," in the loving care of Sisters Celina and Ksawera, until she married. Although she "found love and reverence" there, her behavior nonetheless served as a reminder that the spirit had not fully subsumed the brethren's flesh, nor that the sisters were simply "spirits in a female shell." In April, just as he was contemplating his lecture on the status of women in a Towianist world, Mickiewicz found himself asking the Master to send Gutt to assist him "in many individual matters which [he] was unable to handle . . . , for instance, the brethren's relationships with women." Whether this was a prudent request is another matter. It was becoming increasingly clear that, as Towiański was later forced to admit, Brother Gutt had himself been "a victim of the spirit of lust all his life."[114]

Indeed, matters of Eros were becoming a concern in Mickiewicz's own household, that "smaller arena" where, Towiański believed, "a man must become great" in order to be "great in a greater arena." Earlier that year, in February, as he was "returning from church and thinking about Napoleon," Mickiewicz fell and twisted his hand, as a consequence of which he was forced to cancel his course for several weeks. Like everything else that he encountered now—a glance, a premonition, an ostensible coincidence, to say nothing of a dream—this was indisputably a sign: his "spirit, clearly, had not yet served enough to merit grace." "From this moment," Mickiewicz confessed to Towiański, "I sin through omission, through a lack of vigilance, and through wistfulness," whereupon he added, "I can't recall other temptations, except for temptations for my own wife, with whom, I felt, I should discontinue our sexual relationship for a time." Under the circumstances, Mickiewicz's gesture of (self-)denial was not, perhaps, as severe as it might appear. Celina herself was probably less than eager, having too suffered "a hard fall on the steps of a church" that laid her up for several weeks.[115]

By late March, Mickiewicz could report that "things [were] better with her and will be better." "Great signs have foretold me this," he informed Sister Karolina (as privy to his intimate life as her spouse or, for that matter, Sister Gutt). "I saw [Celina's] spirit.

Henceforth my behavior with her has proceeded with more certain strength and proceeds ever more effectively." That at this point both husband and wife had reached a modus vivendi with Deybel seems to have contributed to a general atmosphere of well-being. The two sisters could sometimes be seen entertaining guests together, the one (Ksawera) singing "in such a way that it was barely possible to recognize any Slavic tones," the other playing "a Polish mazurka" with "a real feel for its folksiness." At the end of that summer, the Mickiewiczes' tenth together, Celina was again pregnant.[116]

Their circle of friends had now shrunk considerably. Although the poet reminded the brethren that "breaking with people, repelling them" for the sake of the Cause was more a sign "of weakness than of strength," over the past year or so he himself had been methodically burning bridges to those he felt "'would judge a man before hearing him and knowing what he doeth [John 7:51].'" In March, indignant with what he characterized as "the aspersions slung at the Master, not to mention at his disciple," by the Czartoryski camp, Mickiewicz resigned from his presidency of the History Section of the Literary Society, the last remaining forum in which he still managed to interact with the emigration in something akin to a normal fashion. When in late spring of that year his old friend Sobolevskii dropped in to Paris for a visit, he "found M. less depressed than last time [1836], but... on bad terms with all of the countless parties dividing the Poles." The poet's friendship with Witwicki, tenuous at best since the conversion, ruptured now irrevocably when Witwicki—"sly, mendacious, not fit to be trusted in anything"—decided to "expose" Towianism in print.* Even Zaleski suffered. During an outing by the Mickiewiczes to Fontainebleau, their old friend complained, "Adam, in his sectarian obstinacy, forgot all about our many years of friendship, he didn't even approach me, although I know that in his heart he can't bear me any ill-will." To be sure, the elderly Vera Khliustin still merited Mickiewicz's attentions, albeit primarily as a recipient of his mystical advice; and he seemed happy enough to host Caroline Olivier when she visited Paris in the first months of 1845, spending nearly every day with her during her stay. But only Quinet and Michelet could count on a friendship that at once internalized and transcended their colleague's sectarianism. As Michelet put it, "As much as we may be *opposed in methodology*, so too we are *united* in our feelings... in our innermost principle."[117]

That fall, however, the edifice that was the Cause began to crack. Deybel, it seems, was acting up again. This time the victim of "the brilliance of Ksawera's eyes" appears to have been none other than Brother Gutt. Driven to nothing short of "physical illness" by her husband's most recent obsession, Sister Gutt insisted that Deybel take a refresher course in Solothurn, where the Towiańskis were now ensconced. Together with her sister-in-law, she made sure that "the Israelite princess" learned "how to maintain *Christ's*

*Stefan Witwicki, *Towiańszczyzna wystawiona i annexami objaśniona* (Paris: Rue de Seine 14, 1844.).

tone with needle, pot, at every step." Sister Ksawera's reeducation at the hands of "the Holy Family" lasted five, no doubt excruciating, months—the same five months during which a far more serious crisis began to perturb the Circle in Paris.[118]

II

Throughout the winter and spring of 1844, Mickiewicz's lectures had provided opportunities enough to keep the brethren mobilized, be it by coming up with suggestions for Brother Adam or "assisting" at them or praying for their success, be it in almost daily meetings and directives in which he revealed to them profundities inaccessible to listeners of the course outwith the Circle. Yet as Mickiewicz reported to Towiański, not all of the brethren seemed to have felt that the professor had "fulfilled . . . the essential" at the Collège; they wanted—needed—something more. In this, Towiański had made his task a little easier (if one may use this word) by producing exclusively for his "beloved" "minister of the Cause" "The Great Period," a new screed in which he elaborated, so to speak, the "tone and vision" of his doctrine.* Surfacing as it did on the heels of Mickiewicz's 19 March lecture—no accident, surely—Mickiewicz sensed, as Towiański knew he would, that something momentous was about to occur, that, as the Master put it so eloquently, "the thread that had been in the realm of the spirit . . . was now cast on the earth."[119]

Much like the release of creative power in Dresden twelve years earlier, the enormous mental exertion that improvising the lectures demanded of him served only to energize Mickiewicz. He gave no thought that spring to his usual escape from the city. After his final lecture, he immediately set about devising a series of projects that the course had, in effect, inspired. Besides directing the brethren to intensify proselytization among both the émigrés and the French (particularly "*ouvriers*" and "soldiers"), he dispatched two of them on a mission to Valais, imagining that this was a "Swiss Poland or Lithuania," hence especially ripe for the Word. At the same time, and partly as a way of involving the French septet in the work of the Circle, he conceived a proposal to a commission recently charged with erecting a monument to Napoleon in Paris. To be modeled on the image of the emperor he had distributed at the final lecture, his project was, Mickiewicz declared, nothing less than what "the genius of France had revealed." (For all his love for Mickiewicz, the sculptor David d'Angers apparently demurred when approached with the idea.)[120]

Nothing came of either initiative. The former, in fact, led to Towiański's expulsion from Solothurn; the latter was ignored. Moreover, two other brothers, whom Mickiewicz had sent to proselytize in the French provinces, were expelled from what the Polish exiles assumed was some sort of republican haven. Perhaps, as the poet wrote to Villemain, "the time had not yet come to understand what must remain a mystery"; perhaps, as he told

*Towiański, "Wielki Period," in *Wybór pism*, 100–122.

the Circle in preparation for their participation in celebrating *les Trois Glorieuses*, only "action in spirit," which "operates invisibly, like an exhalation . . . that can infect an entire region, although it is invisible to the eye," would move the world; but perhaps too, "the continuing failure to realize on earth . . . originate[d] in each of them from a sin of spirit." In any case, as much as Towiański may have approved of Mickiewicz's initiatives, he nonetheless had his own idea for mobilizing the brethren. It was time, he felt, to play the Russian card again and take his mission directly to the tsar. Not at all surprisingly, what the Master concocted as an opportunity for "holding on to the thread and spinning it," contributed, ultimately, to the fraying of the Circle.[121]

In a letter of early June 1844, Towiański announced to his administrator in Paris that "in every contact with Russia it is necessary to act according to the tone with which we will act in the entire Cause." "The power and well-being of Russia," he continued, "are crucial for fulfilling God's Word on earth. . . . I desire to serve Russia on a path that is new and powerful and true." This was certainly not the first time that the Master had articulated such sentiments; indeed, minus the personal note, they were ones the poet himself had put forth often enough in his lectures. To the bitter dismay of his émigré listeners on both the right and the left, he had repeatedly appealed to Russia's spiritual as well as physical might and its providential mission, which together with Poland's would bring about the age of Slavic brotherhood founded in and on the new revelation. It was in part to this end that he had recently attempted to convert the Russian revolutionary Mikhail Bakunin to the Cause, insisting, as the latter recalled later, that "it was enough for one Pole, one Russian, one Czech, one Frenchman, and one Jew to agree to live and act together in the spirit of Towiański in order to overturn and save the world"; and at the moment only a Russian was missing from the equation. What Towiański had in mind, however, was something more grandiose: he would bring about Russia's redemption by converting the emperor himself. Harebrained as the enterprise may have been, the prospect of intervening directly with the despot, of offering him the opportunity to, in effect, save him from himself for the salvation of mankind, was a temptation difficult to resist, particularly when God—and the Master—so willed it.[122]

The fact that it took Brother Adam five months to inform the brethren of the idea nonetheless speaks for itself—as does too the effort he invested in helping Towiański formulate an appropriate appeal to Nicholas (and not only because the Master was none too nimble with French). The two agreed that Brother Chodźko, as a former diplomat of the empire and at the same time someone blindly loyal to Mickiewicz and the Cause, would be best suited to deliver the letter to the Russian embassy in Paris; they also agreed that it would be best if he were the one to sign it.

Given even the sincerity of the beliefs that inspired it, the contents as well as rhetoric of the appeal would be compromising enough; under the circumstances, they were nothing less than scandalous. Addressing Nicholas throughout as "*Sire*" and "*Votre Majesté*," it depicted the emperor as "the greatest instrument of God's will on this earth," while at the same time condemning the Polish uprising as a "deviation from the path desired by God," which "the hand of its own brothers" justly punished now, albeit for the sake of Poland's and by the same token Russia's own salvation. "Under your wing, Sire," the letter declared, "the first step of progress has been taken. . . . Do not reject the fruits of the sacrifice through which Poles offer themselves for the well-being of humanity [this Mickiewicz insisted on adding, since otherwise "earth will misunderstand"], for our Sister-Nation, and for your own well-being [Towiański's original considered only the latter]." The authors assured the tsar that among the Polish exiles there were those who "were permeated with feelings of devotion to God and a sincere love for our brother Russians and for the person of Your Majesty."[123]

Chodźko dutifully deposited the letter, written on paper used expressly for "official correspondence with the ambassador and the tsar," at the Russian embassy in Paris on 15 August. Over the next three months, Mickiewicz attempted to prepare the Circle for what was a fait accompli. Mobilizing the Napoleonic imagery that by now had become rhetorical stock of his allocutions to the brethren, he reminded them that their Master was a "commander in matters of the world, that his orders [should be] obeyed without consideration, just as a soldier obeys the orders of a corporal, and a corporal those of a captain." He played on their impatience, declaring yet again that "the epoch of realization" was indeed nigh and that "today there is no one on this globe besides the Master who could realize the truth in spirit." But he also worked on their guilt and self-esteem, upbraiding them for "seeking easy routes, well-traveled . . . ; yet until [they] find . . . new ones and try them, [they] will never solve any political, administrative, or social problem." In this respect, however, Mickiewicz overplayed.[124]

As it became clear that no answer to Chodźko's initiative at the Russian embassy would be forthcoming, Mickiewicz was approached by Brother Seweryn Pilchowski, who after "a long journey arrived at the feeling that he should go to Russia and appear before the tsar as an envoy of the Cause." This was the same Brother Pilchowski who some weeks earlier had accused Brother Adam of not having been sufficiently assertive in his dealings with Villemain; the same who disapproved strongly of Brother Adam's Gallomania; the same who harbored ambitions of leadership—and a thing for Deybel. Feeling "overwhelmed and ill," Mickiewicz acquiesced and sent Pilchowski to the Master, but not without reservations. As enormous as Brother Seweryn's spiritual power may have been, in Mickiewicz's estimation "he still [did] not have the appropriate tone of the Cause"; indeed, "some alien spirit, or perhaps several of them, had settled in the lower part of his body" and "often seized his thoughts and his mind and his heart." Towiański, however, pronounced "Brother Seweryn's projects . . . pure" and suggested that Mickiewicz work with him "so that what is pure in spirit could be revealed without harm to the Cause." But here the Master, too, miscalculated.[125]

Mickiewicz finally disclosed the contents of Chodźko's letter to the entire Circle on 29 November 1844. That he chose to do so on the fourteenth anniversary of the uprising was, of course, no accident. Declaring that "the revolution" had failed for lack of "the full tone of Christ's love," he proclaimed that only by "loving what is pure and good in Russia . . . and dealing with Russians in this love" would the Cause be consummated. The failure of Chodźko's mission was, in this respect, but a temporary setback; there had appeared, he announced, another brother, who "felt the call" and now "stood at a point from which he should act in deed." "That Brother," Mickiewicz revealed, was "Seweryn Pilchowski," whereupon he "threw himself at Brother Seweryn's feet and Brother Seweryn responded in kind."[126]

All this was disturbing enough in and of itself. The fact that the entire undertaking had been kept from the brethren was doubly so. Their reaction could have been foreseen. Yet, blinded by what can only be described as the hubris of at once unquestioning belief and unquestioned authority, Mickiewicz was genuinely taken aback when those he had heretofore taken to be "sheep" and "fools" rebelled. And in any case, in an atmosphere where intuitions, dreams, coincidences, and premonitions had come to serve as simulacra for the real and the sole measure of consummation, where undertaking any action became, in effect, an exercise in the impossible, something was bound to snap. The entire affair with the letter brought it all to the fore, a symptom of a deeper malaise.[127]

In the first of what would with time become a series of remarkably congruent exposés of the Circle's practices, Brother Mikołaj Kamieński (who before becoming a colonel in this life had apparently spent a previous one "executing the duties of a cow") declared in a letter to Mickiewicz that the appeal to the tsar was nothing more nor less than a desperate attempt on the part of the Circle's "administration" to revive a profoundly moribund organism. A comity that had once united in "blissful prayer, love, and renewal" had become "a tower of *Babel*," wherein the brethren

> were consumed with feigned enthusiasm, were urged to discern in Spirit, [to have] dreams and visions, with the result that each one struggled to attain a state that the administration desired.
>
> There then came *orations*, kissing of feet, the elevation of some brethren and the abasement and degradation of others, there followed a hierarchy of spirits, based on nothing, which then changed by turns.

With this, Kamieński broke with the Circle, proclaiming himself its "avowed opponent." When the administration ignored his letter, he decided to make it public, to the delight, of course, of the entire emigration.[128]

Although no longer an active member of the Circle, Słowacki recognized in Kamieński's protest the "miraculous" "resurrection" of his earlier "veto and negation in spirit...of [the Circle's] Russian tendencies," about which he now felt compelled to remind Mickiewicz. As before, however, he kept his assertion of nonconformity confidential—and he never did publish the poem he wrote on this occasion. In it the Circle was transformed into a "dark lair," "a horrible ruin of minds" ruled by "a *potentate* in a *charlatan's* prophecy foretold," before whom:

> Skeletons of madmen throw themselves—and rattle,
> Abase themselves, and thank him for the honor....
> This one says I, whereupon the spirit of someone else responds.
> Yet another, whom he bullies into exploring his own past,
> Looks and finds someone else's memory in his;
> Yet still another...
> Forgets himself and proclaims that Moscow is his land.
> Another one runs hand through hair and, raising fist into the air,
> Proclaims just like a woman: "Alas, O God! alack!"[129]

By the end of 1844, Mickiewicz's authority among the increasingly restless brethren was beginning to disintegrate. And as it did, individuals inevitably emerged who were ready to reassemble the pieces on their own terms—with the encouragement, it seems, of their manipulative Master. For the next two years, the most powerful "spirits" of God's Cause connived and coerced and abased themselves in a struggle for supremacy, forcing the lesser spirits among them to endure humiliations that made Kamieński's exposé pale in comparison. Looking back on this period of plots, rebellions, reconciliations, and schisms, Goszczyński observed:

> No tongue of man can express nor mind grasp what went on then. The Circle [*Koło*] changed at that time into a tribunal of the Holy Inquisition and into purgatory and maybe even hell; everyone was [caught] in that wheel [*koło*], everyone turned in order to torture others, and everyone experienced judgment and execution; everyone found his executioner in the Circle, and everyone had his victim.

What the brethren referred to as "the pandemonium" had begun.[130]

12

Pilchowski's gambit had paid off. Now that he had obtained Towiański's blessing for the mission to Russia, Mickiewicz had no choice but to pronounce Brother Seweryn "the only one among [them] to have matured," hence someone the brethren were expected to link with and emulate. Pilchowski, however, had greater ambitions. As he went about ostensibly preparing for his journey, he made another dramatic gesture calculated to elevate his status in the eyes of the brethren even more compellingly. On 6 January 1845, "Seweryn Count [self-proclaimed, for added dramatic effect] Biberstein Pilchowski from Terechów" declared that he was recognizing Andrzej Towiański as his Lord and Master, whereby he legally signed his person and all his possessions over to Brother Andrzej, vesting in him "all the rights guaranteed in old Poland to lords over their subjects."[131]

The gesture was more salient than Pilchowski was probably capable of realizing. It made explicit what had become the overarching purpose—or, rather, charge—of every Towianist: to "*renounce* [one's] freedom... and accept as [one's own] the will of *Master Andrzej Towiański*... in all of [one's] doings." Nothing less than absolute obedience and unconditional surrender—of privacy, of conscience, of will, of self—could guarantee absolute freedom, and the Master's unconditional love.[132]

Its implications notwithstanding—and they would, in time, prove grave indeed—Pilchowski's act of submission served to reinforce his standing in the Circle. Mickiewicz himself was forced to recognize this fact, and he directed the brethren to "provide brother Seweryn in writing [an accounting of] their spiritual state... with respect to... their capacity for fulfilling their Christian duty in communion with Christ." For the moment, at least, Pilchowski had succeeded in positioning himself as the Circle's alpha male, in direct competition with Mickiewicz. Never mind that he kept postponing the trip to St. Petersburg, while, as rumor had it, "squandering the 5,000 francs he had collected from Chodźko and the others for the pilgrimage on champagne"; never mind that what he really sought was simply to return to Poland. His readiness to enact, dramatically and zealously, the Master's desire for total subservience impressed a number of his less assertive brethren, upon whom, it seems, Mickiewicz's methods for satisfying Towiański's wishes "in spirit" had palled. It also impressed Sister Ksawera.[133]

Although in November Towiański had proclaimed that "evil had left her" and that Deybel's life was now "purer than before," by March 1845 he was accusing her of having "trampled the laws of spirit and of earth" and of "forfeiting [her] innocence in spirit and in earth." Whatever her transgression, it was egregious enough that Master Andrzej felt compelled to demand that she relinquish her "stained medal" of the Cause and "prepare [her] spirit to accept a pure medal as the mark of a new life." To make sure she worked through her atonement, Towiański charged Brother Adam with guiding her, to which end he expressly forbade her from living with the Mickiewiczes "until she bore the fruit of a new life." For the next few weeks, Mickiewicz worked hard to steer the woman out of her "confusion." But here too, Pilchowski upstaged him. Upon returning from a retreat with Towiański in Einsiedeln, it was Brother Seweryn who managed "in a moment of grace and strength to shatter the fetters that... had been weighing [Deybel] down." The poet suffered this new challenge to his authority with the equanimity of a good servant to the Cause. "Thank God," he wrote to Towiański with news that Sister Ksawera was now living with the family again, "all this is over and done with." This, however, was only the beginning.[134]

Pilchowski had brought with him to Paris a new "summons to action" from Towiański, written expressly for the Easter holiday that year and, in the Master's eyes, a document of unusually profound significance. It was, if anything, more opaque than usual—even his deftest exegete had a hard time divining its meaning for the brethren. According to Mickiewicz's reading, their "Lord and Master" was "summoning [them] again to grasp in spirit the entire totality of the Cause, to embrace it in [their] souls and thus feel [themselves] to be on that rung on which according to God's plan the Lord's Contingent should be standing." Some brethren, however, understood the summons differently (as Towiański had probably intended all along), recognizing it rather as "opening before them . . . a new age, one of deed"; the Master was "only waiting for [them] so the deed could begin." And in this connection, had not Brother Adam himself remarked that "one of the brethren . . . had given [them] an example of the possibility of fulfilling this sacrifice"? Sure enough, three weeks later Pilchowski provided the Guardians with his own interpretation of the screed, in which he charged the brethren—channeling, of course, Towiański's own reflections on the matter—with "grave sin and grave transgression" for not fulfilling the summons. It was not long before Towiański himself informed his minister in Paris that he had "recommended to Brother Seweryn that he should come to [Mickiewicz's] aid . . . in fulfilling this important station of the Holy Cause."[135]

Yet as dissatisfied as he may have been with Brother Adam's administration at this point, Towiański was by no means contemplating demoting his most valuable disciple. Rather, it seems that he felt he could use Pilchowski's assertiveness to "move" Mickiewicz, to extort even more out of him than he was already giving. Despite his disciple's protestations about "losing strength and harming [his] health" as a consequence of his "protracted struggles" with Deybel, Towiański was beside himself upon learning that the poet had allowed her back into his home without his approval. "The fire miraculously inspired is now extinguished," he admonished Mickiewicz, "the force of the Holy Cause has been killed within her." And to drive the knife even deeper, the Master informed Brother Adam that "Brother Seweryn had taken it upon himself to keep vigil over the sister's new road."[136]

By May, Towiański's machinations had produced their intended effect: "summoned by the man of God, [Mickiewicz's] spirit budged." Although he had been planning a visit to Switzerland for some time, the poet was now forced to pay it on the Master's terms. Before leaving, he directed each of the brethren to compose a personal "testimonial" to the Master, which he then appended to a declaration from the entire Circle acknowledging, per Pilchowski's example, "the Master not simply as master, but as the lord of earth and of [them], and placing at his feet [their] souls and [their] bodies in readiness for anything." With this, Mickiewicz told the brethren on the eve of his departure, he was "taking to [their] Lord and Master the fruit of all [their] work so far"—almost a full four years' worth. Having appointed Brother Karol Różycki as his replacement, Mickiewicz set out on 17 May for Towiański's new residence in Richterswil, a small resort town on the Lake of Zurich, not far from Einsiedeln. That he was leaving behind a wife still exhausted from giving birth just five weeks earlier to their fifth child (Jan [for John the Evangelist, patron of the Cause] Gabriel [for the archangel] Donat [for the patron saint of his day of birth]) concerned him little at the moment; in any case, Maria was old enough to help around the house. Of greater concern was Deybel. Although she was now "apparently on better terms with Celina," Mickiewicz nonetheless felt compelled to warn the women that "should there be a major conflict between them, Ksawera would do better to move out until [his] return."[137]

13

It had been nearly two years since Mickiewicz had last basked in the presence of his lord and master. Their reunion, he later reported, sparked the same "emotion that [he] had felt on [their] first meeting." Almost immediately, though, Towiański put him to work, enjoining "the loftiest of Slavic men" to "empty himself, to become a fool for Christ... and like a Lithuanian peasant grandmother... make a pilgrimage to Einsiedeln." During the pilgrimage itself and then for the next four weeks in Richterswil, in interminable sessions and in no less interminable memoranda sent from an adjoining room, the Master by turn flattered and reprimanded, coaxed and threatened Mickiewicz, weaving a babel that was as mesmerizing as it was mind-numbing, as distressing as it was, no doubt, soothing and uplifting. Ordained "the highest Slavic priest, a Peter for the new age" called "to announce and spread the living Word of God," "ancient Israel" had not, it seems, "emptied" himself sufficiently; he had persisted in "submitting to the spirit of the earth"; his spirit and his body were out of sync. Hence his "suffering through the ages"; hence his personal "failures"; hence the confusion among the "lesser spirits" in the Circle, whose "nascent Christian life he killed" with his "fatal" example; and hence also his troubles with Celina, whom he "indulged" for the sake of domestic peace and thus let her drag his spirit down, "muddy [it]..., entice it, weaken it, jerk it around."[138]

In the end, however, the indulgent Master held out hope for his chastened disciple:

> At God's command, O Brother, your way illuminates your life, your ages—you are becoming, as never before, God's slave, a slave of your illuminated way.... Your spirit, having long eluded the essential points of God's thought, touches its base, enters the last circle of God's reckoning—and that reckoning will consist of bearing for God the fruits of received light in every thought, utterance, and deed; of burning ceaselessly at the altar of the Lord the Lord's sacrifices through his high priest; of constantly gathering the

brethren at the altar of the Lord; of exerting the spirit in this as recompense for former dissipation; of building a new and higher church of Christ.

And to encourage him on his new way, Towiański decreed that henceforth it would be Brother Adam who would bear the banner of the Cause, which "for over seventeen years" had been entrusted to Brother Ferdynand. What was intended to serve as a great honor for Mickiewicz marked thus an awful fall for Gutt. As Towiański saw it, his first and most loyal of acolytes had become "a dangerous canal of evil," channeling no less than the lascivious spirit of Louis XIV. How appropriate, then, that Brother Adam should receive that banner from the countervailing spirit of Louise Françoise de La Vallière, Louis XIV's virtuous mistress, inhabiting now the earthly shell of Sister Anna Gutt.[139]

Towiański finally let a physically exhausted but spiritually rejuvenated Mickiewicz go sometime in mid-June. He charged him with delivering a condescendingly gracious answer to the brethren's act of submission as well as an anathema for Brother Ferdynand. He thought it wiser, though, to send a letter encouraging Różycki's "intuitions" under separate cover. About Pilchowski's upcoming visit there was not a word.[140]

Mickiewicz headed back to Paris via Lausanne, not so much out of nostalgia as out of "the conviction" that the Canton of Vaud could become "one of the links" for "fastening the Cause . . . to earth." The city had changed much since his last visit. A radical government had been installed earlier that year and, thanks in part to Scovazzi's energetic proselytizing, was, in Mickiewicz's mind, potentially open to receiving the Word. Certainly the radicals' leader, Henri Druey, gave that impression. In long conversations with the poet, this "man of movement and power . . . evinced complete trust in [him], shared secret notes concerning his person and events in which he participated, in a word, spoke and acted as if he were [their] brother." At one point even, Druey, the future president of the Swiss Confederation, confided "that maybe in a previous life he had been an ox" ("his spirit," it seems, was "more developed than Brother Seweryn Pilch.'s"). But if people new to Mickiewicz seemed "sincerely" drawn to him, acquaintances from years back were markedly cooler. As much as he tried to make amends for behavior "if not necessarily wrong or erroneous according to the Old Covenant, then certainly so according to the spirit of the Cause," he felt as if he were being rebuffed, by the Oliviers, by Melegari, and most painfully, perhaps, by the Jundziłłs.[141]

Lausanne, however, had not forgotten its honorary citizen, whatever his convictions. Upon returning to his hotel one evening, Mickiewicz was met by a throng of "some 400 people"—students from the academy, professors with their wives, even locals—all gathered to listen as a sixty-man chorus serenaded the beloved professor with a "hymn" composed especially for the occasion. Mickiewicz responded with a speech extolling the people of Vaud for sparking "the essence of a new life in the heart of [their] country." "When it will finally be vouchsafed me to see that expected day in my fatherland," he concluded, "even then will I remember your welcoming land and will never forget the reception you arranged for me today." That expected day never came, nor would he ever have the occasion to visit again what might have become his home away from that fatherland.[142]

14

Mickiewicz returned to Paris on 12 July. During his absence, Celina had moved the household, from rue d'Amsterdam to rue du Boulevard in Batignolles, barely a suburb of Paris then, hence markedly more affordable. "For 600 francs a year" she informed her sister, "we have an entire house with a garden . . . ; besides, meat, wine, lighting, and heat are cheaper, and we're only two minutes from the [city] gate." Celina would now occupy a room upstairs next to the children's, while Mickiewicz would have two rooms to himself. One of them opened onto a verandah on which the owner had installed a plaster statue of Napoleon. There was a chicken-coop in the garden, and the poet soon planted a rowan tree nearby, which "reminded him of Lithuania . . . whose bitter berries he also liked for the memories." As for the neighborhood, for better or worse it was teeming with Towianists.[143]

In view of his admonitions to Celina and Ksawera on the eve of his departure, it probably came as no surprise to Mickiewicz that upon his return "Miss Deybel [was] no longer with [them]." No sooner had he left for Switzerland when Ksawera returned to her old ways, "harassing" Celina, "picking on the children," and "neglecting her duties." The conflict became so serious at one point that Różycki, in his role as the Circle's pro tem, felt compelled to intervene. According to Mickiewicz's own, tellingly forbearing, account of the events, Deybel then "vowed to mend her ways, made an effort . . . to give in." This, however, served only to irritate Celina further, to the point that Brother Karol found himself "incapable of maintaining a fraternal and official relationship with her." Although Deybel's ejection from the household seemed to have calmed Celina, the mere mention of Ksawera's name was enough to drive her "into an animal state" (not necessarily figuratively), and "any time there was talk of Celina, Ksawera would leave her senses." There had been problems with Pilchowski as well, who at one point kicked Celina out of his apartment. What Mickiewicz did not realize at first was that all this was in fact a symptom of a more serious problem. In his absence, Brother Seweryn had staged a coup.[144]

Singled out by Mickiewicz himself "as the one who posted the highest movement in the Circle" and encouraged, subtly and otherwise, by the Master, Pilchowski had formed a new "partnership," for which he succeeded in enlisting Różycki, Goszczyński, Wrotnowski, Zan, and even Eustachy Januszkiewicz, among others, as well as Deybel. As Sister Ksawera had explained to Celina, it was time that "someone else from among the brethren should be the Master's stand-in." Mickiewicz, though, was kept in the dark. Indeed, two days after his return, he could still write to Towiański that "everything was better than [he] had left it," as if "the Circle [had been engaged] in constant and great work." But after a few conversations with some of the brethren, the true nature of that work became all too apparent.[145]

On 19 July, Mickiewicz announced at a meeting of the Guardians that, like "a man revitalized," he was back in charge, that "the Master had absolved him of all his faults," and that the only shortcoming for which he must atone had been his failure to recognize "the blessed state in which [Sister Ksawera] had returned from the Master" that past March. He ordered a convocation of the entire Circle for the following day, directing the brethren to prepare themselves "to feel and accept in all simplicity and truth what will be presented to them." On 20 July, the conflict between the administration and the partnership finally erupted. Pilchowski, declared Mickiewicz, had misinterpreted the Master's words [for which, in all fairness, it was unfair to fault him] and as a consequence had "killed the spirit of Sister Ksawera," "repulsed" Brother Adam, "and squeezed the brethren." But instead of responding to Mickiewicz's summons, many of the brethren approached *him* with accusations. "All chaos broke loose, like never before," spilling out onto the dusty streets of Batignolles.[146]

Over the course of the next week, Mickiewicz set about liquidating Pilchowski's partnership and bringing the factious brethren to heel. "Some realized their sin immediately, others grew frightened"—but after "intense work" with Brother Adam "from morning until evening for hours on end," one after another confessed. Their admissions of guilt, signed, delivered to Mickiewicz, and then communicated to the entire Circle, are chilling. "My sin of imprudence," Wrotnowski lamented, "of not running first to the source of grace and light, which flows from our Lord [i.e., Towiański] through you, of not trusting strongly enough that the exact execution of your directives is the simplest way out of our confusion; this grave sin I now see and regret." Januszkiewicz, for his part, chose to make no excuses for his "deviations," faulting himself mightily, instead, "for a lack of feeling for the correct direction" and laying out a seven-point plan for self-improvement. Różycki offered to abdicate his guardianship, "like the most sinful of penitents . . . begging the Lord [i.e., Towiański] and . . . the Lord's viceroy, for succor on this difficult path." All claimed to have been deceived into joining Pilchowski's "unblessed partnership." The Third Section could not have extracted more satisfying admissions of guilt or humiliating declarations of loyalty from its victims.[147]

Not all the brethren, though, proved to be as pliant. Stefan Zan "laid the worst fruit," maintaining that "he had never partnered with" Mickiewicz and would not now. But with the most to lose, it was Pilchowski who also most resisted, not so much as a matter of conscience or even dignity (reflexes, in any case, meaningless under the circumstances), but rather out of a stubbornness reserved for the none-too-bright—or, rather, the desperate. His first impulse was to attack Ksawera; a day later, he offered his hand in marriage, insisting that "he had awakened her life from the dead." Two days after that, in a confrontation with Mickiewicz, he "fell on his knees and admitted that he'd sinned and dragged others into sin with him." But on the following day, he again came to the poet, this time, in the words of Mickiewicz, "in the saddest of shapes," "cold, crass, . . . in total rebellion. . . . Every sign of grace had been erased in him, and what remained was only his old desire of quitting the emigration by any means possible"—and taking the brethren with him. A week later, though, he repeated his wish to marry Ksawera, as "restitution," and then "threatened to take his own life." His efforts to finally "embrace" the brethren through "an act of humility" before the entire Circle proved to be yet another attempt "to master them." By turns contrite and defiant, incapable of any firm resolve, in the brethren's eyes Pilchowski now stood together with the disgraced Brother Gutt (and for much the same reasons) "outside the Circle, beyond the Cause," "tossing about with his shell and his body and carrying a rock inside." Brother Seweryn's "confusion" defied resolution.[148]

But what of the "evil," as Goszczyński put it, "at which the Master directed Pilchowski to shudder with disgust"? What of that "female shell" whose life Brother Pilchowski had "killed" with his "hounding tone" and his "slavishly despotic vibrations"? Deybel quickly grasped that her ambitious lover had been defeated. And despite being deeply implicated in Pilchowski's plot, despite her treatment of Celina and the tumult she had caused in the Mickiewicz household and, by extension, in the entire Circle, she of "the magnetic flow" felt confident that she could count on Mickiewicz's forbearance, and on the Master's as well. She cut her losses with aplomb. Informing Mickiewicz of Pilchowski's proposal of marriage, Deybel insisted that "she did not sense in Brother Seweryn the spark that stirs a Christly life." Although both the Master and his viceroy had decided that there was no longer any need for her to share Towiański's admonitory letter of March with the entire Circle, she nonetheless demonstrated her commitment to the Cause by doing so on her own. She even got Mickiewicz to squeeze out an apology from Celina, whose own spirit, however, still seemed to him "incapable of moving in a straight line." As the liquidation of Pilchowski's partnership was nearing a dénouement, Mickiewicz could report to Towiański not only that Ksawera was "in good shape," but that she "had helped much through her strong and humble resistance to Seweryn." "She will yet," he concluded, "minister to him and other brethren mightily."[149]

And indeed, once it became evident that through his actions Pilchowski had forfeited his special guardianship over Deybel, other brethren came panting in the hope of taking his place. One, "still totally mired in the earth," "fell on his knees" before Mickiewicz "and demanded . . . the thread from [Ksawera's] medal!" Another "took to caring for Sister Ksawera, calling her an angel." And still another, soon enough, was asking for her hand. To Mickiewicz's surprise, the new suitor was Stefan Zan, which at least explained "many of his errant movements." Zan's musical talents notwithstanding, Ksawera turned him down. For the moment she preferred to keep her options open.[150]

"Let us rejoice in the Lord," Mickiewicz reported to Towiański on 24 July, "the evil has been overcome." "I hope," he continued, "that any day now we'll be able to post before you, Lord, a Circle purged and on pure Christian principles reborn." Other than a few "spiritual fasts" and acts of thanksgiving "for the mercy clearly succoring the Cause,"

Brother Adam dealt leniently with the rebels. To be sure, he let them know that he "was not letting them off, that when it came to the most arduous tasks, they would be the first whom [he] would drive." But aside from Pilchowski, who was assigned to perform some unspecified labor by Towiański, the confrontations and confessions appear to have been punishment enough. Henceforth the "password of the day" was to be "*faith and trust*"—and in any case, the Master had already set a new agenda.[151]

15

Throughout the "pandemonium," Mickiewicz had managed to demonstrate yet again his unflinching dedication to the Cause and, in exercising it, extraordinary stamina. Towiański reckoned that he could demand even more. He directed the Circle to renew its work with the emigration (to his delight, the French brethren, all seven or so of them, were flourishing just fine), but also now to make an effort to connect with Jews. They were, after all, a host of spirits at the very heart of his cosmogony. Brother Ram, baptized two years earlier by Sister Deybel and Brother Romuald Januszkiewicz, had already traveled to Jerusalem, Frankfurt, and finally to England in search of converts among his coreligionists. The brethren in Paris, for their part, were called upon to "link and assist [him] in spirit." As usual, though—and just as Towiański knew he would—Mickiewicz insisted on doing more.[152]

On 11 August, the last day of the Three Weeks commemorating the destruction of the Temple, a cohort of Towianists descended on the synagogue at rue Neuve St. Laurent. Having instructed the brethren to "keep [their] heads covered" and "pray without kneeling," Mickiewicz hoped to "commune with the grief of Israel wherever it may find itself on earth lamenting on this day the destruction of Jerusalem," just as Poles lament the taking of Warsaw and the French, the defeat at Waterloo. Not surprisingly, the rabbi presiding at the service became extremely indignant when the poet began "speaking to him of Israel's grief," and this "on behalf of synagogues of the East and the world over." A disappointed Mickiewicz was left opining that the Jews in Paris "want only to have it easy, but to feel pain is what is most difficult for them."[153]

Simultaneously, Brother Adam sent brethren out to proselytize anew among the émigrés, dispatching two to the democrats and two to Czartoryski. Yet despite Mickiewicz's assurances to Towiański that they managed to "move them from their previous stance," both missions returned with predictable results. Although "well-intentioned," supporters of the prince proved to be concerned "only [with] political prospects"; the Democrats, for their part, managed to demonstrate yet again "all the pride of narrow minds and cold hearts." But the same, curiously enough, could not be said of Mickiewicz's own "service" with Fathers Edward Duński and Hipolit Terlecki, Resurrectionists both, who, like their Towianist nemesis, never despaired of prevailing in this contest for spirits. In the course of "a long, free-flowing, and weighty discussion," Duński in particular seemed moved, according to Mickiewicz, "constantly seeking as if to reconcile his bookish theology with the Cause." It would take a while, but by 1847 reconcile the two he did.[154]

There was, nonetheless, something peculiar in Mickiewicz's willingness, after four years of seemingly unbridgeable hostility, to connect with Resurrectionists—or rather, *re*connect, with persons who, after all, before either party had set out on radically different paths of salvation, had been so indebted to each other for spiritual renewal. Indeed, just a few days before his meeting, amid his report documenting how life in the Circle was returning to normal, Mickiewicz wrote to Towiański that his own

> spirit [was] digging a new trough, in a direction opposite to the earlier one, digging tortuously and deviating, but continually heading toward the goal [the Master] had indicated, toward realization.... My impetus is somewhere other than it was before. I feel helpless on the paths of old.

Towiański, it seems, grasped the import of Mickiewicz's words immediately. This was not a self-reproachful avowal of renewed dedication to the Cause. On the contrary, as far as he was concerned his disciple was signaling, not fully consciously, perhaps, but unequivocally, that he was beginning to slip away.[155]

The Master wasted no time in devising a strategy to bring Brother Adam to heel. Within a month of Mickiewicz's pilgrimage to Switzerland, Towiański warned visiting brethren that "whoever has not shuddered with disgust at the pasts of Brother Adam and Brother Seweryn, evil will catch him and subdue him." To make his point clearer, he sent one of them back to Paris with a reproduction of Holbein the Younger's *Crucifixion*. "Some of the brethren explained that the crucifixion... suggest[ed] the Master [was] crucified between two thieves"; others, more percipient, understood it to mean that "in Brother Adam there was a hounding tone, while in Brother Seweryn [Pilchowski] God admitted a despotic tone." Mickiewicz, for his part, interpreted the picture as signifying "the end of a certain period of work in the Circle." That it did, but not in a manner he might have foreseen.[156]

On 1 October 1845, on the slopes of Mt. Etzel, where St. Meinrad founded the monastery of Einsiedeln, Towiański held his second "symposium." His interlocutor this time was Brother Karol Różycki. The Master was not, however, imparting some new revelation. His gibberish concerned the colonel alone, the brother who, as Towiański ostensibly only now realized, "had fulfilled what was necessary for the fullness of God within" him. The session constituted nothing less than an anointing:

> The first Man, Brother, Spirit in the Earth, [links] with the first Man, Brother, Earth in the Spirit, Both Men, Brothers of deed...—*Wieszcz* and Commander both fulfill the path of Service through the Grace given in Brotherly partnership.

Man of inspired deed and man of inspired word, the one of the earth, the other of the spirit, Brother Karol and Brother Adam, over whom hovered the figure of the Man of Destiny—for all of the trinitarian symmetry of the arrangement, Towiański was in effect demoting Mickiewicz. Three weeks later, Sisters Karolina and Anna confirmed what for their purposes was a genuinely inspired decision. On a picture of Jesus in the garden of Gethsemane that they presented to Różycki, the two handmaidens of the Cause inscribed:

> To the brother who . . . , second only to our Master, was the first to fulfill God's will in us women—Received woman into the brotherhood—Called the spirit of woman brother . . . , in his fraternal partnership neither worshipped [woman] idolatrously on account of her shell nor slavishly debased [her].

If there had been any doubts about the reasons for Mickiewicz's fall from grace, they were now dispelled. Somewhere between Celina and Ksawera he had managed to offend the sensibilities of Sister Gutt, whose own marital insecurities had been disrupting relations within the Circle of God's Cause almost from the beginning of its inception.[157]

It was not until 20 November 1845 that Różycki reappeared in Paris, bringing with him an entire packet of letters and directives from Towiański. Mickiewicz's joy at seeing him quickly dissipated upon reading the Master's words, all the more crushing since so callously brutal. Informing the poet that he would now be sharing his "burden" with Brother Karol, Towiański launched into a terrifying critique of Mickiewicz's spiritual state, linked now explicitly with that of Gutt, Pilchowski, and Deybel:

> The tone of sacrifice, the movement of your spirit . . . were brought to a standstill by you, in your purity, and the effects of your hounding tone radiated outward, hampered God's Cause, made your burden heavier, debited your account.

Towiański was henceforth condemning Mickiewicz's spirit not simply to eternal return, but of the most painful and degrading sort. "I saw Israel in the form of a miserable animal," he thundered metempsychotically, "man and animals shuddered before great Israel's life on earth. I saw great Israel fulfilling the will of God in the rocks of the ocean and land." Barely managing to contain himself, the Master concluded with what could be construed as at once curse and, in its own way, consolation:

> You love death, you don't want your life . . . , you regress into your nothingness; sate yourself for ages with your beloved death, with your nothingness in a rock, on the lowest rung of this vale, and sated for the ages with death and nothingness, desire life. . . . I saw great Israel in the shell of a martyr horse, after a tormented life issuing in the moment

> of its death a stirring of the spirit...—at that final verge, earthly laws, earthly considerations, earthly measures, and other such chains binding God's spirits against God's will begin to disappear for great Israel.

But the true nature of Mickiewicz's iniquity was tucked into the middle of Towiański's tirade: "When the banner of spirit's freedom was raised publicly by Brother [*sic*] Anna... the administrators of the spirit stood on the side of earth, and this was written down against them in the book of God."[158]

With the letter to Mickiewicz came epistles to the entire Circle, directing the brethren to "greet as [their] leading brethren two men of Poland, bearing God's Idea for Poland, joined at the apex of God's Thought," while at the same time providing them with what were meant to be devastating characterizations of the nodes of evil within the Circle: "the hounding tone" (Mickiewicz); "the nervous, magnetic tone" (Deybel); "the oriental, despotic tone" (Pilchowski); as well as the ever restless spirit of Louis XIV. Of course the new administrative arrangement constituted yet another "epoch of God's Cause."[159]

But Różycki also brought Mickiewicz another letter from Towiański, one written shortly after having issued his curse, which he now insisted on minimalizing as merely "an administrative note." The Master dared hope that Brother Adam would not hold it against him. Mickiewicz bore even this humiliation with equanimity, ever mindful that pride had always been his greatest sin. He immediately informed the Guardians of the new arrangement and set the Circle an appropriate agenda (essentially identical to the agendas he had been setting for the past four years). To Towiański he responded without resistance, neither defensively nor with resentment nor as a victim—but also as if by rote. He admitted that his "great efforts, both internal and external, had been heading in a direction incompatible with God's thought," and that Towiański's letter had "arrived just in the nick of time, at once like a warning and refreshment." Mickiewicz's letter was terse, its tone dignified yet also somehow resigned and weary. That month, in a rare conversation with Zaleski about Towianism, he observed:

> The inventor of gunpowder thought he could blow up the world; he didn't, but gunpowder nevertheless remained. Something similar can be said about our truth; there's not as much in it as we had hoped, but it persists.[160]

16

1846 began with a series of ostensibly positive developments. Celina, Mickiewicz reported, "had genuinely moved and had already had a moment of life in the Cause. She sighed." Even Brother Pilchowski seemed "freer." (Brother Gutt, alas, persisted "in a sad state.") As far as the Circle was concerned, the new arrangement seemed to suit everyone just fine. If anything, it constituted the kind of deed that among the brethren passed for action, and for the moment, at least, appeared to energize them. At the annual Christmas Eve cum name-day reception at the Hôtel Lambert, the Czartoryski camp's eponymous headquarters on Île Saint-Louis since 1843, both Różycki and Mickiewicz "spoke so eloquently [of the Cause] that those present wept, and even the prince," one of his party noted, "was so moved that... in relating the entire scene his every word betrayed what a powerful impression it had made on him."[161]

As rumors began swirling about "some new revelation," the Brother *Wieszcz* and the Brother Commander redoubled their efforts. Having convinced Towiański to publish his most recent "symposium," they armed the brethren with the new screed and sent them out into the community. Pairs of Towianists could be observed visiting émigrés in their homes and communicating their message "in an exceedingly solemn tone, with a serious and grim demeanor"; leaving the brochure with the "person upon whom they had descended," they would return a few days later to check whether anything had "stirred." Mickiewicz and Różycki, for their part, focused their efforts on the Resurrectionists. Yet despite the "opening" the poet had thought he sensed in his conversation with Fathers Terlecki and Duński, their superiors remained adamant. They insisted that any hope of reconciliation would be contingent upon Mickiewicz's readiness to "condemn completely anything whatsoever in Towiański's *Symposium* and in [his] own lectures that could be construed as being against the teachings of the Roman Catholic Church." In Mickiewicz's eyes, such a response was little more than an expression of "resistance," for which the guilty party "would answer before God."[162]

But beneath this whir of renewed activity, something was amiss. In a diary entry of 30 January, Goszczyński noted with his customary discretion when relating matters concerning trouble within the Circle, "Some of the brethren felt that the main source of our disunity hitherto are the two tones coursing separately among us: the spirit in earth and the earth in spirit." Euphemisms aside, over the previous few months, ever since the installment of the duumvirate, disunity must have evolved into a conflict so serious that Mickiewicz felt compelled to travel to Switzerland again, as did Różycki. Called to take their place this time was "Sister, or, rather, Brother," as Mickiewicz pointedly corrected himself in a letter to Karolina Towiańska, Alix Mollard. A schoolteacher and former Vintrasist, "a woman of great strength," according to Goszczyński, Mollard had made an impression with her own hysterical outbursts at one of Mickiewicz's lectures. More important, though, she was fanatically devoted to Towiański—and to his increasingly dictatorial handmaiden Sister Gutt.[163]

On 4 February, Mickiewicz set off to Zurich to meet his master. The journey took the expected four days. For the poet, however, it spanned a lifetime. Traveling in the company of Eustachy Januszkiewicz, he suddenly opened up—about his family and childhood, his years in Vilnius and Kowno, his experiences in Russia and travels in Italy, his marriage.

Never before had he confided so much to another about his past*—never, that is, except to Towiański. His reflections, it seems, poured out spontaneously, mixing the sweet with the bitter, triumphs together with regrets—life as a story to be told, now, in retrospect, rather than constantly, neurotically relived. Whether he realized it at the moment, Mickiewicz was free. All that remained was to demonstrate his liberation to the man who had done so much to effect it, and to come to terms with the consequences.

What was to be Brother Adam's final, traumatic "session" with his Lord and Master lasted two months, from 8 February until 7 April. It was not, however, strictly *à deux*. Brothers Januszkiewicz and Różycki hovered in the wings throughout, just in case Towiański might need them to exert pressure on the wayward Brother *Wieszcz*. More critically, so too was Sister Anna, the woman who, Mickiewicz felt, "had destroyed and spoiled the work of the Circle" and who was now intent on bringing him to heel for what she perceived as slights against her spiritual self.[164]

It appears that the first confrontation in Zurich was, in fact, between Brother Adam and both sisters Max—or, as they preferred to be addressed, "brethren." The results were predictable. In a note to the two, Towiański assessed Mickiewicz's tone with them as "unchristian." "On account of their female shells, they became not brethren but, as pagan law would have it, . . . tools of the gutter." This said, he commenced working on his wavering disciple directly. He again threatened the poet with eternal return, condemning him to "*a bestial shell*," to "difficult lives," then finally and most devastatingly, to "*rocks* . . . , where movement, life, groaning, desire, love must come into being." For the benefit of the other brethren, he characterized Brother Adam as one of "the four kings of false tones [together with Pilchowski, Ferdynand Gutt, and Deybel], inimical to the tone of Christ," worse even than Tsar Nicholas. "I'd gladly give my left hand to be burnt," Towiański confided to Januszkiewicz, "would that only *the furies* pursue Adam now." He had Różycki renounce him. But just as the Master was hoping that the pressure might break Mickiewicz, events in the world unexpectedly intruded onto his spiritual fantasy, effectively precipitating what both he and the poet by now recognized to be inevitable.[165]

On 18 February 1846, an uprising erupted in the free Republic of Cracow, the only piece of Poland not occupied by any of the three partitioning powers, albeit under their joint protection since the Congress of Vienna. Planned for years by the Polish Democratic Society, the uprising was to have encompassed all of Poland but fizzled everywhere except in the republic. Having succeeded in gaining control of the city, the insurgents set about mobilizing all segments of Polish society in the surrounding Galician countryside against the Austrians. Peasants were promised the abolition of serfdom and enfranchisement; workers, national workshops with higher pay and relief from taxes. But what in some regions

*Januszkiewicz did his best to note down their conversations, which he then published in 1859. Cf. *Rozmowy*, 253–58.

began to resemble a genuine revolution, in others metastasized into a jacquerie. Thanks in part to Austrian agitation, the uprising emboldened Polish peasants to turn on their Polish masters. Peasant mobs pillaged and burned manors, slew their inhabitants, and handed over gentry insurgents to the Austrian authorities. By 4 March, Austrian and Russian forces had recovered enough to quash both the gentry uprising and the rebellious peasants.

News of the uprising reached Paris in the first days of March, stirring émigrés of all political factions to something approaching unity and their French hosts to renewed expressions of support for the Polish cause. Despite its defeat, the uprising seemed to vindicate, at least for the moment, the wisdom of the émigré left. The specter of Polish peasants sawing their fractious Polish masters in half would, however, soon enough come to haunt it irreparably. But if for Mickiewicz all this constituted "a repetition of the same act," wherein "peasants bear oppression for a long while, suffer, and finally massacre their masters," in Towiański's view this only proved that the whole affair was an ill-timed, misbegotten expression "of the earth," "not the fruit of the Father's love, but the fruit of man's iniquity." As far as he was concerned, any "thought of an earthly fatherland not according to God's will [was] a crime." Indeed, he instructed the brethren gathered in his Zurich hideaway, "the highest pinnacle [of the Cause's] steadfastness would be to make a heartfelt vow not to leave the mountains of Switzerland for the remainder of their lives and not ache for Poland if it happened to emerge not according to God's thought." "And it is precisely hell," he continued, "that works to divert the feeling of higher administrators toward something else, to deflect them from this goal." The insinuation was clear enough. It was Mickiewicz, after all, who "in his dreams or desires" (in *Forefathers' Eve*, part 3, to be exact) had once "privileged the well-being of millions over the triumph of God," and, it seems, upon hearing of the uprising, had insisted on doing so again—in the face of the Master's explicit condemnation of this "evil."[166]

To Mickiewicz, Towiański's reaction to the news from Galicia finally exposed the misunderstanding that had fueled his faith in the Master from the very beginning. In his thirst for transforming the world for the sake of Poland, he now grasped that all along he had been mistaking the m(e)an(s) for the ends.

In a last desperate attempt to hold on to his disciple, Towiański struck at him ruthlessly, where he knew he was weakest. The poet's mother, it seems, had appeared to Sister Karolina in a dream, ostensibly condemning her son for his "torpor." "The Lord's summons is nigh," she supposedly warned him, "save yourself! You've lost much, only three days remain." In order to avoid any misunderstanding, Sister Karolina proffered her own (or, what is more likely, her husband's) interpretation of the visitation. "I felt that the Lord's summons," she observed in relating the dream to Mickiewicz, "meant the death of Br[other] Adam."[167]

Mickiewicz was, by all accounts, genuinely terrified. He sincerely believed this to be "the voice of God from the land of the spirit." Certain that "he would die, Adam prepared for death," wrote out a will, and apparently spent a horrific "final" night. But when on the third day he found himself still among the quick, his indignation grew, in proportion, perhaps, to the terror to which he had just been so cravenly subjected. On 27 March, no longer contained by either fear or guilt, he told "the Master the entire truth." To Towiański's accusations that it was his fault "that the Circle was in bad shape, since it was he who was the hounding spirit," Mickiewicz apparently

> expressed his readiness to provide proof of his innocence. Towiański responded that [the poet] had an evil spirit within him. Mickiewicz, in turn, [accused] the Master of listening to old women—"I have my own plans." . . . Upon hearing this, Towiański fell prostrate with his arms outstretched and in a great sweat began reciting a prayer. Mickiewicz too fell to the ground.

The following morning, Towiański informed his disciple that their "past had come to a close." Brother Adam had "repulsed God's will"; five years of "efforts . . . to arouse Christly movement [in him] . . . had proven fruitless." But then just as he had done numerous times before in similar circumstances—and still hoping for the same effect—Towiański appeared to relent. He dispatched Brother Różycki with a letter to Mickiewicz, delivered and accepted kneeling, in which he averred "eternal union" with Brother Adam and insisted that "he continue holding his office." This time, Mickiewicz would not be taken in. "I accept the Lord's missives as I always have, on my knees," he replied, "but I cannot accept the duties of leader unless the Master consents to my executing them according to my own feelings."[168]

The confrontation had become a battle of wills, one in which Towiański still believed his would triumph. After all, Mickiewicz made it clear that he remained devoted to the Cause as such; it was only its ostensible distortion by the Master's servants, himself included, that repulsed him. Towiański ventured a final ploy. Mindful of the poet's respect for Czartoryski, he asked Mickiewicz to undertake another mission to the prince. In the same breath, however, in the appeal he was charging the poet to convey, Towiański called Czartoryski a traitor, in effect forcing Mickiewicz to choose between himself and the prince. After "undergoing a frightful struggle," the poet decided that "he could no longer travel down this road." On 7 April, he informed his "Master and Lord" that he was "compelled to leave immediately." The transference was complete.[169]

CHAPTER TEN

SCISSION (1846–1848)

Mickiewicz arrived in Paris on 10 April 1846. Four days later—it happened to be the Tuesday after Easter, the fifth since the foundation of the Circle of God's Cause—Sister Alix Mollard called a meeting of the brethren, during which Brother Adam was to make some sort of restitution. For whatever reason, Sister Alix was not satisfied. She accused the poet of having "introduced Satan into the Circle." Anyone, she threatened, unwilling to "recognize the Sisters surrounding the Master as Holy" would be "crushed." Mickiewicz responded by announcing that he was breaking with the Circle.[1]

"Just like a plant, gathering new strength as it emerges," Mickiewicz had begun the process of shedding the "old bark."[2]

I

Unlike Słowacki or Kamieński, Mickiewicz was not leaving the Circle an isolated dissident, nor, for that matter, did the rupture in any way constitute a rejection of Towiański's teachings or of the Cause as such. His gesture had the unequivocal support of some twenty brethren—the brothers Chodźko, Aleksander and Michał, Eustachy Januszkiewicz (but not Romuald), Wrotnowski, Zan, among others, and, for the Oedipal touch, Różycki's own son—who too had had their fill of "matriarchy," of the "hounding," "spying and denunciations" with which Sister Gutt and her minions had been "oppressing" the Circle since at least the pandemonium of 1844. Like Mickiewicz, they felt that what had once been a comity marked by "rapture, strength, love, and freedom" had been perverted into "some sort of un-Christian environment"; they too saw themselves "miserably idling away to everyone's indignation." And as much as they continued to insist, by any account sincerely, on their abiding faith in Towiański's teachings, by walking out together with Mickiewicz they also demonstrated that their insistence was, in their eyes, a function of loyalty to the Master's only true disciple. It was, after all, Brother Adam who had "fortified" their faith in Towiański's mission, "when, on the contrary, all other administrators had . . . led [them] into temptation in his name."[3]

As the discontented brethren poured out their grievances on paper, addressed directly—and, for greater effect, sent as a single packet—to the Master, Mickiewicz himself chose silence. The words of those who had suffered most at the hands of the Administration were salient enough to at once explain and justify his decision to break with the Circle; in any case, they served only to corroborate what he had told the Master in person during their last encounter. His gesture that April evening could speak for itself. But if his decision was designed to elicit at the very least a moment of self-reflection on the part of those as culpable as he in distorting the work of the Circle, it fell on ears deaf with the indignation of blind belief. Over the next several months "a terrible storm of evil" convulsed the Circle, with no one certain how it would end.[4]

Unaccountably, Brother Commander Różycki remained in Switzerland, either unwilling or unable to intervene. It was thus left to Sister Mollard and Brother Goszczyński to deal with the crisis. Immediately, however, their predicament was complicated by Brother Pilchowski's decision to finally "hand himself over to the Russian government . . . 'in the spirit of God's Cause, so as to serve the Polish nation.' " Animosities were briefly put on hold as Mickiewicz, still the public face of Towianism in Paris, published a condemnation of the embarrassing apostasy, which had, in any case, been long in the making (and to which he himself had contributed). This notwithstanding, it soon enough became clear to everyone that, despite half-hearted efforts at reconciliation on the part of both factions (a third emerged as well), the rift between those loyal to Mickiewicz and those who out of personal animosity or fear or genuine conviction chose the security of the familiar would not be healed.[5]

As for Towiański, isolated in his Swiss hideaway, it took some time for him to grasp the extent to which "evil had afflicted [his] community," and even then he remained in denial. It was only after receiving the packet of letters from the dissenters in late May, registering their dissatisfaction with the state of the Circle and at the same time defending Mickiewicz, that the Master took steps to salvage the integrity of his mission in Paris. But his emissary, Brother Gutt, back in the Towiański's graces if only for the purpose, failed to patch matters up. Mickiewicz himself remained stubbornly silent. After some thought, he declined to answer Towiański's summons to return to Switzerland and "assume leadership in its fullness." Yet just as it seemed that Towiański might have to resign himself to the defection of his prized disciple, another opportunity presented itself, from an unexpected quarter. For whatever reason—her own doubts, perhaps, regarding Towiański; perhaps genuine concern about the spiritual consequences of her husband's decision or, on the contrary, hopes for the Master's blessing in this regard; or, perhaps, a new flare-up with Deybel—Celina resolved to confront Towiański on her own. Mickiewicz, it seems, construed her decision to be a miracle.[6]

Two days before her departure in mid-September, the poet prepared a note for his wife instructing her how she should comport herself in the presence of the Master. "Stand before [him]," he wrote, "in complete freedom, forgetting that you had or have obligations toward me."

> Be sincere with the Master to the very end. . . . Consider your state at the moment a new miracle, a miracle the full magnitude of which only I alone see and feel, just like the miracle of your cure.

Mickiewicz asked her to leave her wedding band behind as a sign of her ostensible liberation, but also with the expectation that she would return revitalized from her encounter with the Master and thus "a fiancée worthy of [her husband]."[7]

Having assured her family that she would not be away for long, Celina ended up staying in Switzerland for nearly a month, shuttling, for the most part, between Einsiedeln and Towiański's residence in Richterswil. In the course of that month, the Master, his spouse, Sister Gutt, as well as the small circle of brethren-in-residence, subjected this "poor, kithless woman" (as Celina described herself) to psychological pressure that would soften even the most stable of psyches. Their aim, of course, was not so much to reinstill in her a faith that was never particularly stalwart to begin with, but, rather, sufficient self-confidence to confront her rebellious husband. In hour upon seemingly endless hour of prayer and instruction in darkened rooms amid various talismans of the Cause, by turns "revealing" to her all of her and her husband's "shortcomings" and assuring her of his abiding love, threatening the two with regressively baser reincarnations and impressing on her that "God's plan was vested in the one saving the other," Towiański, together with his helpmates, at once shamed and frightened and loved Celina into submission. Her "soul positively wax[ed] listening to [him]." He promised, after all, that if she succeeded in convincing her husband to finally "offer [himself] up to the labors and office determined for him by God and the Master" and "stand before [him] naked, empty, and foolish," "all difficulties in [their] marriage would subside, vanish, and blessings would enter [their] home."[8]

To Mickiewicz, little of what his wife communicated to him in a series of prolix (if in places none too literate) letters was new. The revelations, the diagnoses, the threats, the promises—he himself had heard them all before, just as he himself had nearly yielded a few months earlier to the suasive atmosphere the Master was so adept at conjuring. Celina's, however, was a different, more fragile constitution, a "demented woman," as she herself admitted, and at the same time profoundly insecure about a marriage in which, on Towiański's prompting, she pictured herself as that "single aching finger" of a hand which "it deprives of strength and power." With each letter from Switzerland, it was becoming increasingly evident to Mickiewicz that the Master, but above all his spiritually enlightened sisters, had managed to successfully exploit Celina's vulnerabilities as wife, woman, and cripple.[9]

As days turned into weeks, and as Celina was becoming "so wrapped up in [her] Affair that [she] had forgotten about [him] and the children" (and this just as eighteen-month-old Jan happened to require the care of doctors), Mickiewicz became concerned. Concern turned into alarm when some three weeks into her visit Celina informed him that after an all-night vigil devoted to her salvation she decided to remain in order to "tie the knot of brotherhood" with the Master's circle so that she could have "a point of resistance" in Paris against the "adversities in Spirit and body" that resided there. On top of this she now needed money. Mickiewicz's answer was as unambiguously curt as it was manipulative. Aside from news about Jan (teething painfully, but the doctor "says to be patient") and Helena ("she in particular pines for you"), he informed Celina that he was himself "somewhat weak" (hemorrhoids). As for money:

> I'm sending you seventy fr. I don't have more. What you'd left didn't last until the end of the month. I pawned the watch case. We don't have anything more to pawn.... After paying for bread, milk, beer, etc., I have enough left until the end of the week, after which... I have no idea where to turn.... Extending your stay would leave me in new trouble.[10]

If this rather obvious plea for sympathy and attention was meant to shake Celina out of her enchantment, her immediate response was not encouraging. How could she think of money for milk, bread, and beer when "at the moment [she] had to untangle matters regarding [her] salvation"? How could she tear herself away from a man who enveloped her with such "fatherly kindness and affection" and where "everyone served and hugged [her]"; where time, "strange to say, passed quickly and pleasantly"? And she may have stayed longer had she not learned from one of the brethren in Paris that when he went to call on her husband Deybel had "opened the door and immediately sent him away, saying that [Mickiewicz] was busy." The Master himself shared her apprehension in this regard, reminding her "in no uncertain terms," as she stressed to her husband, that it was her "responsibility to guard [their] home from the evil that had possessed [Ksawera]." "I would ask you," she pleaded with Mickiewicz shortly before departing from Richterswil, "not to allow [Ksawera] to work around or spend time with the children," for which there were "important reasons... not all of this earth."[11]

Yet for all of his ostensible solicitude in this respect, Towiański was not finished with his hostage. He fully approved of Celina's sudden "need" (Deybel, sick Jan, pining Helena notwithstanding) to pay a visit to Brother Różycki on her way back to Paris. The "few hours" she assured Mickiewicz she would be spending in Mulhouse turned into a few days. There too there were prayers and sermons and "services under the white cross planted on French land," all with the aim of strengthening Celina's resolve on the mission with which she had been entrusted. "O God!" prayed Sister Karolina ominously, "succor our first administrator's companion in life, obedient to her calling, but should she be recalcitrant, do with her what Your wisdom and justice betokens."[12]

Celina returned to Paris on 17 October, to rumors (untrue, as it turned out) that Mickiewicz had fought a duel with Pilchowski. She immediately called a meeting of the Circle to share her impressions of her visit and, presumably, inform them of her mission to reconcile her husband with the Master. But although her initial steps in this regard appeared to encourage the circle in Switzerland, by November Sister Gutt and her allies found themselves "waiting impatiently... for good news" about her progress—for that matter, any news at all. Amid the everyday routines of family life, memories of the spiritual bliss she had experienced in Towiański's presence began to fade, and with them the exigency of the resolutions she had made. Indeed, two years later she would recall the "insincerity and cowardice" with which she behaved during her visit in Mulhouse. What mattered now was that she was reunited with her "companion for life," whose spirit she had vowed to serve "in all extremities and dangers... for all his ages." The irony of these words—Towiański's own, as it happened—was not lost on Mickiewicz. He could barely contain himself upon Celina's return, confiding to Bohdan Zaleski that "only now did he have a wife, only now had she begun living an inner life."[13]

2

Efforts to reconcile Towiański with his disciple would continue until the poet's death. Nonetheless, Celina's inconclusive mission that fall appears to have sealed the transformation that had taken place in Mickiewicz's relationship with the Master, and in Mickiewicz himself. The poet, it was noticed, was now once again "getting along well and politely with people," in particular with those whom in his sectarian unforbearance he had shunned for years. All who took it upon themselves to approach him at the time could not help wondering how "greatly changed" he was. "The rift between [Mickiewicz and Towiański] is great," Father Edward Duński reported to his Resurrectionist brethren in Rome, "he condemns his own course [at the Collège], claiming that it was written solely under the influence of [Ferdynand] Gutt." On top of this, the poet expressed unusual enthusiasm for Pius IX, an ostensibly liberal Italian whose election to the papacy that summer raised expectations of a much-desired reorientation in the Vatican's politics. To his erstwhile Catholic adversaries, Mickiewicz's behavior seemed to token "a genuine return to the Church."[14]

The émigré community was soon atickle with the prospect of finally "winning [the poet] back." A few even opened their pocketbooks as an incentive. After all, opined

Zygmunt Krasiński about the man who at once fascinated and repelled and frustrated him over the years, it was "indigence that prevented [Mickiewicz] from seeing things clearly"—and by all accounts he was indeed barely surviving. Now that it appeared he had "changed, grown gentler, that that Israelite pride, that fanatical obduracy had disappeared," Krasiński deemed it appropriate to make Mickiewicz a gift of 1,500 francs. At the same time, the ever solicitous Januszkiewicz, himself now emancipated from the clutches of the Master, succeeded in convincing Cezary Plater to subsidize an advance of 4,000 francs for the completion of that history of Poland which Mickiewicz had begun writing several years earlier (and which he again would never complete). For his part, Father Duński felt content to give catechism lessons to the poet's oldest daughter.[15]

Not everyone, however, was convinced. "Until there is genuine abasement [on Mickiewicz's part]," Dun´ski's Resurrectionist colleague Father Hube insisted to the congregation in Rome, "demonstrated by a public recantation of publicly disseminated errors, I won't believe that God's grace is the author of this transformation." There were good reasons for his wariness. For all of his sudden accessibility, and the break with Towian´ski notwithstanding, Mickiewicz, as Zaleski put it, remained "petrified in his sectarianism."[16]

On 30 November 1846, Mickiewicz and his group of followers met on rue Saint Charles to formally established a circle of their own; the day they chose was the Master's name-day. The rift with Towiański may have been beyond repair; his revelation, however, together with his capacity to inspire and serve as a paragon, remained as vital, as binding, and as "omnipotent" as ever, but with one fundamental—or, as it were, fundamentalist—caveat: the dissidents vowed to "respect only that spirit and that tone [which] was revealed to [them] . . . by the Master during the gatherings in Nanterre"; they would have no other "masters" or "Master" before them. Firm in their belief "that the salvation of [their] souls and the fatherland rest[ed] with the Master's spirit and tone," they declared that they would "preserve that tone and struggle to plant and maintain it."[17]

Flush with their new-found freedom and the vistas it might open before them, the dissidents hastened to jettison what they perceived as the forms of their oppression. Gone now were the septets and tightly scripted convocations, with their services, confessions, labors, and rituals, along with the prostrations and sighing that the old administration had demanded accompany them. Yet old habits died hard (and weren't these forms in fact Mickiewicz's own innovations?). Compulsive as ever when it came to matters of organization, Mickiewicz immediately impressed on his band of emancipated brethren the need for "a certain order." "Devote two days a week," he instructed them,

> Monday and Tuesday, for example, to friendly repasts. Let each of the brethren take turns presiding, in alphabetical order. The leader will . . . either inaugurate a discussion or read some excerpt from the Master's writings or something of his own. The presiding brother has the right to remain silent. . . . In case of disagreement, he

> decides.... Welcome outsiders only on one of those two days. The following two days can be used for normal conversation.... Devote one day, e.g., Saturday, to complete silence; no discussions.
>
> Should a brother feel that he can do something important for the Cause,... let him say so. I shall see to it!

The new regime was certainly less ritualized, more democratic even, and, in view of the trauma they had all experienced, particularly sensitive to an individual's autonomy. But it remained a regime nonetheless, with Mickiewicz as its charismatic point of light. It was for his sake that the brethren had seceded, eager to believe his promise that this would be "the final year of [their] privations."[18]

Yet if Towiański continued to serve as the measure of all things for the dissidents, "the perfect man," whose example they were all called on to realize, it was no longer his voice they heard being channeled in Mickiewicz's homilies to them. Freed from his obligations as the unquestioning agent of the Master's will, the poet set about reforming what was now *his* circle in *his* own image, and this with an urgency and prophetic force that he had not evinced since his most inspired days at the Collège.

"A holy life," he taught his brethren, "was no longer sufficient for the road, for the deed, to which the Master in his love and might had summoned them." What the present moment demanded was, instead, greater engagement with the world, and with Poland above all, which "thread" Towiański had from the very start of his mission deemphasized and which Mickiewicz now felt personally "called... to carry." He bade his "choir" to abandon "the monastery" and contemplate, rather, their "religious relationship to the nation," the "need for a new priesthood," and "how things should be in a future Poland." This would mean reassessing (to everyone's relief, no doubt) their hitherto "Panslavic" stance toward Russia in order "to demonstrate... that the tone in Poland today is loftier and purer." No less crucially, however, this would mean also reassessing their stance toward the Polish peasant, whose "right to the land on which he sits" was given at once by God and, ostensibly, by Polish tradition. "The times," after all, "were full of long awaited political changes"—one needed only to look at the events in Galicia, the recent revolutions in Switzerland, the election of the new pope, the discontent with the current order in France, Italy, and Germany—and times like these demanded from each one of them as individuals new ideas and new directions that would "transform the shape of the world." In this regard, there could be "absolutely no covenant... with the old order of things," be it political, social, or, especially, ecclesiastic. They were being summoned, as disciples of Towiański but, no less fatefully, also as Poles, to "destroy wherever possible all of the cogs [of the old order]," for the sake of "Poland, France, and through them, the entire world, all of mankind," "not with theory," however, and "not with blood, but as Christians." In this way only could they ever hope to "attain [their] Master and [their] Poland." As he would explain a few months later, as Europe was erupting in revolution:

> For a long time the Circle was concerned with solely spiritual work and solely spiritual efforts. Many [brethren], including some in the Master's circle, had confined themselves to this sphere of action, encouraging exertions of the spirit, maintaining tone among the brethren in personal relations, and at the same time neglecting all work aimed at the public, at the masses, and any application of the [Cause's] principles to political deed. This part of our task resides primarily in us, and by executing it with the help of God and by demonstrating purity of deed, as well as through the measure of our spirit, we'll arrive whither our Master summons and awaits us.[19]

The one issue that surfaced with peculiar insistence in Mickiewicz's allocutions that winter, as compelling and at the same time as inextricably intertwined with "the need for a new priesthood" and the question of "the shape of a future Poland," was what he identified as the issue of family, "the relationship of man and wife, of parents and children," in other words, of woman. The present age, he proclaimed to the (handful of) sisters gathered before him, "was the age of the liberation of women":

> Women are summoned to equality; spirits do not have gender, are equal to each other, and in accordance to differences in organization are called to appropriate deeds. You have been slaves until now; you were given an inferior role, one that was most advantageous for men. . . . One must recognize, then, that women are called to brotherhood with men in the Cause, to an important role. . . . Many of our women, after all [and here he recalled Emilia Plater, the woman warrior who fought and died in the 1830 uprising and whom he had immortalized in a poem, as well as his friend Klaudyna Potocka, the benefactress of Polish refugees in Dresden], are, by dint as much of reason as of power of the spirit, more capable of presiding at meetings, in a government, than men!

And no single institution was more to blame for preventing woman from achieving her spiritual potential than the Church, in exactly the same way as it suppressed the gifts of charisma and prophecy. Its bankruptcy in this regard belied its claim to bind here on earth. As if to prove his point, Mickiewicz took it upon himself that February to join in holy matrimony two of his disciples, "according to the laws of Compassion, . . . in the spirit of the new law . . . ," calling the couple "to mutual work on advancing from marital bondage to loving, fraternal equality." He nonetheless insisted on "blessing this act through the service of our Lord Jesus Christ and the devotion and work of his servant, . . . the Master." It would seem that Father Hube's skepticism about Mickiewicz's ostensible return to the Catholic fold was warranted.[20]

Mickiewicz had addressed these issues before, most notably in his final lectures at the Collège; the woman's question was, after all, a central concern for Towiański. And their spiritualist peculiarities notwithstanding, the poet's opinions on the matter were in fact part of a progressive, fiercely anticlerical discourse that since at least the beginning of the decade strove to situate the predicament of modern woman within the broader struggle for sociopolitical emancipation, a discourse as varied as the socialist, communist, Christian, and utopian prescriptions that informed it. In this sense, and for all of their fundamental philosophical differences, his ideas resonated not only with those of George Sand, but also of Marie d'Agoult, who expressed her own views on women in an essay "on liberty" that happened to appear that same winter.* Even before reading it, Mickiewicz graciously assured his friend that being "the work of someone as real and sincere as [she], it could only be in her image."[21]

But then too, strong women, capable of acting independently of—and, indeed, as—men, had always intrigued Mickiewicz, and not only in his poetic imagination. To be sure, his renewed focus on the women's question may have been prompted, in part, by feelings of guilt about his own "unchristian" behavior toward "brethren" in "female shells," above all toward the Master's wife, whom the poet genuinely respected and who, together with Sister Anna, had taught him a thing or two about the spiritual potential of the "new" woman. Yet its urgency that winter was no less a consequence of Mickiewicz's encounter with yet another remarkable woman, a woman as independent and as intellectually, politically, and spiritually evolved as Sand and d'Agoult—of altogether different stock than Celina. Then again, weren't nearly *all* of the other women who had attracted him over the years? Maria, the three Karolinas, Volkonskaia, Anastaziia Khliustin, Konstancja Łubieńska, Potocka, Ksawera?

3

Sometime in mid-February, Mickiewicz received a packet from a Miss Margaret Fuller, the European correspondent for the *New York Tribune*, containing an inscribed volume of Emerson's poetry as well as a letter "asking him to come and see [her]." Her name was no doubt familiar to the poet, if only as the editor of and contributor to the April 1841 issue of *The Dial*, in which he had found Emerson's "Man the Reformer"; perhaps Sand or Chopin, whom she visited at this time, may have recommended her. Although it is unlikely that he was aware of her recently published collection of essays, *Papers on Literature and Art*, like Sand he probably knew the earlier *Woman in the Nineteenth Century*, Fuller's ground-breaking 1844 manifesto of women's rights, which included her own

*Daniel Stern [Comtesse d'Agoult], *Essai sur liberté considérée comme principe et fin de l'activité humaine* (Paris, 1847).

Fig. 25 Margaret Fuller. Engraving after a painting by Alonzo Chappel. Published in Evert A. Duyckinck, *Portrait Gallery of Eminent Men and Women of Europe and America*, vol. 2 (New York, 1872).

apotheosis of Emilia Plater. In her letter of introduction, Fuller praised Mickiewicz's lectures, which, to her regret, she could appreciate only in their published form. What had drawn her attention in them were the Polish professor's observations on Emerson, her Transcendentalist mentor and colleague, with whom she shared a fascination with Christian mystics and Continental romantics as well as a dedication to the struggle for human rights and social justice.[22]

Thirty-seven years old at the time, unmarried, "a blonde but with dark eyes and... a skinny body consumed by spiritual labor and books," this daughter of New England Unitarians was a home-schooled polymath who knew "Greek, Latin, and practically all of the European languages." By the time she traveled to Europe in the summer of 1846, Fuller was a recognized educator, critic, social activist, and writer, the female face of American romanticism. But she was also something of a mystic, capable of "intuiting things," as Aleksander Chodźko noted in his diary,

> and had had visions; she believes that in a future life she'll be a man and that the present age is the age of women's liberation. Her notions about marriage and many of her ideas about life and the destiny of man are notions and ideas completely consonant with those of the Cause.... She feels that either the woman or the man sent for the purpose of bringing about the new age is already here on earth, and the purpose of her visit to Europe was to find this messenger of God.

When she finally met Mickiewicz, on 15 February, "in the company of many other women," it was as if a page of their beloved Swedenborg had come to life. The poet marveled that somehow, on her own, she had come to "a complete knowledge of the Cause"—surely evidence, as Fuller would have put it, of "two halves of one thought." "He made such an impression on her," Aleksander Chodźko noted at the time, "that she sat down on a sofa in a faint."[23]

As she herself reported to Emerson a month later, Fuller had found "the man [she] had long wished to see, with the intellect and passions in due proportion for a full and healthy human being, with a soul constantly inspiring," someone with whom for the first time in her travels (and perhaps ever) she "felt any deep-founded mental connection." As for Mickiewicz, their first encounter was intimate enough, it seems, to inspire him to outline for the American feminist the paths of her spirit:

> Her *foothold* is in the old world, her *sphere of action* is in the new world; her *peace* is in the world of the future.
>
> She is called to feel, to speak, to act in these three worlds....
>
> Your spirit is bound to the history of Poland, the history of France, and is beginning to bind with the history of America.

> You belong to the second generation of spirits.
>
> Your mission is to work toward the liberation of the Polish, French, and American woman.

Intimate enough, in fact, that Mickiewicz dared suggest that "the first step in [her] liberation and the liberation of [her] gender (of a certain class) is to know whether it is permitted that [she] remain a virgin," a notion that Fuller had been wrestling with for years. "My Margueritte, give your spirit, and to those who are ready to receive it, give with it everything." Two weeks after their first encounter, Mickiewicz enjoined his circle of brethren "to beseech God . . . that he give [them] . . . a priestess."[24]

The two managed to see each other often and intensely during the ten days that remained before Fuller had to leave Paris for Italy. But even that did not suffice. She hoped, it seems, that Mickiewicz might detain her. The poet, however, insisted that she go, for the sake of her "happiness and . . . progress"; and in any case, there was no point to staying "unless all of [him] could be with [her]."[25]

She sent him letters from Italy, a number of them, it would appear, although none are extant. In his responses Mickiewicz strove to play the role of an older, spiritually wiser, experienced advisor, urging the younger Fuller to "live as much as possible," to "enjoy what surrounds" her, to "breathe life in through [her] pores." Yet amid the words of counsel, another voice could be seen emerging, no less older and wiser, but now also unexpectedly frank, one that spoke wistfully of old loves (in her travels Fuller had happened to meet Karolina Sobańska), personal disappointments, and regrets. "Life," he admitted to her,

> as long as it lasts, has something intangible and does not permit itself to be enclosed in a dead letter. Especially a life like mine, which has left no trace on the face of the earth, for I have won no battles, I have neither built nor destroyed a city. . . . We lived only in the soul and we have exerted influence only upon souls. Who can know how far this influence extends.

He addressed her as "Chère Amie," as if responding to Fuller's craving for a "purely intellectual and spiritual" friendship, "unprofaned by any mixture of lower instincts," but also sensing that something else lay beneath the sublimated surface.[26]

That spring, Fuller confided to friends:

> You ask me if I love M. I answer he affected me like music or the richest landscape, my heart beat with joy that he at once felt beauty in me also. When I was with him I was happy; and thus far the attraction is so strong that all the way from Paris I felt as if I had left my life behind, and if I followed my inclination I should return at this moment. . . .

But then she added, "Still I do not know but I might love still better tomorrow." She would soon enough, but in a way Mickiewicz may not have been expecting.[27]

Fuller, however, was not the only woman to inspire the poet's dreams of a Towianist "priestess." For ten years, ever since their overwrought parting in 1833, Mickiewicz had had no contact with Konstancja Łubieńska (although she continued to make every effort to subsidize her former lover, either secretly or indirectly). Now, thanks in part to her son, an early (but, in Mickiewicz's assessment, unworthy) convert to Towianism, Łubieńska too had developed a fascination with a spiritual doctrine that spoke to her own notions of a liberated Polish woman—and all the more precious since it was espoused by the man she still cherished deeply. It was probably her openness to the Master's teachings, "the spark of a new life," as Mickiewicz put it, that helped her ease her way back into her beloved's attentions. He did not begrudge them, just as he never begrudged his new-found truths to any potential convert to the Cause. He was convinced, he wrote her, that her "soul must seek a different kind of freedom and joy."[28]

The two had met for the first time again in the fall of 1843, when Łubieńska traveled briefly to Paris, and then once more in 1844, when she settled her daughter, Mickiewicz's godchild, in a Parisian school. Her visits to the city now became more frequent, as did their correspondence—and her gifts of money (to the tune of 3,000 francs on one occasion), which Mickiewicz was finally persuaded to accept. But it was only after her other son's arrest in 1846 in connection with a failed uprising in Poznań that year, followed shortly by the death of her husband, that their renewed relationship stabilized into a spiritual, respectful friendship, transformed by time, circumstances, and the teachings of the Master. (This did not, however, prevent the Prussian police from recording rumors that she had borne the poet's child.)

In her double grief, and constantly under the watchful eye of the Prussian police as well as the disapproving gaze of Poznań society, Łubieńska turned to Mickiewicz for counsel and solace, ample substitutes, it seems, for his affections. For his part, it was another opportunity to impart his truths and thus, perhaps, to save yet another soul from a life they both had shared. "You ought to often feel a need," he chided his "beloved Konstancja" when she turned to him for advice in connection with her son's arrest, "to write to me":

> I know you, that you are inwardly superior to what surrounds you. . . . You have the right to *live*. This one thing I demand of you. . . . Seek everything that makes you happy, that uplifts you, that puts you in a state in which I have often seen you and felt you beside me. Because that is life.
>
> Don't let any person lord over you. Be free. Assess all rights, all means that you have at your disposal, and defend everything, and don't let anyone tear anything away from you. Don't let anyone tear your peace of spirit away.

Mickiewicz missed her between her visits to Paris, but "in a human way," confident that their friendship would become "purer and purer and increasingly salutary for the both of [them]."[29]

There was, however, yet another "exceptional woman" who happened to draw Mickiewicz's attention that winter and spring. Beautiful, multitalented, with a grace and wit that captivated throngs of admirers wherever she lived, Countess Delfina Potocka was as notorious for her romances (with Count Flahaut de la Billarderie, Duke Ferdinand-Philippe d'Orléans, and King Jérôme Bonaparte, among others) as she was worshipped for her powers to inspire the likes of Chopin, Słowacki, and above all Krasiński, whose lover she had been for almost a decade. But it was neither her reputation as "a Don Juan in skirts" nor as a romantic muse that attracted the poet to this "higher spirit." Rather, it was her capacity to at once suffer and transcend her circumstances as a woman. Forced into marriage at the age of fifteen to a despicable magnate, she embodied for Mickiewicz the plight of her gender in a patriarchal system, which to its shame the church sanctioned. He urged her to find the courage to travel to Rome in order to "throw [herself] at the feet of the Holy Father and implore him that no woman after [her] should experience [her] fate." At one point he even went so far as to delegate Celina on a mission to the countess, hoping, perhaps, to win her for the Cause. In the end, to Mickiewicz's great disappointment, Potocka proved unable to transcend her circumstances.[30]

4

A few weeks into 1847, Mickiewicz received a letter from his brother Franciszek. It had been several years since they had made contact, albeit not for a lack of trying (the Prussian police had proved vigilant). The poet's response was a lengthy one. Amid bits of information he had managed to glean about their siblings and kin in the old country (but unaware that their younger brother Jerzy had died seven years earlier), Mickiewicz sketched a painfully terse but nonetheless narcissistically comforting portrait of his own family for Franciszek's benefit:

> I'm healthy. My wife is well, ever since her miraculous recovery. . . . I have five [children]. The oldest is already thirteen. The two boys are in school. The two little ones are at home. My children bear a great and strange resemblance to our family, that is, to me and to you, my brothers. The oldest, Marynia, reminds me of you both in personality and even looks. Władzio, the second, has really taken after me, and everyone sees that in him. Helenka, the third, is pure Aleksander, even blonde like him and round and thrifty, and a stickler for order. The youngest reminds me of Antoś, whom I remember well. And what's stranger, the fourth, Oleś, is by his personality and nature a spitting image of Jerzy. May they be happier than us and may their road in life be easier than ours.[31]

Never one to complain about matters other than health, Mickiewicz wrote nothing about his material condition—and with his salary from the Collège now cut in half (upon his own insistence) to 2,500 francs a year plus the 1,000 he continued to receive through his sinecure at the Bibliothèque Royale, it was tenuous. Visitors that winter were struck by the "extreme poverty and neglect" that haunted the Mickiewicz household: rooms unheated in February; the children as well as parents in shabby, worn-out clothing; increasingly fewer objects to pawn. But, then, neither the poet nor his wife seemed overly concerned, counting as they always did on the appearance of "unexpected income, which had rescued them in similar circumstances many times in the past." And indeed, it was thanks to the generosity of others—not only Łubieńska, Krasiński, and Plater, but also Celina's sister Helena—that the Mickiewiczes were able to begin living somewhat less precariously that spring and summer. Convinced, as Mickiewicz was fond of saying, that "God will always provide," they themselves remained generous to a fault,* always ready to welcome guests to their home in Batignolles, provide accommodations for those in need, and even pay others' debts.[32]

In the beginning of May, after seven months of restraint, Towiański again made an effort to reach out to Mickiewicz. As if sure that time might have worked to cool heads and heal wounds, and still in denial, he dared hope "that hell would not attain victory." "Push everything aside, O my Brother," he appealed to his rebellious disciple, "and concern yourself only with your spirit, recognize and abandon the crooked paths that God opened but did not intend for you—and you can accomplish this with one stirring, like the one you manifested when receiving the medal in Nanterre."[33]

Perhaps it was Towiański's seemingly naïve insistence that all the clocks could somehow be turned back with that single "stirring"; perhaps it was his bald-faced unwillingness to acknowledge that something had gone terribly wrong, but after over a year of stubbornly ignoring the Master's efforts at reconciliation, Mickiewicz could no longer contain his bitterness. In a letter as lengthy as it was devastatingly frank, he reiterated the complaints that the damaged brethren had directed to Towiański a year earlier. But as their erstwhile "chief administrator," Mickiewicz also tried to lay bare what his victims could only intuit from their sufferings. He spared no one, least of all himself. "When you revealed yourself to us," he reminded Towiański,

> everything went from the spirit to souls and from these souls returned immediately to your spirit. Then, others, we ourselves, . . . forced their way between you and your Circle.

*To an almost flighty fault: when in July of that year Celina's uncle died leaving her a bit of money, both she and Mickiewicz agreed to transfer it to her uncle's younger brother, who had only just arrived in Paris and was staying with the Mickiewiczes.

> We oppressed our brethren.—As your administrators, we oppressed our fatherland....
>
> That stirring, which you elicited with your sacrifice..., we reached out for it. We wanted to purchase that stirring for a moment of ardor, ephemeral ardor, and at times *simulated*.... We placed the stirring of souls on exhibit as if to adorn our vanity.... We ordered brethren to rejoice or suffer, to love or hate, often without ourselves having those feelings of pain or joy that we were summoning.
>
> We who summoned, being ourselves without faith,... unable to bear the solitude that... manifested our nothingness to ourselves, set at our brethren. We subjected them to suffering so as to amuse ourselves, tragically, at the sight of their agonies.... We elicited an artificial life: we ordered brethren to move in ways that were often discordant with their inner state. We deprived them of that ultimate freedom, respected by all tyrannies, the freedom of *silence*. The brethren... endured all this in your name, so long as they could remain in the Circle....
>
> Anyone who did not agree with us in everything and anything was proclaimed a mutineer. We instituted the most deplorable dominion to be found on the face of the globe,... because it admits only denunciations and punishments....
>
> We wanted to justify this dominion by linking it to spiritual dominion. That is why we repeated that we command through the spirit, although there was no spirit in us to speak of. We kept frightening the brethren, who were petrified by such commands, with divine punishments... and were pleased when a brother was afflicted with suffering or need; we would push him away, trample on him.

Mickiewicz's use of the first-person plural was deliberately provocative. In view of the refusal on the part of all those he implicated in devising this dictatorship of the spirit to admit any fault, much less express contrition—and was not the Master himself to blame here too, at the very least insofar as he had refused to rein in his minions?—he concluded that it would be "difficult... to return to that atmosphere of trust, to that sincerity with which [he and Towiański] came together years ago." As far as Mickiewicz was concerned (Towiański did not respond), this particular act in their drama was over. The drama itself, however, was far from dénouement.[34]

That spring, just as Celina experienced another, and by all accounts particularly "vehement," relapse connected with some sort of intrigue among the brethren, Mickiewicz decided that instead of their usual vacation in Saint-Germain-en-Laye, the family should spend the summer on the Normandy coast in Langrune, "a still completely undiscovered fishing village" that the poet "chose, hearing it was secluded and inexpensive." For 5.5 francs a person, the seven of them could put a carriage on a train at the Gare Saint-Lazare at 6:00 in the evening, ride the recently inaugurated railway as far as Louviers, and then the carriage to Caen, arriving at 8:00 in the morning; from there it was another two hours to Langrune. "The trip by carriage and railroad, the new sights, finally the sea, glimpsed for the first time" filled the children with "indescribable happiness." Excellent swimmer that he was, Mickiewicz, too, liked the spot.[35]

The family rented an apartment for eighty francs monthly, although it was not particularly comfortable. And instead of economizing, as they had hoped, the Mickiewiczes soon found themselves paying exorbitant prices for basic foodstuffs that were difficult to come by, if at all, on this isolated stretch of Normandy coast. As Maria recalled years later, "they at times came close to suffering from hunger in this hospitable land." But if the lay there was "barren, flat, . . . a sandy steppe without the vastness and poetry of a steppe," for the children, at least, the novelty of the sea, with its bizarre flora and fauna, made up for everything; "the only thing that scared them was the thought that one day they would have to leave Langrune."[36]

Despite his efforts to distract Celina—and himself, for that matter—by having a piano brought in from Caen, Mickiewicz continued to have a difficult time with her throughout the summer. As late as the end of August, he was still complaining to Alojzy Niewiarowicz, the brother most implicated in her recent outburst, that he had "recklessly increased [the poet's] hardships by inciting resistance . . . in a person whose friendship and comity [were] indispensable to [him]." The enforced inactivity and tedium of Langrune only exacerbated matters. What little comfort Mickiewicz found came in the form of letters from Fuller, whose demands on him for spiritual advice elicited desires that Celina was incapable of grasping, much less satisfying. Fuller informed him, most likely, that during her stay in Rome that spring she had met a young man to whom she was now becoming strongly attracted. Mickiewicz responded by urging her to "live and act as [she] write[s]," as the liberated woman she projected in her works:

> Don't forget that even in your private life as a woman you have rights to uphold. Emerson says it well: *give all for love*. . . . The relationships that suit you are those which develop and free your sprit, responding to the legitimate needs of your organism and leaving you free at all times. You are the sole judge of these needs.

Although she found them, as Mickiewicz put it, "*harsch*," Fuller, it seems, took her friend's words to heart, but not, perhaps, as he had intended. Within a few months of receiving them, she found herself pregnant.[37]

It was not without a sense of relief that Mickiewicz felt compelled to cut the vacation short in early September. The political atmosphere in Paris was growing increasingly unpredictable, and several matters needed attention. Łubieńska was about to return home after her most recent stay there, and it had been arranged earlier that summer that she should take Maria with her to the Grand Duchy of Poznań, where the twelve-year-old girl could meet her uncle Franciszek and at the same time experience a native Polish way of life. No less pressing, though, were the demands of the brethren, who were seeking their leader's guidance in these volatile times. In this respect, Mickiewicz felt more confident than ever. He had had a powerful dream in Langrune in which a certain "friend" had dictated to him the words to a song, but admonishing him to reveal its words "only to those who sing its music and dance to it together with [the brethren]." After waking, Mickiewicz apparently "lit a candle and wrote down three or four stanzas of the song in a notebook," which he later gave as a gift to Deybel. He had taken the dream to be a sign that the time for action had finally come.[38]

5

The Mickiewiczes returned to a Paris that was seething. Since at least the fall of 1846, when the worse of two consecutive failed harvests caused famine and an exorbitant rise in prices, leading to widespread unrest, the July Monarchy had been losing what little legitimacy it still had left. Despite an easing of the economic crisis by the spring of 1847, class tensions had become intractable. The poor and the disenfranchised looked with equal hostility at the old aristocracy and a new *haute bourgeoisie*, the primary beneficiaries of a regime whose unofficial slogan was *enrichissez-vous!* The government of François Guizot, servant of the propertied elite, exacerbated matters by steadfastly refusing to extend the franchise. In July 1847, just as the Mickiewiczes were leaving for Langrune, various elements of the French opposition, stymied by Guizot's majority in the House of Deputies, had initiated a series of so-called reform banquets at which speaker after speaker denounced the government for betraying the revolution of 1830. Demands for change in the political order intensified with every toast. Mickiewicz was certainly not alone in his conviction that "the awakening of France was nigh." It was no coincidence, then, that writers as unlike on the ideological spectrum as Alphonse Lamartine, Victor Hugo, and Louis Blanc all appealed to the ideals of the French Revolution that year. Michelet's own intervention in this discussion soon earned him the same fate at the Collège as that of his Polish friend and colleague (Quinet's lectures had already been suspended the previous year).[39]

As in the past at such junctures, expressions of solidarity with Poland, especially timely in the wake of the suppression of the Cracow uprising the previous year, once again became a requisite topos of the rhetoric of French political discontent. Many Polish émigrés responded in kind by lending their support to the reform movement. That summer and fall, however, another cause, just as strongly felt and understood to be no less integral to the universal struggle of peoples, was vying for the attention of all progressives. The Italian peninsula was stirring, and that augured conflict with Austria, a development the emigration had been expecting for years.

Having packed Maria safely off to Poznań with Łubieńska shortly after the family's return from Langrune, Mickiewicz turned his attention to his circle. With many of his predictions about the state of affairs in Europe finally crystallizing into definite contours, he confronted his brethren with a question that had, all individual needs aside, drawn them to Towianism in the first place. "Is the time not approaching," he asked at their first convocation that fall, "for us to resolutely bestir ourselves from emigration, even if our steps be of this earth"? He solicited the brethren's advice in this regard, counting on the power of their "tone" and "rhythm" to provide them with direction; by the same token, he saw "no need to turn first to the Master." Like the words of the song he had dreamt in Langrune, whatever they decided was to remain among them.[40]

Mickiewicz's question, however, was largely moot. Although in the course of the following days he dutifully reviewed the brethren's suggestions, they simply confirmed what his own "instinct" had already answered in the affirmative. On 5 October he informed the brethren of his decision. They were all being "called to secure on earth a state for the spirit"; and since "the building of [such] a state . . . must originate in Rome," Rome is where he now felt "impelled to go." There he would "present all of the ideas drawn from the Master," but "in [his] own way" and "with the eagerness of a martyr: to perish for the holy Cause." For the moment, however, Mickiewicz confided the exact "aim and scope of [his] service" to only two people: his long-time collaborator Feliks Wrotnowski—and Ksawera Deybel, his oneiric friend from Langrune.[41]

By mid-November, Mickiewicz felt sure enough of his plans to inform Fuller that he was hoping to see her in Italy soon, possibly even "before the end of the year." At the same time, he sent word to the Resurrectionists in Rome about his impending arrival and his wish to see the pope. The prodigal son, they assumed, was coming home, "in order to fulfill the duty of his conscience and quench the needs of his soul." Thanks to Kajsiewicz's interpellation, the pope expressed his willingness to oblige: "Let him come, and I'll hear him out—*venga pure.*"[42]

But despite the Resurrectionists' success in collecting funds for the journey, it was not until the second half of January 1848 that Mickiewicz was ready to set out. After closing his account with Januszkiewicz to the tune of 1,350 francs, he asked Edward Geritz, a trusted brother of independent means, to serve as his aide and companion on the trip. Before leaving, Mickiewicz insisted on paying a farewell visit to King Jérôme Bonaparte, his acquaintance from their days in Rome and a talismanic link to the great one himself, "the Godfather," as the Towianists had nicknamed him. Mickiewicz had important information to pass on, which, he assured Napoleon's youngest brother, came from a source that could not be impugned. "Louis Philippe's reign," he revealed to the king, "is ending, your family is returning to power, Guizot, in my eyes, is finished." And so it would shortly come to pass, although not quite as Mickiewicz envisioned it.[43]

On 22 January, Mickiewicz bid farewell to his brethren, leaving them as well as his wife and five small children in the care of Brother Juliusz Łącki. Celina dearly—irrationally, perhaps—wanted to join him, but that was out of the question. On a mission as vital to the Cause, she would only be a hindrance, she was not well, and in any case, they simply did not have the means (the children, it seems, were not an issue). "Guard your spirit," Mickiewicz admonished her, "and keep it free and gentle."[44]

Just as the poet reached the Orléans railway terminal, he was handed a letter from Goszczyński. In it the orthodox brethren expressed alarm at Mickiewicz's mission. How, they asked, could he represent the Cause to the Holy See if he had broken with the man who embodied it? "In what spirit, in whose name would he summon [the Church]?" Until he made amends and returned to the path the Master had limned for him, "the deed [he was] contemplating would constitute nothing less than a coup against the Cause . . . and would be fatal to [him] and those who follow [his] footsteps." Mickiewicz read the letter "with great attention," got on the train, and, in the company of Geritz, set off for Italy—for how long, he himself was not quite sure, but he was determined to continue "perturbing the world."[45]

CHAPTER ELEVEN

POLITICS (1848–1849)

The journey from Paris to Marseilles took over two weeks, "more on foot than by carriage," as Mickiewicz would later recall. From Marseilles it was another two days by boat to Civitavecchia, where as Poles he and Geritz had their passports stamped for free by "sympathetic" Italians—a good thing, no doubt, since upon his arrival in Rome on 7 February the poet had only nine paoli (about five francs) to his name; as always, he was certain "that God would provide."[1]

After a few days in the Hotel di Minerva—and a futile search on Geritz's part in the cold February rain for a place to stay in the vicinity of the Scala Santa—Mickiewicz took a room for the duration of his stay in Rome on the Via del Pozzetto, around the corner from his old haunt on the Via della Mercede and only a few steps away from the Church of San Claudio, headquarters of the Congregation of the Resurrection of the Lord. Waiting for him was a letter from Celina (unfortunately not extant), followed shortly by one from Łącki, who informed Mickiewicz that his wife was still intent on following him to Rome. He was glad his plenipotentiary in Paris managed to restrain her. "Visit her often," Mickiewicz advised, "don't summon her to any service or consultation that might cause her to exert herself, struggle, or resist." Her state must have been precarious indeed when they had parted.[2]

I

Physically, the Eternal City had barely changed after fifteen years of stasis under Gregory XVI. Politically, though, it was a different world. Like the rest of the Italian peninsula, Rome was once again caught up in nationalist fervor, only this time the prospects of risorgimento seemed more hopeful than they had been in years, thanks in large part to the election of Pius IX. During his first year in office, the new pope had embarked on a program of modernization in the Papal States, eased censorship laws, introduced a semblance of representative government, and instituted a civic guard. One of his first acts was to grant amnesty to all political prisoners as well as exiles, many of whom were convinced—misguidedly, as it would turn out—that the Vatican might now also be ready to advance their dream of an independent, united Italy. The goodwill the pope's reforms generated among the inhabitants of the Papal States was as genuine as it was widespread; nor did his actions go unappreciated among liberals throughout Italy, where chants of *Viva Pio Nono!* alternated with *Viva l'Italia!* Calls for reform were soon roiling the entire peninsula, with anti-Austrian sentiment growing proportionally. Metternich's ham-handed attempts at intimidation, which Pius himself resisted, enflamed the situation further. By the time Mickiewicz settled in on the Via del Pozzetta, the Kingdom of the Two Sicilies as well as Tuscany had been granted constitutions; Pius IX had agreed to a secular government for Rome, promising even further liberalization; and Lombardy and Venetia were on the verge of insurrection, with Sardinia threatening to go to war with Austria on their behalf.

The Polish emigration was keenly aware of the possibilities that such a war augured for their own cause. Mickiewicz himself had predicted the previous December that "if Austria intervenes... in Italy, the emigration will go there en masse... and will constitute a legion just as it did in 1793 [*sic*]." The Democrats, however, proved hostile to any Polish formations in Italy, focused as they continued to be on mobilizing resistance in Poland itself. For his part, Prince Czartoryski recognized that tensions on the peninsula might indeed open up a promising arena. Acting, as always, through diplomatic channels, he sent his nephew, General Władysław Zamoyski, to Rome to direct negotiations with the Vatican for the presence of Polish officers in the papal army and at the same time incline the Holy Father toward a more forceful stand on Poland's behalf, something that in their own way the Resurrectionists had been trying to impress on the pope since his election. Once in place, it was hoped that such a corpus, with a Polish general at its head, would at the appropriate moment be ready to constitute a Polish legion, which would come to the aid of Italians struggling for liberation against a common oppressor. What no one counted on was Mickiewicz's intervention in this matter.[3]

2

Mickiewicz had been preoccupied since leaving Paris with "preparing... to commence [his] service before the local administration" and was not particularly eager to make new acquaintances. He posted Geritz at the door to his room like some "Cerberus," "admitting, dismissing, or barring the way." He did not, however, neglect his friends. Most urgent was his desire to see Miss Fuller, whose life, and in some respects their relationship, had taken a dramatic turn. She was carrying a child. She had met Giovanni Ossoli, a young Italian nobleman, the previous spring, and had fallen in love. Yet she had divulged her predicament, which was consuming her, to no one, not even him. Now she told Mickiewicz. In his role as Fuller's self-styled spiritual advisor, the poet did his best to comfort her. Her condition, he told her, was "a very natural, very common ailment" and in any case, God would spare her "suffering" as long as she could establish her "moral strength . . . in such a manner as to dominate the physical." His almost daily visits to Fuller on the nearby Corso seemed to have a powerful effect on his cerebral, melancholy friend, sparking rumors in America to the effect that the poet "wished to divorce himself in order to marry Margaret." As she confided to Emerson that winter, "Mickiewicz is with me, it was him I wanted to see more than any other person, in going back to Paris, and I have him much better here." She was already considering asking him to be the godfather of the child.[4]

There were, however, older friendships to renew as well. Among the first visits Mickiewicz paid upon his arrival—albeit as much, perhaps, out of calculation as out of nostalgia—was to Zinaida Volkonskaia, his Russian guardian angel during those bittersweet years in Rome almost two decades earlier. She and the poet had maintained sporadic contact over the years, corresponding whenever the need arose and meeting during her occasional visits to Paris. The princess had nonetheless been kept well informed about the peripeties of Mickiewicz's life thanks to the close relationship she had developed with the Resurrectionists, whose order owed much to her efforts and generosity. A fifty-nine-year-old widow now, who had consummated her conversion to Catholicism by becoming an oblate nun, Volkonskaia no doubt too rejoiced upon learning of the poet's ostensible desire to reconcile with the church and was eager to use her salon, thriving as always but now devoted more to ecclesiastic matters than the arts, to facilitate his intentions.

But of the friendships Mickiewicz chose to renew that winter none proved more stimulating—because in equal measure maddening and salutary—than that with Zygmunt Krasiński. When Mickiewicz had last seen him in Geneva in 1831, Krasiński was a precocious nineteen-year-old, high-strung, neurotic, and absolutely captivated by the older poet. Thirty-six now, unhappily married, and still in the thrall of a despotic father, he was the author of several brilliant works that in the eyes of Polish readers at once rivaled and challenged those of his idol. Mickiewicz had returned the favor, as it were, by devoting a series of lectures at the Collège to Krasiński's *Un-Divine Comedy* that evinced a genuine, albeit not uncritical, admiration of the younger writer's talent. An unapologetic aristocrat, terrified of social upheaval, and an anti-Semite to boot (Mickiewicz's marriage to Celina had especially offended his sensibilities), Krasiński was at once fascinated and repelled by Towianism, or more accurately, by Mickiewicz's involvement with it. He followed the doings of the Circle with voyeuristic delight, intrigued as much by its everyday pathology as by its doctrine. Mickiewicz was well aware of this interest, all the more so since Krasiński had been willing to at least listen and consider when the rest of the emigration condemned and slandered. He was eager to test this "nervous man," who, as he put it, "trembled in the face of every ordeal." Their first encounter met both men's expectations. Mickiewicz "didn't recognize me at first," Krasiński reported to his lover Delfina Potocka, but suddenly he threw himself at me and hugged me to the point of suffocation, and then in a Mongolian tone said to Geritz . . . : "Get out, leave us to ourselves." The tone reminded Krasiński of his father.[5]

Over the course of the next month, they met almost daily, either at Mickiewicz's or at Krasiński's on the nearby Via del Babuino, conversing and arguing for hours. "49 years old, and he yells like a youth," Krasiński observed, "he jumps up and down, gets fired up, believes, stamps his feet"; then, amid the "squealing and shouting," he "stands before a mirror and just like an actor . . . contorts and arranges his face, throws back his hair, as if he had been studying this for a while now." But it was what informed these performances, what Krasiński referred to as Mickiewicz's "despotism," that most disturbed the irenic author of *Psalms of the Future*. To him it was all of a whole—the imperious tone, the brusque behavior, the uncompromising doctrine. "Surely [Mickiewicz] has subjected himself to Towiański as an instrument," he wrote to Potocka, for "only a slave can be such a despot." His "holy, titanic love for Poland" notwithstanding, Krasiński was convinced that Mickiewicz had let the Master dictate the method for attaining it: an army of saints "arrayed like common soldiers, . . . and led by sergeants, officers, and colonels"—"the Muscovite method in the New Jerusalem." Krasiński was under no illusion. Everything Mickiewicz said and did, down to his ostensibly "unbridled rage against the aristocracy," betrayed "the enormous power of Towiański . . . to bind the soul just as Mongolian discipline can bind the body."[6]

Yet Krasiński also recognized something at once colossally tragic and pathetic about Mickiewicz, "something out of Michaelangelo," as he put it, which at moments mitigated his "savage one-sidedness and all the hardness of his fanaticism." But to Krasiński's amazement, this "courageous" man was also mortified of appearing ridiculous in front of others, just as he feared that some of his more fantastic projects might be misunderstood by "*them*." And it was precisely *them* that Mickiewicz had been preparing to confront in Rome.[7]

The Resurrectionists had been waiting for their nemesis's visit for some two months now. They knew Mickiewicz would be demanding an audience with the pope; they, in turn, were demanding an unequivocal public renunciation of the Master. A few days after his arrival, the poet finally walked into their residence at San Claudio as they were all gathered for their daily recreations. Upon espying Father Aleksander Jełowicki, he declared, "'I have offended you; for the love of God, forgive me!'" To the man who had become his "mortal enemy," it appeared as if their "old friendship, which Mickiewicz had broken off seven years earlier . . . at Towiański's instigation, had been restored." But if Jełowicki took Mickiewicz's expression of personal contrition as a signal of his readiness to atone for more egregious sins, he was mistaken. After several subsequent meetings with the fathers, it became clear that Mickiewicz had come to Rome "more with a desire to teach the pope than to receive his teachings." The Resurrectionists had run up against "the infernal might of Towiański." Any hope of breaking "Adam's fetters," they concluded, rested with the one "power" in Rome ostensibly mighty enough to wrestle with the Master's. That power resided in the person of Makryna Mieczysławska.[8]

3

Three years earlier, in the late summer of 1845, just as Emperor Nicholas I was preparing to visit Rome in connection with an eventual concordat with the Vatican, there appeared in Paris a sixty-some-year-old woman claiming to be the prioress of a Basilian convent in Minsk. Mother Makryna, as she came to be known, brought with her horror stories about the persecution of the Uniate Church in Lithuania at the hands of the Orthodox Russian regime. Her cause was immediately taken up by the Resurrectionists, who provided publicity for her and then dispatched her to Rome to meet with Pope Gregory XVI. Although he did little more than rebuke the tsar for his outrages, the pope seems to have been moved enough by her tales of martyrdom that he gave Mieczysławska permission to establish a convent in Rome. Before long, this semiliterate nun from the Belarusian provinces gained a reputation as something of a seeress, and her chapel at Trinità dei Monti became the object of pilgrimages by pious Poles. The Resurrectionists, but especially her patron Jełowicki, promoted her now as a kind of right-thinking anti-Towiański whom they could utilize in their war against the heresy. For like Towiański, she possessed that special aura of at once other-worldly simplicity and self-assurance that captivated everyone who met her. Unlike Towiański, though, whom the emigration from the beginning had misguidedly accused of charlatanism, it was Mother Makryna who proved to be the fraud.

Whether the Resurrectionists suspected anything in this regard is unclear (it was not until some fifty years after her death in 1869 that she was finally unmasked as having been neither a prioress nor even a nun), although in many ways she certainly was a product of their spin. In any case, it was not long before Mickiewicz received an invitation from the holy woman. Upon seeing him (all this according to Krasiński, who had it second-hand), Mieczysławska said nothing; she just sighed loudly:

> That sigh articulated so much genuine pain that Ad[am] says it pierced him like a knife; then, as in an epic, they exchanged names. "I am Ad[am] Mick[iewicz], an exile from Lithuania."—"And I am that nun, tossed across the entire world, from Lithuania to the land of Italy."

Krasiński's sense of drama notwithstanding, Mickiewicz appears to have been profoundly shaken by the encounter—the Resurrectionists had gauged well their old friend's susceptibility to charismatic personalities. At that first meeting, he "crumbled from his chair, slid to [Mieczysławska's] feet, began to sob and cry savagely, and called out: 'I'll do anything you command..., just save my soul.'" They prayed together, and in the course of prayer she compelled him to repeat: "I renounce Tow[iański]." Caught up in the hysteria of the moment, Mickiewicz apparently complied—though "perhaps," as Krasiński surmised, "despite himself." For the next few weeks, the poet attended mass at Mother Makryna's chapel daily, "in tears, beating his breast, oblivious to those around him, sometimes in nervous convulsions." But he also confided his troubles, how "everyone was hounding him, persecuting him, never had a good word for him, that he was very miserable."[9]

It was precisely this readiness, fostered over the years by his relationship with Towiański, to open up completely and sincerely that the Resurrectionists had been counting on exploiting. Mieczysławska impressed on Mickiewicz that only a full and sincere confession could redeem him, and when on 29 February he finally succumbed to her insistence, "she told him that it just so happened that an acquaintance of his was present at the convent, one who had known him for many years and who had read his works with unalloyed enjoyment over those years, Father Aleksander Jełowicki." This time Krasiński was not hyperbolizing when he imagined the moment as "a drama in the full sense of the word." If abasement on the scale of Mickiewicz's poetic imagination was their aim, the Resurrectionists could not have staged it better. But then too, there was little of Christian mercy in this sadistic, humiliating spectacle that only years of resentment could have engendered.[10]

Mickiewicz's confession before Jełowicki, that "malicious and puny mediocrity," as Krasiński characterized him, that "pompous dwarf," lasted for six and a half hours over two days. "Cries of despair, like the howls of someone being cut with a knife" could be heard in an adjoining hall. On the second day, after four hours in the confessional, Father Jełowicki absolved Mickiewicz of his sins, empowered to do so by the pope on condition that the poet "promise in public to hand over Towiański's works as well as his own on the subject... for the Church's adjudication, to which he would submit." Jełowicki then insisted that the poet take him for his father confessor—"'Mend your ways!'" as Mickiewicz put it some months later, "and, at the same time, 'Submit to me!'" The following day, the poet joined his countrymen in taking communion at the Church of San Claudio. In Jełowicki's estimation, the communicant exhibited the requisite "signs of sincere devotion."[11]

But Krasiński, for one, was not so certain. Mickiewicz's face may have grown "gentler, his mind calmer," but he was still "capable of straying another thirty times," "confessions and renunciations notwithstanding," and he had still to keep his promise of submitting the offending writings to Jełowicki. "Surely," Krasiński remarked in what is perhaps one of the more acute readings of Mickiewicz's behavior at the time, "he must have thought that if he fulfills such a boundless sacrifice, that if he grovels, that if he abases and spiritually humiliates himself, he'll suddenly rise from that confessional like a giant in the face of God!—that boundless contrition will afford him boundless power"—and at the expense of Jełowicki's vanity.[12]

4

On 3 March, a day after Mickiewicz's communion, news reached Rome of the republican revolution in France. Nine days earlier, on 22 February, following the cancellation of what was expected to be a particularly aggressive "reform banquet" in Paris, students, workers, members of secret organizations, and even some Towianists took to the streets, singing the Marseillaise, shouting *À bas Guizot!*, erecting barricades, and showering soldiers and police with cobblestones. The next day, Louis Philippe installed a new government, which in turn triggered a night of fighting and bloodshed. On 24 February, ten-year-old Władysław Mickiewicz found himself amid a throng on the Place de la Concorde. Too small to see, he could only hear shouts of "He's not worth even a single shot" directed at a man hurrying from the Tuileries Palace to the carriage that was about to take him to his exile in England.[13]

Two days after King Louis Philippe's abdication, Polish émigrés in Paris staged a rally in support of the provisional government of the new republic, which included a number of figures perceived to be sympathetic to the Polish cause. But despite the rhetoric, the government of Alphonse Lamartine soon made it clear that it had no intention of realigning French foreign policy. The emigration, for its part, was too badly fractured to make a difference, much less any constructive decisions. Amid the confusion, some urged Mickiewicz to return, "with Polish banner in hand," in order to petition the government for the creation of a Polish legion. A week later, at a ceremony reinstating Michelet and Quinet at the Collège, an empty chair was set on the daïs in their colleague's honor. In their speeches, the two professors repeatedly invoked the name of "dear and great Mickiewicz," "the national poet of fifteen million people," who "despite his absence . . . was among [them], together with the spirit of his brothers, the Poles and Slavs."[14]

Initial hardships notwithstanding, Celina was generally pleased by the course of events. Like other Towianists, she supported the revolutionary government, from which she certainly had nothing to fear. On the contrary, she immediately recognized its installation as an opportunity to petition for the rescission of the 1842 order expelling Towiański from France, a sentiment shared by dissident and loyalist Towianists alike. From Switzerland the Master, too, quickly grasped that the time may indeed have come "to personally serve [his] brother Frenchman."[15]

News of all this reached Rome in dribs and drabs. Although "in throes of ecstasy" about events he claimed he had foretold, Mickiewicz nonetheless had no illusions about the new government, insisting, with his usual prescience, that it was "transitional" and that soon "a strong hand would seize power and . . . crush [it]." He approved of the brethren's participation in events, but at the same time reminded them of their Master's words, that "a Pole has no obligation to work on behalf of the French." Accordingly, his only initiative under the new circumstances was to urge the provisional government to rescind restrictions against Polish émigrés in France. In any case, he had more important concerns in Rome.[16]

Two days after news of the revolution reached Rome, Mickiewicz was ushered into the Quirinal Palace for an audience with the pope. Pius "welcomed him most cordially, like a beloved son," albeit probably as one of a group that day. What they discussed remains a mystery—perhaps an invitation for Towiański?—but according to Jełowicki, the meeting did not go well. "Poor man," the pope apparently remarked after the audience. Although downcast, Mickiewicz was not deterred. He began drafting some sort of letter to the pope, after which he would travel to Switzerland to see the Master. Events that March compelled him to abandon both projects for something immeasurably grander.[17]

On the first day of spring, news reached Rome that the people of Vienna, too, had taken to the barricades, forcing Metternich, the despised architect of the post-Napoleonic order in Europe, to resign. In an outburst of anti-Austrian sentiment, a mob coursed through the streets, "tore down the Austrian coat of arms from the Venetian Palace, and burnt it in the Piazza del Popolo." "Adam Mickiewicz," wrote Fuller in a dispatch for *The New York Tribune*, "the great poet of Poland, long exiled from his country or the hopes of a country, looked on, while Polish women, exiled too, . . . brought little pieces that had been scattered in the streets and threw them into the flames, an offering received by the Italians with loud plaudits." Over the previous few weeks, the spirit of the French revolution had spread rapidly throughout Europe. And as it did, demands for civil liberties and socioeconomic change, for constitutions, national guards, enfranchisement, and the abolition of serfdom, fused with calls for national self-determination. While Germans and Italians called for unification, almost simultaneously, from Bohemia and Hungary and Croatia to Poznań and Galicia, captive nations began confronting their hegemons, some with petitions, speeches, and demonstrations, others with bricks and arms. After months of mounting tensions, the citizens of Venice and Milan rose up to expel their Austrian occupiers, prompting King Charles Albert of Sardinia and Piedmont to proclaim his readiness to march to their defense. As all around him Italians mobilized to aid their countrymen in Lombardy, a few even rallied by Mickiewicz's own words from "The Pilgrim's Litany,"* the poet grasped the sense of his presence in Rome. He had come on a mission that would transcend "this world." Events in this world now transformed it.[18]

*An Italian paraphrase of the litany was printed secretly in Lombardy. W. Mickiewicz, *Mémorial* 1:178–81.

5

With war against Austria seemingly inevitable and as Polish émigrés in Paris were weighing whether to head for Poznań to join the uprising there against Prussia or to Italy to fight the Habsburgs, the idea of constituting a Polish legion in Rome became more timely than ever. But just as both the Hôtel Lambert and the Resurrectionists were intensifying their negotiations with the Vatican, Mickiewicz confided to Czartoryski's agents that now he himself "intended to form a Polish Legion," on his own terms.[19]

In a sense, Mickiewicz had been nurturing dreams to this effect since childhood, ever since the veterans of Dąbrowski's Italian Legion passed through Nowogródek on their way to Moscow with the *Grande Armée*. Over the years, the Polish soldiers who chose emigration after the disappearance of their state in order to fight for their own freedom by fighting for the freedom of others came to epitomize for him the very essence of Polishness: courage, loyalty (to Napoleon as well as to the fatherland), doggedness in the face of adversity, a democratic spirit as well as the spirit of self-sacrifice, and above all, perhaps, the capacity to wed word to deed in a single heroic act. "Those who joined the Legions," Mickiewicz asserted in his lecture of 26 April 1842,

> abandoned everything that was private, everything that tied them to their land, to national tradition; they went into battle not on behalf of any [political] opinion; . . . they sought their fatherland having no idea where to seek it. . . . Governments, forms changed every minute; it was necessary to abandon all concern for form, to disengage oneself from all opinions in order to find the strength that would one day come to the country's aid. . . . The mysterious power that produced this national miracle was precisely that unknown god whose name is—Polish patriotism. (*Dz.* 9:272–73/*LS* 3:184–85)

But then too, the notion of a legion fed into Mickiewicz's abiding fascination with the military, which, after his own failure to join the fight in 1830, guilt had transformed into a powerful compensatory fantasy. He had come to envision the emigration as something akin to a military order, embodying it most saliently in the figure of *Pan Tadeusz's* Father Robak and then in the Polish "pilgrimage"; and had he not repeatedly enjoined the Circle, in the terse cadences of command that he so admired, "to actualize its military spirit" if it were to fulfill the Master's mission? The creation of a legion, with him as its heroic leader, would at once justify and consummate his sixteen years in emigration.[20]

Although the pope refused to sanction the creation of a Polish legion under its own banner within the confines of the Papal States—the Vatican, after all, was not at war—the Resurrectionists nonetheless managed to elicit the pledge of a papal blessing should a formation be constituted beyond their borders. On 23 March, just as Charles Albert finally declared war against Austria, the fathers called a meeting of the Polish community in Rome in order to inform it of the pope's commitment and to discuss how they should proceed. Some present wondered whether a legion was even necessary, to which Mickiewicz responded with anger, "arguing that it was . . . , but also . . . that they should choose its commanders themselves." Father Jełowicki then proposed that Mickiewicz join him and several others in a delegation to the pope, who, it was hoped, would now give his official blessing for the creation of a legion. Their visit was to take place two days later, on the Feast of the Annunciation.[21]

On 25 March, an hour before the scheduled visit, Mickiewicz "arrived at [the Resurrectionists'] in a feverish state." He had, finally, turned over copies of the last two years of his lectures together with other Towianist writings to Father Jełowicki earlier that day. Now he fell on his knees before Father Hube, "asking him for his blessing in preparation for the audience." Then, to the Resurrectionists' dismay, Mickiewicz proceeded to "beseech [them] all to unite [their] spirits with his in what he was about to say to the Holy Father." As Krasiński had predicted, the penitent had had a relapse. Gently, the fathers reprimanded the poet for his Towianist babble, which only irritated him further. As they set off for the Quirinal, the Resurrectionists could not but feel "very perturbed" by their companion's state.[22]

By seven o'clock that evening the entire delegation had gathered for the audience. It constituted something of a microcosm of the Polish emigration: besides Fathers Jełowicki and Hube, it comprised one of Czartoryski's agents, a representative of the Democrats, an aristocrat recently arrived from Warsaw, a leader of the 1830 uprising (Jełowicki's brother, in fact)—and "Mickiewicz as himself." As they waited to be ushered in, the poet could be seen pacing back and forth, "his head held high, with his face flushed, preparing for his speech to the Holy Father." When the doors opened to admit them, it was Mickiewicz who went in at the head of the delegation, as if for some reason everyone took for granted that this was as it should be. His demeanor was that of a man inspired. As the pope stood leaning at a table, the poet began to address him "fervently," and in a loud voice "expounded to the Holy Father that a new age of the spirit had arrived," that the peoples of Europe were stirring, and it was the "responsibility" of the pope to lead them, "for otherwise blood would flow." As he spoke, his voice kept rising, and several times the pope had to ask him to quiet down. Then suddenly, Mickiewicz "grabbed the Holy Father by the hand, shaking it violently and yelling, 'Know that today the spirit of God is in the smocks of the people of Paris!'" Taken aback, Pius responded, "Do not forget, my dear son, to whom you are speaking." The poet retreated, leaving everyone nonplused. Although others now took their turns to argue the case, Mickiewicz's outburst, as embarrassing as it was riveting, had irreversibly transformed the remainder of the encounter. The pope went on to assure the delegation of his sympathies for Poland's plight, but as far as the legion was concerned, he remained noncommittal, suggesting that they speak with his Ministry of Foreign Affairs. "Poland," he concluded, "should arise and as it does I'll give it my blessing, but only to a Poland that is Catholic, *no other!*" To this, Mickiewicz yelled out, "We swear that we are ready to die for the Catholic faith." But as everyone knelt down for the final blessing, the poet continued speaking "so passionately that the pope blushed and cut him off." The audience was over.[23]

Fathers Jełowicki and Hube stayed behind to smooth matters over, reminding Pius of the promise he had made to them earlier regarding the creation of the legion. That evening still, they reported back to their compatriots. Immediately an argument erupted as to who should lead this legion, with Mickiewicz again maintaining that they should insist on choosing their own commander, adding now, though, that it be someone who was "clean, who did not belong to any faction"—certainly not, as some suggested, General Zamoyski, who was, after all, Czartoryski's man, but rather someone like... Karol Różycki. If anyone had any doubts as to Mickiewicz's intentions, this should have put them to rest. That some young Russians he had met with in Rome on several occasions were now "running around like crazy and idolizing him as prophet" certainly did nothing to allay suspicions.[24]

Two days later, practically the entire Polish community in Rome convened again to discuss the matter. Mickiewicz, for his part, had not been idle. He had been frequenting the Caffè Greco, where he managed to make contacts among young émigrés, disaffected artists mostly, on whom his name, to say nothing of his charismatic forcefulness, seemed to work its magic. If there was to be a legion, it would be organized as he saw fit, that is, as he confided to Łącki, "in accordance with the Master's principles."[25]

To the forty or so Poles who gathered on 27 March to decide what shape a legion was to take, Mickiewicz reiterated "that for these new times a leader is needed who would represent the new *idea*," not someone—again Zamoyski—connected to "times irrevocably gone by." And when a few of the assembled objected "that an adherent of heresy would be even worse," Mickiewicz exploded, lashing out at the Resurrectionists, at Jesuits, at aristocrats—at anyone, in other words, who disagreed with him. Tempers flared. Some came to the poet's defense, others accused him of being disingenuous, insinuating that his ideas for the legion were "simply Towiański's teachings in disguise." Mickiewicz screamed in response, "The church has not condemned Towiański's teachings yet [a month later, though, it would], hence I can adhere to them and spread them!" whereupon he reached into his coat, took out a booklet, and declared, "These are the Master's words, which I always carry near my heart." At this point, the meeting turned chaotic. It was obvious by now to most that Mickiewicz had tricked the Resurrectionists and was intent on organizing, as one observer put it, "a Towianist legion." There were, nonetheless, some voices that called for the poet to lead—which he did, storming out with a handful of supporters in tow, the cadre of his Detachment of God.[26]

Among Mickiewicz's most vocal antagonists that day was a twenty-seven-year-old artist and poet from Warsaw, Cyprian Norwid, who with time would be recognized as one of Poland's greatest, a rival—or, rather, an agonistic alternative to—his poetic and intellectual progenitor. Conservative, a devout Catholic, and painfully sensitive to anything he perceived as a slight to his dignity, he had had a run-in with Mickiewicz some weeks earlier. Their confrontation at the meeting only confirmed his first impressions, that "this was a scary man." "I believe," Norwid wrote a few weeks later, still shaken by Mickiewicz's performance,

> that the *coil*, which at the same time is a *bridle*, popped in his constitution. *Good* and *evil* get confused in the subtleties of his mystical formulas—there is nothing one can firmly stand on in relations with him, barring, perhaps, becoming his slave.

As he matured, Norwid's relationship with the older poet would acquire the complex hues and depths of well-aged wood, which only made the knots and cracks more salient. They would meet again, under different circumstances, equally unkind to both. Yet even in his old age, long after Mickiewicz had passed away, Norwid's encounter that March with the man he would compare at various times to Socrates, Dante, Columbus, Camoens, Kościuszko, and Napoleon would continue to haunt him.[27]

6

The accounts vary. At one point there appears to have been thirteen men, then fourteen; some even claimed there were twenty; Krasiński settled on the number twelve for dramatic effect. Ultimately, in the face of "shouts, curses, jibes . . . [and] insults," only eleven chose to tie their fate to that of Mickiewicz, vowing, to "follow [him] anywhere": Edward Geritz; the latter's hunchbacked step brother, on the lam from creditors; seven Polish artists studying in Rome on Russian scholarships; a musician; and Wincenty Jan Nepomucen Siodołkowicz, a sixty-five-year-old lieutenant-colonel who had fought in the Napoleonic wars. After making sure that all went to confession first ("none of them had been practicing before"), Mickiewicz assembled this motley contingent on 29 March in order to finalize on paper the founding of what he called the "*First Polish Detachment* (as a unit of the Lord's host)." Its aim was to "return to the fatherland in union . . . with fraternal detachments of [other] Slavs"; its "lieutenant and provisional leader" was to be Adam Mickiewicz; and its "Set of Principles"—its "Symbol"—was as follows:

1. The spirit of Christianity, in the holy Roman Catholic Faith, manifesting itself through free deeds.
2. The Word of God . . . —the civil and social law of nations.
3. The Church—guardian of the Word.
4. The Fatherland—the sphere of life for the Word of God on earth.

5. The Polish spirit—the servant of the Gospel . . . rises from the dead in the body in which . . . it was laid in the grave a hundred years ago. Poland rises free and independent, and extends its hand to Slavdom.
6. In Poland—freedom of religion and assembly.
7. Free speech, freely manifested. . . .
8. Everyone of the nation a citizen—every citizen equal in rights and before authority.
9. Elected public office, freely bestowed, freely accepted.
10. To Israel, our elder brother, respect, brotherhood, assistance on the way to his eternal and terrestrial good, complete equality of rights.
11. To life's companion, woman, brotherhood, citizenship, complete equality of rights.
12. To every Slav living in Poland—fraternity, citizenship, equality in everything under the law.
13. To every household, its own land, under the protection of the commune; to every commune, communal land, under the protection of the nation.
14. All property, respected and inviolable, to be protected by the national government.
15. Political assistance . . . is owed by Poland to . . . the fraternal Czech people . . . and Russian people. Christian assistance to every nation.[28]

It would seem that what Mickiewicz was trying to formulate here was nothing short of a future constitution for Poland. Yet in merging, in the spirit of Towianism, notions common to various progressive agendas of the day (freedom of speech and religion, universal suffrage, guaranteed rights for women, Jews, and ethnic minorities, the distribution of land, Slavic fraternalism) and ones that took into consideration native traditions (respect for private property and, above all, the leading role of the church) with a mystical belief in the eventual resurrection of Poland as it once was, what Mickiewicz produced, in fact, was yet another brilliant improvisation, articulated now as a political program, but an improvisation nonetheless. To be sure, the "Set of Principles" (or, as Fuller referred to it, Mickiewicz's "declaration of faith") was the culmination of many years of meditation—from *Forefathers' Eve*, part 3, *The Books*, and *Pielgrzym Polski* to the lectures at the Collège de France and his own take on the teachings of Towiański—but not of thought, exactly. Rather, it was a creature of inspiration, more poetic than political, more intuitive than systematic—and yet, somehow, utterly realistic. For all of his instinctive objections to Mickiewicz's vision for Poland—a potential "hell on earth"—Krasiński unwittingly got it right when he observed that "all of this may be in the future."[29]

With the formation of his detachment both in spirit and on paper, Mickiewicz felt that he had fulfilled his mission in Rome. Having gotten the permission of the Vatican censor for the publication of the "Set of Principles" in Italian,* he was ready to lead his

*"Simbolo politico polacco," *Mémorial* 1:501–2.

little band of misfits from Rome through "Florence, Milan, Bohemia to Cracow." In a letter to the brethren in Paris, he encouraged those who could to "prepare to head out" for Italy to join them. But to what end, exactly? It would appear that Mickiewicz was envisioning his contingent as the nucleus of a Polish legion which, in turn, was to lay the foundation for one made up of Habsburg Slavs that would liberate their respective homelands; as for himself, he was intent on "hurrying to the Master," whence he would return to Paris. Yet none of this was particularly clear, nor, for that matter, was it evident how any of it was to be financed. As always, Mickiewicz was content to improvise, to trust his intuition, certain that the good Lord would provide. There were, in any case, other priorities: the detachment required a banner; the banner, a blessing from the pope. The poet's sensitivity to the symbolic, to say nothing of the principles he now espoused, would not have had it otherwise.[30]

He had been hoping that Mother Makryna would design the detachment's banner—her imprimatur for the enterprise had become almost as crucial as the pope's. But despite her sympathies, Mieczysławska's Resurrectionist handlers made sure that Mickiewicz left empty-handed. Not to be deterred, the poet had someone else design a banner to his liking: "on the finial a silver eagle [apparently the lid from Mickiewicz's Czapek & Patek watch], beneath the finial [i.e., on an aquila, à la the Roman, and Napoleonic, legions]: '1. Polish Detachment' on one side; 'Slavdom' on the other; the banner, half red with a white cross, half white with a red cross" (the white for Towianism, the red, apparently, for revolution; the combination of the two, Poland's national colors). Now, however, came the more difficult challenge: securing the papal blessing—Pius IX, after all, had been wary of extending one even to the Resurrectionists.[31]

It just so happened that a few weeks earlier the relic skull of St. Andrew, patron saint of the Slavs, had mysteriously disappeared from its sanctuary in the Church of Sant' Andrea della Valle. On 1 April, just as mysteriously, it reappeared, and the Vatican announced that Pius would hold a special ceremony to celebrate its return. Mickiewicz saw his opportunity. Four days later, under the watchful eye of the papal tribune, the poet and his band of legionnaires joined a host of local fraternities in a procession from Sant' Andrea della Valle to St. Peter's, with Geritz solemnly carrying their banner in the van. "At the tomb of St. Peter . . . the pope stood at the altar and blessed . . . the banner with the head of St. Andrew"—just as he did the banners of all of the Roman fraternities amid which the detachment had positioned itself. But this—perhaps even unknowingly—was as far as Pius was willing to go in public. He agreed, however, to bless just the banner in private, at the same time extending his blessing to "the intrepid Poles" who had borne it and sending them a requisite handful of small metal crosses as a gift. It was all very ambiguous, but for Mickiewicz's purposes precisely enough to legitimate the entire enterprise.[32]

On 10 April, as troops and volunteers from all over Italy were rushing to reinforce Charles Albert in what was now a full-scale war with Austria, Mickiewicz and his "fighting force" prepared to set off for Lombardy as well, with the intention, thereafter, of "returning to Poland immediately." In his order of the day to the contingent, the "leader-in-chief" called for "the spirit in which [they] had all been united" to "manifest itself in [their] pilgrimage, [their] bivouacs, and [their] battles" (*Dz.* 12:12). Yet despite the bravado, Mickiewicz was leaving Rome "a completely broken man": "everything that [he] had counted on had risen up against [him]." He had managed to alienate practically every Pole in the city with his "perfidious and obstinate" behavior—now insisting that he remained "obedient to the pope," now spouting Towianisms and disparaging the Resurrectionists and aristocrats for ostensibly impeding the Polish cause by working against him. Some feared that he was fomenting revolution. Even Mother Makryna seemed to have lost her patience: "Pride, pride, a coward, he'll go down like a fly and won't accomplish a thing." As Krasiński observed on the day of Mickiewicz's departure, "Surely at bottom this at times roaring tiger has a heart full of insecurities ... he is the most *sincerely* deceitful and hence the most dangerous of people"—which apparently did not prevent Krasiński from donating 500 francs to the detachment's coffer (as a security deposit perhaps?). The two antagonists parted on the best of terms.[33]

7

The detachment left Rome for Civitavecchia in two carriages. From there, "in straitened circumstances and beset by hardships," they made it by steamer to Livorno. The sight of a dozen vessels manned by Slavic crews heartened them. Here, after all, was their first opportunity to put their principles to work. But after some initial contacts with "captains of the Slavic ships," the Poles, it seems, were warned by the commander of the local national guard to refrain from anything that might enflame the already restless populace of the Tuscan port. After two days in Livorno, the detachment boarded a train to Empoli for the first leg of its "march" to Milan, whence Mickiewicz was now planning to make his way to Switzerland in order to "stand before the Master." "I hope," he confided to Łącki, "that he'll find me on a better level, both inwardly and outwardly, than I had been two years ago." In a letter to the brethren, he again encouraged those who could to join his detachment. As an official piece of correspondence now, this one demanded official stationary, which Mickiewicz had the foresight to order in Rome: a Polish eagle, sans crown, and a letterhead that read, "Cohorta polacca—Capo conduttore."[34]

Such, it would appear, are the bare facts of the detachment's stay in Livorno. But such is not how Mickiewicz would describe it. A few days after the visit, he informed the government of Modena that "through the captains of the ships, the entire Slavic navy of the port promised ... its help" for his enterprise. In a letter to the French minister of foreign affairs, he wrote that those same captains ("there were twelve of them") "ran" to the Poles, "translated [their] appeal, and promised to remove the Austrian colors and hoist those of Poland." Krasiński, for his part, was given the benefit of even greater detail: not only did the captains "translate" the Set of Principles, but they "understood" and "accepted" them; as for the Polish colors, "they vowed to fly [them] with the addition of twelve stars [symbolizing] the Slavic tribes."[35]

The respective identities of the addressees go a long way in explaining the aim of Mickiewicz's embellishments. To the republican president of Modena, through whose town the detachment was about to pass on its way to Milan, Mickiewicz was intent on portraying his mission as at once legitimate, noble, and a success, just as he was for the benefit of the French republican government, which he was urging to come to the aid of Austria's Slavs by sending a fleet into the Adriatic. As for the letter to Krasiński, he knew full well that all of Rome, to say nothing of his friend's wide circle of correspondents, would soon hear of the detachment's accomplishments, with additional details thrown in for good dramatic measure. After all, as Mickiewicz reminded the French foreign minister, "without propaganda, there is no faith."[36]

As the detachment "marched" by train and carriage and on foot through Empoli, Florence, Bologna, Modena, Parma, and Lodi to Milan, "bivouacking" in hotels, Mickiewicz's letters (*vel* those of his aide-de-camp Geritz) brimmed with accounts of enthusiastic crowds rushing to greet them as they approached each town. "Clergy, army, and folk" "filled the streets with cries of 'Long live Poland, long live Pius IX, long live free Italy!'" (or, more pointedly, "'Long live the Polish martyrs, long live the great Poet, long live the Polish banner, blessed by Pius IX'"). Throngs cheered as Mickiewicz stepped out onto balconies to deliver rousing speeches about Poland's and Italy's common struggle. Towns were illuminated and orchestras played; poets read verses "To Our Polish Brethren," and people stood beneath the hotel windows where the detachment stayed holding torches. "Our march was a continuous triumph," the poet reported to Łącki from Milan:

> In the lands we traveled through, governments would be the first to visit us. Military staffs reported to us. We had numerous guards in front of the house where the banner was kept. We were given military honors.[37]

It is difficult now, as it was then, to separate the facts from spin. And in this regard, newspaper accounts of the events are of little help. On the contrary, the nationalist Italian press had its own agenda in those heady days and was eager to exploit "the noble Polish pilgrims" for its own ends. Needless to say, Mickiewicz was more than willing to oblige. The press legitimized his enterprise, and rather than having to promote it himself, he could now direct his correspondents to the relevant articles in Italian papers, which on occasion he himself fed to their suddenly ubiquitous reporters. But then too, the Italian press was reporting on events that its editors themselves had an active hand in staging. As the Poles moved from town to town, newspaper accounts of their earlier sojourns invariably preceded them. To a large extent it was the press that brought out the crowds and generated the enthusiasm; it quite literally made the news. And it was a win-win proposition: Mickiewicz's detachment got a media event and free publicity; the newspapers got to advance the Italian cause and earn a few francesconi in the bargain. None proved as intrepid in effecting this unspoken arrangement than those of Florence.[38]

On 16 April, the morning after the detachment's arrival in the capital of Tuscany, *La Rivista di Firenze* had the walls of the city plastered with posters announcing the presence of "the Polish émigrés, who are advancing to Lombardy under the leadership of their great poet Adam Mickiewicz to fight . . . alongside [their Italian] brethren for the great principle of national independence, common to Poland and Italy." They invited the citizens of Florence to "gather at one in the afternoon on the cathedral square, whence they would make their way to where Mickiewicz lived." On the following day, all three Florentine newspapers provided lengthy, breathless accounts of the entire spectacle:

> The people of Florence, preceded by the flags of Tuscany, Rome, the Italian tricolor, and the German tricolor, set out in a huge column to the cathedral square and walked in silence to the hotel where the noble pilgrims were staying; there they broke out in sustained applause for Poland, free Germany, and Italy.

After quoting at length from the speeches of various local representatives welcoming "the noble Poles," "pilgrims . . . transformed into warriors," as well as their leader, "the Polish Dante, capable of performing miracles with sword and word," the accounts turned their attention to the man himself as he walked out onto the balcony to thank the people of Florence:

> The thunder of applause that greeted his appearance is impossible to describe. The windows of all the houses were richly decorated; the street was filled with people as far as the eye could see. Adam Mickiewicz made a gesture, and the vast crowd grew silent. We can repeat his words; but it is impossible to describe the majestic figure of the Apostle of Poland, to convey the force of his speech, nor the inspired tone that . . . shook the fibers of his audience's soul.

He spoke in Italian of Poland's sufferings; of Poland's approaching resurrection, and with it of all the Slavic peoples; of Poland's mission to unite all peoples in Christian brotherhood. "You Florentines," Mickiewicz concluded,

> have consummated a Christian deed of brotherhood today. By welcoming foreign pilgrims, who, still unarmed, are threatening the mighty of this world, you've saluted that which in us is immortal—our faith and our patriotism. We thank you, and now we repair to church in order to thank God. (Dz. 12:316)

Fig. 26 Mickiewicz addressing the crowds in Florence, 1848. Drawing by Aleksander Zieliński. Courtesy of the Adam Mickiewicz Museum of Literature, Warsaw.

"To the church," the crowd repeated, "to the church," and everyone, according to *La Rivista di Firenze*, flocked after the contingent of Poles to Santa Croce. As "Adam Mickiewicz humbled himself before God," all of the banners (including now the detachment's own) formed "a canopy over the graying head of the apostle of Slavic nations." "Amen," Mickiewicz said as the priest petitioned God to bless Italy and Poland; "Amen," echoed the throng. The account did not fail to mention that the first group of people to greet Mickiewicz in the hotel that day was a delegation of Florentine reporters.[39]

The detachment's stay in Florence was relatively lengthy—six days in all—and it proved critical to the mission's success. The Florentine papers performed their service masterfully. All of Italy was now aware of the detachment's exploits (such as they were), and Mickiewicz could now direct his brethren in Paris to have the accounts of his ostensible successes reprinted in the French press (which papers in Poland soon picked up as well). To Fuller, too, he suggested that she read the Italian papers for details of his reception, on the assumption that they would eventually make it into a dispatch for *The New York Tribune* (which in fact they already had). But as important as publicity was in legitimating the mission, other aspects of the undertaking were no less urgent. As always, God was willing to provide.[40]

Thanks to the generosity of a successful Polish painter living in Florence and his wealthy English wife, the detachment was outfitted in uniforms: "a dark blue overcoat with an amaranth collar, a Polish cap, a white cross over the heart"—the symbol of God's Cause. But the couple also helped allay what was, perhaps, Mickiewicz's primary concern: continued funding for the mission. It was with this in mind that the detachment's Leader-in-Chief paid a visit to Grand Duke Leopold II, Tuscany's "Daddy" and one of the more liberal rulers on the peninsula. "The prince heard [him] out with kindness, warned [him] of dangers, and assured [him] of his sympathies"—after which "sincere accounting," Mickiewicz accepted the prince's offer to finance the detachment's journey to Bologna.[41]

On 21 April, the detachment set out from Florence, "equipped and partially armed," their coffer a bit fuller, their spirits lifted by a rousing send-off from the city's youth. Before leaving, Mickiewicz wrote to the brethren in Paris, again urging them to join him in Milan but this time singling out Sister Ksawera, who "should decide on her own whether to remain in Paris or make her way" to Italy (she chose not to). In a separate letter, he reminded Celina to remain watchful and free and gentle. He would summon her if they had the means, "but there was no way now." "Say hello to the kids," he concluded, before cautioning her "not to entrammel her spirit."[42]

The contingent's reception in Bologna appears to have taken its cue from those in Empoli and Florence—throngs, delegations of dignitaries, speeches from a hotel balcony, but also a visit to the public library, where Mickiewicz was shown a copy of his works (in Polish). The reception would probably have been even more impressive had it not been for the Easter holiday. Modena too, according to the papers, met the "Polish Tyrtaeus" with the requisite enthusiastic crowds, speeches from a hotel balcony, and a military band providing a festive touch to the occasion. But if in Reggio, the next town on the route, the detachment arrived several hours earlier than the posters announcing the event had led the populace to expect, Parma's local paper had prepared its readers with an extensive account of the detachment's visit in Florence. "The famous Pole Mickiewicz and his noble detachment of compatriots . . . were greeted with loud cheers" as they entered. Here, however, the success of the detachment's visit would not be measured by the size or enthusiasm of crowds, nor by the pathos of speeches given from balconies, nor even by an orchestra. What the duchy had to offer instead was something more precious. The provisional government voted to cover all the costs associated with "the upkeep of the eminent Mr. Mickiewicz and the Poles accompanying him for the course of their stay . . . in the hotels they [were] inhabiting" in Parma (105 francs) as well as "their trip by post to the border" (100 francs). On top of this, it donated an additional 250 francs to the detachment's cause, which effectively financed a good portion of its subsequent stay in Milan. But then too, the "military honors" as well as the "anxious and hopeful cheers and best wishes" with which a crowd saw off "Poland's greatest living poet . . . and his eleven compatriots . . . for the plains of Lombardy" suggest that Parma's generosity may not have been as disinterested as it seemed.[43]

On 29 April, just as Pope Pius IX was announcing his decision not to lend his support to the war with Austria, the contingent finally reached Lombardy, crossing the River Po by means of a pontoon bridge, their carriages following behind. That same day it made it as far as Lodi, where another "enthusiastic" reception awaited it, replete with a young student's declamation of "Ode to Youth" in Italian. "During the entirety of [their] stay," the local paper gushed, "crowds gathered in large numbers and, amidst the singing of national anthems, shared in the general joy of the occasion." Two days later, on 1 May, the detachment was in Milan, the culmination of their march.[44]

For some two weeks now, the citizens of Milan had been reading "the press's fantastical exaggerations," as one of its own later admitted, about "a cohort [of Poles], under the leadership of the great poet Mickiewicz, making its way to Lombardy to fight for [it]." In response, a somewhat nervous municipal government ordered a contingent of police to escort "the Polish crusaders" as they made their way from Lodi to Milan, concerned, ostensibly, that an overenthused crowd might pose a danger to the poet and his men. "A mile from the city," Mickiewicz reported to Łącki on the day of his arrival in the capital of Lombardy,

> an official delegation received us [at the Porta Romana] and throngs of people saw us into the city, where an armed national guard, several thousand strong, was waiting for us. The entire city stirred. No monarch had ever been received quite this way.

"Carriages full of women, crowds of children, all the clergy, . . . the entire city decked out," a marching band—Geritz had "neither seen nor heard nor read anything like it." Nor, for that matter had the Italian journalist Giuseppe Cesana, who many years later recalled how the throng, "expecting to see a long line of warriors dressed like leads in the ballet *Mazeppa*," saw instead a group of

> just eleven individuals—one of them a hunchback—and all in mufti; the only Polish thing about them was a four-cornered carmine hat—*czapska* [*sic*]. And they were on foot.
>
> At the head of the squad marched an old man with an ardent gaze, an expressive face, a white mane down to his shoulders, and a beard, no less white, down to his chest.
>
> This was a genuine disappointment for the public, a disappointment that a few barely concealed and that many vented with less than hospitable gestures and words.[45]

But then Mickiewicz himself could not hide his own disappointment. "Oh, how we would have been welcomed," he bemoaned to Łącki, "had we had a battalion at least." He compensated by giving two rousing speeches that day, one to a spontaneous throng of young people gathered on the Piazza San Fedele, the other from the balcony of the Palazzo Broletto, in the company of journalists and government officials. The Milanesi responded in kind. "Shouts of 'Long live Poland! Long live Mickiewicz! Long live Poland and Italy!' never ceased erupting from all breasts, amidst the growing enthusiasm of the crowds."[46]

8

As a military band serenaded him that evening outside what would be his home for the next month on the Via dei Bossi, Mickiewicz sat down to read the letters that had been accumulating in Milan over the previous three weeks.

Fuller's, it seems, were pleasureless, full of anxiety about her condition. He was grateful to her for arranging his lodgings in Milan and for letters of recommendation, but at the moment he had little time or patience for her neediness. Celina, for her part, was overjoyed to finally have had news from him. She was genuinely pleased with her husband's accomplishments in Rome. "You presented the cause . . . of a reborn, new Poland," she enthused, "Israel and woman have finally won respect." His project for reversing French laws regarding the émigrés, however, had gone nowhere, despite the efforts of Michelet and Quinet. The children were healthy and well behaved, but she sorely missed Maria. In view of the rising tensions between Prussia and Poznań, Celina's "mother's intuition" wished that Łubieńska would send their daughter home already, something that Mickiewicz too now urged his friend to consider. Money, as always, was a problem but, as always, of little concern: she had pawned Mickiewicz's chalices, both the one he had received as a farewell gift in Moscow in 1828 as well the one presented to him as a memento of his Christmas improvisation of 1840. Should the need arise, she wrote, she could always find something else to pawn.[47]

What did concern Celina, though, just as it did those brethren who wrote to him that spring, was the status of Mickiewicz's relationship with the Master. "It'd be a good thing," she chided her husband gently, "if you could let [Towiański] know something about yourself." Karol Różycki's appearance in Paris had made the matter especially urgent. In preparation for the Master's own return to France, Brother Commander had been pressuring the dissidents in a most unbrotherly way to acknowledge him as leader (he even demanded that Łącki turn over the Cause's banner), maintaining that by taking his mission to Italy rather than working for the Cause in France "Br[other] Adam . . . was determining a direction for the Circle altogether different" from what the Master had indicated. But then Różycki himself refused to act outside the Circle, content, as Wrotnowski put it, with wallowing in "the same old methods, the same old work, harassment, and friction." "Better to be with [Tsar] Nicholas," concluded Celina, "than with this torturer of man's spirit and will." Różycki, for his part, complained in his own letter to Mickiewicz that in their "abiding evil" Celina and the other dissident brethren refused to yield to his authority, at the same time reiterating the error of his erstwhile partner's ways. Yet as much as the brethren from rue Saint Charles may have wished for Mickiewicz's return to Paris to "extricate [them] from this misery," they nonetheless put their trust in what they continued to believe was their leader's infallible intuition. Unlike Różycki, Brother Mickiewicz was doing something—and in any case, he had no intention of "altering [his] path for the sake of events that change daily." "Our service in France is apostolic," he reminded Łącki, "in Italy its aim is to secure the first point on earth."[48]

In this respect, however, another letter he read that evening must have given Mickiewicz pause. Father Jełowicki wrote to inform him that the Sacred Congregation of the Index had placed both *L'Église officielle et le Messianisme* and *L'Église et le Messie*, the last two years of his course, on its list of prohibited books.* Even the liberal Vatican censor, who had approved the publication of "The Set of Principles," apparently found the lectures to be "*an olio of every heresy condemned by the Church.*" Yet surely this came as no surprise to the poet, nor even much of a disappointment; after all, he had himself disclaimed the lectures repeatedly (if not necessarily whole-heartedly). As far as Towiański was concerned, however, the Sacred Congregation of the Index was helpless. Since the Master had refrained from publishing anything, there was nothing for it to condemn. For Mickiewicz, this was vindication enough. Potentially more troubling was Jełowicki's contention that Pius was indignant upon learning that the poet was claiming, "falsely," that he had blessed the detachment's banner and that the expedition was undertaken in his name. But Mickiewicz shrugged this off as well. This was Jełowicki's version of events; his own happened to be different—and as copy, certainly more effective.[49]

*An unintended effect of the decision was to reunite Mickiewicz with his former colleague at the Collège Edgar Quinet, whose *Allemagne et Italie* the Congregation happened to condemn at the same session.

Indeed, what Mickiewicz gleaned from the brethren's letters seemed to justify the ends of his half-lies, distortions, and self-promotion. Several of them had heeded his call and chosen to join him in Italy. Most significantly, in this respect, was the change of heart it apparently effected in Colonel Mikołaj Kamieński, who three years earlier had left the Circle in disgust over the letter to Tsar Nicholas. Having retracted his apostasy, he had mobilized a contingent of some two hundred volunteers and set out from Paris in the name of the Cause as he understood it. He was now in Strasbourg, ready to move out should Mickiewicz give the order. The poet did so immediately.

9

Ever since leaving Rome, Mickiewicz had grown increasingly firm in his belief that the only option for Polish émigrés in this time of upheaval was Italy's struggle against Austria. He was convinced (from what little information he had) that those of them who were now "staggering aimlessly in Germany or fighting in the restless provinces of Prussia and Austria, where they have neither ideas nor a banner nor a representative," would sooner or later see things his way, as would those who were still counting on France to make some decisive gesture on Poland's behalf. Despite the doubts and opposition of practically the entire emigration, he had succeeded in making his detachment if not a force to be reckoned with, then at least one that made the news. It was time now to transform it into a genuine legion—just as General Dąbrowski had done fifty years earlier.[50]

Armed with assurances that volunteers were on the way, the poet submitted a proposal to the Provisional Government of Lombardy. The legion's mission, as he presented it, would be two-fold: to fight against Austria alongside Italian forces; and to recruit ethnic Slavic soldiers serving in the Habsburg ranks from among deserters and prisoners of war. His conditions were as follows:

1. The Polish Legion would fly its own banner and be commanded by Poles.
2. The Legion would constitute an auxiliary corpus in the service of Lombardy.
3. The Legion would be used exclusively in war against Austria and its allies.
4. Poles would enjoy all the rights of Lombard citizens for the duration of their service.
5. The Legion would cease its service in the Italian army should it to be summoned to serve in Poland.
6. All Slavic prisoners of war should be dispatched to Milan, where Poles would recruit them for the Italian army. The government should facilitate the spread of Slavic-language propaganda among the Habsburg armies.
7. Success would depend on the expeditiousness with which the government of Lombardy officially proclaimed the formation of the Legion.

A week later, on 9 May, the provisional government "accepted the project with pleasure," that is, provisionally (actually, it approved only point 2 unconditionally and demurred on point 6; the remaining points would require further consideration). What it requested now, before extending its official approval, was a detailed plan of the legion's organization—in other words, proof that it was a viable formation. For the next few weeks, Mickiewicz set about mobilizing every resource available to him in order to make it so.[51]

Although Mikołaj Kamieński continued to tarry in Strasbourg, Brother Michał Chodźko's arrival in Milan in the first days of May, together with Brother Henryk Służalski and three other veterans of the 1830 uprising, eased Mickiewicz's task considerably, not least by replenishing the legion's coffers. He immediately dispatched Służalski to Strasbourg, where he was to facilitate Kamieński's march to Lombardy. The brethren in Paris, meanwhile (including Towiański's own son), set about recruiting volunteers for what they referred to as the "Legion of Polish Crusaders." Those interested were asked "to report to Mrs. Mickiewicz, rue du Boulevard 12, or Mr. Łącki, 72 rue Truffait," whose homes would henceforth serve as the Parisian headquarters for the legion. Within a few weeks, close to thirty "crusaders" were ready to set out for Italy. When in mid-May émigrés in Switzerland put out their own call for the creation of a legion, Mickiewicz responded immediately with arguments on behalf of his formation. "Here in Italy," he wrote to Henryk Nakwaski, his old acquaintance from their days in Lausanne, "Providence is extending the opportunity of uniting us in arms, our banner has been planted here, here the fraternal feelings of people and governments give us succor; here before us is our common enemy—the Austrian army."[52]

By the end of May, with his project close to realization, Mickiewicz was ready to remind the government of Lombardy of the assurances it had given him three weeks earlier. He informed it of Kamieński's imminent arrival in Milan, adding, with his usual enthusiasm, that "numerous contingents [were] arriving from Algeria or [would] turn back from Germany" and, like many other willing Poles, "were but awaiting [the government's] summons." The next day, on 25 May, Mickiewicz received the answer he had been hoping for. Lombardy officially agreed to the formation of a legion of six hundred men, including, eventually, Polish—but only Polish—prisoners of war. As far as the banner was concerned, the provisional government left the decision up to King Charles Albert. That very same day, the Lombard minister of war gave the legion its imprimatur, as it were, by ordering it to the military barracks of San Girolamo.[53]

As satisfying as this agreement may have been under the circumstances, its reservations regarding the project left Mickiewicz leery of tying the fate of his legion solely to Lombardy. His mistrust was fueled, it seems, by his acquaintance that May with Italy's most celebrated revolutionary nationalist, Giuseppe Mazzini. They met thanks to a letter of introduction from Margaret Fuller, for whom the Italian occupied a place in a pantheon of heroes second only to that of Mickiewicz. Mazzini worshipped Mickiewicz as a poet, but it was what he called the Pole's "belief in the religious crusade of Mankind, . . . in the great destiny of brotherhood sent by God," that is, as author of the *Books of the Polish Nation and Pilgrimage*, that marked them as kindred spirits, romantic maximalists both, whose refusal to compromise ideals for the sake of political expediency made them inconvenient to the "realists" they both so despised. Mazzini had little patience with the liberal government of Lombardy, and he urged Mickiewicz to also approach the republican government of Venice with his project, if only for leverage. Although nothing came of it, Mickiewicz now understood Fuller's assessment of the Italian revolutionary, "the only man," as he put it to his American friend, "who ha[d] the political energy necessary for the moment." Several months later, in articles analyzing events in Italy for *La Tribune des Peuples*, Mickiewicz would repeatedly come to the defense of his Italian friend. "In these difficult times," he wrote in a piece entitled "Mazzini and the Mazziniists," "Mazzini demonstrated the rare gift of political self-denial and unselfishness. . . . While [his critics] accuse [him] of serving the revolution badly, they in fact fear that he will serve it only too well!" (Dz. 12:28/TP, 65).[54]

A few days after concluding his agreement with the government of Lombardy, Mickiewicz reported to Prince Czartoryski that he had "successfully constituted a Polish Legion in Milan":

> A dozen of us left Rome with this aim, now our number has grown and we are setting about organizing it. Only in Italy can our countrymen unite in a spirit that is religious and purely national, without submitting to any party. . . . The effort that went into constituting [this legion] was great. Countrymen blocked my way with their suspicions and malicious gossip. . . . Only merciful God came to our aid.

He was now asking Czartoryski to do the same, particularly in view of the collapse of the Polish uprising in the Grand Duchy of Poznań, toward which the prince had chosen to direct his efforts. Mickiewicz sent Michał Chodźko to Paris with conciliatory letters to the Hôtel Lambert and even urged General Zamoyski, his recent antagonist in Rome, to "take his stand together with [the legionnaires] as one of them, forgetting both bygone intrigues and services." At the same time, he also instructed Chodźko to petition the French Ministry of Foreign Affairs for diplomatic support for his enterprise, facilitate passage for those in France wishing to join the legion, and financial backing, together with "a thousand rifles and military equipment." Mickiewicz was already aware that two weeks earlier, French radicals had managed to mobilize a hundred thousand Parisians on behalf of the Polish cause, demanding that the provisional government declare war on Russia and Prussia—and then almost succeeded in toppling it. He was counting, it seems, on the generosity that usually comes with having just dodged a bullet. But then too, the French government was more than happy to accommodate any enterprise that might encourage Polish émigrés to seek their fortunes elsewhere.[55]

On 1 June, Kamieński finally arrived in Milan with his contingent. As one of Czartoryski's agents put it, up until now the government of Lombardy, "had grown used to treating Mickiewicz and his twelve apostles as *pazzi*, since as far as their doctrine is concerned, no one understood it." But the appearance of Kamieński's column, 150 strong (it had shrunk somewhat due to desertions by those unhappy with its leader's Towianist inclinations), consisting of veterans of the November Uprising as well as French adventurers, now made the legion a force to be reckoned with—something the government of Lombardy had feared. As the new arrivals settled into their barracks in Milan, eager for action, the Ministry of War chose to stall. With no official proclamation concerning the formation of the legion forthcoming, much less a decision about engaging it in battle, everyone was growing impatient, and money was running out. The minister's insistence that the legion fly the Italian, rather than Polish, colors produced the intended effect. More desertions ensued, and prospects for further recruitment were clouded.[56]

Unable to commit the government of Lombardy to anything more tangible than approval of the legion's officer corps, Mickiewicz decided to appeal directly, and in person, to Charles Albert, king of Sardinia and Piedmont, with whose realm the people of Lombardy had just voted to unite. Although the patriot king promised Mickiewicz that he would immediately sign a decree proclaiming the formation of the legion (and largely on its leader's terms to boot), he did not do so, fearful, as always, of anything that smelled of revolutionary republicanism; and in any case, the Hôtel Lambert had already approached him about the prospect of forming a legion of its own in Italy, on terms certainly more acceptable to him. Mickiewicz was now forced to play the card Mazzini had dealt him, threatening the government of Lombardy with the prospect of sending his legion to republican Venice. Faced with an embarrassing image problem, to say nothing of the prospect of close to two hundred idle Polish legionnaires milling about Milan, it relented.

By 24 June the legion was armed and outfitted. Mickiewicz's work in Milan was over. In a farewell memorandum to Colonel Kamieński, now officially the legion's commanding officer, Mickiewicz underscored that "Italy [was] at present the only place here on earth... where [a Pole] can for the first time feel independent." Kamieński's "aim," he went on, "should be to serve Italy sincerely, and by supporting its independence as ardently as possible, one could truly serve [the Polish] cause in the future as well." But sincerity is precisely what the memorandum seemed to lack, although it was consistent with what had become a somewhat troubling modus operandi. For, counter to his agreement with the government of Lombardy, Mickiewicz was now suggesting to Kamieński that the legion could in fact serve the Italian cause on the side of "any movement aimed at advancing it, ... even if it came to shattering existing forms of government in Italy." If Venice were to call, the legion was to heed its summons immediately. It would appear that both the provisional government of Lombardy and King Charles Albert had had reason enough to be concerned.[57]

"The formation of the Legion is being realized," Mickiewicz wrote to his patrons in Florence on 25 June, the day of his departure from Milan:

> The first company (some one hundred and twenty men), commanded by Colonel Kamieński, is leaving for the front tomorrow. . . . The second company, already organized, is arriving from France; we are expecting a third from Strasbourg. . . . Knowing as you do the lucklessness of our nation and emigration, you can imagine that all of this came about not without difficulty.[58]

On 27 June, the First Company of the Polish Legion marched to the Austrian-Italian front under orders from the Piedmontese general Giacomo Durando. It would be another six weeks, however, before it would see action. On 6 August, in the village of Carzago, a few kilometers west of the shores of Lake Garda, the legion fired its first shots at the enemy and suffered its first casualties. That same day, near Lonato, the legion fought again, valiantly by all accounts, but also losing its commander to a serious wound. This mattered little, since three days later, on 9 August, King Charles Albert concluded an armistice with Austria.

Another few dozen legionnaires had stayed behind in Milan—together with the legion's banner—under the command of the venerable lieutenant colonel Siodołkowicz. Their mission there was to enlist new recruits from among Slavic deserters and POWs as well as to organize volunteers arriving from France. As the city was falling to the Austrians at the beginning of August, Siodołkowicz spirited the banner away to Piedmont, where he deposited it with the French embassy for safekeeping.

Mickiewicz, for his part, was returning to Paris, ostensibly "on matters connected with the further [organization] of the formation." As far as he was concerned, he had accomplished his mission. He had created the legion—the embodiment here on earth of everything he felt Towiański had instilled in him about the spirit—in the face of resistance, hostility, and ridicule, against both financial and logistical odds, impelled by a conviction that his enterprise was just, and by sheer force of will and guile. After sixteen years in emigration, consumed by guilt and continually grasping and flailing at opportunities to assuage it through deed, he could believe that he had at last achieved a modicum of expiation. But then too, Mickiewicz was in effect leaving the legion to its own devices. To be sure, he would continue to watch over it—recruiting, financing, intervening on its behalf—but at a distance, and with ever increasing disengagement.[59]

10

Mickiewicz was returning to Paris none too soon. He had learned from his correspondents that Brother Różycki's presence had exacerbated the feud between the two circles to unsettling proportions. The decision of seventeen-year-old Jan Towiański, the Master's own son, to volunteer for the legion, and thus side with Mickiewicz, had made matters even worse (the father eventually prevailed). Letters from brethren loyal to Brother Adam as well as from Celina brimmed with desperation. "Come back, dear Brother," Aleksander Chodźko pleaded with his leader, "because only your presence can extricate us from the chaos that Karol has put us in." Shortly thereafter, Towiański himself arrived in Paris, and he too summoned Mickiewicz.[60]

The Master remained unmoved in his opposition to his disciple's enterprise. "Our cause and our sphere of action are here in Paris," he pronounced to the brethren of both circles gathered in his apartment on the Champs Elysées. "Whoever betakes himself hence—is a traitor, commits a sin for which he will suffer through the ages." What Mickiewicz was doing was "for the sake of smoke, for the sake of human glory, and not for Christ." Towiański was sure that the charisma of his physical presence among the brethren, but above all the threat of a withdrawal of his affection, would produce the desired effect, and to some extent they did. Several of the dissenting brethren asked for forgiveness; one kissed the Master's feet, weeping. Yet to Towiański's dismay, several, including Celina, spoke up openly in defense of their leader and his mission. The Master exploded with uncharacteristic fury, lashing out at Celina for being "in league with a powerful evil spirit of Israel," at Łącki for his marriage outside the church, and, of course, at the one whom they defended, the cause of the Circle's perturbation. "'Adam is my enemy!'" he thundered, "God will damn Adam." For the first time, perhaps, the brethren saw both the Master's "might of spirit" and his "human frailties." Yet they remained torn, terrified of finding themselves unloved by the one whose love they craved but at the same time convinced that the course Mickiewicz had taken was nonetheless correct. As two of the brethren put it in a letter to the poet, "We feel that without the Master there is no guarantee that our activity is blessed, but in siding with him without You there is no direct, human work here on earth." They were all imploring Brother Adam to return in order to resolve the conflict once and for all, one way or another. The insurrection in Paris upset everyone's calculations.[61]

On 22 June, enraged by the announcement that the national workshops created by the provisional government as a misguided solution to the unemployment problem would be terminated, some fifteen thousand workers and others dissatisfied by the bourgeois régime of Lamartine took to the barricades. When fighting broke out, Celina happened to be on the other side of the Seine, visiting the Quinets. Fearful for the children, and against the advice of her hosts, she set off for home, navigating barricades, corpses, and invitations to help "dislodge cobblestones." At this moment, at least, she was thankful that neither her husband nor their daughter Maria were in Paris. For the next three days, government forces commanded by the newly appointed dictator General Louis Cavaignac "systematically cleansed" the rebellious *arrondissements*. The suppression of the uprising was bloody, brutal, and effective. The state of siege, with its concomitant terror and repression, remained in effect for another three months. On 11 July, the day after Mickiewicz's arrival in Paris, Towiański and Ferdynand Gutt found themselves among the thousands who had been arrested.[62]

The Man of Providence and his companion were taken to the local *commissariat* and informed that they were being charged with sedition, largely on the basis of "false denunciations, most of which," as Seweryn Goszczyński correctly surmised, "came from the emigration." The next day, the two were transferred to the Conciergerie, where Towiański spent the first few days in the cell once occupied by Marie-Antoinette.[63]

The Circle reacted immediately. After visiting the Master in prison, Różycki called the brethren together in order to pen protests to the authorities. Putting aside his disagreements under the circumstances, he turned to Mickiewicz as well. The poet, however, demurred. "I couldn't confer with them," Mickiewicz explained to one of the legionnaires, "for reasons of which you're aware"; and, as if to justify both his behavior and his cause, he added, "if the Italian Legion stands up and grows, only it will be able to call for the Master's freedom with dignity." It was not until a month later, when Aleksander Chodźko informed Mickiewicz that Towiański and Gutt were about to be deported to Cayenne, in French Guiana, and insisted that "this [they] could not permit," that Mickiewicz finally agreed to intervene. He visited Towiański in prison and asked Quinet and Victor Hugo to intervene with Cavaignac. In a letter to the general, signed by Mickiewicz and nearly every Towianist in Paris at the time, the brethren maintained that "a great sin had been committed against truth and justice by condemning this man, whose entire life is but a continuing series of sacrifices and purest devotion to God, country, and fellowman."[64]

But it was left to Celina to win the day. As her son recalled many years later, she managed to arrange a meeting with Cavaignac thanks to an acquaintance. The general was at first unwilling to listen; then, relenting somewhat, he told her to take the matter up with the prefect of police, who just happened to be sitting in the anteroom. Celina had the prefect called in and, "to Cavaignac's amazement," ordered him to sign a release order for Towiański. The general was apparently later overheard saying that "he had freed [Towiański] unjustly..., that Mrs. Mickiewicz had pulled this off, that, having descended on him like that," she could have freed even the most notorious of the June revolutionaries.[65]

Towiański was freed on 21 September (Gutt would have to wait until November). Yet when the brethren held a thanksgiving service for the Master at Saint-Séverin, Mickiewicz did not attend, nor did he join Różycki in taking communion with him three days later, through which gesture Towiański hoped to "renew [their] fraternal Christian union." Nonetheless, the Master's brush with oblivion seemed to have awakened something akin to feelings of remorse. Over the next few weeks, Mickiewicz began to acquiesce, willing, it seems, to give Towiański the benefit of the doubt when he insisted that "brother deserves complete forgiveness from brother, each must completely forget the past." In a series of retreats with the Master in Paris and Montereau, the poet and Różycki agreed to work toward reconciliation. But the rift proved too deep, too fraught with hurt, resentment, and distrust—and Mickiewicz's new-found sense of freedom and purpose too precious. Four months later, the poet reported to Towiański:

> I don't see any way that I can stand on anything certain with the community of brethren. Whenever I'm alone, the whole thing seems simple and easy, but with each meeting with this or that brother, I see that we're far from converging in a feeling that is alive and fruitful. Many of them brandish the same tone Father Jełowicki used with me in Rome.... There are even those whose amour propre has injected itself into this lengthy inquest against me. To summon them in a way that would move their consciences, make their prejudices disappear, and kindle a desire for brotherhood is beyond my powers. And as for general discussions, wherein everyone agrees in general, such discussions are pointless, just like a Pole and Russian who agree when it comes to their best wishes for mankind but who wish for immediate mutual destruction.

By this time, the Towiańskis and the Gutts were in Avignon, where the Master was preparing for a journey to Italy to try yet again to bear witness before the pope. After a few months, however, with the pope still in exile in Gaeta, Towiański decided otherwise and, together with the Gutts, headed back to Switzerland, where he would remain until the end of his life. Mickiewicz would never again see the man who had changed his life to the core.[66]

II

In mid-September, as he was attempting to resolve his relationship with Towiański and the Circle, Mickiewicz received a disturbing letter from one of the legionnaires in Italy. After the capitulation of Milan and the Salasco ceasefire, Kamieński's men had joined Siodołkowicz's in Piedmont and now, unsure of their status, found themselves at the mercy of a none too sympathetic Charles Albert:

> Everyone's hopes... were... directed toward receiving some instructions from the Creator, the Leader of the Legion, according to which they would move in the direction indicated or, in the absence of the necessary information, derive... enough strength and fortitude to bear further hardships, privations, and abnegation of the fate of each.... The saddest of rumors have begun to circulate (that Mr. Mickiewicz doesn't want to think of us,... that the Legion was created... only to advance Mr. Towiański's teachings, that Mr. Mickiewicz is completely occupied with the imprisonment of his great friend and is no longer concerned with the Legion...).

The truth, as always, lay somewhere in between, but that did not make it any prettier.[67]

Upon his arrival in Paris, Mickiewicz had indeed set about agitating and working for his legion. The state of siege made recruiting difficult, and a lack of funds threatened to undo the entire enterprise. But God smiled again on his fortunate son. In mid-July, the eccentrically patriotic count Ksawery Branicki, scion of two of Poland's most notorious national apostates (and Krasiński's brother-in-law), for whatever reason donated a portion of his enormous fortune to finance the legion—about 20,000 francs "in gold and bank notes," with a commitment of more should it be necessary. For the next two months, Mickiewicz's home was transformed into a recruitment center, quartermaster's office, and logistical headquarters rolled into one, whence men, money, and orders for the legion were sent and wither all correspondence was directed, either to the *Conducteur en chef* himself or to Michał Chodźko, who effectively took charge of the legion's day-to-day affairs. By the middle of August they managed to outfit and dispatch an additional four columns of volunteers, including one commanded by Chodźko himself.[68]

In Italy, though, the legion itself was deteriorating. In the face of hostility from Charles Albert and intrigues on the part of both General Zamoyski and Polish democrats, beset by infighting, desertions, and general demoralization, its existence was becoming untenable. In letter upon letter to Paris, legionnaires painted a sorry picture:

> The majority of our French [volunteers], if not all of them, will leave. We're having a difficult time with them. Their haughtiness, wantonness, lack of respect for anything, and penchant for robbery makes ridding ourselves of some of them vital. Similarly, we're having a very difficult time with the older émigré soldiers. We devoted ourselves to them with all our souls, [but] they refuse to give anything back in return. It's difficult to imagine how human dignity has become completely smothered in some of them, drunkenness is the sole mainspring of their life, dissatisfied with everything, they have ripped the white [Towianist] crosses off [their uniforms], the one thing that gives us comfort, and are ready to abandon everything for the sake of this earth, but they lack the courage even for this.

"Amid these various internal worries, envies and . . . intrigues, amid the garbage and mud, completely cut off from the world," the legionnaires pleaded for direction or at least encouragement from their *conduttore:* "We await a few words from You, Brother Leader, with longing, like that lightening bolt that in the midst of a stormy night shows the way to tireless travelers so that they can continue on for a while."[69]

Mickiewicz tried to allay their concerns by sending money, but not much else. And by the end of September even that source of comfort evaporated. Branicki withdrew his funding, and the leader-in-chief was compelled to shut down operations in Paris. Focused now on organizing the four columns of new recruits, whose passage to Italy required frequent interventions with both French and Italian authorities as well as with Czartoryski,

Mickiewicz seems to have lost interest in those already there. The legionnaires felt as if he had "forgotten [them]" amid "the dirt, the personalities, and the hatreds." Increasingly, they began calling for his return to Italy, "so that he could once again rouse [them] with the spirit of his inspiration." Mickiewicz's response, when it finally came after over a month of silence, was anything but heartening: "The need to tend to matters of the Legion, that is, the finances and the means for dispatching people, perforce keeps me here." As for directives, he suggested that the legionnaires "try making it to Genoa . . . but, if worse comes to worst, head for Livorno or the Papal States . . . , if possible, to Venice." By way of encouragement, he reminded them that "the intention is in the spirit, waging [the struggle] depends on our strength, and the outcome rests with the will of God."[70]

The successful formation that fall of a second company of legionnaires in Tuscany, under the command of Michał Chodźko, served only to complicate matters. In trying to coordinate it with Siodołkowicz's in Piedmont, Mickiewicz was forced to navigate through a tangle of considerations, from the political situation obtaining in Italy and the persistent interference of General Zamoyski to petty rivalries among the legion's officers and empty coffers and more desertions. Having to manage all this from a distance, when letters sometimes took more than a week to reach their destination and when he had to constantly read between the lines of correspondents advancing their own agendas, led to confusion and misunderstandings. By the time the two detachments consolidated in Tuscany that December, Mickiewicz had effectively disengaged.

At the beginning of February 1849, the poet received a letter signed by 105 legionnaires. Having lost faith in Chodźko's command, they asked the poet, as their leader-in-chief, to draw up an agreement in person with the Tuscan government concerning the formation of the legion. "It would be most desirable," they continued, "if you could yourself . . . appear among us, if only for a brief time, in order to determine our direction and succor us in difficulties that are mounting with every day." Mickiewicz did not respond to this letter, nor to any subsequent ones; as for the agreement, after writing a few paragraphs, he abandoned it in mid-sentence. He would leave it for others to complete.[71]

To be sure, Mickiewicz did not neglect the legion entirely. As fighting broke out again that March between Charles Albert and Austria, and as the republics of Tuscany and Rome were preparing to defend themselves, he continued to recruit volunteers and on occasion intervene on the legion's behalf. He remained convinced, as he observed to a prospective recruit, that Poles "should eagerly take advantage of" the Italians' permission "to form a Polish army on their land . . . , since it was only with Polish regiments that [Poles] would win back [their] independence." Nonetheless, when it came to responding to repeated requests on the part of the demoralized legionnaires for at least "a few words, for a single idea in this extraordinary and difficult predicament," Mickiewicz remained silent.[72]

Looking back on the events of 1848 seven months later, when the pandemic of liberation movements that had erupted from Italy to Galicia and Poznań had been contained,

Mickiewicz could see only squandered opportunities. "This was a grand moment," he wrote to Ignacy Domeyko,

> when all roads were open for action. . . . The emigration rushed to [Poland], fleeing misfortune, and found itself in greater misfortune. Those same people who, when one talked to them of moral rights or obligations, about God and faith, scorned all this, calling out for *arms*—they had their arms. They didn't want to fight. The Italian Legion fled, abandoning rifles and returning to France on rumors that the subvention [for émigrés] would be increased. They shamelessly forsook Polish eagles. I was there, and you can imagine how I suffered.

Mickiewicz was exaggerating, of course (only a handful of officers, egged on by hostile Democrats, actually abandoned the legion), but the sense of his disillusionment was not unfamiliar. He had experienced this before, in 1832 with his prescriptions for the emigration and then again in the Circle of God's Cause—transforming others in his own image, driven at once by imagination, guilt, and self-abnegation, proved impossible. To demand "dominion over souls" in an ecstatic trance was one thing; to effect it in a world of more pedestrian imaginations was something else. Although under the circumstances the legion never really had a chance,* its failure was the consequence of what Mickiewicz believed to be its strength: "impracticality, poetry, spirituality." For his efforts, he would have to endure a lawsuit and an attempt at extortion from legionnaires who felt Mickiewicz had defrauded them, as well as a public tongue-lashing from Father Kajsiewicz for "meddling in foreign affairs that did not even have anything remotely to do with the [Polish] cause."[73]

12

At the beginning of September 1848, the Mickiewiczes moved to a home on rue de la Santé (now rue de Saussure), a few blocks north of the apartment they had been occupying in Batignolles for the previous three years. It was "a lovely house, large, comfortable, with two gardens," for the same price as the previous one, and with enough space for the

*After its consolidation in Tuscany, the legion was initially used by the provisional government there to guard against counterrevolution. In April, after the fall of the Tuscan republic, most of the legionnaires set out for Rome to defend the newly created republic against the French, but the agreement it reached with Mazzini's government in May no longer acknowledged Mickiewicz as leader-in-chief. For the next month the legion participated in the defense of Rome. After the defeat of the republic, and with it the collapse of the liberation movement in Italy, the legionnaires hoped to contribute their services to the Hungarian cause, on behalf of which a number of their compatriots were already fighting. On 22 July, 160 of them set off for Corfu but were diverted to Patras instead, where they learned of the defeat of the Hungarian revolution. In 1852, those who had remained in Greece were forced to leave and seek their fortunes elsewhere.

children to afford Mickiewicz some peace and quiet. In June, the French Ministry of Education had renewed his sabbatical at the Collège de France, which meant that, as before, he continued to split the salary—5,000 francs—with his replacement. Count Branicki's donation to the legion permitted the family to at least devote that meager income to their own needs; a gift from Celina's sister Helena in St. Petersburg augmented it somewhat. Despite repeated entreaties on the part of both Celina and Mickiewicz, Łubieńska continued to postpone Maria's trip back to Paris ("she helps me out at home," she explained, "as if she were my beloved daughter"). At one point Celina was even ready to travel to Poznań herself to retrieve her, but was denied a passport. It was not until October that Maria, "kissed and blessed" by her uncle Franciszek, finally made it back to Paris. Presumably she brought back the "piece of Polish bread and... oat flakes and mushrooms" that her mother had requested, items apparently impossible to obtain in Paris. She also, no doubt, had a generous gift to pass on to her father.[74]

As 1848 was drawing to a close, Mickiewicz received an unexpected letter from the painter Wojciech Stattler, in whose company the poet used to while away evenings in smoke and conversation near the Spanish Steps in Rome twenty years earlier. Now professor at the School of Fine Arts in Cracow, Stattler "had been asked to inquire whether [his old friend] might want to assume the chair of the History of Polish Literature" at the Jagiellonian University. Mickiewicz responded immediately in the affirmative, with the caveat, however, that the conditions for accepting the position would not contain anything that might "offend [his] Christian or civic conscience." Having just spent several months organizing a legion to fight Cracow's Habsburg rulers, this should have been the least of Mickiewicz's concerns. Not surprisingly, nothing came of the proposal. Nor, for that matter, did anything come of his request to resume his teaching duties at the Collège; the ministry opted for retaining the status quo. In any case, both issues proved moot.[75]

That same winter, just as Mickiewicz was disengaging himself from both the Towianist experiment in spiritual living and his own experiment in warfare on this earth, an event occurred that gave him impetus for a project he had been contemplating for some time, one more suited to his abilities than playing at military commander or lecturing at a university, to say nothing of rehabilitating emotionally damaged brethren.

On 10 December 1848, Prince Louis-Napoleon Bonaparte, nephew of the great emperor, was elected president of the French Republic with some 75 percent of the vote. Having failed twice earlier to return the Bonaparte family to power by force of arms, the man his mother, Princess Hortense, described as "gently stubborn" succeeded in gaining an overwhelming mandate not so much on the strength of his ostensibly liberal views, as on the magic of his name. Two decades earlier, upon meeting the young prince, Mickiewicz had insisted to his flattered mother "that the star in which Napoleon had believed had not gone out forever." Now, what he had been awaiting—indeed, predicting and expecting—for so many years had finally come to pass: a Bonaparte was again leading the most progressive nation in Europe. Mickiewicz celebrated with a "half bottle of wine" as well as frequent strolls around the column in the Place Vendôme, remarking to anyone who would listen, "Well? Didn't I tell you there'd be a Napoleon?" Four weeks later, he joined a delegation of Polish émigrés to wish the new president success and remind him as much of his responsibilities toward "the Great Nation" as of his ineluctable destiny: "May the sprit of the hero whose name you bear guide You and assist You with its inspiration." Louis-Napoleon's busy schedule prevented Mickiewicz from explaining the hidden meaning of those words in person. Nonetheless, his election that winter made the project the poet had been contemplating especially timely. And once again, Branicki's money made it possible.[76]

Like his eventual backer, Mickiewicz was acutely aware that amid the welter of periodicals of every ideological stripe being published in Paris at the time—from *La Gazette de France*, *Le Journal des Débats*, and *La Presse* to *La Démocratie Pacifique*, *La République*, and *La Populaire*—the situation in Europe demanded a paper with a genuinely internationalist perspective, one that would transcend party politics in order to advance the struggle of the oppressed peoples of Europe. He imagined a periodical in French whose task would be to focus the attention of the new president and the nation chosen by God to consummate his uncle's mission on the fate of all those who "sympathize with everything that is genuinely progressive in the French revolution and genuinely heroic in the Napoleonic age."[77]

Although Mickiewicz had made inquiries about the costs of such an undertaking as early as August, it was not until mid-February 1849 that he finally convinced Branicki to make a commitment—"70,000 francs" by one account, "300,000" by another. (The Russian chargé d'affairs reported at the time that Czartoryski too had some hand in the venture.) With funding now a certainty, Mickiewicz immediately set about realizing his project, guided, to some extent, by his experiences with *Pielgrzym Polski* nearly twenty years earlier. He paid the 24,000 francs that the government required as a security deposit for starting a new publication ("These days," Lamennais observed bitterly, "one needs money, much money, in order to enjoy the freedom to speak") and found a space for the editorial offices on rue Neuve-des-Bons-Enfants 7, steps away from the Palais Royale. These were soon outfitted "with large tables, covered with cloth, and small, slanted writing desks." It was decided that the paper would be a morning paper (later there would be an evening edition as well), appearing seven days a week in large, four-page format, with an annual subscription rate for Paris of 24 francs. Aside from regular front-page pieces devoted to commentaries on what its editors felt were the most important issues of the day, it would also feature news from abroad, a daily recap of political events in France, and, in recognition of the need for drawing a readership, also theater and art reviews, a feuilleton, stock quotes (despite Mickiewicz's loathing for the Bourse), as well as advertisements. The title Mickiewicz chose for the paper was *La Tribune des Peuples*, a nod, perhaps, toward an earlier

Carbonari *Tribune*, but in any case evocative enough: no one would mistake it for anything other than a mouthpiece for progressive internationalism.[78]

Mickiewicz moved just as expeditiously in organizing an editorial staff and board of directors. Having put his daughter Maria to work writing out invitations, each signed with a hearty "*salut et fraternité*," and with his wife and a few musical friends providing entertainment in the evenings, the poet played host to a stream of visitors that February with a view toward determining the direction and make-up of the paper. Over the course of a few weeks, amid smoke so thick that Maria "was forced to wait several minutes at the door before making out what was happening in that cloud," an editorial staff took shape, although not without interference on the part of the paper's benefactor. With himself as editor-in-chief, at a salary of 300 francs a month, Mickiewicz took on the French journalist, and fellow Bonapartist, Eugène Carpentier to serve as managing editor and as secretary the radical Polish writer Edmund Chojecki, who was soon succeeded in this position by another French journalist, Auguste Lacaussade, at a salary of 150 francs. Administrative matters were to be handled by Ksawery Godebski, son of a prominent Polish poet and himself a writer of comedies, who, together with Mickiewicz and, apparently, two or three other prominent Polish émigrés (all with connections to the Hôtel Lambert), also sat on the paper's board of directors.[79]

The remainder of *La Tribune*'s editorial staff, its more or less regular contributors, was as international as the newspaper's profile, and, if overwhelmingly progressive, nonetheless as ideologically pied: French leftists, utopian socialists, and a French feminist (Jean Julvécourt, Jules Lechevalier, Hippolyte Castille, Ange Pechméja, Charles Martin, Pauline Roland) shared the same pages with a German communist (Hermann Everbeck) and Belgian socialist (Hippolyte Colins); Italian republicans (Luigi Frapolli, Giuseppe Ricciardi) and Russian radicals (Ivan Golovin, Nikolai Sazonov) with Polish democrats (Franciszek Grzymała, Leopold Sawaszkiewicz) and a Proudhonist (Chojecki); Romanian revolutionaries (Nicolae Bălescu, Ştefan Golescu) with their Croatian counterparts (Andrija Brilić, Stefan Hrkalović). In addition, the *Tribune* published articles by special correspondents from all over Europe. At one point, the editors of the paper claimed that it "provided for . . . sixty families" (TP (f), 1 September 1849), although surely rather meagerly—"the newspaper [was] not rich."[80]

Surprisingly, this ideological olio in itself was not the cause of tensions in the paper's offices, reflecting as it did the editor-in-chief's own syncretism in this regard. Where disagreements did arise, and this from the very beginning, was on the one issue that also distinguished *La Tribune* from other progressive Paris papers of the day, namely, its editor-in-chief's stance toward Louis-Napoleon.

With the preparatory work for the paper behind them, Edmond Chojecki invited the *Tribune*'s collaborators and friends to an inaugural supper at his home on 23 February. As Aleksandr Herzen, the émigré Russian radical who the poet hoped would collaborate in his enterprise, recalled years later, Mickiewicz seemed withdrawn and distracted that evening, reacting to the "obsequiousness" and "reverence" some of his countrymen manifested toward him with a "*laisser aller*" that Herzen found distasteful. Like others who described the poet in those days, he was struck by a "face weary... with misfortune,... inner pain, and the exaltation of bitterness." When the mostly foreign guests—"from Sicily to Croatia"—finished eating, the host raised a toast to the first anniversary of the revolution, whereupon Mickiewicz rose to say a few words. In a speech so "deft," as Herzen put it, "that Barbès and Louis-Napoleon both could have applauded," the Polish poet declared

> that democracy today is assembling in a new, open camp, headed by France, that *once again* France will rush to liberate all oppressed peoples under the same eagles, the same banners at the sight of which all tsars and governments once paled, and that once again they'll be led by one of the members of that dynasty, crowned by the people, which Providence appointed to lead the revolution on the righteous path of authority and victory.

The words of the new paper's editor-in-chief were met with embarrassed silence. When another guest—a Spaniard—rose to voice his protest, denouncing all tyrannies be they "royal or imperial, Bourbon or Bonapartist," Mickiewicz tried to explain himself, but unconvincingly. An auspicious beginning to the venture this was not. Herzen declined to participate; a few weeks later Chojecki resigned, followed shortly by the Russian Ivan Golovin, who published an open letter in another leftist newspaper criticizing Mickiewicz's stance toward Louis-Napoleon. Mickiewicz, for his part, tacked up a sign in *La Tribune*'s office enjoining employees "from inveighing [...] against the head of state."[81]

On the morning of 15 March 1849, the first issue of *La Tribune des Peuples*, print run unknown, appeared in the cafés and reading rooms of Paris. The programmatic lead article, written by Mickiewicz and, like the remainder of his contributions to the paper over the next 130 issues, unsigned, left no doubt as to the direction of the periodical. Insisting that the "cause of peoples throughout the world" is the "only true cause of France itself," *La Tribune des Peuples* viewed its main task as informing the French public about foreign affairs and thus advancing a "sincere and by the same token completely new relationship between France, which is striving to build its future, and Europe, which is toiling to liberate itself from its past." "As people of the February Revolution," and "in solidarity with the Great Revolution as far as ideals were concerned and with the Napoleonic age with regard to their realization," the paper committed itself to the republic, "heir to Christianity" and the embodiment of France's spirit. Acknowledging "the Christian principle in politics," foreign as well as domestic, it vowed to "always be on the side of those who, faithful to the progressive instinct of the masses, are working toward building a social system corresponding to the new needs of the people" ("Our

Program"; Dz. 13:18–20/TP, 55–58). Two weeks later, above the lead article there appeared for the first time what would henceforth serve as *La Tribune*'s motto, taken from a resolution passed by the National Assembly a year earlier: "Fraternal alliance with Germany; the liberation of Italy; the restoration of a free and independent Poland" (TP (f), 29 March 1849).

Over the course of the next two months, Mickiewicz contributed some sixty pieces to the paper, most of them lead articles, all of them anonymous. They ranged over a wide array of issues, domestic as well as foreign, analytic as well as topical, but always with a view toward explaining their implications for the liberation struggles of Europe: from analyses of the situation in Italy, vigorously championing republicanism against its aristocratic and ecclesiastical foes, to observations on the relationship of political developments in Germany and France; from his own take on the meaning of socialism and the institution of a free press to commentaries on French politics, foreign policy, and political rhetoric in which he invariably singled out a resurgent Orléanism as the single greatest danger to France and, hence, to Europe. And although Mickiewicz avoided touching on the Polish question often or in any great detail, he did devote a number of articles to explicating to his French readers what he understood as the true nature of Russian imperial policies. Here he appears to have had direct access to well-placed diplomatic sources (probably the salon of his old friend Anastaziia Khliustin de Circourt), just as in his discussion of events in Italy he could draw on personal experiences as well as up-to-date information from his correspondents in the legion.*

In this, just as in his work for *Pielgrzym Polski* or in his lectures at the Collège, Mickiewicz proved particularly sensitive to hidden analogies and unexpected connections, often focusing on seemingly minor or otherwise unremarkable developments as ostensible symptoms of some larger malaise. Yet if in this respect his quickness to (over)generalize the particular and reach conclusions that sometimes stretched the evidence may have been the mark of a good journalist of his (or any other) age, it was no less a function of the paranoia intrinsic to his millenarian perception of the world. Whether the subject was socialism or Orléanism, Mazzini's republicanism or the pope's fear of it, Russia's plans for intervening on behalf of Austria or France's unwillingness to do so on behalf of Italy—everything was but a refraction of a fundamental spiritual struggle between, on the one side, the forces of the old world and the status quo, of reaction, egotism, and self-interest, dynasts, Orléanists, the Vatican, the Italian as well as Polish aristocracy, tsar and emperor, "organized for a long time already into something resembling... a secret society [that] has to this day not ceased operating in all corners of Europe according to a plan cunningly framed by their mysterious leaders" ("Germany Explained by France";

*In addition, the issues from 19 and 20 March and 8 and 16 April contained Mickiewicz's translation of Emerson's "Man the Reformer" (L'homme religieux réformateur"; TP, 348–86).

Dz. 12:62/TP, 107); and, on the other, the people, "the worker and soldier" ("Bonapartism and the Napoleonic Ideal"; Dz. 12:104/TP, 149), those "who fight for independence or for the extension of their freedoms" ("[The recent revolutions . . .]"; Dz. 12:107/TP, 151), those "who plow the earth, forge steel, weave linen and silk"—those who, in their collective wisdom, on 10 December cast their vote overwhelmingly for "the name that signified: A FREE EUROPE! Louis-Napoleon Bonaparte" ("Orleanism"; Dz. 12:176/TP, 215). Mickiewicz's political program, if one can call it that, was nothing less, nor more, than an articulation of a revolutionist imagination, a product of affect rather than political reasoning, an arational, intuitive politics of one. As he himself admitted a few years later, he was a socialist insofar as he "sympathized with the February Revolution and the cause of progress, without being connected to any . . . party," while at the same time "seeing in the February Revolution only a vehicle for achieving the Napoleonic ideal."[82]

La Tribune did not go unnoticed by its competition. Even the right-wing *Gazette de France* was willing to give it a chance, and papers on both right and left occasionally cited it as a source, particularly on matters dealing with Russia. At one point, a bomb went off outside its editorial offices, and in April there were rumors that the government was considering deporting the foreigners on its staff. Yet the paper's singular mix of leftist critique and Napoleonism probably bemused more than upset. This changed dramatically, however, after the May 1849 elections, which sharply polarized the National Assembly between a rightist majority and a leftist minority, but perhaps even more critically for the internationalist editors of *La Tribune*, after the French government's refusal to oppose Tsar Nicholas's intention to intervene in Hungary on Austria's behalf. In a lead article of 23 May entitled "The Enemy," *La Tribune* in effect equated the French president with the Russian tsar and openly criticized him for betraying both his name and the republic. As usual, the article (by Jules Lechevalier) was unsigned, but it signaled a rejection on the part of most of the paper's editorial staff of their chief's indulgent treatment of Louis-Napoleon. Mickiewicz, it seems, did not resist, opting, instead, for silence. Although he continued to occupy his position as editor-in-chief, he appears to have been unwilling to take part personally in the paper's increasingly strident attacks on the president and his government. In any case, sometime around 7 June, Mickiewicz became "very ill" and for "several days" was unable to come to work. It just so happened that that week proved fateful for the paper.[83]

On 7 June, it finally became obvious that the expeditionary force Louis-Napoleon had sent to Italy in late April under the pretext of denying Austria greater influence on the peninsula had in fact been directed to crush the Republic of Rome—a cause that Mickiewicz had been espousing from the very inception of *La Tribune* and for which the remnants of his legion were in fact now fighting. The leftist opposition called for the president's impeachment—and then for his overthrow. On 13 June, apparently without its editor's knowledge, *La Tribune* joined the opposition as well as other progressive papers in urging "all the People to rise" (TP (f), 13 June 1849). This time, though, they did not. The demonstrations organized by the left received no support from the heretofore reliable elements of the disaffected—which did not prevent the National Assembly from declaring a state of emergency. *La Tribune* shared the fate of other left-wing papers that night. Its offices were raided, its managing editor and two other employees arrested, and its "doors sealed" (TP (f), 1 September 1849). Some of the staff fled Paris. Its editor-in-chief was forced to go into hiding.

For the next three weeks Mickiewicz disappeared from view, "far from the persecutions and anxieties that ensued," but also that much more secure from the cholera that happened to be ravaging the city. Most of that time he spent on the Left Bank, hunkering down in the apartment of the lawyer Antoine Dessus, one of the many young French admirers he had inspired at the Collège de France. There was a restaurant downstairs on the rue de l'Ancienne Comédie where he could order meals, and in the evenings he got out for strolls, keeping to streets less traveled. Some of those strolls took him as far as Nanterre, where, "so it was rumored, Ksawera Deybel . . . gave birth" that spring to his child.[84]

By the end of July, the situation had eased somewhat, and Mickiewicz felt secure enough to return home, although on occasion he found it prudent to stay at the Oliviers on Place des Vosges. Since the government decided not to press any charges against the paper, he was determined to resume publishing as soon as possible. Nonetheless, like other émigrés, he continued to "remain in the shade." The clamp-down had served to bring to the surface resentments against a community of foreigners who, particularly now, after the tumult of 1848, seemed only to confirm the view of them as troublemakers, bent on fomenting unrest both at home and abroad. In this respect, the lifting of the state of siege in mid-August had absolutely no effect on their predicament. This was brought home to Mickiewicz in no uncertain terms when, just as he began going about the task of restarting *La Tribune* that August, he was warned by the police that any involvement with the paper would result in deportation. For whatever reason, though, Mickiewicz chose to ignore the warning, "intent on doing what [he] must, come what may." As Celina observed, "We are ready to bivouac if that should be [God's] will." Just in case, the poet applied for—and received, few questions asked—a passport from the Canton of Vaud, the one place he thought that he and his family would always be welcome.[85]

With Branicki agreeing, albeit reluctantly this time, to continue funding the venture, Mickiewicz managed to reconstitute *La Tribune* largely unchanged, although a few of his regular collaborators chose to remain abroad. He hoped, however, to bring new correspondents on board, to which end he invited Margaret Fuller to contribute from Italy, "if only with copies of [articles she wrote] for American papers." Despite the radical profile of *La Tribune*, Fuller did not accept the proposition, and in any case the paper soon ceased publication. Nine months later, in the summer of 1850, Fuller, together with her husband and child, perished in a shipwreck off the coast of Long Island.[86]

After a few weeks of "internal and external housekeeping," on 1 September 1849, *La Tribune* began appearing again. It led with an article (anonymous, as usual, but written by Mickiewicz) explaining the circumstances of the paper's closure two months earlier and at the same time disavowing any intent on the part of its editors to foment unrest. On the contrary, it went on, domestic unrest could only be to the advantage of the enemies of freedom, who would see France weak in order to press their nefarious claims on Europe. "Affairs that are persistently referred to as foreign are, for France, domestic"; conversely, "ideas hatched in Paris" have shaken all of Europe. "This antagonism between terrestrial powers abroad and the intellectual activity of France," the article concluded, ostensibly restating *La Tribune*'s program of 15 March,

> can be resolved only by awakening throughout the affect that created and inspired all Christian nations, by awakening Christian affect, by resurrecting the Christian idea and its actual application to the laws governing secular society and material affairs. ("*La Tribune des Peuples* Shares the Fate of the Cause Which It Has Vowed to Defend"; Dz. 12:207/TP, 260)[87]

Yet before Mickiewicz could get comfortable again in the editorial offices, he received another visit from the police, reminding him of their earlier warning. The poet relented, but only to the extent that he stopped coming to work. For the next month, with "the government continually threatening... to deport [him] from France," he performed his duties from home, having friends copy his articles and then deliver them to the paper, where they were edited appropriately in order to throw off police spies. In any case, the twenty or so pieces he managed to contribute over the course of the next few weeks were more restrained now in view of new laws on censorship passed earlier that summer, and at the same time unmistakably elegiac, reflecting the defeats of the revolutions and liberation struggles of the previous year. Nevertheless, Mickiewicz continued to express his belief in the eventual triumph of "the affect of nationality," which he now conflated with republicanism and progress in general ("[The peoples' armies...]"; Dz. 12:210–11/TP, 262–63), and in France's leading role in this regard, which even more than before he associated with the Napoleonic tradition. The emperor, after all, had "grasped the [democratic] spirit of France..., that spirit of expansion which will always attempt to project itself onto Europe despite the official egotism of its governments" ("[The pioneering mission...]"; Dz. 12:225/11 September 1849, TP (f)).[88]

By the end of September, however, Mickiewicz's position was becoming untenable, as was that of all the Poles involved with *La Tribune*; they too had had visits from the police. Threatened with deportation, Branicki pulled his funding. Although this in itself did not seal the fate of the paper, the constant harassment finally forced Mickiewicz and his compatriots on the board of directors to submit to what was by now the inevitable.

On 15 October, the 134th issue of *La Tribune* led with a declaration from its Polish directors "collectively announcing their resignation":

> Unexpected misfortunes . . . befell, by turn, all nationalities whose cause *La Tribune des Peuples* continued to defend. Through its policies, the French government declared itself on the side of the system hostile to this cause. The predicament of foreigners who found refuge in France worsened: drastic measures were taken against many people interested in the newspaper. . . . From the moment [Poles] are denied the right to struggle against the heavens on behalf of their cause, it is their responsibility to retreat from battle. ("Declaration of the Directors of *La Tribune des Peuples*"; *Dz.* 12:291–92/*TP*, 331–32)

For the first time, and the last, the name of Adam Mickiewicz appeared in *La Tribune*, together with that of one of his Polish colleagues. The editors that remained, now exclusively French, vowed to continue the paper and its mission. Yet without funds and unable to survive solely on subscriptions, they were finally forced to discontinue, publishing the final issue on 10 November 1849. Like so many periodicals born of the idealism and revolutionary hopes of 1848, *La Tribune des Peuples* disappeared into the reactionary night that followed.

CHAPTER TWELVE

HIBERNATION (1849–1855)

On the eve of the declaration announcing his resignation from the editorial board of *La Tribune des Peuples,* Mickiewicz decided to break his six-year, Towiański-induced silence to Ignacy Domeyko. "We write to you in difficult times," he confided to his friend in Chile,

> from amidst fog and storm. God's disfavor continues to hang over us and our Fatherland.... The eruption in France that we had foreseen and predicted has ended, plunging the world again into darkness. The emigration is paying dearly for the pride and impudence with which it made such a fuss here.... The fall of the Hungarian cause... ended the moral being of the emigration. Many are accepting amnesty or seeking it, some are leaving for America. I'm hanging on here in Paris so far, but I don't know for how long. The regime is threatening me as well. Everything around me far and wide has either died out or broken with me....
>
> In the emigration, or rather in what's left of it, the material poverty is grim. It haunts us constantly as well, and sometimes makes itself felt. So far, however, we've had a place to live and bread and something to pay with, hence so far we belong to the fortunate.

Amid the unrelenting gloom, Mickiewicz nonetheless found some room for hope. "Truth will not perish," he consoled himself, "and whatever good still remains in our souls will see its moment of rebirth." For the moment, though, there was little to do but go on "living and enduring"—"no small thing in times like these."[1]

I

As Maria Mickiewicz recalled years later, the weeks immediately after her father's resignation from *La Tribune* were particularly difficult. Although the poet continued to receive his half salary from the Collège, he had refused Branicki's offer to pay for the three months the paper had been suspended. At one point, the Mickiewiczes were apparently forced to pawn "all the valuables in the house, one after another." But thanks in part to the occasional gift—from Łubieńska, from Celina's sister in St. Petersburg, and even from some of Mickiewicz's Russian friends in Moscow, who, having heard that he "was living in great penury in Batignolles," managed to pass on five thousand rubles—their situation soon stabilized, enough, at least, for "the more expensive items to make their way back home again." As Celina put it to her sister at the beginning of 1850, they may not have had much, "but [they] were grateful to God even for this," considering the woeful predicament of many of their fellow émigrés.[2]

Of far greater concern to the Mickiewiczes was the increasing precariousness of their status in France. Between the poet's efforts on behalf of republican Italy and his collaboration with French radicals, to say nothing of his ethnic profile, the poet found himself now under constant suspicion from a regime that was growing more repressive with every day. (Denunciations from hostile émigrés accusing the poet of Russian sympathies certainly did not help matters.) Arrest and deportation were a very real possibility, as almost all of the Polish democrats in France quickly learned. Yet despite the choice his recently acquired Swiss passport afforded, Mickiewicz refused to follow the example of those who, sharing his predicament, opted for voluntary exile. He chose to remain, hoping to ride out the reactionary tide by lying low, ready to accept his fate, should it worsen, with Christian resignation. After all, as he wrote to Łubieńska, "the loser is *always guilty*. If things don't work out for us, we should first inquire to what extent we ourselves are the cause and only then consider the external circumstances."[3]

After the whirlwind of events of the preceding two years, Mickiewicz's life now settled into a predictable and narrowly circumscribed flow. Each week now had its set routine. One evening a week was invariably reserved for dinner at Vera Khliustin's, his old Russian friend from Rome and Władysław's godmother. Another was devoted to private concerts either at the Mickiewiczes', the Quinets', or at the home of Alfred Dumesnil, Michelet's son-in-law and an ardent admirer of the poet from his days at the Collège: Adelle Dumesnil would sing, Alfred Dessus, the poet's friend from *La Tribune*, played the violin, Celina the piano, and guest performers were always welcome to demonstrate their virtuosity with pieces by Haydn, Beethoven, Chopin, Henselt, and Mickiewicz's beloved Mozart. On several occasions, old friends passed through Paris—Sobolevskii, Prince Viazemskii, Karolina Sobańska—to remind him of happier days, when the future still teemed with a myriad of unexplored possibilities.

But these were just brief moments of diversion in what was otherwise an "existence" to be "endured." Celina's health—her heart, her lungs—was beginning to deteriorate; on top of this, by the spring of 1850, at the age of thirty-eight, she was pregnant again. Aside from the musical soirées, she "never went out," although doctors counseled her to take a rest by the sea. Mickiewicz, too, rarely visited, preferring to receive guests in his "rather roomy" second-floor study in the house on rue de la Santé, where he found himself playing host with increasing frequency to visitors from Poland eager to meet the illustrious poet-prophet or, as the case may be, notorious heretic and revolutionary. Dressed in his "favorite green capote" and holding a "long Turkish pipe in his hand" while "a pair of his youngest children rolled around on the ground at his feet," Mickiewicz accommodated the celebrity seekers, aspiring poets, and pilgrims with remarkable equanimity, providing them with plenty of tidbits for subsequent reminiscences and, on occasion, an autographed memento. In any case, he was never at a loss for company. Towianists continued to drop by regularly, as did Michelet, the Oliviers, and Prince Czartoryski's close collaborator Karol Sienkiewicz. Someone was always up for a game of chess. And when silence descended on the sometimes gloomy household, Henryk Służalski, the family's imposing, mustachioed factotum, was always there to break it with tales and anecdotes that reminded Mickiewicz of Old Polish raconteurs as distant now in time as they were of place.[4]

It was during these early months of 1850 too that Mickiewicz developed a close relationship with Armand Lévy, a French socialist journalist of partially Jewish origins whose stenographic skills soon earned him a position as the poet's amanuensis.* Almost thirty years Mickiewicz's junior, Lévy considered the charismatic ex-professor the "greatest of all the famous men" he had met, one whose ineluctably "powerful faith" strengthened not only his own dedication to the struggle for the rights of the oppressed but also his Jewish identity. The Mickiewiczes, for their part, were no less taken by this spirited, idealistic young man, whom they were soon treating like one of the family, a relationship Lévy would try to cement two years later by proposing—without success—to Maria. Until the end of his life he would remain devoted to the Mickiewiczes and to the memory of the man whose acquaintance he deemed to be "one of the greatest, most fortunate events of [his] life."[5]

2

In the first days of June 1850, the Mickiewiczes welcomed a new guest in their home in Batignolles. Thirteen years younger than her half-sister Celina, Zofia Szymanowska came

*At one point early in their relationship, Mickiewicz observed to Lévy that it was a good idea "to write down thoughts that came from inspiration; often later one can't retrieve them in their living form" (Armand Lévy, "Rozmowy z Mickiewiczem," *Rozmowy*, 388). Lévy took this advice very much to heart, producing in time a scrupulous record of his conversations with the poet, the most extensive of its kind.

to Paris at once to escape the stifling atmosphere of occupied Warsaw and to pursue a career as a painter. Moody, melancholic, but also headstrong and energetic, she had been warned that the house on rue de la Santé, possessed as it was by "the strange, inexplicable essence of Towianism," might not be the best place for nurturing her talents. And indeed, on entering the Mickiewiczes' home, the twenty-five-year-old Szymanowska "was struck by a sense of general disorder, neglect, a sense of disarray." Closer inspection did nothing to dispel first impressions. "Mrs. Mickiewicz," she wrote four years later in a memoir of her life with her half-sister's family,* "carried on her entire person . . . traces of neglect and dejection, [. . .] as if her mind remained unsound from that memorable illness." The master of the house she found intimidating, his glance so inquisitively piercing as to make her uncomfortable. Nonetheless, the genuine affection with which Celina welcomed her to Paris soon won Szymanowska over, and so too, with time, did the poet's "wisdom, goodness, and profound empathy." As Celina's belly grew that year, Szymanowska found herself becoming an increasingly indispensable member of the household, "a creature," as Celina put it, "at once pleasant and kind and full of devotion, who underst[oo]d [the Mickiewiczes'] predicament."[6]

There were, nonetheless, aspects of the Mickiewicz household that Szymanowska found difficult to accept. As her half-sister was showing her around the house, Szymanowska caught sight of "a woman standing in the vestibule with a child in her arms," her gaze so "penetrating" that she "felt something akin to anxiety mixed with repugnance toward this woman." Celina introduced the woman as Ksawera Deybel, "a friend of the household," where she seemed to "occupy some sort of special and unspoken position." Deybel was by then the mother of two daughters, both born out of wedlock: Claire, the older of the two and presumably the offspring of her Towianist lover Seweryn Pilchowski; and Andrée, "the child sired by Adam" in 1849.[7]

Good Towianist that she was, Deybel lost no time in drawing Szymanowska into "conversations and dialogues" about the Cause. In the process, she also revealed, as Szymanowska's future husband would later put it, all the "dirt and filth of the Towianists' roguery" and, inevitably, all kinds of "scandalous things . . . about Adam's home." Szymanowska felt repelled by the whole arrangement: the constant visits from "ragged émigrés who called Adam and Celina brother and sister," the incomprehensible babble of the Cause, the lack of order in the house, and the "complete neglect" of the children, who lived, as it were, in a state "of nature, but a nature that was somehow wild and murky."

*The fate of Szymanowska's memoir constitutes one of the more shameful episodes in the history of Mickiewicziana. Intent on brushing out anything that might cast a shadow on his father's reputation, Władysław Mickiewicz invested an almost desperate energy, as well as a good deal of money, into obtaining Szymanowska's text, which was, apparently, highly critical of the Mickiewiczes' way of life. Once he did, he destroyed it. Only a few pages survived. The history of the memoir is recounted by Żeleński, *Brązownicy*, 81–118; and Kossak, *Rodzina M.*, 326–37.

She "declared war" on the cult, with the hope of bringing a modicum of normality to the household, if only for the sake of the children. In this Szymanowska quickly found an ally in Maria, who of all of them "made a distinct but pleasant impression" on her, and at the same time earned the life-long enmity of Władysław.[8]

It was at Szymanowska's urging that the Mickiewiczes finally enrolled the boys in school that fall, at first in the Polish National School in Batignolles. When Władysław complained to her about being constantly teased about his parents' Towianist practices and refused to continue attending, it was at her behest that Celina suggested he be transferred to a proper French school. Had his father had his way, he would have sent him, together with his brothers, off to serve as apprentices, to engage in "practical work," as Mickiewicz put it, or, in Władysław's case, even to Domeyko in Chile. Celina, however, insisted, just as she now wanted to see her youngest daughter, Helena, study in a pension. Despite the financial burden all this entailed, twelve-year old Władysław was enrolled that same autumn in the prestigious Collège Sainte Barbe, thanks in part to the efforts of the ever obliging Michelet and the generosity of his godmother, Vera Khliustin. Two years later, the younger boys began attending a French *collège* as well.[9]

For the moment, there was not much Szymanowska could do about Ksawera, and in any case, she needed her help in caring for the pregnant and increasingly fragile Celina. It was Mickiewicz, then, rather than his sickly wife, who ended up spending a month on the Normandy coast that year. Not long after his return, on 20 December, their sixth and last child was born. Two weeks later, with Zofia Szymanowska and Mickiewicz's friend Karol Sienkiewicz standing as godparents and the proud father "looking already like a handsome old man," the boy was baptized Józef (in honor of the two Szymanowskas' father) Teofil (the day's patron saint) Rafał (the archangel). None of the names evoked the Master or the Cause.[10]

Unable to pay the eight months' rent in advance that their landlord on rue de la Santé requested, the Mickiewiczes moved again that February. Their choice of a new apartment on rue de l'Ouest, with its "front gate directly across from the Jardin du Luxembourg" and in close proximity not only to the Collège Sainte Barbe but also to the Michelets', Quinets', and Dumesnils', would indicate that they had decided—or that Szymanowska had succeeded in impressing on Celina—that it was time to distance themselves from the Towianist ghetto in Batignolles. Although the landlord's no children policy meant that they had to smuggle the younger ones in under cover of night, the Mickiewiczes quickly settled into their "comfortable and inexpensive" first-floor apartment on the Left Bank. In June, an evidently stronger Celina informed her sister that she was feeding little Józef, that Władysław was getting good marks at the Collège, that Helena was enrolled in a pension, that the two younger boys were going to school, and that Maria was "studying English, Italian, and making an effort at music, although without much enthusiasm." She "thanked God for Adam, the children, and [her] return to health."[11]

3

Ever since his resignation from the editorial board of *La Tribune*, Mickiewicz had been idle. Besides the musical evenings, conversations about politics, games of chess that sometimes continued into the following day, and the occasional visitor, he had little to occupy himself beyond his circle of family and friends. In March 1851, six years after his Towianist-induced tantrum, he began participating once again in the work of the History Section of Czartoryski's Literary Society, which, as its secretary assured him, "never cease[d] considering [him] a member." He devoted himself with particular energy to what at the moment was the society's most pressing project, namely, the acquisition of a building to house its library. Thanks in part to his fundraising efforts as well as his success in securing the qualified support of Władysław Zamoyski, the society eventually bought a building at quai d'Orléans 6, where it resides to this day.*[12]

Yet aside from helping edit appeals and invitations for the section, and aside from correspondence, Mickiewicz wrote little, if anything. After all, as he repeated on so many occasions since completing *Pan Tadeusz*, the time for writing had passed, that, like his beloved Byron, one must instead "*make poetry!*" Nonetheless, his contention that "were [he] able, [he] would withdraw three quarters of [his] works from circulation" notwithstanding, Mickiewicz was not at all averse to entertaining offers to republish them in new editions, if only in the hope of supplementing his meager income. His last major publication, a five-volume French edition of the entire four-year course at the Collège de France,** had proven to be a disappointment. As his long-time representative in these matters, Eustachy Januszkiewicz, informed him in March, "if sales continue to be as slow as they hitherto have been, another three years would be needed to cover" just the costs of printing. About this same time, though, Mickiewicz was approached by a publisher in Wrocław who offered him 12,000 francs, in twelve annual installments, for a two-volume edition of his works. Januszkiewicz, for his part, succeeded in negotiating a deal with a publisher in Berlin whereby Mickiewicz would receive 3,000 francs in three installments for a complete edition of his works, with an additional 6,000 francs in three installments for the rights to a sequel to *Pan Tadeusz*. Nothing came of either venture (aside from an advance of 1,000 francs)—nor of the sequel. Although Mickiewicz warmed up to the idea for a while and seems to have even begun scribbling something, he "wasn't happy with what [he] wrote." Short on "inspiration" and, as he explained,

*Thanks to his son Władysław, the Bibliothèque Polonaise now also houses the Mickiewicz Museum, the largest repository of Mickiewicziana, including the sixty Roman coins that the poet, a passionate numismatist since his days as Lelewel's student, at one point donated to the society from his own extensive collection.

***Les Slaves. Cours professé au Collège de France par Adam Mickiewicz et publié d'auprès les notes sténographiées*, 5 vols. (Paris: Comptoir des imprimeurs-unis, 1849).

"unable to write on commission," he was forced to admit "that the time for creative writing was over for him."[13]

That July, with little else to do and at about the same time that Szymanowska moved in with the family on rue de l'Ouest, Mickiewicz decided to spend a few weeks in Fontainebleau, where his old friend Józef Bohdan Zaleski had been residing for years. Although Towianism had driven an increasingly deeper wedge between them, neither had allowed it to destroy their friendship irreparably; it was grounded too deeply in mutual affection and respect. During strolls about town and excursions to the forest around Fontainebleau in search of mushrooms, which invariably concluded over a beer or two at some café, they tried to catch up. After years of minimal contact, their conversations now ranged over everything, from religion, politics, and poetry to family and the lot of aging émigrés like themselves. Painfully aware that Mickiewicz had "neither money nor a change of linen" even, Zaleski insisted on inviting his friend home to dinner almost daily, where, "gay and talkative," he would regale his hosts and other guests with anecdotes about Old Poland, "interesting facts . . . about Frankists," "stories about his adventures in Rome and Milan," and seemingly sober thoughts about Towiański and his mission. Mickiewicz's one-month stay nevertheless proved somewhat awkward, at least for Zaleski. As he observed to Goszczyński after the visit, he found it difficult "to resurrect the old harmony that used to exist between [them]."[14]

Mickiewicz returned to Paris in late August, still shaken by news of the death of his Philomath friend Jan Czeczot, about which he learned from Zaleski only now, four years after the fact. But within a week of his return, he was off again, this time to Le Havre in the company of his oldest son. Łubieńska, it seems, had sent another "package," and in a letter to his daughter Maria, Mickiewicz requested that he be sent two hundred francs "without delay" so as to be able to remain by the sea for another month. After all, for the pleasure of swimming in the ocean and walking along the beach he was paying little: "five francs a day" for "breakfast, dinner, a bottle of wine, and lodging," which he split with Władysław.[15]

It was not until the beginning of October 1851, after what turned out to be, in effect, a two-month holiday, that Mickiewicz finally settled back in Paris, a bit under the weather, but nonetheless refreshed by his time away from a household that was evidently in a state of conflict. In her campaign to bring stability to the home, Szymanowska, it seems, had made "a nuisance of herself," disrupting time-worn habits and routines, antagonizing old acquaintances, and even pitting members of the family against each other. For Mickiewicz, her departure for Italy with Maria could not have come soon enough—nor, it would appear, for Maria, whom a traumatic childhood left particularly sensitive to domestic tumult. A few days after their departure on 30 October, Zaleski found Mickiewicz "in a wonderful mood," "healthy and happy" and the most gracious of hosts.[16]

4

Sometime near the end of November, Mickiewicz was struck by what he described as "an idea from on high": "The destiny of the Napoleons depends on the way they conceive of the Polish cause, and their destiny is tied to that of nations." On account of illness, he had been unable to proclaim this idea "on the 27th or the 28th of November" as "commanded." He nonetheless felt compelled to communicate it to Louis-Napoleon, if only now, in mid-December—after the fact.[17]

On the night of 1–2 December 1851, on the forty-seventh anniversary of his uncle's coronation as emperor, President Louis-Napoleon Bonaparte had staged a coup. For over two years, the president and the right-wing National Assembly had been engaged in an increasingly discordant minuet. Although perfectly content with most of the reactionary legislation enacted by the Assembly, Louis-Napoleon had also begun demanding greater authority for himself. Despite his coyness, it was evident that what he sought was the establishment of an imperial presidency, if not the reestablishment of a second Napoleonic empire. Key in this regard was a change in the constitution that would allow him to run for a second term in the upcoming elections, which, he argued, was the only way to guarantee continued stability. After much debate, the Assembly refused. As Mickiewicz remarked at the time, "If the president understood the full force of his name and his tradition, he would . . . throw these chatterers out the door"—which is exactly what Louis-Napoleon now did. Faced with the prospect of losing power, he seized it. Moving with remarkable efficiency, he dissolved the National Assembly, restored universal suffrage, and suspended the constitution. There was, of course, resistance both in Paris and in the provinces—several hundred died and another 26,000 were arrested—but nothing comparable to the events of 1848; in any case, it was precisely the threat of "anarchy" in the future that the coup was ostensibly meant to eliminate. Three weeks later, the French citizenry voted overwhelmingly to approve the coup, investing Louis-Napoleon with the powers of "legal dictatorship." The Bourse showed its approval by rising fourteen percent. In January, under a new constitution he had been empowered to frame, Louis-Napoleon was made president for ten years. Eleven months later he would be crowned emperor for life.[18]

For all his usual prescience, the coup came as something of a surprise to Mickiewicz, but by no means as something ominous. Unlike Michelet, who ran to the poet on the following day, "trembling with anger," or Quinet, who as a member of the opposition in the Assembly was forced to flee, or Lévy, whose republican speeches made him a persona non grata, Mickiewicz welcomed Louis-Napoleon's seizure of power. "What reasons should I have for feeling bad for the Assembly or the constitution?" he wrote to Łubieńska. "The people from whom government was finally wrested were at the helm earlier and showed who they really are." And in a letter he addressed to the president himself (whether he actually sent it is another matter) he declared that "at last the spirit of Napoleon had begun working through [him]," that through his actions the emperor's nephew had "smitten the selfish desire of the French soul to entertain itself with everything" and "dissipated that historical and philosophical smoke that had obscured the history of Christianity and Napoleon"; he even went so far as to praise the president for "ridding French books of the filthy vice with which France had infected the world." When informed that his name might be among those slated for deportation to Cayenne, Mickiewicz remained unmoved: "I will never stop seeing in what the chief of state is doing anything but the salvation of France and the beginnings of its rebirth."[19]

Indeed, the prospects that Louis-Napoleon's coup seemed to afford encouraged Mickiewicz to finally apply again for French citizenship. After all, a government headed by "the Emperor's heir" was the "only one to which a Pole could swear allegiance without ceasing to be faithful to his patriotic duties and honor." In a letter of 22 February 1852, he appealed to the president to approve his request for papers that would "allow [him] to enjoy the rights of a French citizen." The poet, however, overestimated the appeal of his Bonapartism for the Bonapartists actually in power, who at the moment were more concerned with eradicating any vestiges of the spirit of 1848 than with accommodating some Polish mystic obsessed with the figure of the emperor. "Mr. Mickiewicz," wrote the minister of police in one of a series of reports generated by the poet's request, "belongs to that exceptional category of refugees who habitually support numerous publications that are aimed at stoking disorder and propagating socialist doctrines among the working class." "I should add," he continued, "that Mr. Mickiewicz is the most dangerous of all Polish refugees because the resources of his spirit and imagination allow him to propagate, with great success, anarchist and subversive doctrines." It was inevitable, then, that his performance at the Collège de France would become an issue. As another report relayed, although "some Poles have noted that Mickiewicz often praised Emperor Napoleon [and hence] support[ed] the political ideas of the prince-president, the majority... relate[d] that the poet-professor... wanted to make fun of the emperor's name... by pronouncing him a Messiah of new ideas." That this is exactly how Louis-Napoleon himself referred to his uncle in his *Idées Napoléoniennes* seems to have gone unremarked.[20]

The upshot of Mickiewicz's request for naturalization was thus not only a refusal, which was to be expected, but also the unexpected decision to finally relieve him, together with Quinet and Michelet, of his position at the Collège, ostensibly for "not accommodating his lectures to the subject... of the course and in view of the fact that he had been on sabbatical for the past few years." In the stroke of an authoritarian pen, inspired in one part by a desire to rid the republic of seditious elements, in another by complaints from the Russian embassy, and in still another by denunciations from malicious Polish émigrés, Mickiewicz was deprived of his only regular source of livelihood—and this by the man whom he believed to be the blessed descendant of the great Napoleon, if not quite his reincarnation.[21]

Mickiewicz took this display of Louis-Napoleon's benevolence in humble stride. In a letter to the minister of education, he expressed gratitude "to the French Government for the numerous tokens of goodwill that [he] had received from it on various occasions" and his love for a nation "that [he] had served in all good conscience with the loyalty and devotion due to [it]" as Poland's "Sister-Fatherland." In any case, he wrote to Łubieńska, "there's the hope that with time this might all turn out for the better." Celina too accepted this new "trial" with equanimity. "We have the strength to bear it," she comforted her daughter in Rome, "since this is not the greatest of misfortunes that could befall a family as large as ours."[22]

Although the educational establishment, now firmly in the hands of reactionary Catholics, certainly approved of the president's decision, some of Mickiewicz's influential friends were outraged. Both King Jérôme and his son Napoleon (Plon-Plon), a Polonophilic liberal and great admirer of the poet, joined Hortense Cornu, a childhood friend of Louis-Napoleon who knew Mickiewicz from his first stay in Rome back in 1829, and the rector of the Collège Barthelémy Saint Hilaire in urging the president to at least restore the poet's salary until some new position could be arranged. Louis-Napoleon relented, and at the end of June, Mickiewicz was informed that he would once again be receiving his half of the salary from the Ministry of Education. Four months later, thanks to the efforts of his influential friends, he was appointed librarian at the Bibliothèque de l'Arsenal. The irony was surely not lost on him.

5

Although Mickiewicz's "life outside the family [was] sometimes disrupted and threatened, at home it remain[ed] uneventful." Everyone was relatively healthy. "The children," he informed his brother Franciszek that summer, were "studying, some in school, some at home, and [were] growing." Maria was still in Italy with Szymanowska, where they were joined by Armand Lévy, who had fled Paris after the coup. For a time, Mickiewicz nursed plans for a trip to Switzerland, but this time was turned down for a passport. In mid-September, the Mickiewiczes were forced to move yet again on account of the owner's distaste for children. For 1,200 francs, they found "a large and comfortable first-floor apartment [on nearby rue Notre-Dame-des-Champs], with a large and beautiful garden" and "a nice room" for Szymanowska. It would appear that on this occasion Deybel did not join them—she was pregnant again, albeit this time not by the man of the house.[23]

In November 1852, just as the French citizenry was preparing to vote for the restoration of the empire, Mickiewicz began his new career as a librarian at the Bibliothèque de l'Arsenal. He was not unfamiliar with this unique institution, founded in 1757 as a repository for medieval manuscripts and prints, and where in 1831 he had visited its head librarian at the time, the poet and bibliophile Charles Nodier. The pay at the Bibliothèque was not, however, commensurate with its reputation: a miserable 166.65 francs a month, 158.32 after taxes. But what Mickiewicz lost in pay, he gained twice over with an apartment at the Arsenal that came with the position. His duties, as he himself described them, were "more tedious than strenuous"—some in the emigration, though, felt the position was "wretched and demeaning"—three days a week, from ten in the morning until four in the afternoon at the beck and call of users, and often enough as the object of curiosity on the part of "visitors to the Bibliothèque... hoping to catch a glimpse of him." Although at one point he complained to his son that he had been "buried among the dead," he nonetheless saw his new situation as "an omen of something more auspicious for the future."[24]

And so too did he view Louis-Napoleon's accession to the imperial throne that December. Mickiewicz was convinced that the new regime "would result in something good," would "force minds to seek a higher truth," while at the same time "checking the pride of individual people." Shortly after the coronation, as if the renewal of a Napoleonic empire had awoken the slumbering Towianist in him, he sketched a rambling memorandum to the emperor enjoining him to reject the "theories" of "legitimists, Orléanists, republicans, etc." and be instead "a man of deed," "an adventurer," like his uncle, like Caesar, like Alexander the Great; and, like the crusading Capets once did in Syria, to stand for liberty and justice by siding with the Polish cause for the sake of his own dynasty and of humanity itself.[25]

It probably came as no surprise to him, then, that a few weeks later, after three years of silence, he should receive a letter from Towiański, who was just as thrilled by a turn of events that promised a new opportunity for witnessing the Cause in France. It was a conciliatory letter, full of the mellifluously manipulative flattery the Master was so deft at mobilizing when he needed something from his erstwhile disciple:

> The memory of what you, beloved Brother, had done for God's Cause and for me, its servant, lives in me, as does the memory of your pure stirrings, which revealed your Christian as well as Polish essence, ... as does the memory that you, Brother, were the first to take to heart and with conviction ... believe in God's Cause and in my mission, ... that ... through your example you roused many to accept your vision, your way and sacrifice."

Mickiewicz responded graciously and, one might say, even with a sense of relief, apologizing for his own protracted silence. He was also quick to guess what was on the Master's mind. "It appears to me," he responded,

> that everything is trending in the direction of compelling societies and those who rule them to approach the truths of the source that is within you.... The ease with which the word of truth may actively reveal itself is becoming clearer with every day.[26]

Over the course of the next year, Mickiewicz did what he could—more, perhaps, out of a sense of obligation toward the Master than conviction in the efficacy of his plans—to pave the way for the Man of God to bear witness before the scion of his spiritual forerunner. He prepared a "Memorandum in Defense of the Prophet Andrzej Towiański," which he succeeded in relaying to Napoleon III, and then, having apparently piqued the interest of the emperor's entourage, an abstract of Towiański's musings on Napoleon. But before anything could come of these efforts, events in the real world made them irrelevant. As Mickiewicz had once remarked to Zaleski, what had ultimately distanced him from Towiański was his realization that the Master had "lost track of time, i.e., he dream[t] and nothing more."[27]

6

The Mickiewiczes moved into the apartment at the Arsenal in April 1853. Deybel was no longer with them, having decided to finally throw in her lot with the father of her newest child, one Edmond Mainard, an aspiring functionary of the French police who, thanks to his beloved, had become something of a confidant of Mickiewicz.* In their new quarters on rue de Sully 1, the poet's family finally had "clean air" as well as a beautiful view across the Seine toward the Île Saint-Louis (and the Hôtel Lambert), the Pantheon, Les Invalides, and the botanical garden. Although the apartment was large, it was "badly laid out," its windows so low that Mickiewicz was forced to have them fitted with bars for fear his youngest children might fall out. He decorated his own room with "a beautiful etching depicting the archangel Michael after the original at the Capuchins in Rome or the Raphael in the Louvre," a reproduction of the icon of the Holy Mother of Ostrabrama in Vilnius, and "Domenichino's original drawing depicting the communion of St. Jerome." Nearby hung "a small etching of Napoleon I picturing him among his generals, and beneath this a daguerreotype of a graying man, standing upright in a frock-coat buttoned to the top, like one worn by French veterans"—Towiański in his rightful place on Mickiewicz's personal iconostasis.[28]

Besides his new responsibilities and the regular schedule they imposed, Mickiewicz's life changed little. As before, his world revolved around dinners at Vera Khliustin's, musical evenings, the same rather narrow circle of friends for chess and conversation. He was spending more time with the children now, helping Władysław with his Latin homework, taking them on frequent outings in the city. A savvy financial operation a few months earlier had improved the family's material situation to the tune of 3,000 francs—out of which

*Writing under the pseudonym Edmond Fontille, Mainard would go on to produce the first book-length biography of Mickiewicz in French, *Adam Mickiewicz, sa vie et sa croyance. Esquisse biographique, impressions et souvenirs* (Paris: Humbert, 1862). One must assume that, besides his own conversations with Mickiewicz, one of his primary sources of information about the poet and his views was his wife, Ksawera Deybel.

Fig. 27 Mickiewicz in 1853. Photograph by Michał Szweycer. Courtesy of the Adam Mickiewicz Museum of Literature, Warsaw.

Mickiewicz now began sending 100 regularly to the Towiańskis in Zurich, ostensibly as a gift for his godson Kazimierz. In addition to his work in the History Section, which in early 1854 officially merged with the Literary Society to form the Polish Historical-Literary Society, with Mickiewicz as its vice president, the poet was elected to the board of the Polish School in Batignolles, where too he served as vice president. Here as well he devoted most of his energy to fundraising, although he also helped shape aspects of the curriculum, sat in on examinations, and participated in commencement ceremonies. In March 1853, feeling secure and settled, he had applied for French citizenship once again—and once again, despite his explanations and the references he provided, despite the intervention of Prince Napoleon Bonaparte, his application was denied. The police concluded that Mickiewicz's "Napoleonic ideas" smelled too much of "doctrines and theories whose realization could be dangerous."[29]

That summer, with Maria back from nearly nineteen months in Italy, Mickiewicz took the family to Montgeron, a village southeast of Paris, about a third of the way by rail to Fontainebleau, where he rented inexpensive lodgings in a villa owned by an elderly French general. Although until the end of July he had to commute to work almost daily, which "left [him] little freedom," once his own vacation began he spent much time with the children, accompanying them on hikes to surrounding woods and lakes. They were joined that summer by Władysław's best friend from school, the son of Mehmet Ali's personal physician, whom the Mickiewiczes had come to treat as their "seventh child." The arrival in August of Julian Fontana, Chopin's musical executor and himself an internationally renowned pianist, kept the family continually supplied with music. As summer turned to fall and it came time for the boys to return to school, Mickiewicz decided to prolong his stay for another few weeks. Celina had gone back "to Paris in order to install Helena in a pension and prepare the home for winter." Some weeks earlier, she had fallen ill, but only briefly, hence no one paid it much mind, least of all Celina.[30]

7

Mickiewicz returned to Paris that fall to the sight of "new squares, houses, entire streets," with which Haussmann was transforming the city—and to the rumble of war. Tensions between Russia and France over an enfeebled Ottoman Empire had been flaring and subsiding at least since the dénouement of the Springtime of Peoples. An international crisis over Russian demands that Turkey hand over Polish legionnaires who had fled there after the events of 1848 had been narrowly averted. Shortly thereafter, though, what began as a dispute between Orthodox Russia and Catholic France over the guardianship of holy places in Ottoman Jerusalem slowly but intractably began to spiral out of control, fueled as much by Emperor Napoleon III's desire to legitimate his claims to his uncle's imperial legacy as by Emperor Nicholas I's own imperial designs on "the sick man of Europe."

Fig. 28 Prince Adam Czartoryski. After a drawing by an unknown artist, ca. 1850. Courtesy of the Adam Mickiewicz Museum of Literature, Warsaw.

Between shows of force and efforts at compromise, it was evident by the fall of 1853 that a confrontation involving not only Russia, Turkey, and France, but also Great Britain and Austria was imminent. The Concert of Europe, which for some four decades and through sundry crises had somehow managed to keep the competing interests of the Great Powers in check, was on the verge of collapsing. For the first time in years, the Polish emigration sensed an opening. As Mickiewicz had observed to Karolina Towiańska in March, "All around us in this great world things are getting more threatening and acute."[31]

Even before the outbreak of hostilities that November, the eighty-three-year-old Czartoryski had begun remobilizing his efforts to write Poland into any eventual equation that might emerge should the Great Powers go to war. In a stream of brochures and memoranda issuing from the Hôtel Lambert, as well as in private correspondence and through personal contacts, the prince and his agents tried to impress on the governments of France and Great Britain the need for confronting Russia forcefully and by the same token taking the Polish cause into account. At the same time, Czartoryski also turned directly to Turkey, hoping to negotiate with the Porte and its allies the creation of a Christian legion with Polish officers in charge. In this, however, the prince encountered competition from elements of the Polish left, who too had come to recognize in the looming international conflict an opportunity to advance the Polish cause on their own terms. Backed by Prince Napoleon, a potential candidate for the throne of a resurrected Poland, and financed by Ksawery Branicki, a group of dissident Democrats had constituted the so-called Polish Circle in Paris with the aim of footing a legion of their own. But just as they and Czartoryski were setting their respective plans into motion, a third actor was already establishing facts on the ground in Istanbul. Nominally an agent of Czartoryski, Michał Czajkowski, a Polish writer and veteran of 1830 and 1848, a figure as colorful as any in an age teeming with adventurers, had fled to Turkey after the defeat of the Hungarian revolution, where he converted to Islam in order to stave off deportation and thus continue serving the Polish cause. Now, as Sadik Mehmet Pasha, he received permission from the Porte to form a detachment of Ottoman Cossacks to be made up of deserters, prisoners of war, refugees from Russia, and volunteers from Slavic lands. As Józef Bohdan Zaleski observed for the benefit of the Resurrectionists that winter:

> The emigration [was] beginning to boil and bubble chaotically as of old. The apostate Mehmet Sadik is demanding that a scarlet banner be embroidered with St. Michael and a Crescent. . . . Some are setting off to Turkey to become Pashas, others, democratic [Cossack brigands]. . . . The Hôtel Lambert is organizing a dynastic government, and former big shots [from the Democratic Society], a government of the people. Old soldiers and the more hot-headed from among the young, impoverished, and bored, are heading East in droves in order to jump headlong into the fire of battle—at least their sacrifice is pure because it is disinterested.[32]

Amid the ideological antagonisms and personal animosities that from the start marked the émigrés' efforts, what each of these players needed was legitimacy for their respective enterprise, as much with the governments whose sponsorship they sought as with their fellow Poles, both abroad and at home. In this they turned instinctively to Mickiewicz, not by any means for his experience with organizing legions, but rather "for [his] blessing" and "Confirmation," as a figure whose moral authority remained unimpeachable precisely because it was ideologically androgynous.[33]

No sooner had the poet returned from Montgeron than he found himself enlisted in the thankless task of mediating between the Polish Circle and the Hôtel Lambert, the former in the persons of Generals Ludwik Mierosławski and Józef Wysocki, veterans of 1830, 1848, and various conspiracies in between, the latter in the person of his old rival Władysław Zamoyski. His efforts to reconcile the two camps proved as futile as they were high-minded. At a meeting of the two factions the poet managed to arrange that November in his apartment, Wysocki, much like Mickiewicz himself five years earlier in Rome, argued that any future legion should choose its own leader. Zamoyski, for his part, reprised his role as well, insisting that the leader should be one "whom Prince [Czartoryski] appointed in his role as the Nation's Chief and not some demagogic dietine." To this Mickiewicz responded:

> For there to be any form of government in Poland . . . there must be an uprising in Poland. In order for there to be an uprising, there must be at least one Polish regiment. There can be no regiment without a colonel. And seeing that you [Zamoyski] do not have one, you must accept one from the democrats. . . . There is no time for arguments, let everyone, rather, do what they can.

A few weeks later, with Mickiewicz's blessings, Wysocki left for Turkey to organize a legion on the democrats' terms. Zamoyski followed shortly thereafter, hoping to derail Wysocki's mission and at the same time use Czajkowski's influence in order to create a formation of his own—to do, in other words, what he could as well.[34]

From the start, Mickiewicz's sympathies lay with the democrats. Suspicious as always of Zamoyski's intentions, and of the "aristocratic camp" in general, he felt that at least Wysocki was ready to "cast off the influence of factions" and work for the "purely national cause." Yet when he was asked to join the Polish Circle's Finance Committee, he hesitated. For one, there was the question of potential repercussions for collaborating with radicals. Having not so long ago found himself on a list of those slated for deportation, Mickiewicz was "terribly scared of Cayenne"; "our cowardly poet," observed a participant in the events, insisted that he would serve only at the behest of Prince Napoleon himself. But even then he hesitated. He continued to believe that only a committee embracing all of the factions, transcending issues of "aristocracy or democracy" for the sake of "acting and cooperating on the path of concrete actions" made any sense. Anything else would be premature.[35]

By the end of April, though, as the Anglo-French alliance was preparing to go to war against Russia, the issue of the committee was becoming moot. It was growing increasingly clear that Wysocki would be returning from his mission to Istanbul with nothing to show for it and that, thanks to its influence and money and backing (the emperor had recognized Prince Czartoryski as the sole legitimate representative of the emigration), the Hôtel Lambert was emerging as the only player of consequence. Encouraged by Prince Napoleon as well as by emissaries from Prussian Poland, who were all eager to see a legion emerge under a unified command, the Circle agreed to make an effort to come to some sort of understanding with the Hôtel Lambert. Once again, Mickiewicz was persuaded to assume the role of mediator, despite his continuing reservations about the "aristocrats." But soon enough this too became moot. After initially demonstrating a degree of openness, Czartoryski reverted to conducting meetings on his own terms and only with those he felt "command[ed] the public trust." It wasn't long before the Polish Circle grew irrelevant, and the poet found his role as mediator transformed into that of the prince's indispensable enabler.[36]

8

Sometime in January 1854, as Maria was recovering from what was apparently a rather serious illness, Celina suffered a breakdown. Once more, Mickiewicz was compelled to have her institutionalized. In February, "the state of her health was still not normal." It was not until April that she finally recovered sufficiently to come home, just as Mickiewicz was immersing himself in émigré affairs, shuttling back and forth between the Polish Circle, Plon-Plon, and Czartoryski's people. As summer approached, "Mickiewicz and his entire family were feeling well"; he even invested in some stocks, for what would again be a tidy profit. By August, though, it was becoming increasingly evident that Celina was suffering from something more than mental illness—as Goszczyński understood it, a combination of "moral" illness and what apparently was cancer, affecting "now the head, now the breast, now the womb": "during her physical sufferings her moral state [was] . . . fine, but it change[d] for the worse when her sufferings ease[d]; she [would] then behave as if she [were] crazy."[37]

Mickiewicz at first "saw no danger and was full of hope for a speedy recovery," despite doctors' warnings that "the illness might last a while." He sent two of the children to the seashore for the summer in the care of one of Celina's friends and lodged two others in Montmorency with another. As for himself, he remained in Paris with his wife, together with Maria and little Józef.

It was at this time that he penned what in its own way was a remarkable poem. Inspired as much by his son's struggles with his Latin homework as by the Franco-English alliance's capture in mid-August of the Russian Baltic fortress of Bomersundum, the Latin ode was addressed to Napoleon III, in whom,

> For the sake of the downtrodden, returns that man,
> His hand like Romulus's, a terror for the proud—
> Your uncle, Caesar.
> ("Ad Napolionem III Caesarem Augustum. Ode in Bomersundum captum"; *Dz.* 1:416)

At the urging of Aleksander Chodźko, Mickiewicz allowed the ode to appear anonymously in November, just as the French public was beginning to entertain "defeatist" doubts about the sense of the alliance's decidedly less glorious siege of another Russian stronghold, this one on the Black Sea called Sebastopol. A contribution to the war effort on the domestic front, perhaps, or maybe simply a demonstration that his skills as a Latinist had not diminished with age, it was the last poem Mickiewicz would ever publish.[38]

Celina now "rarely left her bed, and her increasingly painful suffering was emaciating her." Agonized groans, loud enough at times to be heard on the street below, would be followed by moments of ease. "The evenings [were] pretty calm, the nights usually good, although [she] still ha[d] to take pills to induce sleep." Until Zofia Szymanowska returned to Paris in late November from a trip to Warsaw, responsibility for Celina's care was almost exclusively in Maria's hands; Mickiewicz, for his part, watched the younger children. On occasion he would relieve his daughter, send her out of the room, and then sit by Celina's bed, caressing her "tiny, withered hand," trying to comfort her with as much optimism as he could muster.[39]

In late December Celina's condition unexpectedly improved. Even the doctors were amazed by what they believed to be signs of recovery. For about a month she felt strong enough to get up every day and even putter around the house. A brief visit from Karolina Towiańska lifted her spirits, as did the presence of Szymanowska. In mid-February, though, on Maundy Thursday, she got up for the last time. The doctors informed Mickiewicz that her condition was hopeless. "Many days earlier" Celina had insisted that he "let her know the moment he understood that the end was drawing near." He did so now, at the very beginning of March. At this, wrote the poet to a mutual friend, "a great change came over her. She prepared for death with great courage and calm." After making all the necessary domestic arrangements and bidding farewell to her children and friends "as if before a journey," Celina asked her husband to make sure to inform Towiański that she had been and continued to be "faithful [to him] in spirit." "In these moments of parting," recalled Mickiewicz a few weeks later, "we were united for the first time. She vowed that she would constantly help me in spirit and be with me." Why, he asked, could she not have always been like this, adding, "I went through hell with her."[40]

On 5 March 1855, two days after hearing that Tsar Nicholas I had just preceded her, Celina asked for a priest, confessed, and received communion. She had spent part of the previous night with Władysław, telling him "moving things" and praying for everyone she knew. Only one more matter needed to be resolved. Shortly before drawing her final breath, she found herself alone with her husband and Szymanowska. Too weak to speak, she motioned for them to take each others' hands and "with her finger made the sign of the cross over their clasped palms," as if betrothing them.* Her dying wish, however, could never be fulfilled. Władysław and even Maria would not countenance it, much less the poet, for whom his sister-in-law's values and way of life were simply incompatible with his. That afternoon, a few months short of her forty-third birthday, Celina Mickiewicz née Szymanowska passed away. Mickiewicz "ripped a mirror from the wall, put it to her mouth," and seeing that there was no breath, said, "Look, the eyes are still staring."[41]

For the next two days, friends and acquaintances, Polish and French alike, filed through the apartment in the Bibliothèque to pay their last respects. Celina was laid out in "a black silk dress... holding a silver crucifix in her hands,... above her head [there hung] only a portrait of Towiański." Mickiewicz "was sad, but emotionally calm." A death mask was made and announcements sent out concerning the funeral, which was to be held on 8 March. That morning, as Władysław and Armand Lévy were about to place the lid on the coffin, Mickiewicz "ran to his office and returned holding some objects that he put... into the coffin without showing anyone." After a mass in the Church of St. Paul on rue Saint-Antoine, a large procession accompanied the coffin to Père Lachaise, where Celina was buried. Mickiewicz broke down in tears, along with everybody else.[42]

After the funeral, on his way to dinner with a few of his closest Towianist friends, Mickiewicz reminisced about his life with Celina. Among other things, he recalled the dream he had had in St. Petersburg years before their marriage in which he had associated the still pubescent Celina with instruments of torture and a wedding.** "Everything came true to a tee!" he sighed. As Celina herself remarked to him days before her death, "Adam, you could have made me happy, but you didn't know how, and I didn't want it."[43]

9

Mickiewicz gathered up some of Celina's things—"6 linen shirts, 1 kaftan, 1 muslin dress, 1 bonnet, 1 barege shawl, 3 collars,... 1 scarf, 1 sheet, 1 skirt"—and sent them to a needy

*Such was Szymanowska's version of the event, recorded in 1858 in her "Description of My Betrothal to Adam Mickiewicz" written for her "family's information and as evidence in the future." According to Władysław, Celina took Szymanowska's hand and said simply, "I leave my six children in your care" (*Żywot* 4:393), while Maria records her mother as saying to her, "You will be [little Józef's] mother, you and Zosia" (Gorecka, *Wspomnienia*, 139).

**See chapter 3, p. 120.

friend, together with forty francs. Szymanowska too took it upon herself to go through her half-sister's belongings; in the process, whether accidentally or not, she shattered the portrait of Towiański. The Master's presence, however, was not so easily exorcised. A few weeks later, Mickiewicz received a letter of condolence from Towiański himself. Although unable to restrain himself from expressing disappointment that Celina's "tone" never produced the proper "sacrifice," he nonetheless recalled with melodramatic gratitude her efforts on his behalf in 1848 and hoped that now, after her death, her spirit would join with Mickiewicz's in order to "consummate what [they] had hitherto not consummated." "Death," he wrote, "does not give a divorce. God's common will . . . must be consummated in common, if not in this vale, then in the next."[44]

The poet's most immediate concern was for the children, particularly the youngest. No sooner had Celina been buried than he received a proposition from Piotr Falkenhagen-Zaleski, the financier who handled his stock transactions, to take in four-year old Józef. Mickiewicz agreed, remarking that "had Queen Victoria wanted to bring up Józef, [he] would feel less at ease." As for the others, Jan and Aleksander continued boarding at the Collège Louis-le-Grand, while the rest remained for the moment with their father and Szymanowska at the Bibliothèque. The ordeal of the preceding months had left Mickiewicz "shaken and weary." Yet most everyone agreed that he looked "hearty and strong," if stouter and greyer. He had long ago learned to confront misfortune by stoically suppressing the temptation to regret.[45]

A few days after the funeral, Mickiewicz received an unexpected letter from Henrietta Ankwicz (now Kuczkowska), the girl he had hoped to marry during those carefree days in Rome some twenty-five years earlier and whom he had subsequently immortalized as Zosia in *Pan Tadeusz*. Overjoyed at hearing from her after a silence of some seven years, he responded with a letter that was at once wistful and strangely full of hope—just as he remembered her to be:

> Today I'm happy . . . to be beginning the first day of resurrection and spring in your dear name. Ever since I bid you farewell . . . my life has been almost a constant interring of someone or something. Out of the generation with which I've lived and grown accustomed to suffering want, some have left us forever, others are living out their funereal days that are no better than death. . . . You . . . lived under another and therefore, perhaps, better star.

He went on to inform her briefly of his situation: that after many years of wandering, he was now working in a library, that he was the father of a large family, of a nineteen-year-old daughter, a fifteen-year-old (*sic*) son, the rest younger and attending school. But not a word about Celina, as if her death was like any other in a life spent "constantly interring," and then moving on.[46]

CHAPTER THIRTEEN

REBIRTH AND DEATH (1855)

In May 1851, as Mickiewicz retreated from the public arena after his frenzy of activity in 1848–1849, Zygmunt Krasiński predicted to one of his correspondents, "Just wait and see, he'll soon throw himself once again into something else *with fervor.*" It would take another four years, but Krasiński once again proved that there were few who understood Mickiewicz better.[1]

I

On 28 April 1855, an embittered Italian patriot took a shot at Napoleon III as he was riding down the Champs Élysées. A week later, Mickiewicz joined Prince Adam Czartoryski and a handful of his loyal followers in a visit to the Tuileries Palace to thank Providence for the emperor's miraculous escape. Napoleon was moved. In hushed tones he "expressed his sympathies for Poland to the prince, but then raising his voice in order to be heard by palace aides, he added, 'I can do nothing for her.'" Mickiewicz was not pleased by what he felt was the emperor's hypocrisy. To Armand Lévy that evening he remarked, "Of the two—the true prince was the Pole."[2]

Over the years, the relationship of prince and poet had been an uneasy one, informed as much by temperament as by generational sensibility. Ideologically, they had never seen eye to eye, or, rather, their respective conceptions of the world were simply incommensurable, the one rational and calculatingly realistic, the other impulsively intuitive, driven by a hypertrophied imagination that continually strove to transcend ideology for the sake of action, however unrealistic. Yet as profound as their differences may have so often been, be it over Towianism or the Italian Legion, indeed, over the very essence of the Polish cause, Mickiewicz's respect for the person of the prince—the godfather, after all, of his oldest son—was too deeply felt, too filial, to affect their relationship irreparably. Some two and a half years earlier, at the annual name-day ball for the prince, which on this occasion had been organized by graduates of the Polish schools the prince once supervised, Mickiewicz had risen with "his face aflame" and, "combing his gray hair back with a noble gesture," let forth "a brilliant improvisation." Referring repeatedly to Czartoryski as "the supreme leader," he had declared that the prince's willingness "to sacrifice his high position, his wealth and his entire future for the sake of the national idea" had inspired an entire generation. It behooved those who were once his charges, who chose "the path that the Prince in his wisdom drew and traced continuously," "to keep spinning the national thread that Prince Adam had initiated and which he had conscientiously preserved for half a century amidst the storms that buffeted Poland" (Dz. 13:332–33). By the spring of 1855, as events in the East raised the hopes of Poles for a reconfiguration of the status quo, Mickiewicz conceded that only the prince was in a position to initiate any meaningful action on behalf of their cause.[3]

In a series of conversations with Ludwik Lenoir-Zwierkowski, Czartoryski's agent for the Near East who was now tasked with winning the poet over for the Hôtel Lambert, Mickiewicz admitted that the prince's efforts with regard to the current situation "deserved admiration." Artfully egged on by Zwierkowski, he at one point volunteered that if he had the means and could be assured that his children would be cared for, he would "gladly" go to the East in support of Czartoryski's activities in Turkey:

> Once [the Poles there] see that I, with a gray head but with an ardent heart, am going where it directs me, just as my mind does, not a sophisticated mind, but simply that of a peasant, that one can find Poland and hence one must look for it, then the young and the more able, since they are soldiers, would perhaps no longer dare to rot, beg, and not fulfill their sacred duty. There is no other way to address the emigration, only that I go myself where I'm obliged.[4]

As Zwierkowski reported to Czartoryski, "Mr. Adam's inclination in this regard is perhaps the best means by which to extricate [the Hôtel Lambert] out of . . . the revulsion that the emigration and some [in Poland] exhibit toward [its] activities." More to the point, "this man's magical name and well-intentioned desires" might be precisely what the Hôtel Lambert needed to gain the cooperation of the independently minded, and suspicious, Michał Czajkowski for its efforts to create Polish formations under the patronage of England and France, with General Zamoyski as their commander. Mickiewicz, it seems, approved of this project, fully aware, however, that he would find himself once again having to cope with the intrigues of his nemesis.[5]

Genuinely pleased by the poet's apparent readiness "to serve the common weal," which the Hôtel Lambert at the same time took to be "a pact with [its] politics and with [the prince's] . . . family," Czartoryski and his people went to work immediately. Assuring Mickiewicz that he would retain his librarian's salary and that his family would be accommodated, they concocted an ostensibly scholarly mission for the poet whereby he would be traveling to the East with the aim of "determining the influence of France on the Slavic population of Turkey." On 11 June, Napoleon III agreed in principle to Czartoryski's proposal. All that was needed now was to procure the necessary funds as well as the approval of Mickiewicz's employer, the French minister of education Hippolyte Fortoul. Fortoul, however, was not particularly well disposed toward an employee who had embarrassed the ministry on more than one occasion. He was perfectly content to hold off with a decision in the matter, and the prince, for reasons of his own, saw no cause to prompt him. In late July, Mickiewicz informed Łubieńska, "I had hoped to obtain a sabbatical for a long period of time, having received instructions to make a distant scholarly journey. All of these plans are on hold."[6]

2

Mickiewicz could do little but wait. Knowing that a decision might come at any minute and he would have to decamp immediately, he "could think of nothing else." An incident occurred, however, that briefly disrupted this uncertainty in a rather extraordinary manner. Tytus Działyński, one of Prussian Poland's leading citizens, had been persuaded by the Russian ambassador in Berlin to send out feelers to the emigration. Near the end of July, Działyński descended on Paris, where he met with several leading émigrés, Mickiewicz among them. Hoping to exploit the emigration's disappointment with French and English policies toward Poland, he suggested that it may be high time for Poles to come to some sort of understanding with Russia, a Slavic nation after all, whose new ruler, Alexander II, seemed ready to abandon the reactionary politics of his father. Mickiewicz no longer had any illusions about Russian intentions—nor the Master there to shape them. He vigorously objected. However reprehensible the behavior of the Western powers may have been, what distinguished them from Poland's enemies was their willingness to allow the emigration to "create national formations to free [the country] from its yoke." To be sure, Russia was Poland's natural ally against the Germans. Yet although such a "union could be the beginning of a new era for humanity, morality, and civilization," it could become a reality only if Russia recognized Poland's "right to existence, being, and national life." Until that time, Poles would continue to ally themselves with the West, above all Napoleonic France, with whom Poland is linked through "ties and memories deeply rooted in the nation." Działyński left Paris empty-handed.[7]

With summer quickly passing and news of allied successes in the Crimea heartening a war-weary nation, Fortoul continued to delay. As Mickiewicz reported in August to Edmond Mainard in Toulouse—or, more accurately, to his wife of four months, Ksawera

Deybel—"There is nothing new regarding my personal projects. The same constant uncertainty." Even Zwierkowski began complaining to his boss that it was only thanks to "his patience" that Mickiewicz was "not losing courage and abiding by his plans to go." At home, life continued uninterrupted. In July, Maria went south to Royan for a few weeks with her aunt, leaving only Władysław, Helena, and, for the summer, little Józef at the Arsenal. There were moments when Mickiewicz felt the earthly absence of "poor Celina," but only vaguely. In any case, she "often appear[ed] to [him] in dreams . . . showing [him] much kindness and promising to *work* for [him]." Everyone was healthy, including the poet. A visiting Wojciech Stattler, his painter friend from Cracow who had not seen him since their days in Rome together some twenty-five years earlier, described him as "having gained weight . . . , but without a wrinkle on his brow. His brow was even higher than before, because his eyebrows had sunk. . . ." But then too, "he had a look on his face as if on it were written: 'His mission had been completed.'"[8]

In mid-August, with still no official decision forthcoming from Fortoul, Mickiewicz sent the children to Fontainebleau, where he joined them a few days later for what he projected would be a six-week stay. With Zaleski he could talk of little else but his plans for the journey east and of "the troubles and difficulties he was experiencing at the French ministries in connection with this journey." "He was pensive," his friend recalled some twenty years later, "and his face was sad, but he was as talkative and expressive as ever"—and rarely passed up an opportunity to look for mushrooms in the surrounding woods. His favorite by far was the saffron milk cap, *Lactarius deliciosus*, which the plainclothesman sent to tail him could not have failed to notice.[9]

Upon returning to Paris on 31 August to pick up his paycheck, Mickiewicz received the news he'd been awaiting for over two expectant months. Fortoul approved the proposal for a scholarly mission to the East. Mickiewicz would continue drawing his salary, but an additional 1,500 francs to cover travel expenses would be reimbursed only in the following fiscal year. The Hôtel Lambert, for its part, was willing to throw in another 3,000 francs. As Zwierkowski wrote to Czajkowski at the beginning of September informing him of Mickiewicz's now imminent arrival, this sum would suffice for a "decent" voyage. He was sure, he went on, that the poet "would like Istanbul, but he would have to be pampered, given good food, tea with good chamomile, etc. . . . for he [was] a proud piece of work and one needs to know how to treat him."[10]

Earlier that summer, Mickiewicz had asked Armand Lévy and the family's factotum, Henryk Służalski, to accompany him were the mission to materialize, the first in the capacity of a secretary, the second as an aide cum batman; both readily agreed. He was now informed, however, that they would be joined by Czartoryski's twenty-seven-year-old younger son Władysław, whom his father had decided to delegate to Istanbul in order to further his plans regarding the creation of military formations. It was a decision of which

General Zamoyski wholeheartedly approved; Mickiewicz, for his part, later compared it to "someone... wishing [him] something none too pleasant."[11]

Although the exact day of their departure had still not been set, nor, for that matter the exact length of the mission, there was little time to waste and much to do. The poet made a quick trip to Fontainebleau to bid farewell to the Zaleskis and to bring back Maria and Szymanowska, who had stopped there on their way back from the south. Together they decided that with the exception of Józef, who would remain with the Falkenhagen-Zaleskis, the remaining children would be left in the care of their aunt. Mickiewicz's salary would continue to support them, out of which Szymanowska was to give Aleksander and Jan "3, 4 sous a week" in allowance, "Helen 10 sous a week, Maria 5 francs a week." Aware of the tensions between Władysław and his aunt, and in order to avoid any unpleasant misunderstandings, the boy was to receive an allowance directly from Zwierkowski. Nonetheless, Mickiewicz admonished his son to treat Szymanowska with the respect due to her, letting him know in no uncertain terms that if he did not, "he would suffer greatly for it." In any case, all of these arrangements were only temporary, as he assured those who were not altogether pleased with them, good only until his return from the East.[12]

"The next few days passed quickly in preparations for the road," Maria later recalled, "amidst visits and farewells to friends and acquaintances." Lévy was tasked with finishing editing an abridged version of the Collège lectures that the poet hoped to publish after his return, while the veteran Służalski was delegated to outfit the trio for the journey. When he brought home the tent Mickiewicz was to use during his travels, the poet immediately pitched it in his living room. Squatting in it, he turned to his friends with a smile, saying, "Now I'm at home, I'm a genuine citizen, I have a roof over my head and wherever I pitch my tent, at least this bit of earth will belong to me," whereupon he began to imagine Cossacks, Tatars, and Bedouins, open spaces and speeding horsemen giving chase to "laurels, gazelles, or even hares." What he had dreamt of since his days in Russia seemed on the verge of becoming a reality. Mickiewicz felt alive again.[13]

It was amid this preparatory bustle that Mickiewicz learned that his dear classmate from Vilnius, the gentle, mystical, unbalanced Tomasz Zan, who had returned to Lithuania from exile in Russia in 1841, was eager to hear from him after so many years of silence. Taking advantage of an opportunity to have a letter delivered by hand, the poet scribbled a few lines in which he hinted carefully at his upcoming journey, provided some bits of information about Tomasz's brother Stefan, and shared with him his grief over the death of their friend Jan Czeczot eight years earlier. What Mickiewicz did not know was that Zan too was already dead, having passed away a few weeks earlier.

In his letter, Mickiewicz recalled a recurring dream he had had "around the time" of Czeczot's death in which his friend was searching for him all over Paris, while he, in turn, "forgot to find out where [Czeczot] lived." Perhaps it was premonition, then, a "kind of last will," as his daughter insisted years later, but just as likely prudence that compelled the poet to sit down at his desk a few days later together with his oldest son and go through his papers—letters, "quite a few of his own manuscripts, even many poems." Mickiewicz hesitated occasionally over this or that piece of paper, but then tossed it in the fire, declaring, "This I'll never finish." He spared his archive relating to the Cause, just as he did material connected with the Italian Legion. "These," he concluded, "will be of use."[14]

On 7 September, after a meeting with a seemingly "indifferent" Alexandre Walewski, Napoleon Bonaparte's half-Polish illegitimate son and now his nephew's minister of foreign affairs, Mickiewicz was handed a diplomatic passport guaranteeing him free entry into countries friendly to France, along with letters of introduction to French diplomatic agents in Belgrade, Bucharest, and Istanbul. Since he would be traveling, in effect, as an official representative of the Republic of France, Mickiewicz felt that a better opportunity to apply again for French citizenship would probably never present itself. Shortly before his departure, he asked Czartoryski to intercede on his behalf with the Ministry of Justice. "Were this to succeed," he argued, he "would have greater freedom to serve the common cause." The issue, however, would soon prove to be moot.[15]

Mickiewicz's passport had been the final hurdle. The mission was now scheduled to depart from Paris on 11 September. To underscore the importance of the event, the Hôtel Lambert hosted a lavish farewell dinner for Czartoryski's son and his traveling companion. Near the end of the meal, the poet rose to toast Prince Adam, praising his "energy, perseverance, and steadfastness in the face of obstacles" and encouraging all present to emulate his capacity for hope. The prince, in turn, toasted Mickiewicz as "a name that speaks for itself, and his departure together with [Władysław] imbue[d] their . . . journey with national importance."[16]

On the morning of their departure, as Paris was abuzz with news that after a brutal one-year campaign Sebastopol had finally fallen to the Alliance, the Hôtel Lambert organized yet another event publicizing its own, now somewhat belated, contribution to the war, this time with a breakfast at La Tour d'Argent, at which some twenty-five people gathered. Over the clinking of champagne glasses and the slurping of oysters, there again followed toast after toast—to the success of the mission, to the prince, and by Mickiewicz to Michał Czajkowski-Sadik Pasha, in recognition of his efforts to create the detachment of Ottoman Cossacks, his tenacity, his sacrifices, his " 'work and the cross he bore,' " and in defense of his decision to convert to Islam as "the last means of serving Poland." How many among those gathered joined the poet in raising a glass at this moment remains uncertain.[17]

A "lively, energetic, and healthy" Mickiewicz arrived at the Gare Chemin de Fer de Lyon sometime before eight o'clock that evening, accompanied by his children, Służalski,

Władysław Czartoryski and his new wife, the countess of Vista Alegre, who would be traveling with them as far as Lyons, as well as a crowd of émigrés to see them off. Lévy was to join them in Lyons for the remainder of the journey east. As the children were not permitted to enter the *salle d'attente*, they bid farewell to their father at the entrance. "He hugged [them all] and quickly said good-bye, as if guarding himself against emotion, and walked into the hall; but at the door he looked around once more and waved, before disappearing."[18]

3

The party traveled by train to Lyons, where it was met by Lévy, and then continued on to Marseilles by carriage, encountering along the way "a few omnibuses packed with wounded soldiers returning from the Crimea." Although Służalski assured the children that their father was "chained to [them] with all his heart," he could not help remarking that from the moment he had left Paris, Mickiewicz was feeling "increasingly free, lively, and hardy." Prince Władysław seemed pleased with his companion, who assured him of his loyalty to the Hôtel Lambert and promised "to help [him] in everything he were to undertake." The next morning, on 12 September, they were already in Marseilles, where Lévy and Służalski—"the happiest man on earth at the moment"—began rushing about town making final arrangements for the voyage. The poet, for his part, sat down to catch up on correspondence. He wrote to Szymanowska to inform her of his safe arrival in Marseilles and pass on some last-minute admonitions to the children. He wrote two other letters just before embarking, both, as it happened, to women he loved. The first was to Henrietta Ankwicz, with whom he had renewed contacts after Celina's death. It was as if with it a burden had been lifted, allowing memories of youth, of what was and could have been, to come flooding back. The journey that lay ahead seemed to suggest that nothing was irrevocable. "Be so kind," he implored Ankwicz emphatically, "as to write to me now and again!" The second letter was to Deybel (via her husband), his Towianist lover and mother of his child. To her he expressed "great regrets" that he would be unable to visit the family in Toulouse before his journey, but also how thrilled he was by the mission he was about to undertake, which he hoped would improve both his health and his "situation." Neither Ankwicz nor Deybel would ever hear from him again.[19]

On 13 September the party boarded the steamer *Tabor*—"named to commemorate who knows what"—that would take them across the Mediterranean to Istanbul. Concerned that Mickiewicz should travel in comfort, Lévy had managed to secure for him a first-class berth. They set sail at ten that morning in the company of a detachment of French soldiers heading for the Crimean front, a few Poles intent on joining Czajkowski's Cossacks, a Polish nurse, "several horses, two American women in men's hats, four English officers . . . , an Italian woman in a green dress, also two parrots, a few rams, and cabbage." For much of the nine-day journey they "had good but very hot weather," and for Mickiewicz, at least, seasickness had never been a problem. Nights he often chose to spend on deck, together with his companions, "wrapped in [their] coats . . . enjoying . . . the breeze, the sight of stars, and the roar of the waves."[20]

From Marseilles, on a sea teeming with porpoises, they sailed through the Straits of Bonifacio, between Sardinia and Corsica—the island "on which . . . the greatest man of the age was born"—around Sicily, to Malta. On account of cholera, they were not permitted ashore and were forced to pass their time on the deck of the steamer, conversing and "reading a bit of Turkish" from a primer Mickiewicz had helped Aleksander Chodźko publish. After leaving Malta, the steamer "made for the shores of Lakonía, with a view toward Crete in the distance and Mount Ida, and then around the Cape of Matapan." As they entered the Aegean, wending their way through the Cyclades toward Ilium, they passed landmark after ancient landmark—Cythera, Paros, Siros, Delphi, Chios, Lesbos, Pergamum, Knidos—each in its own way evoking the names of gods and heroes, temples and graves, all so familiar to someone who had spent countless hours as a student, then as a professor, and then finally as a father over the texts of Homer and atlases of the ancient world. Some were now barren, like Delos, where the steamer dropped off the body of a passenger who had died.[21]

Izmir, however, evoked an entirely different set of associations, at once of the exotic and of the nostalgically familiar. Allowed to disembark for the first time during their journey, Mickiewicz and his companions encountered the Orient, with its caravans of camels, women in veils, Turks in cafés sitting on pillows smoking hookahs, and Sephardic Jewish merchants, their wives in yellow slippers, "wrapped from neck to knee in Venetian chains." For all their exotica, however, the sights and smells of the stalls in the narrow streets and muddy squares "reminded Mr. Adam completely of Nowogródek." "I was told that Homer's grave was supposed be in Smyrna," he remarked later to an acquaintance, "but what did I care?"

> I stared at something else. A pile of manure and junk lay there, remains all mixed together: manure, garbage, slops, bones, a shattered skull, a piece of sole from an old slipper, some feathers—now that I liked! I stood there for a long while, because it was exactly like the yard of a tavern in Poland.

And just as in Nowogródek, there were synagogues, "where classically serious old men read prayers . . . from Bibles."[22]

After a brief stop in Gallipoli, which to Służalski's eyes seemed "even stranger and more Oriental than Smyrna," the *Tabor* entered the Golden Horn on the morning of

22 September, "escorted by porpoises." Before the travelers, "its every window and minaret gilded by the Eastern sun," shone Istanbul.[23]

4

As the steamer pulled into the harbor, Mickiewicz and his companions gazed at a city in the midst of transformation, an upshot of Sultan Abdülmecid's sweeping social, political, and economic reorganization of his realm, which was, in part, the (willing) price he was paying for Western help in keeping it intact. Although the foreign loans his English and French patrons began floating the previous year would eventually bankrupt the empire, they were now driving the modernization of his cosmopolitan capital. The medieval mosques, *madrasahs*, and palaces that had determined its skyline over the past few centuries had begun to compete with clock towers and Western-style royal residences, as interpreted for the sultan by his Armenian architects. Police and fire stations were springing up in every quarter, together with post offices, sewers, and gas lighting. Instead of the turban, outlawed years earlier by royal decree, Turks walked the new sidewalks of the city in fezzes, dressed in a variant of the European frock coat over tight slacks, whose effect was to force them from pillows onto chairs. Their wives, though—and the European-educated emperor had twenty-one of them—still wore veils, but now alongside those who appeared in public in elaborate, brightly colored turbans, flaunting the newest Parisian fashions. Wooden buildings still lined the narrow, curving streets and still caught fire with alarming frequency, terrifying the armies of cats and dogs that roamed every square and alley of Istanbul. Begging dervishes still jostled kilt-wearing Greeks and pistol-packing Albanians and Georgians in pointy shoes. Like the smells wafting from the market stalls and the calls to prayer from minarets, like the sedan chairs, the white slaves, and the rampant corruption, they seemed impervious to modernization.

Mickiewicz and his companions landed in Pera, the predominantly Christian quarter across the strait from the old city, now more awash than ever with Frenchmen, Englishmen, and other foreigners drawn to—or, like the thousands of wounded, transported to—Istanbul by the war. Companionship and princely generosity notwithstanding, Prince Władysław went off to a hotel, while one of his father's agents escorted Mickiewicz, Lévy, and Służalski to thriftier lodgings in the Vincentian monastery in Galata, not far from the British embassy. These consisted of three corners of a single room, where "instead of beds there were mattresses and a sofa, and coats replaced comforters. One trunk served as a dining table, the other, [Mickiewicz's], as a sofa for guests, and a saddle for a night table." For the next six weeks, they shared this hovel with "a cloud of fleas, bedbugs, and mosquitoes" "de-civilizing," as Lévy put it, "with an ease [. . .] and joy that surprised [them]."[24]

Istanbul proved as familiarly exotic as Izmir. To Mickiewicz, parts of the city "seemed to completely resemble those of [his] native town in Lithuania." "Imagine if you will," he wrote to Vera Khliustin,

> a public square, covered with a layer of manure and feathers, where chickens, turkeys, and all kinds of creatures walk tranquilly amid groups of dogs. But to get to this place, one needs to take streets that seemed . . . primitive and colorful . . . , past piles of dead rats and squashed cats, past dead drunk Englishmen and Turkish porters who hermetically seal both sides of the street.

But what particularly amazed him on his jaunts in the neighborhood was "the honesty and modesty of the merchants": no soliciting, no announcements or advertising. "For the first time in my life," Mickiewicz admitted, "I felt like doing some shopping."[25]

Yet aside from a brief excursion "to see the real Constantinople on the other side of the huge pontoon bridge spanning the strait," there was little time for sightseeing. From the very first day of their arrival, Mickiewicz was besieged by visits from Polish émigrés, mostly military sorts and adventurers, some of them converts to Islam like Czajkowski, and almost all complaining about the disarray among the Ottoman Cossacks and the tensions between their commander and General Zamoyski. Neither, however, was in Istanbul at the time. The latter had gone to England to negotiate the formation of a legion; Czajkowski, to his camp in Burgas, some 125 kilometers up the Bulgarian coast from Istanbul. Mickiewicz seemed a bit disoriented at first. What he knew about the situation when still in Paris did not fully correspond to facts—or, rather, gossip—on the ground.[26]

He chose to make his first visit a social one, to an acquaintance of Ksawery Branicki living in Bebek, more for the sensation, perhaps, of sailing up the Bosphorus in a boat than for anything else. His unexpected arrival so flustered the lady of the house as to nonplus Mickiewicz. "So this is how much you love me?" he asked. "What would you extend to saints, then? Don't forget, I'm not a saint!" The following day, on 26 September, he accompanied Prince Władysław on his first official visits, again up the Bosphorus to Terapia, to the British and then French embassies. Although the poet himself was greeted with a degree of gracious curiosity by the British ambassador, from the "more than cold" reception Stratford de Redcliffe extended to the young prince it was obvious that the matter of a Polish legion was by no means as certain as the Hôtel Lambert had been led to believe. In fact, "England," as Mickiewicz later reported to Lévy, "did not want to and would not do anything for Poland." The French ambassador, Édouard de Thouvenel, proved just as unresponsive. On their return to Istanbul that evening, Mickiewicz and the prince learned that Czajkowski was "intent on seeing [them] both" in his camp in Burgas as soon as possible.[27]

The very next day, without waiting for Czartoryski, Mickiewicz called on Czajkowski's wife Ludwika Śniadecka, a woman no less intrepid and rebelliously adventurous than her

Muslim mate but also more intelligent and polished. The ostensible purpose of his visit to her residence in Beşiktaş was to get some sense of Czajkowski's predicament and the task that he would be facing. What drew him, though, were memories of Vilnius. Mickiewicz had encountered Śniadecka years ago while still a student, in the company of her father Jędrzej and her uncle Jan, his classicist antagonists at the university. "He was sincere," she wrote describing the poet's visit to Zwierkowski,

> and I with him.... It was nice to see him, although he was so very pale and somewhat "materialisé." He immediately took both my hands and spoke to me with feeling, that he would like to know me not only for Sadik's sake, but for who I am, since he knew my father and my uncle.... I didn't want to let him go.

Both in their fifties now, both wanderers in a foreign and hostile world on behalf of a cause to which both had dedicated their lives, they embodied for each other a place and time that there, on the shores of the Bosphorus, both seemed desperate to preserve, if only by pooling their memories.[28]

5

On 5 October, Czartoryski, Mickiewicz, Lévy, and Służalski boarded the English steamer *Patrick* that would take them to Czajkowski's camp in Burgas. Sailing past the nearly completed palace of Dolmabahçe and the wooden mansions of Istanbul's elite lining the western shore of the Bosphorus, the steamer entered the Black Sea, its "air heavy," its "shores desolate," the gray waters "reflecting a leaden sky." After a twenty-hour voyage, the steamer, flying the Polish flag at the behest of Prince Władysław, weighed anchor in Burgas Bay.[29]

On arriving at the Cossack camp a few kilometers south of the town, the visitors were told that Czajkowski had gone off hunting, but that their tents had been prepared for them. They were quartered with the first regiment, the so-called irregulars, made up of a pied assortment of Poles, Russian Old Believers, "Ukrainian, Dobrujan, and Kuban" Cossacks, as well as a number of Jews, all "very attached to [Sadik Pasha]." The second regiment consisted exclusively of Poles and was considered to be loyal to General Zamoyski. That evening, after Czajkowski's return, the guests were treated to a Cossack welcome: "a lavish dinner, [Sadik Pasha's] entire officer staff at his table like children with a father," replete with "singing, then music... on fiddles, banduras, and drums." "Mr. Adam was very happy."[30]

For the next twelve days Mickiewicz and his companions were treated with all the generosity, openness, and hospitality that only these somewhat wild, devil-may-care warriors could muster. Each morning they were up at 5:00 to observe the Cossacks taking "orders, drilling, ... marching past for review," their formation stretching out "for several kilometers." Mickiewicz was particularly impressed by their horsemanship and "the natural strength of these uncivilized Cossacks," but also by their "discipline," enforced as it was by corporal punishment. On the almost daily hunts for rabbits, the poet, riding a lively steed lent to him by Sadik Pasha, with a borzoi at his side, managed to keep up with the best of the Cossacks. Exhilarated and hungry after the hunt, the companions would return to camp for dinner, sharing their hosts' mutton stew and enjoying "the music, the Cossack dances, ... and even a Cossack theater on hobby horses." As Czajkowski recalled years later: "Adam Mickiewicz told me that only now, in our camp, had he come to life again, that here he ... genuinely wanted to join the irregular Cossacks." For their part, both Służalski and then Lévy did just that.[31]

Yet as enjoyable as life with the Cossacks proved to be for Mickiewicz, and pleased as he was by "the camp and ... Sadik and his staff and the entire way of life there," the divisions he now observed riving it "worried and grieved" him deeply. As he reported to Prince Adam, no one was more to blame for this than General Zamoyski, who, according to Mickiewicz, was intent on destroying Czajkowski's work by assuming command of the Cossacks and placing them under British control, all for the sake of "positions in the military, ... high pay, and rapid promotions." Prince Władysław, for his part, appeared content to view everything "through General Zamoyski's eyes." As the Hôtel Lambert's man in Istanbul, he was proving to be weak, ineffectual, and "preoccupied with trifles having nothing to do with the reason ... for his trip." When the poet confronted him one night, accusing him of acting "not as a representative or one of the representatives of the Polish cause, but as a trusted agent of Zamoyski, sent to cause harm to Sadik Pasha," Czartoryski cut his visit to Burgas short and returned to Istanbul.[32]

Shortly after his departure, Czajkowski's regiment of Cossack irregulars declared openly and unanimously that they would rather disband than serve as "mercenaries" under the British flag, material blandishments, Zamoyski's intrigues, and pressure by the Turkish government notwithstanding. Mickiewicz was "moved by their gallantry and high-mindedness," but no less so by the sight of the some two hundred Jewish volunteers, mostly deserters from the Russian army or former prisoners of war, who joined the others in proclaiming their loyalty to a Polish convert to Islam and his Polish cause. It struck Mickiewicz that here might be the nucleus of a potential Jewish legion, whose "participation in the Polish effort could influence the behavior of their fellow believers in Poland." The Towianist in him—and perhaps the Jew—for whom the emancipation of Polish Jewry was a cardinal point in the Set of Principles of 1848, continued to believe that "without the liberation of the Jews and the development of their spirit Poland would be incapable of rising."[33]

Lévy grasped Mickiewicz's idea of a Jewish military formation immediately, eager as he was, in Śniadecka's words, "to in this way elevate his humiliated nation and restore its military reputation." Czajkowski did as well, at least ostensibly, authorizing Lévy to "speak to Jewish elders...about the possibility of increasing the number...of their coreligionists serving in the Cossack unit." Privately, though, he had his doubts, treating the project, initially, with the instinctive scorn of a Polish gentryman. What "an unheard of absurdity," he wrote to his wife, "to see armed Jews side by side with Cossacks commanded by a Polish noble." But to his credit, when confronted later by a Mickiewicz infuriated by his reference to "lousy Jews," Czajkowski apologized for this "whim of a gentry imagination." He conceded that a regiment made up of Jews might indeed be "important, very necessary, and even vital for the cause" and expressed qualified support for Lévy's and Mickiewicz's efforts to this end. To demonstrate his good intentions, not only did Czajkowski forbid attempts by his Cossacks to force conversions as well as derisive remarks about others' beliefs, but also instituted the practice of allowing "Muslims to observe Fridays..., Jews, Saturdays, and Western and Eastern Christians, Sundays, each according to his tradition." As Mickiewicz remarked in this regard, with his usual hyperbole, "This is the first time since the scattering of the Jews that something like this has occurred."[34]

For all its spiritually restorative joys, however, the poet soon learned that life in a military camp could be parlous physically, particularly for a man about to turn fifty-seven. The days spent on horseback under a blazing sun and the cold, damp nights on hard ground, the "cabbage with venison" shared in a tent with singing and dancing Cossacks may have fired his romantic imagination, but they also wreaked havoc on a constitution unused to such conditions. At first he attempted to ride out the cramps, the diarrhea, and the fever, steeling himself with the sight of "others sicker than [him] out hunting rabbits." Nonetheless, his companions' concern for his health soon prevailed. On 17 October, Mickiewicz, together with Lévy and Służalski, boarded the Austrian steamer *Persia* to Varna, where they transferred to the French ship *Pericles* for the voyage back to Istanbul.[35]

Had it been physically possible, Mickiewicz would have stayed. He felt that in Burgas he had been transported back "onto the bosom of his fatherland." As one observer noted wryly, Mickiewicz "had completely flipped, he even likes the whippings.... [Czajkowski] managed to play to his weaknesses, it took just a few singers and melancholy Ruthenian songs not only to win him over, but to completely captivate him. O poets!"[36]

6

Mickiewicz returned to Istanbul "very...ill...with dysentery," and neither the room in Galata nor the diet he kept—home-made chicken pilau, but more often meals at local establishments, where the water was bad, the bread coarse, and the wine acidic—were particularly conducive to a rapid return to health. Nor was his insistence on conducting his daily routine as if there were nothing wrong. While his friends scoured the city for more amenable accommodations so that "Mr. Adam could have some free time and a bit of a rest," he answered the stack of letters waiting for him on his return, wrote reports to the Hôtel Lambert, drafted official memoranda concerning the Jewish legion, received visitors almost daily, and even ventured out, on one occasion as far as Beşiktaş to visit Śniadecka and on another to Terapia to sign a document at the French embassy. Each day he would go to bed exhausted.[37]

It was only at the very beginning of November, when the three companions abandoned their cubicle in the Vincentian monastery and moved to a hotel until something more permanent could be found, did the poet finally regain his strength. "As fit as the moment he left Paris," Służalski informed the family in Paris on 3 November. (As it turned out, assurances in this regard were largely *ad usum domesticum*.) A few days later, after being forced to abandon plans for a promising apartment on account of protests by local "mullahs" unhappy about the presence of giaours, the trio finally found a place owned by a German-Polish couple in Pera on Yeni Şehir (now, more or less, Serdar Ömer Pasa Sokagi) at the bottom of Kalyoncu Kulluk. It was not much of an improvement: the neighborhood was "squalid," the apartment "small, damp but inexpensive." As "unhealthy" as the place may have been, Służalski reported that Mickiewicz was very pleased with it.[38]

The poet's mission, however, was proving frustrating. To be sure, the project of a Jewish legion was "developing propitiously," thanks in large part to Lévy, for whom it had become something of an obsession. After his initial reservations, Czajkowski too seemed enthusiastic, particularly when Lévy's memoranda to the Turkish Ministry of War met with a positive response. But Mickiewicz's promise to Prince Czartoryski "to work with all [his] might to reconcile Sadik and Zamoyski" was nowhere near fulfillment. On the contrary, Zamoyski's "fatal influence" and "deceitful behavior" had effectively ruined Czajkowski's hard-won enterprise. With the permission of the Porte, the general succeeded in luring one of the Cossack regiments into service under the British flag, with the aim, it seems, of compromising Czajkowski and arrogating command of the Polish force to himself. "Mr. Zamoyski," observed Mickiewicz in a report to the prince that was as frank as it was bitter, "always began with *himself* and finished with *himself*." As for the prince's son, he had been less than helpful, tacitly enabling Zamoyski with his fecklessness. In tandem, they had managed to place the Hôtel Lambert's project in the East at risk. The whole affair reminded the poet of a prostitute who, asked why she had not conceived a child, replied, "What one begins, the other spoils." "I don't know what Mr. Zamoyski began," concluded Mickiewicz to Prince Adam, "but everybody knows how much he's already spoiled." By mid-November, Mickiewicz no longer saw any reason to expend energy on Czartoryski's behalf. He stopped seeing Prince Władysław, who left Istanbul on 19 November without even bidding good-bye to the poet. Mickiewicz had decided to throw in his lot with Czajkowski.[39]

7

The weather in Istanbul had turned "foul," with "constant rain," so that Mickiewicz now rarely went out to eat in the afternoon as was his custom. He had not been feeling well for several days, often waking up in the middle of the night, unable to fall back asleep. His mood, though, seems to have been jolly, if somewhat morbid. In a brief dramatic sketch he penned in French at the time, a Hungarian aide-de-camp mocks his Polish superior who is suffering from a bout of cholera. "Colonel, colonel," the former observes as the latter tries to down some medication between fits of vomiting, "You'll kick the bucket tonight like a plucky old dog. This is it, the end. . . . You're pursing your lips like a young lady and flashing your teeth. It's all over, you old coot." "That'll be the day, you good-for-nothing," replies the colonel, who, the reader subsequently learns, is still alive and well at age seventy ("Conversation de malades"; *Dz.* 5:259/*Żywot* 4:CXXIX).[40]

On 25 November, Mickiewicz ate a dinner of "grilled chicken" washed down with "half a bottle of Bordeaux," after which he joined Lévy to practice writing Turkish. At ten o'clock they parted for the night. Around midnight Mickiewicz got up to make himself a cup of tea. Lévy, himself under the weather, thought nothing of it and went back to sleep. The next morning, on 26 November, the poet woke up feeling nauseous, but when Służalski asked him to show him his tongue, Mickiewicz laughed it off, comparing his friend to little Józef, who during his mother's illness would ask every visitor to show him their tongue. When the mail arrived, he lay down on his bed to read it, feeling, it seems, somewhat better. Hipolit Kuczyński, another Polish convert to Islam and an aide-de-camp in the Egyptian army, dropped by soon after, and the four chatted for a while. In connection with the current state of affairs, Mickiewicz remarked that "even had [he] known that [he] should die from cholera somewhere in Turkey, [he] would still have gone." "Better to be a secretary in some regiment of Polish Cossacks," he declared, "than a chancellor of a French institute." They were soon joined by Emil Bednarczyk, a veteran of 1830 and a Democrat whom Mickiewicz had been eyeing as a potential commander for the Jewish legion. Shortly after ten o'clock, Mickiewicz indicated to his friends that he needed a nap. Neither Lévy nor Służalski seemed overly concerned—they had seen this before—and soon left to run some errands. Not feeling well himself, Bednarczyk decided to stay behind.[41]

Around noon, Bednarczyk went to check on Mickiewicz. To his horror, he saw the poet "dressed only in his shirt, as pale as a corpse, standing in the door of his room in bare feet and holding on to the frame so as not to fall, since he was bent over backward." Leaping to hold him up, Bednarczyk asked what he wanted. Mickiewicz could only motion with his head to the bathroom, but then changed his mind. When Bednarczyk tried to escort him to bed, however, the poet refused to let go of the door. With one arm wrapped around Mickiewicz's waist, Bednarczyk struggled to release his grip and the two went crashing to the floor, the poet's head striking something hard. Hearing the racket, the landlady came rushing into the room. She helped Bednarczyk put Mickiewicz to bed, and "since he was as cold as ice," they began "rubbing him with their hands and with brushes." The landlady ran to the other room to make a chamomile infusion, but when she returned with it, Mickiewicz refused to drink. "'Get a doctor,'" she yelled at Bednarczyk.[42]

He found one in the person of a Dr. Gembicki, who on hearing a description of the symptoms declared, "This is cholera of the most violent sort... there's no saving him." To Bednarczyk's pleas, the doctor replied that since there was nothing he could do, treating a man as famous as Mickiewicz might be later misconstrued as an attempt on his life. Desperate, Bednarczyk put a pistol to Gembicki's head and marched him off to Mickiewicz's apartment, after which he himself ran off to fill the prescription for laudanum Gembicki had written.[43]

Gembicki found Mickiewicz barely conscious. Although the doctor knew that it was futile, he ordered some water to be boiled in stone pots, which he then proceeded to place around the poet's body. Mickiewicz came to briefly, and seeing an unknown face standing over him, asked, "What does this man want from me? I didn't do him any harm... here I was... dreaming I was in heaven, and then this bad man comes along and wakes me up." He continued to refuse to drink, much less take the medicine Bednarczyk had by now brought, and would spit out everything forced into his mouth. Having finally been persuaded to swallow a few drops of laudanum, Mickiewicz fell back into a feverish sleep.[44]

Służalski did not return until later that afternoon, whereupon Bednarczyk, exhausted by his ordeal, went home. Lévy arrived a short while later only to hear from the landlady, whom he met on the stairs, that things looked bad. He found Slużalski standing over Mickiewicz next to the doctor, crying, but whether out of grief or remorse is difficult to say. Gembicki repeated what he had told Bednarczyk, that there was little hope. Mickiewicz slipped in and out of consciousness, while the doctor continued to warm his body with pots and rubs and mustard plasters. But his hands and feet were growing colder, his fingers stiff. Asked by Służalski at one point if he had anything to tell the children, the poet said weakly, "Tell them to love each other." By this time, two more doctors had arrived. Mickiewicz was writhing in pain from cramps, yet he refused to, or simply could not, take any more medicine. He turned to Lévy and said, "They don't even know what's wrong with me,... they want to warm me up, but I'm burning all over." Someone sent for a Polish priest, who arrived around six o'clock, together with a fourth doctor, Stanisław Drozdowski. The poet was no longer able to speak. "A few minutes before 9:00," shortly after receiving Extreme Unction, Adam Mickiewicz took his last breath, twenty-nine days short of his fifty-seventh birthday.[45]

These appear to be the facts. Służalski and Lévy, independently of each other, described Mickiewicz's final hours somewhat differently. They both seem to have come to feel that their lack of concern on that final day for the man they both worshipped and for whom they were both, in a sense, responsible may have contributed to his death. The accounts they sent to the family in Paris were, as a consequence, full of self-justificatory—and, one should

Fig. 29 Mickiewicz on his deathbed. Photograph. Courtesy of the Adam Mickiewicz Museum of Literature, Warsaw.

add, mutually recriminatory—inconsistencies, if not downright lies. It was only a matter of time, then, before their convoluted narratives, together with those of Drozdowski, Kuczyński, and then of their interlocutors in Istanbul, muddled the picture and, like most earnestly self-serving cover-ups, gave rise to all manner of rumor. The fact that the official death certificate filed the following day at the French embassy by Dr. Drozdowski did not list the cause of death only exacerbated matters. Dr. Gembicki's apprehensions were in this regard quite prescient. As late as the 1930s, people were still debating whether Mickiewicz had been poisoned, the price he ostensibly may have paid for his involvement in émigré intrigues. The poet died of a food- or water-borne toxin, malignant cholera perhaps, compounded by the injury to his head. Like his beloved Byron, he perished, so to speak, more aspirationally than operationally.

8

Lévy, Służalski, and Kuczyński remained alone with the body. The priest went to sleep in another room. Służalski was bereft: "What will I do now," he moaned, "I've lost everything, I'm a body whose soul has escaped.'" From that moment, he refused to leave the corpse's side, keeping vigil over it day and night. The following morning, on 27 November, an artist was summoned to draw the deceased, in whose features Służalski recognized Napoleon's. A few hours later a plaster death-mask was cast and then a photograph taken. After informing both the French and British embassies about the death, Lévy and Służalski telegraphed Prince Czartoryski:

> On the twenty-sixth, at 9:00 in the evening, Adam Mickiewicz passed away after a brief illness. We intend to accompany him shortly to Paris. Inform the family, gently.

To Władysław, Lévy wrote a brief note of condolence:

> Dear child! How can I comfort you when I myself am heartbroken? Courage. Such was the will of God.... We should never crumble under the weight of a blow, as your father and mother, who suffered so much, always repeated to us.... I have only strength enough to cry with you.[46]

Almost immediately, mourners began filing through the small house on Yeni Şeri. "We gazed at that noble head," one recalled, "on which the white hair lay tousled all about, and at the half-open blue lips, as if ready to speak, and we were as silent as the silence of the grave." That night the corpse was embalmed—against Mickiewicz's wishes, who did not want "doctors to see what was going on in his body." The heart was left in place.[47]

But even this moment of national grief did not pass without a to-do among the émigrés. Some in the city's Polish community—with the support of none other than General Zamoyski—insisted that the poet's remains be buried in Turkey. Lévy forcefully objected, not only on account of the family, but also for strategic reasons. "One needs to find a resting place," he argued, "by taking into consideration the influence it might exert." France was the only option.[48]

The final preparations proceeded swiftly, particularly since neighbors were already grumbling about the "danger of keeping a corpse in the house for too long." Lévy dressed the body in a "frock-coat, pants, and a black vest," and then a "fur coat that [Mickiewcz] wore on chilly days"; a blue Polish insurgent's cap (*konfederatka*) was placed on the head. After cutting a few locks of hair for the children, Lévy helped lay the body in a zinc coffin that had been lined with balsam branches to prevent it from being jostled during the voyage. Over the heart he placed a portrait of Celina, a long letter from Maria, a scrap of paper with a few words from Władysław, a lock of little Józef's hair, and a heavy Russian coin Mickiewicz had come upon in Istanbul that had reminded him of his mother. The corpse was covered with flowers, its face veiled. At the last moment, Lévy placed a crucifix in its hands. Of Mickiewicz's personal possessions—mainly papers, including scenes from an unfinished play and fragments of stories, as well as official letters for what was to be the remainder of the poet's mission—which the French embassy had ordered sealed, he kept only Celina's watch, the one the poet had used on his journey east, to give to Władysław as a memento. Mickiewicz's saddle, tent, and rifle, his indispensable possessions on the visit to Czajkowski's camp, he gave to Śniadecka. The zinc coffin was subsequently placed into one made of pine. When a third, oak coffin arrived later that day, it "proved too big for the narrow stairway leading up to the apartment." The only solution was to bring the two inner coffins containing the body down from the apartment and place them in the large outer one, which would remain parked near the entryway to the building for over a month. Służalski was forced to continue his vigil on the stairs. Beside the coffin, "two funeral candles burned continuously, night and day."[49]

Permission from the appropriate authorities to transport the body back to France proved frustratingly difficult to obtain. In the face of the efforts on the part of local Poles to have the poet interred in Turkey, the French ambassador at first refused to release the corpse to Lévy and Służalski without receiving some sort of instructions in the matter from the family. Disgusted, however, by the émigrés' "disgraceful" squabble over the remains and without waiting for a response from Paris, Thouvenel acceded to the importunities of the poet's companions. On 6 December, he ordered the coffin sealed for the journey back to France. All that remained now was to book passage. This, however, proved no less frustrating. Since it was assumed that Mickiewicz had died of cholera, and in view of the quarantine in Marseilles, no shipping company, neither British nor French, was willing. It was not until 26 December, after exhausting a variety of different options, that Lévy finally received a reply from the Service Maritime des Messageries Impériales informing him that "the *Euphrate*, leaving on Monday, would accommodate the casket of A. Mickiewicz."[50]

Lévy and Służalski immediately arranged a funeral mass for that Sunday, 30 December. Mourners were to gather at ten in the morning at the house on Yeni Şeri (there would be someone on Kalyoncu Kulluk to "provide the necessary directions"), whence at ten thirty the cortège would proceed to the Church of St. Anthony on Istiklâl Caddesi, the main street of Pera. "Out of respect for the will of the deceased," they announced, "no speech, secular or ecclesiastic, will be pronounced over the coffin." "Everyone was wanting to appropriate him for themselves," recalled Lévy, unaware that at the moment he was predicting the fate of Mickiewicz's afterlife.[51]

"It was a December day," recalled one participant in the event, "gloomy and foggy, the fog occasionally turning to drizzle." A crowd of Poles, both military and civilian, gathered in front of the house. Zamoyski had ordered his Polish regiment to accompany the coffin of Poland's "*wieszcz*, whose songs . . . roused it to unshakable loyalty, to duty, and to enduring struggle with its enemies." The casket was placed on a cart and draped with a shroud. It lurched forward, preceded by priests, flanked on both sides by the soldiers, their "rifles bearing signs of mourning . . . their drums covered with crêpe," up the steep, muddy street packed with people. When the cortège reached the top of the street it became apparent that not only Poles were mourning the passing of one of their own:

> Like a river trapped in the bed of the street, there flowed a crowd of people dressed in turbans. The head of this column abutted ours, the rear was lost somewhere in the indiscernible distance. The people walked in silence.... It was the Bulgarians who had prepared this surprise for us. In the person of the deceased they were honoring a genius of Slavic poetry.... But they were not the only ones who from among the peoples of Constantinople appeared at the funeral service.... Except for [Turks], all nationalities had their representatives in the funeral cortège... Serbs, Dalmatians, Montenegrans, Albanians, Greeks, Italians.

After the funeral service, for which an agent of Prince Czartoryski donated 2,000 francs, the cortège proceeded down the hill of Galata to the quays of Tophane, where a boat was waiting to take the coffin and its two escorts, Służalski and Lévy, to the *Euphrate*. The steamer set sail for France on the following day.[52]

9

The children had been informed of their father's death on 30 November. That very same day, as he was hurrying to a meeting at Karol Różycki's to celebrate Towiański's name-day, Seweryn Goszczyński ran into an acquaintance who had just heard the news from Czartoryski's people. The Towianists received it "in a Christian frame of mind," deploring, though, "that death caught up with [Mickiewicz] on a path inappropriate for him, that his end was the consequence of his having renounced his mission." They nonetheless ordered a mass for his intention, which Father Duński celebrated that Sunday at the Church of St. Méry. In his sermon, he assured the fifty or so Towianists present that Mickiewicz's spirit would now "aid God's Cause immensely." Goszczyński went home that evening and wrote a "funeral ode" memorializing "the *wieszcz* of *wieszczes*." It was the first of a flood of tributes that would soon begin flowing from the pens of poets and poetasters, Polish and otherwise, lamenting the passing of "the prophet of song," "the guardian of his people," the "pilgrim," and "martyr," whose words would one day "resurrect the nation" just as their creator had "inspired Poland with his breath."[53]

As condolences began pouring in from friends and strangers, a committee was constituted almost immediately to organize a fund drive on behalf of the Mickiewicz orphans, albeit with the usual émigré bickering. By the end of December, it had collected nearly 75,000 francs, with Ksawery Branicki proving to be by far the most generous; in mid-January it had some 104,000 francs at its disposition, donated by émigrés and contributors from Poland alike—a sum that would have taken Mickiewicz another fifty years to earn at the Arsenal. In addition, Prince Napoleon Bonaparte, who, as *La Presse* reported, "had honored the poet with his friendship," personally "assumed the costs of educating Mickiewicz's two [youngest] sons." A Guardians' Council was established to care for the orphans. The pied nature of its membership—Ludwik Wołowski, Piotr Falkenhagen-Zaleski, Michelet, King Jérôme Bonaparte, Aleksander Chodźko, Ksawery Branicki, Armand Lévy—guaranteed, however, that there would be little agreement over the future course of the children's lives, for whose well-being, in any case, Szymanowska still felt directly responsible.[54]

Their suffering, as Władysław later put it, had now become "exacerbated by an eruption of general grief." News of the poet's death spread quickly throughout the émigré community in Paris, and from Paris to Poland and to every corner of Europe, at first by word of mouth and in private correspondence, then in the press. On 3 December, *La Constitutionnel* reported "the sad news of the death of Mr. Adam Mitzkiévitch, the great Polish poet, former professor of Slavic language and literature at the Collège de France and, most recently, librarian at the Bibliothèque de l'Arsenal," who in the course of "a scholarly mission to the East... was struck down by cholera." For its part, the Catholic *L'Univers* made sure to add, somewhat disingenuously, that "sensing he was about to die, the famous Polish poet had a Polish priest called, who dispensed the Holy Sacraments and all the consolations that may be found in the Christian religion. His death was that of a fervent Christian."[55]

Shortly thereafter, newspapers in Poznań, Cracow, and Lwów began publishing more extensive obituaries (mention of Mickiewicz's name was still prohibited in the Russian Empire):

> The nation felt the pain of the loss of its *wieszcz*, whose song had been transfused by the profoundest of national feelings. Oh, let us cry over his grave, for the more deeply we feel this loss, the more appropriate will be the honor we extend to his merits and memory!... In all of Europe there was and is no poet whom the entire nation cherished with such respect and love.

These sentiments were echoed simultaneously in the Slovak, Italian, Czech, Bulgarian, and Serbian press, all of which bemoaned, in the words of the *Deutsches Museum*, the loss "of not only the premier poet of his nation, but one of the premier poets of Europe, and even the world." As Mickiewicz's friend Caroline Olivier wrote in *Le Revue Suisse:*

> After having reaped its harvest far and wide on the fields of battle and in the broad population through war and epidemics, death comes to strike, blow by blow, many heads who

> rise above the throng or who are, at least, not simply a unit, a cipher, an unknown number, but have a name that evokes memories. . . . Thus it has finally taken not only a great poet, but a great heart and a great spirit, a man who truly embodied the notion of genius through the depth and original compass of his thought, through his extraordinary insight and simplicity . . . With him, a great light has been extinguished.[56]

By the middle of January, obsequies had been held in Inowrocław and Lwów in Poland, and in Berlin. A memorial mass was held in Rome as well, but not with the participation of the Resurrectionists, who continued to express doubts about "what religion Mickiewicz had died in." In Poznań, however, Father Aleksy Prusinowski pronounced a sermon as sincere in articulating the nation's loss as it was pathetic:

> His name? There is no name for him, for each is too trivial! Where was he born? The bowels of the fatherland were his maternal womb, his cradle, the bed of pain on which an exhausted nation lies. Where did he live? He lived in the air that our breasts breathe, in the thoughts that want to burst through our temples, in the feelings that exert our hearts. Who was he? Don't ask! For this is the greatest of pain, he was the soul and the thought, the word of the nation. And now he's dead! Oh! not dead. . . . He has only fulfilled his calling, which God had bestowed on the nation as a mission that people chosen by Providence accept, and this is his greatness.[57]

Privately, the immediate reactions of friends and acquaintances were mixed. "For people of my generation," Krasiński wrote from Baden on 8 December,

> he was honey and milk and bile and spiritual blood. We all stem from him. He had swept us away on a wave of inspiration and cast us into the world. He was one of the pillars supporting a vault made not of stone, but of so many living and bloody hearts—a gigantic pillar he was, although itself cracked. . . . The greatest *wieszcz* not only of the nation, but of all Slavic tribes no longer lives.

Zaleski, for his part, was not as generous. As Goszczyński noted in his journal, "That Bohdan, ostensibly so sensitive and soft-hearted, attacked Adam, his pride, his shortcomings . . . with a fervor and doggedness that I had never had the occasion to see in him." Old General Skrzynecki, Towiański's first convert and then first antagonist in the West, seemed almost relieved. "However lamentable the loss of the great Poet," he wrote to Prince Czartoryski, "as far as the future is concerned . . . *il y aura une force perturbice demain*—and besides, he was very conceited, full of pride, and was as stubborn as a Jew." "Mickiewicz, what had you done to people?" Norwid asked plaintively.[58]

10

On 7 January the steamer carrying the poet's remains docked in Marseilles, where the authorities granted permission for the coffin to proceed. By 9 January the coffin was in Paris. Władysław Mickiewicz went out to meet it at the Gare de Lyon at four o'clock that morning, whence, accompanied by Aleksander Chodźko, Służalski, Lenoir-Zwierkowski, Lévy, and Celina's relative Ludwik Wołowski, it was transported on a carriage "drawn by two white horses, one saddled, with a coachman in the saddle," to the Church of St. Mary Magdalene, the neo-Classical temple on the place de la Concorde designed to the glory of Napoleon's army. The funeral was to take place on Monday, 21 January. Invitations were sent out to the Polish community in Paris on behalf of the "orphaned children and friends of the deceased." In accordance with Mickiewicz's wishes, he was to be buried alongside his wife, not at Père Lachaise, however, but in the émigré cemetery in Montmorency.[59]

The service began shortly before eleven and ended an hour later. Minutes before it was to commence, a disaffected émigré had at General Zamoyski on the steps of the church with a cane. Despite what many at the time took to be a political protest directed at a man some felt had been betraying the Polish cause, the attack was a purely personal affair, having nothing to do with politics or, for that matter, with Mickiewicz—which made the incident all the more distasteful, confirming, as it ostensibly did, the émigré malaise before the entire world, its "domestic shame," as Norwid called it.[60]

Too heavy for the catafalque, the coffin was placed on the floor of the church. Although *Wiadomości Polskie*, the house organ of the Hôtel Lambert, insisted that "many foreigners, friends, and admirers" had come to bid farewell to the Polish poet, the only French in attendance besides Lévy were Michelet, a group of Mickiewicz's auditors at the Collège, coworkers from the Arsenal, and Mme Rossignol, one of the family's closest friends. "Practically every Pole in Paris," however, "hurried to pay his last respects to the deceased": Towianist friends and foes alike, Aleksander Biergiel, Aleksander Chodźko and his brother Michał, Eustachy Januszkiewicz, Henryk Służalski, Feliks Wrotnowski, Stefan Zan; colleagues, and enemies, from the Hôtel Lambert, Prince Adam Czartoryski, Ludwik Lenoir-Zwierkowski, and Władysław Zamoyski; the Wołowskis; Józef Bohdan and Józef Zaleski; and perhaps even, but incognito and from a distance, Zygmunt Krasiński. There as well, recently arrived from Poznań, was Konstancja Łubieńska, Mickiewicz's erstwhile lover and confidante of his last years. As she was "turning tables" on her estate, the poet's "spirit" had appeared to her and ordered her to come to Paris for the funeral.[61]

As in Istanbul, no one was asked to give a sermon or speech; the potential for controversy was just too great. The service lasted a little over an hour, concluding sometime after noon. The coffin was placed in a hearse, which then made its way through Paris north to Montmorency, in its wake "a long line of carriages." Celina's coffin, exhumed a few days earlier from Père Lachaise, was waiting for it at St. Martin's, the parish church in Montmorency. So too was a crowd of people who had chosen to travel by rail to this little town where Mickiewicz and Celina had spent some of their first married days together in the company of their friend and protector Julian Ursyn Niemcewicz, now to be their neighbor in death. After a brief service, a group of youths hoisted the coffins on their shoulders and began wending their way on foot to the cemetery, some distance away. The road being "very steep, those carrying the huge coffin [containing Mickiewicz] had to change places often, halting the cortège a number of times." It took them nearly an hour. The weather had cleared and "the air was very gentle" as the two coffins were lowered into the ground.[62]

Only the ostensibly sensitive and soft-hearted Zaleski had been asked by the guardians of the family to say a few words over the grave of his friend. Bidding him farewell in the name of his Lithuania and "all of Poland from sea to sea," in the name of his "homeless" émigré community, in the name of his family and his "dearest and nearest from the banks of the Niemen, Wilija, and the whole world wide," Zaleski eulogized Mickiewicz as "unquestionably... superior to poets of the age" in whom

> a great mind and great affect were conjoined... and balanced with stalwartness of character and readiness for deed. But above all Adam Mickiewicz was a Polish patriot, on active civic duty for his nation.... For an entire age he pilgrimaged to the grave of his Mother-Country—in order to breathe life into her corpse for its resurrection.

It was for its sake that "he became inflamed, flew into rabid passion, sinned much, but loved no less." With this, as had become the custom among the émigrés, Zaleski threw a handful of Polish earth from "somewhere on the Dnieper's banks" onto the coffin and concluded, paraphrasing Mickiewicz's invocation to *Pan Tadeusz*,

> O Holy Virgin, you who guard bright Częstochowa,
> And shine in the Sharp Gate of Vilnius. You who protect
> The castle town of Nowogródek, with its faithful inhabitants,
> *Conduct the* Wieszcz *back by some miracle to his Native Land!*[63]

POSTSCRIPT

For they will open Your grave yet again,
And proclaim Your achievements in a different way,
Ashamed of the tears they shed today,
They will shed tears *to the power of two* . . .

—Cyprian Norwid[1]

On 27 June 1890, as a delegation of dignitaries from Poland, a handful of émigrés, and surviving members of Mickiewicz's family looked on, the poet's remains were disinterred in preparation for their translation to Poland. Upon opening the coffin, the gravediggers found

> a covering of rotten grass . . . , which [they] began to rake away with pitchforks and to place into wheelbarrows. After two or three more clumps of soppy grass were moved, a pair of shoes appeared and then the skull . . . and the remains, which were difficult to examine satisfactorily on account of the herbs sticking to them. They were moved in this state to a metal casket with the greatest of care. As they were being lifted, the shoes fell off and the skull slipped. They were laid [in the new casket] in the same position as they had been found, covered with ash, and bespread with flowers.

Among the herbs, the workers also came across "a metal figurine of Christ, from a cross, apparently, with its right arm broken off, as well as a rusty copper coin . . . and a white porcelain button, which objects Władysław Mickiewicz kept as mementos." With the transferal completed, the gravediggers immediately set to cutting up the original zinc coffin into little pieces, to sell, like so many holy relics, as souvenirs at what for Poles would be one of the most momentous events of the century.[2]

I

Much had changed in the thirty-five years following Mickiewicz's death. What had not was Poland's predicament. The efforts the Hôtel Lambert had invested in what has since come to be known as the Crimean War proved but an irritant in the face of the Great Powers' desire for stability. The Peace Congress of Paris, concluded in March 1856, in effect restored the post-Vienna order, and at the same time disposed of the Polish emigration once and for all as a factor to be reckoned with, if it ever really was. Seven years later, the January Uprising of 1863 in Russian Poland, bloodier and more futile than those that preceded it, sealed its fate. Although largely a home-grown affair, it was nonetheless the work of a generation brought up on the ideals of the Great Emigration, on romantic poetry, messianism, conspiracies, and a concomitant willingness to sacrifice blood, if only for the sake of demonstrating the will to exist. With nothing to show for it, however, but yet another crop of martyrs and repression even more brutal than before, the insurrection left the nation exhausted, and questioning the romantic politics that had precipitated the disaster. For the next two decades, as the focus of Polish national life shifted back to the homeland, Poles in all three partitions settled into a state of unwilling acquiescence, turning inward and pinning their hopes of survival on "sensible" cooperation with the partitioning powers while continuing to test, whenever possible, the policies put in place to demoralize them. In this uneven contest, in which cultural artifacts, perforce, functioned as simulacra for national institutions, the figure of Adam Mickiewicz, domesticated and adapted to the new environment, came to serve Poles as a constant point of reference—the nation's *wieszcz*, the first and the greatest, whose life and works at once shaped and embodied the ethos of modern Poland.

The idea of transferring Mickiewicz's remains to Poland first surfaced as a possibility after 1866, and was guided as much by political realities as by the potential for a symbolic statement. Whereas in dealing with his Polish population Bismarck had settled on a campaign of expulsion and deracination, and tsarist Russia continued to suppress ruthlessly any untoward expressions of national sentiment in its Polish provinces, Austria had opted for extending a measure of autonomy to its (Galician) portion of the old Commonwealth. Polish national identity was allowed to flourish, together with limited self-rule, in return for the loyalty of the land's conservative aristocracy to the Habsburg throne. Were Mickiewicz's "bones" to indeed find "a grave . . . in [his] land" ("Pilgrim's Litany"; *Dz.* 5:62), from a practical perspective Cracow was the only option. With its medieval royal castle and cathedral on Wawel Hill as seemingly indestructible reminders of Poland's independence, its symbolic function as the nation's old capital was indisputable. That the poet had never set foot in the Galician city was beside the point. When approached with the project by a Galician newspaper, Mickiewicz's son Władysław had no objections. "It was never [the family's] idea," he responded, "that the remains of our beloved father should find their final grave in a foreign albeit welcoming land in Montmorency." If reburial in Cracow was indeed the "desire of the general public," Władysław continued, "the family's wishes yield when it comes to disposing of the remains of the man who belongs more to the entire country than to them." Władysław's only condition was that his father be interred in the Royal Cathedral, "alongside Kościuszko and [Prince Józef] Poniatowski," modern Poland's greatest military heroes.[3]

It was not until the 1880s, however, after a good deal of resistance on the part of Galicia's cautious conservative elite, that the project finally began to acquire realizable shape, thanks largely to the efforts of Cracow's liberals and above all its youth. By June 1890, all of the preparatory work for the event was in place, whereupon responsibility for seeing it through was handed over to—co-opted by, rather—a committee headed by the land's Polish authorities. The event was henceforth to be official, paid for with Galician government funds rather than donations (which, it should be noted, now totaled nearly 10,000 guldens, gathered from all parts of Poland). Nonetheless, when the committee approached Franz Josef for permission, the Austrian emperor balked, not having forgotten that Mickiewicz had once described his great-great-grandmother Maria Theresa as nothing less than "a proud she-devil," and "godless" to boot (*Books of the Polish Nation*; Dz. 5:16). It was only after his two highest civil servants in Galicia threatened to resign did the emperor relent, not quite capable of grasping "the importance that [these two loyal Poles] attached to the [event]." In any case, it was understood by all involved that the Galician authorities would do everything necessary to prevent the occasion from turning into a political demonstration.[4]

The reinterment at Wawel was set for 4 July.

2

When the workers opened the grave in Montmorency that early summer day in 1890, Mickiewicz's metal casket was found lying beneath the rotting wooden coffin of his wife. Beside them lay five others. Two contained the remains of their sons. The older coffin, dating back to 1864, was that of Aleksander, the fourth-born. A polyglot and a promising journalist who was just beginning to cut his teeth under the guidance of Armand Lévy with articles for the French press on the January Uprising, Oleś was only twenty-two when he died in Berlin of tuberculosis—not what his father would have expected from a boy he had described as "tough of body... capable of being a soldier." The fresher coffin housed the remains of Aleksander's younger brother Jan. Jean, as he was usually referred to (Mickiewicz had nicknamed him Pippin after the founder of the Carolingian dynasty), was intelligent, quick-witted, but also restless and unpredictable. At the age of eighteen he had made his way to Cracow with hopes of participating in the uprising, which, it seems, he never did. Shortly after his return to Paris in 1864 his increasingly erratic behavior compelled even his siblings to admit that he had inherited their mother's genes. The son Mickiewicz was sure "would always manage" spent the last seventeen years of his life in and out of the mental institution in Charenton outside of Paris, where he passed away in 1885, "dead to the world" long before then.[5]

Of the remaining children, Maria, Władysław, Helena, and Józef all lived to witness the reinterment of their father's remains, as did Helena's husband and Władysław's wife, together with a handful of Mickiewicz's grandchildren. Whether Andrée Mainard did as well remains a mystery (she would have been forty-three in 1890). In any case, this would have made little difference. Maria and Władysław had made sure that their illegitimate half-sister should be consigned to oblivion, along with her recently (1889?) deceased mother. Ksawera Deybel-Mainard's periodic entreaties for some form of recognition for her daughter and herself—Władysław at one point called them "blackmail"—had been callously dismissed after Mickiewicz's death by the embarrassed keepers of his flame.[6]

Fifty-year-old Helena, whose "purely Slavic" slowness and naïve sincerity had once so charmed her father, was about to leave France for the first time in thirty years in order to participate in the solemnities in Cracow. Since 1862, she had been living a prosaic, contented life outside of Paris as the wife of Ludwik Hryniewiecki, a railroad engineer, and as the mother of their four surviving children. She was as unremarkable as Mickiewicz had, in his own way, always hoped she would be.[7]

Witnessing the exhumation that day together with his brother Władysław was forty-year-old Józef, everyone's beloved Zizi, who as the youngest of the Mickiewicz children was barely five when he was orphaned. Brought up by the doting Falkenhagen-Zaleskis and then the object of contention between them and his siblings, he too, it seems, had inherited a dose of his mother's genes, although there was something of his father in him as well. Drawn equally to piano and pen, over the years he had turned into an absent-minded, eccentric misanthrope, never quite able to find a niche in life and acutely uncomfortable with his status as a son of Poland's *wieszcz*. Since 1874, he had been working for the Administration Générale de l'Assistance Publique in Paris, a job that only went so far in satisfying his sense of social justice. The income, though, allowed Józef to indulge his journalistic vein, which he expended on researching and writing virulently anticlerical tracts, few of which were ever published—not quite what Mickiewicz had in mind when he once characterized his youngest son as having been "created to be a poet."[8]

It was Maria and her younger brother Władysław who, since Mickiewicz's death, had presumed to represent his legacy to the world. They did so with a dogged sense of reverential purpose that effectively determined the content, if not quite the shape, of the poet's image for generations.

Marynia, as Mickiewicz called his favorite child, had married in 1857, more out of a desire for independence than love. Her marriage of eleven years to the artist Tadeusz Gorecki, the son of Mickiewicz's friend, the poet and erstwhile Towianist Antoni, was not a happy one, all the more so since her brothers were never able to come to terms with her choice of husband. Of the four children she had had with Gorecki, only one, a son, still survived. Scarred for life by her mother's illness as well as years of Towianist experiments in child-rearing, Maria had grown into a haughty, stubborn, and bitterly intolerant woman, a devout Catholic who sought to compensate for her childhood traumas by projecting a domesticated image of her father as a national poet devoted to the national cause—and "a Catholic to the core." As far as she was concerned, the messy details and contradictions of his private life, to say nothing of his heterodoxy and revolutionism, were irrelevant in this larger scheme of things, suppressed as they had to be for the sake of his role as an edificatory icon for the nation. On this point, Maria found herself waging a life-long battle with her brother, just as she did over the material artifacts that she possessed as her inheritance from her parents.[9]

Władysław, for his part, was still experiencing the thrill of having just seen the first volume of his Polish biography of his father come out in print (the remaining three would follow over the next five years). As a title for what he considered the culmination of his own life's work, Władysław had chosen *Żywot*—a word which for a Polish reader immediately evoked the "life" of a saint—*Narrated on the Basis of Material He Himself Had Gathered as well as His Own Recollections.** The title effectively epitomized Władysław's way. From the moment of his father's death, he had devoted his own life to preserving and promoting Mickiewicz's legacy—as he understood it, and as he saw fit.

Encouraged and aided at each step of that way by Armand Lévy, first as mentor, then as more of a brother (and perhaps even lover) than friend, and finally as business partner, Władysław made it his mission to collect every artifact, every quote, every reminiscence, thought, and scrap of paper relating to his father, in the process traveling to every place associated with his name. That journey, first undertaken in 1859–1862, eventually took him to St. Petersburg, where, as if attempting to literally relive Mickiewicz's life through his own, he fell deeply in love with Maria Malewska, the daughter of his father's closest Philomath friend Franciszek and his mother's sister, Helena. The cousins were married in 1863. One of their two surviving daughters was with them at the graveside at Montmorency. Two of the other coffins unearthed that day contained the remains of Adam and Celina, children of Władysław and Maria who had died in infancy. (The fifth was that of Maria Gorecka's first child, also named Celina.)

To be sure, Mickiewicz was not the sole focus of Władysław's public life. Over the years, he had worked as a journalist, editor, translator, and political activist, in time assuming the role of unofficial ambassador of all things Polish in Paris. To this end, in 1866 he and Lévy had founded the Librairie du Luxembourg, which in the course of its twenty-three years of ruinously unprofitable existence published some two hundred volumes in Polish and French, everything from cheap editions of the Polish classics to political pamphlets, and provided employment for members of the Mickiewicz clan. Nonetheless, it, like each one of Władysław's endeavors, was invariably driven by a single impulse and framed by a single consideration: to promulgate his father's legacy. In this, however, it was not so much that a good deal of Władysław's efforts were devoted to publishing

**Żywot Adama Mickiewicza, podług zebranych przez siebie materiałów, oraz z własnych wspomnień opowiedział*, in four volumes (1890–1895). A second, expanded edition of the first two volumes appeared in 1926.

the writings of the poet,* but rather that they, like the entire enterprise, were intended to demonstrate—uncritically, defensively, anachronistically—the wisdom and continuing relevance of Mickiewicz's political thought and of a life devoted to its realization.

It was this aspect of her younger brother's tribute to their father that the ultramontane Maria found difficult to stomach. Yet the incongruity of their respective takes on Mickiewicz's legacy notwithstanding, Władysław was just as intent as his sister on projecting him as a flawless paragon of the Polish cause, in effect "a monument of bronze," as one critic in the 1920s would famously put it, erected to serve "the interests of the nation." And although Władysław may have been more willing than Maria to give his father's Towianism a sympathetic hearing, Deybel, Pilchowski, illegitimate children, and, for that matter, Celina's mental illness were something else entirely. On these points, family honor, no less than Victorian sensibility and the exigencies of the national struggle, demanded discretion, if not silence. Celina's condition was to be dealt with euphemistically; some of the Towianists more outré practices were to be ignored; Deybel's name had to be expunged from both narrative and archive; and anything that might besmirch, diminish, or even cast the merest shadow upon Mickiewicz's achievements or the wisdom of his ways was to be categorically—and, in many instances, simply dishonestly—dismissed.[10]

3

Acceding to the wishes of the committee in charge of the translation, Władysław had agreed to make the appropriate arrangements for the French portion of the event himself. On the morning of 28 June 1890, "a large crowd... dressed... in mourning..., made up of women, old men, young people and children, Poles, Frenchmen, Hungarians, Czechs, and Russians," many bearing wreaths on behalf of various organizations and institutions, arrived at Montmorency by train from Paris for the official exhumation, accompanied by a gaggle of reporters from both the French and Polish press.[11]

Thanks to Władysław, the program at the graveside was ideologically ecumenical. Much to the displeasure of some in attendance, he had personally invited Ernest Renan to speak on behalf of the Collège de France. The notorious author of *The Life of Jesus* opened the solemnities with a farewell to his "great and illustrious colleague," who together with Michelet and Quinet, "had become a symbol [of the institution],... an inseparable part

*Including several editions of his father's works (*Dzieła*, 4 vols [1868, 1869–1870, 1876]); *Dzieła*, 11 vols. [1880–1885]); several editions of his correspondence (1870–1872, 1871–1873, 1875–1876); a new edition of the Parisian lectures (1866); *La Politique du dix-neuvième siècle* (1868), being a collection of Mickiewicz's political writings; *Mélanges posthumes*, 2 vols. (1872–1879), which collected Mickiewicz's French-language works; *Współudział Adama Mickiewicz w sprawie Andrzeja Towiańskiego. Listy i przemówienia*, 2 vols. (Paris, 1877), a collection of materials relating to Mickiewicz's activity as a Towianist; and *Mémorial de la Légion polonaise de 1848 créée en Italie par Adam Mickiewicz* (1877). In addition, Władysław also had published a one-volume French-language biography of his father in 1888, *Adam Mickiewicz, sa vie et son œuvre*.

of [its] past glories and past joys." France, he went on, would never forget this "great idealist" "who believed... in the divine spirit that animates all those who carry the breath of life and, despite dark clouds, saw a brilliant future where downtrodden humanity would find consolation for its sufferings." Renan's speech was followed by a few words from a representative of the Association Littéraire et Artistique Internationale, and then, on behalf of the Polish Historical-Literary Society in Paris, the last vestige of the Hôtel Lambert, by a farewell from Prince Władysław Czartoryski, who thirty-five years earlier had so disappointed Mickiewicz during their joint mission to Istanbul. Addressing him now as "the king of inspiration and national feelings," sent "by Providence" to instill his unfortunate nation with "faith in [its] viability and hope for a better future," Czartoryski bid him return "to the land that [he] loved on behalf of millions."[12]

After a representative of the Cracow committee thanked France for the "hospitality" it had extended to Poland's greatest poet and Renan for his eloquent tribute, what followed gave many at the ceremony uncomfortable pause. Aware that this would be their only opportunity to pay their last respects, Polish socialists took their turn in honoring the man they considered to be their "forerunner." As Bolesław Limanowski, one of their most prominent representatives, put it in his speech that day, "Out of all his socialist contemporaries [Mickiewicz] understood best what genuine internationalist socialism should be, condemning the egotistical isolation of nations but respecting the freedom and autonomy of each and believing all nations to be a single family." For their part, representatives of students from both Poland and abroad reminded the crowd that the poet had always "steadfastly stood on the side of the disinherited and exploited" and that only "when [his] remains rest in a free and independent land" would this tribute to him be consummated. Władysław, it seems, had made his point—but so too did the Polish collective: henceforth Mickiewicz's legacy was to be up for grabs, with every emergent ideological formation hoping to "drag him over to its side" as an unimpeachable source of legitimation.[13]

The ceremony concluded on a less controversial note, with tributes from representatives of Polish women in the emigration, ethnic Lithuanians, the Czecho-Slovak Association of Paris, and the local Hungarian community. Borne on the shoulders of the young people who had done so much to make the occasion possible, the new coffin containing the poet's remains was taken to the parish church for a memorial service, where it was serenaded by students of the Polish School in Batignolles, still in existence forty-eight years after its founding. As in life, so in afterlife, Mickiewicz was leaving his wife and children behind.

That evening the poet's remains were placed on a train at the Gare de l'Est to commence their final journey. As the crowd gathered around the car containing the coffin, depositing wreath upon wreath into the compartment, sixty-three-year-old Armand Lévy, "Mickiewicz's longtime and dearest friend, a witness of his last minutes in Istanbul, and always an ardent admirer of his genius," gave witness "'before those dear remains'" of

France's abiding love for Poland, which he sealed with "a fraternal kiss" on the cheek of one of the student delegates accompanying the poet's coffin to Poland. Lévy, however, remained on the platform that evening, watching the car carrying the remains of the man he worshipped fade into the darkness. As an unrepentant freethinker, socialist, and staunch defender of the rights of Jews, he had not been invited to Cracow.[14]

Some twenty-four hours later the train rolled into Zurich. The throng that met Mickiewicz's remains was made up of Poles and Swiss as well as assorted foreigners who had found refuge in this haven for the politically incorrect, among them the handful of Andrzej Towiański's disciples that still clung to the Master's teachings eleven years after his death there in 1879. Nine speeches—in Polish, French, German, Italian, Russian, and Bulgarian—and a forest of torches paid tribute to the Polish poet and honorary professor of the Academy of Lausanne, who had come ever so close to making Switzerland his home away from home.

The reception in Vienna was a different matter altogether. The Austrian authorities had made it clear that no public tributes would be permitted. Just to make sure, they had the coffin transferred from the French train to an Austrian one in the middle of the night, without the knowledge of even the family. And when a group of some one hundred people gathered at the station the following morning, they were told that the train had been delayed and would not be leaving until the day after.

On the evening of 3 July 1890, the train carrying Mickiewicz's remains, accompanied by Władysław, his wife, and younger daughter, finally pulled into Cracow, where some eighteen members of the poet's family, including Helena, together with her husband and one of their daughters, Maria and her son Ludwik, as well as Władysław's other daughter were waiting to meet it.

4

For days, the city had been preparing for the event. Flags and bunting, garlands and wreaths were hung from practically every building and balcony along the route from the train station to Wawel. Torches and urns on pylons of various shapes, sizes, and faux surfaces cropped up on streets and squares, together with stands for choirs and orchestras and dignitaries. Poles from every corner of Poland and beyond descended on Cracow—10,000 from Lwów, Warsaw, and Vienna in a single day; another 2,500 packed into an eighteen-wagon train, with three more to follow on the eve of the solemnities—"gentry, townsfolk, peasants, merchants, artisans, guilds and associations..., young people and veterans, women and children," and, of course, nearly everyone who was anyone making a living with pen, brush, chisel, or musical score. Every available space in the city was mobilized to accommodate the throngs. Medical personnel were stationed along the parade route just in case. By early in the morning of 4 July, some one hundred thousand people had

Fig. 30 Mickiewicz's reinterment in Cracow. Photograph published in *Złożenie zwłok Adama Mickiewicza na Wawelu dnia 4go lipca 1890 roku* (Cracow, 1890).

gathered in Cracow to witness Mickiewicz's coffin make its way from the railroad warehouse where it had been housed overnight through the center of the Old Town to Wawel Cathedral.[15]

At eight that morning, after a brief funeral service, "the modest lead coffin" was placed on a pyramid-shaped hearse covered with dark red plush and "a baldachin of the same material towering over the coffin," to which was affixed a sign bearing a verse from Mickiewicz's "Pilgrim's Litany": "For a grave for our bones in our land, we beseech you, O Lord!" (The baldachin would have to be lowered later in order to let the carriage pass under telegraph wires.) In what would be the first of a series of speeches that day, Władysław Mickiewicz thanked the students of Cracow and the organizing committee for making the occasion possible, and, on behalf of "the unfortunate nation" as well as the family, also "the Monarch" "for honoring their most ardent desires." As bells rang out from the city's many churches, the provincial marshal of Galicia accepted the poet's remains, remarking that in the nation's current predicament "the only bright ray of comfort is the thought that at least this portion of Polish land will be allowed to pay homage to the ashes of Adam Mickiewicz . . . and to lay them to rest where for centuries our nation has been accustomed to burying its kings and heroes."[16]

"A splendid sun shone down on the city" when, to the accompaniment of Chopin's funeral march, an enormous procession surged forward along the prescribed route. First an orchestra, then a detachment of firemen, then one hundred and fifty peasants bearing forty-four wreaths—the mystical number of Poland's "savior" from *Forefathers' Eve*, part 3—some from as far as the poet's native Lithuania, that spelled out, one letter at a time, "TO ADAM MICKIEWICZ, FROM THE FOLK OF ALL THE LANDS OF POLAND." There followed delegation upon delegation representing all manner of Polish associations, organizations, and institutions—students, teachers, journalists, public employees, pharmacists, entrepreneurs, craftsmen, shopkeepers, waiters, clerks, Polish mothers, daughters, and virgins, printers, plumbers, doctors, booksellers, sculptors and painters, veterans, oil workers, lawyers—from all three partitions and from practically every country with a Polish presence, decked out in an array of modern and traditional dress, bearing wreaths made of every imaginable symbolic material, some on satin pillows, others with sashes featuring appropriate verses from the *wieszcz*'s poetry. A delegation from Warsaw, the "land of tears and misery," carried a silver wreath bearing the line (from *Pan Tadeusz*), "Born in bondage, shackled at birth"; shepherds from the Tatra Mountains bore a wreath made of dwarf mountain pine; a wreath carried by a delegation of Polish Jews, one among several, proclaimed, quoting again from *Pan Tadeusz*, that they "loved the fatherland like Poles." Delegations from Lithuania and the Grand Duchy of Poznań, from Polish Silesia, Bukovina, and the Ukrainian provinces of the Old Commonwealth announced themselves to all be "children of one fatherland." Carrying wreaths of their own in a tribute to Mickiewicz's great friendships were the families of Tomasz Zan, Antoni Edward Odyniec, and

Józef Bohdan Zaleski. There were Czech, Serb, and Ukrainian delegations as well, hailing "the great poet of the fraternal Polish nation," but for whatever reason, none representing Russia, Germany, Italy, France, or Switzerland. By 1890, Mickiewicz had become, it seems, largely a "minor" Slavic phenomenon.[17]

Over an hour passed before the carriage bearing the coffin, drawn by six horses, finally started on its way. Preceding it were members of the Polish Academy of Sciences and a full complement of professors from Galicia's two universities, followed by the Armenian and Roman Catholic bishops of Cracow accompanied by some five hundred priests. In its wake walked Mickiewicz's family, together with the highest dignitaries of the land. As the hearse made its way down Warszawska Street, through Matejko Square, and along Basztowa and Sławkowska Streets, its retinue of ceremonial pallbearers continually changing so as to give as many notables as possible their moment of contact with charisma, showers of flowers streamed down from windows and balconies packed with onlookers. The procession paused briefly in the Market Square, where it was serenaded by a choir of two hundred in front of St. Mary's Cathedral, then proceeded down Grodzka Street, which was bedecked with banners, rugs, and tapestries. As one of Władysław's daughters recalled:

> Cracow was transformed unrecognizably. . . . The procession wended its way slowly for hours. The innumerable throng seemed to be a single feeling creature. . . . A kind of madness, fervor seemed to possess everyone. . . . Peasants, upon learning that the *Wieszcz*'s family was passing before them, threw themselves at our knees. Mothers, young ladies publicly kissed my Father's hand, some Jewess almost forced some trifle on me as a souvenir.

Gazing at the throng crowding every inch of sidewalk around him, Maria's son Ludwik "kept shaking his head . . . and repeating in his French-accented Polish, 'I had no idea that my grandfather was so popular.'"[18]

When the hearse reached the foot of Wawel Hill, a group of students hoisted the coffin onto their shoulders for the final leg of its journey. Turning to address the poet's remains, their spokesman, Włodzimierz Lewicki, a Polonized Ruthenian, promised "the great bard" that Poland's youth "would march forward inspired by [his] slogans . . . and would demolish . . . the already collapsing structures of egotism, ignorance, and caste in order to build on these ruins a better future in the name of *liberty, equality,* and *fraternity!*" With Wawel's giant Zygmunt Bell tolling from on high, the students carried the coffin up the steep hill to the entrance of the cathedral, where it was met by Adam Asnyk, one of the most prominent poets of the post-1863 generation. "After the loss of our independence," he intoned from the cathedral steps, "when we were deprived of our ancient kings and hetmans, when the royal seal . . . perished on the battlefield of history and when . . . arms proved inadequate in [Poland's] defense, Providence sent a new leader for its abased and grieving people."

> This leader lifted the falling banner of a defeated nation, bore it away from the confusion of battles lost . . . and transported it from a land of tears . . . to the immortal country of the spirit, where it must rise above brute force and fickle fate, above corporeal suffering, and even above the momentary doubt of the heavy burden of stumbling generations.
>
> This leader was Adam Mickiewicz. . . .
>
> However much conditions of existence, currents of thought, and conceptions may change, the essential idea of the *wieszcz* will stand immovably above the ephemeral slogans of the day. For he is not the property of one age, one generation, one party, one class, or segment of the nation, but belongs to all of suffering Poland as it struggles for life.[19]

Asnyk was followed by the rector of the Jagiellonian University, Count Stanisław Tarnowski, the most eloquent spokesman of Galicia's conservative, Catholic elite, and its arbiter of taste in all things cultural—who had worked hard over the months to minimize the students' contribution to the event as well as block the participation in it of Galicia's peasants and workers. Unhappy with the tone of Lewicki's speech (which he thought he had managed to censor beforehand), Tarnowski made no effort to conceal his ressentiment. "Our century," he ventured,

> began in great confusion, confusion of conscience, mind, and intercourse, and it now concludes no differently. . . . In this chaos of ideas, aspirations, sufferings, and events, in which it would have been easy to break apart or, what's worse, decompose . . . we have at least survived with soul intact and scatheless. God's will and grace preserved [our nation], as did our own will and merit; but we had help and sustenance from those great ones among us who guarded that soul's unity and essence, its consciousness of self and its responsibility. . . . Such was Mickiewicz. This is his royal heritage, and his right to rest in these royal tombs.

As a professor of literature at the Jagiellonian University and author of countless articles and monographs on Polish romanticism, it was Tarnowski who more than anyone, perhaps, had been responsible for the tamed, Catholicized image of Mickiewicz that, despite the students' efforts, was on display that day in Cracow.[20]

At the conclusion of Tarnowski's speech, the students carried Mickiewicz's remains into Poland's national sanctuary, where for some five hundred years, until its disappearance from the map of Europe, the nation's kings and queens had been crowned and interred, alongside its bishops, notables, and heroes. Accompanied by priests singing funeral dirges, the coffin was placed on a towering catafalque, at its head on one side a reproduction of the icon of Our Lady of Częstochowa, Poland's protectoress and queen, and on the other an image of Our Lady of Ostrabrama in Vilnius, which, as Mickiewicz had written in the invocation to *Pan Tadeusz*, "would by some miracle return [him and his people] to the bosom of the fatherland" (*Dz.* 4:11). The mass—Mozart's *Requiem*—was celebrated by Cracow bishop Albin Dunajewski, who only days earlier had been elevated to cardinal. Cracow's star preacher, Father Władysław Chotkowski, gave the sermon, which effectively consummated Mickiewicz's domestication within the church from which he had become so alienated during his lifetime. "We wanted to have him among the graves of our kings," Father Chotkowski proclaimed, because he "nourished the nation in its days of spiritual hunger, braced its energy, strengthened its hopes, and hoisted its hearts aloft"—but only insofar as "he was a Catholic," who "through his songs contributed to the salvation of souls in our nation."

> And although no one can be forbidden from participating in this general expression of grief, one must beware should anyone who has renounced Christ and the Catholic Church want to appropriate him or consider him as one of their own.[21]

It was just before three o'clock in the afternoon when Father Chotkowski concluded his nearly hour-long sermon. Cardinal Dunajewski led the clergy in performing the final ceremonies. Once again the students hoisted the coffin onto their shoulders. They eased it down the narrow stairs leading to a recently renovated chamber where a sarcophagus, made of limestone from Częstochowa, its bottom strewn with sand from the Niemen River and earth from Nowogródek, awaited the poet's remains. To the tolling of the Zygmunt Bell, Adam Mickiewicz's coffin was lowered into its final resting place among the kings and heroes of Poland.

NOTES

PREFACE

1. Zygmunt Krasiński to Adam Sołtan, 8 December 1855, in *Listy do Sołtana*, ed. Sudolski, 617.
2. See Siwicka, *Zapytaj Mickiewicza*.
3. Green, "Polish Hip-Hop."
4. de Lautréamont, *Les Chants de Maldoror*, 318.
5. Weintraub, *Poetry of Adam Mickiewicz*; Welsh, *Adam Mickiewicz*.
6. Jastrun, *Adam Mickiewicz*; Pruszyński, *Adam Mickiewicz*; Dernałowicz, *Adam Mickiewicz*.
7. Coleman, *Young Mickiewicz*.
8. Gardner, *Adam Mickiewicz*.
9. Weintraub, "Adam Mickiewicz (1798–1855)."
10. See Bibliography, Kronika Życia i Twórczości Mickiewicza.

CHAPTER 1. CHILDHOOD (1798–1815)

1. Aleksander Mickiewicz to Franciszek Mickiewicz, 1860, *Korespondencja AM* 1:308 n. 1.
2. Zygmunt Krasiński to August Cieszkowski, 13[–14] July 1848, *Listy do Cieszkowskiego* et al. 1:358. Branicki, quoted in Rymkiewicz, *Kilka szczegółów*, 29. Varnhagen von Ense, *Tagebücher*, 276. Rybczonek, "Przodkowie Adama Mickiewicza po kądzieli."
3. Mickiewicz to Józef Jeżowski, [end of February] 1830, *Dz.* 15:24. Ludwika Śniadecka to Michał Czajkowski-Sadik Pasha, 16 January 1856, quoted in Rawita-Gawroński, "Sadyk-Pasza," 223–24.
4. As recalled by Maria Gorecka (1875), *Wspomnienia*, 100.
5. Franciszek and Aleksander Mickiewicz to Mickiewicz, 25 November/7 December 1819, *AF K* 1:308–9; A. Mickiewicz to Mickiewicz, 6/18 June 1820, *AF K* 2:146.
6. Skulski, "Studia szkolne."
7. As recalled by Aleksander Biergel, *Rozmowy*, 319.
8. As recalled by Władysław Mickiewicz, *Żywot* 1:22.
9. Nieuważny, *My z Napoleonem*, 103–4. As recalled by W. Mickiewicz, *Żywot* 1:22.
10. As recalled by Jules Michelet, *Rozmowy*, 267.
11. Quoted in *Żywot* 1:368.

CHAPTER 2. YOUTH (1815–1824)

1. *Lzp* 1:268.
2. Morawski, *Kilka lat*, 60–61.
3. Bujakowski, *Z młodości*, 15–16.
4. Franciszek Malewski to Mickiewicz, 23 November[–1 December/5–13 December] 1819, *AF K* 1:307. As noted down by Eustachy Januszkiewicz (1846), *Rozmowy*, 254–55.
5. As noted down by Aleksander Chodźko (1844), *Rozmowy*, 224. *Lzp* 1:262, 258–59.
6. Mickiewicz to Onufry Pietraszkiewicz, 6/18 February 1821, *Dz.* 14:177. Malinowski, *Księga wspomnień*, 35.
7. Czeczot to Mickiewicz, 6/18 October 1819, *AF K* 1:155.
8. As recalled by Antoni Edward Odyniec (1875–1878), *Rozmowy*, 47; as noted down by Franciszek Malewski (1827), ibid., 61.
9. "Prawidła dla uczniów lekcyj publicznych w Imperatorskim Uniwersytecie wileńskim" (1817), quoted in Chmielowski, *Adam Mickiewicz* 1:77–78.
10. *Rekonstrukcja*, 669.
11. "Ustawy [ogólne] Towarzystwa Filomatycznego wileńskiego," *AF M* 2:1–2.
12. Malinowski, *Kilka lat*, 210. "Sprawozdania sekretarza" (1 October 1817–1 January 1818), *AF M* 1:30–41, 231–40, 126.
13. Organizational matters, *Dz.* 6:9–115; reviews, critiques, and reports, Dz. 6:117–82. "Remarks on Dyzma Bończa-Tomaszewski's *Jagiellonida*," *Pamiętnik Warszawski* 13 (1819), *Dz.* 5:81–106.
14. Jeżowski, "[Przemowa na posiedzeniu Wielkim 1 styczni 1818]," *AF M* 1:17. *Dz.* 2: 205–51. Wolff, *Inventing Eastern Europe*, 215.
15. Jeżowski, "[Przemowa na posiedzenių Wielkim 1 styczni 1818]," *AF M* 1:17.
16. "Onufrowe," *AF P* 2:85–106.
17. Mickiewicz to Malewski, 19 June/1 July 1820, *Dz.* 14:134.
18. Mickiewicz to Jeżowski, ca. 10/22 February 1821, *Dz.* 14:181. Michał Czarnocki, "Krótka wiadomość o tajnych towarzystwach uczniów Uniwersytetu Wileńskiego," in *Z filareckiego świata*, 156.
19. Czeczot to Mickiewicz, 20 [Dec. 1820/1 Jan. 1821], *AF K* 3:95. Malewski to Mickiewicz, 20 [Dec. 1820/1 Jan. 1821], ibid., 92. Czeczot to Mickiewicz, 20 [Dec. 1820/1 Jan. 1821], ibid., 95–96.
20. Mickiewicz to Rector Szymon Malewski, *Dz.* 14:36. Czeczot to Mickiewicz, 8/20 April 1820, *AF K* 2:19.
21. Mickiewicz to Józef Jeżowski, [24 November/6 December 1819], *Dz.* 14:74. Mickiewicz to Jeżowski, [5/17 May 1820], ibid., 107. Mickiewicz to Jeżowski, [27 January/8 February 1820], ibid., 98.
22. Mickiewicz to Jeżowski, [24 November/6 December 1819], *Dz.* 14:74; Mickiewicz to Jeżowski, [19/31 January 1820], ibid., 97. Mickiewicz to Jeżowski, [ca. 10/22 January 1821], ibid., 164.
23. Onufry Pietraszkiewicz to Mickiewicz, 23 February/7 March [1821], *AF K* 3:165.
24. Tomasz Zan to Mickiewicz, 10/22 Dec. 1822, *AF K* 4:370; Czeczot to Mickiewicz, 7/19–11/23 Oct. [1820], ibid., 2:328.
25. Malewski to Mickiewicz, 26 January/7 February 1821, *AF K* 3:125.
26. Malewski to Mickiewicz, 9[–13–14/21–25–26] June 1820, *AF K* 2:156. Baworowski, "Notatka," 153–54. Mickiewicz to Jeżowski, 10/22 January 1821, *Dz.* 14:164.
27. As noted down by A. Chodźko (1847), *Rozmowy*, 232.
28. As noted down by A. Chodźko (1844), *Rozmowy*, 225. Kazimierz Piasecki to Mickiewicz, 1/13 December 1821, *AF K* 4:81. Zgorzelski, "Materiały."
29. Mickiewicz to Malewski, June 15/27 1822, *Dz.* 14:215. Pietraszkiewicz to Mickiewicz, August 5/17 1822, *AF K* 4:218. Czeczot to Mickiewicz, 26 November/8 December 1822, ibid., 359.
30. Anonymous note in the journal *Wanda*, *Mwow*, 49. Malewski to Mickiewicz, 11 November 1822, Korespondencja. Zan to Mickiewicz, 7/19 February 1823, *AF K* 5:40–41. As noted down by A. Chodźko (1844), *Rozmowy*, 225.

31. Mickiewicz to Zan, 13/25 May 1820, *Dz.* 14:124–25. As noted down by A. Chodźko (1845), *Rozmowy*, 225.
32. Mickiewicz to Czeczot, ca. 25 June/7 July 1817, *Dz.* 14:13–14. Czeczot to Mickiewicz, 15/27 December 1819, *AF K* 1:349.
33. Malewski to Mickiewicz [30–31 Jan./11–12 Feb. 1821], *AF K* 3:127. Odyniec, *Wspomnienia*, 225, 232.
34. Mickiewicz to Czeczot, 15/27 [January–18/30 January 1820], *Dz.* 14:89. Mickiewicz to Czeczot, [19 February/2 Marc 1820], ibid., 101. Mickiewicz to Pietraszkiewicz, [26 June/8 July 1821], ibid., 195.
35. Mickiewicz to Jeżowski 5/17 May 1820, *Dz.* 14:107.
36. Mickiewicz to Jeżowski, 29 November/11 December 1820, *Dz.* 14:159.
37. Malewski to Jeżowski, 6–7/18–19 April, 20 April/2 May 1821, *AF K* 3:258.
38. Czeczot to Pietraszkiewicz, 25 April/7 May 1821, *AF K* 3:279–80; Jeżowski to Mickiewicz 4/16 May 1821, ibid., 291.
39. Mickiewicz to Czeczot, 20 April/2 May 1821, *Dz.* 14:188. Mickiewicz describes this glen in great detail in a letter to Czeczot and Zan, 10/22 May 1820, ibid., 111.
40. Odyniec, *Wspomnienia*, 228n.
41. Zan to Pietraszkiewicz, 23 August/4 September 1820, *AF K* 2:248–49.
42. Mickiewicz to Jeżowski, 29 November/11 December 1820, *Dz.* 14:160. Czeczot to Pietraszkiewicz, 25 April/7 May 1821, *AF K* 3:275; Malewski to Jeżowski, [6–7/19–19 April, 20 April/2 May 1821], ibid., 258.
43. Domeyko, "O młodości," 151. Maria Puttkamer to Zan, 27 March/8 April [1822], *AF K*, 4:183. M. Puttkamer to Zan, 11/23 November [1822], ibid., 332.
44. M. Puttkamer to Zan, [12/24 April 1822], *AF K* 4:196.
45. Mickiewicz to Pietraszkiewicz, 6/18 [February 1821], *Dz.* 14:177–78.
46. Mickiewicz to Czeczot 25 July/6 August 1821, *Dz.* 14:198.
47. Mickiewicz to Czeczot, 25 July/6 August 1821, *Dz.* 14:199.
48. Mickiewicz to Pietraszkiewicz, 13/25 September [1821], *Dz.* 14:201.
49. Mickiewicz to Pietraszkiewicz, 13/25 September [1821], *Dz.* 14:201–2.
50. Zan to Mickiewicz, 22 October/3 November 1822, *AF K* 4:308. Mickiewicz to Zan, [16/28 October 1822], *Dz.* 14:235.
51. M. Puttkamer to Mickiewicz, 18[/30 August 1822], *AF K* 4:229–30.
52. M. Puttkamer to Zan, 29 September/11 October [1822], *AF K* 4:268. Mickiewicz to M. Puttkamer, 17/29 [October 1822], *Dz.* 14:237–39. Gąsiorowski, *Adam Mickiewicz*, 101–7.
53. Czeczot to Mickiewicz, 28 September/10 October [1822], *AF K* 4:265–66. M. Puttkamer to Mickiewicz, [June or October 1822 or May 1823], Korespondencja. M. Puttkamer to Zan, [1/13 May 1823], *AF K* 5:195; Mickiewicz to Zan, [16/28 September 1822], *Dz.* 14:225. Czeczot to Malewski, 30 May/11 June 1823, *Korespondencja Filomatów*, 450.
54. Mickiewicz to Czeczot and Antoni Edward Odyniec, [18/30 June 1823], *Dz.* 14:300. M. Puttkamer to Zan, [1/13 May 1823], *AF K* 5:196.
55. *Żywot* 1:69 n. 1.
56. Mickiewicz to Malewski, [ca. 23 January/4 February 1822], *Dz.* 14:206.
57. Odyniec, *Wspomnienia*, 190. *AF M* 2:431.
58. Mickiewicz to Malewski, 20 November/2 December [1822], *Dz.* 14:245. Mickiewicz to Zan, [10/22 October 1822], ibid., 233; Mickiewicz to Jeżowski, 1/13 February [1823], ibid., 258. Mickiewicz to Czeczot, [23 August/4 September 1823], ibid., 308. Mickiewicz to Zan, [10/22 October 1822], ibid., 233.
59. Mickiewicz to Czeczot, 9/21 April [1823], *Dz.* 14:291.
60. Mickiewicz to Odyniec, 22 February/6 March 1826, *Dz.* 1:346.
61. Zan to Mickiewicz, 13/25 May 1823, *AF K* 5:219–20.
62. Walerian Krasiński to Czeczot, 27 May/8 June 1823, *AF K* 5:239. Kajetan Koźmian, quoted in Syga, *Te księgi*, 26. Fr[anciszek] Grzymała, "Poezje Adama Mickiewicza" (*Astrea*, 1823), *Mwow*, 52.

63. Report of Rector Twardowski to Governor-General Aleksandr Rimskii-Korsakov, 9/21 May 1823, *Rekonstrukcja*, 72–74. Grand Duke Constantine to Emperor Alexander I, 14/26 May 1823, ibid., 87.
64. Grand Duke Constantine to Emperor Alexander I, 14/26 May 1823, *Rekonstrukcja*, 87.
65. Morawski, *Kilka lat*, 261.
66. Edward Tomasz Massalski, "Z pamiętników," in *Z filareckiego świata*, 288–89, 296–97. Malinowski, *Księga wspomnień*, 36.
67. Massalski, "Z pamiętników," in *Z filareckiego świata*, 289.
68. Mickiewicz to Czeczot, 5/17 January 1827, *Dz.* 14:383.
69. *Rekonstrukcja*, 337–38. Ibid., 624–25. Ibid., 679.
70. Domeyko, "Filareci i Filomaci," in *Z filareckiego świata*, 102. Mickiewicz to Czeczot, 5/17 January 1827, *Dz.* 1:385.
71. *Rekonstrukcja*, 680.
72. Mickiewicz to Malewski, [14/26 July 1824], *Dz.* 14:318.
73. Otto Ślizień, "Z pamiętnika (1821–1824)," in *Z filareckiego świata*, 140.
74. *Rekonstrukcja*, 717–18. Nikolai N. Novosiltsov to Minister of Education Aleksandr S. Shishkov, 23 October/4 November 1824, ibid., 733.
75. Odyniec, *Wspomnienia*, 291–92. Receipt to Petr Shlykov, 24 October/5 November 1824, *Dz.* 14:325. Mickiewicz to Lelewel, 16/28 January [1829], ibid., 548.
76. Authorization for Marian Piasecki, 24 October/5 November 1824, *Dz.* 14:325. Domeyko, "Filareci i Filomaci," in *Z filareckiego świata*, 103–4.

CHAPTER 3. EXILE (1824–1829)

1. Pietraszkiewicz to Stanisław Kozakiewicz, [end of November 1824], *AF Nz* 1:50–51.
2. Pietraszkiewicz, "Opisanie Rossyi, jej mieszkańców, stolicy Petersburga i Moskwy w roku 1824–1830," in *AF Lzz* 1:39–63.
3. Shishkov to Jan Witt, 16/28 December 1824, *K biografii*, 27. Mickiewicz to Shishkov, [18/30 November 1824], *Dz.* 14:326. Shishkov to the Ministry of National Education, 16/28 December 1824, *K biografii*, 30; Shishkov to Witt, 16/28 December 1824, *K biografii*, 28.
4. Bujakowski, *Z młodości*, 30–31.
5. Ivan S. Turgenev and Aleksandr I. Herzen, quoted in Pedrotti, *Józef-Julian Sękowski*, 2, Mickiewicz to Odyniec, [ca. 24 April/6 May 1829], *Dz.* 14:587.
6. Przecławski, "Kaleidoskop wospominanii," cols. 1889–1900, 1931–37.
7. Pushkin, *Polnoe sobranie* 8:411; 11:214. Wincenty Pełczyński to Jeżowski [17/29 November 1820], *AF K* 3:19–20. Mickiewicz to Bułharyn, [13] June [1829], *Dz.* 14:600.
8. Rettel, "Aleksandr Pushkin," 210.
9. *Ss*, 613.
10. Malewski to Maria Malewska, 24 January/4 February 1825, *AF Lzz* 1:113.
11. Malewski to M. and Zofia Malewska, 10/22 December 1824, *AF Lzz* 1:108.
12. Mickiewicz to Herman Hołowiński, [13/25 May 1825], *Dz.* 14:338. Mickiewicz to Odyniec, [end of February 1825], *Dz.* 14:333.
13. Witt to the Administration of the Richelieu Lycée, 2/14 February 1825, in *K biografii*, 31–32. Malewski to M. and Z. Malewska, [after 17 February/1 March] 1825, *AF Lzz* 3:116.
14. Mainard, *Le Prophète national*, 16–18. Vigel, *Zapiski*, 231–33, 299.
15. Jeżowski et al. to Pietraszkiewicz, [4/16 March 1825], *AF Nz*, 78; Mickiewicz to Odyniec, [end of February 1825], *Dz.* 14:334.
16. Quoted in Herlihy, *Odessa*, 123.
17. Mickiewicz to Lelewel, 7/19 January 1827, *Dz.* 14:392; Mickiewicz to Odyniec, 22 February/6 March [1826], ibid., 346.
18. Vigel, *Zapiski*, 300.

19. Mickiewicz to Margaret Fuller, 26 April [1847], *Dz.* 16:427–28.
20. Vigel, *Zapiski*, 301. Lee, *The Last Days*, 11. Kaczkowski, *Wspomnienia*, 115–17.
21. Mickiewicz to Z. Malewska, 2/14 May 1825, *Dz.* 14:337–38. Novosiltsov to Grand Duke Constantine, 30 May/12 June 1825, in Mościcki, "Z pobytu," 142. Dudrovich to S. I. Mogilevskii, 30 June/11 July 1825, *K biografii*, 43–44. Witt to Alexander I, 1/13 August 1825, "Mezhdutsarstvie," 149.
22. Gorecka, "Ze wspomnień," 239–40.
23. Witt to Alexander I, 13 August 1825, "Mezhdutsarstvie," 149. For his 1842 lecture on the Decembrists, Mickiewicz supplemented his personal knowledge of the events with information he drew from the official report on the uprising, *Conspiration de Russie. Rapport de la Commision d'enquête de St.-Pétersbourg à S. M. l'Empereur Nicolas I*... (1826). He was the first, however, to expose Boshniak's role in the affair.
24. Gorecka, *Wspomnienia*, 119.
25. Mickiewicz to Lelewel, 7/19 January 1827, *Dz.* 14:392.
26. Olizar, "Z pamiętników," 15.
27. Mickiewicz to Witt, 26 March/7 April 1825, *Dz.* 14:335; Mickiewicz to Witt, 28 June/10 July 1825, ibid., 339–40. Mickiewicz's diploma and rank, *K biografii*, 51–53; Wierzbowski, *Z badań*, 72–73.
28. Dmitrii V. Golitsyn to Shishkov, 19 September/1 October 1825, in *K biografii*, 47.
29. Mickiewicz to Hołowiński, 23 June/5 July 1826, *Dz.* 14:358.
30. Daniłowicz to Lelewel, 21 February[/5 March] 1825, *AF Lzz* 3:699. Mickiewicz to Odyniec, 22 February/6 March [1826], *Dz.* 14:346.
31. *Żywot* 1:234.
32. Cyprian Daszkiewicz to Lelewel [24 March/5 April 1826], *AF Lzz* 1:310. Szymanowska-Malewska, *Dziennik*, 21, 24. Pietraszkiewicz, "Opisanie," *AF Lzz* 1:42–43, 49–50.
33. Mickiewicz to Odyniec, 22 February/6 March [1826], *Dz.* 14:346; Malewski to M. and Z. Malewska, [29 March/10 April 1826], *AF Lzz* 3:136
34. Mickiewicz to Zan, 9/21 June [1826], *Dz.* 14:355–56. Aleksander Mickiewicz to Lelewel, 10/22 November 1827, quoted in *Żywot* 1:289.
35. Malewski to M. and Z. Malewska, *AF Lzz* 3:145; Mickiewicz to Joanna Zaleska, 27 September/9 October [1826], *Dz.* 14:366–67.
36. Novosiltsov to Golitsyn, 9[/21] November 1826, *K biografii*, 69.
37. Mickiewicz to Odyniec, [March 1826 (?)], *Dz.* 14:353. Mickiewicz to Zan, 9/21 June [1826], ibid., 356.
38. F[ranciszek] S[alezy] Dmochowski, "Uwagi nad teraźniejszym stanem, duchem i dążnością poezji polskiej," *Mwow*, 57.
39. Mickiewicz to Czeczot and Zan, 5/17 January 1827, *Dz.* 14:386. Mickiewicz to Odyniec, [beginning of November] 1827, ibid., 426–27. Mickiewicz to Odyniec, 14/26 April 1827, ibid., 406.
40. Polevoi, *Zapiski*, 167–69.
41. Polevoi, *Zapiski*, 153; Pietraszkiewicz, "Opisanie," *AF Lzz* 1:50. As recalled by S. D. Poltoratskii, quoted in Berezina, "Mitskevich," 472.
42. Avraam S. Norov to Petr A. Viazemskii, 9 November 1825, quoted in Mitskevich, *Sonety*, 242 (Norov, the brother of a Decembrist and future minister of education, met Mickiewicz during the latter's last weeks in Odessa).
43. Viazemskii, "Mitskevich o Pushkine," 326–27.
44. Barsukov, *Zhizn' i trudy*, 48.
45. Malewski to M. and Z. Malewska, 27 September/9 October 1826, *AF Lzz* 3:146.
46. Wincenty Pełczyński to Jeżowski, 17/29 November 1820, *AF K* 3:21.
47. Mickiewicz to Odyniec, March 1827, *Dz.* 14:401. A fragment of this letter, in which Mickiewicz provides an overview of the Russian literary scene, soon appeared in a Warsaw periodical.
48. Mickiewicz is quoting Pushkin's own characterization of his hero Eugene Onegin (*Polnoe sobranie* 6:23). Sergei T. Aksakov to Stepan P. Shevyrev, 26 March 1829, in "Iz bumag," 50. Polevoi, *Zapiski*, 171.
49. Viazemskii, "Mitskevich o Pushkine," 327.

50. Malewski to M. and Z. Malewska, 21 December/2 January 1827, *AF Lzz* 3:152.
51. Mitskevich, *Sonety*, [51–52], 304. Mickiewicz to Odyniec, 14/26 April 1827, *Dz.* 14:406. For help in navigating the Polish, Topçi-Başa employed the services of Aleksander Chodźko, a Philareth exile and student of oriental languages who in 1829 published a Polish translation of the preface and of the Persian paraphrase in a Warsaw periodical (*Mwow*, 213–15).
52. Lelewel to Mickiewicz, 21 April 1827, Korespondencja. Mickiewicz to Odyniec, [June 1827], *Dz.* 14:413. Mickiewicz to Józef Kowalewski, 9/21 June [1827], ibid., 411.
53. Mickiewicz to Lelewel, 7/19 January 1827, *Dz.* 14:392. Malinowski, *Dziennik*, 48. F[ranciszek] S[alezy] Dmochowski, "Uwagi na 'Sonetami' Pana Mickiewicza," *Mwow*, 77, 76. Kajetan Koźmian to Franciszek Morawski, [March 1827], ibid., 334–35.
54. M[aurycy] Mochnacki, "O 'Sonetach' Adama Mickiewicza," *Mwow*, 84, 86.
55. Viazemskii, "Sonety Mitskevicha," 326–28.
56. Koźmian to Morawski, 22 December [1827], in *Mwow*, 341. Zan to Mickiewicz, July 1827, *AF Lzz* 2:263. Mickiewicz to Czeczot and Zan, 5/17 January 1827, *Dz.* 14:382–83.
57. Malewski to M. and Z. Malewska, 14/26 April 1827, *AF Lzz* 3:159. K. D. Kavelin, in *Literaturnye Salony*, 326.
58. S. Shevyrev, in *Literaturnye Salony i Kružki*, 172–75. Malewski to Katarzyna Malewska, [7/19 February 1826 (*sic*)], *AF Lzz* 3:131. Malewski to M. and Z. Malewska, [17/29 January 1827], ibid., 153. Volkonskaia's salon made a somewhat different impression on the English traveler Frederick Chamier: "The party was doomed to listen to the recital of poems [including Volkonskaia's own] concocted during the week, each speaking in his turn, and each occupying, as much as possible, the time and patience of his neighbour. It was a most miserable, dull, and stupid business . . . [a] preposterously ridiculous affair." Chamier, "Anecdotes of Russia," 76. Chamier's reportage also contains renderings of two excerpts from *Konrad Wallenrod*, the first in English, (76–79).
59. Malewski to M. and Z. Malewska, 10[/22] November 1827, *AF Lzz* 3:172. Zinaida A. Volkonskaia, "Portrait de Mickiewicz," in Mickiewicz, *Mélanges*, 331–32. Volkonskaia to Mickiewicz, 8 June 1832, Korespondencja.
60. Mickiewicz to Odyniec, 14/26 April 1827, *Dz.* 14:406. Malewski to M. and Z. Malewska, 15/27 August 1828, quoted in *Żywot* 1:286.
61. Malewski to M. and Z. Malewska, 29 May/10 June 1827, *AF Lzz* 3:164–65. Malewski to Lelewel, 4/16 July 1827, ibid., 370.
62. Volkonskaia to Mickiewicz [2/14 April 1827], Korespondencja. Mickiewicz to Odyniec, [beginning of November] 1827, *Dz.* 14:426. The text of the improvisation, which Daszkiewicz wrote down that evening, was found among Pietraszkiewicz's papers during his arrest in 1831. It was among the evidence that earned the Philomaths' archivist a sentence of death, which was subsequently commuted to exile in Siberia.
63. Mickiewicz to Odyniec, [beginning of November] 1827, *Dz.* 14:426. Aleksander Mickiewicz to Lelewel, 10/22 November 1827, quoted in *Żywot* 1:289.
64. Malewski to M. and Z. Malewska, 10[/22] November 1827, *AF Lzz* 3:172.
65. Morawski, *W Peterburku*, 176, 169.
66. Szymanowska-Malewska, *Dziennik*, 24.
67. Mickiewicz to M. Szymanowska, 2/14 November 1828, *Dz.* 14:520.
68. Mickiewicz to Odyniec, [beginning of November] 1827, *Dz.* 14:425.
69. "Program czasopisma 'Iris,'" *Dz.* 6:184.
70. Mickiewicz to Marian Piasecki, [ca. mid-November 1827], *Dz.* 14:433.
71. A. Chodźko to Odyniec, 14/26 December 1827, *Dz.* 14:438 n. 2. Mickiewicz to Zan, 3/15 April [1828], ibid., 459.
72. Mikołaj Malinowski to Lelewel, 28 December 1827/9 January 1828, *AF Lzz* 3:750.
73. Podolinskii, "Vospominaniia," 860.

74. Morawski, *W Peterburku*, 9.
75. Polevoi, *Zapiski*, 174, 172. Mickiewicz to Odyniec, 22 March/3 April 1828, *Dz.* 14:454.
76. Mickiewicz to Odyniec, 22 March/3 April 1828, *Dz.* 14:454. Avdotia P. Elagina to Vasilii A. Zhukovskii, 30 November/12 December 1827, in ibid., 454 n.18. Polevoi, *Zapiski*, 173. Mickiewicz to Lelewel, 12 June [1829], *Dz.* 14:598.
77. Mickiewicz to Zan, 3/15 April [1828], *Dz.* 14:459.
78. Malinowski, *Dziennik*, 45, 64. Przecławski, "Kaleidoskop," 1921. Allocution to the Guardians of the Septets and the Brethren Whom They Summoned, 21 November 1844, *Dz.* 13:189.
79. Malinowski, *Dziennik*, 56–60. Malinowski to Lelewel, 7/19 February 1828, in *Mwow*, 350. Immediately after the event, Malinowski sent a letter describing the evening to a friend in Warsaw. Somehow (via Odyniec?) paraphrased excerpts from the letter made it into Warsaw's *Gazeta Polska* (1828, no. 71). It was not long before the ever vigilant Novosiltsov construed the publication of the letter as well as its contents as yet another manifestation of Polish fractiousness—and yet another example of the lax treatment being accorded Mickiewicz in Russia. Bułharyn's own report of the incident to the secret police spared both the poet and Malinowski any further repercussions. And, of course, news of the improvisation garnered Mickiewicz even more renown.
80. Malinowski, *Dziennik*, 60.
81. Mickiewicz to Daszkiewicz, [beginning of January 1828], *Dz.* 14:443.
82. Daszkiewicz to Lelewel, 26 February/9 March 1828, *AF Lzz* 1:332. Bułharyn, quoted in Syga, *Te księgi*, 49. Mickiewicz to Lelewel, [end of July 1828], *Dz.* 14:493.
83. Novosiltsov to Grand Duke Constantine, 10 April 1828, in *Mwow*, 207–12. Bulgarin [Bułharyn], *Vidok*, 313–18. Rettel, "Aleksandr Pushkin," 212–13.
84. K. Koźmian to Morawski, [ca. 30 March 1828], in *Mwow*, 353. Andrzej Edward Koźmian to Morawski, 5 April 1828, in ibid., 358. K. Koźmian to Morawski, quoted in Chwin, "Wstęp," CXXII.
85. Spazier, *Geschichte*, 127. Józef Bohdan Zaleski to Odyniec, 30 March 1828, in *Mwow*, 352. As recalled by M. Darowski, in ibid., 384.
86. Mochnacki, *Powstanie* 1:254 (italics added). From an anonymous article in a January 1831 issue of *Nowa Polska*, quoted in Chwin, "Wstęp," CXVII.
87. Polevoi, *Zapiski*, 173.
88. [Polevoi], review of *Konrad Wallenrod*, *Moskovskii telegraf* 19 (1828):436–37.
89. Mickiewicz to Odyniec, [beginning of November] 1827, *Dz.* 14:426. Mickiewicz to Odyniec, 22 March/3 April 1828, ibid., 452. As recalled by Edward Chłopicki (1876), *Rozmowy*, 339. As recalled by Walery Wielogłowski (1875), ibid., 283.
90. Words spoken by either Leonard Chodźko or Ludwik Nabielak, quoted in Chwin, "Wstęp," CXVIII.
91. Mickiewicz to Zan, 3/15 April [1828], *Dz.* 14:460.
92. Mickiewicz to Zan, 3/15 April [1828], *Dz.* 14:460. Malewski to M. and Z. Malewska, 25 July/6 August 1827, *AF Lzz* 3:166. Malewski to M. and Z. Malewska, 10/22 October 1827, ibid., 169.
93. Zaleska to Daszkiewicz, 21 April/3 May 1828, *AF Lzz* 1:431. Zaleska to Daszkiewicz, 11/23 May 1828, ibid., 431; Zaleska to Mickiewicz, 21 April/3 May 1828, Korespondencja (in a mixture of Polish and French). Mickiewicz to Zaleska, 20 August/1 September [1828], *Dz.* 14:505.
94. Quoted in Iazykov, *Stikhotvoreniia i poèmy*, 542.
95. Daszkiewicz to Lelewel, 6/18 July 1827, *AF Lzz* 1:328. Mickiewicz to Karl Jaenisch, [23 December] 1828/[4 January] 1829, *Dz.* 14:538. Karolina Jaenisch-Pavlova to W. Mickiewicz, 20 April 1890, quoted in *Żywot* 1:271. Mickiewicz to Karolina Jaenisch, 26 March/7 April [1827], *Dz.* 14:395–97.
96. Mickiewicz to Daszkiewicz, 30 July/11August [1828], *Dz.* 14:497. Jaenisch-Pavlova to W. Mickiewicz, 20 April 1890, quoted in *Żywot* 1:271.
97. Mickiewicz to Daszkiewicz, [23 April/5May 1828], *Dz.* 14:468. Mickiewicz to Daszkiewicz, [mid-July 1828], ibid., 486–87. Mickiewicz to Daszkiewicz, [ca. 15/27 August 1828], ibid., 502–3.

98. Mickiewicz to Daszkiewicz, [end of January 1829], *Dz.* 14:550–51. Mickiewicz to Daszkiewicz, [first half of February 1829], *Dz.* 14:554.
99. Jaenisch to Mickiewicz, 19 February/3 March 1829 (in French, with the last three words in Polish), Korespondencja.
100. Pushkin to the Third Division, 7/19 January 1828, *Ss*, 616. Mickiewicz to Zan, 3/15 April [1828], *Dz.* 14:460. Mickiewicz to Golitsyn, 12/24 April 1828, ibid., 463, 465.
101. Szymanowska-Malewska, *Dziennik*, 44–45. Viazemskii to V. F. Viazemskaia, 8[/20] February 1828, *Ss*, 620.
102. Kireevskii, *Polnoe sobranie* 2:210. Baratynskii, *Polnoe sobranie*, 101. Mickiewicz to Odyniec, 28 April/10 May, *Dz.* 14:471. Malinowski to Lelewel, 25 April/6 May 1828, "Listy . . . do Lelewela," 159.
103. Mickiewicz to Daszkiewicz, [beginning of May 1828], *Dz.* 14:474. Viazemskii to Viazemskaia, 24 April/5 May 1828; 4/16 May 1828, *Ss*, 624.
104. Leonard Chodźko to Mickiewicz, 3 May 1828, Korespondencja. L. Chodźko's preface, quoted in Syga, *Te księgi*, 66.
105. Mickiewicz to Lelewel, [end of July 1828], *Dz.* 14:492. Piasecki to Odyniec, 20 February/3 March 1828, *AF Lzz* 2:559. Mickiewicz to Odyniec, [beginning of July 1828], *Dz.* 14:485.
106. Józef Muczkowski to Lelewel, 2 May 1828, "Listy . . . do Lelewela," 158.
107. Juliusz Adolf Munk to Lelewel, 18 July 1828, "Listy . . . do Lelewela," 161. Mickiewicz to Józef Muczkowski, 5/17 March [1829], *Dz.* 14:578. Muczkowski to Lelewel, 3 September 1829, "Listy . . . do Lelewela," 169.
108. Mickiewicz to Daszkiewicz, [first half of February 1829], *Dz.* 14:553. Viazemskii, "Mitskevich," 328; Viazemskii to V. F. Viazemskaia, 2/14 May 1828, *Ss*, 624–25. *Lzp* 1:39.
109. Kern, *Vospominaniia*, 60; Mickiewicz to Daszkiewicz, [beginning of May 1828], *Dz.* 14:474.
110. Przecławski, "Kaleidoskop," 1901. Mickiewicz to Daszkiewicz, [ca. 15/27 January 1829], *Dz.* 14:545. As recalled by Gorecka, *Rozmowy*, 270. As recalled by Józef Przecławski, *Rozmowy*, 44.
111. *Lzp* 1:34. Morawski, *W Peterburku*, 126, 129, 123; Przecławski, "Oleszkiewicz," 81.
112. Malinowski, *Dziennik*, 36–37. The list of mystics is Mickiewicz's own, from his 1842 lecture at the Collège de France on the Masonic movement in Russia (*Dz.* 9:340–42/*LS* 3:265–68).
113. *Lzp* 1:37.
114. Mickiewicz to M. Szymanowska, 2 June [1829], *Dz.* 14:593. Szymanowska-Malewska, *Dziennik*, 207. Morawski, *W Peterburku*, 169. As recalled by Aleksander Biergiel (1870s), *Rozmowy*, 324.
115. *Lzp* 1:130. Odyniec situates the ride in a season other than the one in which "The Faris" was most probably written, i.e., the winter of 1828. Mickiewicz must have been quite pleased with the poem, since he himself translated it into French several times.
116. Quoted in Syga, *Te księgi*, 84. N. A. Polevoi, review of *Poezye*, 30–31.
117. Mickiewicz to Lelewel, 16/28 January [1829], *Dz.* 14:546. K. Koźmian to Morawski, [April 1829], in *Mwow*, 360; F. S. Dmochowski, "Odpowiedź na pismo P. Mickiewicza 'O krytykach i recenzentach warszawskich,'' in *Mwow*, 241. Lelewel to Malewski, 22 April 1830, *AF Lzz* 3:643. Mickiewicz to Odyniec, [ca. 24 April/6 May 1829], *Dz.* 14:586.
118. Mickiewicz to Benkendorf, [December 1828], *Dz.* 14:533. Benkendorf to Constantine, 7/19 February 1828, in Fiszman, *Mickiewicz w Rosji*, 63–64. Daszkiewicz to Lelewel, 20 March/1 April 1829, *AF Lzz* 1:341.
119. Mickiewicz to the Collegium of Foreign Affairs, [19 February/3 March 1829], *Dz.* 14:568.
120. Malewski to Sz. Malewski, 13/25 March [1829], *AF Lzz* 3:191.
121. Barsukov, *Zhizn'*, 304.
122. Pushkin, *Polnoe sobranie* 3:331.
123. Mickiewicz to Malewski, 31 March/12 April 1829, *Dz.* 14:584. Jaenisch to Mickiewicz, 5/17 April 1829, Korespondencja; Pavlova, "10 November 1840," *Polnoe sobranie*, 90. Jaenisch-Pavlova to W. Mickiewicz, 20 April 1890, quoted in *Żywot* 1:273.

124. Mickiewicz to Jeżowski, [end of February] 1830, *Dz.* 15:25.
125. Mickiewicz to Odyniec, [ca. 24 April/6 May 1829], *Dz.* 14:585.
126. Malewski to Lelewel, 20 May/1 June 1829, *AF Lzz* 3:373. Mickiewicz to Malewski, 11/23 May 1829, *Dz.* 14:589–90; *Lzp* 1:42–43.
127. *Lzp* 1:48. M. Szymanowska et al. to Mickiewicz [14/26 May 1829], *AF Lzz* 3:344.
128. N. Polevoi, review of *Poezye*, 30.
129. U[shakov], "O russkom perevode," 349. *Lzp* 1:41.
130. Malewski to Lelewel, 11/23 September 1829, *AF Lzz* 3:380.
131. Viazemskii to P. I. Bartnev, 6 March 1872, quoted in Ospovat and Timenchik, "*Pechalnu povest sokhranit*," 29.
132. As recalled by Biergiel, *Rozmowy*, 321.

CHAPTER 4. THE GRAND TOUR (1829–1831)

1. Mickiewicz to Malewski, 2 June [1829], *Dz.* 14:595. Mickiewicz to M. Szymanowska, 2 June [1829], ibid., 593.
2. Mickiewicz to Malewski, 2 June [1829], *Dz.* 14:595. Mickiewicz to Lelewel, 12 June [1829], ibid., 597.
3. Mickiewicz to Bułharyn, [13] June [1829], *Dz.* 14:599. Mickiewicz to Szymanowska, [13] June [1829], ibid., 603.
4. Karl Friedrich Zelter to Johann Wolfgang von Goethe, 12 June 1829, in Goethe, *Briefwechsel*, 1242.
5. Eulogiusz Zakrzewski, in *AMwppo*, 100. Wojciech Cybulski, cited in Bełza, *Kronika potoczna*, 90.
6. Mickiewicz to Malewski, [13] June [1829], *Dz.* 14:601–2. As recalled by Wojciech Cybulski (1870), in Bełza, *Kronika potoczna*, 91. Malewski to Lelewel, 11/23 September 1829, *AF Lzz* 3:379.
7. As recalled by Wincenty Pol (1871), *AMwm*, 220.
8. As recalled by Cybulski (1870), in Bełza, *Kronika potoczna*, 92. *Allgemeine Preussische Staats-Zeitung*, 21 June 1829, quoted in Witkowski, "Z pobytu," 34.
9. As recalled by Cybulski (1845), *AMwm*, 106–8. As recalled by Karol Libelt (1874, 1849), in *DzW* 1.4:106–9.
10. *DzW* 1.4:109. Mickiewicz to Malewski, [13] June [1829], *Dz.* 14:601; Mickiewicz to Malewski, 30 November [1829], ibid., 612.
11. As recalled by Cybulski (1870), *AMwm*, 107. Mickiewicz to Malewski, [ca. 10 July 1829], *Dz.* 14:606. Malewski to Lelewel, 11/23 September 1829, *AF Lzz* 3:379.
12. Mickiewicz to Malewski, [ca. 10 July 1829], *Dz.* 14:606–7.
13. Ludwik Jabłonowski, quoted in Kallenbach, *AM* (1923) 1:418. Malewski to Lelewel, 11/23 September 1829, *AF Lzz* 3:379.
14. Šafařík, *Geschichte*, 466.
15. Čelakovský to Josef Vlastimil Kamarýt, 26 July 1829, in Čelakovský, *Korespondence*, 12. As recalled by Lucjan Siemieński (1865), *Rozmowy*, 134. Václav Hanka to Malewski, 7 August 1829, *AF Lzz* 3:546.
16. Jean de Carro, *Almanach de Carlsbad*, quoted in Szyjkowski, *Polskie peregrynacje*, 311. Mickiewicz to Malewski, 30 November [1829], *Dz.* 14:613. Quoted in Szyjkowski, *Polskie peregrynacje*, 321. Mickiewicz to Łubieńska-Wodopolowa, 26 July [1855], *Dz.* 17:335.
17. Mickiewicz to Jeżowski, [end of February] 1830, *Dz.* 15:24. Mickiewicz to Odyniec, [14 February 1834], ibid., 260. Mickiewicz to Malewski, 2 February 1830, ibid., 17. Odyniec's reminiscences of his acquaintance and travels with Mickiewicz first appeared in skeletal (and thus perhaps more reliable) form as part of Wójcicki's *Wspomnienie o życiu Adama Mickiewicza* (1858). Beginning in 1867, however, Odyniec began publishing them serially in the form of suspiciously extensive letters to friends, written, ostensibly, during the course of his travels and chronicling it in no less suspiciously minute detail. Although probably based on authentic correspondence, their serialized version (published eventually in book form as *Listy z podróży* [1875–1878]) is very much a case of retrospective projection gone wild. Full of memory lapses, inaccuracies, and outright

invention, it is, in other words, a partially fictionalized account by a superb storyteller with an ebullient imagination. And yet, not only does a biographer have little choice in the matter considering that in most instances Odyniec is the only source of information for this period in Mickiewicz's life, but, as one scholar felicitously remarked, "Had Odyniec, for instance, invented but half of the opinions on art he attributed to Mickiewicz, he would have to be considered among the leading lights of [art] criticism" (Kołaczkowski, "Mickiewicz," 123). Much the same can be said for Odyniec's book of reminiscences, *Wspomnienia z przeszłości* (1884), which narrates in part his acquaintance with Mickiewicz in Lithuania as well as their days together in Dresden in 1832, although as a memoir it effectively finesses questions of accuracy and credibility. Just to be on the safe side, however, for information concerning their travels, I have chosen to rely whenever possible on the rawer Odyniec of Wójcicki's *Wspomnienie*.

18. *Wspomnienie*, XLIII. Johann Wolfgang von Goethe to Zelter, 20 August 1829, in Goethe, *Briefwechsel*, 1260.
19. Ottilie von Goethe to Mickiewicz, 3 March 1830, Korespondencja. Holtei, *Vierzig Jahre*, 141–42 (and *Wspomnienie*, XLV).
20. *AMaydF*, 35–37. *Wspomnienie*, XLIV.
21. Holtei, *Vierzig Jahre*, 149n (and *Wspomnienie*, XLV). Mickiewicz to Odyniec, 28 September [1835], *Dz.* 15:302.
22. Mickiewicz to Flora Laskarys, [5 March 1830], *Dz.* 15:27.
23. Szymanowska to Friedrich von Müller, 10/22 December 1827, quoted in Czajkowska, "Wokół wizyty," 294. In her letter to von Müller, Szymanowska had requested Goethe for an autograph for Mickiewicz. Although he never sent it, Goethe's archive contains a couplet addressed to the Polish poet, together "with a used quill": "I devote myself to a poet who has proved himself / And sang downright amusing praises to our friend [Szymanowska]" (Goethe, *Sämtliche Werke* 2:823).
24. Mickiewicz to O. Goethe, 16 December 1829, *Dz.* 14:618. *Lzp* 1:247. Mickiewicz to Jeżowski, [end of February 1830], *Dz.* 15:23–24.
25. Dernałowicz, "Przekład *Farysa*," 39. David d'Angers, *Carnets* 1:60–61.
26. Mickiewicz to A. Chodźko, 1 April [1842], *Dz.* 16:62. In Odyniec's account, it is Mickiewicz, not a bull, who slips while trying to dislodge a rock into the Rhine and manages to save himself by grasping a tree (*Wspomnienie*, XLVI–XLVIII; *Lzp* 1:339–40).
27. M. Puttkamer to Mickiewicz, 1 November [1830], Korespondencja. Mickiewicz to I. Domeyko, 4 January [1832], *Dz.* 15:129.
28. Mickiewicz to Malewski, 30 November [1829], *Dz.* 14:613.
29. *Wspomnienie*, XLVIII.
30. Szymanowska to Mickiewicz, 29 May/10 June 1829, Korespondencja. *Wspomnienie*, XLVIII. Mickiewicz to Jeżowski, [end of February] 1830, *Dz.* 15:24.
31. Mickiewicz to Jeżowski, [end of February] 1830, *Dz.* 15:24. *Wspomnienie*, XLVIII–XLIX. Volkonskaia to Mickiewicz, 16 October 1829, Korespondencja.
32. Mickiewicz to Maria Mickiewicz, 19 December 1851, *Dz.* 17:152.
33. Anastaziia S. Khliustin de Circourt, quoted in *Żywot* 2:87; A. Khliustin de Circourt to Mickiewicz, 13 July [1830], Korespondencja. Mickiewicz to Sobolevskii, 19 January 1830, *Dz.* 15:10.
34. Volkonskaia to Mickiewicz, 24 November 1831, Korespondencja.
35. Mickiewicz to Malewski, [end of November–beginning of December 1829], *Dz.* 14:614–15.
36. Szymanowska to Thorvaldsen, 24 May 1829, in "Miscellanea," 193.
37. *Lzp* 2:43.
38. Stattler, "Przypomnienie," 214. Mickiewicz to Ankwicz-Kuczkowska, [8 April] 1855, *Dz.* 17:325.
39. Mickiewicz to Malewski, 2 February 1830, *Dz.* 15:16. Mickiewicz to Malewski, [end of November–beginning of December 1829], ibid., 14:614 (Malewski published excerpts of this letter in the Polish-language newspaper he was editing in St. Petersburg at the time).

40. Mickiewicz to Malewski, 2 February 1830, *Dz.* 15:17. Quoted in Siemieński, *Ewunia*, 33–34. "Wyjątek z listów prywatnych pisanych do Lwowa," in *Mwow*, 269–70.
41. As recalled by Vera Khliustin, in *Żywot* 2:68.
42. W. Mickiewicz, *Pamiętniki*, 1:182. *Lzp* 2:61. Anastaziia Khliustin's diary, quoted in *Żywot* 2:106, 72. Mickiewicz to A. Khliustin [September–beginning of October 1830], *Dz.* 15:69.
43. A. Khliustin's diary, quoted in *Żywot* 2:86. W. Mickiewicz, *Pamiętniki*, 1:175.
44. *Mwow*, 311.
45. Cooper, *Pages*, 230. Cooper, "To the American People," *Letters and Journals*, 128. Sobolevskii to Shevyrev, 10 August 1830, in "Vyderzhki," Shevyrev, 485.
46. Mickiewicz to Khliustin, [31 March 1830], *Dz.* 15:29. Stattler, "Przypomnienie," 230.
47. *Wspomnienie*, LI.
48. Mickiewicz to Sobolevskii, 19 January [1830], *Dz.* 15:10. Mickiewicz to Lelewel, 6 February [1830], ibid., 20. Mickiewicz to Jeżowski, [end of February] 1830, ibid. 15:24. Mickiewicz to Malewski, 30 November [1829], ibid., 14:612. Mickiewicz to Malewski, 2 February 1830, ibid., 16.
49. Stattler, "Przypomnienie," 214. Mickiewicz to Jeżowski, *Dz.* 15:24. Stattler, "Przypomnienie," 230.
50. Stattler, "Przypomnienie," 214. Odyniec to Jan Korsak, 7 April 1832, in Pług, "Odyniec," 41:118. Garczyński, *Wiersze do Aliny*, quoted in Szeląg, "Garczyńskiego 'Wiersze,'" 92. Mickiewicz to Garczyński, [23 May 1833], *Dz.* 15:210.
51. *Lzp* 2:129.
52. Przecławaski, "Kaleidoskop," 1927. *Lzp* 1:37.
53. *Lzp* 2:306.
54. Mickiewicz to Z. Ankwicz, 13 June [1830], *Dz.* 15:43. Odyniec to Malewski, 15 May 1830, *AF Lzz* 3:555.
55. Mickiewicz to Malewski, 27 June [1830], *Dz.* 15:49.
56. *Wspomnienie*, LIII. Mickiewicz to Malewski, 27 June [1830], *Dz.* 15:48–49.
57. *Lzp* 2:377.
58. Mickiewicz to I. Domeyko, [23 June 1830], *Dz.* 15:45–46.
59. In a review of a translation of Goethe's *Wilhelm Meister*, *Journal des debats*, 2 January 1830. *Lzp* 2:406.
60. *Lzp* 2:65.
61. D'Herbelot, in *AMaydF*, 43. Burgaud des Marets, in *AMaydF*, 39.
62. *Le Globe*, 25 April 1830, in *AMaydF*, 41. Mickiewicz to L. Chodźko, 10 July 1830, *Dz.* 15:59–60. D'Herbelot, in *AMaydF*, 47.
63. Mickiewicz to Z. Ankwicz, *Dz.* 15:52–53. Siemieński, *Ewunia*, 55 (at some point later, Henrietta scratched out the name "Adam" in the entry and replaced it with "my brother"). Mickiewicz to Z. Ankwicz, *Dz.* 15:53.
64. *DzW*, 1.3:107. As noted down by Władysław Zamoyski (February 1830), in Sudolski, "Mickiewiczowskie wspominki," 93.
65. *Lzp* 2:453–54.
66. *Lzp* 2:475. Mickiewicz to A. Chodźko [9 October 1830], *Dz.* 15:72.
67. *Wspomnienie*, LV.
68. Mickiewicz to S. Khliustin, [ca. 12 August 1830], *Dz.* 15:63.
69. Mickiewicz to Z. Ankwicz, 14 August [1830], *Dz.* 15:65–66.
70. Zygmunt Krasiński to Wincenty Krasiński, 5 September 1830, in Krasiński, *Listy do ojca*, 187–88.
71. Mickiewicz to Malewski, 20 November [1830], *Dz.* 15:82. Mickiewicz to Czeczot, [9 October 1830], ibid., 73–74. Krasiński to W. Krasiński, 5 September 1830, in Krasiński, *Listy do ojca*, 193.
72. A. Khliustin to Mickiewicz, 23 August 1830, Korespondencja.
73. Mickiewicz to Sobolevskii, [6 November 1830], *Dz.* 15:77; Mickiewicz to A. Khliustin [4 September–10 October 1830], ibid., 69.
74. Krasiński, *Dzieła*, 240. Mickiewicz to S. Khliustin, [ca. 12 August 1830], *Dz.* 15:63.
75. Krasiński to W. Krasiński, 22 October 1830, in Krasiński, *Listy do ojca*, 196. Mickiewicz to A. Chodźko, [9 October 1830], *Dz.* 15:72.

76. Mickiewicz to Odyniec, 19 November [1830], *Dz.* 15:79–80. Mickiewicz to Malewski, 20 November [1830], ibid., 82.
77. Mickiewicz to Odyniec, 19 November [1830], *Dz.* 15:79.
78. Mickiewicz to S. Khliustin, 30 December 1830, *Dz.* 15:85. Mickiewicz to Malewski, 20 November [1830], ibid., 82. Krasiński to W. Krasiński, 5 December 1830, in Krasiński, *Listy do ojca*, 214. Mickiewicz to Odyniec, 19 November [1830], *Dz.* 15:79.
79. Mickiewicz to Malewski, 20 November [1830], *Dz.* 15:82.
80. Mickiewicz to Malewski, 20 November [1830], *Dz.* 15:82. Mickiewicz to Julia Rzewuska, [27 March 1832], ibid., 142.
81. Mickiewicz to Odyniec, 19 November [1830], *Dz.* 15:79.
82. S. Khliustin to Mickiewicz, 22 November 1831, Korespondencja.
83. Quoted in *Żywot* 2:143.
84. Sobolevskii to Malewski, 24 December/5 January 1868, *AF Lzz* 3:606.
85. Mickiewicz to S. Khliustin, 30 December 1830, *Dz.* 15:84. Mickiewicz to A. de Circourt, 31 December [1830], ibid., 86. Mickiewicz to Wojciech Stattler, 19 April [1830], ibid., 98.
86. Mickiewicz to M. Szymanowksa, 20 February [1831], *Dz.* 15:91. Mickiewicz to Garczyński, 2 March [1831], ibid., 93–94.
87. Mickiewicz to F. Mickiewicz, 4 April [1831], *Dz.* 15:95.
88. Felix Mendelssohn-Bartholdy to his family, 15 March 1831, in Mendelssohn-Bartholdy, *Letters*, 119. Sobolevskii to Malewski, 24 December/5 January 1868, *AF Lzz* 3:606 (Sobolevskii noted not without some ironic satisfaction that "in this way he supplied [Russia] with one more enemy"). Mickiewicz to Stattler, 19 April [1831], *Dz.* 15:98. Mickiewicz's passport in Ruszkowski, " 'Jutrznia,' " 123 n. 1.
89. Mickiewicz to M. Szymanowska, 16 May 1831, *Dz.* 15:102. Mickiewicz to S. Ankwicz, 22 July [1831], ibid., 108.
90. Sobolevskii to Malewski, 24 December/5 January 1868, *AF Lzz* 3:606.
91. Mochnacki, *Powstanie* 2:109. Koźmian, *Pamętniki*, 362. Gosławski, in *AMwppo*, 119–20.

CHAPTER 5. CRISIS AND REBIRTH (1831–1832)

1. Mickiewicz to Malewski, 4 April [1831], *Dz.* 15:95. Siemieński, *Ewunia*, 84. Kajsiewicz, "Pamiętnik," 407.
2. Sobolevskii to Shevyrev, 7 May 1[831], in "Vyderzhki," 480.
3. Reeve to Krasiński, 25 May 1831, in Krasiński, *Listy do Henryka Reeve*, 2:327. Mickiewicz to S. Ankwicz, 27 July [1831], *Dz.* 15:109.
4. Krasiński to Reeve, 7 July 1831, in Krasiński, *Listy do Henryka Reeve*, 1:262. Mickiewicz to Lelewel, 23 March 1832, *Dz.* 15:139.
5. Mickiewicz to Lelewel, 23 March 1832, *Dz.* 15:139. Mickiewicz to S. Ankwicz, 27 July [1831], ibid., 108.
6. As recorded by Niemcewicz, *Dziennik* 1:16. Mickiewicz to S. Khliustin, 16 [July 1831], *Dz.* 15:104–5. Mickiewicz to S. Ankwicz, 27 July [1831], ibid., 108–9.
7. Mickiewicz to Jan Korwin Piotrowski, 20 November [1831], *Dz.* 15:117. Gorecki, in *AMwppo*, 117. Gorecki to L. Chodzko, [28 July 1831], *Dz.* 15:112 n. 6.
8. Mickiewicz to S. Ankwicz, 27 July [1831], *Dz.* 15:110.
9. Mickiewicz to V. Khliustin, [23] November [1832], *Dz.* 15:174. In the album of Honorata Skórzewska, August 1831, ibid., 17:519. As recalled by A. Chodźko (1850s), *Rozmowy*, 244.
10. As recalled by E. Januszkiewicz (1846), *Rozmowy*, 257. Mickiewicz to I. Domeyko, 4 January [1832], *Dz.* 15:129.
11. Mickiewicz to Józef Grabowski, 15 September [1832], *Dz.* 15:167. Garczyński to Mickiewicz, 17 April 1833, Korespondencja. Łubieńska would go on to refract her affair with Mickiewicz in the novella "The Unbeliever," which she published in 1842. Allusions to the affair can also be found in the works of other writers published in the 1840s.

12. Mickiewicz to J. Rzewuska, [27 March 1832], *Dz.* 15:142. G . . . , "Wyjątek z pamiętników," 101.
13. As recalled by Józef Taczanowski, *Rozmowy*, 490. Skałkowski, "Z pamiętnika Adama Turno," 190.
14. Maria Bnińska to Mickiewicz, [March 1832], Korespondencja. Mickiewicz to Volkonskaia, [16 April 1832], *Dz.* 15:149.
15. To Taczanowski, [16 April 1832], *Dz.* 15:146. Dezydery Adam Chłapowski to Walerian Wielogłowski, 28 October 1848, in "Listy," ed. Jabłoński, 131; Malewski to Mickiewicz, 14/26 November [1831], *AF Lzz* 3:353.
16. Mickiewicz to F. Mickiewicz, 12 December [1831], *Dz.* 15:122.
17. Garczyński, foreword to *Wiersze do Aliny*, quoted in Szeląg, "Garczyńskiego 'Wiersze,'" 92. Mickiewicz to Lelewel, 23 March 1832, *Dz.* 15:139. *DzW* 1.3:158.
18. Skałkowski, "Z pamiętnika Adama Turno," 190.
19. Announcement of the edition, *Gazeta Wielkiego Księstwa Poznańskiego*, 14 January 1832, quoted in Maciejewski, *Mickiewicza*, 391.
20. 1847 report of the Prussian police, quoted in Maciejewski, *Mickiewicza*, 492.
21. Mickiewicz to J. Rzewuska, [27 March 1832], *Dz.* 15:142. Mickiewicz to Flora Laskarys, [20 March 1832], ibid., 137.
22. I. Domeyko, *Moje podróże*, 1:94. Platen, "An einen deutschen Fürsten," *Werke*, 167.
23. I. Domeyko to Jan Siemieński, 26 October 1880, *Korespondencja AM* 4:5. S. Khliustin to Mickiewicz, 22 November 1831, Korespondencja.
24. Mickiewicz to Lelewel, 23 March 1832, *Dz.* 15:138. I. Domeyko to J. Siemieński, 26 October 1880, *Korespondencja AM* 4:5.
25. I. Domeyko to J. Siemieński, 26 October 1880, *Korespondencja AM* 4:5. Mickiewicz to Rzewuska, [27 March 1832], *Dz.* 15:142.
26. Mickiewicz to Lelewel, 23 March 1832, *Dz.* 15:139.
27. As recalled by Odyniec, in Siemieński, *Religijność*, 146. As recorded by Seweryn Goszczyński (1840s), *Rozmowy*, 169.
28. As recalled by Odyniec, in Siemieński, *Religijność*, 147. As recorded by Burgaud des Marats (1830s), *Rozmowy*, 266. As recorded by Goszczyński (1840s), *Rozmowy*, 168–69.
29. As recorded by Kajsiewicz (1830s), *Rozmowy*, 125.
30. As recorded by Jan Nepomucen Niemojowski (1845), 252, *Rozmowy*. As recorded by Goszczyński (1839?), ibid., 169. *Lzp* 1:37.
31. Mickiewicz to Grabowski, 29 April 1832, *Dz.* 15:152.
32. As noted down by Adolf Skarbek-Malczewski, *Rozmowy*, 108. Pol, *Pamiętniki*, 192. Perhaps the general was echoing Mickiewicz's own words from *Konrad Wallenrod*, in which Konrad rebukes his guardian Halban: "Alas, all too much to your songs did I listen! . . . You've won! war is a triumph for a poet!" (*Dz.* 2:116).
33. Mickiewicz to Lelewel, 23 March 1832, *Dz.* 15:139.
34. Mickiewicz to Odyniec, [beginning of November] 1827, *Dz.* 14:426.
35. Mickiewicz to F. Mickiewicz, 29 April [1832], *Dz.* 15:154. Mickiewicz to Volkonskaia, [16 April 1832], ibid., 149. Mickiewicz to Lelewel, [mid-May (?) 1832], ibid., 156.
36. Mickiewicz to Odyniec, 28 January [1833], *Dz.* 15:189. Domeyko, *Moje podróże*, 1:96–97.
37. Sobańska to Benckendorf, [November 1832], quoted in Czapska, "Karolina i szef żandarmów," *Szkice*, 90.
38. As noted down by Skarbek Malczewski, *Rozmowy*, 107. Domeyko, Moje *podróże*, 1:97–98; Pol, *Pamiętniki*, 191. Odyniec, *Wspomnienia*, 433.
39. Gregory XVI, "Cum primum."
40. Mickiewicz to Volkonskaia, [16 April 1832], *Dz.* 15:149. Mickiewicz to F. Mickiewicz, 29 April [1832], ibid., 154. Mickiewicz to Volkonskaia, [16 April 1832], ibid., 149; Mickiewicz to

Grabowski, 19 June [1832], ibid., 159. Mickiewicz to Lelewel, [middle of May (?) 1832], ibid., 155. Mickiewicz to Lelewel, 23 March 1832, ibid., 138.

41. Mickiewicz to F. Mickiewicz, 19 June [1832], *Dz.* 15:162, 161. Volkonskaia to Mickiewicz, [6 June 1832], Korespondencja.
42. Mickiewicz to Odyniec, [10 (?)] July 1833, *Dz.* 15:224. Mickiewicz to Odyniec, [21 April 1833], ibid., 203. Mickiewicz to F. Mickiewicz, 29 April [1832], ibid., 154. Mickiewicz to Odyniec, [14 February 1834], ibid., 261. Mickiewicz to Volkonskaia, 10 July [1832], ibid., 163.

CHAPTER 6. EMIGRATION (1832–1834)

1. Jełowicki, *Moje wspomnienia*, 288.
2. Domeyko to J. Siemieński, 26 October 1880, *Korespondencja AM* 4:5–6. Aleksander Jełowicki to Ksaweryna Chodkiewicz, 2 July 1832, in Jełowicki, *Listy do Ksaweryny*, 38. Henryk Nakwaski, "Pamiętniki," 28 June 1832, in Kallenbach, *AM* (1897), 2:403.
3. Domeyko, *Moje podróże* 1:103.
4. Domeyko, *Moje podróże* 1:104. "Ze Lwowa," *Rozmaitości*, 25 August 1832, 285.
5. Mickiewicz to Augustin Choppin d'Arnouville, prefect of Bas-Rhin, 14 July 1832, *Dz.* 15:165. Domeyko, *Moje podróże* 1:116. Description of Mickiewicz, quoted in Borejsza, "Adama Mickiewicza przyjazd," 59.
6. Domeyko, *Moje podróże* 1:110–11.
7. Domeyko, *Moje podróże* 1:114.
8. Domeyko. *Moje podróże* 1:116–18.
9. Fryderyk Chopin to Norbert Alfons Kumelski, 18 November 1831, in Chopin, *Korespondencja* 1:187. Jełowicki to Chodkiewiczowa, 11 September 1832, in Jełowicki, *Listy do Ksaweryny*, 59.
10. Population figures: Kramer, *Threshold of a New World*, 25–26.
11. Bohdan Zaleski to Władysław Mickiewicz, last days of October 1874 ["Adam Mickiewicz podczas pisania i drukowania *Pana Tadeusza*], *Korespondencja AM* 2:XIV.
12. Mickiewicz to Lelewel, [middle of May (?) 1832], *Dz.* 15:155.
13. Henryk Nakwaski, "Pamiętniki," 4 October 1838, in Kallenbach, *AM* (1897) 2:406.
14. Compatriots from Besançon to Mickiewicz, 8 August 1832, Korespondencja. The letter, which accompanied the gift of a ring, was from émigrés in the Besançon *dépôt*, most of whom were former students at the University of Vilnius. Mickiewicz responded ([1–8 October 1833]) by proclaiming the ring "a wedding band," proof that he had been "from childhood trothed to the fatherland" (*Dz.* 15:169).
15. Mickiewicz to Domeyko, 28 August [1833], *Dz.* 15:231. J. B. Zaleski to W. Mickiewicz, 8 April 1869, *Korespondencja JBZ* 4:122. Mickiewicz to J. B. Zaleski, [26 December 1840], *Dz.* 15:596.
16. Stanisław Egbert Koźmian to Jan Koźmian, 5 August 1832, in "Listy o AM," 64. Hieronim Kajsiewicz to Leonard Niedźwiecki, 24 May 1836, in B. Zaleski, "Ks. Hieronim Kajsiewicz," 281.
17. Juliusz Słowacki to Salomea Bécu, 3 September 1832, in Słowacki, *Korespondencja*, 1:137 (Słowacki here himself proudly cites Mickiewicz's opinion, blind, it seems, to its implications), 134–35.
18. Statute of the Society of Lithuanian and Ruthenian Lands (10 December 1831), quoted in Wasilewski, "Mickiewicz i Słowacki," 92.
19. Elizabeth Marlay to James Fenimore Cooper, 4 September 1832, *Correspondence of Cooper* 1:287.
20. Mickiewicz to Lelewel, [first half of May (?) 1832], *Dz.* 15:156. Słowacki to Bécu, 4 October 1832, in Słowacki, *Korespondencja* 1:144.
21. J. B. Zaleski to Ludwik Nabielak, 4 December 1832, *Korespondencja JBZ* 1:44. Mickiewicz to Odyniec, 28 January 1833, *Dz.* 15:189.
22. J. B. Zaleski to August Bielowski, November 1832, *Korespondencja JBZ* 1:38. J. B. Zaleski to Nabielak, 3 November 1832, *Korespondencja JBZ* 1:38, 42. Tańska-Hoffmanowa, *Pamiętniki* 2:114.

Jan Skrzynecki to Janusz Czetwertyński, 22 July 1833, *Korespondencja AM* 4:68. Charles de Montalembert to Félicité de Lamennais, 6 March 1833, in Montalembert, *Lettres*, 66.

23. Mickiewicz to Odyniec, 28 January [1833], *Dz.* 15:189. *Pielgrzym Polski*, 13 Jan. 1833: 3–4.
24. Mickiewicz to Odyniec, [14 February 1834], *Dz.* 15:261. Mickiewicz to Niemcewicz, [ca. 14 March 1833], ibid., 195. J. B. Zaleski to W. Mickiewicz, last days of October 1874, *Korespondencja AM* 2:XXV.
25. Garczyński to Mickiewicz, 16 October 1832, Korespondencja; Mickiewicz to Garczyński, 5 March [1832], *Dz.* 15:192. Garczyński to Mickiewicz, 17 April 1833, Korespondencja.
26. Mickiewicz to Grabowski, 15 September [1832], *Dz.* 15:167. J. B. Zaleski to Nabielak, 3 November 1832, *Korespondencja JBZ* 1:40; Domeyko to Jan Siemieński, 26 October 1880, *Korespondencja AM* 4:6. Mickiewicz to Garczyński, 12 January [1833], *Dz.* 15:187.
27. Mickiewicz to Odyniec, [8 December 1832], *Dz.* 15:177. Karol Sienkiewicz to Czartoryski, 12 August 1832, *Rozmowy*, 147.
28. As recorded by A. Chodźko (1840s), *Rozmowy*, 228.
29. My renditions from the *Books* are based on the translation by Dorothea Prall Radin, in Mickiewicz, *Poems*, 369–415.
30. Mickiewicz to Odyniec, [8 December 1832], *Dz.* 15:178. Mickiewicz to Krystyn Ostrowski, 13 November [1840], ibid., 583. Krasiński to Konstanty Gaszyński, 16 December 1833, *Listy do Gaszyńskiego*, 68.
31. Anonymous to Mickiewicz, 18 May 1833, quoted in *Żywot* 2:252. *Uwagi o użyciu najkorzystniejszym czasu w emigracji wraz z projektem stowarzyszenia się wychodźców polskich* (1833), in ibid., XIX–XXIII. Figures from the fall 1833 election to Dwernicki's Committee of the Polish Emigration are from Gadon, *Wielka Emigracja*, 434.
32. Hipolit Błotnicki, *Dziennik*, November 1832, quoted in Wójcicka, "Hipolit Błotnicki," 211. From a public critique by the radical Jan Czyński (July 1833), quoted in Pigoń, *O "Księgach,"* 116. Breve of Gregory XVI to the bishop of Rennes, 5 October 1833, quoted in *Żywot* 2:211 n. 3. Domeyko, *Moje podróży* 1:167. Mickiewicz to Odyniec, 28 January [1833], *Dz.* 15:189.
33. Publication figures: Syga, *Te księgi*, 111–17, 128–34.
34. Stanisław Roplewski, "O literaturze polskiej na emigracji" (1840), quoted in Pigoń, *O "Księgach,"* 119–20.
35. Montalembert to Lamennais, 2 January 1833, in Montalembert, *Lettres*, 34. Montalembert to Henrietta Ankwicz, 22 February 1833, in Siemieński, *Ewunia*, 145. The German translation, "unter den Augen des Verfassers getreu in Deutsche übertragen," by P. J. Gauger, appeared in Paris at the end of March 1833, in two editions; the English, by Krystyn Lach Szyrma, appeared in London in late spring of 1833.
36. From Sainte-Beuve's review of Montalembert's translation (1833), in *AMaydF*, 148. Giuseppe Mazzini to his mother, 18 [November 1834], Mazzini, *Scritti* 10:215; from Pierre Ballanche's review of Lamennais' *Paroles d'un croyant* (1834), *AMaydF*, 155. Thomas Carlyle to John Carlyle, in Carlyle, *New Letters* 1:184. From Lamennais's correspondence (1833), in *AMaydF*, 145. As Lamennais was following the progress of Montalembert's translation, he himself was working on *Paroles d'un croyant*, arguably his most famous work, published in 1834. Itself a biblical stylization, it too envisioned an immanent revolution that would revitalize Europe's social order according to the principles of Catholic Christianity. The spiritual progenitor's indebtedness to his spiritual son is undeniable.
37. Domeyko, *Moje podróży* 1:167.
38. Mickiewicz to Odyniec, [21 April 1833], *Dz.* 15:202. Mickiewicz to Odyniec, 19 April 1834, ibid., 266. Stefan Witwicki to Odyniec, 24 July 1836, in Odyniec, *Wspomnienia*, 378–79.
39. Walery Wielogłowski, *Emigracja polska wobec Boga i narodu* (1848), quoted in Sudolski, "Adam Mickiewicz w pamiętnikach Bogdana Jańskiego," 93.
40. Mickiewicz to Niemcewicz, [ca. 14 March 1833], *Dz.* 15:195. Błotnicki, *Dziennik*, November 1832, quoted in Wójcicka, "Hipolit Błotnicki," 211.

41. Mickiewicz to Niemcewicz, [ca. 14 March 1833], *Dz.* 15:196. Eustachy Januszkiewicz to W. Mickiewicz, 4 November 1874, quoted in *Żywot* 2:238.
42. *Pielgrzym Polski*, 7 Dec. 1832: 3, 4. *Pielgrzym* had also published Mickiewicz's appeal on behalf of the Lithuanian-Ruthenian Society for memoirs of the uprising (2 December 1832).
43. "Oświadczenie," *Pamiętnik Emigracji Polskiej*, 6 June 1833 (*Zygmunt I. Jagiellończyk*): 8. "Nasi krytycy," *Feniks*, no. 3 (*Pierwej być, a potem rządzić jak być potrzeba*): 14.
44. Ludwik Plater to Czartoryski, 12 April 1833, quoted in *Kronika 1832–1834*, 187. *Feniks*, 15 June 1833, quoted in *Żywot* 2:XIX.
45. Mickiewicz to Garczyński, [8 April] 1833, *Dz.* 15:200. Mickiewicz to Niemcewicz, [end of May 1833], ibid., 214.
46. Marlay to Cooper, 4 September 1832, in Cooper, *Correspondence* 1:287. Mickiewicz to F. Mickiewicz, [16 November 1832], *Dz.* 15:172. Mickiewicz to Garczyński, [8 April] 1833, *Dz.* 15:200. Garczyński to Mickiewicz, 17 April [18]33, Korespondencja.
47. Mickiewicz to F. Mickiewicz, 14 February [1833], *Dz.* 15:191. Mickiewicz to Garczyński, 5 March [1833], ibid., 192. Mickiewicz to Garczyński, [8 April] 1833, ibid., 200. Mickiewicz to Odyniec, [8 December 1832], ibid., 178. Mickiewicz to Odyniec, [21 April 1833], ibid., 203.
48. Mickiewicz to Odyniec, [8 December 1832], *Dz.* 15:178. Mickiewicz to Niemcewicz, [end of May 1833], ibid., 213.
49. Mickiewicz to Odyniec, 2 July [1834], *Dz.* 15:269. Mickiewicz to Z. Ankwicz, [24 November 1832], ibid., 177. Z. and H. Ankwicz to Mickiewicz, 11 March 1833, Korespondencja.
50. Mickiewicz to Odyniec, 28 January [1833], *Dz.* 15:189. Mickiewicz to Garczyński, [8 April] 1833, ibid., 200. Mickiewicz to Garczyński, 6 May [1833], ibid., 207.
51. J. B. Zaleski to W. Mickiewicz, last days of October 1874, *Korespondencja AM* 2:XVII, XIII. Mickiewicz to Odyniec, [21 April 1833], *Dz.* 15:202.
52. Mickiewicz to Odyniec, 23 May [1833], *Dz.* 15:212. Zaleski to W. Mickiewicz, last days of October 1874, *Korespondencja AM* 2:XVII–XVIII. Niemcewicz, *Pamiętniki* 2:181 (23 November 1833). Mickiewicz to Odyniec, 23 May [1833], *Dz.* 15:213.
53. Garczyński to Mickiewicz, 26 November [18]32, Korespondencja. Garczyński to Mickiewicz, 9 January [18]33, ibid.
54. Mickiewicz to Garczyński, 6 May [1833], *Dz.* 15:206. Mickiewicz to Garczyński, [23 May 1833], ibid., 209. *DzW* 1.3:158.
55. Mickiewicz to Garczyński, 12 January [1833], *Dz.* 15:186–87.
56. Garczyński to Mickiewicz, 25 February 1833, Korespondencja. Garczyński to Mickiewicz, 14 May [18]33, ibid. Mickiewicz to Garczyński, [23 May 1833], *Dz.* 15:208.
57. Mickiewicz to Achille de Broglie, [mid-June 1833], *Dz.* 15:215. Three years later, though, this declaration would come back to haunt him.
58. J. B. Zaleski to W. Mickiewicz, last days of October 1874, *Korespondencja AM* 2:XXIII n. 1. Mickiewicz to Stattler, 21 March 1836, *Dz.* 15:316. Contract, quoted in Syga, *Te księgi*, 259–60. Mickiewicz to F. Mickiewicz, [10?] July [1833], *Dz.* 15:221. Mickiewicz added that he also had "a small sum" for his brother, "enough for a comfortable life at least for a year."
59. Mickiewicz to Domeyko, [10(?) July 1833], *Dz.* 15:218. Potocka to Odyniec, 2 August 1833, quoted in Pług, "Odyniec," 41:170. Mickiewicz to Odyniec, [10 (?)] July 1833, *Dz.* 15:223–24.
60. Garczyński to Wincenty Turno, 8 August 1833, *Korespondencja AM* 2:284. Mickiewicz to Domeyko, 26 or 27 [July 1833], *Dz.* 15:225. Mickiewicz to Domeyko, 2 August [1833], ibid., 227. Mickiewicz to Odyniec, 11 November [1833], ibid., 243.
61. Mickiewicz to Domeyko, 12 August [1833], *Dz.* 15:228. Mickiewicz to Domeyko, 28 August [1833], ibid., 31. Mickiewicz to Domeyko, 28 August [1833], ibid., 231. Mickiewicz to Domeyko, 7 September [1833], ibid., 232. Mickiewicz to Odyniec, 22 September [1833], ibid., 236–37.

62. Mickiewicz to Domeyko, 22 September [1833], *Dz.* 15:235. Potocka to Odyniec, 2 August 1833, quoted in Pług, "Odyniec," 41:170.
63. Mickiewicz to Odyniec, 11 November [1833], *Dz.* 15:242. Mickiewicz to F. Mickiewicz, 28 September [1833], ibid., 238.
64. Mickiewicz to Odyniec, 23 May [1833], *Dz.* 15:212. Mickiewicz to Domeyko, 2 August [1833], ibid., 227. Mickiewicz to Odyniec, 11 November [1833], ibid., 242.
65. Mickiewicz to Odyniec, 11 November [1833], *Dz.* 15:242. Mickiewicz to Potocka [end of November (?)–December (?) 1833], *Dz.* 15:248.
66. Mickiewicz to Odyniec, [14 February 1834], *Dz.* 15:261. Niemcewicz, *Pamietniki* 2:181 (23 November 1833). Mickiewicz to Kajsiewicz, [second half of November (?) 1833], *Dz.* 15:246. Błotnicki, *Dziennik*, 1 June 1834, quoted in Wójcicka, "Hipolit Błotnicki," 217. Mickiewicz to F. Mickiewicz, 19 April [1834], *Dz.* 15:264.
67. J. B. Zaleski to W. Mickiewicz, last days of October 1874, *Korespondencja AM* 2:XX. Mickiewicz to Odyniec, [14 February 1834], *Dz.* 15:261.
68. J. B. Zaleski to W. Mickiewicz, last days of October 1874, *Korespondencja AM* 2:XXI. Niemcewicz, *Pamiętniki* 2:280 (15 March 1834).
69. J. B. Zaleski to W. Mickiewicz, last days of October 1874, *Korespondencja AM* 2:XXIII. J. B. Zaleski to Kajsiewicz, 22 June 1834, *Korespondencja JBZ* 1:66.
70. As recorded by Kajsiewicz (1830s), *Rozmowy*, 125.
71. Stanisław Worcell to Mickiewicz, 7 November 1838, Korespondencja. Słowacki, *Dzieła wszystkie* 7:82.
72. Słowacki, "[Notatki różne z 'Raptularza']," *Dzieła wszystkie* 15:469. Cyprian Norwid to Józef Ignacy Kraszewski, [ca. 15] May 1866, in Norwid, *Pisma wszystkie* 9:223.
73. Niemcewicz to Witwicki, 15 July 1837, *Korespondencja AM* 4:70.
74. Mickiewicz to F. Mickiewicz, 19 April [1834], *Dz.* 15:264. J. B. Zaleski to W. Mickiewicz, last days of October 1874, *Korespondencja AM* 2:XXI. Mickiewicz to Odyniec, [14 February 1834], *Dz.* 15:261.
75. J. B. Zaleski to W. Mickiewicz, last days of October 1874, *Korespondencja AM* 2:XXIV. Mickiewicz to Odyniec, 19 April 1834, *Dz.* 15:265.
76. Mickiewicz to Kajsiewicz, 27 July [1834], *Dz.* 15:273–74. Jełowicki to Chodkiewiczowa, 19 March 1834, in Jełowicki, *Listy do Ksaweryny*, 145–46.
77. J. B. Zaleski to Kajsiewicz, 5 February 1834, *Korespondencja JBZ* 1:60. J. B. Zaleski to Kajsiewicz, 22 June 1834, ibid., 1:66.
78. Ilnicka, "Łucja z książąt Gedroyciów Rautenstrauchowa," 163. Rautenstrauchowa, *Wspomnienia moje o Francji* (1839), in *Wspomnienia o Mickiewiczu*, 30.
79. As recorded by Aleksandra Faucher, quoted in *Kronika 1832–1834*, 316.

CHAPTER 7. DOMESTICITY (1834–1839)

1. Mickiewicz to Odyniec, 2 July [1834], *Dz.* 15:269. Morawski, *W Peterburku*, 174. Szymanowska-Malewska, *Dziennik*, 342.
2. C. Szymanowska to H. Szymanowska, 29 February 1832, quoted in *PS*, 149. C. Szymanowska to H. Szymanowska, 6 March 1832, quoted in ibid., 15–51. C. Szymanowska to H. Szymanowska, 24 May 1832, quoted in ibid., 153.
3. C. Szymanowska to H. Szymanowska, October 1832, quoted in *PS*, 155.
4. M. Szymanowska to Mickiewicz, 14/26 May 1828, Korespondencja.
5. Mickiewicz to Malewski, 20 November [1830], *Dz.* 15:82. M. Szymanowska to Mickiewicz, 14/26 May 1828, Korespondencja. Odyniec, *Listy* 1:48; Mickiewicz to Malewski, 2 February 1830, *Dz.* 15:17. Mickiewicz to Malewski, 20 November [1830], ibid., 82. Mickiewicz to M. Szymanowska, 20 February [1831], ibid., 92.

6. J. Koźmian to Kajsiewicz, 29 August 1834, in *Korespondencja między Koźmianem a Kajsiewiczem*, 7. Mickiewicz to F. Mickiewicz, [ca. 5 August 1834], *Dz.* 15:276. Mickiewicz to Kajsiewicz, 27 July [1834], ibid., 272.
7. Mickiewicz to Odyniec, 2 July [1834], *Dz.* 15:269. As recalled by A. Chodźko (1859), *Rozmowy*, 243–44.
8. H. Szymanowska to M. and Z. Malewski, 27 July 1834, quoted in *PS*, 170. Declaration of Celina Szymanowska's Majority, in *Żywot* 2:XXVII. As noted by E. Januszkiewicz, quoted in *Żywot* 2:295.
9. E. Januszkiewicz to W. Mickiewicz, 24 July 1874, quoted in *Żywot* 2:296.
10. Adam Mickiewicz's Marriage Certificate, in *Żywot* 2:XXVIII. Domeyko to Maria Gorecka, 5 July 1875, quoted in *PS*, 172. As recalled by Biergiel, *Rozmowy*, 325.
11. Niemcewicz, *Dziennik pobytu* 2:428. Domeyko to Maria Gorecka, 5 July 1875, quoted in *PS*, 172. C. Mickiewicz to Franciszek and Barbara Wołowski, 22 July 1834, quoted in ibid., 172. Jełowicki to Chodkiewicz, 25 July 1834, in Jełowicki, *Listy do Ksaweryny*, 153.
12. Niemcewicz, *Dziennik pobytu*, 2:428 (Witkowska, *Celina i Adam*, 79, suggests that Niemcewicz was himself the author of the epigram). Karol Hoffman, *Dziennik*, quoted in *Kronika 1834–1840*, 32. Krasiński to Gaszyński, 23 August 1834, in Krasiński, *Listy do Gaszyńskiego*, 86. Klementyna Tańska-Hoffmanowa, in Kacnelson, "Zapiski," 58. Maurycy Mochnacki to Bazyli Mochnacki, 25 July 1834, in Mochnacki, *Listy*, 253.
13. Karol Hoffman, *Dziennik*, quoted in *Kronika 1834–1840*, 32.
14. Tańska-Hoffmanowa, in Kacnelson, "Zapiski," 56–58. Mickiewicz to Potocka [ca. 25 August 1834], *Dz.* 15:281.
15. Jełowicki to Chodkiewicz, 25 July 1834, in Jełowicki, *Listy do Ksaweryny*, 154. Eugenia Larisch to E. Januszkiewicz, 25 August 1834, quoted in *Kronika 1834–1840*, 42.
16. Mickiewicz to Kajsiewicz, 27 July [1834], *Dz.* 15:272.
17. Mickiewicz to F. Mickiewicz, [ca. 5 August 1834], *Dz.* 15:276. Mickiewicz to Odyniec, [ca. 12 August 1834], ibid., 278. C. Mickiewicz to H. Malewski, 29 August 1834, quoted in *PS*, 175.
18. C. Mickiewicz to H. Malewski, 29 August 1834, quoted in "Mm" 5.18:163; Mickiewicz to Odyniec, [ca. 12 August 1834], *Dz.* 15:278; Tańska-Hoffmanowa, in Kacnelson, "Zapiski," 58. C. Mickiewicz to Julia Wołowska, 19 October 1834, quoted in "Mm" 5.18:164. Mickiewicz to Odyniec, [ca. 12 August 1834], *Dz.* 15:278. C. Mickiewicz to Julia Wołowska, 21 August 1834, quoted in "Mm" 5.18:162. Tańska-Hoffmanowa, in Kacnelson, "Zapiski," 58–59.
19. Mickiewicz to Odyniec, [ca. 12 August 1834], *Dz.* 15:278. Tańska-Hoffmanowa, in Kacnelson, "Zapiski," 58. Ludwik Nabielak, *Dziennik*, quoted in Zawadzki, *Ludwik Nabielak*, 100.
20. C. Mickiewicz to the Odynieces, 25 January 1835, in *Księga pamiątkowa* 1:23; C. Mickiewicz to H. Malewska, 29 August 1834, quoted in "Mm" 5.18:163. E. Januszkiewicz to Eugenia Larisch, 30 April 1835, in Sudolski, "Mickiewiczowskie wspominki," 95. E. Januszkiewicz to Larisch, 18 August 1836, in ibid., 95.
21. Mickiewicz to Odyniec, 28 September [1835], *Dz.* 15:302; Mickiewicz to Odyniec, 16 August [1837], ibid., 376. Mickiewicz to Domeyko, 14 June [1838], ibid., 403; C. Mickiewicz to H. Malewska, 18 September 1835, quoted in "Mm" 5.18:165. C. Mickiewicz to H. Malewska, 24 February 1836, quoted in ibid., 167. Niemcewicz, 4 June 1836, *Dzienniki 1835–1836*, 311.
22. Mickiewicz to Domeyko, 4 [October 1837], *Dz.* 15:380; Bohdan Jański to J. B. Zaleski, 19 June 1838, in Sudolski, "Adam Mickiewicz w pamiętnikach," 99.
23. Jełowicki to Chodkiewicz, 9 June 1836, in Jełowicki, *Listy do Ksaweryny*, 223. E. Januszkiewicz to Larisch, 3 October 1836, in Sudolski, "Mickiewiczowskie wspominki," 96. Mickiewicz to Odyniec, 18 July [1836], *Dz.* 15:323–24.
24. Mickiewicz to Odyniec, [ca. 12 August 1834], *Dz.* 15:278. Mickiewicz to Cezary Plater, [25 September 1834], ibid., 283. Witwicki to Odyniec, 26 August 1836, in Odyniec, *Wspomnienia*, 379. Błotnicki, *Dziennik*, 18 May 1835, in Wójcicka, "Hipolit Błotnicki," 219.

25. Mickiewicz to Rzewuska, [end of July–August 1835], *Dz.* 15:294. E. Januszkiewicz to Larisch, 18 August 1836, in Sudolski, "Mickiewiczowskie wspominki," 95; Nakwaski, "Pamiętniki," 8 April 1840, in Kallenbach, *AM* (1897) 2:408. Mickiewicz to Odyniec, 18 July [1836], *Dz.* 15:234.
26. Kajsiewicz to Victor Pavie, 18 May 1836, quoted in *Żywot* 2:357. Mickiewicz to Kajsiewicz, [29 January 1838], *Dz.* 15:389; Mickiewicz to Domeyko, 4 [October 1837], ibid., 381.
27. Jełowicki to Chodkiewicz, 15 October 1836, in Jełowicki, *Listy do Ksaweryny*, 233.
28. Mickiewicz to F. Mickiewicz, [end of December 1836–beginning of January 1837], *Dz.* 15:341. Mickiewicz to Odyniec, [end of December 1836–beginning of January 1837], ibid., 343.
29. Mickiewicz to Odyniec, [end of December 1836–beginning of January 1837], *Dz.* 15:344.
30. As recalled by Wojciech Grzymała, quoted in Kallenbach, *AM* (1923) 2:258; Mallefille to W. Mickiewicz, 2 August 1867, in *MP* 1:15. D'Agoult to Mickiewicz, [second half of May 1837], Korespondencja; Sand to Mickiewicz [ca. 22 May 1837], ibid. Mallefille to W. Mickiewicz, 2 August 1867, in *MP* 1:15. Sand to Mickiewicz [ca. 22 May 1837], Korespondencja.
31. *Tygodnik Literacki*, 21 May 1838: 64. Mickiewicz to Sand, June 3 [1837], *Dz.* 15:363.
32. Mickiewicz to de Vigny, [15 March 1837], *Dz.* 15:349. Vigny to Mickiewicz, 1 April 1837, Korespondencja. Stern (d'Agoult), "Journal," 8 June 1837, in *Mémoires* 2:117. Mickiewicz to de Vigny, 1 July [1837], *Dz.* 15:367–68. Mickiewicz to Odyniec, [end of December 1836–beginning of January 1837], ibid., 344.
33. Sand, *Œuvres autobiographique* 2:438. Sand, "Essai sur le drame fantastique, Goethe. Byron. Mickiewicz" (1839), in *AMaydF*, 91. Sand to Charlotte Marliani, [13 March 1839], in Sand, *Correspondance* 4:600.
34. Leon Szuman to Piotr Semenenko, 11 November 1837, quoted in *Kronika 1834–1840*, 307. Tańska-Hoffmanowa to the Nakwaskis, 11 March 1838, quoted in Kallenbach, *AM* (1923) 2:271–72. Mickiewicz to E. Januszkiewicz, [Fall 1835 (?)], *Dz.* 15:304.
35. Mickiewicz to Odyniec, [after 20 July 1835], *Dz.* 15:295; as noted down by A. Chodźko (1848), *Rozmowy*, 241. His paraphrases of another forty apothegms and sayings, including some taken from Baader and Benjamin Franklin, were published posthumously.
36. Mickiewicz to Kajsiewicz, 31 October [1834], *Dz.* 15:285.
37. Mickiewicz to Kajsiewicz and Leonard Rettel, 16 December [1833], *Dz.* 15:250–52.
38. As recalled by Walerian Kalinka, quoted in *HZZP* 1:41. "[Act of Foundation of The Society of United Brethren]," 19 December 1834, quoted in *Żywot* 2:259.
39. Jański, "Dzienniki," 13 June 1835, quoted in Micewski, *Bogdan Jański*, 250.
40. Kajsiewicz to Leonard Niedźwiecki, 24 May 1836, quoted in Br. Zaleski, "Ks. Hieronim Kajsiewicz," 286. Mickiewicz to F. Mickiewicz, [end of December 1936–beginning of January 1837], *Dz.* 15:340–41; Mickiewicz to J. B. and Józef Zaleski, [ca. 14 May 1838], ibid., 399.
41. "Kongregacja katolicko-papieska," *Pólnoc*, 12 Oct. 1835, 64. Review of Kajsiewicz's *Nunc dimittis Domine*, *Nowa Polska* 3 (1836): 477.
42. Mickiewicz to J. B. and J. Zaleski, [ca. 14 May 1838], *Dz.* 15:398.
43. Karol Wodziński to J. B. Zaleski, 14 July 1836, quoted in *Żywot* 2:362. Witwicki to Wodziński, 7 October 1836, quoted in *Żywot* 2:369.
44. Sobolevskii to Malewski, 24 December 1868/5 January 1869, *AF Nz* 3:607. Mickiewicz to Sobolevskii, [6 April 1837], *Dz.* 15:352.
45. Mickiewicz to Viazemskii, [first half of March (?) 1839], *Dz.* 15:464.
46. Witwicki to Odyniec, 15 April 1837, quoted in Odyniec, *Wspomnienia*, 381–82; Niemcewicz, "Dzienniki," quoted in *Kronika 1834–1840*, 266; Gorecka, *Wspomnienia*, 2; C. Mickiewicz to H. Malewska, 15 October 1837, quoted in *Żywot* 2:393–94.
47. Mickiewicz to C. Mickiewicz, [11 September 1837], *Dz.* 15:379. Mickiewicz to Domeyko, 4 [October 1837], *Dz.* 15:381.
48. Mickiewicz to Odyniec, 16 August [1837], *Dz.* 15:376.

49. Mickiewicz to F. Mickiewicz, 20 February 1839, *Dz.* 15:461. Odyniec to Mickiewicz, 10 September 1837, Korespondencja. "We've received letters from Odyniec or, rather, from his daughter" (Mickiewicz to F. Mickiewicz, [3 or 23] March 1841, *Dz.* 15:611).
50. Mickiewicz to J. B. and J. Zaleski, [end of July 1838], *Dz.* 15:412. C. Mickiewicz to H. Malewska, 27 June 1839, quoted in "Mm," 5.18:170. W. Mickiewicz, *Pamiętniki* 1:204 n. 1.
51. Mickiewicz to C. Mickiewicz, 20 October [1838], *Dz.* 15:424. Scovazzi, quoted in *Żywot* 2:408–9.
52. Mickiewicz to C. Mickiewicz, 20 October [1838], *Dz.* 15:424–25.
53. A. Khliustin de Circourt to Augustin de Candolle, 28 October 1838, in *Żywot* 2:XXXVI. Charles-Augustin Sainte-Beuve to Charles Monnard, 7 July 1838, in Sainte-Beuve, *Correspondence générale* 2:469.
54. Nakwaski, "Pamiętniki," 4 November 1838, in Kallenbach, *AM* (1897) 2:404. Board of Public Education to the Council of State, 7 November 1838, in Ferretti, "Adam Mickiewicz," 166–67. "Extrait des procès-verbaux de l'Académie," in *Żywot* 2:XL.
55. Błotnicki, "Dziennik," 18 May 1835, quoted in Wójcicka, "Hipolit Błotnicki," 219. Niewiarowicz, *Wspomnienia*, 90–91.
56. Niemcewicz, "Dzienniki," 1 November 1838, quoted in *Kronika 1834–1840*, 390. Błotnicki, "Dziennik," 11 November 1838, quoted in Wójcicka, "Hipolit Błotnicki," 224. E. Januszkiewicz to Niedźwiecki, 8 November 1838, quoted in Jasińska, "Celina Mickiewiczowa," 289.
57. E. Januszkiewicz to Niedźwiecki, 8 November 1838, quoted in Jasińska, "Celina Mickiewiczowa," 289. Niedźwiecki to Bertold Wierciński, 18 November 1838, quoted in ibid., 290. E. Januszkiewicz to Larisch, 20 November 1838, quoted in Pigoń, "'Wiek klęski," 537 n. 7.
58. E. Januszkiewicz to Larisch, 20 November 1838, quoted in Pigoń, "'Wiek klęski," 537 n. 7.
59. Séance du Conseil de l'Instruction Publique, 17 November 1838, in Feretti, "Adam Mickiewicz," 169. Mickiewicz to Domeyko, [7 December] 1839, *Dz.* 15:504; E. Januszkiewicz to Larisch, 20 November 1838, quoted in Pigoń, "'Wiek klęski," 537 n. 7. E. Januszkiewicz to Larisch, 24 December 1838, quoted in Pigoń, "'Wiek klęski," 537.
60. E. Januszkiewicz to Larisch, 20 November 1838, quoted in Pigoń, "'Wiek klęski," 537 n. 7. Sainte-Beuve to Caroline Olivier, [25 November 1838], *Correspondance* 2:485.
61. Mickiewicz to C. Mickiewicz, [ca. 27 December 1838], *Dz.* 15:438–39. Mickiewicz to C. Mickiewicz, [ca. 6 February 1839], ibid., 453. Mickiewicz to C. Mickiewicz, 15 February [1839], ibid., 458–59.
62. Tańska-Hoffmanowa to Karolina Nakwaska, 4 April 1839, quoted in Kallenbach, *AM* (1923), 2:274–75.
63. Sainte-Beuve to the Oliviers, 26 November 1838, *Correspondance* 2:509. Mickiewicz to Domeyko, 7 [February] 1839, *Dz.* 15:456, 455. Mickiewicz to F. Mickiewicz, 20 February 1839, ibid., 460. The Academy of Lausanne to the Board of Public Education, 24 November 1838, in *Żywot* 2:XL.
64. Mickiewicz to C. Mickiewicz, [first half of January 1839], *Dz.* 15:448; Mickiewicz to C. Mickiewicz, [beginning of March 1839], ibid., 463.
65. Tańska-Hoffmanowa to Karolina Nakwaska, 4 April 1839, quoted in Kallenbach, *AM* (1923) 2:274. C. Mickiewicz to H. Malewska, 2 April 1839, quoted in "Mm," 5.18:171 Witwicki to J. B. Zaleski, 11 May 1839, quoted in *Żywot* 2:424. Witwicki to Klementyna Grabowska, 25 February 1839, "Nieznane listy," 549.
66. Barsukov, *Zhizn'*, 5:279–80.

CHAPTER 8. ACADEME (1839–1841)

1. C. Mickiewicz to Łucjan Stypułkowski, 18 June 1839, quoted in *Żywot* 2:429.
2. Mickiewicz to J. B. Zaleski, [ca. 30 June–3 July (?) 1839], *Dz.* 15:478. Mickiewicz to J. B. Zaleski, 20 September [1839], ibid., 495. Mickiewicz to Domeyko, 11 August 1839, ibid., 481. Mickiewicz to J. B. Zaleski, 20 September [1839], ibid., 495.

3. J. Olivier to C. Olivier, [14 August 1839], in Ferretti, "Adam Mickiewicz," 175. The Academy to the Council of Public Education, 31 July 1839, in *Żywot* 2:XLIV.
4. C. Mickiewicz to Stypułkowski, 3 [actually 9] July 1839, quoted in "Mm" 5.18:173; Mickiewicz to Domeyko, 11 August 1839, *Dz.* 15:481. Nakwaski, "Pamiętniki," 11 September 1839, in Kallenbach, *AM* (1897) 2:407. Gorecka, *Wspomnienia*, 17.
5. Mickiewicz to Kajsiewicz and Piotr Semenenko, 13 March [1840], *Dz.* 15:534.
6. [Meeting of the Council of State, 24 September 1839], in Ferretti, "Adam Mickiewicz," 177–78. Mickiewicz to André Gindroz [vice president of the council of state], 6 October 1839, *Dz.* 15:497.
7. Mickiewicz to J. B. Zaleski, 20 September [1839], *Dz.* 15:495.
8. As recalled by J. Olivier, quoted in *Żywot* 2:434. Witwicki to J. B. Zaleski, 26 November 1839, *Listy SW*, 23. Report of the Academy, 27 February 1840, in *Żywot* 2:LV. Nakwaski, "Pamiętniki," 8 April 1840, in Kallenbach, *AM* (1897) 2:408. Mickiewicz to Domeyko, [7 December] 1839, *Dz.* 15:505.
9. Mickiewicz to J. B. Zaleski, 29 November [1839], *Dz.* 15:503. Mickiewicz to Domeyko, 15 February 1840, ibid., 519. Mickiewicz to C. Olivier, [12 November 1839–first half of July 1840], ibid., 500. Mickiewicz to C. Nakwaska, 22 [December 1839], ibid., 511.
10. Faculty of Letters, Private Observations on Several Fields of Study, 15 February 1840, in *Żywot* 2:XLIX. From the memoirs of Władysław Orpiszewski, quoted in *Kronika 1834–1840*, 508. Report of the Cantonal College, 26 February 1840, in *Żywot* 2:LII. Monnard, Report to the Academy, 27 February 1840, in ibid., LIV.
11. [Director] Solomiac, Report to the Cantonal College, 26 February 1840, in *Żywot* 2:LII. Monnard, Report to the Academy, 27 February 1840, in ibid., LVI. Students' Petition, 9 March 1840, in ibid., LIX.
12. Mickiewicz to August Jaquet, 21 March 1840, *Dz.* 15:537. Mickiewicz to Léon Faucher, 13 March [1840], ibid., 528. In an earlier letter to Faucher ([8] March 1840), Mickiewicz had written that he was being offered "a salary of 3,500 francs; taking into account how inexpensive the country is, this sum is worth 5,000 francs of what you would spend" (ibid., 522). To Franciszek (13 March [1840]), he wrote that he would be earning "4,500 francs" (the first printed edition of the letter [no autograph extant] has "4,800" [*Korespondencja AM* 1:142]), without indicating that this was in *French* francs (*Dz.* 15:535).
13. Mickiewicz to Domeyko, 15 February 1840, *Dz.* 15:519–20.
14. Mickiewicz to J. B. Zaleski, 2 July [1840], *Dz.* 15:549; Gorecka, *Wspomnienia*, 7–15. Mickiewicz to J. B. Zaleski, 29 November [1839], *Dz.* 15:503. Mickiewicz to Tekla Wołowska, 8–9 March [1840], ibid., 526.
15. Mickiewicz to Domeyko, 15 February 1840, *Dz.* 15:519. Kajsiewicz to Mickiewicz, 2 April 1840, Korespondencja.
16. Gorecka, *Wspomnienia*, 16–17. Mickiewicz to J. B. Zaleski, 7 January [1840], *Dz.* 15:515.
17. *Courrier suisse*, 23 June 1840, in *Żywot* 2:LXXIX. Mickiewicz to Faucher, 25 May 1840, *Dz.* 15:547; Niedźwiecki to Ignacy Jackowski, 21 April 1842, quoted in Jasińska, "Celina Mickiewiczowa," 296.
18. "Installation de M. Adam Mickiewicz," *Courrier suisse*, 30 June 1840, in *Żywot* 2:LXXIX–LXXXI. Meeting of the Council of the Faculty of Sciences and Letters, 18 June 1840, in Ferretti, "Adam Mickiewicz," 192. Mickiewicz never did manage to prepare the improvised lecture for publication, as the academy requested. It is extant only thanks to a stenogram (*Dz.* 7:243–52, in Polish translation).
19. Discours de M. [Emmanuel] de la Harpe, in *Żywot*, 2:LXXXI. Discours de M. Ch. Monnard, in ibid., LXXXIX–XC.
20. *Le Courrier français*, 21 April 1840. Mickiewicz to Domeyko, [7 December] 1839, *Dz.* 15:505.
21. Faucher to Mickiewicz, 5 March 1840, Korespondencja. Faucher to Mickiewicz, [ca. 10 March 1840], ibid.
22. Mickiewicz to Faucher, [8] March 1840, *Dz.* 15:522–23. Sainte-Beuve to C. Olivier, 19 March 1840, *Correspondance* 3:251.

23. Victor Cousin to Mickiewicz, 10 April 1840, Korespondencja. Cousin, "Exposé des motifs," *Moniteur universel*, 20 and 21 April 1840, in *Żywot* 2:LXVIII–LXX.
24. Mickiewicz to Cousin, 15 April 1840, *Dz.* 15:540–41.
25. A. Czartoryski to Mickiewicz, 24 July 1840, Korespondencja.
26. Mickiewicz to J. B. Zaleski, 2 July [1840], *Dz.* 15:549. Mickiewicz to Faucher, [17 April 1840], ibid., 543. Mickiewicz to Cousin, 16 August 1840, ibid., 557.
27. [Order of] Cousin, 8 September 1840, in *Żywot* 2:C.
28. J. B. Zaleski to Seweryn Goszczyński, 11 August 1840, *Korespondencja JBZ* 1:175. Mickiewicz to J. B. Zaleski, 4 September [1840], *Dz.* 15:560.
29. C. Mickiewicz to Mickiewicz, 2 September [1840], Korespondencja. Mickiewicz to J. B. Zaleski, 4 September [1840], *Dz.* 15:560. Mickiewicz to J. B. Zaleski, 19 September 1840, ibid., 561. C. Mickiewicz to H. Malewska, 9 November 1840, quoted in "Mm" 5.18:400. Sainte-Beuve to J. Olivier, 20 September [1840], *Correspondance* 3:356.
30. Mickiewicz to Jacques van Muyden, 23 September 1840, *Dz.* 15:564–65.
31. Council of Public Education to Mickiewicz, 9 November 1840, Korespondencja.
32. Nakwaski, "Pamiętniki," 5 October 1840, in Kallenbach, AM (1897) 2:409. Mickiewicz to A. Czartoryski, 17 July [1840], *Dz*, 15:551. Mickiewicz to Domeyko, [23 or 24 December 1840], ibid., 593.
33. Nakwaski, "Pamiętniki," 5 October 1840, in Kallenbach, AM (1897), 2:409.
34. *Le Courrier suisse*, 9 October 1840, in *Żywot* 2:CIII–CIV.
35. Nakwaski, "Pamiętniki," 5 October 1840, in Kallenbach, AM (1897) 1:409. C. Mickiewicz to H. Malewska, 9 November 1840, quoted in "Mm" 5.18:400.
36. Mickiewicz to Jundziłł, 8 October 1840, *Dz.* 15:571; Mickiewicz to Luigi Melegari, 8 October [1840], ibid., 572. Mickiewicz to Stypułkowski, 9 October [1840], ibid., 575.
37. Witwicki to J. B. Zaleski, 14 October 1840, *Listy SW*, 40. Gorecka, *Wspomnienia*, 18; C. Mickiewicz to H. Malewska, 9 November 1840, quoted in "Mm" 5.18:400. Witwicki to J. B. Zaleski, 1 November 1840, *Listy SW*, 40.
38. Mickiewicz to Jundziłł, 18 October [1840], *Dz.* 15:576–77. Mickiewicz to Domeyko, 7 May [1841], ibid., *Dz.* 15:619. *Mloda Polska*, 25 September 1840, quoted in *Żywot* 2:476; "Pan Adam Mickiewicz i słowiańszczyzna," *Nowa Polska* 4 (1840), quoted in ibid., CIX–CX.
39. E. Januszkiewicz to Larisch, 19 December 1840, in Kallenbach, "Z epoki," 468. Mickiewicz to Domeyko, 7 May [1841], *Dz.* 15:618; Witwicki to J. B. Zaleski, 1 November 1840, *Listy SW*, 40.
40. Sainte-Beuve to C. Olivier, 19 February 1841, *Correspondance* 4:50.
41. "Pan Adam Mickiewicz i słowiańszczyzna," *Nowa Polska* 4 (1840), quoted in *Żywot* 2:CX. Mickiewicz to F. Mickiewicz, [3 or 23] March 1841, *Dz.* 15:611. Pavel Josef Šafárik [Šafařík] to Pogodin, 31 October 1840, in Šafařík, *Korespondence* 1.2:623.
42. Mickiewicz to J. B. Zaleski, [26 December 1840], *Dz.* 15:595. Witwicki to J. B. Zaleski, 26 November 1840, *Listy SW*, 41; J. B. Zaleski to Lucjan Siemieński, 3 December 1840, quoted in *Żywot* 3:8. Mickiewicz to J. B. Zaleski, [2 December 1840], *Dz.* 15:588. J. B. Zaleski to Mickiewicz, 4 December 1840, Korespondencja.
43. As noted down by Aleksandr Turgenev (22 December 1840), quoted in Larionova, " 'Kogda narody,' " 36. Witwicki to J. B. Zaleski, 26 December 1840, *Listy SW*, 45.
44. Witwicki to J. B. Zaleski, 26 December 1840, *Listy*, 44–45.
45. As noted down by Turgenev (22 December 1840), quoted in Larionova, "'Kogda narody,'" 36. Witwicki to J. B. Zaleski, 26 December 1840, *Listy SW*, 45.
46. Witwicki to J. B. Zaleski, 26 December 1840, *Listy SW*, 44–45. As noted down by Turgenev (22 December 1840), quoted in Larionova, "'Kogda narody,'" 36. E. Januszkiewicz to Larisch, 28 December 1840, quoted in *Żywot* 3:21. "Ouverture du cours d'Adam Mickiewicz au Collège de France," *Le Constitutionel*, 24 December 1840, in *AMaydF*, 190. "Ouverture du cours d'Adam Mickiewicz," *Le Siècle*, 24 December 1840, in ibid., 193.

47. Witwicki to J. B. Zaleski, 26 December 1840, *Listy SW*, 46. Mickiewicz to Domeyko, [23 or 24 December 1840], *Dz.* 15:593; Mickiewicz to J. B. Zaleski, [26 December 1840], ibid., 595. Mickiewicz to Melegari, 27 December 1840, ibid., 597.
48. Nakwaski, "Pamiętniki," December 1840, in Kallenbach, *AM* (1897) 2:410.
49. J. Koźmian, quoted in Edward Duński to Walery Wielogłowski, 6 February 1841, in "Listy o AM," 76. E. Januszkiewicz to Larisch, 28 December 1840, in Sudolski, "Mickiewiczowskie wspominki," 97. J. Koźmian to S. E. Koźmian, 4 January 1841, in "Listy o AM," 72. E. Januszkiewicz to Larisch, 28 December 1840, in Sudolski, "Mickiewiczowskie wspominki," 98.
50. J. Koźmian to S. E. Koźmian, 4 January 1841, in "Listy o AM," 72. E. Januszkiewicz to Larisch, 28 December 1840, in Sudolski, "Mickiewiczowskie wspominki," 98. There exist twenty-three accounts, some communicated privately shortly after the event, others published not long after, still others recounted after many years. See *Kronika 1840–1844*, 50–51, for a complete list.
51. Witwicki to J. B. Zaleski, 28 December 1840, *Listy SW*, 48.
52. E. Januszkiewicz to Larisch, 28 December 1840, in Sudolski, "Mickiewiczowskie wspominki," 98–99. E. Januszkiewicz to Larisch, 7 January 1841, in ibid., 99.
53. E. Januszkiewicz to Larisch, 7 January 1841, in Sudolski, "Mickiewiczowskie wspominki," 100.
54. Sand, *Journal intime*, December 1839 [*sic*], in *AMaydF*, 95.
55. Sand, *Journal intime*, December 1839 [*sic*], in *AMaydF*, 93. N. O. "Improwizatorowie," *Tygodnik Literacki*, 22 February 1841, in Zakrzewski et al., *Sądy współczesnych*, 130. Słowacki, *Dzieła*, 5:138.
56. Mickiewicz to Zaleski, [26 December 1840], *Dz.* 15:596; Mickiewicz to Jan Skrzynecki, 22 March 1842, ibid., 16:55.
57. Gorecka, *Wspomnienia*, 63–64. *Dziennik Narodowy*, 1841, quoted in Pigoń, "Dramat dziejowy," 459. E. Januszkiewicz to Larisch, 20 January 1841, in Kallenbach, "Z epoki," 469; Niedźwiecki to Władysław Zamoyski, 28 June 1841, quoted in "MwkN," 219. *Le Siècle*, 24 December 1840, in *AMaydF*, 193.
58. "S," "Korespondencja z Paryża," *Orędownik Naukowy* 10 (1841), 80. Witwicki to J. B. Zaleski, 13 February 1841, *Listy SW*, 58.
59. Louis Loménie, "M. A. Mickiewicz," in *AMaydF*, 111.
60. Jules Michelet to Mickiewicz, 22 December 1840, Korespondencja. Mickiewicz to Michelet, 23 December [1840], *Dz.* 15:591–92.
61. Witwicki to Zaleski, 13 February 1841, *Listy SW*, 58.
62. Mickiewicz to F. Mickiewicz, [3 or 23] March 1841, *Dz.* 15:611. Henryk Jakubowski, quoted in Seweryn Goszczyński to J. B. Zaleski, 16 January 1841, *Listy SG*, 116–17. "Pan Adam Mickiewicz profesor," *Nowa Polska* 4 (1841), 2. Mickiewicz to Feliks Wrotnowski, [26 May 1841], *Dz.* 15:621.
63. Loménie, "Mickiewicz," in *AMaydF*, 111 (the biography appeared originally in the twenty-ninth issue of *Galerie des contemporains illustres par un homme de rien*). Mickiewicz to Krystyn Ostrowski, 21 March [1841], *Dz.* 15:614.
64. Mickiewicz to Domeyko, 7 May [1841], *Dz.* 15:618. Loménie, "Mickiewicz," in *AMaydF*, 111.
65. Mickiewicz to J. B. Zaleski, 23 June [1841], *Dz.* 15:624. Niedźwiecki to Zamoyski, 20 July 1841, in Finkel, "Z korespondencji," 286.
66. Mickiewicz to Jundziłł, [23 February 1841], *Dz.* 15:606. Niedźwiecki, "Zapiski," 2 March 1841, quoted in Jasińska, "Celina Mickiewiczowa," 291.
67. Witwicki to J. B. Zaleski, 28 January 1841, *Listy SW*, 52. Mickiewicz to Jundziłł, [6 September 1841], *Dz.* 15:654.
68. Walerian Chełchowski to Domeyko, 9 October 1841, *WAM* 1:8 n. 1. As noted down by A. Chodźko (26 April 1843), quoted in *Żywot* 3:86. As related to W. Mickiewicz by Rettel (27 September 1877), quoted in ibid., 87. As noted down by Franciszek Szemioth, quoted in Siemieński, *Religijność*, 150. As related to W. Mickiewicz by Scovazzi (8 August 1871), quoted in *Żywot* 3:88. Mickiewicz to Melegari, 12 September [1842], *Dz.* 16:97.

CHAPTER 9. SECTARIANISM (1841–1846)

1. Mickiewicz to Skrzynecki, 23 March 1842, *Dz.* 16:55.
2. Dominik Iwanowski, "Ważniejsze chwile początków misji A. T.," quoted in Pigoń, "Zręby," 168. Andrzej Towiański to Duński, 7 July 1849, *WAM* 2:134. Skrzynecki to Mickiewicz, 3 April 1842, Korespondencja. It might be noted that Towiański, "an eminent Polish patriot and mystic," is included among exemplars of "sainthood" in William James's *Varieties of Religious Experience*, 308 n. 2.
3. Massalski, "Z pamiętników," 272–73. Ferdynand Gutt to Walerian Pietkiewicz, 14 February [18]36, in Pigoń, "Zręby," 224–25.
4. Krasiński to Delfina Potocka, 26 [November] 1841, *LdDP* 1:366. Odyniec to Siemieński, 20 April 1871, in Siemieński, *Religijność*, 150.
5. Allocution to the Guardians of the Septets and the Brethren Whom They Summoned, 21 November 1844, *Dz.* 13:190. As noted down by Wrotnowski (beginning of October 1844), *Rozmowy*, 249.
6. Allocution to the Guardians of the Septets, 1 June 1844, *Dz.* 13:154.
7. Towiański, "Praca nad ludem," in *Wybór pism*, 40. Wołodko, "Wspomnienie," 578–79.
8. Iwanowski, "Ważniejsze chwile," quoted in Pigoń, "Zręby," 168. Towiański to the Peasants of Antoszwińcie, 2 November 1867, in *Wybór pism*, 47.
9. Towiański, "Biesiada," in *Wybór pism*, 53–69.
10. Mickiewicz to Towiański, [16 August 1845], *Dz.* 16:343.
11. Witwicki to Mickiewicz, 20 February 1844, Korespondencja.
12. Mickiewicz to C. Mickiewicz, [3 August 1841], *Dz.* 15:630; Towiański, "Grzechy nowej epoki," in *Wybór pism*, 201; Towiański, "O ofierze troistej," in ibid., 189. Mickiewicz to C. Mickiewicz, 8 August [1841], *Dz.* 15:635; Mickiewicz to J. B. Zaleski, 15 August 1841, ibid., 638. As noted down by A. Chodźko (1843), *Rozmowy*, 206. My understanding of Mickiewicz's conversion—and I should stress "understanding" since to this day, for most Mickiewicz scholars the poet's Towianism still remains something of an embarrassing enigma—owes much to Ullmann, *The Transformed Self* ("haven of last resort," pp. 3–25); and Rambo, *Understanding Religious Conversion*.
13. Mickiewicz to Juliusz Grużewski, 19 January 1842, *Dz.* 16:20. "Coup d'œil sur le *Dziady*," *Dz.* 5:271/*MP* 2:219. As noted down by Karol Edward Wodziński (1835–1836), *Rozmowy*, 130–31. *LzP* 1:419–20. "O przyszłym wielkim człowieku, tudzież dodatek do artykułu o konstytucji powstańskiej," *Dz.* 6:292. Mickiewicz to Skrzynecki, 23 March 1842, ibid., 16:55.
14. Mickiewicz to Jundziłł, 26 January 1842, *Dz.* 16:30. Mickiewicz to Skrzynecki, 23 March 1842, ibid., 56. Mickiewicz to Jundziłł, [6 September 1841], ibid., 15:654. Mickiewicz to Domeyko, 12 October [1841], ibid., 666. Allocution to the Circle, 21 August 1844, ibid., 13:177.
15. Ostrowski, "Wspomnienia" (October 1841), 99. Towiański to Mickiewicz 4–16 October 1841, Korespondencja. Towiański to Mickiewicz, 29 August 1841, ibid. S, "Allgemeine Verhältnisse." *Allgemeine Zeitung des Judenthums*, 26 July 1838: 362. According to Mickiewicz's own exegesis, by "Israelite" Towiański meant "the oldest spirits . . . that is, spirits of Israel regardless of what bodies they inhabit," Jewish, French, or Slav (Allocution to the Circle, 19 March 1845, *Dz.* 13:214).
16. Towiański to Mickiewicz 4–16 October 1841, Korespondencja.
17. Mickiewicz to Jundziłł, 26 January 1842, *Dz.* 16:30; Mickiewicz to Jundziłł, [6 September 1841], ibid., 15:654. Towiański, [Słowianin w ucisku], *WAM* 1:2–3; E. Januszkiewicz to Larisch, 14 August 1841, ibid., 2:165; Towiański to Mickiewicz, Antoni Gorecki, and Izydor Sobański, 27 August 1841, ibid., 1:5.
18. Mickiewicz to Olizarowski, 30 August [1841], *Dz.* 15:645; E. Januszkiewicz to Larisch, 14 August 1841, *WAM* 2:165. Mickiewicz to J. B. Zaleski, [11] August 1841, *Dz.* 15:637–38. The poem appeared a month later in an émigré periodical, submitted, apparently, by Mickiewicz himself; it was said that he also composed music to the words.

19. Mickiewicz to J. B. Zaleski, 10 August [1841], *Dz.* 15:638. Ludwik Plater to A. Czartoryski, 12 August 1841, quoted in Kallenbach, *AM* (1926) 2:360. Ostrowski, "Antoniego Ostrowskiego wspomnienia" (October 1841), 92.
20. Mickiewicz to F. Mickiewicz [first half of September 1842], *Dz.* 16:100–1.
21. Niedźwiedzki to Zamoyski, 16 August 1841, quoted in "MwkN," 223; Goszczyński, 12 August 1841, *Dziennik SB* 1:22; Niedźwiecki to Ignacy Jackowski, 12 August 1841, quoted in "MwkN," 222. Witwicki to Mickiewicz, 28 August 1841, Korespondencja. Walerian Chełchowski to Domeyko, 9 October 1841, *WAM* 1:8 n. 1. Mickiewicz to Jundziłł, [6 September 1841], *Dz.* 15:654. Ostrowski, "Antoniego Ostrowskiego wspomnienia" (October 1841), 86; Karol Sienkiewicz to A. Czartoryski, 20 August 1841, quoted in Kallenbach, *AM* (1926) 2:360–61.
22. Mickiewicz to Domeyko, 12 October 1841, *Dz.* 15:666–67. Mickiewicz to Jundziłł, [6 September 1841], ibid., 654. Mickiewicz to J. B. Zaleski, [15 November 1841], ibid., 672.
23. Mickiewicz to Jundziłł, 26 January 1842, 16:30.
24. Mickiewicz to E. Januszkiewicz, 25 September [1841], *Dz.* 15:661; Mickiewicz to countrymen in Paris, 25 September [1841], *Dz.* 15:662. As described by Hipolit Błotnicki, quoted in Kallenbach, "Towianizm" 163:24–25. Niedźwiecki to Jackowski, 30 September 1841, in "MwkN," 226. Chełchowski to Domeyko, 9 October 1841, *WAM* 1:8 n. 1; E. Januszkiewicz to E. Larisch, 5 October 1841, *WAM* 2:166.
25. J. Koźmian to Semenenko, 30 September 1841, quoted in *HZZP* 4:8. Chełchowski to Domeyko, 9 October 1841, *WAM* 1:8 n. 1. *Demokrata Polski*, 27 October 1841, quoted in *Żywot* 3:110. Alojzy Biernacki to Mickiewicz, 27 September 1841, Korespondencja.
26. Witwicki to Mickiewicz, 1 July 1842, Korespondencja. J. Koźmian to Semenenko, 30 September 1841, *HZZP* 4:9.
27. Kajsiewicz to Domeyko, 12 December 1843, quoted in *Kronika 1840–1844*, 532.
28. Witwicki to Mickiewicz, 1 July 1842, Korespondencja. Undated note by Zaleski, in *Korespondencja JBZ* 2:11. Zaleski to Mickiewicz, [11 November 1841], Korespondencja. Mickiewicz to Zaleski, [15 November 1841], *Dz.* 15:672.
29. Witwicki to Mickiewicz 19 August 1841, Korespondencja; Witwicki to Mickiewicz, 5 November 1841, ibid. Witwicki to Zaleski, 16 March 1842, *Listy SW*, 86. Witwicki to Zaleski, 24 November 1841, ibid., 77. Witwicki to Mickiewicz, 20 February 1844, Korespondencja.
30. E. Januszkiewicz to Larisch, 14 August 1841, quoted in *Kronika 1840–1844*, 140. A. Chodźko to Mickiewicz, 13 February 1842, Korespondencja.
31. Skrzynecki to Mickiewicz, 3 April 1842, Korespondencja. Witwicki, *Towiańszczyzna*, 8. Niedźwiecki to Jackowski, 30 September 1841, quoted in "MwkN," 226.
32. *Narodowość*, 22 January 1841. Towiański, "Wezwanie do emigracji polskiej," in *Wybór pism*, 78–79. Unlike the first, this appeal was published almost immediately (whether it was also dictated by God and whether it was subsequently redacted is unclear). Wańkowicz's painting hangs in Saint-Séverin to this day.
33. Towiański to Mickiewicz, 29 August 1841, Korespondencja. Towiański to Mickiewicz, 4–16 October 1841, ibid.
34. Gorecka, *Wspomnienia*, 34. Niedźwiecki, "Zapiski," 19 October 1841, quoted in "MwkN," 228.
35. Adolphe Lèbre, "Cours d'Adam Mickiewicz au Collège de France," *Le Semeur*, 22 December 1841, in *AMaydF*, 199–200. A. Czartoryski to Mickiewicz, 20 December 1841, Korespondencja; J. Koźmian to Semenenko, 27 December 1841, quoted in *HZZP* 4:19. Goszczyński to Siemieński, 21 December 1841, *Listy SG*, 133; Niedźwiecki to Zamoyski, 16 December 1841, quoted in "MwkN," 230.
36. J. Koźmian to Semenenko, 7 February 1842, quoted in *HZZP* 4:30. Witwicki to J. B. Zaleski, 13 April 1842, *Listy SW*, 90. Turgenev to K. S. Serbinovich, 21 April 1842, quoted in *Adam Mitskevich v russkoi pechati*, 227. J. Koźmian to Semenenko, 7 February 1842, quoted in *HZZP* 4:30. J. Koźmian to C. Plater, 7 January 1842, in Trojanowicz, "Listy Jana Koźmiana," 484.

37. J. Koźmian to C. Plater, 15 April 1842, in Trojanowicz, "Listy Jana Koźmiana," 495. Mickiewicz to A. Chodźko, 7 May 1842, *Dz.* 16:72.
38. Niedźwiecki to Zamoyski, 4 May 1842, quoted in "MkwN," 239; J. Koźmian to Stanisław Egbert Koźmian, 4 May 1842, in "Listy o AM," 87. Witwicki to J. B. Zaleski, 8 May 1842, *Listy SW*, 91. *Dziennik Narodowy*, 7 July 1842. I quote from the first of two extent records of the speech.
39. Niedźwiecki to Zamoyski, 4 May 1842, quoted in "MkwN," 239.
40. Mickiewicz to Napoleon Bońkowski, 19 May 1842, *Dz.* 16:77. Mickiewicz to Jełowicki, [24 or 25 February 1842], ibid., 46. Motty, *Przechadzki* 2:430–31.
41. *Pszonka*, 3.11/12 [1842], 41. Although *Pszonka* was a satirical journal, its description here of Towiański's recruiting methods is by and large credible, corroborated as it is by other sources.
42. Duński to Wielogłowski, 6 July 1842, "Listy o AM," 92. Towiański, "Z przemówienia na zebraniu sług Sprawy Bożej," in *Wybór pism*, 80–81. Concluding prayer quoted in *Żywot* 3:139.
43. Wrotnowski to Domeyko, 14 November 1842, quoted in *Żywot* 3:189.
44. Goszczyński, 27 November 1842, *Dziennik SB* 1:44. Begun in 1841 and kept until practically the end of his life in 1876, Goszczyński's "Diary of God's Cause" constitutes one of the most valuable sources of information about the sect.
45. Słowacki to Bécu, 2 August 1842, in Słowacki, *Korespondencja* 1:491. Goszczyński, 2 August 1842, *Dziennik SB* 1:36.
46. Goszczyński, 9 September 1843, *Dziennik SB* 1:112. Towiański, "O ofierze troistej," in *Wybór pism*, 185–86.
47. Nikolai D. Kiselov to Benkendorf, 26 March/7 April 1842, in Fiszman, "Andrzej Towiański," 132. Towiański to Mickiewicz, [not before 10] June 1842, Korespondencja. Towiański, "Odezwa do Koła przed wyjazdem z Francji," in *Wybór pism*, 81. Allocution in the Circle, 27 December 1842, *Dz.* 13:17; Mickiewicz to Towiański, 11 September [1842], ibid., 16:95.
48. Iwanowski to Tomasz Nielubowicz [both Towianists], 2 July 1842, quoted in Więckowska, "Z propagandy," 215.
49. Słowacki to Bécu, 24 September 18842, in Słowacki, *Korespondencja* 1:496. Mickiewicz to Towiański, 11 September [1842], *Dz.* 16:94–95. Towiański to Mickiewicz, 18 September 1842, Korespondencja.
50. Mickiewicz to Towiański, [ca. 12 October 1842], *Dz.* 16:105. "Słowa Chrystusa," ibid., 1:417–18; "Słowa Panny," ibid., 1:418–19.
51. Mickiewicz to F. Gutt, [18–19 June 1843], *Dz.* 16:181.
52. Mickiewicz et al. to Charles Duchâtel, *Dz.* 16:85. Mickiewicz to Towiański, [ca. 25 November 1842], ibid., 123.
53. Mickiewicz to Domeyko, 24 October 1842, *Dz.* 16:110–11. "Słówko o cudach," *Pszonka* 4.9/10 (1843), 38; [lead article], ibid., 3.11/12 [1842], 46, 47, 44.
54. Mickiewicz to Domeyko, 24 October 1842, *Dz.* 16:111. Jełowicki to Mickiewicz, 2 May 1842, Korespondencja; Jełowicki to Semenenko, 30 March 1843, quoted in *HZZP* 4:137. Kajsiewicz to Semenenko, 21 September 1842, quoted in ibid., 73. Duński to Semenenko, 11 October 1842, quoted in ibid., 78. Duński to Semenenko, 29 August 1842, quoted in ibid., 67. Towiański to Mickiewicz, 30 October 1842, Korespondencja. Mickiewicz to Towiański, 3 November 1842, *Dz.* 16:115.
55. Kajsiewicz, Dziennik, 29 November 1842, quoted in *HZZP* 4:95. Goszczyński, 29 November 1842, *Dziennik SB* 1:46. Allocution to the Circle, 27 November 1842, *Dz.* 13:13. Notes from Conversations with the Master and Their Oral Explanations, 4 November 1843, ibid., 70.
56. Kajsiewicz to the Resurrectionists in Rome, n.d., quoted in *HZZP* 4:97–98. Mickiewicz to Towiański, 3 November 1842, *Dz.* 16:113–14. Allocution to the Circle, 27 December 1842, ibid., 13:17.
57. Towiański to Mickiewicz, 10 March [1843], Korespondencja.
58. Allocution to the Circle, 11 April 1843, *Dz.* 13:26.

59. Allocution to the Circle, 14 October 1842, *Dz.* 13:9. Allocution to the Circle, 18 February 1843, ibid., 22. Allocution at the Confession of the First and Sixth Septets, 2 and 6 July 1843, ibid., 47–49. Mickiewicz to Towiański, 5 July 1843, *Dz.* 16:190.
60. Directives to Goszczyński, 16–20 [?] July 1843, *Dz.* 13:55. Note to the Septets, 27 May 1843, ibid., 34; Allocution to the Guardians of the Septets, 27 May 1843, ibid., 35. Allocution to the Guardians of the Septets, 18 November 1843, ibid., 77; Allocution to the Guardians of the Septets, Together with an Explanation of Questions of One of the Brethren and Towiański's Answers, 25 November 1843, ibid., 80; Allocution to the Guardians of the Septets, 30 December 1843, ibid., 93.
61. Note to the Septets, 27 May 1843, *Dz.* 13:34. Allocution at a Meeting at Władysław Plater's, ibid., 308.
62. Allocution at a Session of the Polish Literary Society, 3 May 1843, *Dz.* 13: 313. Goszczyński, 5 August 1843, *Dziennik SB* 1:103.
63. Allocution to the Circle, 17 May 1843, *Dz.* 13:31. Towiański to the Brethren, 10 March 1843, *WAM* 1:77. Towiański to the Brethren, 14 March 1843, ibid., 79. Allocution to the Circle, 11 May 1843, *Dz.* 13:29. [Towiański to the French], *WAM* 2:300.
64. Mickiewicz to F. Gutt, 15 [June 1843], *Dz.* 16:178. Towiański to Mickiewicz, 27 August 1843, Korespondencja. Adam Mickiewicz's Commentary on a Letter from Towiański, 10 September 1843, *Dz.* 13:69.
65. Alfred Dumesnil to Eugène Noël, 6 March 1847, quoted in *Żywot* 3:454. Allocution to the Circle, 11 May 1843, *Dz.* 13:29–30. Mickiewicz to F. Gutt, 29 May 1843, ibid., 16:170.
66. Towiański to the Brethren, 10 March 1843, *WAM*, 1:77. Goszczyński, 17 May 1843, *Dziennik SB* 1:65. Mickiewicz to F. Gutt, 3 [June] 1843, *Dz.* 16:172.
67. Allocution to the Circle, 17 May 1843, *Dz.* 13:31. Towiański, "Z przemówienia na zebraniu sług Sprawy Bożej" (4 May 1842), in *Wybór pism*, 81. Słowacki to Mickiewicz, [after 1 December 1844], Korespondencja.
68. Towiański to Mickiewicz, [March . . . April 1843], Korespondencja. Towiański to Mickiewicz, 16 July [1843].
69. Jełowicki to Semenenko, 30 March 1843, quoted in *HZZP* 4:136–37. Mickiewicz to Huber (?), [20 January 1843 (?)], *Dz.* 16:136. Towiański to Mickiewicz, 5 December 1842, Korespondencja. Mickiewicz to Towiański, 5 July 1843, *Dz.* 16:189.
70. Allocution and Prayer at the Ceremony of Bestowing Medals of God's Cause, 3 June 1843, *Dz.* 13:36. Mickiewicz to F. Gutt, 29 May 1843, ibid., 16:170.
71. C. Mickiewicz to Kazimiera Wołowska, 28 June 1842, qtd. in *Kronika 1840–1844*, 304. Słowacki, "Chór duchów izraelskich," *Dzieła* 12.1:322. As noted down by E. Januszkiewicz (12 February 1846), qtd. in Kallenbach, "Towianizm," 169:336.
72. As noted down by E. Januszkiewicz (12 February 1846), quoted in Kallenbach, "Towianizm," 169:336. Allocution to the Brethren, 28 June 1843, *Dz.* 13:45.
73. J. Koźmian to C. Plater, 4 June 1842, in Trojanowicz, "Listy," 502. Mickiewicz to Towiański, [ca. 12 October 1842], *Dz.* 16:105. Towiański, as noted down by Goszczyński, 26 June 1847, *Dziennik SB* 1:338.
74. Instruction for Goszczyński, 16–20 [?] July 1843, *Dz.* 13:54. Allocution and Prayer at the Ceremony Bestowing Medals of God's Cause, 3 June 1843, ibid., 37; Mickiewicz to Goszczyński, 28 [July 1843], ibid., 16:195. Towiański to Mickiewicz, 24 July [1843], Korespondencja.
75. Witwicki to the Resurrectionists, 26 August 1843, quoted in *HZZP* 4:133.
76. Towiański to Amschel Mayer Rothschild, 15 August 1843, *WAM* 2:195.
77. Mickiewicz to C. Mickiewicz, [after 6 August–end of August 1843], *Dz.* 16:200; Allocution to the Circle, 1 November 1843, ibid., 13:63–64. Mickiewicz to C. Mickiewicz, [after 6 August–end of August 1843], ibid., 16:199.
78. Goszczyński, 23 August 1843, *Dziennik SB* 1:108.

79. Goszczyński, 23 August 1843, *Dziennik SB* 1:108. Towiański to Mickiewicz, [8 September 1843], in *WAM*. 1:109–10.
80. Towiański to the Brethren, 5 August 1843, in *WAM* 1:107. Caroline Olivier, "Journal," 5 March 1842, quoted in Wellisz, *Une Amitié*, 105.
81. Malewski to Mickiewicz, 12 October [1843], Korespondencja.
82. Towiański to the Brethren, 10 September 1843, *Dz.* 13:68. Allocution to the Guardians of the Septets, 18 November 1843, ibid., 78, 75–76.
83. Allocution to the Circle, 1 November 1843, *Dz.* 13:65. Letter to the Septets, 7 December 1843, ibid., 84.
84. Towiański to Mickiewicz, 9 November 1843, Korespondencja; Towiański to Mickiewicz, 24 November [1843], ibid. Allocution to Representatives of the Septets, 16 December 1843, *Dz.* 13:87. Towiański, "Biesiada," in *Wybór pism*, 61.
85. Niedźwiecki to Zamoyski, 29 June 1843, referring to an article in the ultramontane *L'Univers*, quoted in "MwkN," 255.
86. Michelet, *Journal*, 1:510. Niedźwiecki to Zamoyski, 29 June 1843, quoted in "MwkN," 255. Mickiewicz to Towiański, 5 July 1843, *Dz.* 16:190.
87. Niedźwiecki to Zamoyski, 29 June 1843, quoted in "MwkN," 255; A. Turgenev to Viazemskii, 23/11 March 1843, *Ostaf'evskii arkhiv*, 225. Kopitar to Mickiewicz, 30 January 1844, Korespondencja; Kollár to Antoni Mark, 23 May 1843, quoted in Batowski, "Dwie polemiki," 104 (Kollár was referring specifically to Mickiewicz's lecture of 27 December 1842 [*Dz.* 9:38–51/*LS* 4:51–73], devoted in part to the Czech scholar). Niedźwiecki to Zamoyski, 8 June 1843, quoted in Kallenbach, *AM* (1926) 2:419.
88. Niedźwiecki to Zamoyski, 29 June 1843, quoted in "MwkN," 255. Michelet, in *Paris-Guide par les principaux écrivain et artistes de la France* (1867), in *AMaydF*, 273–74.
89. George Sand, "De la littérature slave," in *AMaydF*, 207, 209, 210. Quinet, *L'Ultramontanisme*, 37.
90. Mickiewicz to F. Gutt, 29 May 1843, *Dz.* 170. Mickiewicz, *Vorlesungen* 1:VIII.
91. Gołembiowski, *Mickiewicz odsłoniony*, 51. A. Chodźko to Towiański, 21 May 1846, in *DpM*, 140. Allocution to the Guardians of the Septets, 13 January 1844, *Dz.* 13:98. Allocution to the Guardians of the Septets, 16 March 1844, ibid., 120. Michelet's words according to a police report, quoted in *Żywot* 3:265.
92. D'Agoult to Franz Liszt, 10 January 1844, in *AMaydF*, 260; Julian Fontana to S. E. Koźmian, 5 February 1844, in Fontana, "Wybór listów," 193. Witwicki to Skrzynecki, "Listy o AM," 103.
93. A. Passy to Villemain, 24 March 1844, in *AMaydF*, 279. As noted down by Armand Lévy (1850s), *Rozmowy*, 391. Mickiewicz to F. Mickiewicz, 9 May [1844], *Dz.* 16:243–44.
94. Mickiewicz to Towiański, 15 March 1844, *Dz.* 16:221. Mickiewicz to F. Gutt, 20 March [1844], ibid., 223. A. Turgenev to Zhukovskii, 4 April 1844, in Fiszman, "Andrzej Towiański," 112.
95. A. Turgenev to Zhukovskii, 4 April 1844, in Fiszman, "Andrzej Towiański," 112. Augustin Bonnetty, "Les Verbes nouveaux, M. Mickiewicz, M. Towiański, M. Quinet," *Annales des philosophie chrétienne* 52 (1844), in *AMaydF*, 230; Kajsiewicz, "Pamiętnik" (1844), quoted in *HZZP* 4:151. Mickiewicz to F. Gutt, 20 March [1844], *Dz.* 16: 223.
96. Mickiewicz to F. Gutt, 20 March [1844], *Dz.* 16:233. Goszczyński to Nabielak, 10 April 1844, *Listy SG*, 170. Bonnetty, "Les Verbes nouveaux," in *AMaydF*, 231. Gołembiowski, *Mickiewicz odsłoniony*, 51; Goszczyński to Nabielak, 10 April 1844, *Listy SG*, 170. Mickiewicz to F. Gutt, 20 March [1844], *Dz.* 16:223; Kajsiewicz, "Pamiętnik" (1844), quoted in *HZZP* 4:151; *Pszonka* 6.6–7 [1844]: 28.
97. Quinet, "Leçon au collège de France de 20 mars 1844," in *AMaydF*, 222–23. Mickiewicz to Karolina Towiańska, 21 March [1844], *Dz.* 16:226.
98. Passy to Villemain, 24 March 1844, in *AMaydF*, 279.
99. A. Turgenev to Zhukovskii, 4 April 1844, in Fiszman, "Andrzej Towiański," 112. Dumesnil to Noël, 30 March 1844, in *AMaydF*, 263. Mickiewicz to Michelet, [22 April 1844], *Dz.* 16:239.

100. Towiański to Mickiewicz, 11 April [1844], Korespondencja.
101. *Dziennik Narodowy*, 27 April," quoted in *Żywot* 3:292–93.
102. "Nieludzka komedia, *Pszonka*, 4.6–7 [1844]: 23. Gabriel Delessert to Villemain, 4 May 1844, in *AMaydF*, 246.
103. André Jacoby [Symphorien Vaudoré], *Liberté d'enseignement. Les nouveaux Montanistes au Collège de France* (1844), quoted in W. Mickiewicz, "O zawieszeniu," 230–31. J. B. Zaleski to Kajsiewicz, 23 May 1844, *Korespondencja JBZ* 1:271.
104. Police report, 21 May 1844, quoted in *Żywot* 3:303. *Dziennik Narodowy*, 25 May 1844, quoted in ibid., 298.
105. Goszczyński to Nabielak, 3 June 1844, *Listy SG*, 174. Allocution to the Guardians of the Septets, 20 January 1844, *Dz.* 13:101.
106. Goszczyński to Adam Piwowarski, 24 August 1844, *Listy SG*, 182. Fedor Chizhov, "Diary," 28 May 1844, quoted in Fiszman, "Pokłosie," 15.
107. Mickiewicz to Towiański, 29 May 1844, *Dz.* 16:248. As noted down by S. Zan (11 July 1844), quoted in *Żywot* 3:299. *Dziennik Narodowy*, 1 June 1844. Villemain to the Delessert, 31 May 1844, in W. Mickiewicz, *Adam Mickiewicz*, 345.
108. Tomasz Kantorbery Tymowski to Walery Wielgłowski, 27 July 1844, "Listy o AM," 111; *Dziennik Narodowy*, 19 April 1845.
109. Passy to the Minister of the Interior et al., 26 June 1844, in *AMaydF*, 248. Alexandre Dufai, "La Sorbonne et le Collège de France," *Revue de Paris*, 12 June 1845; *L'Univers*, 10 July 1844, both quoted in *Żywot* 3:367, 327. *Moniteur Universel*, 10 July 1844, in *AMaydF*, 253–54; *Le Constitutionnel*, 10 July 1844, quoted in Michelet, *Journal* 1:876 n. 3. As noted down by Chodźko (7 June 1844), *Rozmowy*, 217.
110. Mickiewicz to Villemain, 4 October 1844, *Dz.* 16:276–77.
111. Mickiewicz, *Pisma* 1:v–vi.
112. Allocution to the Guardians of the Septets, 13 January 1844, *Dz.* 13:96. Allocution to the Guardians of the Septets, 2 March 1844, *Dz.* 13:109. Allocution to the Guardians of the Septets, 20 January 1844, ibid., 100. Allocution to the Guardians of the Septets, 13 January 1844, ibid., 99. Allocution to the French Circle, 5 May 1844, ibid., 145; Instructions to the Fourth Septet, 7 March 1844, ibid., 111. Allocution to the Guardians of the Septets, 2 March 1844, ibid., 109. Allocution to the Guardians of the Septets, 24 February 1844, ibid., 106.
113. Goszczyński to Nabielak, 10 April 1844, *Listy SG*, 168.
114. Towiański to Mickiewicz, 3 April [1844], Korespondencja. Mickiewicz to Towiański, [19 February 1844], *Dz.* 16:213. Towiański to K. Towiańska and Anna Gutt, 11 February 1846, in *WAM*, 2:26. Mickiewicz to Towiański, [8 April 1844], *Dz.* 16:232. Towiański to Mickiewicz, 31 July 1845, Korespondencja.
115. Towiański to Mickiewicz, 2 June 1845, Korespondencja. Mickiewicz to Towiański, [19 February 1844], *Dz.* 16:214; Mickiewicz to K. Towiańska, 21 March [1844], ibid., 226. Mickiewicz to Towiański, [8 April 1844], ibid., 231.
116. Mickiewicz to K. Towiańska, 21 March [1844], *Dz.* 16:226–27. Chyzhov, Diary, 12 July 1844, quoted in Fiszman, "Pokłosie," 23.
117. Allocution to the Guardians of the Septets and to the Brethren Whom They Summoned, 21 November 1844, *Dz.* 13:188; Speech to the History Section, 6 March 1844, ibid., 314. Sobolevskii to Malewski, 24 December 1868/5 January 1869, *AF Lzz* 3:607. Witwicki to Mickiewicz, 16 January 1845, Korespondencja. J. B. Zaleski to J. Koźmian, 11 November 1844, *Korespondencja JBZ* 1:295. Mickiewicz to Scovazzi, 29 July 1845, *Dz.* 16:334. Michelet to Mickiewicz, [28 February 1845], Korespondencja.
118. Towiański, as noted down by E. Januszkiewicz (winter 1846), in Kallenbach, "Towianizm," 169:336.

119. Towiański to Mickiewicz, 29 March [1844], Korespondencja. Mickiewicz to Towiański, [8 April 1844], *Dz.* 16:233. Towiański to Mickiewicz, 1 June [1844], Korespondencja.
120. Allocution to the Guardians of the Septets, 24 June 1844, *Dz.* 13:161; Mickiewicz to Towiański, 29 May 1844, *Dz.* 16:249. Mickiewicz to the Members of the Former Commission Charged with Examining Projects for a Monument in Memory of Napoleon, [before 12 July 1844], *Dz.* 16:263.
121. Mickiewicz to Villemain, 4 October 1844, *Dz.* 16:276; Allocution to the Guardians of the Septets, 29 July 1844, *Dz.* 13:173–74; Allocution to the Guardians of the Septets and Those Whom They Summoned, 21 November 1844, ibid., 192. Towiański to Mickiewicz, 1 June [1844], Korespondencja.
122. Towiański to Mickiewicz, [first half of June 1844], Korespondencja. Bakunin, "Confession" [July–beginning of August 1851], *V tiurme*, 112–13.
123. A. Chodźko to Nicholas I, 15 August 1844, *WAM* 2:223–29; Mickiewicz to Towiański, [ca. 26 July 1844], *Dz.* 16:270.
124. Mickiewicz to A. Chodźko, [before 15 August 1844], *Dz.* 16:273. Allocution in the Circle, 11 June 1844, *Dz.* 13:156. Allocution to the Guardians of the Septets and to the Brethren Whom They Summoned, 21 November 1844, ibid., 186, 190, 192.
125. Mickiewicz to K. Towiańska, 1 November [1844], *Dz.* 16:283. Mickiewicz to Towiański, 13 November 1844, ibid., 286. Towiański to Mickiewicz, 22 November [1844], Korespondencja.
126. Allocution to the Circle, 29 November 1844, *Dz.* 13:198–201.
127. Słowacki, "Notatki różne z 'Raptularza,'" *Dzieła*, 15:471.
128. Budzyński, *Wspomnienia* 1:329. Declaration of Mikołaj Kamieński, 19 February 1845, in *DpM*, 118–19.
129. Słowacki, "To the Entire Circle of So-Called Towianists," *Dzieła* 15:258. Słowacki, "Matecznik," ibid., 12.1:192–93.
130. Goszczyński, February 1854, *Dziennik SB* 1:512–13.
131. Allocution in the Circle, 29 November 1844, *Dz.* 13:200–201. [Declaration of Pilchowski's Subjugation], 6 January 1845, in *DpM*, 120.
132. "Oświadczenie w sprawie Mikołaja Kamieńskiego," 19 March 1845, *Dz.* 16:308.
133. Official Letter of Brothers Adam Mickiewicz and Seweryn Pilchowski to the Guardians of the Septets, 11 February 1845, *Dz.* 13:205. Krasiński to Cieszkowski, 23 January 1846, in Krasiński, *Listy do Cieszkowskiego et al.* 1:210–11.
134. Towiański to Mickiewicz, 5 November [1844], Korespondencja. Towiański to Deybel, 4 March 1845, in Kallenbach, *Towianizm*, 187–88. Towiański to Mickiewicz, 7 March 1845, Korespondencja. Mickiewicz to Towiański, 1 April [1845], *Dz.* 16:312.
135. Towiański to Mickiewicz, 28 May 1845, Korespondencja. Mickiewicz to Towiański, [17] April [1845], *Dz.* 16:313. Allocution in the Circle, 19 March 1845, ibid., 13:211. Goszczyński to Nabielak, 27 May 1845, *Listy SG*, 195. Goszczyński, 8 April 1845, *Dziennik SB* 1:229–30. Towiański to Mickiewicz, 11 April 1845, Korespondencja.
136. Mickiewicz to Towiański, 1 April [1845], *Dz.* 16:312. Towiański to Mickiewicz, 23 April [1845], Korespondencja.
137. Goszczyński to Nabielak, 27 May 1845, *Listy SG*, 195. Allocution to the Circle, 16 May 1845, *Dz.* 13:220. Mickiewicz to Towiański, 14 July 1845, *Dz.* 16:323.
138. Mickiewicz to Towiański, [16 August 1845], *Dz.* 16:343. Towiański to Mickiewicz, 24 May 1845, Korespondencja; Towiański to Mickiewicz, 4 June 1845, ibid.; Towiański to Mickiewicz, 2 June 1845(a), ibid. Towiański to Mickiewicz, 2 June 1845(b), ibid.
139. Towiański to Mickiewicz, 4 June 1845, Korespondencja. Towiański to Mickiewicz, 12 June 1845, ibid. Towiański to F. Gutt, 1 July 1845, Korespondencja, n. 1.
140. Towiański to Karol Różycki, 14 June 1845, *WAM* 1:251.
141. Mickiewicz to Towiański, 1 July 1845, *Dz.* 16:317.
142. Romuald Januszkiewicz to [?], 28 June 1845, *Extraits de lettres*, 16. Speech to the Youth of Lausanne, *Dz.* 13:318–19.

143. C. Mickiewicz to H. Malewska, 12 July 1845, quoted in "Mm" 5.19:119. Gorecka, *Wspomnienia*, 36–39.
144. C. Mickiewicz to H. Malewska, 12 July 1845, quoted in "Mm" 5.19:119. Mickiewicz to Towiański, 14 July 1845, *Dz.* 16:323.
145. Feliks Wrotnowski to Mickiewicz, 21 July 1845, Korespondencja. Mickiewicz to Towiański, 14 July 1845, *Dz.* 16:324, 321–22. Mickiewicz to Towiański, 27 July [1845], ibid., 329.
146. Summons to the Guardians of the Septets, 19 July 1845, *Dz.* 13:226; Allocution to the Guardians of the Septets, 19 July 1845, ibid., 227–28. Goszczyński, 10–11 July 1845, *Dziennik SB* 1:249. Mickiewicz to Towiański, [24] July 1845, *Dz.* 16:326.
147. Mickiewicz to Towiański, [24] July 1845, *Dz.* 16:326; Mickiewicz to Towiański, 27 July [1845], ibid., 331. Wrotnowski to Mickiewicz, 23 July 1845, Korespondencja; E. Januszkiewicz to Mickiewicz, 23 July 1845, ibid. Różycki to Mickiewicz, 26 July 1845, ibid.
148. Mickiewicz to Towiański, [24] July 1845, *Dz.* 16:327; Mickiewicz to Towiański, 22 July 1845, ibid., 325. Mickiewicz to Towiański, 27 July [1845], ibid., 329–30. Mickiewicz to Towiański, [2 August 1845], ibid., 341. Mickiewicz to Towiański, [16 August 1845], ibid., 344. Mickiewicz to Towiański, 17 September 1845, ibid., 355; Towiański to Mickiewicz, 5 August [1845], Korespondencja.
149. Goszczyński, 10–11 July 1845, *Dziennik SB* 2:249. Towiański to Pilchowski, 10 July 1845, quoted in *Kronika* 1844–1847, 166; Towiański to Mickiewicz, 31 July 1845, Korespondencja. As noted down by E. Januszkiewicz, 16 February 1845, quoted in Kallenbach, "Towianizm," 169:337. Mickiewicz to Towiański, 22 July 1845, *Dz.* 16:325. Mickiewicz to Towiański, 27 July [1845], ibid., 331. Mickiewicz to A. Gutt, 13 October 1845, ibid., 367. Mickiewicz to Towiański, [24] July 1845, ibid., 327.
150. Mickiewicz to Towiański, 27 July [1845], *Dz.* 16:329. Mickiewicz to A. Gutt, 23 October [1845], ibid., 371.
151. Mickiewicz to Towiański, [24] July 1845, *Dz.* 16:326–27. Allocution to the Guardians of the Septets, 19 July 1845, ibid., 13:228. Summons to the Brethren, 23 July 1845, ibid., 229. Mickiewicz to Towiański, [2 August 1845], ibid., 16:342. Summons to the Brethren, 23 July 1845, ibid., 13:229. Reveille from the Administration, 27 July 1845, ibid., 231.
152. Allocution to the Brethren, 1 August 1845, *Dz.* 233.
153. Order of Service in the Synagogue, 11 August 1845, *Dz.* 13:235. Mickiewicz to Towiański, [16 August 1845], ibid., 16:344.
154. Mickiewicz to Towiański, [16 August 1845], *Dz.* 16:344. Mickiewicz to A. Gutt, 13 October 1845, ibid., 366. Mickiewicz to A. Gutt, 7 September 1845, ibid., 350.
155. Mickiewicz to Towiański, 27 July [1845], *Dz.* 16:331.
156. Towiański to Dominik Iwanowski, 20 August 1845, quoted in *Kronika*, 1844–1847, 194. Goszczyński, 27 August 1845, *Dziennik SB* 1:263. Mickiewicz to A. Gutt, 7 September 1845, *Dz.* 16:349.
157. "Biesiada z bratem Karolem," *WAM* 2:240, 245. From E. Januszkiewicz's notebook, quoted in *Kronika* 1844–1847, 213.
158. Mickiewicz to Towiański, [ca. 25 November 1845], *Dz.* 16:374. Towiański to Mickiewicz, 31 October 1845, Korespondencja.
159. Towiański to the Circle, 29 October 1845, *WAM*, 1:306, 307. Towiański to Różycki, 13 November 1845, *WAM* 2:8.
160. Towiański to Mickiewicz, 9 November 1845, Korespondencja. Mickiewicz to Towiański, [25 November 1845], *Dz.* 16:374. Chełchowski to Domeyko, 3 December 1845, quoted in *Żywot*, 3:394.
161. Mickiewicz to K. Towiańska, 13 January [1846], *Dz.* 16:385, 384. S. E. Koźmian to Zofia Chłapowska, "Listy o AM," 113.
162. *Dziennik Narodowy*, 7 February 1846: 1013–14. Józef Hube to Mickiewicz, 3 January 1846, Korespondencja. Mickiewicz to K. Towiańska, 13 January [1846], *Dz.* 16:384.

163. Goszczyński, 30 January 1846, *Dziennik SB* 1:271. Mickiewicz to K. Towiańska, 13 January [1846], *Dz.* 16:384. Goszczyński, 24 May 1844, *Dziennik SB* 1:179.
164. As noted down by A. Chodźko, 10 May 1846, quoted in *Żywot* 3:409.
165. Towiański to K. Towiańska and A. Gutt, 11 February 1846, *WAM* 2:24. As noted down by E. Januszkiewicz, 12 February [1846], quoted in Kallenbach, "Towianizm," 169:335. Towiański to Mickiewicz, 12 February 1846, Korespondencja.
166. As noted down by A. Chodźko, 18 May 1846, quoted in *Żywot* 3:422; Words of Andrzej Towiański [to the brethren gathered in Zurich], 17 March 1846, *WAM* 2:28, 29, 30, 32.
167. K. Towiańska to Mickiewicz, 20 March [1846], Korespondencja.
168. K. Towiańska to Mickiewicz, 20 March [1846], Korespondencja. As noted down by A. Chodźko, 10 May 1846, quoted in *Żywot* 3:409–10. Niedźwiedzki, Diary, 7 July 1846, quoted in "MwkN," 272. Towiański to Mickiewicz, 28 March 1846, Korespondencja. As noted down by A. Chodźko, 10 May 1846, quoted in *Żywot* 3:410.
169. E. Januszkiewicz to Larisch, 15 May 1846, *WAM* 2:247. Mickiewicz to Towiański, 7 April [1846], *Dz.* 16:388.

CHAPTER 10. SCISSION (1846–1848)

1. Edward Geritz to Towiański, 21 May 1846, in *DpM*, 131.
2. Allocution to the Brethren, 27 February 1847, *Dz.* 13:266.
3. Hieronim Bońkowski to Towiański, 21 May 1846, in *DpM*, 129; E. Januszkiewicz to Towiański, 21 May 1846, in ibid., 133; Henryk Służalski to Towiański, 21 May 1846, in ibid., 131. Ignacy Chodkiewicz to Towiański, 21 May 1846, in ibid., 137.
4. Goszczyński to Nabielak, 7 August 1846, *Listy SG*, 209.
5. Mickiewicz, Declaration Concerning the Matter of Seweryn Pilchowski, 23 August 1846, *Dz.* 16:390.
6. Towiański to the Circle, 15 August 1846, *WAM* 2:39. Towiański to the Circle, 15 August 1846, ibid., 41.
7. Mickiewicz to C. Mickiewicz, 10 [September 1846], *Dz.* 16:393. C. Mickiewicz to Mickiewicz, 18–19 September 1846, Korespondencja.
8. C. Mickiewicz to Mickiewicz, 18–19 September 1846, Korespondencja; C. Mickiewicz to Mickiewicz, 14 September 1846, ibid. C. Mickiewicz to Mickiewicz, 22 September 1846, ibid.; C. Mickiewicz to Mickiewicz, 28 September 1846, ibid.; C. Mickiewicz to Mickiewicz, 18–19 September 1846, ibid.
9. C. Mickiewicz to Mickiewicz, 6 October 1846, Korespondencja; C. Mickiewicz to Mickiewicz, 2 October 1846, ibid.
10. C. Mickiewicz to Mickiewicz, 28 September 1846, Korespondencja. C. Mickiewicz to Mickiewicz, 2 October 1846, ibid. Mickiewicz to C. Mickiewicz, 2 October [1846], *Dz.* 16:397.
11. C. Mickiewicz to Mickiewicz, 6 October 1846, Korespondencja. C. Mickiewicz to Mickiewicz, 2 October 1846, ibid.; C. Mickiewicz to Mickiewicz, 6 October 1846, ibid. C. Mickiewicz to Mickiewicz, 2 October 1846, ibid.; Towiański to a Meeting of Brethren . . . in Richterswill, 1 October 1846, *WAM* 2:54.
12. C. Mickiewicz to Mickiewicz, 6 October 1846, Korespondencja. According to notes by E. Januszkiewicz, quoted in *Kronika 1844–1847*, 320–21.
13. Iwanowski et al. to C. Mickiewicz, 19 November 1846, quoted in "Mm" 5.19:123; C. Mickiewicz to Mickiewicz, 14 April 1848, Korespondencja. Towiański to Mickiewicz, 1 October 1846, ibid. J. B. Zaleski to Witwicki, 7 November 1846, *Korespondencja JBZ* 2:59.
14. Duński to Kajsiewicz (quoting C. Plater), 27 November 1846, quoted in *HZZP* 4:166. Hube to Kajsiewicz (quoting Wielogłowski), 27 November 1846, quoted in ibid., 165.

15. J. Koźmian to Wielogłowski, 21 January 1847, quoted in *Kronika 1844–1847*, 353. Krasiński to Cieszkowski, 15 January 1847, *Listy do Cieszkowskiego* et al., 1:261. Krasiński to Cieszkowski, 2 January 1847, ibid., 258.
16. Hube to Kajsiewicz, 27 November 1846, quoted in *HZZP* 4:165. J. B. Zaleski to Domeyko, 7 December 1847, *Korespondencja JBZ* 2:82.
17. Act of Foundation of a Separate Circle of the Cause, 30 November 1846, *Dz.* 13:254.
18. Allocution to the Brethren, 26 January 1847, *Dz.* 13:259. Allocution to the Brethren, 31 December 1846, ibid., 256.
19. Allocution for Leonard Rettel's Circle, 5 March 1847, *Dz.* 13:278–79. Allocution to the Brethren, 27 February 1847, ibid., 269. Allocution to the Brethren, 27 February 1847, ibid., 265, 268; Allocution to the Brethren, 31 December 1846, ibid., 256. Allocution to the Brethren, 26 January 1847, ibid., 258. Allocution to the Brethren, 27 February 1847, ibid., 268; Allocution to the Brethren, 9 March 1847, ibid., 286. Allocution to the Brethren, 9 March 1847, ibid., 287; Allocution to the Brethren, 4 March 1847, ibid., 276–77. Allocution to the Brethren, 27 February 1847, ibid., 266. Allocution to Leonard Rettel's Circle, 5 March 1847, ibid., 283; Allocution to the Brethren, 27 February 1847, ibid., 266. Allocution to the Brethren, 27 February 1847, ibid., 267. Mickiewicz to Kamieński, 9 May 1848, *Dz.* 16:549.
20. Allocution to the Brethren, 26 January 1847, *Dz.* 13:258. Allocution to Leonard Rettel's Circle, 5 March 1847, ibid., 283–84. Allocution to the Brethren, 4 March 1847, ibid., 274. Act of Marriage, Bestowed on Julian and Aleksandra Łącki, 15 February 1847, ibid., 260, 262.
21. Mickiewicz to d'Agoult, 3 March 1847, *Dz.* 16:418.
22. Margaret Fuller to Ralph Waldo Emerson, 15 March 1847, in Fuller, *Letters* 4:261.
23. A. Chodźko, Diary, 26 February 1847, quoted in *Żywot*, 3:451–52; Fuller, *Woman*.
24. Fuller to Emerson, 15 March 1847, in Fuller, *Letters* 4:261. Mickiewicz to Fuller, [after 15 February 1847], *Dz.* 16:415–16. Allocution to the Brethren, 4 March 1847, ibid., 13:275.
25. Mickiewicz to Fuller, [end of March 1847], *Dz.* 16:424.
26. Mickiewicz to Fuller, 26 April [1847], *Dz.* 16:427–28. Margaret Fuller, Journal Fragment, 22 January [1840], quoted in Kornfeld, *Margaret Fuller*, 28.
27. Fuller to Marcus and Rebecca Spring, 10 April [1847], *Letters* 4:263.
28. Mickiewicz to Konstancja Łubieńska, 5 October [1845], *Dz.* 16:358. Mickiewicz to Łubieńska, 13 February 1845, ibid., 299.
29. Mickiewicz to Łubieńska, [ca. middle of December 1846], *Dz.* 16:403. Mickiewicz to Łubieńska, [end of September–beginning of October 1847], ibid., 468.
30. Krasiński to Potocka, 9 February 1848, *LdDP*, 3:648. Krasiński to Adam Sołtan, 31 December 1838[–1 January 1839], in Krasiński, *Listy do Sołtana*, 258. Krasiński to Potocka, 20[–21] February 1848, *LdDP* 3:680.
31. Mickiewicz to F. Mickiewicz, [22 January 1847], *Dz.* 16:413.
32. Meissner, *Geschichte*, 1:245. W. Mickiewicz, *Pamiętniki* 1:33. Krasiński to Potocka, 27 February 1848, *LdDP* 3:699.
33. Towiański to Mickiewicz, 1 May 1847, Korespondencja.
34. Mickiewicz to Towiański, 12 May 1847, *Dz.* 16:432–34.
35. Mickiewicz to Alojzy Ligęza Niewiarowicz, 21 August 1847, *Dz.* 16:460. Gorecka, *Wspomnienia*, 43–44. Mickiewicz to V. Khliustin, 13 July [1847], *Dz.* 16:443.
36. Gorecka, *Wspomnienia*, 44–45. Mickiewicz to V. Khliustin, 13 July [1847], *Dz.* 16:443.
37. Mickiewicz to Niewiarowicz, 31 August 1847, *Dz.* 16:460. Mickiewicz to Fuller, 3 August 1847, ibid., 451–53. Mickiewicz to Fuller, 16 September [1847], ibid., 461.
38. Allocution to the Brethren, 27 September 1847, *Dz.* 13:297. As recalled by J. B. Zaleski (1877–78), ibid., 601.
39. Report of the Paris Police, 20 December 1847, *Rozmowy*, 276.

40. Allocution to the Brethren, 27 September 1847, *Dz.* 13:295–96.
41. Epistle to the Brethren, 5 October 1847, *Dz.* 13:299. As recorded by Michał Chodźko (2 November 1847), *Rozmowy*, 297–98. Mickiewicz to Juliusz Łącki, 12 February 1848, *Dz.* 16:487.
42. Mickiewicz to Fuller, 17 November 1847, *Dz.* 16:473. Wielogłowski to Kajsiewicz, 8 January 1848, quoted in *HZZP* 4:179. Kajsiewicz, Pamiętnik, quoted in ibid., 181–82.
43. Mickiewicz to Łącki, 9 March [1848], *Dz.* 16:491 and n. 10. As told to W. Mickiewicz by Biergiel and Lévy, in *Żywot* 3:492.
44. Mickiewicz to C. Mickiewicz, 19 April [1848], *Dz.* 16:517.
45. Goszczyński et al. to Mickiewicz, 18 January 1848, *Listy SG*, 241–42. Teodor Ernest Rutkowski to Goszczyński, 22 January 1848, quoted in Kostenicz, "Słowacki," 545. Mickiewicz to Grabowski, 22 January 1847, *Dz.* 16:409.

CHAPTER 11. POLITICS (1848–1849)

1. As noted down by Ludwik Zwierkowski (1852–1855), in Czajkowski, *Kozaczyzna*, 255. Krasiński to Potocka, 27 February 1848, *LdDP* 3:699.
2. Mickiewicz to Łącki, 12 February 1848, *Dz.* 16:488.
3. As noted down by the Paris police (December 1847), *Rozmowy*, 276. Mickiewicz to Łącki, 12 February 1848, *Dz.* 16:487.
4. Krasiński to Potocka, 7[–8] February 1848, *LdDP* 3:644. Mickiewicz to Łącki, 12 February 1848, *Dz.* 16:487. Mickiewicz to Fuller, 4 May 1848, *Dz.* 16:541. Emerson, *Journals*, 503. Fuller to Emerson, 14 March 1848, in Fuller, *Letters* 5:55.
5. A noted down by Teofil Lenartowicz (1874), *Rozmowy*, 353. Krasiński to Potocka 9[–10] February 1848, *LdDP.* 3:647–48. Krasiński's frequent and prolix letters from the period, above all to Delfina Potocka, to whom he wrote daily, paint an unsurpassed portrait of Mickiewicz in Rome, richly detailed, vivid, and full of high emotion, but one that also tends toward hyperbole and literary stylization, often projecting the poet through the prism of Mickiewicz's works as well as Krasiński's own at times overwrought imagination. The entire corpus reads as if he were composing a drama.
6. Krasiński to Potocka, 17–[18] February 1848, *LdDP* 3:674; Krasiński to Potocka, 8 March 1848, ibid., 728. Krasiński to Potocka, 20[–21] March 1848, ibid., 754; Krasiński to Potocka, 14 February 1848, ibid., 659. Krasiński to Potocka, 17[–18] February 1848, ibid., 673. Krasiński to Potocka, 17[–18] February 1848, ibid., 673.
7. Krasiński to Potocka, 15[–16] February 1848, *LdDP* 3:664–69.
8. Jełowicki to Skrzynecki, 29 March 1848, quoted in *HZZP* 4:185; Krasiński to Potocka, 1 March 1848, *LdDP* 3:706. Hube to S. E. Koźmian, 17 February 1848, quoted in *Kronika 1848–1849*, 51. Krasiński to Potocka, 20[–21] February 1848, *LdDP* 3:679.
9. Krasiński to Potocka, 22 February 1848, *LdDP* 3:685–86. Krasiński to Potocka, 27 February 1848, ibid., 699. Krasiński to Potocka, 22 February 1848, ibid., 686.
10. Quoted in *Jenerał Zamoyski* 5:70. Krasiński to Potocka, 1 March 1848, *LdDP* 3:707.
11. Krasiński to Potocka, 1 March 1848, *LdDP* 3:707; Krasiński to Potocka, 2 March 1848, ibid., 712. Krasiński to Potocka, 1 March 1848, ibid., 706. Mickiewicz to Towiański, 25 February 1849, *Dz.* 17:23. Jełowicki to Skrzynecki, 29 March 1848, quoted in *HZZP* 4:185–86.
12. Krasiński to Potocka, 3 March 1848, *LdDP* 3:716; Krasiński to Gaszyński, 2 March 1848, in Krasiński, *Listy do Gaszyńskiego*, 494. Krasiński to Potocka, 1 March 1848, *LdDP* 3:707.
13. W. Mickiewicz, *Pamiętniki*, 1:53.
14. Anna Geritz to E. Geritz, 26 February 1848, *Korespondencja AM* 4:321. Michelet, *Cours* 2:404; Quinet's speech quoted in *Żywot* 4:35.
15. Towiański to Różycki, 16 May 1848, *WAM* 2:110.

16. Zamoyski to A. Czartoryski, March 1848, quoted in *Jenerał Zamoyski* 5:83. Grabowski to F. Mickiewicz, 7 March 1848, *Korespondencja AM* 4:73. Mickiewicz to Łącki, 9 March [1848], *Dz.* 16:490.
17. Grabowski to F. Mickiewicz, 7 March 1848, *Korespondencja AM* 4:73. Jełowicki to Skrzynecki, 29 March 1848, quoted in *HZZP* 4:185–86.
18. Łubieński, *Mickiewicz w Rzymie*, 8. [Margaret Fuller], "Things and Thoughts in Europe: Foreign Correspondence of *The Tribune*, no. XXIII," *New York Tribune*, 4 May 1848.
19. As noted down by Ludwik Orpiszewski (22 March 1848), quoted in *HZZP* 4:196.
20. Allocution to the Guardians of the Septets, 1 September 1844, *Dz.* 13:179–80.
21. Zamoyski to A. Czartoryski, 24 March 1848, quoted in *Jenerał Zamoyski* 5:91.
22. Jełowicki to Skrzynecki, 29 March 1848, quoted in *HZZP* 5:186.
23. Jełowicki to Skrzynecki, 29 March 1848, quoted in *HZZP* 5:185. Allocution at the Audience with Pope Pius IX, *Dz.* 13:322–24 (Jełowicki to Skrzynecki, 29 March 1848; as noted down by Orpiszewski [March 1848]; Orpiszewski to the Hôtel Lambert, 28 March 1848).
24. As noted down by Orpiszewski (March 1848), quoted in *HZZP* 4:197. Krasiński to Potocka, 31 March 1848, *LdDP* 3:778.
25. Mickiewicz to Łącki, 2 April [1848], *Dz.* 16:498.
26. Jełowicki to Skrzynecki, 29 March 1848, quoted in *HZZP* 4:188–89. Orpiszewski to the Hôtel Lambert, 28 March 1848, in *Legion Mickiewicza*, 44. As noted down by Orpiszewski (1848), quoted in *HZZP* 4:197–98. Jełowicki to Skrzynecki, 29 March 1848, quoted in ibid., 189. Orpiszewski to the Hôtel Lambert, 28 March 1848, in *Legion Mickiewicza*, 44.
27. Cyprian Norwid to Skrzynecki, 15 April 1848, *Pisma* 8:60.
28. Mickiewicz to Łącki, 2 April [1848], *Dz.* 16:497; Orpiszewski to the Hôtel Lambert, 28 March 1848, in *Legion Mickiewicza*, 45. Mickiewicz to Łącki, 2 April [1848], *Dz.* 16:498. "Skład zasad," ibid., 12:10–11 ("Principes de la Pologne renaissante," *Mémorial*, 1:69–70).
29. [Fuller], "Things and Thoughts in Europe: Foreign Correspondence of *The Tribune*, no. XXIV," *New York Tribune*, 15 June 1848. Krasiński to Potocka, 5 April 1848, *LdDP* 3:791; Krasiński to Potocka, 4 April 1848, ibid., 788.
30. Mickiewicz to Łącki, 2 April [1848], *Dz.* 16:498.
31. E. Geritz to A. Geritz, 19 April 1848, *Ll*, 13.
32. E. Geritz to A. Geritz, 19 April 1848, *Ll*, 13. Giuseppe Galetti, Minister of the Papal Police, to Mickiewicz, 9 April 1848, Korespondencja.
33. Mickiewicz to Galetti, 6 April 1848, *Dz.* 16:500; Krasiński to Potocka, 10 April 1848, *LdDP* 3:805; Mickiewicz to Łącki, 2 April [1848], *Dz.* 16:497. Orpiszewski to the Hôtel Lambert, 8 April 1848, in *Legion Mickiewicza*, 55–56; Krasiński to Potocka, 7[–8] April 1848, *LdDP* 3:801. Krasiński to Potocka, 10 April 1848, ibid., 805.
34. Mickiewicz to Krasiński, [23 April 1848], *Dz.* 16:526. Mickiewicz to Łącki, [12 April 1848], ibid., 505. Mickiewicz to the Brethren in Paris, 12 April 1848, ibid., 503–4.
35. Mickiewicz to Giuseppe Malmusi, President of the Government of Modena, 17 April 1848, ibid., 510. Mickiewicz to Jules Bastide, [ca. 22 April–28 April] 1848, ibid., 521. Mickiewicz to Krasiński, [23 April 1848], ibid., 526.
36. Mickiewicz to Bastide, [ca. 22 April–28 April] 1848, *Dz.* 16:522.
37. Mickiewicz to Krasiński, [23 April 1848], *Dz.* 16:526; E. Geritz to A. Geritz, 19 April 1848, *Ll*, 13–14; E. Geritz to A. Geritz, 3 May 1848, ibid., 17. *Mémorial* 1:496. Mickiewicz to Łącki, 1 May [1848], *Dz.* 16:529.
38. *La Patria*, 17 April 1848, quoted in *Mémorial* 1:228.
39. *La Patria*, 17 April 1848, quoted in *Mémorial* 1:228–38, 503-4. *Rivista di Firenze*, 17 April 1848, quoted in ibid., 241–45.
40. Mickiewicz to the Brethren in Paris, [19 April 1848], *Dz.* 16:515. Mickiewicz to Fuller, 19 April [1848], ibid., 517–18. Fuller's article, "Things and Thoughts in Europe: Foreign Correspondence

of *The Tribune*, no. XXIV," *New York Tribune*, 15 June 1848, was dated 19 April, the same day as Mickiewicz's letter to her from Florence.

41. E. Geritz to A. Geritz, 3 May 1848, *Ll*, 17. Mickiewicz to Krasiński, [23 April 1848], *Dz*. 16:527.
42. Mickiewicz to Krasiński, [23 April 1848], *Dz*. 16:527. Mickiewicz to the Brethren in Paris [19 April 1848], ibid., 514–15. Mickiewicz to C. Mickiewicz, 19 April [1848], ibid., 517.
43. *L'Italie Centrale*, 27 April 1848, quoted in *Mémorial* 1:356. *La Gazzetta di Parma*, 28 April 1848, quoted in ibid., 378. Provisional Government of Parma, 28 April 1848, quoted in *Żywot* 4:IX; Provisional Government of Parma, 5 May 1848, quoted in ibid., X; *Gazzetta di Parma*, 29 April 1848, quoted in *Mémorial* 1:378.
44. *Gazzetta di Lodi*, 2 May 1848, quoted in *Żywot* 4:135–36.
45. Cesana, *Ricordi*, 229; *Gazzetta di Milano*, 28 April 1848, quoted in *Mémorial* 2:2. Provisional Government of Milan to Police Chief Giuseppe Toccagni, 1 May 1848, quoted in *Mémorial* 2:8. Mickiewicz to Łącki, 1 May [1848], *Dz*. 16:529; E. Geritz to A. Geritz, 3 May 1848, *Ll*, 18, 17. Cesana, *Ricordi*, 228–29.
46. Mickiewicz to Łącki, 1 May [1848], *Dz*. 16:530. *Voce de Popolo*, 2 May 1848, quoted in *Mémorial* 2:11.
47. C. Mickiewicz to Mickiewicz, 13 April 1848, Korespondencja.
48. C. Mickiewicz to Mickiewicz, 13 April 1848, Korespondencja. Feliks Wrotnowski to Mickiewicz, 14 April 1848, ibid. C. Mickiewicz to Mickiewicz, 14 April 1848, ibid. Różycki to Mickiewicz, 18 April 1848, ibid. A. Chodźko to Mickiewicz, 13 April 1848, ibid. Mickiewicz to Łącki, [16 May 1848], *Dz*. 16:564.
49. Jełowicki to Mickiewicz, 27 April 1848, Korespondencja. Jełowicki enclosed a copy of the papal decree, dated 15 April 1848 (*Żywot* 4:VI–VII).
50. Mickiewicz to Mikołaj Kamieński, 9 May 1848, *Dz*. 16:549–50.
51. Mickiewicz to the Provisional Government of Lombardy, 3 May 1848, *Dz*. 16:533–35. Provisional Government of Lombardy to Mickiewicz, 9 May 1848, Korespondencja.
52. Announcement quoted in *Mémorial*, 2:197. Mickiewicz to Nakwaski, [13] May 1848, *Dz*. 16:558.
53. Mickiewicz to the Provisional Government of Lombardy, 24 May 1848, *Dz*. 16:568.
54. Giuseppe Mazzini to Mickiewicz, [2 May 1848], Korespondencja. Mickiewicz to Fuller, 4 May 1848, *Dz*. 16:541.
55. Mickiewicz to A. Czartoryski, [28 May 1848], *Dz*. 16:576. Mickiewicz to Zamoyski, 28 May 1848, ibid., 578. Mickiewicz to Bastide, 30 May 1848, ibid., 582.
56. Józef Sobolewski to Zamoyski, [end of June–beginning of July] 1848, quoted in *Jenerał Zamoyski* 5:131.
57. Mickiewicz to Kamieński, [ca. 23 June 1848], *Dz*. 16:602–3.
58. Mickiewicz to Edmund Boratyński, 25 June 1848, *Dz*. 16:604–5.
59. Mickiewicz to Boratyński, 25 June 1848, *Dz*. 16:605.
60. A. Chodźko to Mickiewicz, 19 May 1848, Korespondencja.
61. A. Chodźko to Mickiewicz, 31 May 1848, Korespondencja. Łącki to Mickiewicz, 8 June 1848, ibid. Wrotnowski and E. Januszkiewicz to Mickiewicz, 6 June 1848, ibid.
62. As recalled by W. Mickiewicz, "Mm" 5.19:280–81.
63. Goszczyński to Erazm Zaremba, 31 July 1848, *Listy SG*, 260.
64. Mickiewicz to Józef Dziekoński, [12 July 1848], *Dz*. 16:606. A. Chodźko to Mickiewicz, [8 August 1848], Korespondencja. Thirty-Six Brethren to General Louis Cavignac, 12 August 1848, *Dz*. 17:430.
65. As recalled by W. Mickiewicz, "Mm" 5.19:283; *Żywot* 4:198. Mickiewicz to Towiański, 25 February, 1848, *Dz*. 17:24.
66. Towiański to Mickiewicz, 26 September [1848], Korespondencja. Towiański to Mickiewicz, 1 October 1848, ibid. Mickiewicz to Towiański, 25 February 1849, *Dz*. 17:23.
67. Józef Orłowski to Mickiewicz, 10 September 1848, Korespondencja.
68. Mainard, *Adam Mickiewicz*, 142.

69. Dziekoński to Mickiewicz, 19 August 1848, Korespondencja. Ignacy Klukowski and Dziekoński to Mickiewicz, 5 September 1848, ibid.
70. Józef Witkowski to Mickiewicz, 4 September 1848, Korespondencja. Wincenty Siodołkowicz to Mickiewicz, 15 September 1848, ibid. Mickiewicz to Klukowski, 1 September 1848, *Dz.* 16:646.
71. 105 Legionnaires to Mickiewicz, 22 January 1849, Korespondencja. Project of an Agreement with Lodovico Frapelli, Representative of the Republic of Tuscany, [1–5 March 1849], *Dz.* 17:414.
72. As noted down by Aleksander Fijałkowski (1858), *Rozmowy*, 309. Dziekoński to Mickiewicz, 31 May 1849, Korespondencja.
73. Mickiewicz to Domeyko, 14 October 1849, *Dz.* 17:62. Klukowski to Mickiewicz, 23 March 1848, Korespondencja. Kajsiewicz, *O duchu narodowym*, 26.
74. Marie Chodz´ko to M. Chodz´ko, 8 September 1848, quoted in "Mm" 5.19:285. Łubien´ska to C. Mickiewicz, 21 September 1848, quoted in ibid., 287. F. Mickiewicz to Mickiewicz, 26 September 1848, Korespondencja. C. Mickiewicz to M. Mickiewicz, 21 September 1848, quoted in "Mm" 5.19:288.
75. Stattler to Mickiewicz, 17 December 1848, Korespondencja. Mickiewicz to Stattler, 27 December 1848, *Dz.* 16:689.
76. *Lzp* 2:43; Maria Mickiewicz to F. Mickiewicz, 26 December 1848, quoted in *Żywot* 4:210. Krasiński to Bronisław Trentowski, 18[–19] December 1848, in Krasiński, *Listy do Cieszkowskiego* et al. 2:156. Allocution to Prince Louis Napoleon, President of the French Republic, *Dz.* 13:329.
77. Allocution to Prince Louis-Napoleon, President of the French Republic, *Dz.* 13:329.
78. Herzen, *Byloe i dumy* 10:37; Nikolai D. Kiselov to Karl Nesselrode, 17 February/1 March 1849, quoted in Borejsza, "'Potwór,'" 69 (the Russian chargé d'affairs in Paris reported, probably inaccurately, that there were other donors as well). Lamennais, 11 July 1848, quoted in Livois, *Histoire de la Press*, 236. Herzen, *Byloe i dumy* 10:38.
79. As recalled by W. Mickiewicz, *Żywot* 4:226. Gorecka, *Wspomnienia*, 57.
80. Mickiewicz to Fuller, 9 September 1849, *Dz.* 17:50.
81. Herzen, *Byloe i dumy* 10:38–41. As recalled by W. Mickiewicz, *Tribune*, 17.
82. Mickiewicz to Police Commissioner Hébert, 15 August 1852, *Dz.* 17:189.
83. Jules Lechevalier to Jules Dufaure, Minister of the Interior, 21 June 1849, quoted in *TP*, 28.
84. Antoine Dessus to W. Mickiewicz, 2 June 18[93], quoted in *Żywot* 4:252–53; Goszczyński, 20 June 1849, *Dziennik SB*1:429.
85. Mickiewicz to Fuller, 9 September 1849, *Dz.* 17:50. C. Mickiewicz to Dessus, 6 August 1849, quoted in "Mm" 5.19:380.
86. Mickiewicz to Fuller, 9 September 1849, *Dz.* 17:50.
87. Mickiewicz to Ksawery Godebski, 23 August 1849, *Dz.* 17:44.
88. Mickiewicz to Godebski, 2 October 1849, *Dz.* 17:54.

CHAPTER 12. HIBERNATION (1849–1855)

1. Mickiewicz to Domeyko, 14 October 1849, *Dz.* 17:62–63; Mickiewicz to Salomea Dobrzycka, [beginning of September 1849 or June 1850], ibid., 48.
2. B[artenev], "[Note]," 224. Gorecka, *Wspomnienia*, 61–62. C. Mickiewicz to H. Malewska, 4 January 1850, quoted in "Mm" 5.19:382.
3. Mickiewicz to Łubieńska-Wodopolowa, 27 October [1850], *Dz.* 17:92.
4. Mickiewicz to Łubieńska-Wodopolowa, 6 September 1851, *Dz.* 17:138. C. Mickiewicz to H. Malewska, 4 January 1850, quoted in "Mm" 5.19:382. Chłopicki, "W dworku," 210; Falkowski, *Wspomnienia*, 173.
5. Armand Lévy, "Rozmowy z Mickiewiczem," *Rozmowy*, 377–79.
6. Zofia Szymanowska, "Zapiski emigrantki," quoted in Żeleński, *Brązownicy*, 103. Szymanowska, "Zapiski," quoted in *Żywot* 4:273. C. Mickiewicz to H. Malewska, 19 June 1851, quoted in "Mm" 5.19:386.

7. Szymanowska, "Zapiski," quoted in Żeleński, *Brązownicy*, 107. Teofil Lenartowicz to Józef Ignacy Kraszewski, [after 8 August 1870], in Kraszewski and Lenartowicz, *Korespondencja*, 183. As Szymanowska's eventual husband, Lenartowicz had read her memoir.
8. Lenartowicz to Kraszewski, 21 September 1870, in Kraszewski and Lenartowicz, *Korespondencja*, 186. Lenartowicz to Kraszewski, [after 8 August 1870], ibid., 183. As recalled by W. Mickiewicz, *Żywot* 4:273–74; Szymanowska, "Zapiski," quoted in Żeleński, *Brązownicy*, 106.
9. Szymanowska, "Zapiski," quoted in *Żywot* 4:275. Mickiewicz to Domeyko, 7 July 1850, *Dz.* 17:82.
10. Jełowicki to Domeyko, 9 April 1851, quoted in *Żywot* 4:283.
11. Gorecka, *Wspomnienia*, 85–86. C. Mickiewicz to H. Malewska, 19 June 1851, 29 June 1851, quoted in "Mm" 5.19:387.
12. Karol Sienkiewicz to Mickiewicz, [ca. 1 February] 1851, Korespondencja.
13. Mickiewicz to A. Chodźko, 8 February 1842, *Dz.* 16:38. As recalled by Hieronim Napoleon Bońkowski (1883), *Rozmowy*, 468. E. Januszkiewicz to Mickiewicz, 9 March 1851, Korespondencja. Mickiewicz to Zygmunt Schletter, 16 March 1851, *Dz.* 17:108. E. Januszkiewicz to Mickiewicz, 4 April 1851, Korespondencja. As recalled by W. Mickiewicz (1900), *Rozmowy*, 512. Franciszek Szemioth to Bronisław Zaleski, 10 December 1874, ibid., 513.
14. J. B. Zaleski, Dziennik, 8 August, 26 July, 3 August, 28 July 1851, in *Korespondencja JBZ* 2:181–84. J. B. Zaleski to Goszczyński, 16 September 1851, ibid., 191.
15. Mickiewicz to Maria Mickiewicz, 18 September 1851, *Dz.* 17:139–40.
16. As recalled by W. Mickiewicz, in "Mm" 5.19:389. J. B. Zaleski, Dziennik, 8 November 1851, quoted in *Żywot* 4:300; J. B. Zaleski to Goszczyński, 15 November 1851, *Korespondencja JBZ* 2:194.
17. Mickiewicz to Louis-Napoleon Bonaparte, [4–15 December 1851], *Dz.* 17:151.
18. As noted down by Lévy (1851), *Rozmowy*, 394.
19. As noted down by Lévy (1851), *Rozmowy*, 395. Mickiewicz to Łubieńska-Wodopolowa, 22 December [1851], *Dz.* 17:155. Mickiewicz to Louis-Napoleon, [4–15 December 1851], ibid., 150. As recalled by Edmond Mainard [Fontille] (1862), *Rozmowy*, 310.
20. Mickiewicz to Police Commissioner Hébert, 15 August 1852, *Dz.* 17:190. Mickiewicz to Louis-Napoleon, 22 February 1852, ibid., 170. Charlemagne de Maupas to Minister of Justice Jacques Abbatucci, 20 March 1852, in Fiszman, "Materiały," 477–78. Paris Police Prefect Pierre Petri to Minister of Education Hippolyte Fortoul, 29 March 1852, in *Żywot* 4:L; Napoleon III, *Napoleonic Ideas*, 35.
21. Louis-Napoleon, Decree of 12 April 1852, in *Żywot* 4:XL.
22. Mickiewicz to Fortoul, 18 April 1852, *Dz.* 17:173–74. Mickiewicz to Łubieńska-Wodopolowa, 30 April 1852, ibid., 179. C. Mickiewicz to M. Mickiewicz, 16 April 1852, quoted in "Mm" 5.19:393.
23. Mickiewicz to F. Mickiewicz, 14 June 1852, *Dz.* 17:181. C. Mickiewicz to M. Mickiewicz, 21 September 1852, quoted in "Mm" 5.19:397–98. W. Mickiewicz, *Pamiętniki*, 78.
24. Mickiewicz to Łubieńska-Wodopolowa, 1 May 1853, *Dz.* 17:227. Gorecka, *Wspomnienia*, 116. Mickiewicz to Łubieńska-Wodopolowa, 4 January 1853, *Dz.* 17:209.
25. Mickiewicz to Łubieńska-Wodopolowa, 4 January 1853, *Dz.* 17:209. [Memorandum to Napoleon III], *Dz.* 12:301–2/*La Politique*, 283–84.
26. Towiański to Mickiewicz, 28 December 1852, Korespondencja. Mickiewicz to Towiański, [17 January 1853], *Dz.* 17:212.
27. Mickiewicz to Emperor Napoleon III, 17 December 1853, *Dz.* 17:262–66. Zaleski, Dziennik, 26 July 1851, in *Korespondencja JBZ* 2:181.
28. Gorecka, *Wspomnienia*, 124. Norwid, "Czarne Kwiaty," *Pisma wszystkie* 6:184.
29. A[bbatucci], Note on Mickiewicz, 15 April 1853, in Fiszman, "Materiały," 485.
30. Mickiewicz to K. Towiańska, 31 August 1853, *Dz.* 17:248. Gorecka, *Wspomnienia*, 125, 129.
31. Mickiewicz to K. Towiańska, 31 August 1853, *Dz.* 17:248. Mickiewicz to K. Towiańska, 24 March 1853, ibid., 224.

32. J. B. Zaleski to Kajsiewicz, 26 January 1854, *Korespondencja JBZ* 2:223.
33. Ludwik Mierosławski to Mickiewicz, [13 December 1853], Korespondencja.
34. Ludwik Mierosławski to the Polish Democratic Society, 7 December 1853, in Knapowska, "Mickiewicz w latach 1853/5," 73. As recalled by Zamoyski (1856), *Rozmowy*, 301–2.
35. Mickiewicz to Józef Wysocki, 2 May 1854, *Dz.* 17:290. Seweryn Elżanowski to Wysocki, 7 April 1854; 12 April 1854; 23 May 1854, quoted in Handelsman, *Mickiewicz*, 21–22, 26.
36. Hôtel Lambert, Confidential Memorandum, 1854, quoted in Handelsman, *Mickiewicz*, 30.
37. Mickiewicz to A. Rossignol, 25 February 1854, *Dz.* 17:285. Władysław Laskowicz to Domeyko, 15 April 1854, quoted in Odrowąż-Pieniążek, "List," 112. Goszczyński, 16 September 1854, *Dziennik SB* 1:506.
38. W. Mickiewicz, *Pamiętniki* 1:76.
39. Gorecka, *Wspomnienia*, 133. M. Mickiewicz to Szymanowska, 2 November 1854, quoted in *Żywot* 4:387. Gorecka, *Wspomnienia*, 133–34.
40. Duński to K. Towiańska, 6 March 1855, in Duński, *Listy*, 284. Mickiewicz to Niewiarowicz, [9–15 March 1855], *Dz.* 17:321. Mickiewicz to Łubieńska-Wodopolowa, 18 May 1855, ibid., 327; Różycki to K. Towiańska, 6 March 1855, in Duński, *Listy*, 285.
41. As recalled by W. Mickiewicz, in *Żywot* 4:393. Szymanowska, "Opis zaręczyn moich z Adamem Mickiewiczem dla wiadomości rodziny mojej i śladu w przyszłości," quoted in Żeleński, *Brązownicy*, 198. A Chodźko, Diary, quoted in *Żywot* 4:394.
42. W. Mickiewicz, *Pamiętniki* 1:77. *Żywot* 4:395. J. B. Zaleski, Dziennik, 7 March 1855, in *Korespondencja JBZ* 2:238.
43. As recalled by Biergiel, *Rozmowy*, 323. Różycki to K. Towiańska, 6 March 1855, in Duński, *Listy*, 286.
44. Mickiewicz to Niewiarowicz, [9–15 March 1855], *Dz.* 17:321. Towiański to Mickiewicz, 17 March 1855, Korespondencja.
45. Maria Falkenhagen-Zaleski to W. Mickiewicz, [n.d.], quoted in *Żywot* 4:400. Mickiewicz to Łubieńska-Wodopolowa, 18 May 1855, *Dz.* 17:327. *Żywot* 4:396.
46. Mickiewicz to Henrietta Kuczkowska, [8 April] 1855, *Dz.* 17:324–25.

CHAPTER 13. REBIRTH AND DEATH (1855)

1. Krasiński to Cieszkowski, 7 May 1851, in Krasiński, *Listy do Cieszkowskiego* et al. 1:595.
2. As noted down by Lévy, *Rozmowy*, 409.
3. As recalled by Piotr Falkenhagen-Zaleski, quoted in *Żywot* 4:342.
4. As noted down by Ludwik Lenoir-Zwierkowski, 2 June 1855, *Rozmowy*, 439–41.
5. Zwierkowski to A. Czartoryski, [2] June 1855, *Rozmowy*, 434 n. CI.
6. As noted down by Lenoir-Zwierkowski, 4 June 1855, *Rozmowy*, 445; Lenoir-Zwierkowski to A. Czartoryski, [end of August?] 1855, quoted in Handelsman, *Mickiewicz*, 51 n. 3. Mickiewicz to Łubieńska-Wodopolowa, 26 July [1855], *Dz.* 17:334.
7. Mickiewicz to T. Zan, 2 September 1855, *Dz.* 17:345. As noted down by Tadeusz Morawski, 31 July 1855, *Rozmowy*, 431–32.
8. Mickiewicz to Edmond Mainard, 10 August 1855, *Dz.* 17:340. Lenoir-Zwierkowski to A. Czartoryski, 3 September 1855, quoted in Handelsman, *Mickiewicz*, 65. Mickiewicz to Mainard, 25 June 1855, *Dz.* 17:330. Stattler to Karol Estreicher, 3 February 1860, quoted, in Kallenbach, AM (1926) 2:469.
9. J. B. Zaleski to Zdzisław Morawski, 15 September 1876, *Rozmowy*, 348.
10. Fortoul to Mickiewicz, 5 September 1855, Korespondencja. Lenoir-Zwierkowski to Michał Czajkowski, 1 September 1855, in Fijałek, ed., "Z papierów," 293.
11. As recalled by Biergiel, *Rozmowy*, 325.
12. Note to Szymanowska, 10 September 1855, *Dz.* 17:545. Mickiewicz to Szymanowska, 12 September 1855, ibid., 355.
13. Gorecka, *Wspomnienia*, 147. As recalled by Lenoir-Zwierkowski (1857), *Rozmowy*, 446–47.

14. Mickiewicz to T. Zan, 2 September 1855, *Dz.* 17:345. Gorecka, *Wspomnienia*, 148. As recalled by W. Mickiewicz, *Żywot* 4:419.
15. As noted down by Lévy, quoted in *Żywot* 4:408. Mickiewicz to A. Czartoryski, [11 September 1855], *Dz.* 17:351.
16. As noted down by A. Chodźko (9 September 1855), quoted in *Żywot* 4:414.
17. As noted down by A. Chodźko (11 September 1855), quoted in *Żywot* 4:420.
18. Gorecka, *Wspomnienia*, 148.
19. Henryk Służalski, Diary, 11 and 12 September 1855, in *Żywot* 4:CXIV. Służalski to Z. Szymanowska, 12 September 1855, in ibid., CI. Władysław Czartoryski to A. Czartoryski, 12 September 1855, quoted in Handelsman, *Mickiewicz*, 67. Mickiewicz to Mainard, 13 September 1855, *Dz.* 17:358. Mickiewicz to Kuczkowska, 13 September 1855, ibid., 357. Mickiewicz to Mainard, 13 September 1855, ibid., 358.
20. Służalski, Diary, 15 September 1855, in *Żywot* 4:CXIV, CI–CII. Mickiewicz to M. Mickiewicz, 3 October [1855], *Dz.* 17:361. Lévy to W. Mickiewicz, 15 September 1855, in *Żywot* 4:LXIX.
21. Lévy to W. Mickiewicz, 15 September 1855, in *Żywot* 4:LXIX; Lévy to W. Mickiewicz, 16 September 1855, in ibid., LXXI. Mickiewicz to M. Mickiewicz, 3 October [1855], *Dz.* 17:361.
22. Służalski, Diary, 20 September 1855, in *Żywot* 4:CXXI–CXXII. Służalski to Z. Szymanowska, 19 [*sic*] September 1855, in ibid., CII. As recalled by Karol Brzozowski (1883), *Rozmowy*, 452. Służalski, Diary, 20 September 1855, in *Żywot* 4:CXXI.
23. Służalski, Diary, 21 September 1855, in *Żywot* 4:CXXII. Służalski, Diary, 22 September 1855, in ibid., CXXIII.
24. Lévy to W. Mickiewicz, 1 November 1855, in *Żywot* 4:LXXXIX–XC. Lévy to W. Mickiewicz, 23 September 1855, in ibid., LXXII.
25. Mickiewicz to V. Khliustin, 21 October 1855, *Dz.* 17:364–65.
26. Lévy to W. Mickiewicz, 23 September 1855, *Żywot* 4:LXXII.
27. As recalled by Brzozowski (1883), *Rozmowy*, 451. As noted down by Lévy, ibid., 416. Czajkowski to W. Czartoryski, 25 September 1855, quoted in Kijas, *Michał Czajkowski*, 32.
28. Śniadecka to Lenoir-Zwierkowski, 1 October 1855, *Rozmowy*, 455.
29. Lévy to W. Mickiewicz, 20 October 1855, in *Żywot* 4:LXXXIII.
30. Mickiewicz to A. Czartoryski, 25 October 1855, *Dz.* 17:369. Służalski to Z. Szymanowska, 7 October 1855, in *Żywot* 4:CVI.
31. Służalski to Z. Szymanowska, 20 October 1855, in *Żywot* 4:CVI–CVII. Lévy to W. Mickiewicz, 20 October 1855, in ibid., LXXXIV; Mickiewicz to Czartoryski, 25 October 1855, *Dz.* 17:369. Służalski to Z. Szymanowska, 20 October 1855, in *Żywot* 4:CVII. Czajkowski, Pamiętnik, quoted in Rawita-Gawroński, "Sadyk-Pasza," 217.
32. Mickiewicz to Lenoir-Zwierkowski, 25 October 1855, *Dz.* 17:374. Mickiewicz to A. Czartoryski, 25 October 1855, ibid., 369–70. Mickiewicz to A. Czartoryski, 13 November 1855, ibid., 390. Mickiewicz to W. Czartoryski, 19 November 1855, ibid., 403.
33. Czajkowski, Pamiętnik, quoted in Rawita-Gawroński, "Sadyk-Pasza," 219. As noted down by Lévy, *Rozmowy*, 417. Lévy to Emil Bednarczyk, [end of 1855], quoted in Brandstaetter, "Legion," 24.
34. Śniadecka to Jan Ludwik Grudowicz, 30 January 1856, quoted in Rawita-Gawroński, "Sadyk-Pasza," 220; Czajkowski to Lévy, 16 October 1855, quoted in Brandstaetter, "Legion," 24. Czajkowski, Pamiętnik, quoted in Rawita-Gawroński, "Sadyk-Pasza," 219–20. Śniadecka to Czajkowski, 16 January 1856, quoted in ibid., 223–24; Czajkowski to Mickiewicz, 15 November 1855, Korespondencja; Czajkowski, Order of the Day, 25 October 1855, quoted in Brandstaetter, "Legion," 30–31. Lévy to Czajkowski, ca. 29 November 1855, quoted in ibid., 31.
35. Śniadecka to Lenoir-Zwierkowski, 22 October 1855, quoted in Czapska, *Ludwika Śniadecka*, 328. Mickiewicz to A. Czartoryski, 13 November [1855], *Dz.* 17:391.
36. Mickiewicz to A. Czartoryski, 25 October 1855, *Dz.* 17:369. Brzozowski to Elżanowski, 1 November 1855, quoted in Handelsman, *Czartoryski* 3.2:550.

37. Stanisław Drozdowski to Śniadecka, 21 December 1855, in Kallenbach, AM (1926) 2:510. Służalski to Z. Szymanowska, 3 November 1855, in *Żywot* 4:CX.
38. Służalski to Z. Szymanowska, 3 November 1855, in *Żywot* 4:CX. Lévy to W. Mickiewicz, 4 November 1855, in ibid., XCI. Drozdowski to Lenoir-Zwierkowski, 21 December 1855, in Kallenbach, AM (1926) 2:510.
39. Mickiewicz to Czajkowski, 5 November 1855, *Dz.* 17:382. A. Czartoryski to Mickiewicz, 27 October 1855, Korespondencja. Mickiewicz to Seweryn Gałęzowski, 19 November 1855, *Dz.* 17:401. Mickiewicz to A. Czartoryski, 13 November [1855], ibid., 389–92.
40. As recalled by Służalski (1859), in "Prawda," 77.
41. As recalled by Lévy (22 September 1856), quoted in *Żywot* 4:448. As recalled by Hipolit Kuczyński, in "Prawda," 85.
42. As recalled by Emil Bednarczyk (1877), in "Prawda," 91–92.
43. As recalled by Bednarczyk (1877), in "Prawda," 92–93.
44. As recalled by Bednarczyk (1877), in "Prawda," 93.
45. Lévy to W. Mickiewicz, 3 December 1855, in "Prawda," 83. As recalled by Służalski (January 1856), in ibid., 78. Lévy to W. Mickiewicz, 3 December 1855, in ibid., 83; as recalled by Służalski (January 1856), in ibid., 78.
46. As recalled by Lévy (1855 or 1856), quoted in *Żywot* 4:455. Telegraph quoted in ibid., 455. Lévy to W. Mickiewicz, 29 November 1855, in ibid., XCV.
47. As recalled by Hipolit Kuczyński, "Prawda," 88. Ludwika Groppler to the Nakwaskis, 8 December 1855, in ibid., 70.
48. As recalled by Lévy (1855 or 1856), quoted in *Żywot* 4:456.
49. Służalski to Z. Szymanowska, 24 December 1855, in *Żywot* 4:CXII. As recalled by Lévy (1855 or 1856), quoted in ibid., 457–58, 474, 478.
50. Lévy to W. Mickiewicz, 10 December 1855, in *Żywot* 4:XCIX. Service Maritime des Messageries Impériales to Lévy, 26 December 1855, in ibid., CXXXII.
51. Lévy and Służalski, Invitation to Mickiewicz's Funeral, in *Żywot* 4:CXXXIII. As recalled by Lévy (1855 or 1856), quoted in ibid., 476.
52. As recalled by Teodor Tomasz Jeż [Miłkowski] (1885), quoted in *Żywot* 4:480–81. Zamoyski to the Division of Ottoman Cossacks, 12 December 1855, in ibid., CXXXIV.
53. Goszczyński, 30 November 1855, *Dziennik SB* 1:539–40. Duński to the Brethren in Zurich, 1 December 1855, in Duński, *Listy*, 314. AM*wppo*, 221ff.
54. *La Presse*, 25 January 1825.
55. As recalled by W. Mickiewicz, *Pamiętniki* 1:97. *Le Constitutionnel*, 3 December 1855. *L'Univers*, 14 December 1855.
56. Jan Dobrzański, *Nowiny* (Lviv), 15 December 1855, quoted in Kawyn, "Cześć, 599. *Deutsches Museum*, 27 December 1855, quoted in Werner, "Niemiecki nekrolog, 201. C. Olivier, quoted in *Korespondencja AM* 4:238 n. 1.
57. Kajsiewicz, quoted in W. Mickiewicz, *Mémorial* 1:174. Prusinowski, *Mowa*, 5–6.
58. Krasiński to Sołtan, [8 December 1855], in Krasiński, *Listy do Sołtana*, 617. Goszczyński, 7 December 1855, *Dziennik SB* 1:541. Skrzynecki to A. Czartoryski, 23 December 1855, in Kallenbach, AM (1926) 2:511. Norwid, "[Coś ty Atenom zrobił, Sokratesie]," *Pisma wszystkie* 1:236.
59. As noted down by A. Chodźko, quoted in *Żywot* 4:482. Funeral announcement quoted in *Kronika 1850–1855*, 541.
60. Norwid, "Duch Adama i skandal," *Pisma wszystkie* 1:237.
61. *Wiadomości Polskie*, 10 and 11 January 1856, quoted in *Żywot* 4:482–83; Wrotnowski to NN, 21 January 1856, quoted in Pigoń, *Z dawnego Wilna*, 146.
62. *Wiadomości Polskie*, 10 and 11 January 1856, quoted in *Żywot* 4:483.
63. Zaleski, "Mowa," *Dzieła*, 182–87.

POSTSCRIPT

1. Norwid, ["Coś ty Atenom zrobił, Sokratesie"] (1856), *Pisma wszystkie* 1:236.
2. As reported by Władysław Laskowicz (28 June 1890), quoted in Rosiek, *Zwłoki*, 243. As reported by Stanisław Kraków (28 June 1890), quoted in Hordyński, "Sprowadzenie," 352.
3. W. Mickiewicz to the Editors of *Kraj*, 17 May 1869, in Stachowska, "Materiały," 183. W. Mickiewicz, *Pamiętniki* 1:269.
4. W. Mickiewicz, *Pamiętniki* 3:306.
5. As recalled by Służalski (1856), *Rozmowy*, 459. W. Mickiewicz to Kraszewski, 1 May 1885, quoted in Kossak, *Rodzina M.*, 281.
6. W. Mickiewicz to Ksawera Mainard, 29 June 1858, quoted in Kossak, *Rodzina M.*, 196.
7. Niedźwiecki to Jackowski, 21 April 1842, in Jasińska, "Celina Mickiewiczowa," 296.
8. As recalled by Służalski (1856), *Rozmowy*, 459.
9. Maria Gorecka to W. Mickiewicz, 25 March 1877, quoted in Borejsza, Sekretarz, 293.
10. Żeleński, *Brązownicy*, 81.
11. Hordyński, "Sprowadzenie," 352.
12. Ernest Renan, "Discours prononcé au nom du Collège de France á l'exhumation des cendres d'Adam Mickiewicz, au cimetière de Montmorency, le 28 Juin 1890," in *AMaydF*, 360–62; W. Czartoryski, quoted in Hordyński, "Sprowadzenie," 357.
13. Bolesław Limanowski, quoted in Świątecka, "Sprowadzenie zwłok," 47; Bouffał, quoted in ibid., 48. Żeleński, "'Pomnikomania' krakowska," *Słówka*, 213.
14. *Kurier Lwowski*, 4 July 1890, quoted in Borejsza, *Sekretarz*, 337.
15. Hordyński, "Sprowadzenie," 377.
16. Hordyński, "Sprowadzenie," 373–75.
17. *Le Monde*, 15 and 16 July 1890, in *AMaydF*, 364. *Złożenie zwłok*, 50–61, 77–95, 126–36.
18. Helena Mickiewiczówna to Lenartowicz, 21 July 1890, in Lenartowicz, *Korespondencja*, 214. Żeleński, *Brązownicy*, 325.
19. Włodzimierz Lewicki, quoted in Hordyński, "Sprowadzenie," 379. Adam Asnyk, quoted in ibid., 380–83.
20. Stanisław Tarnowski, quoted in Hordyński, "Sprowadzenie," 384.
21. Władysław Chotkowski, quoted in Hordyński, "Sprowadzenie," 389–90.

BIBLIOGRAPHY

UNPUBLISHED SOURCES

Korespondencja Adama Mickiewicza. Edited by Elżbieta Jaworska et al.*

CHRONICLE OF MICKIEWICZ'S LIFE AND WORKS

Dernałowicz, Maria. *Od "Dziadów" części trzeciej do "Pana Tadeusza." Marzec 1832–czerwiec 1834. Kronika życia i twórczości Mickiewicza*. Warsaw: PIW, 1966.

——. *Paryż, Lozanna. Czerwiec 1834–październik 1840. Kronika życia i twórczości Mickiewicza*. Warsaw: IBL, 1996.

Dernałowicz, Maria, Ksenia Kostenicz, and Zofia Makowiecka. *Kronika życia i twórczości Mickiewicza. Lata 1798–1824*. Warsaw: PIW, 1957.

Kostenicz, Ksenia. *Legion Włoski i "Trybuna Ludów." Styczeń 1848–grudzień 1849. Kronika życia i twórczości Mickiewicza*. Warsaw: PIW, 1969.

——. *Ostatnie lata Mickiewicza. Styczeń 1850–26 listopada 1855. Kronika życia i twórczości Mickiewicza*. Warsaw: PIW, 1978.

Makowiecka, Zofia. *Brat Adam. Maj 1844–grudzień 1847. Kronika życia i twórczości Mickiewicza*. Warsaw: PIW, 1975.

——. *Mickiewicz w Collège de France. Październik 1840–maj 1844. Kronika życia i twórczości Mickiewicza*. Warsaw: PIW, 1968.

WORKS CITED

Adam Mickiewicz aux yeux des Français. Edited by Zofia Mitosek. Warsaw: PWN, 1992.

Adam Mickiewicz w poezji polskiej i obcej 1818—1855—1955 (Antologia). Edited by Jerzy Starnawski. Wrocław: Ossolineum, 1961.

Adam Mitskevich v russkoi pechati, 1825–1955. Bibliograficheskie materialy. Moscow and Leningrad: Akademiia Nauk SSSR, 1957.

Adama Mickiewicza wspomnienia i myśli. Edited by Stanisław Pigoń. Warsaw: Czytelnik, 1958.

Archiwum Filomatów. Part 1, *Korespondencja, 1815–1823*. Edited by Jan Czubek. 5 vols. Cracow: PAU, 1913.

——. Part 2, *Materiały do historii Towarzystwa Filomatów*. Edited by Stanisław Szpotański and Stanisława Pietraszkiewiczówna. 3 vols. Cracow: AU, 1920–1921.

*Available on request from the author: koropeck@humnet.ucla.edu.

Archiwum Filomatów. Part 3, *Poezja Filomatów*. Edited by Jan Czubek. 2 vols. Cracow: PAU, 1922.

——. *Listy z więzienia*. Edited by Zbigniew Sudolski. Warsaw: Ancher, 2000.

——. *Listy z zesłania*. Edited by Zbigniew Sudolski. 3 vols. Warsaw: Ancher, 1997–1999.

——. *Na zesłaniu*. Vol. 1. Edited by Czesław Zgorzelski. PAN Komitet Nauk o Literaturze Polskiej, Materiały Literackie, 3. Wrocław: Ossolineum, 1973.

Bakunin, Mikhail A. *V tiurme i ssylke, 1849–1861*. Vol. 4 of his *Sobranie sochinenii i pisem 1828–1876*. Edited by Iu. M. Steklov. 1935. Reprint, Düsseldorf: Brücken-Verlag; Vaduz: Europe-Printing, 1970.

Baratynskii, Evgenii A. *Polnoe sobranie stikhtvorenii*. Edited by L. G. Frizman. St. Petersburg: Akademicheskii proekt, 2000.

Barsukov, Nikolai. *Zhizn' i trudy M. P. Pogodina*. 22 vols. 1888–1906. Slavistic Printings and Reprintings, 162. The Hague: Mouton, 1969–72.

B[artenev], [P]etr [I]. "[Note to 'Stikhi I. V. Kireevskogo Mitskevichu']." *Russkii arkhiv* 12.2 (1874): 223–24.

Batowski, Henryk. "Dwie polemiki." In his *Przyjaciele Słowianie*. Warsaw: Czytelnik, 1956, 85–112.

Baworowski, Wiktor. "Notatka o liście." *Pamiętnik Towarzystwa Literackiego im. Adama Mickiewicz* 2 (1888): 153–54.

Bełza, Władysław. *Kronika potoczna i anegdotyczna z życia Adama Mickiewicza*. 2d ed. Warsaw: Familia, 1998.

Berezina, V. G. "Mitskevich i 'Moskovskii telegraf.'" In *Adam Mitskevich v russkoi pechati, 1825–1955. Bibliograficheskie materialy*. Moscow: AN SSSR, 1957, 471–79.

Bilip, Witold. *Mickiewicz w oczach współczesnych. Dzieje recepcji na ziemiach polskich w latach 1818–1830. Antologia*. Wroclaw: Ossolineum, 1962.

Borejsza, Jerzy W. "Adama Mickiewicza przyjazd do Francji." In his *Piękny wiek XIX*. Warsaw: Czytelnik, 1984, 46–59.

——. "'Potwór niewdzięczności—Mickiewicz.'" In his *Piękny wiek XIX*. Warsaw: Czytelnik, 1984, 60–73.

——. *Sekretarz Adama Mickiewicza (Armand Lévy i jego czasy, 1827–1891)*. 2d ed. Wrocław: Ossolineum, 1977.

Borowczyk, Jerzy. *Rekonstrukcja procesu filomatów i filaretów, 1823–1824*. Uniwersytet im. Adama Mickiewicza w Poznaniu, Filologia Polska, 75. Poznań: UAM, 2003.

Brandstaetter, Roman. "Legion żydowski Adama Mickiewicza (Dzieje i dokumenty)." *Miesięcznik Żydowski* 2.1 (1932): 20–45, 112–32, 225–48.

Budzyński, Michał. *Wspomnienia z mojego życia*. 2 vols. Poznań: Jan Konstanty Żupański, 1880.

Bujakowski, Zygmunt. *Z młodości Mickiewicza. Nieznane szczegóły z lat 1815–1825*. Warsaw: Gebethner and Wolff, 1914.

Bulgarin [Bułharyn], F. V. *Vidok Figliarin. Pis'ma i agenturnye zapiski F. V. Bulgarina v III Otdelenie*. Edited by A. I. Reitblat. Novoe literaturnoe obozrenie, 1998.

Canonico, Tancredo. *André Towiański*. Turin: Vincent Bona, 1897.

Carlyle, Thomas. *New Letters*. Edited by Alexander Carlyle. Vol. 1. London: John Lane, 1904.

Čelakovský, Frant[išek] Ladislav. *Korespondence a zápisky*. Edited by František Bílý. Vol. 2. Prague: ČAN, 1910.

Cesana, Giuseppe A. *Ricordi di un Giornalista (1821–1851)*. Milan: Bortololotti di Giuseppe Prato, 1890.

Chamier, Frederick. "Anecdotes of Russia." *The New Monthly Magazine and Literary Journal*, 1830, part 2:73–81.

Chłopicki, Edward. "W dworku na Batignolles. Ze wspomnień." *Bluszcz* 12 (1876): 209–10, 217–18, 227–28.

Chmielowski, Piotr. *Adam Mickiewicz. Zarys biograficznoliteracki*. 2 vols. Warsaw: Gebethner and Wolff, 1886.

Chopin, Fryderyk. *Korespondencja*. Edited by Bronisław Edward Sydow. 2 vols. Warsaw: PIW, 1955.

Chwin, Stefan. "Wstęp," to *Konrad Wallenrod*, by Adam Mickiewicz. Biblioteka Narodowa I:72. Wrocław: Ossolineum, 1991.

Cooper, James Fenimore. *Correspondence*. Edited by James Fenimore Cooper. 2 vols. New Haven: Yale University Press, 1922.

——. *The Letters and Journals of James Fenimore Cooper*. Edited by James Franklin Beard. Vol. 2. Cambridge, Mass.: The Belknap Press of Harvard University Press, 1960.

——. *Pages and Pictures from the Writings of James Fenimore Cooper*. Edited by Susan Fenimore Cooper. New York: W. A. Townsend, 1861.

Czajkowska, Krystyna. "Wokół wizyty Mickiewicza w Weimarze." *Ruch Literacki* 23.5–6 (1982): 283–99.

Czajkowski, Michał [A. K. O.]. *Kozaczyzna w Turcji. Dzieło w trzech częściach*. Paris: L. Martinet, 1857.

Czapska, Maria. *Ludwika Śniadecka*. Warsaw: Czytelnik, 1958.

David d'Angers, Pierre-Jean. *Carnets. Edited by* André Bruel. 2 vols. Paris: Librairie Plon, 1958.

Dernałowicz, Maria, ed. "Przekład *Farysa* i list do Pierre-Jean Davida d'Angers odnalezione przez Leszka Kuka." *Blok-Notes Muzeum Literatury im. Adama Mickiewicza* 12/13 (1999): 33–44.

Domeyko, Ignacy. *Moje podróże. Pamiętniki wygnańca*. Edited by Elżbieta Helena Nieciowa. 3 vols. Wrocław: Ossolineum, 1962.

——. "O młodości Mickiewicza. "In *Księga pamiątkowa na uczczenie setnej rocznicy urodzin Adama Mickiewicza (1798–1898)*. Vol. 1. Warsaw: Bronisław Natanson, 1898, 145–55.

Duński, Edward. *Listy (1848–1856)*. Edited by Attilio Begey and Józef Komenda. Turin: Vincente Bono, 1915.

Emerson, Ralph Waldo. *The Journals and Miscellaneous Notebooks*. Vol. 11, 1848–1851. Edited by A. W. Plumstead et al. Cambridge, Mass.: The Belknap Press of Harvard University Press, 1975.

Falkowski, Juliusz. *Wspomnienia z roku 1848 i 1849*. Poznań: J. K. Żupański, 1879.

Ferretti, Giovanni. "Adam Mickiewicz à l'Académie de Lausanne." *Études de Lettres* 14 (1940): 127–99.

Finkel, Ludwik. "Z korespondencji Leonarda Niedźwieckiego." In *Rok Mickiewiczowski. Księga pamiątkowa wydana staraniem Kółka Mickiewiczowskiego we Lwowie*. Vol. 1. Lviv: H. Altenberg, 1899, 284–87.

Fiszman, Samuel. "Andrzej Towiański w świetle dokumentów." In his *Archiwalia Mickiewiczowskie*. Wrocław: Ossolineum, 1962, 122–44.

——. "Materiały Mickiewiczowskie w paryskich Archives Nationales." *Pamiętnik Literacki* 56.3 (1965): 465–503.

——. *Mickiewicz w Rosji. Z archiwów, muzeów, bibliotek Moskwy i Leningradu*. Warsaw: PIW, 1949.

——. "Pokłosie Mickiewiczowskie z archiwów moskiewskich." *Twórczość* 3.1 (1947): 5–24.

——. *Z problematyki pobytu Mickiewicza w Rosji*. Warsaw: PIW, 1956.

Fontana, Julian. "Wybór listów . . . do Stanisława Egberta Koźmiana." Edited by Józef Fijałek. *Rocznik Biblioteki Polskiej Akademii Nauk w Krakowie* 1 (1955): 187–266.

Fuller, Margaret. *The Letters of Margaret Fuller*. Edited by Robert N. Hudspeth. Vols. 4–6. Ithaca: Cornell University Press, 1987–1994.

——. *Woman in the Nineteenth Century*. New York, 1845. *American Transcendentalism Web*. 27 Feb. 2003. http://www.vcu.edu/engweb/transcendentalism/authors/fuller/woman1.html.

G . . . [Gabriela Puffke]. "Wyjątek z pamiętników mojej cioci z roku 1832" *Kurierek Poznański* 12 July 1865: 101–2.

Gadon, Lubomir. *Wielka Emigracja po powstaniu listopadowym*. Paris: Księgarnia Polska, n.d.

Gąsiorowski, Albert. *Adam Mickiewicz i pisma jego do roku 1829*. Cracow: Kraj, 1872.

Gilles-Maisani, Jean-Charles. *Adam Mickiewicz, poète national de la Pologne. Ëtude psychanalytique et caractérologique*. Montreal: Bellarmin, 1988.

Goethe, Johann Wolfgang. *Briefwechsel zwischen Goethe und Zelter in den Jahren 1799 bis 1832*. Vol. 20.2 of *Sämtliche Werke nach Epochen seines Schaffens*. Edited by Edith Zum und Sabine Schäfer. Munich: Carl Hanser Verlag, 1998.

——. *Sämtliche Werke. Briefe, Tagebücher und Gespräche.* Vol. 2, *Gedichte 1800–1832.* Edited by Karl Eibl. Frankfurt am Main: Deutscher Kalssiker Verlag, 1988.
Gołembiowski, Władysław. *Mickiewicz odsłoniony i towiańszczyzna.* Paris: Maulde and Renou, 1844.
Gomolicki, Leon. *Przygoda archiwalna.* Wrocław: Ossolineum, 1976.
Gorecka, Maria. *Wspomnienia o Adamie Mickiewiczu opowiedziane najmłodszemu bratu.* 3d ed. Warsaw: Published by author, 1897.
——. "Ze wspomnień o moim ojcu." *Pamiętnik Towarzystwa Literackiego im. Adama Mickiewicza* 2 (1888): 238–40.
Goszczyński, Seweryn. *Dziennik Sprawy Bożej.* Edited by Zbigniew Sudolski et al. 2 vols. Warsaw: PAX, 1984.
——. *Listy (1823–1875).* Edited by Stanisław Pigoń. Archiwum do Dziejów Literatury i Oświaty w Polsce, 19. Cracow: PAU, 1937.
Grabowicz, George G. [Hrabovych, Hryhorii]. "Symvolichna avtobiohrafiia u Mitskevycha i Shevchenka." In his *Shevchenko iakoho ne znaiemo (Z problematyky symvolichnoï avtobiohrafiï ta suchasnoï retseptsiï poeta).* Kyiv: Krytyka, 2000, 52–67.
Green, Peter S. "Polish Hip-Hop Rocks the Homies on the Blok." *New York Times,* 5 April 2002, late ed., A4.
Gregory XVI, Pope. "Cum primum." *Papal Encyclicals Online.* http://www.papalencyclicals.net/Greg16/g16cumpr.htm.
Handelsman, Marceli. *Adam Czartoryski.* 3 vols. Rozprawy Historyczne, 23–25. Warsaw: TNW, 1948–1950.
——. *Mickiewicz w latach 1853–1855.* Warsaw: F. Hoesick, 1933.
Herlihy, Patricia. *Odessa: A History, 1794–1914.* Cambridge, Mass.: Harvard Ukrainian Research Institute, 1986.
Herzen, Aleksandr I. *Byloe i dumy.* Vols. 8–11 of *Sobranie sochinenii v tridtsati tomakh.* Moscow: AN SSSR, 1956–1957.
Holtei, Karl von. *Vierzig Jahre.* Vol. 4. Breslau: Eduard Trewendt, 1862.
Hordyński, Zdzisław. "Sprowadzenie zwłok Adama Mickiewicza na Wawel." *Pamiętnik Towarzystwa Literackiego im. Adama Mickiewicz* 4 (1890): 341–402.
Iazykov, N. M. *Stikhotvoreniia i poèmy.* 3d ed. Leningrad: Sovetskii pisatel', 1988.
Ilnicka, Maria. "Łucja z książąt Gedroyciów Rautenstrauchowa." *Bluszcz* 22 (1886): 145–46, 154–56, 161–63.
"Iz bumag Stepana Petrovicha Shevyreva." *Russkii arkhiv* 16.2 (1878): 47–87.
James, William. *The Varieties of Religious Experience: A Study in Human Nature.* New York: The Modern Library, 2002.
Januszkiewicz, Romuald. *Extraits de lettres et documents (1844–1865).* Vol. 1 of *Action et souvenirs de quelques serviteurs de l'Œuvre de Dieu.* Edited by Attille Begey. Turin: Vincent Bona, 1913.
Jasińska, Stanisława. "Celina Mickiewiczowa w zapiskach Leonarda Niedźwieckiego." *Pamiętnik Biblioteki Kórnickiej* 6 (1958): 286–300.
Jełowicki, Aleksander. *Listy do Ksaweryny. Listy do Ksaweryny Chodkiewiczowej z lat 1832–1839.* Translated by Maria Fredro-Boniecka. Edited by Franciszek German. Warsaw: Pax, 1964.
——. *Moje wspomnienia.* Warsaw: Pax, 1970.
Jenerał Zamoyski. 6 vols. Poznań: Biblioteka Kórnicka, 1910–1930.
Kacnelson, Dora. "Zapiski Klementyny z Tańskich Hoffmanowej o Mickiewiczu i Celinie z lat 1833, 1834, 1835 i 1842." *Blok-Notes Muzeum Literatury im. Adama Mickiewicza* 11 (1994): 51–62.
Kaczkowski, Karol. *Wspomnienia z papierów pozastałych po ś. p. . . .* Vol. 1. Lviv: Gubrynowicz and Schmidt, 1876.
Kajsiewicz, Hieronim. *O duchu narodowym i duchu rewolucyjnym, mowa . . . miana dnia 29 listopada 1849 roku w Kościele Matki Boskiej Wniebowziętej (de l'Assomption), w Paryżu.* Paris: L. Martinet, 1849.
——. "Pamiętnik o początkach Zgromadzenia Zmartwychwstania Pańskiego." In his *Pisma.* Vol. 3. Cracow: Uniwersytet Jagielloński, 1872, 402–96.

Kallenbach, Józef. *Adam Mickiewicz*. 2 vols. Cracow: Spółka Wydawnicza Polska, 1897.
——. *Adam Mickiewicz*. 2 vols. 3d ed. Lviv: Ossolineum, 1923.
——. *Adam Mickiewicz*. 2 vols. 4th ed. Lviv: Ossolineum, 1926.
——. "Towianizm na tle historycznem." *Przegląd Powszechny* 163 (1924): 18–30; 164 (1924): 110–247, 229–44; 165 (1925): 160–75; 169 (1926): 194–203, 331–44; 170 (1926): 32–51.
——. *Towianizm na tle historycznym*. Cracow: Przegląd Powszechny, 1926.
——. "Z epoki emigracyjnej (1833–1841)." *Lamus* 1.3 (1909): 440–70.
Kawyn, Stefan. "Cześć pozgonna dla Mickiewicz wśród poetów Lwowskich (1855–1856)," *Pamiętnik Literacki* 48.4 (1957): 593–608.
Kern (Markova-Vinogradskaia), A. P. *Vospominaniia o Pushkine*. Moscow: Sovetskaia Rossiia, 1987.
Kireevskii, I. V. *Polnoe sobranie sochinenii v dvukh tomakh*. Edited by M. Gershenzon. 2 vols. Moscow: IMU, 1911.
Kijas, Juliusz. *Michał Czajkowski pod urokiem Mickiewicza*. Cracow: Uniwersytet Jagielloński, 1959.
Kleiner, Juliusz. *Mickiewicz*. Rev. ed. 2 vols. Lublin: Towarzystwo Naukowe KUL, 1995.
Knapowska, Wisława. "Mickiewicz w latach 1853/5 w świetle dokumentów emigracyjnych." *Kwartalnik Historyczny* 62.6 (1955): 71–89.
Kołaczkowski, Stefan. "Mickiewicz jako człowiek. Glosy." In his *Portrety i zarysy literackie*. Vol. 1 of *Pisma wybrane*. Edited by Stanisław Pigoń. Warsaw: PIW, 1968, 75–130.
Korespondencja między Janem Koźmianem a Hieronimem Kajsiewiczem. Edited by Franciszek Chłapowski. Part 1, *25 listów od 28-go sierpnia 1833 do 8-go maja 1836 r*. Poznań: Ruch Kulturalny, 1915.
Kornfeld, Eve. *Margaret Fuller: A Brief Biography with Documents*. The Bedford Series in History and Culture. Boston: Bedford Books, 1997.
Kossak, Ewa. *Rodzina M*. Warsaw: Czytelnik, 1991.
Kostenicz, Ksenia. "Prawda i nieprawda w relacjach o śmierci Mickiewicza." *Blok-Notes Muzeum Literatury im. Adama Mickiewicza* [1] (1975): 42–95.
——. "Słowacki wobec 'służby' Goszczyńskiego dla Mickiewicza na początku 1848 roku." *Pamiętnik Literacki* 58 (1967): 543–53.
Koźmian, Jan. *Pisma*. Vol. 3. Poznań: Jarosław Leitgebr, 1881.
Koźmian, Kajetan. *Pamiętniki*. Edited by Marian Kaczmarek and Kazimierz Pecold. 3 vols. Wrocław: Ossolineum, 1972.
Kramer, Lloyd S. *Threshold of a New World: Intellectuals and the Exile Experience in Paris, 1830–1848*. Ithaca: Cornell University Press, 1988.
Krasiński, Zygmunt. *Dzieła literackie*. Vol. 3. Edited by Paweł Hertz. Warsaw: PIW, 1973.
——. *Listy do Adama Sołtana*. Edited by Zbigniew Sudolski. Warsaw: PIW, 1970.
——. *Listy do Cieszkowskiego, Jaroszyńskiego, Trentowskiego*. Edited by Zbigniew Sudolski. 2 vols. Warsaw: PIW, 1988.
——. *Listy do Delfiny Potockiej*. 3 vols. Edited by Zbigniew Sudolski. Warsaw: PIW, 1975.
——. *Listy do Henryka Reeve*. Edited by Paweł Hertz. 2 vols. Warsaw: PIW, 1980.
——. *Listy do Konstantego Gaszyńskiego*. Edited by Zbigniew Sudolski. Warsaw: PIW, 1971.
——. *Listy do ojca*. Edited by Stanisław Pigoń. Warsaw: PIW, 1963.
Kraszewski, Józef Ignacy, and Teofil Lenartowicz. *Korespondencja*. Edited by Wincenty Danek. Wrocław: Ossolineum, 1963.
Landa, S. S. "Mitskevich nakanune vosstaniia dekabristov (Iz istorii russko-pol'skikh obshchestvennykh i literaturnykh sviazei)." In *Literatura slavianskikh narodov, 4, Iz istorii literatur pol'shi i chekhoslovakii*. Moscow: Izdatelstvo AN SSSR, 1959, 91–185.
——. "Do jednego ze 'spółuczniów, spółwięźniów, spółwygnańców . . .' (nieznana improwizacja Mickiewicza)." In *Archiwum Filomatów. Na zesłaniu*. Vol. 1. Edited by Czesław Zgorzelski. PAN Komitet Nauk o Literaturze Polskiej, Materiały Literackie, 3. Wrocław: Ossolineum, 1973, 205–17.
Larionova, E. O. "'Kogda narody, raspri pozabyv, . . .' (A. I. Turgenev na paryzhskikh lektsiiakh Mitskevicha, 1840–1842 godov." *Russkaia literatura* 2 (1998):35–45.

Lautréamont, comte de [Isidore Ducasse]. *Les Chants de Maldoror* [1868–69]. Translated by Guy Wernham. New York: New Directions, 1965.

Lee, Robert. *The Last Days of Alexander and the First Days of Nicholas (Emperors of Russia)*. 2d. ed. London: Richard Bentley, 1854.

Legion Mickiewicza. Wybór źródeł. Edited by Henryk Batowski and Alina Szklarska-Lohmannowa. Wrocław: Ossolineum, 1958.

Łempicki, Stanisław. "Tak zwany 'Heinrech' w autografie *Ksiąg Pielgrzymstwa Polskiego* Adama Mickiewicza." In his *Wiek złoty i czasy romantyzmu w Polsce*. Edited by Jerzy Starnawski. Warsaw: PWN, 1992, 669–724.

Lenartowicz, Teofil, and Helena Mickiewiczówna. *Korespondencja*. Edited by Józef Fert. Lublin: Towarzystwo Naukowe KUL, 1997.

Listy legionistów Adama Mickiewicza z lat 1848–1849. Edited by Hanna Lutzowa. Wrocław: Ossolineum, 1963.

"Listy o Adamie Mickiewiczu i jego towarzyszach, pisane do Joachima Lelewela w latach 1819–1829." Edited by Maurycy Stankiewicz. *Pamiętnik Towarzystwa im. Adama Mickiewicza* 1 (1887): 145–71.

"Listy o Adamie Mickiewiczu w zbiorach rękopiśmiennych Biblioteki PAN w Krakowie." Edited by Zbigniew Jabłoński. *Rocznik Biblioteki Polskiej Akademii Nauk w Krakowie* 1 (1955): 48–185.

Literaturnye salony i kružki. Pervaja polovina XIX [v]eka. 1930. Edited by N. L. Brodskii. Reprint, Hildesheim: Georg Olms, 1984.

Livois, René de. *Histoire de la presse française*. Vol. 1, *Des origines à 1881*. Lausanne: Éditions Spes, 1965.

Łubieński, Edward. *Mickiewicz w Rzymie. Odpowiedź na list bezimienny umieszczony w* Dzienniku Polskim. Poznań: Księgarnia Katolicka, 1850.

Maciejewski, Jarosław. *Mickiewicza wielkopolskie drogi. Rekonstrukcje i refleksje*. Poznan: Wydawnictwo Poznańskie, 1972.

Mainard [Fontille], Edmond. *Adam Mickiewicz. Sa vie et sa croyance. Esquisse biographique, impressions et souvenirs*. Paris: Humbert, 1862.

———. *Le Prophète national de la Pologne*. 2d ed. Paris: Humbert, 1864.

Malinowski, Mikołaj. *Dziennik*. Translated and edited by Manfred Kridl. Vilnius: Księgarnia Stowarz. Nauczycielstwa Polskiego, 1921.

———. *Księga wspomnień*. Edited by Józef Tretiak. Źródła do Dziejów Polski Porozbiorowej, 3. Cracow: AU, 1907.

Mazzini, Giuseppe. *Scritti editi et inediti*. 94 vols. N.p.Imola, 1906–.

Meissner, Alfred. *Geschichte meines Lebens*. Vol. 1. Vienna: Karl Prochaska, 1884.

Mendelssohn-Bartholdy, Felix. *Letters from Italy and Switzerland*. Translated by Lady Wallace. London: Longman, Green, Longman, and Roberts, 1862.

"Mezhdutsarstvie v Rossii s 19-go noiabria po 14-e dekabria 1825 goda. Istoricheskie materialy." *Russkaia starina* 35 (1882): 147–216.

Micewski, Bolesław. *Bogdan Jański, założyciel zmartwychwstańców 1807–1840*. Warsaw: Ośrodek Dokumentacji i Studiów Społecznych, 1983.

Michelet, Jules. *Cours au Collège de France, 1838–1851*. Edited by Paul Villaneix et al. 2 vols. Paris: Gallimard, 1995.

———. *Journal*. Edited by Paul Villaneix. 2 vols. 2d ed. Paris: Galiimard, 1959.

Mickiewicz, Adam. *Cours de littérature slave professé au Collège de France*. 5 vols. Paris: L. Martinet, 1860.

———. *Dziadów część III w podobiźnie autografu*. Edited by Józef Kallenbach. Cracow: PAN, 1925.

———. *Dzieła* (Wydanie Rocznicowe [Anniversary Edition]). 17 vols. Warsaw: Czytelnik, 1993–2006.

———. *Dzieła wszystkie*. Vols. 1, 4. Edited by Konrad Górski. Wrocław: Ossolineum, 1969–.

———. *Korespondencja*. Edited by Władysław Mickiewicz. 4th ed. 4 vols. Paris: Księgarnia Luxemburgska, 1874–1885.

——. *Mélanges posthumes*. 2 vols. Edited by Władysław Mickiewicz. Paris: Librairie du Luxembourg, 1872–1879.

——. *Pan Tadeusz. Podobizna rękopisów*. Edited by Tadeusz Mikulski. Wrocław: Ossolineum, 1949.

——. *Pisma*. Vol. 1. Paris: Eustachy Januszkiewicz, 1844.

——. *Pisma prozaiczne francuskie*, Edited by Tadeusz Makowiecki et al. Vol. 7, part 1 of *Dzieła wszystkie* (Wydanie Sejmowe). Warsaw: Skarb Rzeczypospolitej Polskiej, 1933.

——. *La Politique du dix-neuvième siècle*. Edited by Władysław Mickiewicz. Paris: Librairie du Luxembourg, 1870.

——. *Poems*. Edited by George Rapall Noyes. Translated by various hands. New York: The Polish Institute of Arts and Sciences in America, 1944.

——. *Przemówienia*. Edited by Stanisław Pigoń. Vol. 13 of *Dzieła wszystkie* (Wydanie Sejmowe). Warsaw: Skarb Rzeczypospolitej Polskiej, 1936.

——. *Rozmowy z Adamem Mickiewiczem*. Edited by Stanisław Pigoń. Vol. 16 of *Dzieła wszystkie* (Wydanie Sejmowe). Warsaw: Skarb Rzeczypospolitej Polskiej, 1933.

——. *Les Slaves: Cours professé au Collége de France*. 5 vols. Paris: Comptoir des imprimeurs-unis, 1849.

——[Mitskevich]. *Sobranie sochinenii*. Vol. 5. Edited by M. S. Zhivov et al. Moscow: Khudozhestvennaia Literatura, 1954.

——[Mitskevich]. *Sonety*. Edited by S. S. Landa. Leningrad: Nauka, 1976.

——. *La Tribune des Peuples*. Edited by Władysław Mickiewicz. Paris: E. Flammarion, 1907.

——. *Vorlesungen über slawische Literatur und Zustände, gehalten im Collège de France*. Translated by Gustav Siegfried. 2 vols. Leipzig: Brockhaus and Avenarius, 1843.

——. *Wiersze . . . w podobiznach autografów*. Part 1, 1819–1829. Edited by Czesław Zgorzelski. Wrocław: Ossolineum, 1973.

Mickiewicz, Władysław [Ladislas]. *Adam Mickiewicz: Sa vie et son œuvre*. Paris: Nouvelle Librairie Parisienne, 1888.

——. *Mémorial de la Légion Polonaise de 1848 créée en Italie par Adam Mickiewicz*. 3 vols. Paris: Libraire du Luxembourg, 1877.

——. "Moja matka." *Przegląd Współczesny* 5.18 (1926): 145–75, 395–406; 5.19 (1926): 119–31, 280–90, 380–409.

——. "O zawieszeniu wykładów Adama Mickiewicz w Collège de France." In *Rok Mickiewiczowski. Księga pamiątkowa wydana staraniem Kółka Mickiewiczowskiego we Lwowie*. Vol. 1. Lviv: H. Altenberg, 1899, 225–32.

——. *Pamiętniki*. 3 vols. Warsaw: Gebethner and Wolff, 1926. *Polska Biblioteka Internetowa*. http://www.pbi.edu.pl/site.php?s=NmU1ZDAxZWMwOTY4&tyt=pami%C4%99tniki&aut=mickiewicz&x=0&y=0.

——. *Żywot Adama Mickiewicza podług zebranych przez siebie materiałów oraz z własnych wspomnień*. 4 vols. Poznan: Dziennik Poznański, 1892–95.

——. *Żywot Adama Mickiewicza podług zebranych przez siebie materiałów oraz z własnych wspomnień*. 2d ed. 2 vols. Poznan: Poznańskie Towarzystwo Przyjaciół Nauk, 1929–1931.

Mickiewicziana w zbiorach Tomasza Niewodniczańskiego w Bitburgu. Edited by Maria Danilewicz Zielińska and Janusz Odrowąż-Pieniążek. 2 vols. Darmstadt: Deutsches Polen Institut, 1989.

"Miscellanea mickiewiczowskie." *Blok-Notes Muzeum Literatury im. Adama Mickiewicz* 12/13 (1999): 193–217.

Mochnacki, Maurycy. *Listy*. Vol. 1 of his *Dzieła*. Poznań: Jan Konstanty Żupański, 1863.

——. *Powstanie narodu polskiego w roku 1820 i 1831*. Ed. Stefan Kiniewicz. 2 vols. Warsaw: PIW, 1984.

Montalembert, Charles de. *Lettres de Montalembert à Lamennais*. Edited by Georges Goyau and P. de Lallemand. Paris: Desclée, De Brouwer, 1932.

Morawski, Stanisław. *Kilka lat mojej młodości w Wilnie*. Edited by Adam Czartkowski and Henryk Mościcki. Warsaw: PIW, 1959.

——. *W Peterburku. 1827–1838. Wspomnienia pustelnika i Koszałki Kobiałki*. Edited by Adam Czartkowski and Henryk Mościcki. Poznań: Wydawnictwo Polskie, n.d.

Mościcki, Henryk. "Z pobytu Mickiewicza w Odessie." In his *Pod znakiem orła i pogoni. Szkice historyczne*. Warsaw: Gebethner, 1915, 137–44, 284–85.

——. *Wilno i Warszawa w "Dziadach" Mickiewicza*. 2d ed. Warsaw: Rytm, 1999.

Motty, Marceli. *Przechadzki po mieście*. 2 vols. Edited by Zdzisław Grot. Warsaw: PIW, 1957.

Napoleon III. *Napoleonic Ideas. Les Idées Napoléoniennes par le Prince Napoléon-Louis Bonaparte*. Edited by Brison D. Gooch. New York: Harper and Row, 1967.

Niemcewicz, Julian Ursyn. *Dzienniki 1835–1836*. Edited by Izabella Rusinowa. Warsaw: WUW, 2005.

——. *Pamiętniki . . . Dziennik pobytu mego za granicą. Od dnia 21 lipca 1831 r. do 20 Maja 1841 r*. 2 vols. Poznań: Jan Konstanty Żupański, 1876.

Niewiarowicz, Alojzy Ligenza. *Wspomnienia o Adamie Mickiewiczu*. Lviv: Gubrynowicz and Schmidt, 1878.

Norwid, Cyprian. *Pisma wszystkie*. 11 vols. Edited by Juliusz W. Gomulicki. Warsaw: PIW, 1971–1976.

Oberlaender, Ludwik. "Kompleks żydowski Adama Mickiewicza." *Miesięcznik Żydowski* 3.1 (1932): 467–74.

Odrowąż-Pieniążek, Janusz. "List do Ignacego Domeyki do Mickiewicza z roku 1850." *Twórczość* 22.11 (1966): 111–14.

Odyniec, Antoni Edward. *Listy z podróży*. 2 vols. Edited by Marian Toporowski. Warsaw: PIW, 1961.

——. *Wspomnienia z przeszłości opowiadane Deotymie*. Warsaw: Gebethner and Wolff, 1884.

Olizar, Gustaw. "Z pamiętników" (1892). In *Pamiętniki dekabrystów*. Vol. 3, *Sprawy dekabrystowskie w pamiętnikarstwie polskim*. Edited by Wacław Zawadzki. Warsaw: PIW, 1960, 5–87.

O'Meara, Patrick. *K. F. Ryleev: A Political Biography of the Decembrist Poet*. Princeton: Princeton University Press, 1984.

Ospovat, A. L., and R. D. Timenchik. *"Pechal'nu povest' sokhranit' . . ."* Moscow: Kniga, 1987.

Ostaf'evskii arkhiv kniazei Viazemskikh. Vol. 4, *Perepiska knizia P. A. Viazemskogo s A. I. Turgenevym, 1837–1845*. Edited by V. I. Saitov. St. Petersburg: M. M. Stasiulevich, 1899.

Ostrowski, Antoni. "Antoniego Ostrowskiego wspomnienia o Mickiewiczu i Towiańskim." Edited by Elżbieta Z. Wichrowska. *Blok-Notes Muzeum Literatury im. Adama Mickiewicza* 12/13 (1999): 69–117.

Pavlova, Karolina. *Polnoe sobranie stikhotvorenii*. Moscow-Leningrad: Sovetskii pisatel', 1964.

Pedrotti, Louis. *Józef-Julian Sękowski: The Genesis of a Literary Alien*. University of California Publications in Modern Philology, 73. Berkeley: University of California Press, 1965.

Pigoń, Stanisław. "Dramat dziejowy polsko-rosyjski w ujęciu Mickiewicz." In his *Zawsze o Nim. Studia i odczyty o Mickiewiczu*. 2d ed. Warsaw: Rytm, 1998, 446–68.

——. *O "Księgach narodu i pielgrzymstwa polskiego" A. Mickiewicza*. Cracow: G. Gebethner, 1911.

——. *"Pan Tadeusz." Wzrost, wielkość i sława. Studium literackie*. Cracow: Universitas, 2002.

——. "Wiek klęski." In his *Zawsze o Nim. Studia i odczyty o Mickiewiczu*. 2d ed. Warsaw: Rytm, 1998, 520–47.

——. *Z dawnego Wilna. Szkice obyczajowe i literackie*. Biblioteczka Wileńska, 2. Vilnius: Magistrat M. Wilna, 1929.

——. "Zręby 'Sprawy Bożej.' Źródła i pokrewieństwa kilku idei podstawowych towianizmu." In his *Z epoki Mickiewicza. Studia i szkice*. Lviv: Ossolineum, 1922, 163–240.

Platen, August von. *Werke*. Vol. 1, *Lyrik*. Munich: Winkler, 1982.

Płoszewski, Leon. "Mickiewicz w korespondencj i zapiskach Leonarda Niedźwieckiego." *Pamiętnik Biblioteki Kórnickiej* 6 (1958): 189–285.

Pług, Adam [Pietkiewicz, Antoni]. "A. E. Odyniec." *Kłosy* 40 (1885): 65–66, 86–87, 151–52, 234–35, 254–55, 283, 286, 299, 318–19, 339–38, 346–47, 361, 364, 373, 376; 41 (1885): 45–46, 106, 117–19, 140–41, 150–51, 170–71, 182–83, 199, 202, 222, 253–54, 295, 298.

Podolinskii, A. I. "Vospominaniia." *Russkii arkhiv* 10.1 (1872): 856–65.

Pol, Wincenty. *Pamiętniki*. Edited by Karol Lewicki. Cracow: WL, 1960.

Polevoi, Ksenofont Alekseevich. *Zapiski*. St. Petersburg: A. S. Suvorin, 1888.

Polevoi, Nikolai A. Review of *Poezje Adama Mickiewicza*. In his *Literaturnaia kritika. Stat'i i retsenzii, 1825–1842*. Edited by V. Berezina and I. Sukhikh. Leningrad: Khudozhestvennaia literaturara, 1990.

——. Review of *Konrad Wallenrod*, by Adam Mickiewicz. *Moskovskii telegraf* 19 (1828): 436–38.

Prusinowski, Aleksy. *Mowa żałobna na nabożeństwie za duszę Adama Mickiewicza odprawiona w Poznaniu w kościele ś. Marcina dnia 15. styczni 1856 r.* Grodzisk: Augustyn Schmaedicki, 1856.

Przecławski, Józef [Tsiprinus]. "Kaleidoskop vospominanii II. Adam Mitskevich." *Russkii arkhiv* 10.9 (1872): cols. 1887–1954.

——. "Józef Oleszkiewicz (Ze wspomnień Petersburga)." *Pracy do Komisji Badań nad Historią Literatury i Oświaty* 1 (1914): 77–91.

Pushkin, Aleksandr S. *Polnoe sobranie sochinenii*. 19 vols. 1937–1959. Reprint, Moscow: Voskresen'e, 1994–1997.

Quinet, Edgar. *L'Ultramontisme ou l'Église romaine et la société moderne*. 3d ed. Paris: Comptoir des Imrimeurs-Unis, 1845.

Rawita-Gawroński, Franciszek. "Sadyk-Pasza i Adam Mickiewicz." In *Rok Mickiewiczowski. Księga pamiątkowa*. Lviv: H. Altenberg, 1899, 216–24.

Rettel, Leonard. "Aleksandr Pushkin." *Zven'ia* 3–4 (1934): 204–14.

Rosiek, Stanisław. *Zwłoki Mickiewicza. Próba nekrografii poety*. Gdańsk: Słowo/Obraz Terytoria, 1997.

Ruszkowski, Janusz. "'Jutrznia oswobodzenia nad Litwą,' czyli Mickiewicz w czasie powstania listopadowego." In *Nie tylko o Norwidzie*. Edited by Jolanta Czarnomorska et al. Poznańskie Towarzystwo Przyjaciół Nauk. Wydział Filologiczno-Filozoficzny. Prace Komisji Filologicznej, 38. Poznań: PTPN, 1997, 123–39.

Rybczonek, Sergiusz. "Przodkowie Adama Mickiewicza po kądzieli." *Blok-Notes Muzeum Literatury im. Adama Mickiewicza* 12/13 (1999): 177–87.

Šafařík [Šafárik], Pavel Jozef. *Geschichte der slawischen Sprache und Literatur nach allen Mundarten*. 1869. Reprint, Bautzen: VEB Domowina-Verlag, 1983.

——. *Korespondence*. Vol. 1, *Vzájemné dopisy . . . s ruskými učenci (1825–1861)*, part 2. Edited by V. A. Francev. Prague: Česka Akadmia Věd a Uměni, 1928.

Sainte-Beuve, [Charles Augustin]. *Correspondence générale*. Edited by Jean Bonnerot. Vols. 2–6. Paris: Librairie Stock, 1936–1938.

Sand, George. *Correspondance*. Vols. 3–7. Edited by Georges Lubin. Paris: Garnier Frères, 1967–1970.

——. *Œuvre autobiographiques*. Edited by Georges Lubin. 2 vols. N.p.: Gallimard, 1971.

Sapieha, Leon. *Wspomnienia (z lat od 1803 do 1863 r.)*. Edited by Bronisław Pawłowski. Lviv: H. Alenberg, G. Seyfarth, E. Wende, n.d.

Shevyrev, Boris S., ed. "Vyderzhki iz zagranichnykh pisem S. A. Sobolevskogo k S. P. Shevyrevu." *Russkii arkhiv* 47.2 (1909): 475–511.

[Siemieński, Jan]. *Ewunia (Henrietta Ewa z hr. Ankwiczów I-voto Sołtykowa, 2–voto Kuczkowska), 1810–1879*. Tarnów: Józef Pisz, 1886.

Siemieński, Lucjan. *Religijność i mistyka w życiu i poezjach Adama Mickiewicza*. Cracow: Władysław Jaworski, 1871.

Sinko, Tadeusz. *Mickiewicz i antyk*. Wrocław: Ossolineum, 1957.

Skałkowski, A. M., ed. "Z pamiętnika Adama Turno." In *Fragmenty*. Edited by A. M. Skałkowski. Poznań, 1928, 82–195.

Skulski, Ryszard. "Studia szkolne Adama Mickiewicza (Część I)." *Życie i myśl* 1.6 (1952): 287–316.

Słowacki, Juliusz. *Dzieła wszystkie*. Edited by Julius Kleiner. 17 vols. Wrocław: Ossolineum, 1952–1975.

——. *Korespondencja*. Edited by Eugeniusz Sawrymowicz. 2 vols. Wrocław: Ossolineum, 1962.

Smolikowski, Paweł. *Historia Zgromadzenia Zmartychwychstania Pańskiego. Podług źródeł rękopiśmiennych*. 4 vols. Cracow: Spółka Wydawnicza Polska, 1892–1896.

Śniadecki, Jan. "O pismach klasycznych i romantycznych." In *Polska krytyka literacka (1800–1918). Materiały*. Edited by Jan Zygmunt Jakubowski. Vol. 1. Warsaw: PWN, 1959, 152–64.

Spazier, Richard Otto. *Geschichte des Austandes des polonischen Volkes in den Jahren 1830 und 1831*. Vol. 1. Altenburg: Literatur-Comptoir, 1832.

Stachowska, Krystyna. "Materiały." In *Kraków Mickiewiczowi. Praca zbiorowa*. Edited by Danuta Rederowa. Cracow: WL, 1956, 181–223.

Stattler, Wojciech Kornel. "Przypomnienie starych znajomości. Na pamiątkę Klementynie z Zerbonich Stattler." *Kłosy* 17 (1873): 197–98, 213–14, 229–31, 246–47, 266–67, 282–83.

Stern, Daniel (Comtesse d'Agoult). *Mémoires, souvenirs et journaux*. Edited by Charles F. Dupêchez. 2 vols. Temps Retrouvé, 58–59. Paris: Mercure de France, 1990.

Sudolski, Zbigniew. "Adam Mickiewicz w pamiętnikach Bogdana Jańskiego. *Rocznik Towarzystwa Literackiego im. Adama Mickiewicza* 3 (1968): 93–104.

——. "Mickiewiczowskie wspominki." *Rocznik Towarzystwa Literackiego im. Adama Mickiewicza* 8 (1973): 91–109.

——. *Panny Szymanowskie i ich losy. Opowieść biograficzna*. Warsaw: LSW, 1986.

Świątecka, Maria. "Sprowadzenie zwłok Adama Mickiewicz do kraju." In *Kraków Mickiewiczowi. Praca zbiorowa*. Edited by Danuta Rederowa. Cracow: WL, 1956, 27–87.

Syga, Teofil. *Te księgi proste. Dzieje pierwszych polskich wydań książek Mickiewicza*. Warsaw: PIW, 1956.

Szeląg, Zdzisław. "Stefana Garczyńskiego 'Wiersze do Aliny.'" *Miscellanea z lat 1800–1850*, 2. Archiwum Literackie, vol. 11. Wrocław: Ossolineum, 1967, 88–119.

Szeliga, Dr. [Józef Bieliński]. "Proces Filaretów w Wilnie. Dokumenta urzędowe z 'Teki' rektora Twardowskiego." *Archiwum do Dziejów Literatury i Oświaty w Polsce*, vol. 6. Cracow: AU, 1890, 170–332.

Szpotański, Stanisław. *Działalność polityczna Mickiewicza*. Vol. 3 of *Adam Mickiewicz i jego epoka*. Warsaw: J. Mortkowicz, 1922.

Szyjkowski, Marian. *Polskie Peregrynacje do Pragi i Karlowych Warów. Od Augusta Mocnego do Adama Mickiewicza*. Bydgoszcz: Biblioteka Polska, 1936.

Szymanowska-Malewska, Helena. *Dziennik (1827–1857)*. Edited by Zbigniew Sudolski. Warsaw: Ancher, 1999.

Tańska-Hoffmanowa, Klementyna. *Pamiętniki*. 3 vols. Berlin: B. Behr, 1849.

Towiański, Andrzej. *Pisma*. 3 vols. Turin: Vincent Bona, 1882.

——. *Wybór pism i nauk*. 2d ed. Edited by Stanisław Pigoń. Biblioteka Narodowa 1:8. Cracow: Krakowska Spółka Wydawnicza, 1922.

Tretiak, Józef. *Młodość Mickiewicza (1798–1824). Życie i poezja*. 2d ed. Vol. 2. St. Petersburg: K. Grendyszyński, 1898.

La Tribune de Peuples. Édition phototypique. Edited by Henryk Jabłoński. Wrocław: Ossolineum, 1963.

Trojanowicz, Zofia. "Listy Jana Koźmiana do Cezarego Platera (Mickiewicz—wykłady paryskie—towianizm)." *Miscellanea z okresu romantyzmu*, 2. Edited by Jarosław Maciejewski. Archiwum Literackie, 15. Wrocław: Ossolineum, 1972, 475–511.

Turner, Victor. *Dramas, Fields, and Metaphors: Symbolic Action in Human Society*. Ithaca: Cornell University Press, 1974.

——. *The Ritual Process: Structure and Anti-Structure*. Ithaca: Cornell University Press, 1977.

U[shakov], V. "O russkom perevode sonetov Mitskevicha." *Moskovskii telegraf* 30 (1829): 336–57.

Varnhagen von Ense, Karl August. *Tagebücher*. Vol. 14. Leipzig: Hoffmann and Lampe, 1870.

Viazemskii, Prince P. A. "Mitskevich o Pushkine." In his *Polnoe sobranie sochinenii*. Edited by Count S. D. Sheremetev. Vol. 7, 1855 *g*.–1877 *g*. St. Petersburg: Stasiulevich, 1882, 304–32.

——. "Sonety Mitskevicha." In his *Polnoe sobranie sochinenii*. Edited by Count S. D. Sheremetev. Vol. 1, 1810 *g*.–1827 *g*. St. Petersburg: Stasiulevich, 1878, 326–36.

Vigel', F. F. *Zapiski*. Edited by S. Ia. Shtraikh. Vol. 2. 1928. Memoir Series, 10. New York: Oriental Research Partners, 1974.

Walka romantyków z klasykami. Edited by Stefan Kawyn. Biblioteka Narodowa, I:183. Wrocław: Ossolineum, 1960.

Wasilewski, Zygmunt. "Mickiewicz i Słowacki jako pamiętnikarze." In his *Mickiewicz i Słowacki.* Warsaw: Gebethner and Wolff, n.d., 86–111.

Wellisz, Léopold. *Une Amitié polono-suisse: Adam Mickiewicz, Juste et Caroline Olivier et l'épisode Lèbre-Towianski, avec des documents inédits.* Lausanne: F. Rouge, 1942.

Werner, Ryszard M. "Niemiecki nekrolog Mickiewicza." *Pamiętnik Towarzystwa Literackiego im. Adama Mickiewicza* 5 (1891): 201–2.

Więckowska, Helena. "Z propagandy towianistycznej w Towarzystwie Demokratycznym Polskim. Na marginesie nieznanego listu Juliusza Słowackiego." *Przegląd Współczesny* 135/136 (1933): 212–24.

Wierzbowski [Verzhbovskii], Teodor. *K biografii Adama Mitskevicha v 1821–1829 godax.* St. Petersburg: Imperatorska Akademiia Nauk, 1898 [= *Sbornik otdeleniia russkogo iazyka i slovesnosti Imperatorskoi Akademii Nauk* 66.5].

——. *Z badań nad Mickiewiczem i utworami jego.* Warsaw: Jan Cott, 1916.

——. *Mickiewicz. Słowo i czyn.* 2d ed. Warsaw: PWN, 1998.

Witkowski, Michał. "Z pobytu Mickiewicza w Berlinie." *Przegląd Zachodni* 12, nos. 1/2 (1956): 29–42.

Witwicki, Stefan. *Listy . . . do Józefa Bohdana Zaleskiego.* Edited by Dionizy Zaleski. Lviv: Dionizy Zaleski, 1901.

——. "Nieznane listy Stef. Witwickiego do Klem, Grabowskiej." Edited by W. Francew. *Pamiętnik Literacki* 22/23 (1925–1926): 544–55.

——. *Towiańszczyzna wystawiona i aneksami objaśniona.* Paris: Rue de Seine 14, 1844.

Wójcicki, K. W. *Wspomnienie o życiu Adama Mickiewicza.* Warsaw: J. Jaworski, 1858.

Wójcicka, Zofia. "Hipolit Błotnicki o Adamie Mickiewiczu (w 'Dzienniku' z lat 1832–1855)." *Pamiętnik Literacki* 71.1 (1980): 209–36.

Wolff, Larry. *Inventing Eastern Europe: The Map of Civilization on the Mind of the Enlightenment.* Stanford: Stanford University Press, 1994.

Wołodko, Edward. "Wspomnienie o Towiańskim." Edited by Henryk Mościcki. *Biblioteka Warszawska* 265.1 (1907): 575–82.

Współudział Adama Mickiewicza w sprawie Andrzeja Towiańskiego. Listy i przemówienia. 2 vols. Paris: Księgarnia Luksemburgska, 1877.

Wspomnienia o Mickiewiczu. London: Orbis, 1947.

Zakrzewski, Bogdan, et al. *Sądy współczesnych o twórczości Słowackiego, 1826–1862.* Wrocław: Ossolineum, 1963.

Zaleski, Bronisław. "Ks. Hieronim Kajsiewicz" (Wyciąg z listów i notat zmarłego) (1812–1873). *Rocznik Towarzystwa Historyczno-Literackiego w Paryżu* 1 (1873–1878): 254–419.

Zaleski, Józef Bohdan. *Dzieła pośmiertne.* Vol. 1. Cracow: Czas, 1891.

——. *Korespondencja.* Edited by Dionizy Zaleski. 5 vols. Lviv: H. Altenberg, 1900–1904.

Zawadzki, Władysław. *Ludwik Nabielak. Opowieść historyczna.* Lviv: Gubrynowicz and Schmidt, 1886.

Żeleński (Boy), Tadeusz. *Brązownicy i inne szkice o Mickiewiczu.* Vol. 4 of *Pisma.* Warsaw: PIW, 1956.

——. *Słówka.* Cracow: WL, 1983.

Z filareckiego świata. Zbiór wspomnień z lat 1816–1824. Edited by Henryk Mościcki. Warsaw: Biblioteka Polska, 1924.

Zgorzelski, Czesław. "Materiały do dziejów wileńskiej edycji 'Poezyj' Mickiewicza." *Pamiętnik Literacki* 57 (1966): 624–51.

Zielińska, Marta, ed. *Korespondencja Filomatów (1817–1823).* Warsaw: PIW, 1989.

Złożenie zwłok Adama Mickiewicza na Wawelu dnia 4-go lipca 1890 roku. Książka pamiątkowa. Cracow: Drukarnia Związkowa, 1890.

"Z papierów po Michale Czajkowskim i Ludwice Śniadeckiej (1841–1867). Cz. I. Korespondencja z lat 1854–56." Edited by Józef Fijałek. *Rocznik Biblioteki Polskiej Akademii Nauk w Krakowie* 10 (1964): 253–311.

SELECTED BIBLIOGRAPHY

Aizenshtok, I. Ia. "Do perebuvannia Mitskevycha na Ukraïni (Adam Mitskevych i P. Hulak-Artemovs'kyi)." In *Mizhslov'ians'ki literaturni vzaiemyny (Zbirnyk statei)*. Kyiv: AN URSR, 1958, 97–110.

Arnaud, René. *The Second Republic and Napoleon III*. Translated by E. F. Buckley. London: William Heineman, 1930.

Bartoccini, Fiorella. *Roma nell'ottocento. Il Tramonto della "Città Santa." Nascita di una capitale*. Vol. 16 of *Storia di Roma*. Bologna: Cappelli, 1985.

Batowski, Henryk. *Przyjaciele Słowianie*. Warsaw: Czytelnik, 1956.

Bazylow, Ludwik. *Polacy w Petersburgu*. Wrocław: Ossolineum, 1984.

Beauvois, Daniel. *Lumières et societé en Europe de l'est: L'Université de Vilna et les écoles polonaises de l'Empire Russe*. 2 vols. Lille: Atelier Reproduction des Thèses, 1977.

Binyon, T. J. *Pushkin: A Biography*. London: HarperCollins, 2002.

Bordet, Gaston. *La Pologne, Lamennais et ses amis 1830–1834*. Paris: Éditions du Dialogue, 1985.

Borowy, Wacław. "Poeta przeobrażeń." In his *O poezji Mickiewicza*. Vol. 2. Lublin: Towarzystwo Naukowe KUL, 1958, 191–212.

Coleman, Marion Moore. *Young Mickiewicz*. Cambridge Springs, PA: Alliance College, 1956.

Collingham, H.A.C. *The July Monarchy: A Political History of France, 1830–1848*. London: Longman, 1988.

Corbet, Charles. *L'Opinion française face à l'inconnue russe (1799–1894)*. Paris: Marcel Didier, 1967.

Czapska, Maria. *Szkice Mickiewiczowskie*. Londyńska Biblioteka Literacka, 18. London: B. Świderski, 1963.

Dabrowski, Patrice M. *Commemorations and the Shaping of Modern Poland*. Bloomington: Indiana University Press, 2004.

Dernałowicz, Maria. *Adam Mickiewicz*. Warsaw: Interpress, 1981.

———. "'Avant que Mickewicz n'entre au Collège de France. . . .'" In *Mickiewicz 1798–1998: Bicentenaire de la naissance*. Spec. issue of *Actes de la Société Historiques et Littéraire Polonaise* 4 (1998): 43–52.

Desmettre, Henri. *Towianski et le messianisme polonais*. 2 vols. Lille: Faculté de Théologie, 1947.

Dubiecki, Marian. "Pierwsze miesiące pobytu Adama Mickiewicza zagranicą." In *Księga pamiątkowa na uczczenie setnej rocznicy urodzin Adama Mickiewicza (1798–1898)*. Vol. 2 Warsaw: Bronisław Natanson, 1898, 5–11.

Dunajówna, Maria. *Tomasz Zan. Lata uniwersyteckie, 1815–1824*. Vilnius: Towarzystwo Przyjaciół Nauk w Wilnie, 1933.

Fairweather, Maria. *The Pilgrim Princess: A Life of Princess Zinaida Volkonsky*. London: Constable, 1999.

Fortescue, William. *France and 1848: The End of Monarchy*. London: Routledge, 2005.

Galanter, Marc. *Cults: Faith, Healing, and Coercion*. New York: Oxford University Press, 1989.

Gałęzowska, Irène. *Bibliothèque Polonaise de Paris, 1839–1939*. Paris: [Bibliothèque Polonaise], 1946.

Gardner, Monica. *Adam Mickiewicz: The National Poet of Poland*. 1911. Reprint, New York: Arno Press, 1971.

Gomolicki, Leon. *Dziennik pobytu Adama Mickiewicza w Rosji. 1824–1829*. Warsaw: Książka i Wiedza, 1949.

Hass, Ludwik. *Wolnomularstwo w Europie środkowo-wschodniej w XVIII i XIX wieku*. Wrocław: Ossolineum, 1982.

Henry, Martin. *Histoire de la Bibliothèque de l'Arsenal*. Paris: Librairie Plon, 1900.

Holt, Edgar. *Risorgimento: The Making of Italy, 1815–1870*. London: Macmillan, 1970.

Izmailov, N. V. "A. A. Bestuzhev do 14 dekabria 1825 g." In *Pamiati dekabristov. Sbornik materialov*. Vol. 1. Leningrad: AN SSSR, 1926, 1–99.

Jastrun, Mieczysław. *Adam Mickiewicz*. Warsaw: Polonia, 1955.

Kalembka, Sławomir. *Wielka Emigracja. Polskie wychódzstwo polityczne w latach 1831–1862*. Warsaw: Wiedza Powszechna, 1971.

Kamza, Paweł, and Janusz Ruszkowski. *Wiara i propaganda. Legion Mickiewicza 1848–1998*. Poznań: PTPN, 1999.

Kawyn, Stefan. *Ideologia stronnictw politycznych wobec Mickiewicza, 1890–1898*. Lviv: Filomaty, 1937.

Kieniewicz, Stefan. "Histoire de 'La Tribune des Peuples.'" In his *L'indépendance et la question agraire. Esquisses polonaises du XIXe siècle. Opera Minora*. Wrocław: Ossolinuem, 1982, 117–82.

Kłossowski, Andrzej. *Ambasador książki polskiej w Paryżu Władysław Mickiewicz*. Wrocław: Ossolineum, 1971.

Kopczyński, Krzysztof. *Mickiewicz i jego czytelnicy. O recepcji wieszcza w zaborze rosyjskim, 1831–1855*. Warsaw: Semper, 1994.

Korbut, Gabriel. "Przyjaciel rzymski Mickiewicza (O autorze 'Snu w Podhorcach')." In his *Szkice i drobiazgi historyczno-literackie*. Warsaw: Kasa im. Mianowskiego, 1935, 15–24.

Koropeckyj, Roman. "Orientalism in Adam Mickiewicz's *Crimean Sonnets*." *Slavic and East European Journal* 45 (2001): 660–78.

——. *The Poetics of Revitalization: Adam Mickiewicz between* Forefathers' Eve, part 3 *and* Pan Tadeusz. East European Monographs, 536. Boulder: East European Monographs, 2001.

Kossak, Ewa K. *Boskie diabły*. Warsaw: Czytelnik, 1996.

Krzyżanowski, Ludwik. "Cooper and Mickiewicz: A Literary Friendship." In *Adam Mickiewicz: Poet of Poland*. Edited by Manfred Kridl. New York: Columbia University Press, 1951, 245–58.

Kukiel, M. *Czartoryski and European Unity, 1770–1861*. Princeton: Princeton University Press, 1955.

Lewak, Adam. "Czasy Wielkiej Emigracji." In *Polska. Jej dzieje i kultura od czasów najdawniejszych do chwili obecnej*. Vol. 3, *Od roku 1796–1930*. Warsaw: Trzaska, Evert and Michalski, 1927, 193–233.

Lincoln, W. Bruce. *Sunlight at Midnight: St. Petersburg and the Rise of Modern Russia*. New York: Basic Books, 2000.

Lotman, Ju. M. "The Decembrist in Everyday Life." In Lotman and B. A. Uspenskij, *The Semiotics of Russian Culture*. Edited by Ann Shukman. Michigan Slavic Contributions, 11. Ann Arbor, 1984, 71–123.

Makowski, Krzysztof A. "Wątek żydowski w badaniach nad Mickiewiczem." In *Księga Mickiewiczowska. Patronowi uczelni w dwusetną rocznicę urodzin 1798–1998*. Edited by Zofia Trojanowiczowa and Zbigniew Przychodniak. Poznań: Wydawnictwo Naukowe UAM, 1998, 419–50.

Makowski, Stanisław. *Świat sonetów krymskich Adama Mickiewicza*. Warsaw: Czytelnik, 1969.

Mansel, Philip. *Constantinople: City of the World's Desire, 1453–1924*. London: John Murray, 1995.

——. *Paris between Empires, 1814–1852*. London: John Murray, 2001.

Markiewicz, Zygmunt. *Polsko-franzuskie związki literacki*. Warsaw: PWN, 1986.

Mężyński, Kazimierz. *Gotfryd Ernest Groddeck profesor Adama Mickiewicza. Próba rewizji*. Gdańskie Towarzystwo Naukowe, Wydział I Nauk Społecznych i Humanistycznych, 48. Gdańsk: Gdańskie Towarzystwo Naukowe, 1974.

Mocha, Frank. "Tadeusz Bułharyn (Faddej V. Bulgarin), 1789–1859: A Study in Literary Maneuver." *Antemurale* 17 (1974): 60–209.

Mucha, Bogusław. *Adam Mickiewicz czasów emigracji i Rosjanie*. Łódź: Uniwersytet Łódzki, 1997.

——. *Rosjanki w życiu Adama Mickiewicza*. Katowice: Śląsk, 1994.

Nechkina, M. *Griboedov i dekabristy*. 3d ed. Moscow: Khudozhestvennaia literatura: 1977.

Nicod, Françoise. "Lausanne capitale (1803–1845). In *Histoire de Lausanne*. Edited by Jean Charles Biaudet. Toulouse: Privat; Lausanne: Payot, 1982, 259–302.

Niesiołowska-Rothertowa, Zofia. "Portrety Mickiewicza." *Wiedza i Życie* 22 (1955): 236–51.

Ordon, Edmund. "Mickiewicz and Emerson." In *Mickiewicz and the West*. Edited by B. R. Bugelski. Special issue of *University of Buffalo Studies* 23.1 (1956): 31–54.

Perrot, A.-M. *Petit atlas pittoresque des quarante-huit quartiers de la ville de Paris*. 1834. Reprint. Edited by Michel Fleury and Jeanne Pronteau. N.p.: Les Éditions de Minuit, n.d.

Pertek, Jerzy. "Bałtycka podróż Mickiewicza." *Przegląd Zachodni* 12.1/2 (1956): 10–28.

Podhorski-Okołów, Leonard. *Realia Mickiewiczowskie*. 2d ed. Warsaw: Rytm, 1999.

Polski słownik biograficzny. Cracow: Gebethner and Wolff, 1935–.
Price, Roger. *The French Second Empire: An Anatomy of Political Power*. Cambridge: Cambridge University Press, 2001.
Pruszyński, Ksawery. *Adam Mickiewicz: The Life Story of the Greatest Polish Poet*. London: Polish Cultural Institute, 1955.
Rambo, Lewis R. *Understanding Religious Conversion*. New Haven: Yale University Press, 1993.
Reychman, Jan. "Zainteresowania orientalistyczne w środowisku mickiewiczowskim w Wilnie i Petersburgu." In Marian Lewicki et al., *Szkice z dziejów polskiej orientalistyki*. Edited by Stefan Strelcyn. Warsaw: PWN, 1957, 69–93.
Royle, Trevor. *Crimea: The Great Crimean War, 1854–1856*. London: Little, Brown, 1999.
Rutkowski, Krzysztof. *Braterstow albo śmierć. Zabijanie Mickiewicza w Kole Bożym*. Paris: Libella, 1988.
——. "Miejsce Xawery Deybel w rodzinie Mickiewiczów." In *Tajemnice Mickiewicza*. Edited by Marta Zielińska. Warsaw: IBL, 1998, 29–62.
——. *Stos dla Adama, albo kacerze i kapłani*. Warsaw: Bellona, 1994.
Rymkiewicz, Jarosław Marek. "Jeszcze coś o *podróżnych* (i Awdotii Guriew)." *Arcana* 24 (1998): 47–54.
——. *Kilka szczegółów*. N.p.: Arcana, 1994.
——. *Baket*. London: Aneks, 1989.
——. *Żmut*. Paris: Instytut Literacki, 1987.
Rymkiewicz, Jarosław Marek, Dorota Siwicka, Alina Witkowska, and Marta Zielińska. *Mickiewicz. Encyklopedia*. Warsaw: Horyzont, 2001.
Rzążewski, Adam [Aër]. "Mickiewicz w Odessie." *Ateneum* 33.1–3 (1884): 500–527.
Sedler, M. J. "Falret's Discovery: The Origin of the Concept of Bipolar Affective Illness." *American Journal of Psychiatry* 140 (1983): 1127–33.
Sendich, Munir. "Karolina Jaenisch (Pavlova) and Adam Mickiewicz." *The Polish Review* 14.3 (1969): 68–78.
Siwicka, Dorota. *Zapytaj Mickiewicza*. Gdańsk: słowo/obraz terytoria, 2007.
Skurnowicz, Joan S. *Romantic Nationalism and Liberalism: Joachim Lelewel and the Polish National Idea*. East European Monographs, 83. Boulder: East European Monographs, 1981.
Słownik języka Adama Mickiewicza. 11 vols. Edited by Konrad Górski and Stefan Hrabec. Wroclaw: Ossolineum, 1962–1983.
Stearns, Peter N. *Priest and Revolutionary. Lamennais and the Dilemma of French Catholicism*. New York: Harper and Row, 1967.
Stefanowska, Zofia. "Geniusz poety, geniusz narodu. Mickiewicz wobec powstania listopdowego." *Teksty Drugie* 36 (1995): 19–31.
——. "Mickiewicz o 'Wacława dziejach' Garczyńskiego." In her *Próba zdrowego rozsądku. Studia o Mickiewiczu*. 2d ed. Warsaw: Rytm, 2001, 215–44.
Straszewska, Maria. *Życie literackie Wielkiej Emigracji we Francji, 1831–1840*. Warsaw: PIW, 1970.
Sudolski, Zbigniew, ed. *Korespondencja Filomatów. Wybór*. Biblioteka Narodowa, I:293. Wrocław: Ossolineum, 1999.
Świrko, Stanisław. *Z Mickiewiczem pod ręką czyli życie i twórczość Jana Czeczota*. Warsaw: LSW, 1989.
Syga, Teofil, and Stanisław Szenic. *Maria Szymanowska i jej czasy*. Warsaw: PIW, 1960.
Szpotański, Stanisław. *Andrzej Towiański. Jego życie i nauka*. Warsaw: Kasa im. Mianowskiego, n.d.
Szyndler, Bartłomiej. *Mikołaj Nowosilcow (1762–1838). Portret carskiego inkwizytora*. Warsaw: DiG, 2004.
Thackery, Frank W. *Antecedents of Revolution: Alexander I and the Polish Kingdom, 1815–1825*. East European Monographs, 67. Boulder: East European Monographs, 1980.
Urban, Jan. *Makryna Mieczysławska w świetle prawdy*. Cracow: Przegląd Powszechny, 1923.
Ullmann, Chana. *The Transformed Self: The Psychology of Religious Conversion*. New York: Plenum Press, 1989.
Walicki, Andrzej. *Mesjanizm Adama Mickiewicz w perspektywie porównawczej*. Warsaw: IBL, 2006.

——. *Philosophy and Romantic Nationalism: The Case of Poland*. Oxford: Clarendon Press, 1982.

Weintraub, Wiktor. "Adam Mickiewicz (1798–1855)." In *European Writers: The Romantic Century*. Edited by Jacques Barzun. Vol. 5, New York: Scribners, 1985. 607–34.

——. "Adam Mickiewicz, the Mystic-Politician." *Harvard Slavic Studies* 1 (1953): 133–78.

——. "Bakunin—Mickiewicz." In his *Mickiewicz—mistyczny polityk i inne studia o poecie*. Edited by Zofia Stefanowska. Warsaw: IBL, 1998, 140–62.

——. "A Duel of Improvisations." In *Studies in Russian and Polish Literature, in Honor of Wacław Lednicki*. Edited by Zbigniew Folejewski. The Hague: Mouton, 1962, 142–59.

——. *Literature as Prophecy: Scholarship and Martinist Poetics in Mickiewicz's Parisian Lectures*. The Hague: Mouton, 1959.

——. *Poeta i prorok. Rzecz o profetyzmie Mickiewicza*. [2d ed.] Warsaw: Biblioteka Narodowa, 1998.

——. *The Poetry of Adam Mickiewicz*.'S-Gravenhage: Mouton, 1954.

——. "The Problem of Improvisation in Romantic Literature." *Comparative Literature* 16 (1964): 119–37.

——. *Profecja i profesura. Mickiewicz, Michelet i Quinet*. Warsaw: PIW, 1975.

Wellisz, Léopold. *The Friendship of Margaret Fuller D'Ossoli and Adam Mickiewicz*. New York: Polish Book Importing Co., 1947.

Welsh, David. *Adam Mickiewicz*. New York: Twayne, 1966.

Witkowska, Alina. *Celina i Adam Mickiewiczowie*. Cracow: WL, 1998.

——. *Rówieśnicy Mickiewicza. Życiorys jednego pokolenia*. Warsaw: Wiedza Powszechna, 1962.

——. *Towiańczycy*. Warsaw: PIW, 1989.

Vatsuro, V. È. "Mitskevich v stikhakh Lermontova." In *Dukhovnaia kul'tura slavianskikh narodov. Literatura, fol'klor, istoriia. Sbornik statei k IX Mezhdunarodnomu s'ezdu slavistov*. Leningrad: Nauka, 1983, 109–29.

Zielińska, Marta. "Tajemnica przyjaźni z Margaret Fuller." In *Tajemnice Mickiewicza*. Edited by Marta Zielińska. Warsaw: IBL, 1998, 63–78.

Złożenie zwłok Adama Mickiewicza na Wawelu dnia 4go Lipca 1890 roku. Książka pamiątkowa. Cracow: Drukarnia Związkowa, 1890.

INDEX

Page numbers of figures are in italics